# A History of Glengarry

by
## Royce MacGillivray
and
## Ewan Ross

Mika Publishing Company
Belleville, Ontario
1979

A History of Glengarry
Copyright © Mika Publishing Company, 1979
ISBN 0-919303-32-3
Printed and bound in Canada

# CONTENTS

# ACKNOWLEDGEMENTS

So many people have assisted us in gathering the material for this history that it is impossible to list them all here, but we must not let this volume go to press without expressing our gratitude to Mrs. Harriet I. MacKinnon, Miss Ethel Ostrom, Sister Clair McDonald, Mr. and Mrs. Earl Munro, Mr. and. Mrs. Archie P. Munro, Mr. and Mrs. George R. Arnott, Mr. and Mrs. Howard Pattingale, Mrs. Evelyn van Beek, Sister Mary Electa, Mrs. Donald Emberg, Mrs. Gertrude Snyder Wood, Dr. and Mrs. Norbert Ferré, Mrs. Ranald McDonald, Mrs. Roderick McRae of Maxville, Mrs. Jean MacIntosh, Mrs. J.T. Smith (Dorothy Dumbrille), Mr. Campbell Fraser, Mr. Melvin Ferguson, Mrs. Donald MacDougall, Mr. Eugene Macdonald, former editor of the *Glengarry News*, Mrs. Elizabeth Blair of Toronto, Alex W. Fraser of the Glengarry Genealogical Society.

Mr. Grant MacGillivray, Mrs. John Forney, Mrs. Mabel Maclean, Mrs. Dorothy McKee, Mrs. Ruth Mowat, Mrs. Mabel Mossop, Mr.Hugh P. MacMillan, Professor Paul Cornell, Mrs. Rory MacGillivray, Mrs. Ewan Ross, the staff of the *Glengarry News*, of the National Library, and of the National and Ontario Archives, and of the University of Waterloo Library, and the late Rhodes Grant, D.A. Condie, and Emma Urquhart. We are grateful, too, for the care and diligence of Mrs. Adelheid Bender who did research work and proofreading for us and of Mrs. Susan Shantz who typed our manuscript.

We are grateful to the following for permission to print copyright material: The Champlain Society for extracts from *Lord Selkirk's Diary 1803-1804* (Champlain Society 1958); Dorothy Dumbrille and Progress Books for extracts from Dorothy Dumbrille, *All This Difference* (Toronto, Progress Books, 1945) in our Chapter XVI; The Earl of Dundonald for extracts from his grandfather's *My Army Life*; the Executors of Rhodes Grant for extracts from Rhodes Grant's histories of Martintown; Sandra Gwyn for a passage (in our Chapter XVI) from her article in *Saturday Night* of July/August 1975; Rt. Hon. J.W. Pickersgill for Mackenzie King's remarks on the 1945 Glengarry election; *The Review* (Vankleek Hill, Ont.) for the use in our Chapter XVI of passages on Sandy Fraser which first appeared as an article in *The Review* of 31 March 1976; the *Standard-Freeholder* (Cornwall, Ont.) for passages from the autobiography of James Begg which were published in the *Standard-Freeholder*; the University of Toronto Library for material from the King's College records; the University of Toronto Press for the passage from John Porter's *Vertical Mosaic* (University of Toronto Press, 1969) pp. 425-426; Gertrude Wood for her poem "Reminiscence,".

# PREFACE

The present one-volume history of Glengarry is the first of what we hope will be three or possibly even four books on Glengarry. At the same time as this history or shortly afterwards, we hope to issue a book-length *Bibliography of Glengarry County* which will analyze the sources for the history of the county and list the books and articles relating to the county which have been published since the 1780's. The next book, to appear (if at all) a few years from now, will be a *Dictionary of Glengarry County*, containing short lives of all eminent Glengarrians from the earliest times and short encyclopedia-type articles on the history of the Glengarry towns and villages and on such subjects as Glengarry contractors, newspapers, shantymen, and Indian Lands, and explaining terms relating to the history and geography of Glengarry such as the Moccasin (train), "Bonach night", "The Little Fourth", and "Little Russia". It is possible, finally, that we will, some years further on, issue a *Chronology of Glengarry County*, listing events in the county month by month from the 1780's to the time of publication. This will be a local history version of such works as Neville Williams' *Chronology of the Modern World 1763 to the Present Time*. We mention the preparation of this chronology, however, as something just within the limits of possibility, and dependent upon, among much else, a favourable public reception for the present volume.

For the two authors, preparing the present volume has been an arduous but at the same time an exciting enterprise. Our separate interests in Glengarry history go back many years, and long before we decided to combine for the writing of Glengarry's history, we were deeply curious about the history of this most remarkable and interesting (as it seems to us) of all the Ontario counties. Our labours of research and writing have been a means of satisfying this curiosity and have left us, also, with the sensation that we were in a sense preparing our own autobiographies, as we probed into the history of a county which has left the strongest marks upon us—as it has done upon so many Glengarrians. We will not believe that this book has been well done unless some of our readers also feel that in reading it they have come better to understand themselves by understanding the historical processes of which they and their ancestors have been a part.

One plea for understanding we must put before our readers. It has long been the custom among certain well meaning writers of local histories to omit much of what is harsh or depressing in their subject, in the belief that it is possible to have a valid history even after the troubles and misfortunes which are so inescapable a part of human life have been filtered out. In this volume, we have broken with this tradition. We have included things which are to the discredit of the county as well as things that are to its credit, have remembered evil events as well as good, have even included things which (in a phrase which no historian should ever utter or allow to pass uncensured in his hearing) were "better forgotten".

For this, we have the following reasons. First, the practice of the fullest candour is simply one of the iron rules by which the historian is bound. Anyone who wishes to write history but finds that he is unable to submit to this iron rule should lay down the pen and go and do something else. Secondly, even if this were not true, and the historian had the opportunity, with a clear conscience, to omit or include as he pleased, it would be totally unworthy of Glengarry County to write a history which only included the good things about it. When the achievements of a person, or an institution, or a place, are genuinely important, as we believe those of Glengarry are, it only diminishes their reputation when one pretends that these good things were the whole story, that there was nothing bad besides. It is only when the history of Glengarry is written on the same principles of impartiality as that of Canada as a whole, that it will be seen how much Glengarry has contributed to the development of Canada.

A word about the scope of this history. In a sense, there have always been two Glengarries. There has been the geographical Glengarry, which corresponded to the geographical boundaries of the county, and there has been the larger, the spiritual or ethnic Glengarry, which extended beyond these boundaries to include the Scottish areas of Stormont County, of Caledonia Township, and of the Quebec border. The references one sometimes finds in nineteenth century newspapers to Cornwall as a town in Glengarry are in one sense simply errors, but in another sense they are founded on fact, for in the nineteenth century Cornwall was, in feeling, a part of this larger Glengarry. The present history will concern itself only with the geographical Glengarry, though from the circumstance that one of the present authors (though born in Alexandria) grew up in Caledonia Township, just outside the Glengarry border, it may readily be believed that they are not unsympathetic to the claims of the larger Glengarry.

When Robert Sellar published his incomparable history of Huntingdon County ninety years ago, he complained in his preface that ''The work of interviewing was not only laborious, but too often disagreeable, for my reception was not always gracious. That a sane man should neglect his business and spend his substance on horse-hire to collect old-world stories, and above all, to do so from disinterested motives, was beyond the comprehension of many, and curt answers, suspicious questions, and downright refusals were sometimes my reward for a cold and fatiguing drive over bad roads''. The present authors are happy to say that their experience has been so much the opposite, that they have seldom received a repulse or an unkind word from a Glengarrian or anyone else in their work of gathering the material for this history. Instead, we have received a degree of cooperation which surprises and awes us as we look back upon it. It seems, in fact, as if local historians, or historians of Glengarry at least, are universal favourites, for archivists, librarians, and individuals have done us innumerable kindnesses in our search for information. If the reader wants to be well treated, let him become a reseacher, at least in Glengarry history! Many a time in opening a letter of information in reply to one of our many requests, in newspapers and letters in Canada and elsewhere, we have known how kings and emperors must feel all the time.

Necessity did something to those who came to Glengarry. Clan feuds, so much a part of life in the old land were almost entirely forgotten in practice and became only tales to be told and retold. Religious differences which had often led to violence in the old land were placed far in the background in the new land and a neighbour became a neighbour even when different clans and religions were involved. The different groups even helped build each others' churches. Priests and ministers comforted the dying and baptized the babies according to need; the literate wrote letters and did legal work for the illiterate.

In Glengarry, as in few other places, the people came to believe they could continue to be Scots and to live in peace. In time their Gaelic gave way to English. The two main religions continued to be firmly established but with almost every clan having members in both churches. French Canadians came into their communities and became neighbours and part of a way of life, an everyday faith based on hard work and frugal living bringing its own reward. The settlement grew and produced enough and a bit to spare and its numbers increased. When the third generation came along it was necessary for many of its members to leave Glengarry to make a living. The county had reached the limit of the numbers it could support.

We have decided that Glengarry has a "mystique" — a

sense of something special about it— and we believe its genesis was in this belief in hard work, frugal living, and a sense of responsibility to yourself and to your neighbours. Inevitably this sense of responsiblity led many of Glengarry's people, young and old, elsewhere to earn a living. When in the early years of this century Ralph Connor wrote his "Glengarry books" he was merely saying what a lot of North America already knew: "Glengarry produces good men."

To us, the people who left Glengarry have, at least for the present, moved off-stage and our work has largely been with those who remained in the area. Each generation marrying and producing a fresh generation reared them as they themselves were reared and the cycle repeated itself; many left home but a nucleus remained to produce another generation in their turn. On those who stayed in Glengarry fell the whole burden of building an educational system, a farming system, a church system, a transportation system, a mercantile system, a social system, a recreational system, and everything else that would provide for their own needs and the education of their young, in what they considered was the path "in which they should go."

Our search for evidence has led us far afield. We feel that our list of the evidence, published along with this history, is a very considerable part of what we have accomplished. In some few areas access to records was denied to us, among them the Diocese of Alexandria-Cornwall. We hope this shortcoming in our search was at least partly compensated for by the splendid cooperation of the Archdioceses of Ottawa and Kingston. In some other areas lack of records and confused records led to hours of frustration. Anyone who tries to sort out early land transactions in Glengarry could easily wind up muttering to himself as could the person who tries to prove just when it became possible for the Rev. John Bethune to perform a marriage legally.

We didn't find all the answers and mayhap we didn't try to answer all the questions. We did try to be honest with ourselves and with those who are hoping our *History of Glengarry* will really be definitive.

This is not a story of mighty deeds, though building Glengarry's stone churches might properly be so considered, but the story of a determined struggle by ordinary men and women over a two hundred year period, with only one object in view, that the children of each succeeding generation might have a better life than their parents.

We believe the evidence indicates the people of Glengarry won.

Here we are not so much concerned with ethnic origins as with what happened to the ordinary people on the concessions and in the small towns and hamlets. Nor have we devoted too much space to the ''big names'' of our folklore unless in some way they contributed to the enrichment of the lives of the ordinary people of Glengarry. Thus J.T. Schell, as a major employer in Glengarry for thirty years, is given more space than Col. Alexander Fraser of Fraserfield, and ''Big Jim'' Rayside and Hugh Munro are more important to us as industrialists than as politicians. In fact, of the 66 politicians (27 in provincial assemblies pre-Confederation, 17 M.L.A.'s since Confederation, 20 M.P.'s in Ottawa and two senators) who have represented Glengarry in our various legislative groups, we found very few whose contribution to Glengarry's weal was noticeable. We have tried to note these exceptions. In one case, that of the Sandfield family, for lack of space we have left unsaid much that could be said.

In the second last chapter of this work (Chapter XVIII) we depart from writing of history in order to attempt the fictional reconstruction of the life of a Glengarry farmer who was born in 1905 and is assumed to be still living at the time of writing. Our reason for doing so, in violation of the custom by which historians do *not* present part of their subject in fictional form, is that we felt that in this we could more effectively present to the reader our impression of what it has been to be a Glengarrian in this century. This chapter may perhaps meet with a variety of views. To some its content will seem so obvious that they will find it difficult to imagine why we thought it necessary to write it at all. To others, it may seem very strange. To some few, we believe (or rather, hope with an intensity equal almost to belief) it will lead to a better understanding of a Glengarry (the county, perhaps, of their ancestors) which they have seen but have not known with intimacy or in detail. To some few, we are sorry to say, it may seem that the life we have described was narrow and disappointing — a great, but understandable error. The fact is, the people who lived such quiet lives in Glengarry often lived out a fuller range of the possibilities that are inherent in being human than their contemporaries who lived in cities. The man we described may seem to have been lacking in feeling, but we suggest that part of the fascination and charm of Glengarry and one of the qualities which so often make life elsewhere seem mean and bleak by comparison is the intensity of emotion with which behind quiet facades such as this one so many Glengarrians live out their lives.

It would be an interesting experiment to try to write a series of several connected lives reconstructing a chain of Glengarrians from the days of the earliest settlement to the present, but unfortunately the materials are not sufficient to make it possible to write such lives with anything approaching satisfactory completeness of details for any period earlier than about 1890.

The chapter of imaginary biography has been put near the end of the book for chronological reasons, but we make bold to suggest to those of our readers who are not Glengarrians that they turn to this chapter first of all and read it before entering upon the rest of the book.

# Chapter I
# "The Land We Live In and the Land We Left"

Readers whose Glengarry links are non-existent or a number of generations in the past may find a brief sketch of the geography of the county useful.

Glengarry is one of the Eastern Ontario counties. It is usually considered the easternmost county in the province, though it beats Prescott for this position by so short a margin that the claim should perhaps not be emphasized. It would be more fair to say that there are *two* easternmost counties, of which Glengarry is one.

The gateway to God's country.

Glengarry is bounded on the east by Quebec Province, on

1

the north by Prescott County, and on the west by Stormont County. Its southern boundary runs through the middle of the widening of the St. Lawrence known as Lake St. Francis; this boundary divides Glengarry from Huntingdon County, P.Q.

The area of the county is 307,840 acres or 481 square miles. The population is small—only 19,270 in the 1976 census. The population was higher in the last century, reaching its highest ever recorded level of 22,447 in the census of 1891.

Among Glengarry's towns and villages, only one, Alexandria (population 3,498 in 1976) has grown large enough to become an incorporated town. The next in size, the village of Maxville, has a population of about 850.

In ethnic origins, as defined for the purposes of the census, about one half of the population is French Canadian, and perhaps about one quarter is Scottish. At an earlier date, the population was almost wholly Highland Scottish. French is widely spoken in Glengarry today, but the visitor will rarely meet a French-speaker who is not also fluent in English.

Politically, Glengarry is part of the municipality of the United Counties of Stormont, Dundas and Glengarry (abbreviation: SDG). Oddly, Glengarry's county town is outside the county, being the city of Cornwall in Stormont County. But Alexandria conveniently situated at almost the centre of Glengarry has long been Glengarry's honorary capital, and in the past it has aspired unsuccessfully to being the county town of a Glengarry separated from its partnership with Stormont and Dundas.

Now, let us see how it all came about.

For a short time, Glengarry extended from the St. Lawrence River to the Ottawa River.

The county was established by Lieutenant Governor Simcoe in a Proclamation of 16 July 1792. The proclamation divided the Province of Upper Canada (newly created by an Order in Council of the year before) into nineteen counties. "...the first of the said counties," the proclamation declared, shall be "hereafter called by the name of the county of Glengary.*'" It was laid down that this county was to be bounded on the east by the lines dividing Upper from Lower Canada, on the south by the St. Lawrence River, on the west "by the easternmost boundary of the late township of Cornwall, running north twenty-four degrees west until it intersects the Ottawa or Grand River," and on the north by the Ottawa River. "The said county is to comprehend all the islands in the said river St. Lawrence nearest to the said county, and in the whole or greater part fronting on the same."

The huge tract of Canadian wilderness which thus received the name of a Scottish Glen was divided approximately in half by a statute of 1798 to create a new county on the north, to be called Prescott. By the same statute, the southern portion, which inherited the name of Glengarry, was awarded or confirmed in the possession of the tract of land on its western border which is now known as "Indian Lands." Since this date, Glengarry has retained its boundaries essentially unchanged. There have, however, been minor adjustments of the boundary lines in the east, west, and south — none of which we will need to mention later.

When Glengarry received its name and its first boundaries in Simcoe's Proclamation, the southern half, the half which is now called Glengarry, had already received at least two substantial groups of settlers.

When the holders of great land grants in New York Province in America wanted tenants for their land, several of them, including Sir William Johnson and Walter Butler, brought out Scottish Highlanders to clear and cultivate their land. Most of the people who were eventually to settle in Glengarry as United Empire Loyalists came to the Mohawk Valley in New York Province as tenant farmers in 1773. They came to an area remote from the mainstream of American colonial life — an area where intercourse was limited to others like them-

*Glengary and Glengarry were both standard spellings till about Confederation.

3

selves and where their main source of information was their landlord.

Not only Scots had become tenant farmers of the big landlords in the Mohawk Valley. In the long drawn out wars with France for predominance in North America, Britain had raised many regiments composed of soldiers drawn from the possessions of the British monarchs along the Rhine and other German-speaking groups allied to them. From time to time, as circumstances permitted, some of these German-speaking groups were disbanded in New York Province, and the discharged soldiers became tenants of the great landholders there. The result was that the settlement pattern of the Mohawk Valley was a mixture of Gaelic-speaking Highland Scots and German speakers with English-speaking landlords. Most of the landlords enrolled their tenants in the local militia and as their colonels secured a personal oath of loyalty from them.

Very shortly after Wolfe took Quebec in 1759 and all of Eastern North America became British territory, Britain started to have trouble with the colonial legislatures over various matters, the chief of which was taxation without representation. No colony sent members to sit in the British Parliament at Westminster and mercantile interests in the great American seaports of Boston and New York and Philadelphia had become a force to be reckoned with between 1700 and 1775.

In 1775 British soldiers and American patriots fired on one another; open war was now a real possibility and the time had come to choose sides. The great landlords held their grants from the King; there was little doubt as to where their loyalties must be placed. The tenant farmers had as militia men sworn an oath to their commanding officers who were also their landlords, so they had limited choice in the matter, nor could they have had much information on which to make a different choice. During the winter of 1775-1776, things came to a head in the Mohawk Valley. Orders went out to arrest the leading Loyalists (known to the rebels as ''Tories'') among

4

them Sir John Johnson, who had succeeded to his father's estates on the latter's death in 1774.

Sir John received enough warning of his imminent arrest to make his escape along with a few of his tenants. They headed for Canada, but fearing the Lake Champlain route would be under rebel control they went north up the valley of the Sacandaga, crossed the height of land at Indian Lake, and followed the valley of the Raquette River to the St. Lawrence at St. Regis, from which they made their way to Montreal.

Here Sir John was promptly gazetted a Lieutenant Colonel and given the task of forming a battalion from those of his settlers who had escaped with him. As month followed month and the war continued more and more of Johnson's settlers made their escape from the Mohawk Valley and eventually joined his battalion. This grew large enough to be split into two battalions which formed a regiment officially known as the King's Royal Regiment of New York and unofficially called the Royal Yorkers or Johnson's Greens.

These battalions were mobilized through the following seven years of the war and were disbanded on Christmas Eve 1783. In the course of the war they had done garrison duty at Carleton Island and at Isle aux Noix and had made several raids into the Mohawk Valley, carrying fire and sword to those who had taken over their lands and homes there.

With the war over, the Loyalist problem was a major headache to the British government. There were thousands of these Loyalists, men, women and children; they were definitely not welcome back in their old homes in the newly formed United States, nor did many of them wish to go back. Neither the common men nor their leaders understood or wanted a government such as was being formed in the United States— a government without a king or a hereditary nobility—a chaos as they saw it.

Different measures to deal with the situation were evolved in Britain, the Maritime Colonies, and in Quebec Province. We are concerned here only with the Quebec part of it, and to deal with these refugees on his hands, the Governor General, Sir Frederick Haldimand, on 26 May 1783 gave orders to his surveyor general Samuel Holland to lay out new townships along the St. Lawrence River beginning at Point au Baudet, the western boundary of M. de Longueuil's seigneury. The disbanded soldiers and their families were collected in a camp at St. Laurent and in the spring they were sent up the St. Lawrence in batteaux to Pointe Maligne, now part of the townsite of Cornwall.

Here, sometime in June 1784 (the exact date is not recorded) the former tenants of Sir John and Sir William Johnson drew the numbers of the lots of their new homes in Canada from a hat. They appear to have traded among themselves so that old neighbours in the Mohawk Valley could again be neighbours in Canada.

Major Samuel Holland, Surveyor General for Canada, had given the task of doing the surveying in what would eventually be Upper Canada to his deputy John Collins, who in turn gave the task to various surveyors. The man who did the work in Glengarry for the purposes of the Loyalist settlement was Patrick McNiff. He laid out the fronts of the first two concessions of the Lake Township (now Lancaster Township) and the first two concessions of Township No. 1 (now Charlottenburgh Township), and in this township he also ran the front lines of lots along both banks of the River Raisin and its South Branch tributary. In 1786 McNiff presented a map of this area to Sir John Johnson, with each Loyalist's name on the land he had drawn. This map is one of the most pertinent of our early land documents. There, in McNiff's crabbed handwriting, are the names of the founders of Glengarry's Loyalist families.

Altogether, perhaps 1000 Loyalists settled in Glengarry in 1784, occupying some 250 farm lots out of the approximately 3000 into which Glengarry was ultimately divided.

Here we must take note of a persistent oral tradition that exists in Glengarry. A few families, also Loyalist, claim that their ancestors settled in Glengarry prior to 1784 but after

1776. To date we know of no shred of written evidence to reinforce this tradition. To all appearances, the settlers of 1784 were the first white settlers in Glengarry.

Once on their land the Loyalists were provisioned with army rations for three years and given necessary tools and implements. Provision was made for their sons and daughters to get land for a nominal sum (£2) when they reached the age of 21.

Though the size of the land grants varied with army rank, in actual practice each family occupied one hundred acres or at most two hundred acres, with one end of the property no more than a mile and a quarter from either the St. Lawrence or the Raisin as the rivers were the only possible highways.

One notable exception to this rule of one hundred acres effectively occupied by a family was the large grant given to Sir John Johnson. This grant stretched from Lake St. Francis at what was then called Point Johnson (now Fraser's Point Park) through Williamstown to the present King's Road. Johnson built two houses on the property, one on the lake, the other, a manor house which still stands, at Williamstown. Also at Williamstown he built that most needful of all things to the pioneer settlers, a grist mill. Williamstown was named after Sir John's father but was known for many years to the settlers in the area as "Moulain an Sir Ian" — Sir John's mill.

Lists have been compiled of the Loyalist settlers in Glengarry for several reasons, such as provision lists, clan names, and clan numbers, but for our purpose here perhaps it is only necessary to mention three families of MacDonells: those of Aberchalder, Leek, and Collachie. These families, including their blood relatives and relatives by marriage, had much to do with the administration of affairs, civil, religious, and military, not only in Glengarry and Stormont but in the larger field of Upper Canada and indeed of the British Empire.

Also among the prominent Glengarry Loyalists we must mention the Reverend John Bethune who not only brought organized Presbyterianism to Glengarry but left descendants who have done good work in several fields in this troubled world since he came to Glengarry in 1787.

Veronica (Mrs. Rev. John) Bethune

The Loyalists were soon joined by a large group of emigrants from Knoydart in Scotland. These arrived in 1786 accompanied by their priest, the Reverend Alexander Macdonell of Scotus, and were the founders of the parish of St. Raphaels. The following notice from the *Quebec Gazette* of 7 September 1786 undoubtedly refers to their ship. ARRIVALS: — ''Ship M'Donald, Robert Stevenson, in 61 days from Glasgow. Passengers, Messrs. Ronald M'Donald, Alexander M'Donald, Ensign M'Donald of late 71st regiment, Rod. M'Donald, Lieut. M'Donald of late 71st regt. and Mr.

M'Serven; Mrs. M'Donald, Miss Isabella M'Donald, Miss Mary M'Donald, and Miss Ann M'Donald, besides 520 Steerage-passengers; being, (as is said) the *whole* inhabitants of a parish in the North of Scotland, who emigrated with their Priest, in hopes of bettering themselves at Cataraqui and its environs.''

If the emigrants originally intended to settle in the Cataraqui(Kingston)area, they were no doubt persuaded to change their minds by the fact that the Townships of Charlottenburgh and Lancaster were closer at hand and that there was already a nucleus of Roman Catholic Scots settled about St. Andrews, north of Cornwall.

The correspondence of Sir John Johnson and General Haldimand in 1784 suggests how this Roman Catholic concentration came about. Johnson wrote to Haldimand in April, passing on a request from his Roman Catholic and Protestant followers that they be allowed "to settle in separate Bodies for the Benefit of their religion." To this Haldimand replied, stating that he had no objection and suggesting as a means by which the desired end could be effected the exchange of the lots the settlers drew for land. These Roman Catholics must have been without the regular ministrations of a pastor as late as 1785, for in June of that year the Reverend Roderick Macdonell was given permission by the government to join the Roman Catholic Highlanders of the new settlements as their clergyman. Father Roderick Macdonell was priest at St. Regis and St. Andrews till his death in 1806.

Readers of Carrie Holmes Macgillivray's novel *The Shadow of Tradition* will remember that in that novel the ship MacDonald had begun its voyage accompanied by another ship which was driven by storms into the port of Philadelphia. From there, after many hardships, the settlers made their way overland to Glengarry where they settled along with their original companions. This story appeared in print in a historical article as early as 1881—a date at which some of the children of the 1786 emigrants must still have been alive.

More recently it has been retold in Dorothy Dumbrille's *Up and Down the Glens*.

A somewhat different version of this tale appears in a York (Toronto) newspaper, the *Upper Canada Gazette*, of 20 January 1827. The paper noted the recent death at Glengarry of Allan M'Donald, Esquire, and asserted that "This gentleman was the last survivor of a party of about three hundred Highland Emigrants whom he headed, and with whom he sailed from Greenock in the summer of 1784, for the Port of Quebec. After a passage of seventeen weeks they were driven by stress of weather into Philadelphia. Though distant from the place of their destination, and assailed by offers which were sufficiently advantageous to induce them to settle in the United States, Mr. M'Donald's influence over them so prevailed that not an individual remained behind, or departed from his Allegiance. After great privations, and at a considerable expense, the party settled in Glengarry, where their numerous posterity are now enjoying the fruits of his persevering Loyalty, and in the midst of whom Mr. M'Donald was in the Commission of the Peace for thirty years enjoying to the last moment, the affection, the respect, and the confidence of all around him."

Further light is thrown on this matter by a petition of 9 December 1835. Dating his petition at Alexandria, Angus McDonell, Lieutenant of the late Glengarry Fencibles, announced that he was the son of Allan MacDonald of the article in the *Upper Canada Gazette*, and that the article had been written by Bishop Macdonell. The fact that the father's name was given as M'Donald and the son's as McDonell we may regard as of no importance; newspapers of this time treated the two names as interchangeable. In the petition, Angus laments the destruction of his stone house in a fire and his family and financial misfortunes, and asks to be assisted with government grants of land, which he believes to be due to him on account of the services of his father and himself. In submitting a copy of the *Upper Canada Gazette* article and retelling the story of his father in his petition, Angus corrects the date of the expedition to 1785. He adds the detail that the ship arrived in Philadelphia in January, which if his dates are correct would put the arrival of the settlers in Glengarry in 1786 at the earliest.

What is the true story of the two ships and their relationship to each other? A search of the Philadelphia press for this period has thrown no light on the problem. Unfortunately, we do not even know the name of the ship which is said to have gone to Philadelphia. It does not seem unreasonable to suppose that there were indeed two groups of settlers arriving in Glengarry about 1786, but we need not decide whether they set out together, nor need we decide which reached Glengarry first — the settlers who came on the MacDonald or the settlers who came by way of Philadelphia.

At any rate, the new accessions had created a sufficiently large Scottish bloc on the upper St. Lawrence to serve as a powerful magnet for other arriving Scots. We learn that in the later months of 1790 a ship called the British Queen arrived in Quebec with twenty families, "amounting to Ninety souls" from the Scottish Highlands. They were necessitated to leave their own country by the oppression of their landlords, and arrived in distressed condition, and some or all of them needed aid if they were to escape starvation the following winter. Their wish was "to go up above Montreal where many of their Country men, who arrived here Passengers four years ago, are already settled. And are willing to establish themselves on the Lands of the Crown on the same terms and considerations on which Lands were granted to their Country men before mentioned." They were also being tempted to settle in the District of Montreal and perhaps did so; there seems no evidence that they reached Glengarry, at least as a body. The provincial government, irritated by this appearance of Highland poverty on its doorstep, and disturbed by reports that another shipload of Highlanders was on its way, ordered an investigation into immigration.

Alexander Macdonell (Greenfield) is said to have brought a number of settlers to Glengarry in 1792.

In 1794 a group of MacLeods, MacGillivrays, and others from the Highlands of Scotland arrived in what is now Lochiel Township. They are usually considered to have been the first settlers of this township. More than forty years later, one of their number, Alexander McLeod, of the 6th Concession of Lochiel, presented a petition to the Lieutenant Governor of Upper Canada asking to be rewarded for having organized the emigration of these settlers and outlining their history. He reported that he had gathered 150 settlers from Glenelg, Glenmorriston, Strathglass, and Knoydart, and that the ship he had chartered for them set sail on 15 June 1793. The emigrants had got nearly half way across the Atlantic when they were forced to return to Scotland by storm damage to their ship; the next vessel in which they set sail was also forced to return to Scotland by storm damage. The consequence of these misfortunes was that the migrants arrived in the New World so late in the fall that they were unable to continue up the St. Lawrence to Quebec and had to spend the winter in Prince Edward Island. In 1794 they continued their journey and began their new life in Glengarry where they received grants of 200 acres of land for each family.

The year 1802 also saw the arrival of a number of Highland emigrants in Glengarry. We find the arrival of several shiploads of Highlanders described in the **Quebec Gazette** of that year. The ship Neptune, nine weeks out from Loch Nevis, carried as "Passengers 600 Highlanders men, women and children." Many of them presumably were destitute, as a public subscription had to be taken up for them immediately upon their arrival. The ship Jane and the brig Albion, both eight weeks out from Fort William, carried respectively 250 and 167 Highlanders. The ship Eagle, two and a half months out from Greenock, had 21 men, women, and children, and the brig Friends, which had sailed a week later from Fort William had 136; it is not specified that these were Highlanders, but it may be guessed from the points of origin that they were.

Among these settlers, perhaps in the above named ships

from Fort William, was a group of emigrants organized by two cousins, Archibald and Alan MacMillan. The customs officials at Fort William had written to their superiors in May, drawing their attention to the plans of these MacMillans "to carry 400 or upwards, of this country People to the Province of Canada." Some of the MacMillans who came with Archibald and Alan settled in Lochiel Township; others helped to open the new Township of Finch in Stormont County and others sought their fortunes elsewhere in Ontario and Quebec.

There is also a tradition that two or three immigrant ships which arrived in Canada in 1802 brought the discharged soldiers of a Highland regiment, the 1st Glengarry Fencibles, and that these settled in Glengarry as a group. Our investigation of whether this tradition is based on fact brings us at the outset to the consideration of the man who was to be one of the best known Glengarrians, and best known Canadians, of the nineteenth century—Father (later Bishop) Alexander Macdonell, the organizer of the Glengarry Fencibles.

Father Alexander Macdonell was born in 1762 in Invernesshire, Scotland. After an education in Scotland, France, and Spain, he was ordained to the priesthood in 1787. While serving as a missionary priest in the Scottish Highlands, he was a spectator of the misery caused to the simple folk of the Highlands by the policy of the "clearances," by which the landlords expelled their tenants to free the land for sheep farming. Seeking a solution to this problem, he arranged to have a body of the dispossessed Highlanders come to Glasgow to work in the mills of the early industrial revolution. In this move there was much danger; the Highlanders in question were Roman Catholics, and their religion was unpopular and even—though the laws were not strictly enforced—against the law. They had the further disadvantage of being ignorant of the English language. In the face of these disadvantages, but with the aid of the tactful management of Father Macdonell, the Highlanders did well in Glasgow till they were thrown out of work in the economic upheavals which followed the beginning of war with France in 1793.

Their pastor next arranged to have the men of this group form a fencible regiment, roughly the equivalent of modern militia, of which he became the chaplain. The Glengarry Fencibles, or the 1st Glengarry Fencibles as we should call them to distinguish them from the Glengarry Fencibles later raised in Canada, served first in Guernsey, and afterwards fought as part of the British government's forces in the Irish Rebellion of 1798. They were unusual in being a Roman Catholic corps at a time when the British army was, officially, wholly Protestant. When the war between Britain and Napoleonic France ended in 1802 with the short-lived Peace of Amiens the Glengarry Fencibles were disbanded, and their chaplain again turned his thoughts to making provision for their livelihood. This time the solution he found was immigration. The military services of the Fencibles entitled them to the favour of the government, but the authorities preferred that the favour be given in the form of assisting their settlement in Trinidad; Father Macdonell and the men, however, favoured emigration to Upper Canada, where they already had friends and relatives. Bowing to the demand, Lord Hobart, the Secretary of State, wrote to the Lieutenant Governor of Upper Canada on 1 March 1803, stating that "A Body of Highlanders mostly Macdonnels and partly disbanded soldiers of the late Glengarry Fencible Regiment with their families and connections" were on the point of migrating to Upper Canada, that they would be accompanied by Father Macdonell, and that they were to be granted "in the usual manner a Tract of the unappropriated Crown Lands in any part of the Province where they may fix in the proportion of Twelve hundred acres to Mr. Macdonnel and Two hundred acres to every family he may introduce into the Colony."

It is one of the established beliefs of Canadian history that the Glengarry Fencibles came to Canada where they settled together in Glengarry County and received their allotments of land as promised in Lord Hobart's letter. Their role as one of the principal founding groups of Glengarry County is as firmly fixed in professional historical writing as it is in legend. The present authors must confess, however, that as they have sifted the evidence they have come at first to suspect and at last to believe that only one half, at most, of this belief is true. That the Glengarry Fencibles, or many of them at least, came to Canada can hardly be denied, but that more than a relatively small number of them settled in Glengarry seems most improbable.

What exactly happened after the Fencibles decided they wanted to emigrate to Canada is uncertain. It has been believed that they arrived in Canada in 1802, but Lord Hobart clearly implies in the above letter of 1 March 1803 that at this time they were still in Britain. A little more than a year later, on 7 April 1804, he again wrote to the Lieutenant Governor about the Fencibles, stating that "Circumstances" had prevented them "from carrying into execution the resolution communicated to you in my letter of the 1st March, 1803, of proceeding in a Body to Canada." By saying that they had abandoned the idea of going in a body to Canada, it will be noted that he did not assert that they had abandoned the idea of emigrating to Canada, or even deny that they may already have reached Canada. From certain accounts of their emigration which may have been based on Father Macdonell's own recollections, we learn that they arrived in Canada in 1803 and in the same year as himself, 1804. We may further date their emigration from certain remarks of Father Macdonell's. About this time, the Scottish landlords promoted a bill to restrict emigration, which became effective on 1 July 1803. Father Macdonell says that "Fortunately, however, for the disbanded soldiers of the Glengarry Fencibles, the greater part of them had got away before the bill came into operation." As late as 20 June 1804, however, when Lieutenant General Hunter replied to Hobart's letter of 7 April, Hunter appeared quite unaware that any of them were within his territory. Instead, he remarked with regret that "I should... have been very glad to have seen the disbanded soldiers of the Glengarry Fencible Regiment settled in Upper Canada. That Regiment served some short time under my command in Ireland in 1798, when I found them to be a remarkably well behaved and well disposed set of people."

That some of the Glengarry Fencibles eventually ended up in Glengarry is certain. There are in existence the names of 16 or 17 men of the regiment who were in Glengarry in the 1820's and later, but these were (with one probable exception) all men who had still not received the 200 acres of land to which they were entitled — not men who had been given land in Glengarry at the time of or shortly after their arrival in Canada. It was, in any case, inevitable that some of the Glengarry Fencibles, wherever they settled in Canada, should eventually make their way to such a mecca for Scotsmen as the Canadian Glengarry had become. Possibly these men who had not received their land grants were living with relatives. Two of them were eventually assigned land in Durham County and one was assigned land in Simcoe County. Why these men did not receive their land grants earlier is probably explained in a plea of Father Macdonell's in 1817. Writing to Earl Bathurst, he reported that "There are about twenty of those of the reduced soldiers of the 1st Glengarry Fencible Regt., who followed me to Canada that never received lands from Government, because too poor at the time to pay the Patent fees," and he asked that the fees be waived for them.

Our further reasons for supposing that the Glengarry Fencibles did not settle as a group in the Canadian Glengarry, and that those who did permanently settle there did not amount to a large number, are these. 1. While the Loyalists and the other emigrant groups of 1786, 1794, and 1815 stand out prominently in the records of the early settlement of Glengarry and their descendants can be found in innumerable Glengarrian families of the present, the 1st Glengarry Fencibles, if they really settled in Glengarry, left surprisingly little trace in the records and have left unaccountably few, and perhaps no descendants in Glengarry. It is hard to see how this contrast could ever have come about if the Fencibles had settled in Glengarry in the large numbers sometimes alleged. 2. Bishop Alexander Macdonell often spoke of the Glengarry Fencibles he brought to Upper Canada, but we are not aware of any statement in which he claimed that he brought them to Glengarry. 3. The emigration of 1786 to Glengarry is easily confused with the emigration of the Glengarry Fencibles to Upper Canada less than twenty years later, especially as both groups of emigrants were headed by a priest called Alexander Macdonell.

In this connection, it is important to notice one of the earliest and most circumstantial of the reports that the Glengarry Fencibles settled in Glengarry, Canada. In 1887 John McLennan "by the Lake," a man of intellectual interests, and recently M.P. for Glengarry, published an essay on the early history of the county. In this he stated that "In 1802 three vessels came from Fort William to Quebec, emigrant laden. Among them were the disbanded soldiers of the Glengarry Fencibles...They were granted free land, and were accompanied by their chaplain, the Reverend Alexander McDonell, afterwards Bishop of Kingston...His influence over the men who were his clansmen as well as his flock was deservedly great. They formed a compact colony in the centre of the country (i.e., county?) and built the fine church of St. Raphaels. The object of the Bishop was good and patriotic, but it is probable that the people would have advanced more rapidly if scattered among other settlers. Time, however, has made good farmers of many of their descendants."

McLennan is a most respectable authority because of his known abilities, his opportunities to gather information, and the fact that when he wrote a few people who came over with the Fencibles as children must still have been alive. However, the value of McLennan's great authority seems, in this matter, to be dashed to nothing by a curious omission in his essay. In a fairly detailed account of the early settlement of the county, he simply omits all mention of the huge 1786 emigration group or groups. Presumably in his mind he merged the 1786 emigration with the 1803-1804 emigration, and the settlement of St. Raphaels which he describes should properly have been the settlement of 1786. J.F. Pringle, writing a few years later, seems unwilling to reject the weighty authority of McLennan, and equally unable to accept it. He reaches a compromise in a statement strangely confused for a writer ordinarily so lucid and thoughtful. *"Several of them,"* he says of the Glengarry Fencibles, "settled about St. Raphaels, where they built the large stone church, that still remains a monument to their industry and zeal." (our italics) J.G. Harkness' principal allusions to the 1803-1804 settlement again seem to be based mostly on McLennan, and he seems to have no independent knowledge of the Bishop's settlers. And of numerous other writers who have spoken of the settlement of the Bishop's followers in Glengarry, none, so far as we know, has ever cited a single piece of valid evidence in favour of his claim.

Let us get an idea of what Glengarry County looked like in the year we have now reached, 1804. At this date, the eastern half of the county was still occupied by the undivided Township of Lancaster, which stretched from the St. Lawrence in the south to the border of Prescott County in the north. In the western half of the county, Indian Lands and the Townships of Charlottenburgh and Kenyon occupied the same positions as today. In Indian Lands, the crown was not granting land to settlers. Elsewhere in the county, there was also land which was not available to claimants, namely the Clergy Reserves and the Crown Reserves. The Clergy Reserves had been established by the Constitutional Act of 1791 to provide financial support for a "Protestant clergy." The disposal of these lands, and even the meaning of the phrase "Protestant clergy," were to be bitterly fought over in Upper Canada for many a year. The Crown Reserves had been established by the British government the year after the passing of the Constitutional Act. Their purpose was to provide a fund for the support of the colonial government.

The rule followed in establishing the Clergy and Crown Reserves was that in every township one-seventh of the land was to be Clergy Reserves and one-seventh of the land was to be Crown Reserves. These reserves were to be, as nearly as possible, distributed evenly throughout the township. In Glengarry, however, presumably because settlement was so well advanced before the system of reserves was established, nothing like the intended pattern of distribution was achieved.

Charlottenburgh and what is now Lancaster Township had a small quantity of Clergy Reserves, and the 9th of Lancaster had a few Crown Reserves, but most of the reserves were squeezed into the north and north-east of the county. The whole of the 9th concession of Kenyon and more than half of the 8th concession were Clergy Reserve land; there were other Clergy Reserves as well in Kenyon, but no Crown Reserves. What is now Lochiel Township contained all the Crown Reserves of the county, except for those in the 9th of Lancaster, and a good deal of Clergy Reserve land as well; altogether, about 40 per cent of Lochiel was tied up in these reserves, and in some parts of the township Clergy and Crown Reserves alternated in checkerboard fashion. Though not at first available for purchase, the reserves were open for leasing, and they were attractive to squatters; thus in one way or another they often had occupants.

It is an important question for our purposes how much of the land of Glengarry was occupied by settlers. It would appear that by this time there was settlement throughout practically the whole of the county, though more land was claimed or patented than was actually under occupation by settlers. The reader who will turn to Appendix I of this volume will find there a detailed chart showing concession by concession the number of lots of land claimed or patented, occupied by Crown or Clergy Reserves, or apparently without claimants, as of 13 May 1801.

It appears from these figures that the flow of settlement or at least of claims and proprietorship in Glengarry proceeded quickly north from the Loyalist settlements on the Raisin River in Charlottenburgh into Kenyon and into what is now Lochiel Township, and more slowly into what is now Lancaster Township. The relative unattractiveness of the latter township to settlers is easily explained by the swamps of that area; in 1784 Sir John Johnson questioned how much the Lake Township would be worth cultivating. The relative attractiveness of the western half of the county to claimants and settlers doubtless explains why the original Township of Charlottenburgh was divided in two at the early date of 1798 to create the new Township of Kenyon in the north, while the original Township of Lancaster remained undivided until an act of Parliament in 1818 cut off the northern part to create the new Township of Lochiel.

From the foregoing survey of the first twenty-one years of Glengarry (1784-1804) it will be evident that much of the history of the earliest settlement is far from clear. It is indeed sobering to a historian to reflect how little is really known about Glengarry and the Glengarrians of that time. Those days are only two long lifetimes away, and already even the commonest details, which were once known to thousands of people, have been irrecoverably lost.

It is not known, for example, what were the motives of most of the settlers for leaving Scotland. There have been studies, of course, of why people left Scotland at this time (the clearances, etc.), but the reasons why people in general left Scotland do not tell us, of course, why these people in particular left. A few traditions about the reasons have come down in a few families in Glengarry; nothing more. When we do not even know the numbers which arrived, it is especially in vain to speculate on their reasons for going, but we may suppose, from several clues, that one powerful motive for migration was that others of the same family and neighbourhood were doing so. Considering how greatly Glengarrians of later generations valued kinship ties, we can guess that it must have been difficult for a Scot of the time to live on that side of the Atlantic which the majority of his relatives had deserted.

Nor do we know what clothes the settlers wore at the time of their arrival, or what clothes they wore for workaday purposes. Most likely the Highland "national dress" worn by a group of "the principal inhabitants" of Glengarry who greeted Mrs. Simcoe in 1792 was only the ceremonial dress worn by the elite on a few special occasions such as this. Presumably the average settler never wore kilts, and presumably Cyrus Cuneo's well known painting of the kilted Glengarry Highlander guiding the plow is merely in error. For church-going, good suits of English cloth of a kind which would not have seemed out of place in an American city were probably standard for men, at least towards the end of this period, and women probably wore equally conventional and respectable dresses of good purchased material.

As to food, potatoes seem to have been prominent; at this time the Highlands of Scotland had come, like Ireland, to rely heavily on the potato. At St. Raphaels at least, corn meal was much used. Porridge may not have been common; when young James Begg came to Glengarry in 1827 he discovered that "there was no oatmeal in Canada then." From the streams and the forest, fish and game should have been readily available, but were they used? Tradition would suggest that these were not sources from which the early Glengarrians readily sought their foodstuffs, and in the last few generations at least — those within living memory — the Glengarrians have been to an extent perhaps unusual among Canadians not a fishing or hunting people.

For the nature of the countryside which the settlers found when they arrived in Glengarry, we have also only poor evidence. The uncertain voices of tradition seem unanimous, however, in reporting that the county was densely covered with forest. It is very probable that a little wood-cutting had taken place along the Front and the Raisin before the arrival of the Loyalists. The occasional settler was doubtless happy to find a natural clearing on his lot; the Reverend William McKillican a little later found that his land had "a fair meadow, bearing heavy crops of wild hay," where beavers had killed trees by flooding. Possibly here and there, especially as settlement progressed, the settler found that fire had cleared the forest from his land. From our knowledge of the relatively domesticated Glengarry woodlots of a later date, we are hardly able to guess what it was like to walk through the primeval forest of those days. Was there dense underbrush? Or none? Was the forest floor a tangled mass of fallen tree trunks — or did recurrent fires set by lightning or the swift processes of decay keep the forest floor clean? But even at its best, the forest must have been intimidating to people who came, as these did, from the treeless Highlands. And everywhere there were swamps to impede settlement — swamps which sometimes turned out to be excellent land when they were drained. Slowly, as the years passed, the very appearance of the land changed; fields replaced forest; swamps receded; high dry hills which because of their dryness attracted the first efforts at cultivation proved when stripped of their forest cover to be unexpectedly stony; streams shrank; and with the retreat of the forest the pioneers' eyes measured for the first time the contours of the hills and the valleys, the flats and the streams of their newly acquired land. From this land there issued every spring almost intolerable clouds of mosquitoes; the surveyors who abandoned the attempt to survey Finch Township in 1815 cited as one of their reasons the mosquitoes. Whether this plague of mosquitoes got better or worse as clearing progressed we can hardly now determine. In the summer and fall, the air must have been dark with smoke from the fires used in land clearing; in the autumn there was the glory of the autumn leaves for those who cared for such spectacles; and finally, for months on end, there were the long, savage winters of Glengarry for which settlers from the relatively temperate Highlands must have been in every way unprepared.

As a searchlight into the darkness of this period, we do fortunately have an excellent traveller's account — that of Lord Selkirk, who visited Glengarry in January 1804. Summarizing the history of the settlement, he mentions the Loyalists, the settlers of 1786 and of "1791 or 92", and the newly arrived emigrants of 1802, though he seems to assume that most of these latter were only residing in Glengarry till they could take up their intended lands in Finch Township. Though some of the Glengarry Fencibles are said to have arrived in Canada as early as 1803, it is noteworthy that he does not mention the existence of any of them in Glengarry. He reports that in Glengarry the "successive recruits have taken up and settled most of 18 concessions, as far as the 10th or 12th — settled almost every lot, behind not so close, as the loyalists at first had only 100 acres on the front, and afterwards received additional lots..." Part of the front, however, was not at first occupied, "being reputed uninhabitable from Swamps." Writing in a series of jottings appropriate to a diary, he says that "Mr. B. [Rev. John Bethune, of Williamstown] etc. reckon 30 or 40 acres the common run of clearing on an old settled lot—from 50 to 100 bushels of Wheat annually sold—with 3 or 4 fat hogs—a good deal of Butter & or Maple Sugar—they have generally 3 or 4 Cows—always a pair of horses & generally Oxen also. —They also raise 150 or 200 bushels of Potatoes usually on new cleared land—also some Pease and Oats for home consumption—no barley—The Beef raised is consumed in the Settlement. —The Pork is bought at Montreal for the North West Trade—formerly there was no other supply & they got 5d or 6d per lb. —of late the competition from Vermont has brought it down to 2d or 4d— Butter sells at 8d Wheat costs ¼s. per bushel to carry to Montreal on Slays. —

"Mr. Bethune speaks of the Settlers in Glengarry as labourious and economical—sending to market many articles which the English Settlers consume—they use less flesh meat, & less bread, more Potatoes, garden vegetables, milk etc.— The old Settlers do not equal the Americans, but the young men who have come over children are as expert as any at the axe—They all he thinks are more assiduous at work than the Amns. [Americans] & allow themselves less indulgence—yet from the want of habit they have not got thro' the work that might have been done—perhaps in part from their living all together which has given them less opportunity of learning soon the modes of carrying on work, adapted to the country."

He found that the older settlers lacked frame houses, but had good houses of square logs, with chimneys and stoves and a garret or half second story, and that their "original log house, of a much poorer appearance, is generally remaining at a short distance."

While settlers elsewhere in Glengarry were becoming owners of their lands, those who had settled in the Indian

Lands strip or corridor on the western fringe of Glengarry had to become tenants — or squatters. How had this come about?

The story of how Indian Lands was established takes us back to several years before the naming of Glengarry County. In March of 1784, when the Canadian authorities were planning the events of the busy summer ahead, in which the Loyalists were to be settled in their new homes, an unexpected and annoying difficulty arose. The Indians of St. Regis informed Sir John Johnson that they considered themselves the owners of a wide tract of land on the north shore of the St. Lawrence, extending from the River au Raisin (i.e., from the present site of South Lancaster) "to a Creek a little above the Long Sault." This news was most unwelcome to Johnson, for this tract included land on which he intended to settle some of his Loyalist followers and found his new town of New Johnstown, now Cornwall. The Indians alleged that they had once had papers or a deed for this tract, but that these had been destroyed in a fire. Johnson's immediate opinion was that the claim was worthless, but it was obviously one which had to be taken seriously. General Haldimand, on being informed of the difficulty, had the records of the province searched, and concluded that no such grant had ever been made to the Indians. Nevertheless, he decided that for a number of good reasons, including the fact that the Indians had been accustomed to consider these lands as their own, they should be treated with consideration. The Indians, too, proved ready for compromise, and by May at the latest an agreement had been reached by which the original wide strip they demanded had been reduced to about the present width of Indian Lands. Presumably about the same time the length of the strip was also established — about 25 miles. The final agreement was made with the Indians by a Colonel Campbell, Sir John Johnson having withdrawn from the negotiations for fear they would injure his standing with the Indians.

The government intended at this time to give the Indians a formal grant for this strip, but no deed ever seems to have been issued. In 1798 the Indians asked to be given copies of the documents by which they held the Indian Lands strip. In 1815, when the subject was again under discussion, Sir John Johnson stated that as far as he knew, no deed had been issued for them. In 1816, when the government investigated the question of who owned Indian Lands, it concluded "that the Land Reserved for the use of the St. Regis Indians, between Cornwall and Charlottenburgh, never did belong to them, but was Reserved from Settlement for their use as Hunting Ground."

There appear to have been no Indians living in Glengarry at the time of arrival of the white settlers, and the Indians of St. Regis, who were, in any case, not very numerous, were not interested in living on their Indian Lands strip. They also found the strip unsuitable for hunting, or superfluous to their hunting needs. The land being otherwise idle, they turned to leasing it to incoming white settlers. In a schedule of rents and arrears of the year 1812, we find tenants officially listed for locations as far north as the 15th concession—which lies about two miles south of the present-day village of Maxville. The compilers of the list were doubtful, however, that there had actually been any cultivation by the tenants listed for the 14th concession, so perhaps the 14th and 15th were where settlement was just beginning. There is a petition of 1821 from the tenants of concessions 14 to 21; 21 is the northernmost concession of Indian lands, so by that date settlement had rolled through all the concessions of this narrow corridor.

We have a valuable glimpse of the state of Indian Lands in the year 1815. The Reverend John Bethune, Father Joseph Marcoux, Neil McLean, and an Alexander McDonell, probably the future bishop, presented to the government the results of their examination of Indian Lands and its settlers from concessions 4 to 14. They found that with few exceptions the tenants had tickets of occupation or leases, which the members of the examining committee seemed to consider as practically identical in effect. Leases were for 99 years, and were renewable to 999 years. Each lot consisted of 90 acres and was to pay a yearly rent of 1½ bushels of wheat and five shillings cash. The Indians were defrauded in the collection of these rents both by their own number and by agents. The examining committee also reported that an error by Patrick McNiff in making the original survey of a part of the western boundary of Indian Lands had shorn off a portion of the tract and given it to Stormont County; on some pretext, Charlottenburgh also got a section of the land.

In 1809, Indian Lands was resurveyed by Jeremiah McCarthy. By this time, it had acquired the name of Nutfield by which it was to be called for the next generation or a little more.

St. Raphaels church from north of King's Road before road was gravelled (c. 1910).

# Chapter II
# Bishop Macdonell's Glengarry

In the fall of 1804 there arrived in Canada Father Alexander Macdonell, the chaplain of the Glengarry Fencibles—a man who impressed himself more vividly than anyone else has ever done on the imagination of the Glengarrians. His name-sake, the first Father Alexander Macdonell of St. Raphaels, had died the year before. As the chaplain of the Glengarry Fencibles journeyed to York in late October to present himself to Lieutenant Governor Hunter, he carried with him a letter in which the Bishop of Quebec stated that an Irish priest had just been assigned to the Scots Catholics of Glengarry. This was a Father Fitzsimmons, whose stay at St. Raphaels was to be short, as he was succeeded in 1805 by Father Macdonell. For the next quarter century, while Father Macdonell resided at St. Raphaels, that pioneer village had the best claim to be the centre of Roman Catholicism in Upper Canada. In 1819, Father Macdonell was appointed Bishop, but without an episcopal city in Canada. In 1826 this lack was supplied, when he became Bishop of Regiopolis (Kingston) or, as we usually say, Bishop of Upper Canada. The boundaries of his diocese were the same as those of Upper Canada. Tiny St. Raphaels enjoyed for some dozen years the honour of having a bishop, who was also by this time one of the best known men in the province, but about 1832 the bishop moved to York and a few years later to Kingston, where he made his permanent residence.

Though on intimate terms with the English rulers of the province, Bishop Macdonell was a Highland Scotsman through and through, and was always particularly concerned with the prosperity of his fellow Highlanders in Canada. He was proud of the work he had done in diverting the flow of migrating Scots Catholics from the United States to Canada, and he noted in 1817 that thousands of Scots Presbyterians and innumerable Irish Catholics who had gone to the United States in recent years "would have proved excellent subjects in the British Colonies." By modern standards, however, his ideas of the role the Highland Scots were to play in Upper Canada seem somewhat over-protective. In his early years at least in Canada, he had the idea of creating a massive Celtic Scots group in Eastern Ontario—almost a nation within the colonies of British North America.

The Rt. Hon. and Rt. Rev. Alexander Macdonell (1762-1840), first Roman Catholic Bishop of Upper Canada. No one looms larger in both the folklore and history of Glengarry than this man.

In a letter of 1806, he noted that the most extensive settlement of Highland Catholics in the province was that of Glengarry, Stormont, and Prescott, where the population already exceeded 10,000 "and is growing in a wonderful manner both by the uncommon increase of its own population and by the annual addition of emigrants from Scotland." But to keep the Highlanders pure from the ideas of American republicanism, they should, he went on to argue, be kept distinct from other settlers. This could be all the more easily done because they had their own language. What was required from the government to achieve this end was to provide, for the Catholics at least, government financed pastors and school-masters. In the same letter he asserted that "all the grantable lands" in the Highland Settlement of the Eastern District (Stormont, Dundas, and Glengarry) had already been taken up, with the result that as young men came of age, they were forced to take up lands among American-born settlers and so absorbed republican ideas. As a remedy, he suggested that the Townships of Alfred, Clarence, and Plantagenet, in the Ottawa District, should be reserved "for the exclusive occupation of Highlanders." Obviously, Glengarry did not develop along these lines. Its destiny was to become, although very slowly, Canadian. But at the time Father Macdonell wrote, a sense of Canadian nationality among English Canadians was still far in the future. Probably few of the Glengarrians of his generation, unless they went to the United States and became Americans, ever regarded themselves as anything but Scottish Highlanders living abroad.

At St. Raphaels, Bishop Macdonell (as we may conveniently call him even when referring to a period before he actually became a bishop) was surrounded by his beloved Highlanders, but his field of activity, from the very beginning of his period in Canada, was immensely wider than this single parish. He was responsible for the spiritual welfare of Roman Catholics scattered throughout the whole of what was then Upper Canada — roughly that part of Ontario which now lies east of the Great Lakes. At the beginning of his ministry in Upper Canada, the only other two priests were the Irish Father Fitzsimmons, who left soon after, and a French Canadian at Windsor who knew no English. Towards the end of his career, Bishop Macdonell declared that for the first ten years, without assistance, he "had to travel over the country from Lake Superior to the province line in Lower Canada, in discharge of my pastoral functions, carrying the sacred vestments, sometimes on horseback, sometimes on my own back, and sometimes in Indian birch canoes, living with savages and without any other shelter or comfort but what their fires and their fares and the branches of trees afforded and crossing the Great Lakes and even descending the St. Lawrence in their dangerous crafts. Nor were the hardships and privations which I endured among the new settlers and emigrants less than what I had to encounter among the savages themselves in their miserable shanties, exposed on all sides to the weather and destitute of every comfort." From his arrival in Canada until 1832, he stated, he had seldom travelled less than 2000 miles a year. For his toil, he had a sure reward. As he wrote to one of his priests, "We must not expect... that missions will be founded by the followers of Christ without privations and difficulties and it is in struggling against those with courage and bearing them with patience that the greater part of our merit consists." There was also the wonder, the ever unfolding mystery of the little known land in which he found himself a traveller. Reviewing twenty-four years of his travels in the province, he remarked that "I have no hesitation in saying that very little more than the borders of some of the lakes and the courses of the principal rivers have been yet explored and the inexhaustible resources and capability of those interminable forests remain yet to be discovered." To aid him, his scattered flocks could contribute little, but he received a salary from the government, various grants of land, and sums of state money for church building.

He wrote modestly that his own role had been "to lay the foundation of religion in these vast regions and leave to others the satisfaction of raising the superstructure." But as his life neared its end, much had been achieved: by 1839 the province had 35 priests, and 48 churches in progress or completed had succeeded to the two wooden and one stone church he had found in the province on his arrival in 1804.

The building which the "Big Bishop" (Fr. Alexander Macdonell, first Bishop of Upper Canada) built for a convent at St. Raphaels but which was never actually used as such. It still stands but not on its original site, which was east of the stone church.

At St. Raphaels an impressive stone church arose to replace the wooden church (remembered as the Blue Chapel, from its blue ceiling) which had been constructed by the settlers of 1786. Destroyed by fire in 1970, the Bishop's church survives today as a stone shell — one of the few North American equivalents of the monastic ruins which fascinate travellers to Britain. The building is said in two early biographies of the bishop to have been constructed in expectation of the arrival from England of a priest from a wealthy and distinguished family, the Reverend Thomas Weld, who in 1826 was consecrated Bishop and coadjutor to Bishop Macdonell. However, there is obviously an error here; Thomas Weld was not ordained to the priesthood till 1821, and the stone church at St. Raphaels was begun by 1819 or earlier. In the end, Bishop Weld never did come to Canada to join Bishop Macdonell, though it is said that he continued to plan to do so even after he was raised to the rank of cardinal in 1830.

Stone Church at St. Raphaels, built by the parishioners under the leadership of their priest Fr. Alexander Macdonell, first Bishop of Upper Canada.

In 1822 Bishop Macdonell had the pleasure of being able to report that "the walls of our church are within a few feet of their height and the roof very nearly finished and ready to be put on." In 1826 the church was opened for services. Bishop Macdonell contributed more than £3600 of his own money to its construction, and at one stage he had assumed personal responsibility for the parishioners' debt of over £3000 for the church. Collecting the money for the new church proved difficult and it was perhaps for this reason that the Bishop in 1832 spoke unhappily about the injustice and ingratitude of the Catholics of Glengarry towards him. If he read the letter of reproach which his contemporary and friend the Rev. John Bethune, the Presbyterian minister of Williamstown, addressed to his Presbyterian flock a few days before his death in 1815, he may have reflected that the Roman Catholic and Protestant Scots of Glengarry were alike a troublesome folk to their pastors. At St. Raphaels the Bishop also erected a good stone presbytery, and a seminary for the training of priests which also doubled as a boys' school.

Within view from St. Raphaels and from much of the southern one third of Glengarry County are the Adirondack Mountains of New York State.So near at hand and so much a presence in the county is the territory of the republic from which the Loyalists fled, and to which such great numbers of Glengarrians were later to emigrate. From the beginning of the Glengarry settlement, there was trade with the United States across Lake St. Francis, and we may be sure that before long the American pedlars who were a familiar sight in most parts of backwoods Canada were also bringing welcome supplies of news and of small household items to pioneer families buried in even the deepest recesses of the Glengarry bush. Except to a few aging Loyalists and their children, the Americans cannot have been objects of either fear or revulsion. Nevertheless, in the years 1812-1814, the people of Upper Canada, and the Glengarrians among them, found themselves at war with the United States.

The war with the United States was a development of the long war between Britain and Napoleonic France. The British were determined to prevent the Americans from aiding the French with their commerce, and the Americans resented British interference with their trade and impressment (for service in the navy) of men from American ships. The more truculent Americans were pleased with the prospect of a war with Britain because, they reasoned, the large but weakly defended British North American colonies would readily fall into their possession. American valor, it was thought, would be seconded by a widespread eagerness among the settlers to shake off the British yoke. In fact, in some areas where American-born settlers who had come in after the Loyalists were numerous, there was disaffection enough to cause the colonial authorities in Canada much anxiety, but the bulk of the population either supported the British cause or took refuge in neutrality. On the American side, the wealth and men put into the struggle bore only a poor proportion to the ready resources which even at that stage in its history the United States possessed.

On the Canadian or British side, the core of the defence force was the regular British troops stationed in Canada, but these were vigorously seconded by Canadian soldiers, including those from Glengarry. The Glengarrians who fought in this war belonged to one of two distinct kinds of troops, which must be clearly distinguished: the Glengarry Militia, and the Glengarry Light Infantry Fencibles. Throughout Upper Canada, males between the ages of 16 and 60 were required to enrol in the citizen army, called the Militia, but received little training. The Glengarry Militia did good service in several operations in the war, but inevitably it was a body which could not be expected to do the work of regular troops. The Glengarry Light Infantry Fencibles, or 2nd Glengarry Fencibles as they are also called, were recruited in 1812, and were given proper training and put on the regular British Army establishment. Father Macdonell was active in recruiting them, and their name echoes that of the Fencibles he had formed in Scotland. When the earliest proposals to raise this new corps had been made back in 1807, they were projected as a corps of Glengarry Highlanders, but in the end General Prevost seems to have been correct in saying of them that ''not a sufficient portion had been raised in Glengarry to give the Corps claim to bear that name.'' But however that may be, they gave glory to the Glengarry name while they served with courage and success through many engagements, including Ogdensburg, Chateauguay, and Lundy's Lane. After the war, there were hopes that the Glengarry Fencibles would be continued as a regular regiment of the British Army, but they were dissolved in 1816.

Father Macdonell was a passionate upholder of the British cause during the war, and one of the most prominent officers in the war was also intimately associated with Glengarry. Lt. Col. John Macdonell (Greenfield) came to Canada in 1792 with his father Alexander Macdonell (Greenfield) and grew up in Glengarry. He was aide-de-camp to General Brock, with whom he was killed at the Battle of Queenston Heights in 1812. At the time of his death he was Attorney-General of the province and Member of the Legislative Assembly for Glengarry.

The impact of the war on the lives of the ordinary people in Glengarry is a subject which remains and probably must always remain obscure. It may be speculated, though not with the strongest confidence, that the failure of any tradition of upheaval, distress, or widespread loss of life to come down to us is evidence that the war had much less impact in Glengarry than either World War I or World War II. In 1813, when Cornwall was threatened by invading Americans, refugees with about 150 wagons loaded with government stores poured into Glengarry. They are said to have got as far as the River Delisle when the happy news of the victory at Crysler's Farm turned them homeward again. A pleasing old story says that the schoolchildren at Martintown were disturbed in their lessons by the thunder of guns at Crysler's Farm—or in another version, at Hoople's Creek. Apart from what may occasionally have happened on the Glengarry Islands in Lake St. Francis, no invading American soldier ever stood on Glengarry soil. We get some glimpses of the non-combattant military services provided by the Glengarrians. When the Reverend John Bethune and the other commissioners mentioned in Chapter I were making their examination of Indian Lands, they found that in the most southerly concessions of the Indian Lands tract during the winter "the transport of Public Stores and Provisions hardly left a Man at home until [the] intelligence of Peace rendered their services no longer necessary."

Once the war was over, the British government set in motion an imaginative scheme of emigration which is usually remembered as the especial project of Lord Bathurst, Secretary of State for War and the Colonies. The experience of the war had shown that the loyalty of many of the Americans who had settled in Upper Canada could not be depended upon. The need for additional loyal subjects in the thinly populated province with its long frontier so dangerously exposed to the United States was pressing — why, therefore, not bring them in from Britain? The British government accordingly formed a plan by which a select group of emigrants was to be given free passage to Canada in the transport ships which would — conveniently — be going to Canada in any case in 1815 to bring back soldiers from the recent war.

Prospective emigrants were invited by proclamation of February 1815 to come forward and take advantage of this scheme. It was required that every male aged above 16 was at the time of departure to deposit £16 in the hands of government agents; for wives the deposit was two guineas, and children under 16 were to travel free. These sums were to be refunded two years later in Canada, provided that the travellers had shown their good faith by settling on their land. The purpose of the deposits was to prevent unscrupulous persons from using the scheme merely to get free passage to the United States. After arriving in Canada, each family of settlers was to be given one hundred acres of land; their male children, on reaching the age of 21, were each to get a similar grant. For the first six or eight months, rations were to be supplied to the settlers. Applicants were to supply evidence of good character. At a later stage, undischarged bankrupts and persons known to have been defrauding the revenue by illicit distilling were expressly barred from sharing in the scheme.

The £16 deposit was a considerable amount of money at this time, and must have ensured that most prospective emigrants from the poorest ranks of society were barred. We can probably picture the emigrants who assembled at Glasgow in the spring of 1815 as being, by the usual standards of nineteenth-century emigration to this continent, a relatively elite group in economic terms. With perhaps a few among them who were, or once had been, well to do, they must have been predominantly sober and industrious folk from the lower middle class and the upper ranks of the poor. It is probably indicative of their standing as an elite that when they were forced to wait idly at Glasgow for the ships assigned to them, a group of 140 petitioned the government for a schoolmaster to teach their children.

Departure was originally scheduled for April, but it was July and August before the four ships assigned to them — the Atlas, the Baltic Merchant, the Dorothy, and the Eliza — had sailed from Scotland. It was about the beginning of October before the ships had all reached Quebec. The emigrants, who had already consumed their money and tried their patience through long delays, saw themselves faced with further months of inactivity. It was now far too late in the season to begin their new farms in the new world. The authorities found themselves faced with the task of providing for these people during the long Canadian winter which was now approaching. Unmarried men from the group were given employment on the King's Works at Kingston. The other settlers were lodged at Brockville, Cornwall, and other points on the St. Lawrence, including River Raisin (South Lancaster Village) where some of them occupied a barracks.

Three locations had been assigned for the farms of the settlers; one was along the Rideau River and one at the head of the Bay of Quinte, but we need concern ourselves here only with the third, which was in Lochiel Township. The provisional Lieutenant Governor, F.P. Robinson, writing to Lord Bathurst in the summer of 1815, remarked that "The Lands in the vicinity of Glengarry in the Eastern District, I wish to reserve for the new settlers expected from Scotland. They will be more comfortable, and will prosper more rapidly, under the friendly assistance and Local Knowledge of their countrymen, than if dispersed over more distant parts of the country, and the Eastern District when fully located will be a powerful support to the Province in either Peace or War." This was a sound view of the interests and advantages of the Lochiel-bound settlers. They were not going into a completely inhospitable wilderness. There was already a well established settlement in

Lochiel, and neighbours could be depended upon to give a helping hand. The Township Papers in the Ontario Archives show that emigrants from all four of the Atlas, the Baltic Merchant, the Dorothy, and the Eliza settled in Lochiel Township. From the Township Papers and other sources, it can be shown that they settled in at least eight of the nine concessions of Lochiel. Our list of the settlers is far from complete, but in every instance known to us, they were settled on Crown Reserve lots. By this time probably there was little good, unclaimed land in Lochiel except in the Crown and Clergy Reserves. Among these settlers of 1815-1816 were the founders of Breadalbane. In a centenary history of the Breadalbane Baptist church, published in 1916, we are told that the founders travelled on the Dorothy, that they held religious services on ship-board in Gaelic, that they spent the winter of 1815-1816 "in the southern portion of the county, where some of the new-comers possessed friends who had settled there a number of years earlier," and that at the early date of August 1816 they, or some of them, organized the first Baptist Church in the Ottawa Valley.

About the same time, and probably in the same year, there settled in Lochiel discharged soldiers of the 2nd Glengarry Fencibles. These, again, appear to have been all settled on Crown Reserve lots. In May of 1816, a government depot of provisions and tools was in existence "in Lancaster." Whether Lancaster in this sense means the port town of Lancaster or the "long" township of Lancaster of which Lochiel was still part, is not specified. Wherever the location, it was doubtless intended to serve both the new arrivals from Scotland and the discharged soldiers. Some further surveying was still necessary at this late date, but by the middle of June Duncan McDonell, Deputy Surveyor, was able to report that despite such hardships as having to wade with his party through water, he had just finished the survey of the Crown Reserves in Lancaster (present Township of Lochiel).

Unfortunately for the new settlers, they had begun their farms at a most unpromising moment. And the old, established Glengarry settlers, who had made sacrifices during the last war, were faced with sacrifices still more painful. A period of several years of hardship was begun by a poor harvest in 1815, and 1816 was the notorious "Year without a Summer." The ensuing distress found voice in two Glengarry petitions of October 1816. One was from some of the settlers who had arrived from Scotland the previous year. Their crops of Indian corn and potatoes had been destroyed by the severe frosts of the summer and they asked for further aid in the form of government rations. The other petition was from Glengarrians of Lancaster Township who declared that they had never yet received government aid but needed it now in the form of a loan of flour, their crops of last year having been injured by the frost and this year being almost entirely ruined. In March of 1817, the provincial parliament considered a petition which had been sent from Glengarry to the Lieutenant Governor, and in which the petitioners spoke of "the horrible prospect of approaching starvation." They alleged "that no less than five hundred and fifty families within this County are sufferers, from the total failure of the crops, the greater part of whom have not at this moment provisions sufficient for the support of their families for one week," and that "the early frosts which have unfortunately destroyed the crops in many other parts of the Province have entirely ruined the crops of every kind in the back parts of this County." They asked for assistance in the form of a loan rather than an outright gift, but the assembly refused their request. Conditions were again disastrous in Glengarry in 1820, when Bishop Macdonell twice referred in letters of July of that year to members of his parish at St. Raphaels as "literally starving." He said that within the month he had had to give to distressed families flour, money, and credit to the value of £40 to 50. Upwards of 3,000 barrels of flour had already been bought this summer in the parish. These misfortunes had temporarily ended the ability of the parishioners to contribute to the financing of the new church at St. Raphaels.

Such conditions remind us how close to the subsistence level our Glengarry ancestors remained at this time. Life on

Glengarry farms in the 1930's and even the 1940's and 1950's of this century was often bleak enough, but it is inconceivable that a harvest failure then could possibly have pushed Glengarrians to the brink of starvation. But a Glengarry farm of 1815-1820 was mostly a unit to support a family with bread, meat, wool, etc.; there being little outlet for sale of surplus produce even in the best times, production was normally limited to the needs of one family rather than extended to meet the opportunities of a ready market, and every contraction meant immediate hardship without cash reserves to alleviate it.

This was not the first period of distress for Glengarrians, nor was it to be the last. The "Hungry Year" of 1788, which was caused by a partial failure of the crops in the preceding year and the cutting off of government aid to the Loyalists, was long remembered in Glengarry. There were crop failures in Glengarry in 1827 and 1828, and at this time or a little later were the "Dumpling Years" — so remembered, at least at St. Raphaels, because of the enforced reliance of the inhabitants on cornmeal dumplings. There appear to have been hard times again in 1841, and in the spring of 1855 D.A. Macdonald, the brother of John Sandfield Macdonald, wrote that "this is the hardest year I ever saw for the people of Glengarry." Again in the 1860's crop failure forced sufferers to rely on cornmeal.

It was in this unhappy post-war period that Alexandria, the principal town of the county, had its beginning when Bishop Macdonell took advantage of the convenient waterway of the Garry River to establish water-powered mills at that point. A statute of 1869 remembered the date as "about" 1818, but there is a receipt of 4 March 1817 for building a bridge "at the mill." The most remarkable previous fact about this locality, so far as is known, is that it was the site of one of the largest land grants given to an individual in Glengarry — the huge block of 2200 acres lying on the east side of what is now Main Street, Alexandria, bestowed on Captain John McDonell of the King's Royal Regiment of New York. There were, or had been recently, mills in the 1st concession of Lochiel just two miles from the Bishop's new mills; these are mentioned in a will of 1816. By 1823, the Bishop's mill site had accumulated a total of 12 buildings. The name Alexandria (from the Christian name of the Bishop) was in use by 1825; in this year, the village also had a postmaster. The village had an alternative name of Priest's Mills, or in Gaelic, Moulain an t' Saigart. Older Glengarrians can still remember the Gaelic name being used. In 1828 the Bishop spoke about insuring his grist and saw mills for £600, and specified their location at this time as being on lot 37, 2nd concession of Lochiel. At a later date the Alexandria mills were re-located on lot 38.

At the time when Alexandria was founded, there was no village anywhere in Glengarry north of it. In the more developed south, there were Lancaster Village (South Lancaster today), Martintown (founded about 1801), Williamstown, and St. Raphaels. Just outside the boundaries of the county was Cornwall, with a few hundred inhabitants. Settlers in the northern part of Glengarry found themselves drawn to L'Orignal, Hawkesbury, and Point Fortune along the Ottawa River, and to Vankleek Hill, which had been founded by a United Empire Loyalist a generation earlier.

In the lives of the Glengarrians at this time there was a great deal that to modern eyes would be rough and displeasing. We have from this period several accounts from visitors which give us some impression of the quality of life.

Lieutenant Governor Maitland reported sadly to Lord Bathurst in 1818 that he had visited the Glengarry settlement and was "disappointed...There is but little cleared, and the people are not so comfortably housed as I had in my imagination fancied they would be. They are very poor, and the Priest McDonell says there are great portions of uncleared lands the property of absentee individuals which is very injurious to the actual settlers. The people are of a good sort, but they brought neither funds nor notions of comfort from the Highlands." Perhaps the most noteworthy thing in this passage is that the good Governor *expected* something better; even at this early date, the legend of Glengarry was apparently beginning to stir.

The naturalist John Goldie, who passed through Glengarry a year later, contented himself with the less provocative statement that "the Inhabitants of Glengarry retain all the appearances & customs of the highlanders of Scotland."

One of our best early accounts of Glengarry is from John Howison, who visited Glengarry in 1818. He contrasted the "polished and interesting peasantry of Lower Canada" unfavourably with the "blunt and uncultivated inhabitants of Glengarry." "As our road lay through the settlement," he says,

I had an opportunity...of seeing it, and was rather disappointed, the improvements bearing no proportion to what I had anticipated. The majority of its inhabitants were indeed very poor when they commenced their labours, and had a variety of discouraging circumstances to contend with, the principal of which were, the peculiarities of the climate, the almost inaccessible situation of their farms, the badness of the roads, and the immense woods which encumbered the soil. They have, in some degree, surmounted the greater number of these difficulties; but still the settlement is not in a very flourishing state, and its inhabitants seem too unambitious to profit by the advantages of their condition. A very great majority of the houses are built of logs, and contain only one apartment; and the possessors display no inclination to improve their mode of life, being dirty, ignorant, and obstinate. Few of the settlers have more than sixty or seventy acres cleared, and the generality only thirty or forty; yet how many comforts, and even luxuries might persons of moderate industry derive from a domain of this extent!

While they were preparing breakfast, at the tavern at which I had stopped, I strolled out for amusement. Diminutive log-houses, surrounded with a few acres of cleared land, presented themselves in various directions; and the feeble vestiges of civilization which these objects exhibited, seem to be derided by the clumps of immense oaks that everywhere waved their colossal boughs, as if threatening destruction to all below. A profusion of decayed and half-burnt timber lay around; and the serpentine roots of trees blown down by tempests stretched into the air in the most fantastic forms. In different places, piles of blazing timber sent forth columns of smoke, which enveloped the forests far and wide. Axes rung in every thicket, and the ear was occasionally startled by the crashing of trees falling to the ground. I attempted to ascertain the age of an oak that had recently been cut down, by counting the circumgirations of the wood, and found it had flourished at least two hundred and sixty-seven years. Its size, however, was very moderate, when compared with that of many others which grew beside it, and which, from their dimensions, I judged to be five or six hundred years old.

We have a valuable, and less condescending view of early Glengarry in the autobiography of James Begg. In 1827, at the age of 12, James Begg arrived in Quebec from Scotland with his step-mother and two other children. His father had preceded them to Canada. Since the father was not at hand in Quebec when they arrived, young Begg was sent in search of him. On the St. Lawrence River boats, he met his first Glengarrians — "a number of raftsmen from Glengarry," who befriended him — and picking up his father's trail in Ottawa, he learned that he had gone to Glengarry, and so young Begg followed him. He spent a night at Vankleek Hill and in the morning "we started for Lochiel through a new cut road. It was then daybreak and the logs were lying just as they had been cut. It had not been cleared off and I can tell you I did not make very good time climbing over the logs...My friend had to wait very often on me until I could come up to him which I am sure was not pleasant as the flies were very bad. We arrived some time in the afternoon at the home of my guide where we received a true highland welcome and where I was tenderly cared for...An old woman...was particularly kind. Seeing my face all bitten with the flies and much swollen, she washed it with buttermilk and bathed my feet in warm water and put me to bed...When I awoke, the house was full of people who had gathered in to a merrymaking on account of the man I came with who I suppose was an older son of the family. They kept up the dance the most part of the night but it did not disturb me for I slept most of the time. I do not remember the name of the people but I will ever remember their kindness. The old woman in particular with her endearing words of Gaelic (My Rouah) or something like that she called me. They were making potash.'' The next day he was on the road to Martintown and passed the Bishop's new church at St. Raphaels along the way. ''A certain woman afterwards asked me if there were any churches in Edinburgh as fine as St. Raphael's. I laughed at her and did not think it worth answering as there were fine churches in Edinburgh.'' Some of the people he met could not speak English. Someone teasingly pointed ''to a field of Indian corn and asked if I knew what that was. Yes, I said, it was leeks. I suppose if I did not know corn, he did not know leeks.'' He found his father at last in the 9th of Charlottenburgh, in a ''small log building'' where he was ''sitting on the four posts of poverty, as the loom was called in Scotland.'' He was weaving for an Irishman, on the halves.

When the family were reunited, they moved to the 20th of Indian Lands, where they worked for a widower—the mother as housekeeper, the father as weaver, and young James as general labourer. James afterwards remembered the unappetizing, monotonous diet, his employer's irritable old father who ''was always afraid that I did not work enough,'' and his employer's ''four fine hogs...of the old land sharks kind,'' which were so fierce that when they escaped from their pen they ''killed a fine dog.'' His father next took:

> two hundred acres, a yoke of oxen, and four cows, on shares.* He was to get half the proceeds of the grain and 60% of butter from each cow. You would think it a fine chance for an immigrant today [1887], but it was very different then. I don't think the cows gave 60 lbs. of butter altogether, they had no pasture and sometimes we would

*We do not know the exact location of this farm. It appears from the context to have been in Glengarry, but even if it was over the border in Stormont we may assume that conditions were basically the same there as on Glengarry farms of the period.

lose them for two or three days at a time in the bush. Many a sore foot I had going through the woods after the cows. I had got well trained in my former place and could not grumble about being barefoot as the master went barefoot all summer. He must have been about 40 years of age...A neighbour hired me to go and help him log a piece of new ground which he had chopped...for this hard work I got a pound of maple sugar per day, worth about four cents at that time. But things did not prosper, the family getting larger, Father getting old, and I wanting to do something for myself. The place was too small, that was the clearing part, and the bush was hard to clear being low land. My father thought if he had a good large farm he could make something out of it, so he took a good large farm at Williamstown. All the family went there but myself, I was left on the home place to make what I could out of it. I had a team of horses, cow, and heifer, I put in the crop barefooted—could not get any boots, no stores nearer than 15 or 16 miles distant and no store boots then. I put in a pretty hard time milking my cow and made my own butter, a neighbour made my bread. The harvest was the worst, I had to get hands to help. I had to work with the men and cook besides, sometimes up all night. The family only stayed away one year when they came back and I was well pleased to have it so for I had a great many troubles.

"It would hardly be believed," Begg thought, the way we had to live at one time, before we got a mill at the Scotch River which a Mr. McLaren built. We had to go about 17 miles to Martintown and about half the way was swamp so we had to go about in zig-zag trail. It was a good day's work to go to Martintown and back the same day, when we ran out of flour—we did not go very often to the mill but lived on potatoes. I mind we got new potatoes on 17th July and we did not eat much bread after that until the beginning of December, and that was a common thing with everyone. There was nothing for supper then but mashed potatoes and milk. One example, my father and I were sawing boards for a man, we had to take our dinner in the bush and all we got was some kernel bread and skimmed milk. His descendants would not like to be told that today.

Young Begg bought land in the Township of Roxborough, and in the spring of 1839 he and his newly married wife "left the Indian Lands for our own home [in Roxborough] on foot, I carrying a bundle of bed clothes, and her carrying some dishes. We arrived in the evening, tired and weary. There was a bunch of snow lying in the fireplace [of the "small house, 14 x17, hewed inside and round out, covered with Elm

Hon. John McGillivray (1778-1856), a wintering partner in the North West fur trading company. He is representative of several of the partners of this company who retired to Glengarry. McGillivray took an active part in local administration and owes his title of "Honourable" to his appointment to the Legislative Council of Upper Canada.

Isabella McLean (1798-1876), wife of Hon. John McGillivray and daughter of Neil MacLean and Isabella Macdonell (Leek). Isabella's brother Archibald became Chief Justice of Upper Canada and her mother's people were prominent legislators, administrators, priests, and soldiers in early Upper Canada.

bark'' which he and his brother had built on the lot the year before] but I soon made a fire, got some supper, made our bed and soon slept the sleep of the weary if not of the just.'' James Begg passes out of the history of Glengarry at this point, and we must take our leave of his recollections of times when ''Money was scarce, produce cheap, clearings small,'' with the heartiest regret that other Glengarry residents of his generation did not write similar autobiographies.

In view of the rough conditions which as we have seen existed in early Glengarry, it is a paradox that the county in those days had so many eminent men associated with it. We have already noticed some of these, and have now to probe the connection between Glengarry and the men of the great fur trading company which makes so brilliant a part of the early history of Canada, the memorable North West Company.

A modest though hardly a major Glengarry connection can be claimed with David Thompson, Sir Alexander MacKenzie, and Simon Fraser, the three greatest explorers associated with the North West Company. Thompson lived for some years at Williamstown, where he or his sons kept a general store. MacKenzie's uncle, who had probably also been his guardian, settled in Glengarry in 1784. Sir Alexander may never have resided in Glengarry but he was a landowner in the county and received the patents for over 800 acres of Glengarry land. He gave a bell to the Presbyterian Church at Williamstown and was a pew-owner there. Fraser lived for over four decades at St. Andrews, just west of Glengarry. From that base, he had every opportunity to know at least a part of Glengarry intimately. Residents of St. Andrews, we trust, will not be annoyed to be told that St. Andrews has, in any case, always had the status of being an "honorary" Glengarry village.

Some of the Norwesters retired to Glengarry, no doubt reasoning that they would feel more at home in this place where they would have Scotsmen all about them than anywhere else in Canada. Williamstown became the home of Hugh McGillis, who purchased the property of Sir John Johnson there, and of the Hon. Duncan Cameron, who was elected as a Glengarry member for the Legislative Assembly. The latter was father of the late nineteenth century shipping magnate, Sir Roderick Cameron. Near Williamstown lived the Hon. John McGillivray, who like McGillis and Cameron had attained the rank of partner in the company. In Glengarry he served for many years as government land agent. He was appointed to the Legislative Council of Upper Canada, an appointive body, corresponding to the present Senate, of which Bishop Macdonell was also a member. In his later years McGillivray inherited the title and some of the property of the

Chief of the Clan McGillivray, though the claim was not fully cleared at law till the time of his son, Neil John, the 12th Chief. Three distinguished reference works agree in stating that John Macdonald of Garth, another partner in the company, retired to Glengarry, but the truth is that his place of retirement was at Gray's Creek in Stormont County, just across the border from Glengarry. All four men enjoyed a long retirement from their exertions in exploration and the fur trade, as they retired at dates ranging from 1815 to about 1820, and died at dates ranging from 1848 to 1860. Their average period of retirement was about 35 years.

Finnan McDonald (1782-1851), called Big Finnan the Buffalo, was with the North West Co. and the Hudson's Bay Co., 1804-1827. He traded furs and explored in southern British Columbia and the north-western United States. When he retired in 1827 he settled in Charlottenburgh Township and he is buried at St. Raphaels (his tombstone was removed and buried during cemetery reconstruction work some years ago). Finnan's authenticated feat of wrestling a buffalo to its death has ensured him a place not only among Glengarry folk heroes but also in the legends of Canada and the United States.

Among the less important Norwesters who retired to Glengarry, we must not forget the colourful Finnan McDonald, called Big Finnan of the Buffalo from a wrestling match which he had with a wounded buffalo in his fur trading days. Finnan came to Glengarry with his parents in the emigration of 1786. In 1828, after 23 years and many adventures in the fur trade, he bought a farm in Charlottenburgh where he settled with his children and his Indian wife. Finnan had never risen to the level of partner in the company. It may be guessed that this rough, inarticulate big man was never considered a gentleman in the social sense that McGillis, McGillivray, Cameron, and Macdonald of Garth enjoyed the secure unquestioned rank of "gentleman" in Glengarry and Stormont.

Among the Norwesters who grew up in Glengarry, we seem to be safe in claiming on grounds of the dates involved Angus Bethune, the son of the Rev. John Bethune and great-grandfather of the famous Dr. Norman Bethune of China. Angus himself twice visited China on behalf of the North West Company.

The Hon. William McGillivray, who was the chief director of the North West Company, narrowly missed becoming the greatest landowner Glengarry has ever seen. Beginning around 1809, he conducted a long struggle to gain possession of Indian Lands. The Indians of St. Regis were willing to let him have the lands on a perpetual lease in return for a modest annual sum. The government was inclined to concur but insisted on the important point that the lands must be surrendered first by the Indians to the Crown, after which they could be reconveyed to McGillivray. A completed surrender to the Crown seems actually to have occurred in 1815 for this purpose, but in the end McGillivray did not get his land. Perhaps the evident resentment of the white settlers in the tract gave the royal officials second thoughts. A lesser scheme to give McGillivray only a portion of the tract also came to nothing, and the grant of 6000 acres in Plantagenet Township which McGillivray was given in 1823 may have been compensation for his disappointment in respect of Indian Lands.

Col. Alexander Fraser of Fraserfield(1776-1853), politician, administrator, farmer, militia colonel, and central figure in a network of marriage relationships including the Pringles of Cornwall and the Sandfield Macdonalds of Glengarry. He was M.L.A. for Glengarry 1824-1834, Legislative Councillor 1838-1853, Warden of SDG 1841-1849, and Registrar for Glengarry 1841-1853.

Bishop Macdonell's friendships among the men of the North West Company existed even before he left Scotland, and in 1827 he was able to say that "Several of that company were my sincere and dear friends and their memory I shall cherish to the last moment of my existence." One of his Norwester friends was the Hon. John McGillivray, who handled some of his business affairs for him and helped to collect the money due to him from the parishioners at St. Raphaels for the building of the church. McGillivray was a Presbyterian, as was another Norwester friend, the Hon. Duncan Cameron. In 1831 Bishop Macdonell mentioned that the Hon. Duncan Cameron and his sister were "the persons in whose society I feel most at home most free and most happy." The Bishop saw with good sense how valuable the produce needs of the North West Company could be to the Glengarrians. In 1820 we find him writing from Glengarry to Thomas Thain, "As you want a great deal of butter for the N.W. Co. will you try to throw your custom in the way of this parish provided we can furnish you on as reasonable terms and with as good quality as others."

Col. Alexander Fraser of Fraserfield was not associated with the North West Company (though his brother Paul was) but he occupied a position in Glengarry comparable to that of the most prominent of the retired fur traders. He was born in Scotland but came to Glengarry with his parents in the early nineteenth century. In the War of 1812 he was quartermaster of a Lower Canada fencible regiment. After the War he settled in Glengarry, near St. Raphaels and Williamstown, on a 1000 acre estate called Fraserfield. The beautiful fieldstone house, almost a mansion, which he built there is still one of the choicest buildings in Glengarry County. Like the Bishop's church, it was the product of a daring concept, and boldly rose above the backwardness of the society in which it was shaped. Col. Fraser represented Glengarry for many years in Parliament, first in the House of Assembly of Upper Canada and then in the Legislative Council of Upper Canada and the United Canadas. He served as government land agent, and the researcher in the early land records of Glengarry will find many letters from the Colonel dealing with the land transactions of the settlers. He was an emotional man, and often showed himself surprisingly deeply involved as he described the problems of the settlers that the chances of business drew to his attention.

Glengarry was also linked in these early times with a number of eminent men through the Glengarry-based Highland Society of Canada. This organization, rather similar to the service clubs of the present day, was founded at St. Raphaels in 1818 as an offshoot of the prestigious Highland Society of London, England. Hon. William McGillivray, Bishop Macdonell, Col. Alexander Fraser, and an eminent man of early Stormont County, the Hon. Neil McLean, were among the founding members. The society continued to meet as late as 1825, and after a period of dormancy was revived in 1842 by John Macdonald of Garth and lasted at least till 1857.

It is not likely that the ordinary Glengarrian of these times found it remarkable that so many eminent men were associated with his county. It was the natural state of affairs back in Scotland for great lords and other powerful men to overshadow humbler men in their neighbourhoods. In Glengarry, Canada, these eminent men provided ideals to follow in social, intellectual, and educational matters. Intensely Scottish though most of them believed themselves to be, these men from the great world outside were also anglicizing forces, bearing down on the Scottish traditions of a people who were just beginning to be North Americans.

Square timber

# Chapter III
# Towards the Canadian Nation, 1837 - 1867

## The Rebellion of 1837-1838

In the 1830's, while Bishop Macdonell was settling down in his new home, first in Toronto and then in Kingston, political discontent was growing disturbingly in Upper and Lower Canada. In each province there were people who felt that the government was unresponsive to the needs of the people and dominated by a self-interested clique of men who had learned how to control the governor. In Upper Canada, there was the sore grievance of the Clergy Reserves, which committed a fair portion of the good land of the province to remain idle or in the hands of tenants while the labours of surrounding owner-farmers enhanced its value by the improvements they added to their own land. There were also grievances in Upper Canada over the exclusive claims of the Church of England and the backwardness of the province in education and roads. In Lower Canada, the old undissolved bitterness over the Conquest was again coming to the fore. To many of the discontented of either province, the United States seemed a country which offered a workable alternative to the British way of doing things. It seemed that the Americans had developed institutions which corresponded more closely to North American conditions than those which the Canadians had acquired from the British. In Upper Canada, the leader and spokesman of the discontented was William Lyon Mackenzie, a fiery Toronto-based Highlander who edited a radical newspaper and who had been a member of the House of Assembly since 1828. In Lower Canada the leader was the eloquent and aristocratic L.J. Papineau, who became dominant in that province's House of Assembly in the 1820's.

The rebellion which these men did so much to ignite was a disorderly affair which began in Lower Canada with fighting in November and December of 1837 and in Upper Canada with Mackenzie's ill-fated attempt to stage a revolution at Toronto in December 1837, and it was drawn out into late 1838 by raids mounted by Canadian rebels and American sympathizers from across the American border. Mackenzie and Papineau both early took refuge in the United States, but when feelings had cooled they were allowed to return to Canada, where they spent a quiet old age. Some of their humbler followers, less fortunate, were hanged. Once the outbreak began, the most loyal, or most conservative persons in the two provinces vigorously supported the royal governments, and moderate reformers, setting aside for the moment their sympathy with some aspects of the rebels' cause, showed themselves every bit as eager to restore the royal authority. Thus persons whose views ranged over a wide part of the political spectrum closed ranks as they cooperated to restore peace to the badly shaken provinces.

The Glengarrians acted with such zeal to suppress the rebels, and gained so signal a reputation for loyalty by doing so, that it may seem superfluous, and in sons of the county even disloyal, to enquire whether they had been in any way previously infected by the discontent of the radicals. Nevertheless, readers will agree that one of the duties historians owe to them is to try to see beneath the surface of things. It has also been one of the principles of the writers of the present work wherever possible to elbow aside the eminent men who were so much associated with Glengarry County at this time, and to try, as nearly as possible, to see what the ordinary people were doing and thinking — a task which, admittedly, can only be most imperfectly done with this early stage of Glengarry history. This being said, what evidence is there of discontent or radical influence in Glengarry before the Rebellion?

We can probably place only very limited emphasis on the fact that there were believed to be radicals at Vankleek Hill, where someone ordered troops to search their houses. Even at that early stage Vankleek Hill, a few miles outside Glengarry's boundary, probably had an Anglo-Saxon outlook which distinguished it from the Scottishness of Glengarry. Whether the radicalism of Vankleek Hill, supposing it to have existed at all outside the minds of excited local conservatives, found any followers in the Breadalbane area, with its close contacts with Vankleek Hill and by Upper Canada standards an articulate population, is an interesting question which can probably not be answered today, so many years later. Coincidentally, if there was anywhere in Glengarry that the Clergy Reserves were felt to be a grievance in the 1830's, it should have been in this corner of the county and along the northern border of Kenyon, because that was where the reserves were found. Interestingly, there is a petition of 1829 from the Breadalbane area protesting about the Clergy Reserves.

More concretely, a few bits of evidence of radicalism elsewhere in the county come to light. Mackenzie addressed a meeting at Williamstown in October 1831, and afterwards Glengarrians signed one of his petitions. Or at least Glengarry names appeared on the petition; what the signatures were worth may be questioned. For we find Bishop Macdonell complaining in 1833 that Mackenzie got Glengarrians to sign his petitions by telling them that the object of the petitions was to obtain more land from the Crown for their children, and we find the Bishop similarly complaining in 1835 that Mackenzie's agents had filled up one of his petitions in Glengarry with forged signatures. Bishop Macdonell also denounced as an insufferable political radical his "worthy cousin" Col. Alexander Chisholm, a former officer in the Royal Africa Corps and near relative of the chief of the Chisholm Clan. Chisholm became one of the Glengarry's two representatives to the House of Assembly in 1834 and kept his seat till 1841. One of Chisholm's radical acts was to oppose state aid to the Roman Catholic clergy, though he was himself a Roman Catholic. Dr. James Grant of Martintown, who was often a candidate but never a victor in Parliamentary elections, had a reputation in the 1830's and 1840's as a radical. An almost legendary figure in the history of Martintown, his reputation as a boon companion is summed up in an incident reported by Rhodes Grant. "No Puritan, he and Duncan McMartin were boon companions all their days. One night after an evening of hard drinking they got into a fight and the doctor's glasses got broken. Until he got new ones he had to doctor his patients 'By guess and by gosh' as his patients said". A letter from Lancaster late in November 1837 quoted in the Montreal *Morning Courier* asserted the willingness of the Glengarrians to fight for the loyal cause and boasted that "in Lancaster and near our place particularly, they are all to a man, ready; even those we used to call Radicals, are ready to turn out; they say although they are radical for reform, they never will fight against Britain". Perhaps even people of very moderate opinions were called radicals in Glengarry; nevertheless, this shows that it was certainly not a county of just one political opinion.

Lastly, we have an interesting real life example of a discontented Glengarrian in a Mr. William Gillespie of South Lancaster, who was interviewed long afterwards by the Montreal **Witness**. Speaking of the rebellion, he admitted, "I must say that at that time my loyalty was not very strong. I took a deep interest in the doings of William Lyon McKenzie and Papineau, but the feeling of loyalty was so great among the Highlanders of Glengarry, that it was not safe to say much, so I had to yield or, as the saying is 'had to dig out'." He reluctantly shouldered his musket and served as a "loyal" soldier.

The obstacles in the way of such private opinions giving rise to an organized movement in Glengarry were formidable. Newspapers were scarce; the Gaelic language isolated people from the outside world; the interest of eminent men such as

Col. Alexander Fraser of Fraserfield was great; the Highlanders lacked a national tradition of free speech and representative institutions; and there was a trait which that perceptive student of his people, Bishop Macdonell, noted in 1827. Though the Highlanders, he said, "listen with pleasure to a man while he promises to save them from taxation yet if they find him in opposition to the Government they immediately lose their confidence in him let him be who he will. A strong instance of the truth of this occurrence has lately occurred in regard to Donald McDonald, the member for Ottawa District whose opposition to Government had been so obnoxious to the people of this county that they threaten if they get hold of him in Glengarry that they will tar and feather him." To anyone who has known the Glengarrians of a later date—not only Scots Glengarrians but French as well—the Bishop's statement has the convincing ring of truth. It has been in the nature of our people in this century to uphold the established order firmly with their votes and actions—while also combining this highly conservative attitude with considerable violence of private opinion on political and social questions. But one would like to know how far in the 1820's and 1830's the blind loyalty the Bishop described was combined with opinions critical of the established order.

In helping to suppress the rebellion the Glengarrians did important service to the Crown. As early as two years before the rebellion began, a writer in the *Cornwall Observer* ("Tullochgorum" from Charlottenburgh) proposed an attack of the Highlanders on Lower Canada. Now this wish became reality, when during the rebellion the Glengarrians intervened twice in Lower Canada. In the winter of 1838, two regiments of Glengarry militia were stationed in that province, one at St. Philippe, Co. Laprairie, and the other at Napierville. These returned home in the spring without having taken part in any fighting. In November 1838, when the rebellion in Lower Canada broke out anew, the Glengarry militia men were a second time ordered into Lower Canada and helped to drive out the rebels who had seized the village of Beauharnois. The Glengarrians were soon ordered back to Upper Canada, which had been invaded by American sympathizers of the rebels. Glengarry militia took part in the Battle of the Windmill at Prescott and did garrison duty at Cornwall and Coteau du Lac, remaining at the latter place till 1843.

Sadly the Glengarrians got a reputation from their second foray into Lower Canada for plundering and destruction. A British officer who observed them at this time spoke of their "leaving a trail, to use their own expression, of six miles wide as they came along...burning and pillaging. Colonel Fraser [Col. Alexander Fraser, of Fraserfield], who commands them, says they are looked upon as savages, to which I could not help answering that I thought by his own account, they deserved it. His justification was that this was the second time they had been brought from home in this manner, and that the third time it will be worse." The success of the Glengarrians in "liberating" horses for themselves at this time seems to have particularly struck the imagination of contemporaries.

In a book called *Canadian Pen and Ink Sketches* (1890) by John Fraser, a near kinsman of Col. Fraser of Fraserfield, there are valuable recollections of the Glengarrians of this time, including some observations which go far to explain the zeal with which they threw themselves into militia service. He remarks that "At the time of which we write, the old martial feeling prevailed and predominated in Glengarry. Both young and old took more delight in recounting or listening to the stories and the glories of past wars than in 'venerating the plough,'..." Looking back over the years at this early Glengarry, he recalled that "Not one-half, we believe, of the young men could now be found in the old County of Glengarry as were there at the time of the Rebellion of 1837, when nearly two thousand fighting men were mustered in one week." To investigate this statement a little, we may note that the figure of "one-half" is based on a personal impression, but that the figure of two thousand is supported by independent evidence; upwards of two thousand Glengarry militia men assembled at Lancaster in December of 1837 in expectation — mistaken, as it turned out — of being ordered into Lower

Canada at that time. The population of Glengarry was given as 12,517 in 1837, and two thousand men would be a bit less than one third of the male population. The contrast that Fraser notes is all the greater because the population of Glengarry at that time when he was writing was not far under twice as large as that of 1837. We may suppose that the Glengarrians threw themselves with joy into the exciting campaigns in Lower Canada not only because they had thrilled since childhood to stories about their warlike ancestors in Scotland, but because in this era of large families and a sluggish and unproductive Canadian economy Glengarry had a great pool of underemployed young (and not so young) men ready for work or fun or mischief or war.

The rebellion had emphasized the defects of the existing parliamentary system in the two Canadas, with the result that the Canadas got a new one. Upper and Lower Canada were merged into one province with a single parliament. French Canada was to have parliamentary representation as before, but now its elected members were to be restrained by having to work with the elected members of the English-speaking west. Upper Canada received the new name of Canada West, and Lower Canada the new name of Canada East, but the old names continued to be used along with the new. The first elections to the Legislative Assembly of the new parliament were in 1841.

For Glengarry, the election marked the rise of a remarkable business and political family. The county now had only one member to elect (instead of two, as under the old system), and the lucky candidate, who easily defeated Dr. Grant, was a promising 28-year old Cornwall lawyer, John Sandfield Macdonald. John Sandfield was born at St. Raphaels, the son of an emigrant from Knoydart. He attended the Eastern District Grammar School at Cornwall, qualified as a lawyer, and set up his practice in Cornwall. He represented Glengarry in the Legislative Assembly till 1857; he was then succeeded by his brother Donald Alexander, commonly known in Glengarry as Donald Sandfield, who represented Glengarry till 1875.

Together, the "Sandfields" represented Glengarry for 34 years. John Sandfield entered politics as the chosen candidate of Col. Alexander Fraser and the Hon. John McGillivray. Though he thus had a link with the old, great men of the county, he was a more plebeian figure than they or many of the men, with their aristocratic pretensions, who had formerly represented the county. They were unmistakably gentlemen; John Sandfield was a gentleman too, but only in the sense that many self-made frontier lawyers not unlike him who went into American politics at this time were accepted as "gentlemen" in the society that produced them. He later described himself as a former "poor Glengarry boy." He was only the first or second Glengarry M.P. to be born in Canada.

The election of 1841 also brought excitement for a number of Glengarrians to whom it offered an opportunity to interfere in the voting in Canada East. There were grave fears in loyal minds at this time as to the probable outcome of the voting in some of the Canada East constituencies. Governor Sydenham himself vigorously pulled all strings to get the desired results in certain critical ridings. There still survived at this time an eighteenth-century and early nineteenth-century practice of bringing gangs of bullies to the scene of voting to intimidate the opposition voters. There is evidence that about 150 Glengarry men appeared in this role in the County of Vaudreuil to influence the **voting** there. And a group of between 80 and 100 Glengarry men travelled in a procession of some 18 cutters and sleighs from Williamstown to support Dr. Michael McCulloch in the important election in the County of Terrebonne, where he was running against the influential French nationalist, L.H. Lafontaine. The Glengarrians did not in fact reach the scene of voting, having turned back a few miles from the polling place on learning that the election was over. In their absence Dr. McCulloch had won the election, though with the support of a squad of "stone-breakers" borrowed from their regular work on road construction in Montreal. The outrages in the Canada East elections were carefully investigated by the new Legislative Assembly—a

John Sandfield Macdonald (1812-1872), native of Charlottenburgh Township. He was M.L.A. for Glengarry 1841-1858, Premier of the United Canadas 1862-1864, and first Premier of Ontario after Confederation 1867-1871. Also notable as a local lawyer (in Cornwall), landowner in SDG, and owner of the Cornwall *Freeholder*. His home in Cornwall became the first Hotel Dieu Hospital.

body which, from shortly after its meeting, included Lafontaine, elected by a radical Toronto constituency. A certain Angus McDonell, a carpenter and farmer from Glengarry, was interrogated, and his testimony is in print, from which we learn that he was recruited for the expedition to Terrebonne by a Montreal **merchant** called Neil McIntosh, and that he was paid all expenses and the respectable sum of one dollar a day.

A final convulsion resulting from the Rebellion of 1837 took place in April 1849, when the governor, Lord Elgin, signed the controversial bill compensating persons who had lost property in the rebellion in Canada East. A mob of conservatives, angry at what they believed to be a policy of rewarding rebels, stoned the governor and burned down the Parliament Buildings, which at that time were in Montreal.

The Glengarrians had gained a reputation for loyalty in 1837-1838, but it was not clear what should be called "loyalty" in the Glengarrians or in anyone else in these renewed troubles. To be loyal to the Crown, as represented by Lord Elgin, seemed to involve gross disloyalty to the British connection. A Montreal newspaper, reporting a few days after the burning of the Parliament Buildings on the indignation against Lord Elgin then sweeping across Canada West, noted a rumour "that the brave Highlanders of Glengarry are arming by thousands to come to the assistance of the British population of Lower Canada, if need be." Col. Fraser of Fraserfield, attending a meeting of the Legislative Council in Montreal, deplored the "disastrous advice" given to Lord Elgin. But it was soon reported that a meeting of 1100 men at Alexandria had backed Lord Elgin; subsequent reports in the opposition press reduced the size of the meeting to several hundred men, and fully half of these, it was asserted, were from Canada East, while a large proportion of the rest were non-electors. Sandfield Macdonald, in whose interest the meeting was probably held, supported Lord Elgin. Formerly Fraser's political protégé, he now felt strong enough to differ from him. The real attitude of Glengarrians was perhaps an enigma to observers of the time. In July, a Montreal newspaper reported a belief that an influential government supporter in Glengarry had just been asked to state in writing how many Glengarrians could be brought to Montreal in defence of the government in case of further anti-Elgin outbreaks.

One wonders whether the Glengarrians had not begun to question some aspects of their behaviour in the Lower province in 1838 and 1841. Perhaps the proposals for a further military use of the Glengarrians caught the county not only in a mood of uncertainty about the nature of loyalty but in a state of painful recovery from the delicious intoxication of the days of the rebellion.

## The North

The northern two townships of the county developed more slowly than Charlottenburgh. Because of a certain traditional tendency to divide Glengarry into two portions, one lying south and the other lying north of Alexandria, one is tempted to speak of a slowly developing north as opposed to an early developed south, but in fact Lancaster Township seems not to have developed any more quickly than its two northern sisters of Lochiel and Kenyon. Virtually all of the eminent men we have already noted as residents of Glengarry made their homes in a single township, Charlottenburgh. But Col. Alexander Chisholm, rather surprisingly, settled in Alexandria as early as the 1820's, and we have now to notice two other men who similarly chose the north and helped to open it economically.

Donald Cattanach was born in Badenoch, Scotland, in 1779. As a young man he was employed in England, but his family emigrated to Canada, and in 1826 he followed them, and we next find him established as a merchant in Alexandria. Opportunities beckoned further north, and in 1832 he settled on some lands he had purchased in Kenyon, on the Lochiel border. He called the place Laggan, after his boyhood home. For the next fifty years the Squire of Laggan, as he has been called, was a prominent figure in his neighbourhood and far beyond it as store keeper, road commissioner, postmaster, magistrate, school superintendent, temperance reformer, Sabbath School teacher, Presbyterian elder, and adviser to the settlers in legal matters. He appears to have found his first years at Laggan difficult, and we find him lamenting in 1833 that ''I did not make nor receive on Barrell of potash, & you may judge of the scarcity of Cash in this part'' and offering to sell his property back to its previous owner. In 1835 he wrote: ''I have been told you regretted selling me this Land so Cheap. I have only to say that I regrett having bought it at all and I am daily looking out for a purchaser for it.'' By this time he had ''got another very handsome place to go to, where I Can Carry my views to effect to much better advantage.''

But it is the later patriarch rather than the struggling young merchant that we will prefer to remember, and of the patriarch we have a portrait in a memoir written by a friend of the family:

> His hospitality was unbounded, his thoroughly Highland welcome made his house a place of free quarters. There might be met the Rev. William Fraser, the Baptist minister mhor of Breadalbane, well known as one valiant for truth; the Rev. Mr. McKillican, Congregationalist, strong in faith and doctrine; the mild-voiced, polite French Canadian missionaries from Lower Canada; his own favorite minister, the Rev. Alex. Cameron, now of Ardershire, Scotland; Rev. Daniel Gordon and many another well known and well beloved name. At his house, for a few short weeks, we heard the voice of the saintly William Burns, who ended his labours in China; and the pleadings for God of the beloved James Drummond, who by God's grace, lit a fire in Glengarry that still burns. We heard there those men of God, Dr. McLaughlin and Alexander N. Somerville, John Roy Fraser and Mr. McTavish, Dr. McLeod, Dr. Burns, and many another eloquent divine, whose praise is in all the churches, and we have not forgotten the privilege. At sacrament time, that white house on the hill had an expansive power that would have done credit to an eastern caravansary. No one ever saw it too full, or found that the excellent housemother was unable to accommodate more guests. ...No one ever saw Mr. Cattanach at his best until they saw him king in the bosom of his family.

Donald's brother Angus, a land surveyor, was a prominent settler at Dalhousie Mills.

About a dozen years after Donald Cattanach settled at Laggan, Alexandria got a "Squire" in the form of John Sandfield Macdonald's younger brother, Donald Alexander. In 1844, when he was 26 years old, he purchased the mill property in Alexandria from Archibald McDonald ("Archie Breach"). Within a few years Donald had in operation in Alexandria a grist mill, a saw mill, a carding and fulling mill, a general store, and "a large ashery on the banks of the mill pond." Young though he was, before he came to Alexandria Donald had already had an important contract on the construction of the Beauharnois Canal. When the Irish labourers at the canal site rioted, Donald narrowly escaped death at their hands, though the particular workers involved in the disturbance apparently had no personal grievance against him. Later he built a large aqueduct for the Montreal waterworks, on which he had 500 employees working in 1855. In 1856 he installed a steam engine in his mill in Alexandria, the Garry River being often too low in the summer to serve the needs of the waterwheel. Even under the new regime which the dynamic younger Sandfield brought to Alexandria, it continued to be hampered by its lack of access for trade purposes to the outside world by either rail, water, or good roads.

We find a grim view of the roads in northern Glengarry in a letter which appeared in the *Cornwall Observer* of 11 April 1834 — this being the time when Donald Cattanach was establishing himself at Laggan and ten years before Donald Sandfield came to Alexandria. The writer calls himself "An Inhabitant" and dates his letter at L'Orignal. "I beg leave to call the attention of the public to the abominable state of the roads between Vankleek hill & Alexandria, and to ask why a country like that, possessing every advantage for improvement, materials for repairing roads near, soil good and thickly populated, should be so far behind almost every other settlement in the Province in that all important article — 'good roads.'

Hon. D.A. Macdonald (1817-1896), also known as Donald Sandfield Macdonald. Brother of John Sandfield Macdonald. His ability as a contractor when a young man made him his first money. His decision to settle at Alexandria and go into business there did much to hold the county together. Warden SDG, 1856; M.L.A. for Glengarry 1858-1867; Postmaster General of Canada, 1873-1875; Lieutenant Governor of Ontario 1875-1880.

"The roads on that route during Spring and Fall are almost impassable — sums of money have been frequently granted by the Legislature to improve them which is squandered without the public deriving much benefit; the statute labour it appears,....if laid out at all, has never been laid out to advantage; old trees have been suffered to lie across the middle of the road for a season, without being removed, and in short the state of the roads denote the greatest sloth and indolence of the inhabitants.

"In passing through the Townships of Lochiel and Kenyon, we see as good a tract of land as ever the sun shone upon, settled in some measure for twenty years, with almost every lot taken up, and an actual settler upon it. We see agriculture carried on in a slothful manner, scarcely a wheel carriage of any kind owned on the route, and instead of the country's improving like other infant settlements of the Province, we see it returning almost to its state of nature—'and why?'—Because the people are hemmed in to their bark-covered huts, and half cultivated farms without having any access to, or communication with other parts of the Province." The writer's answer to this state of affairs is the spending of enough money to complete a passable stage road between L'Orignal and Cornwall. Such a road would tend "to raise the ambition and energy of the inhabitants of those might-be flourishing Townships."

Breadalbane. This engraving from Cox and Hoby's *The Baptists in America* (1836) is probably the oldest picture of a Glengarry scene. We have no way of assessing its accuracy, though the details in general seem to ring true.

A more favourable view of some parts of the northern townships and a most venomous opinion of the young Alexandria appear in the travel journal of a Baptist minister called F.A. Cox who visited Glengarry in 1835. When he arrived at Breadalbane, where there had recently been a religious revival, measures were taken, he wrote:

> to collect the people. It is a Gaelic settle-
> ment, and in that language their valued minister,
> Mr. Fraser, always preaches to them, though both
> he and they are acquainted with English. This
> happily facilitated our intercourse, while it was
> occasionally necessary to refer, through their
> pastor, to their own modes of expression, in order
> to ascertain with accuracy, the idea intended
> to be conveyed.
>
> . . . .
>
> "Breadalbane is a place never to be forgotten.
> My interview with the people was brief, but
> delightful. Their narratives, their emotions,
> their simplicity, were charming. I conversed
> with them, prayed with them, wept with them,
> and bade farewell—but no;—they followed
> from the house, they overtook and surrounded
> me, the willing captives of a pure and spiritual
> affection! The horses were preparing at some
> distance, and though the sun was intense,
> religion, awakened into exercise by converse
> as we walked along, was "as the shadow of a
> great rock in a weary land." The horses were
> not ready. They paused; and forming themselves
> into a semicircle, of which I was accidentally
> the centre, I remarked, "Instead of parting,
> you seem to collect as if a sermon were to be
> preached." "And may we not have one?" they
> asked. The appeal was irresistible; and while
> I discoursed for a short time on the words—
> "I, if I be lifted up, will draw all unto me" -

they listened - wept - and welcomed a doctrine, ever old, yet ever new, - the attractive efficacy of the cross. We parted again - perhaps for ever in this life; but with the blessed and oft-expressed expectation of finally associating in the perfect and blessed state!

"I had now enjoyed the fairest possible opportunity of witnessing the influence of religion on unsophisticated minds. It was the first growth of piety in hearts untrained by the refinement, and unseduced by the deceptions of society; and it was truly refreshing and instructive, to see the genuine teachings of the Spirit, sanctifying the passions, and elevating the soul above the world. The effect was a wonderful transparency of mind, and an extraordinary combination of humility, zeal, and holy love. Oh, how finely did these lilies and roses grow in this garden of the Lord in the desert!

"Mr. Fraser accompanied us on foot, six miles through the forest to Glenelg [Kirk Hill], where we found a lodging at the house of a Highlander who had come two-and-forty years before, to carve out a subsistence for himself in the then unexplored wilderness. He could not speak English intelligibly, nor we Gaelic; so we speedily retired to rest.

"At another place in our further advance through this wild region, called *Priest's Mills*, a very different state of things existed from that which we had recently witnessed at Breadalbane. The corderoy roads were but in harmony with the rude and barbarous condition of the people. Vice and superstition go hand in hand there, and spread moral ruin. In the sober seriousness of folly they assemble annually to practise one of the greatest absurdities that ever entered into the

human mind. Magistrates and people alike in-
fatuated go forth in battle array, penetrate the
forest, and with all the farcical solemnity of a
savage barbarism, proceed with muskets *to fire*, as
they express it, *at the devil*; and then *fence with
swords*, as if it were a real and visible contest.
Their ignorance and irreligion are such, that they
will fiddle and sing Highland songs even when the
priest is in the pulpit, and as a part of worship.
It seems as if superstition sat here at ease on her
throne, as conscious of security amidst the fast-
nesses of the inaccessible wilderness.''

What were the military exercises that the Rev. Mr. Cox
described as taking place at Alexandria? Pretty obviously,
this is a badly distorted report of the practising of the Lochiel
militia. Like so much of the Canadian militia of the time,
the Lochiel regiment no doubt took advantage of its training
days to have a thorough good time. It must be said in defense
of this regiment that it was under the command of a well qualified officer, Col. Alexander Chisholm, and that there is no
reason to suppose it was any less ready than the rest of the
Glengarry militia to do the Crown service when an urgent
need arose a few years later.

As for the fiddling in the church at Alexandria, there was
no reason why there should not have been and a very good
reason why there should have been. The history of stringed
instruments as part of sacred music goes back at least as far
as David and his harp in the Old Testament. Many great
medieval composers wrote sacred music especially for strings
and the tradition has never quite died out in the Roman
Catholic church. In 1835 the church building at Alexandria had
been in use for less than two years and it is doubtful if the
congregation could have afforded an organ, even if they had
felt the need of one or had somebody to play it. But a Scottish
congregation would certainly have had fiddlers who were
familiar from childhood with the old hymns of the church
and the old songs of the Highlands, which even today, six
or seven generations removed from Scotland we regard as

at least semi-sacred. For instance, what Scot would call Mean Cridhe (Let Us Travel Home) or Tag **Outthun** Nan Beann (Take It to the Hills) profane music and not fit for a church? In 1835 most of the people in the Alexandria area looked on Scotland as home and any part of the music of Scotland as sacred.

What the good Baptist Divine did not know, or if he knew would not admit, was that there were other ways of praising God with music than the strictly vocal efforts that some of the Protestant churches insisted on from the time of the Reformation until shortly before 1900.

As the Rev. Mr. Cox journeyed through the southern half of Glengarry, from Alexandria to Lancaster by way of Williamstown, he seems to have found less to awaken his interest, and reported merely that "In the midst of fine forests were frequent *clearances*, and excellent farms".

An engraving of "Breadalbane in Glengarry" which appears in the printed account of Mr. Cox's tour is probably the earliest surviving picture of a Glengarry scene and is reproduced elsewhere in the present volume.

We also get some glimpses of Breadalbane about the 1820's in a remarkable book which is now little known to Glengarrians, the Rev. James Drummond's *A Forest Flower or a Memorial of Daniel M'Killican, Who Died in the 14th Year of His Age*, which was published in Philadelphia by the Presbyterian Board of Publication about the early 1850's. This is a religious tract of 74 pages in which the biography of a real-life resident of Breadalbane, Daniel McKillican, the son of the Rev. William McKillican, a well known Congregationalist minister of pioneer Glengarry, is re-told in the form of a novel. It has some claim to be therefore both a novel *and* a biography, and as a novel it stands at the beginning of the impressive succession of novels on Glengarry, of which Ralph Connor's are the best known. The *Forest Flower* is not quite the first appearance of Glengarry in creative literature, however; the Scottish poetess Ann Cuthbert Knight included a little tepid description of Glengarry in her *A Year in Canada, and Other Poems*, published in 1816. A reference to the *Forest Flower* in a newspaper interview of 1894 seems to take for granted that the novel would be known to many of the newspaper's readers. Be that as it may, it is now so rare that the present writers have only been able to discover two surviving copies. It is written in a style so simple and effective that little of the intensity of religious feeling with which it was written has been lost over the years. Some organization concerned with reprinting the more vivid documents of the Canadian past might do much worse than to reprint it.

The author, the Rev. James Drummond, was a missionary preacher of the Free Church of Scotland in Glengarry about 1847-1848. He seems to have been known there for powerful evangelical preaching and is mentioned in the passage quoted a few pages back on the hospitality of Donald Cattanach. As a Presbyterian, Drummond was of a different denomination from the McKillicans, but this denominational difference never intrudes in the *Forest Flower*.. Drummond was born in Scotland in 1822, and studied at the University of Glasgow and New College, Edinburgh. About 1850 he went as a missionary to Madras, India, but ill health forced him to return home. He is described on the title page of the novel as "Missionary of the Free Church of Scotland, Madras". In 1854 he settled as minister at Clackmannan, Scotland, and he was still senior minister of his congregation there when he died in 1898. He seems to have published only one book—on the subject of communion—besides the *Forest Flower*.

The narrative of the *Forest Flower* is of the plainest and most straightforward kind. At almost the beginning, we are told that Daniel's father, a minister in Scotland, emigrated to Canada with a part of his flock, fearing that if he let them go alone, they would suffer for lack of spiritual advisers. Still loving their old home in Scotland, the emigrants "named their new home amid the woods of Glengarry, Breadalbane". Young Daniel, who was born in Canada, was a precocious and deeply religious child. His religious conversion was hastened by a serious illness which struck him when he was about ten years old. The novel tells of Daniel's concern for his own soul and the souls of his brothers and sisters and other children, and it describes his conversation with his mother and others, the decline of his health, the last stages of a horrifying illness, and his death at the age of 13. This framework of events is used throughout the novel to emphasize the need for religious conversion, especially among the young. Despite his youth, and despite the didactic aims of the novel, young McKillican emerges as a fully rounded, convincing human being; but as was inevitable in so short a novel, the other characters remain relatively undeveloped.

Unfortunately, we cannot be sure how far Drummond's portrait of Daniel is faithful to the original. Daniel died in 1830 or 1832 many years before Drummond came to Canada. Drummond is said to have got his information about him from the neighbours. Apart from this lack of personal acquaintance, it is disturbing to read on the title page of the novel that it was "Revised by the Committee of Publication". What has been changed or lost? For whatever reason, the portrait of Daniel displeased his brother, who complained years later that the book never did Daniel justice.

Every glimpse we can get of life of the Glengarrians of this period is precious, and it is agreeable to record that the novel does contain a fair amount of social detail. Whatever changes the revisers in Philadelphia may have made in the original manuscript  may not have extended to the substance of Drummond's remarks on life and customs of the Glengarrians.

We get some views on the toil of winning a new home in the forest. When the pioneers first arrived at their settlement of Breadalbane, they found neither houses, fields, nor roads, but only woods and the wild animals in them. Each settler "took his broad axe and entered the deep forest to clear a spot for a dwelling, —a little hut, built with logs and roofed with bark or with shingles". As the trees were cut, they were rolled into piles and burned. One of Daniel's acts of self-denial was to accept the task of driving the oxen home after a logging bee and thereby miss the sport of feeding the flames with the other boys.

The labours of the Rev. Mr. McKillican are described. Though a minister, he "had to labour with his hands to get bread for himself and his children" during the six work-days of the week. On the Sundays "he went many miles through the thick woods to preach the gospel to the people scattered over the settlement".

In one passage of the novel, Daniel recalls from his sick bed how in the days of health he and his brother would be out in the fields making hay. "When I got tired leaping about, I threw myself upon the hay on the sleigh, and let the oxen draw me along in the sunshine". Here the author breaks in to remark that "For the sake of those who do not live in Canada, I have to explain that a sleigh is a sort of cart without wheels, which is used to bring home corn and hay from places that are too soft or too rough for the wagon. It is light, and glides smoothly along the ground". This use of a sledge for hay-making seems surprising, but our readers have already seen a bit of evidence that suggests that the passage is based on Drummond's observations and is not an interpolation of his revisers. The critic of Lochiel and Kenyon whose letter in the Cornwall Observer has already been noticed complained about the lack of wheel carriages, and seems to associate this lack with his complaint about the slothful agriculture of those parts. That humble but all purpose sledge the "stone boat" was of course to have a long and honorable history on Glengarry farms. And at the time of which Drummond was writing, when a wheel was an expensive luxury and only the most elementary ditching had begun to drain Glengarry's fields, a sledge was doubtless a very useful farm vehicle.

Another contemporary practice that at first surprises is Daniel's activity in distributing religious tracts. In a pioneer society where money is scarce and every manufactured thing is precious, one does not expect the free distribution of reading matter. Yet here again, we may be in contact with genuine historical fact. At an unspecified date within a decade after Drummond's work in Glengarry, Donald Cattanach employed a young Glengarrian (who, incidentally, had been converted by Drummond's preaching) to distribute religious tracts. Where the distribution took place is not stated, but the fact of these Glengarrians being involved in tract distribution at this time suggests that tract distribution in Daniel McKillican's Glengarry of one generation earlier need not be rejected as historically improbable. The tracts that Cattanach's employee distributed were those of the Philadelphia publishers of the *Forest Flower*. Was the *Forest Flower* published early enough, one wonders, for it to be included among the tracts distributed?

As the foregoing pages have been devoted to tracing the role of the northern concessions in the development of nineteenth-century Glengarry, it is a little disconcerting to have to report that there was a secession movement about this time in the northern portion of Glengarry. In 1820 a notice was given that at the meeting of the next provincial Parliament there would be an attempt to incorporate Lochiel Township into the District of Ottawa. As part of Glengarry, Lochiel was in the Eastern District. If it was united with the Ottawa District (composed then of the Counties of Prescott and Russell) presumably its connection with Glengarry would be ended. In 1831, a petition presented to the provincial Parliament from 235 inhabitants of the Townships of Lochiel and Kenyon asked to have these townships and a portion of Indian Lands attached to the Ottawa District. A ·petition of 12 July 1837 — perhaps not the most propitious date, in view of the country being on the brink of a rebellion — from about 350 inhabitants of the five northern concessions of Lochiel Township and the four northern concessions of Kenyon Township asked to have those nine concessions united into a new township, to be incorporated into Prescott County in the Ottawa District. For the new township the petitioners proposed the name of Glenelg. The greater number of them, they explained, were "emigrants, or descendants of emigrants, from the estate of Glenelg, in the Highlands of Scotland, and... their feelings and recollections are dearly entwined round a name which has been for ages the 'gathering cry' of their forefathers''. Other petitions in favour of a break followed in 1842 and 1843. The latest effort in this project which we have noticed was a statement in the official *Gazette* of 13 September 1845 that application would be made to the provincial Parliament at its next meeting to have the above mentioned five concessions of Lochiel and four concessions of Kenyon added to Prescott County in the Eastern District.

What were the motives behind these attempts? From two draft counter-petitions prepared by the Warden and Councillors of the Eastern District, one dating probably from 1843 and the other dated in 1845, it appears that these gentlemen wished to interpret the secession movement as an aggressive design on the part of the Ottawa District rather than as a real grass-roots movement in the north of Glengarry. It may well be that the leaders of the Ottawa District were anxious to see the secession movement succeed, but there were also good reasons why the inhabitants of the northern portion of the county, and more especially of its north-eastern tip, should want to join the Ottawa District. In the petition of 1837, the signers complained about their remoteness from Cornwall, which was the "metropolis" of the Eastern District and the site of the court house and other public offices. They asserted "their principal connections of business and interest are to be found almost exclusively in the adjoining District of Ottawa, which is the great market for their farming produce and stock, and to which they have to convey their grain to be ground for domestic use; and...the lumber trade, in which many of your petitioners are engaged during winter, leads them generally to the Ottawa River, the northern frontier of that District; while their connection with the southern frontier of the Eastern District is chiefly limited to their attendance at the public offices, or as jurors, suitors, or witnesses at the Courts of Justice in Cornwall''. They could avoid expenses, inconvenience, and loss of time if L'Orignal rather than Cornwall were their county town. The village of

Alexandria, even with its grist mill, apparently lacked attraction for these pioneers. We can more clearly grasp why this was so when we remember that these five northern concessions of Lochiel and four northern concessions of Kenyon were divided from the rest of the county, including Alexandria, by a broad band of swamps running right across Glengarry. In the milder seasons of the year, the primitive roads to the south were likely to be bad. When frost the ''roadmaker'' had improved the roads , the mill wheels were likely to be frozen in.

If Glengarry had lost these nine northern concessions, it would have lost much that is interesting and colourful in its history and the remainder would have been a weaker base to sustain, if it could have sustained at all, the legend Glengarry built for itself. Among other things, if the secessionists had carried away with them into Prescott County the adjacent portion of Indian Lands, in which *The Man from Glengarry* and *Glengarry School Days* are set, those novels would have had to be re-titled, and Glengarry would have lost the distinction of its connection with them.

Before leaving the settlers of the north-east of Glengarry to concentrate for a while on those of the area of Indian Lands in which Ralph Connor set the novels, we must note that in 1828 Lochiel obtained a large scale landlord in the form of King's College, the Toronto college which later became the University of Toronto. Twelve of the remaining lots of Crown Reserve land were given by the government to King's College to be part of its endowments. If each of these lots had been of the standard 200-acre size, the college would have got 2400 acres, but as one or two of the lots were under-sized, the actual acreage was something under 2350. Settlers were allowed to occupy these lands as tenants, and the lands were eventually sold to private owners. King's College received no lands in any other part of Glengarry.

## Ralph Connor
About 1866, the American Sunday-School Union, of Philadelphia, issued a novel of 410 pages called *Shenac's Work*

Rev. Daniel Gordon and Mrs. Gordon, parents of Ralph Connor (Charles W. Gordon).

*at Home.* Set in the area of the present-day Maxville and St. Elmo, it told the story of a hardworking and resourceful pioneer girl, Shenac (Gaelic for Janet) MacIvor, who found herself the principal breadwinner of the family after the death of her father. As part of the background of Shenac's struggle the customs of the Glengarrians are described. Shenac is converted in a religious revival which takes place in her neighbourhood and at the end of the novel she marries a clergyman. Though little known now, this novel seems to have been a success in its day. At least five editions were published, the last recorded being 1904.

The author of *Shenac's Work at Home* was Margaret Murray Robertson. She was born in Scotland in 1823, came to Canada with her father, a Congregationalist minister, when she was a child, and died unmarried at Westmount, Quebec, in 1897. She was a prolific novelist at a time when Canadian literature was just struggling into existence. Her sister Mary married a Presbyterian minister, the Rev. Daniel Gordon, who was the famous minister of Indian Lands, Glengarry. He was of course the father of Glengarry's most celebrated son, the novelist Charles W. Gordon, who wrote under the penname of Ralph Connor. Miss Robertson knew the Glengarrians through her Gordon connections and we may imagine her as being a visitor at the Manse in Indian Lands. Whether she knew Drummond's *Forest Flower* and whether it gave her the idea of writing about the Glengarrians we do not know. A crippled boy who appears in her novel may possibly have been suggested to her by the invalid Daniel McKillican in Drummond's novel.

When his aunt's novel appeared, Ralph Connor was about six years old. He was born at what is now St. Elmo in 1860. In view of the copious detail with which he enriches his Glengarry scenes, it is striking to learn that he left Glengarry in 1871, when he was merely ten years old. His father had at that time accepted a new pastorate at Harrington in Zorra, in Western Ontario. He appears to have relied — and relied successfully — chiefly on what he called his "photographic quality of mind" for his reconstruction of these early scenes. His personal impressions were probably reinforced by hearing other members of the large Gordon family exchange their recollections of Glengarry during the years which followed at Zorra. There appears to be no evidence for the legend that he revisited Glengarry to do research for the Glengarry novels and his personal acquaintance with Glengarry in his adult years, was, at best, exceedingly slight.

Connor chose to follow in the professional footsteps of his father and was ordained as a minister in the Prebyterian church in 1890. Though he was one of the most successful

Ralph Connor (Charles W. Gordon) (1860-1937), minister in Presbyterian and United Churches, church statesman, labour conciliator, army chaplain, and, at the height of his popularity as an author, perhaps the best known living Canadian. Author of *The Man from Glengarry, Glengarry School Days,* and many other books.

novelists Canada has produced, he seems always to have considered himself as in first place a clergyman. He believed that novels were among the means that he had to teach and to improve others. In the novel as an art form he was not interested. In his first few years in the ministry, he served as a missionary to miners, settlers, and lumbermen in the Canadian North West. Afterwards, he settled as a minister at Winnipeg, the city which was his home for the remainder of his life. He began to write relatively late in life. His first book was not published till he was 37. Thereafter volume followed volume, year after year. He served with distinction as a chaplain in the First World War. At this time he discovered that a negligent or dishonest friend who was killed in the war had squandered most of the wealth he had acquired through his writing. In the 1920's and 1930's his literary popularity declined, as fashions changed and the generation which had admired him was replaced with a new. He died at Winnipeg in 1937. In recent years, with the growth in the study and teaching of Canadian literature in schools and colleges, his reputation has revived somewhat, and a few of his best works seem likely to have a permanent place among the "standard works" of Canadian literature.

What did Ralph Connor write about Glengarry? He described his early days in the county in his excellent autobiography, *Postscript to Adventure*. He used the same materials in three substantial novels which he set in Glengarry, *The Man from Glengarry*, *Glengarry School Days* and *Torches through the Bush*. Another novel, *The Girl from Glengarry*, has despite its title only a marginal connection with Glengarry and we need not notice it further here. There are Glengarry references in a few other of his novels. As far as is known, he wrote no short stories or articles about Glengarry.

*The Man from Glengarry* (1901), the first of Connor's novels set in Glengarry and almost certainly his greatest work, tells the story of Ranald Macdonald, a shy but talented boy from the shanties and backwoods who is introduced to the ideas and customs of civilization by the kindly and saintly Mrs. Murray, the wife of the minister of Indian Lands. Mrs. Murray is based on Connor's own adored mother, and the Rev. Mr. Murray is based on the Rev. Daniel Gordon. The Glengarry background is drawn in minute and loving detail with especially fine descriptions of a sugaring-off, a wake, a Glengarry Sunday, a logging-bee, and a fight between a group of Glengarry shantymen and their rivals at the junction of the Scotch River and the South Nation, about a dozen miles north west of St. Elmo. While Connor seems at one point to state that the novel is set in the 1850's, one of its events is a real historical event, the religious revival of 1864-1865, and we may accept it as actually being set in the 1860's, the decade which Connor spent in Glengarry.

*Glengarry School Days* (1902), Connor's next novel, shows signs of having been intended especially as a novel for children but its earliest chapters contain nevertheless some of his best writing. As in *The Man from Glengarry*, the quality of the writing declines badly towards the end. If Connor had been able or willing to do equally good work throughout, Canadian literature would hardly have had a more accomplished masterpiece than *Glengarry School Days*. Probably what we are faced with here is a failure of interest on the part of the author. He gives the impression of being a writer of outstanding gifts who could never be bothered to use them consistently with anything like the degree of care that the great English novelists lavished on their best works. The hero of *Glengarry School Days* is Hughie Murray, the son of the Rev. and Mrs Murray; Hughie, obviously patterned on Connor himself, had appeared briefly the year before in *The Man from Glengarry*. The setting in time is indicated by the fact that the religious revival is referred to as an event of the recent past. The novel contains many excellent passages on Glengarry life and customs, but will always survive as an incomparable picture of pioneer school life. In a country with a population as diverse as Canada's, there are understandably no scenes in Canadian literature in which Canadians can recognize an experience common to all of them, but the description of the spelling match in *Glengarry School Days* comes nearer to filling that role than any other.

Connor's third and last novel set in Glengarry, called *Torches through the Bush*, followed a full generation later in 1934. It is little known compared with the other Glengarry novels. When it appeared Sandy Fraser, the once well known *Farmer's Advocate* columnist from Glengarry County, thought it disappointing compared with the two earlier Glengarry novels. Although it is certainly not quite as good as the others, the difference in quality is too small to explain the great difference in reputation. Probably what has sunk *Torches* is simply that it appeared in the decline of Connor's reputation. If it had followed the other Glengarry novels in, say, 1903, it would have been seen as a good third volume in what would have been regarded ever after as the Glengarry trilogy. This time Connor abandoned the old Maxville-St.Elmo setting in Indian Lands for a new setting in the north-east of the county. It is tempting to identify this new location with Kirk Hill, but in fact, the local details of the area seem to be simply fictitious, and the setting is to all appearances just the old Maxville-St.Elmo setting lightly disguised. Just for good measure, however, Connor brings in Indian Lands as a separate territory, and Indian Lands' Mr. and Mrs. Murray are again enrolled among his characters, and the religious revival is one of the events of the novel.

Let us now try to work out the geographical and religious background of Connor's three Glengarry novels so far as these relate to Indian Lands. In *Shenac's Work at Home* the geographical and religious background are stated with less attention to concrete detail than in Connor's novels, but our findings will apply, though in a more general way, to Miss Robertson's novel as well as Connor's.

To begin, let us imagine ourselves at St.Elmo in the year of Connor's birth, 1860. We would have no difficulty in spotting one landmark familiar to us, namely the small log church, "unpainted and without a steeple", which still stands, a cherished historic building, at the St.Elmo crossroads. This is not the church of which the Rev. Mr. Gordon was pastor, nor was it the school house described in *Glengarry School Days.* This was a Congregationalist church, and one of the pastors who preached in it was the late Rev. William McKillican, the father of Daniel the "Forest Flower". Relations between the Presbyterians and the Congregationalists at St.Elmo were excellent, at least among the adults, but Ralph Connor describes in his autobiography, how one day he and his brother, inflamed by partisan zeal, smashed most of the windows of the "Little Church" as it was called.

"Nothing that I can think of could be a finer testimony both to the high esteem and affection in which our parents were held by the Congregational community and to the spirit of Christian forebearance shown by the members of the Little Church than the fact that the windows were quietly repaired without a word of complaint to the parents of the offenders". A landmark of today which we would miss is the fine brick church, austere but impressive on its hill, called the Gordon Free Church. The Presbyterian manse was at St.Elmo, but the Presbyterian church was several miles further south, at a site within the grounds of what is now the Protestant cemetery just south of the present-day village of Maxville.

If we followed the road, a good part of it in those days through swampy countryside, from St.Elmo south to the Presbyterian church, we would not see Maxville, which did not yet exist, but if we continued south past the Presbyterian church we would come, within a mile or two, to a sprawling pioneer settlement called Notfield. Known later in honour of the new Dominion as Dominionville, it is not mentioned in either Miss Robertson's novel or Connor's novels. Today, as if fact had followed the lead given by fiction, only the merest fragment of it remains as the tiny hamlet of Dominionville.

In this tour we would probably not be at all impressed with the appearance of the Presbyterian church, at least if it has been accurately described by the novelists who have written about it. Margaret Murray Robertson called it "the great gray, barn-like house of worship", and her nephew, who is almost always more descriptive and detailed than she, wrote: "The most enthusiastic member of the congregation could scarcely call the old church beautiful, and to Maimie's eyes it was positively hideous. No steeple or tower gave any hint of its sacred character. Its weather-beaten clapboard exterior, spotted with black knots, as if stricken with some disfiguring disease, had nothing but its row of uncurtained windows to distinguish it from an ordinary barn".

This church, removed from its original foundations and covered with brick, still survives as the Anglican church in Maxville.

To continue our sketch of the geographical background of the novels, let us move on a few years. The Rev. Mr. Gordon's congregation in the old church which we have just described was divided by the controversy, which was troubling Canadian Presbyterians at this time, between the Free Church of Scotland and the state Church of Scotland. Mr. Gordon had been a firm supporter of the Free Church since his student days. When he and his Free Church followers lost control of the old church building, they built a new brick church which has been known since the year of its opening as the Gordon Free Church, near the manse at St. Elmo. For the minister, it must have been convenient to have the manse and the church at last close to each other, but for the children it meant the end of such exhilarating rides to church as that described in the 9th chapter of *The Man from Glengarry*. The work of building the church was in progress in 1863, and the opening ceremonies were held on 20 July 1864.

Before we examine in some detail how these opening ceremonies were connected with the religious revival, we must take one more tour of imagination in the neighbourhood that Ralph Connor knew in his childhood and described in his novels. About a mile north of the manse, and in the 20th concession of Indian Lands, stood a "little log schoolhouse, of great hewn pine logs, plastered at the cracks". This humble structure was the most famous school building in Canadian history — the schoolhouse of *Glengarry School Days*.

We realize that not all our readers can do as the present writers can — turn in our chairs and pick *Glengarry School Days* off a shelf and turn to the pages where physical descriptions of the building are given and to other pages that describe its idyllic sylvan setting. But many of our readers have been or will be in Upper Canada Village, and there stands the old "20th" school. No, it is not the one that Ralph Connor attended; that one burned and was replaced with an almost exact duplicate that in due course was moved to its present site as part of the historical wealth of the area.

When first opened at its present site it was a shame to those who restored it (it had desks in orderly rows like a modern school room) but in a few years someone who knew early schools was given an opportunity and today Mr. Craven, Archibald Munro, or Hughie Murray would feel very much at home in the building, except that it is rather too well maintained. The mortar is never allowed to fall out of the cracks so the pupils (if there were any) could watch the squirrels through the cracks.

Readers, go to Upper Canada Village, sit on a bench in that old building and ponder on the faith in the future that prompted the teaching and the learning of the Pons Asinorum (Euclid Book I, Proposition 5) in a building like this in the Glengarry bush 115 years ago.

The Great Revival is so prominent in *The Man from Glengarry* that this revival must be considered as an event in Canadian literature as well as in Glengarry history. There is therefore a double reason for examining it carefully here. There were religious revivals in Glengarry before this time, and there were to be religious revivals there afterwards, so the revival of the 1860's which we will be examining is by no means a solitary phenomenon in Glengarry history. It would appear, however, that Glengarry has had no revivals since the early years of this century. As we examine the religious history of Glengarry at this time, we find that the revival described by Ralph Connor was only one of at least three revivals taking place in Glengarry at approximately the same time. This produces a problem of terminology. Should the term "Great Revival" be used to cover all three of these — and any others which have failed to leave documentary evidence or which we have failed to trace — or should it be restricted to the only real-life revival which Ralph Connor notices, that in the Rev. Mr. Gordon's church? We will perhaps occasion least perplexity if we leave the term "Great Revival" to designate the one revival Ralph Connor applied it to, that in the Rev. Mr.

Gordon's church, while we regard the other contemporary revivals as movements parallel to the Great Revival. Let us see, now, what these three revivals were.

i. The Rev. John Anderson became minister of the Free Church Presbyterian congregations at Lancaster and Dalhousie Mills in 1854. The Rev. Mr. Anderson is one of the few

Rev. John Anderson (1823-1908). In the summer of 1852 he came to south Glengarry as a student minister of the Presbyterian Free Church and he continued on as an ordained minister of the Free Church congregations of Lancaster and Dalhousie Mills. Dalhousie Mills became a separate charge in 1869 and Anderson left Lancaster in 1870. His autobiography *Reminiscences and Incidents* tells us much about those years.

nineteenth-century Glengarry clergymen that the modern reader has a chance to know intimately, on account of his well written, deeply moving, and painfully candid autobiography,

*Reminiscences and Incidents*, published in 1910 two years after his death. By any standards, *Reminiscences and Incidents* is one of the best books ever written by anyone connected with Glengarry. In this autobiography, he describes a religious revival which took place in his congregations and which, he says, "was well known throughout the whole county of Glengarry." Before this revival, he was depressed by what he regarded as the spiritual torpor of his flock, and he was torn by religious disquiets of his own. Though he never apparently ceased to be fully a religious believer, he was tormented by the possibility that the arguments of religious scepticism might be true. Looking back on his grim experiences of the year 1863, he remarked about his "spiritual foes" that "I knew something of their power before, but my knowledge of them was vague compared with what I experienced in that year of conflict." He began to feel that he would have to abandon the ministry.

While struggling with these anxieties, he decided to hold a week of prayer in his Lancaster church during the first week of January 1864. Possibly he was moved by the consideration that in times of deep perplexity any action is likely to bring a degree of relief simply because, as something new, it changes the problem at least slightly. The response the first night was poor, the sole audience in attendance being "Three...individuals who lived near the church...Two of them were widows, and the hair of one of them white with the snows of many winters; the other a maiden lady, mentally very weak, but a regular attendant at the church services."

But from this very first meeting, his appeals met with a response, and the week of prayer gave way to a major revival characterized by the same scenes of packed church attendance at the revival services, conversions, deep personal soul searching, and massive neighbourhood involvement in the revival that are described in *The Man from Glengarry* and *Torches through the Bush*. The revival was concentrated at Lancaster but extended into Dalhousie Mills and attracted an audience from all over Glengarry. It appears to have lasted at least into the spring of 1865. Anderson describes its conclusion: "But the shower of Divine grace with which the people had been so highly favored gradually ended. It was indeed a fine shower, in many ways resembling a natural shower, beginning with a drop here and there, increasing in number and weight, until a flood was formed which covered the whole country, sweeping away a great deal of dead and decayed rubbish, and turning the barren fields of God's own heritage into fruitfulness." Describing the state of affairs at the beginning of this revival, he remarks that "revival meetings were then unknown among Presbyterians."

ii. The revival next to be considered brings to our attention a neglected figure from nineteenth-century Glengarry history, the Rev. Erastus Rainboth, pastor of the Baptist Church at Notfield. A revival took place in his church in 1864 which, it has sometimes been assumed, spread north and set in motion the revival in the Rev. Mr. Gordon's church. As at Lancaster, the revival began in a week of prayer held in the first week of January. The prayer meetings were extended to last throughout January and February, but for a time the results were discouraging, and the conversion of three little girls, about twelve years old, is believed to have been important in producing the fully developed revival which followed. We are told that daily, at noon, the three little girls "retired to a grove near the school-house, and engaged in earnest and united petitions for a work of grace in the hearts of their young companions. Their prayers of faith were not long unanswered—one and another of their companions became convinced of their lost condition, and joined their praying circle, whilst many others, true to the spirit of the world, mocked and derided, inflicting on those praying ones their juvenile persecutions." The Rev. Mr. Rainboth being absent at this time, Mrs. Rainboth undertook to supervise meetings of these children in her home. When these meetings attracted a large attendance they were replaced by regular revival services, under the supervision of Mr. Rainboth and (later) an assistant, in the Baptist chapel at Notfield.

iii. We come thirdly, then, to the revival in the Rev. Mr. Gordon's new brick church at St.Elmo — the revival so memorably described in *The Man from Glengarry*. From contemporary accounts of the revival, we seem to be justified in assuming that it began in three stages. In the first stage, there were prayer meetings which began with a week of prayer in January 1864, were discontinued when the roads broke up in the spring, and then were resumed and continued all summer. These prayer meetings were themselves a repetition of similar prayer meetings of 1862 and 1863. In the second stage, religious meetings were held in July 1864 in preparation for the opening of the new church later that month. For these, the Presbyterians were allowed to use the log Congregationalist chapel at St. Elmo. The third stage, which saw the beginning of the fully developed revival, began with the opening of the new church on 20 July 1864. The nightly meetings of the revival continued into 1865, and in April of 1865 Mr. Gordon was able to write that no twenty-four hours had "yet passed since the opening of the church in which its walls have not resounded with the voice of praise and prayer." In the following passage he describes the scenes which, two generations later, gave rise to the title of his son's third and final novel about Glengarry *(Torches through the Bush).* As the autumn of the first year of the revival advanced, "the roads became almost impassable, yet it did not occur to any one that the nightly meetings could be discontinued. It was with even renewed astonishment that I saw what numbers of young men and old, through darkness, rain, and mud, found their way to the house of prayer. The scene often presented at the close of the meeting was both picturesque and interesting, as in different directions the eye could trace the progress of the various groups of pedestrians by the blaze of the burning torches carried by the young men to guide them safely through the darkness." Mr. Gordon's health broke under the strain of the continued services. He left for Scotland in August of 1865, leaving his wife and family at St. Elmo, and he was still absent in March of the following year. If his absence was not initially caused by his bad health, his return was at least delayed for that reason. In his absence, the religious meetings of the revival continued on a reduced scale, but by this time the main period of the revival was over.

One result of the Great Revival in the Rev. Mr. Gordon's congregation was the establishing of classes in which young men who wished to enter the ministry and others who merely wished to improve themselves could continue their education to college-entrance level. Subjects taught included classics, mathematics, English, and military drill. To this educational project was given the name of the Bethel Hill Seminary.

We have already commented on the similarities as to setting and events between Miss Robertson's *Shenac* and Ralph Connor's Glengarry novels. Did Ralph Connor know his aunt's novel, and did it influence the writing of his Glengarry novels? Unfortunately, it does not seem possible to answer these questions decisively, but it is interesting and possibly significant that two passages in *The Man from Glengarry* may be echoes of passages in *Shenac.* Miss Robertson writes about the first settlers, ''And though there were those among the aged or the discontented who never ceased to pine for the heather hills of the old land, the young grew up strong and content, troubled by no fear that, for many and many a year to come, the place would become too strait for them or for their children.'' Connor wrote in *The Man from Glengarry,* ''By their fathers the forest was dreaded and hated, but the sons, with rifles in hand, trod its pathless stretches without fear, and with their broadaxes they took toll of their ancient foe.'' So too in describing the opening of the new church, Miss Robertson wrote, ''A few of those to whom even the dust of Zion is dear, seeking to consecrate the house, and with it themselves, more entirely to God's service, met for prayer for a few nights before the public dedication; and from that time for more than a year not a night passed in which the voice of prayer and praise did not arise within its walls. All through the busy harvest-time, through the dark autumn evenings, when the unmade roads of the country were deep and danger-ous, and through the frosts and snows of a bitter winter, the people gathered to the house of prayer.'' And her nephew wrote in *The Man from Glengarry,* "For eighteen months, night after night, every night in the week except Saturday, the people gathered in such numbers as to fill the new church to the door. Throughout all the busy harvest season, in spite of the autumn rains that filled the swamps and made the roads almost impassable, 'in the face of the driving snows of winter, through the melting ice of the spring, and again through the following summer and autumn, the great revival held on." It may or may not be a matter of coincidence that the minister of Indian Lands is given the surname of Murray, which was Miss Robertson's middle name. The evidence that Ralph Connor was influenced by his aunt's novel is a little stronger than the evidence that she was influenced by the *Forest Flower,* but as before we must say—not proven.

## Confederation and Its Background

The uneasy legislative union between Upper and Lower Canada which began in 1841 lasted for little more than a quarter of a century. During this time, John Sandfield Macdonald was premier of the United Canadas in 1862-1864. By the time of his premiership, he had become the member for Cornwall. Our county (represented now by Donald Sandfield) could therefore claim the honour of having been the birthplace of the premier but not of being his present constituency. As the rivalries of Upper and Lower Canada began to make the legislative union difficult to work, enterprising politicians began to turn their eyes towards a confederation of the British North American colonies as a solution to the problem of governing the two Canadas. But the two Sandfield brothers firmly opposed Confederation, and we therefore cannot count them or indeed any other Glengarrians among the Fathers of Confederation.

If the union of the Canadas had proved unsatisfactory, Canadians could at least console themselves for a few years with the thought that their troubles were, at worst, tiny compared with those of their much envied neighbour, the United States. In the years 1861-1865 the United States fought the great Civil War, as the northern states tried to prevent their southern brethren from leaving the union.

In its early stages, the war brought economic distress to Canadians, and interrupted the Canadian recovery from the serious depression which had begun in 1857. Later, the immense demands for merchandise created by the war caused a much welcomed boom in Canada, and there seems no need to doubt the tradition that the war brought great prosperity to Glengarry County. Even a half year after the war had ended, it was reported from Glengarry that "the Yankees are buying up almost everything & animal they can get." But with the end of the war demand, and with the end in 1866 of the reciprocity treaty, which had allowed many Canadian products entry into the United States free of customs duties, hard times were felt in Canada. According to Rhodes Grant: "An old man told me that it was a strange thing; when times began to get hard they got hard all at once. It seemed like overnight. People were comfortable, the first thing they knew they were poor. It seemed as if they became poor as soon as they thought they were poor."

Sandfield Macdonald spoke in Parliament of the "immense number" of young men from Upper Canada who were fighting in the American armies of the Civil War. We have only been able to trace about a dozen Glengarrians who fought in the war, but doubtless there were many more. Visitors to the historic Baptist cemetery at Breadalbane will find there a reminder of the Civil War in the form of the tombstone of Captain James A. Lothian, of the 26th Regiment of Michigan Infantry, who died in hospital at Alexandria, Virginia, in July 1864, of a wound received in action before Petersburg, Florida, a few weeks earlier. An ingenious Glengarrian called Dugald Macdonald, who later published two books outlining his own very personal theories of astronomy and pyramidology, is stated to have covered the Civil War as a journalist for the *New York Daily News*. Sandfield Macdonald had a personal connection with the struggle in that his American brother-in-law, Eugene Waggaman, was a colonel on the

Southern side in the war and was one of the officers who surrendered with Lee at Appomattox.

The American Civil War is also connected with our subject through the Fenian Raids. Numbers of Irish soldiers in the Northern armies belonged to the Irish revolutionary organization called the Fenians which was working in Ireland, Britain, and North America to free Ireland from British rule. As these men had received military training in the American war, ardent Irish nationalists formed the idea of using them to injure Britain by attacking Canada, a British possession, from across the American border. The Fenian Raids, as they were called, which took place in 1866 and 1870, were total failures as far as the aims of the Fenians were concerned, but they caused much alarm in Canada. The Fenian threat was one of the lesser forces acting to bring about Confederation, and the successful actions of the Canadians in their own defense encouraged Canadians' pride in themselves and their nation.

The Glengarrians played a less active role in the Fenian troubles than they had done in the 1837 rebellion. In the spring of 1866 interest was so low that the Cornwall *Freeholder* complained that "Every County in the Province but Glengarry has turned out its quota to protect the frontier... Has the martial spirit of the ancient Gael forsaken Glengarry?" But the answer was clearly no, for a little later the four battalions of the Glengarry militia offered their services to the Governor General in a loyal address, and Volunteer Infantry Companies organized at Lancaster and Williamstown were soon drilling to ready themselves to meet all attackers. When the Fenian threat re-emerged in 1870, the men of the Lancaster and Williamstown Infantry Companies and of a similar company formed at Dunvegan in 1868 by Dr. Donald McDiarmid were among those who turned out to protect Cornwall and the waterfront area near it. As in 1866, the Glengarrians on this occasion took no part in actual fighting against the Fenians.

# Chapter IV
# Glengarry in 1871

For Glengarry in the year 1871 statistical information is available from the first census taken after Confederation — known as the Census of 1871 or, sometimes, as the census of 1870-1871. 1871 is well suited to a survey of Glengarry such as we propose to make because at that time Glengarry stood on the brink of two of the few economic revolutions it has undergone — the rise of the cheese factories, and the building of the Canada Atlantic Railway through the northern concessions.

Confederation in 1867 had united Canada East and Canada West (now renamed Quebec and Ontario) with Nova Scotia and New Brunswick. In 1870, the developing province of Manitoba was added to the new nation, and in 1871 the far-off province of British Columbia was added. In the new dominion, a sense of Canadian nationality had, largely, still to be created. Those who remember Glengarry of the 1940's will agree that even at that late date Scottish Glengarrians thought of themselves as primarily Scottish Highlanders. It may be guessed, therefore, that little sense of ''Canadianism'' had yet emerged in the Scottish Glengarrians of the 1870's. They were attached to the soil of their county and they prided themselves on their loyalty to the Crown — and beyond that, who could know in any case that the union of 1867 would be any more lasting than the union of 1841?

For Glengarrians who had an interest in world affairs, 1871 was an exciting year. As it began, the Franco-Prussian War was in progress and Paris was under siege by the German armies. The French authorities surrendered before the end of

January, and the peace terms were signed in the spring. Communists and other revolutionaries in Paris seized the opportunity created by the weakness of the defeated French government to set up the revolutionary "Commune." Hailed by Karl Marx as the first working class revolutionary government in the world, it was crushed by the French government with the utmost savagery. Meanwhile, the German states which had cooperated to defeat France united early in 1871 to form a new nation in Europe—the German Empire, of which William I, the King of Prussia, was made the first emperor. Thus came into being the "Germany" of the First World War. Awesome in its military might from the very beginning, it was not many years before the new empire had made itself one of the world's top industrial powers. Before 1871 was out, newspaper readers had thrilled to the story of a much lesser event, which nevertheless made a great impression in its day and is still well remembered—the great Chicago fire. And for a few people throughout the world to read, and for many to hear about, there was a new book by Charles Darwin, the celebrated author of the *Origin of Species.* In *The Descent of Man* (1871), he joined the debate, which was already some years in progress, on the development of the human race from ape-like ancestors.

In October, Glengarry was violently linked with the outside world. A Cornwall newspaper reported on the forest fires which had swept through Peshtigo and other settlements in Wisconsin, the Saginaw Valley, and along the Lake Michigan shores, and asserted that "All these villages were filled with young men from Canada, and from many a home in these counties goes up tonight a wail for the loved ones burnt to death in these western towns and woods." The newspaper observed that of the 2000 inhabitants of Peshtigo, about 1200 were Canadians, "the great majority" of which were from the United Counties. It is pleasing to be able to report that, on the basis of such scanty evidence on this subject as we have been able to uncover, these statements and implications about the tragedy which struck Glengarry remain unverified.

Within Glengarry, by contrast, 1871 was a quiet year.

Sir Edward Peacock (1871-1962), son of Congregational minister in Indian Lands and Jane McDougall of Maxville. Began life as schoolmaster in Canada. In England he rose to the very top of the world of finance. Knighted 1934.

Nothing happened remotely comparable in importance to the great storms of the winter of 1869. That winter, which must still have been a lively topic of conversation, was to go down in legend as the Winter of the Deep Snow. There was talk in 1871 of the new railroad which the M.P. for the county, Donald "Sandfield" Macdonald was promoting, and which was to run through the back townships. Presbyterians and others in Glengarry mourned the death in February of the Rev. Hugh Urquhart, of Cornwall, who had for some decades been one of the most eminent Presbyterian clergymen in Ontario. As headmaster of the Cornwall grammar school, one of his pupils had been John Sandfield Macdonald. In 1871 there was the excitement of a provincial election, in which James Craig was re-elected M.L.A., defeating Archibald McNab. It may be feared that less attention was drawn to a competition, held in connection with the games of the Caledonian Society of Glengarry, for the best poem on Glengarry. Professor Daniel Wilson, of University College, Toronto, was the judge, and the prize, a silver medal, was awarded to Mr. John Reed of the Montreal *Gazette*.

Fairfield. Though altered in form and with a wing added (not visible in picture) this house built by John A. (Cariboo) Cameron after his return from the Cariboo goldfields still stands on the north side of Highway No. 2, a bit west of Summerstown. The present owners, the Sacred Heart Order, bought it for a school in 1946.

At what is now St. Elmo, the most newsworthy event of 1871 was the departure of the Rev. Daniel Gordon for his new pastorate in Western Ontario. At St. Elmo, too, in 1871 was born the future Sir Edward Peacock (died 1962) who would be a prominent financier in England and a director of the Bank of England. His father was the congregationalist minister of the log church at St. Elmo and his mother was of a Glengarry family of MacDougalls.

In 1871, Glengarrians were basking in the glory of having a fellow Glengarrian as premier of Ontario, but there was another Glengarrian whose deeds had sounded perhaps even more loudly through the country—the famous Cariboo Cameron.

John A. (Cariboo) Cameron tried his success as a gold miner in the California gold rush, but his lucky strike was made in the Cariboo gold rush of the 1860's. Two months before he and his group made their discovery of gold in December 1862, his wife, who had accompanied him to the gold fields, died at the desolate mining camp of Richfield. With the aid of a fellow Glengarrian, Robert Stevenson, whose writings provide us with our best information on Cameron, he hauled his wife's body 400 miles through the wilderness to Victoria. In 1863 he brought her body back to Cornwall, where it was buried. To preserve it for transportation, it had been enclosed in a metal tank full of alcohol. Besides being generous to his relatives, Cameron built himself a fine house at Summerstown, the cornerstone of which was laid in 1865. A well known Glengarry landmark, it is used today as a school.

Even before his wife was reburied in Cornwall, rumours were afoot that her body was not really in the sealed coffin. As long as he could, Cameron ignored the speculations about the contents of the coffin and about the real sources of his wealth. But when a paper in Syracuse, New York, stated that his wife was still alive and that he had sold her to an Indian chief for his gold claim, he was forced into action. He published a newspaper announcement of the date on which the body would be disinterred. On 10 August 1873, in the presence of a large crowd of spectators, the coffin of Sophia Cameron was opened in Cornwall, and her features, well preserved in the alcohol, fully disproved the charges which had so afflicted her husband. Afterwards, the body was re-interred in the cemetery near her husband's new house at Summerstown. A Montreal newspaper account of the proceedings speaks of the coffin of Sophia's child also being disinterred with that of its mother. This child had died in Victoria, shortly after Cameron's arrival in B.C. Tradition is silent on whether Cameron brought her body to Cornwall at the same time as her mother's or whether he had it moved at some later date.

Cameron's misfortunes did not end here. His business ventures proved unsuccessful, and his wealth melted away. Late in life he again went to British Columbia, where fortune had once so memorably shone upon him, and he died at Barkerville near the scene of his gold mine in 1888.

Cariboo Cameron's reputation is still fresh today, but another Glengarry worthy who received some attention about this time is totally neglected. In 1868, the *Cornwall Freeholder* reported that there was "at the present time, living within two miles of the village of Dunvegan" an old lady named McLean, who had been born in 1751 and was therefore 117 years old. In the following year, it was reported that a woman in Glengarry, whose name was given as Annie Campbell was 126 years old, and that she "frequently during the past summer milked as many as twelve cows daily." In September 1872, Annie Campbell died, and the prestigious Montreal *Witness* reported that she had reached the age of 131 years, having been born on the Isle of Skye in 1741, and that she had emigrated to Canada in 1828. "She was able up to the Monday preceding her death, to follow her former occupation of milking cows." The *Witness* appended some reminiscences of her by the Rev. R.F. Burns, a prominent clergyman, who stated that her pastor had verified her age from the parish registers in the Isle of Skye. Her death was recorded in the vital records of the province of Ontario, where her age was given as 123 years and her occupation as "Dairy Maid." A Glengarry diarist, Angus MacMillan, gave her age at death, more soberly, as 110, and added the useful infomation that she died on lot 30 in the 9th of Kenyon. We get a last glimpse of Annie Campbell in 1890, when the

*Glengarrian* , of Alexandria, reported the death of her daughter, Mrs. K. McLennan ("commonly called Big Jennet") on the same Kenyon lot. "The deceased was the daughter of the oldest woman that ever lived in this part of the country, her age being said to be 131 years when she died. The daughter must have been about 100 years old when she died last week."

There appears at this late date to be no possibility of ascertaining the truth about Annie Campbell's age, and we may pass by at this point the pretty legend of which she was the centre in the interests of leading our readers into some of the statistics which are available for Glengarry in 1871.

To begin, the population figures. In Glengarry in 1871, according to official data, 185 people died, and 499 were born. In 1871, the population of the county was found to be 20,524 — about 1,250 more than it is today. In 1824, the population had been 7,084, in 1831, 10,333, in 1841, 12,546 and in 1851-52, 17,596. In 1860-61 a population of 21,187 is recorded, which was higher than that of 1871, but the figures for Glengarry in 1860-61 seem sufficiently out of line with nineteenth-century Glengarry population figures to make one suspect an error. In 1871, Charlottenburgh, with 6,331 persons, had the largest population of the four townships, and Lancaster the smallest, with 4,415. As there were as yet no incorporated towns or villages, no census figures were published for subdivisions smaller than the four townships. Some comparisons will help to bring out the significance of these figures. In 1871 the total population of Ontario was 1,620,851. About 1¼% of the population of Ontario therefore resided in Glengarry County. In 1871, Montreal was, by Canadian standards, a giant city, with a population of 107,225. Toronto had 56,092, and Ottawa had 21,545. Glengarry had thus a little less than one-fifth of the population of Montreal, had something over one-third the population of Toronto, and had nearly as large a population as the national capital. It is a curious historical fact that Toronto did not pass Glengarry in population size till the late 1830's.

These figures had political and social weight. So long as the Glengarry population compared favourably with that of other populous areas within the province, the county would, inevitably, attract general notice. If Glengarry has almost sunk out of sight in Ontario today, it is partly because our population figures have contracted while those elsewhere in the province have exploded.

In 1871, about two fifths of the Glengarry population was aged under 16. Figures are not available today for exactly the same age groups as in 1871, but about two fifths of the Glengarry population today is aged under 20. Given the fact that a fully adult state of life today, because of prolonged schooling, begins later than it did in most communities a hundred years ago, it seems not unreasonable to say that children and adolescents—the "under-aged" generally— made up about the same proportion in Glengarry society in 1871 as today.

In the census figures for 1871 describing the ethnic origins of the people of Glengarry, we find that the largest group by far, numbering 15,899, was "Scotch". The second largest group, numbering 2,607, was French. The third, fourth, and fifth groups in order of size were Irish (1,279), English (509), and German (122). All other groups were insignificant in size. Included were 17 Negroes.

Figures are also available for the birthplaces of the people of 1871 by countries. No less than 18,295 or 89% of the people of Glengarry were born in Canada, 16,740 or 81½% of them in Ontario. Those born in Scotland numbered 1,648 or a trifle over 10% of the number of persons of Scottish origin. Overwhelmingly, then, by 1871 Glengarry had become a community of native-born North Americans, and natives of Scotland had become a tiny minority—an ever dwindling, fast disappearing link with the country three thousand miles away of which most Scottish Glengarrians knew only by report.

In religion, the largest group was the Roman Catholics, who numbered 10,404 or one half of the population of the county. Presbyterians, subdivided into four different groups, numbered 9012. Baptists were the third largest group, with 544 adherents. Church of England adherents made a surprisingly large showing with a total of 311, largely from the Township of Charlottenburgh. Congregationalists numbered 133, Jews 39, and Methodists (subdivided into three different groups) 38. Only a handful of people did not fall into one or the other of these categories.

From the analysis of the Glengarrians by profession in the Census of 1871, we learn that Glengarry then had 3218 farmers, 854 labourers, 92 servants (11 male and 73 female) 89 blacksmiths, 72 shoemakers, 67 teachers, 66 merchants, 54 weavers, 28 hotel keepers, 20 tanners, 18 tailors, 16 clergymen, 9 doctors, 7 government employees, 4 lawyers, 2 photographers, 1 dentist, 1 fisherman, and 1 gentleman of private means, but no artists or "litterateurs," and no architects, auctioneers, bankers, booksellers, brewers, judges, locksmiths, policemen, professors, or veterinary surgeons.

A new age dawned for the county in 1855 when the Grand Trunk Railway line opened for traffic between Montreal and Brockville, with Lancaster being then or becoming shortly one of its stations. In 1856, the line was opened to Toronto. It may well have been that a few of the Glengarry United Empire Loyalists were still alive to see the first locomotives pass through their county.

The arrival of the railway age brought a new twist to a problem of names which had dogged Lancaster Township and Lancaster Village from the beginning. The reseachers in the history of early nineteenth-century Glengarry will from time to time be puzzled to know whether references to something or someone being in "Lancaster" refer to the township or the village. When the Grand Trunk Railway passed a mile or so north of the village, a new village began to grow up about the station, and the new village became known as New Lancaster and, at last, as Lancaster Depot or Lancaster. The shift of the old name to the new village created the problem of what to call the original Lancaster. It was known variously as The Lower Village, Riviere Raisin, and Kirktown, and finally as South Lancaster. To most people from the north of the county, the two villages together form "Lancaster", though one is an incorporated village (since 19 October 1887) and the other is not, and the initiated or merely careful observer will still detect a distinct break between them. To follow out the complications of this problem to the end, it must be noted that by 1845 the hamlet of North Lancaster, which is in about the centre (rather than the north) of Lancaster Township, had received its name, and that in course of time a railway passing two miles away from it gave rise to another hamlet called North Lancaster Station.

A log house in Glengarry. Log houses in an unrestored state are rare in Glengarry at the time of writing but as recently as the end of World War II they could be found in any concession road and every built-up area in the county. In this one the original small window panes have given way to large ones. Otherwise it could be, and probably is, the same in appearance as when it was built at any time between 1800 and 1880.

Lancaster Village was apparently not without its attractions in 1871. We read that when a railway accident in December caused the train passengers to alight at Lancaster, they "were well entertained at the different hotels in the village".

Vying with Lancaster in 1871 for the role of the most important village in Glengarry, but unhappily without a railway, was Alexandria, reported in at least two books of that year to have a population of about 800. Perhaps a more realistic estimate of the population would be that it amounted to at least 600. Predominantly, the village was Scottish and Roman Catholic. Alexandria had had a bank (the Ontario Bank) for some years, but it had closed by 1871. Nor in this year does there appear to have been any bank elsewhere in Glengarry. 1871 brought an important advance to Alexandria in the arrival of the telegraph, which about that time also reached Martintown and several other centres in the county.

Elsewhere in the county important local service villages had grown up. Williamstown, St.Raphaels, and Martintown were now in their third generation of settlement. Charlie Stackhouse's mills at the north-east corner of Lancaster Township had become a busy little place called Dalhousie Mills. Munro's general store and trading post in the 8th of Charlottenburgh had become the busy hamlet of Munro's Mills. We have mentioned Notfield already, but George MacDonell's business enterprises where the west branch of the Scotch River crosses the 20th of Indian Lands must not be ignored. In 1871 the hamlet of Athol was a busy spot. It had had a post office for 20 years, boasted wooden sidewalks and the usual complement of skilled workers in wood, and blacksmiths and a store. The principal industries, however, were the saw mills, the store, and Urquhart's nearby grist and flour mill.

Kenyon boasted, in addition to the places mentioned, Dunvegan, Skye, Baltic's Corner, Kenyon Town Hall (now Greenfield), and James Fraser's busy hamlet at the west end of Loch Garry, which was important enough to get a post office as early as 1860, even though most of its edifices were built of logs. At Dunvegan, 1871 was important as the year in which the cornerstone of the present stone Presbyterian church was laid.

In Charlottenburgh Glen Donald, Cashion's Glen, Glen Brook, Glen Gordon, Camerontown, and Glen Walter were forming hamlets that soon would boast a cheese factory, a general store, and at least one blacksmith, and in Lancaster Glen Norman, Bainsville, and Curry Hill were taking form.

In the south-east corner of Lochiel the usual crossroads community was growing up on the road between concessions 1 and 2 at lot 8. It was known as Charlie Roy's Corner in 1871 but in 1874 would become a post office village under its present name of Glen Robertson and like all of northern Glengarry anxiously awaited the building of the Montreal and City of Ottawa Junction Railway.

Dalkeith grew up on the crossroad closest to Robertson's Mills on the Rigaud River and got its name from the home area of the Robertson family in Scotland. Dalkeith got its post office in 1867 and in 1871 was the metropolis of north east Lochiel, as it is today.

Oddly enough, the only area in Glengarry that failed to produce "towns with a potential growth" in this period was Breadalbane. Search as we will, we have found in Breadalbane only a school, a cheese factory, a church, post office, and Fraser's tannery, and these were widely separated. No hamlet ever developed with the usual blacksmith and general store in that area.

The years immediately after Confederation showed a beginning of "urbanization" in Glengarry. The beginning unfortunately could not be followed up with sustained growth. Many of the places mentioned above, once busy hamlets, no longer exist, and the rest, except for Alexandria, were doomed to remain small villages. There was not the necessary productivity in their areas to support the services towns provide.

Cornwall, just outside the Glengarry boundaries, was

important for Glengarrians. Its size in 1871 (a little over 2000 souls) meant that it had a large range of shops, businesses, and other facilities. Today, when Cornwall is almost 25 times larger, it is hard to picture how primitive it must have been then. In the spring of 1881, the editor of a Cornwall newspaper complained that "The cows have located themselves for the summer on our principal streets and best sidewalks" In the fall of the same year, the newspaper renewed its complaint about the cows roaming Cornwall streets, and lamented that a Cornwall house of prostitution, which had been raided in August, had revived and that its "inmates...make night hideous with their drunken yells"

Cornwall was the county town for the United Counties. In the early days of the province, local government had been by justices of the peace assembled in Quarter Sessions. This system had been replaced in the early 1840's by government by elected councils, with one council for each district. Glengarry was in the Eastern District, which contained also Stormont and Dundas. In 1849, the old division of the province into districts was abolished. A system of local government by towns, townships, and counties, which is virtually the same as that in use in the United Counties today, was established in 1850. Under the new system, Stormont, Dundas, and Glengarry continued to govern themselves as a unit, and the union of the United Counties can be said to be simply a continuation of the Eastern District under another name. In 1871 a Glengarrian, Peter Kennedy of Notfield, was the Warden of the United Counties.

Among the places that mattered in the lives of Glengarrians at this time, we must now mention one which except as a name has all but vanished from the earth. Early in the nineteenth century, four remarkable mineral springs were discovered in the north of Caledonia Township. In an age of belief in the curative power of such springs, here was a chance to establish a Canadian equivalent of Bath, Cheltenham, Baden Baden, or Mallow. Such places had always provided recreation as well as opportunities to drink and to bathe in the waters. At the site of these springs, there soon arose a health and holiday resort, known as Caledonia Springs. An exuberant newspaper stated in 1842 about the springs and the resort proprietor Mr. Parker that "The public spirit and enterprise of Mr.Parker has rendered the forests of Caledonia a second Elysium, and where a few years ago was the unvisited and unmolested haunt of bears, wolves and other ferocious animals, hundreds of rational beings may now be seen enjoying 'Life at the Springs' ''. As early as 1833, a pair of newlyweds from Alexandria went to Caledonia Springs for their honeymoon. Those who did not care for the inconvenience of a long trip to secure their share of the beneficient waters were catered to, for in 1837 we read that Caledonia Springs water was on sale at the post office in Cornwall. Through the remainder of the nineteenth century, the more affluent Glengarrians are often mentioned as holidaying at Caledonia Springs. Glengarrians of humbler means paid the Springs day visits and brought home containers of the water. The youthful invalids in the *Forest Flower* and *Shenac's Work at Home* both visited the springs in an attempt to recover their health.

In the part of our story on "Churches" we will go into detail that we will not attempt here, but an interesting anomoly in Glengarry's churches and its people in 1871 is worth mentioning. It will be noted as we stated above that half of Glengarry's population in 1871 was Roman Catholic. They had churches at St.Raphaels, Williamstown, Alexandria, and Lochiel and a chapel on lot 26-3rd Kenyon—five in all. The Protestants with the other half of the population had 21 churches—three in Martintown, two in the second of Lancaster, two at Dalhousie Mills, two at St.Elmo, two in the Lancaster villages, two at Kirk Hill, and one at each of Summerstown, Williamstown, Alexandria, Dunvegan, Notfield, Brodie, and Breadalbane. The Auld Kirk Presbyterians at the north end of Indian Lands still had their "white church", though in 1871 there was no village of Maxville to the north of it.

From this one can judge the Protestant Glebe had its

practical uses — most of the ministers had to grow some of their own food if they were to support their families because the congregations were so small, especially in the more rural areas.

There had never yet been a newspaper published in Glengarry, but for those who wanted a newspaper, a large variety was available elsewhere. In Cornwall, John Sandfield Macdonald's newspaper, the lively *Freeholder* defended his political interests, and the anti-Sandfieldite newspaper was the *Gazette*. Among Protestant readers, the Montreal *Witness* was a favourite. Sandy Fraser, the *Farmer's Advocate* columnist, who was born in 1876, later said that he "was, in a way o'speaking, raised on it, in sae far as religion and politics and a few ither things were concerned". A blacksmith in Lochiel who picked up the mail for his neighbours was nicknamed "Witness" Denovan because he brought the *Witness*. Whoever wishes to understand the outlook of English Canada in the disappointing decades from Confederation to the mid-nineties, when economic depression and the continued flight of population to the United States cruelly mocked the hopes of the new nation, can hardly do better than to read the bleak, sour pages of the *Witness*. The *Witness* was valued by the Canadian business community for its commercial news, but it is an interesting question how much its bitterly negative attitudes did to paralyse initiative in that very community. For Catholic readers, there was the Montreal *True Witness*; for years, the *Witness* and the *True Witness* battled each other fiercely through their editorial columns. The Glengarry-born poet J.J.Macdonald was a great admirer of the *True Witness*. Other Montreal newspapers were the *Gazette, Herald, Star, La Minerve and Le Nouveau Monde*. Some Glengarrians devoted to the Reform cause in politics may have read the Toronto *Globe*.

It is most likely however, that the great majority of Glengarry families took no newspaper at all. Some of these, of course, were able to borrow copies which came to their neighbours and circulated from hand to hand in the community. In a picture taken of the congregation at the 75th anniversary service at Columba Church, Kirk Hill, a large rock can be seen in the centre of the picture and in the immediate foreground. Traditions and the memory of people still living twenty years ago tell us this rock was used as a rostrum from which a leading member of the church read out or otherwise passed on items of news and information after church services.

Many Canadian newspapers at this time were openly the propaganda organs of political parties. A subscriber would choose a paper which agreed with his politics, and he might feel strongly about the evil done by the opposition press.

One can trace a number of Glengarry family connections about this time with the newspaper world. John McPhee, a son of one of the earliest settlers of Lochiel, was bookkeeper and cashier of the *Transcript* (Montreal, ceased publication 1865) and afterwards of the *Witness* and his niece married the senior proprietor of the *Witness*. Donald McDonald, proprietor of the *Transcript*, who died in 1870, emigrated to Canada in 1815; while he settled in Montreal to work in the *Gazette* office, his family settled in Lochiel. Oscar McDonell, said to be a native of Glengarry County, was editor and publisher of *Le Canada* (founded Ottawa 1879). At a later stage he was editor of *Le Temps* (Ottawa). Charles Sinclair of St. Elmo mentions in his autobiography that his uncle Duncan Robertson, a school teacher, was editor of the Ottawa (Bytown) *Daily News*.

As to circulation of magazines in Glengarry at this time, little is known. The Cornwall *Freeholder* complained in 1865 that there were ''only 71'' Glengarry subscribers to the *Canada Farmer*, a handsomely illustrated agricultural periodical published by the editor of the Toronto *Globe*. However, these figures contrast favourably with those for Stormont and Dundas, where there were only 10 and 43 subscribers respectively. The religious periodicals of the various denominations may be assumed to have had Glengarry subscribers. A Gaelic and English periodical called *An Gaidheal*, which began in Toronto in 1871, had a subscription agent (D.F. Maclennan) in Williamstown. A few enlightened families may have subscribed to overseas periodicals such as the *Quarterly* or *Edinburgh Review*, which were advertised in the *Freeholder* in 1866 as available through a New York dealer.

Agriculture was the main economic activity in Glengarry in 1871, but it was supplemented by a number of small businesses of the processing or manufacturing kind. Glengarry then had 21 carriage-making establishments employing 66 hands, 18 sawmills employing 106 hands, 14 tanneries employing 27 hands, 8 flour and grist mills, 4 carding and fulling mills, 1 brickyard, and 2 cheese factories employing 3 men and 2 women.

In a review of the economy we must pay especial attention to the potash industry. Potash was made from a lye leached from wood ashes, and was made sometimes by individual farmers and sometimes by entrepreneurs in small businesses called "asheries" to which the farmers sold their ashes. Ashes were produced abundantly as a by-product of the destruction of the forest in land clearing. Sometimes timber seems to have been burned solely to produce ashes for this purpose, without land clearing being intended. At a later date, when less land clearing was taking place, ashes were still available from the household use of wood as a fuel. In an age when cash was scarce in Glengarry and farmers had relatively few saleable products, potash produced a welcome income. Two prospective land purchasers in 1829 complained to a government official that the lots they were thinking of buying in the north of Lochiel were of "very indifferent land, besides there is not any timber on either lot that is anywise fit for making pot ash, and as that is the only way we have of paying for the same, we cannot think of offering at such a high rate..."

An observer of the Lochiel militiamen at the time of the 1837-38 rebellion recalled that, "The sleighs made with high boxes for carrying ashes filled with the volunteers as close together as they could stand were the mode of conveyance. I remember well seeing them passing by Laggan along the Military Road, only their heads and shoulders with the muzzles of their muskets visible, on their way to the front.''

The successive census reports give a profile of the maturity and fall of the Glengarry potash industry. In 1851-1852, Glengarry had 5 potash and pearl asheries (pearl ash was a refined form of potash). In 1871, Glengarry had 10 potash and pearl asheries, employing 30 hands. In 1881 Glengarry had 7 potash and pearl asheries employing 12 hands. By 1891, only three asheries remained in the county, with a total of three employees. Production figures only (70 barrels) are given for pot and pearl ashes in Glengarry in 1901; thereafter, the census returns do not notice potash production. When Farquhar Dewar, who had run an ashery before the First World War, died in 1974, there snapped one of the last links with the old Glengarry potash industry.

For a short time in the 1860's, there was a possibility that Glengarry might develop an oil industry. The Canadian oil industry had begun in Lambton County in 1855. In June of 1865, the *Freeholder* announced that ''a party from the oil regions in the Western part of the province'' had purchased land in the Township of Lancaster ''for the purpose of boring for oil.'' By late summer, boring was under way, and it may have been still in progress a year later. The well attained a depth of some 500 feet, and although no oil was found, there are said to have been indications of gas. The well was on lot 21, in the 2nd of Lancaster, near Bainsville. The name associated in our sources with the venture was that of Thomas H. McLean, presumably the same man as the T.H. McLean who immediately afterwards appears in the news as the Lancaster-based proprietor of a patent medicine called Oleum Kalamos. In the *Freeholder* of 15 March 1867, we read that it is unequalled ''for removing pain of almost any kind,'' and that as a dentifrice it is so effective that a few drops on a brush will make the teeth ''white and clean, no matter how black they may have been.'' We have not been able to trace either McLean's origins or his ultimate fate. The association with patent medicine may or may not — readers must decide — cast doubt on the bona fides of the oil well project. Oleum Kalamos, it may be noted, translates roughly as "pen oil" (= Pennsylvania oil? The Pennsylvania oil fields were being developed at this time and were much in the news).

In 1965, a few years after Glengarry was excited by the possibility of oil in the McCrimmon area, an oil company again sank a hole near the site of McLean's oil well.

Oil, unhappily, has never become one of Glengarry's exports, but let us enquire how the goods which were exported from Glengarry farms and manufactories in 1871 found their outlet. One of the main outlets, and probably the most important, was the Grand Trunk railway station at Lancaster. A.W. McDougald, who wrote an excellent history of Glengarry in the *Glengarry News* in the 1930's, wrote of the importance of Lancaster Station in the decade before the opening of the railway through Alexandria, a period to which his memory reached back:

Lancaster station was the great gateway and commercial entrepôt for all of Glengarry lying east and north of the River aux Raisins, namely for more than two-thirds of the county. It was the point of ingress for all supplies which came into that territory from outside markets and of egress for all commodities to be marketed abroad. Here flourished a number of very substantial trading firms — MacPherson & Alexander, Duncan and George McBean and brothers. Large general merchants were William and David McPherson and Donald McNaughton. It was no uncommon spectacle on a crisp winter's morning for these traders to find a queue of farmers' sleighs a half mile or more in length lined up upon the Military Road laden with the produce of the North Country from as far distant as Caledonia, Skye, Dunvegan, Scotch River [Athol] and even from Vankleek Hill. The staple articles of commerce in this market were dressed hogs, oats, peas and barley and dairy products. Though a declining product in the latter years potash was delivered in the Lancaster market in considerable quantity from the potash mills or "asheries" at Alexandria.

Perhaps this exaggerates the extent to which Lancaster station absorbed the produce of northern Glengarry. It is hard to believe that farmers of the Vankleek Hill area would favour Lancaster in the face of outlets on the Ottawa River. As McDougald's article indicates, the trade of the southern part of Charlottenburgh Township was drawn to the Cornwall station. For a long time in the nineteenth century, Glengarry produce also found an outlet by way of the sleighs which brought goods to Montreal when the snow had improved the roads. The arrival of the Glengarry sleighs was a much awaited event for householders in Montreal about the 1840's. The history of the Glengarry sleigh trade is interesting, but lacks documentation. An eloquent tribute to the Glengarry sleighs appeared in John Fraser's *Canadian Pen and Ink Sketches* of 1890. He speaks of the sleigh trade as being by this time long extinct.

What kinds of crops and livestock were found on the Glengarry farms of 1871? Oats was the principal grain crop, far outdistancing in importance both wheat and barley. Only insignificant amounts of corn were grown. Peas were a field crop of considerable importance and were used both domestically and for pig feed. As in pioneer times, large amounts of potatoes were grown — certainly for domestic use, possibly for purposes of trade. Many farms prior to 1870 had a herd of cows, numbering usually about 7 or 8, to provide milk for the family, and butter and cheese for the family and to sell; after 1870 practically all had as many cows as they could winter. Farms often also had a few pigs, and a flock of hens, which did not lay eggs during most of the winter; and geese for meat, eggs and feathers; and sheep for meat and wool. Perhaps nothing more sharply distinguishes this system of farming from that in use at present than the lack of cash in the former. In 1871, a farm yielded food, fuel, and clothing with reasonable generosity for its occupants, but it generated relatively little cash — partly because the volume of the goods sold was not large, and partly because so large a fraction of goods sold was disposed of in return for other goods, or for credit, or to pay debts incurred by past purchases. For example, a farmer who wished to buy a pair of boots might pay the shoemaker in wheat for them. Or he might bring jars of his wife's good butter to the local store and receive credit for them against which he and his wife could purchase tea, salt, pots, pans, and other household commodities over the following months. Or he might make the purchases at the store first, running up a bill which he would slowly discharge by bringing produce to the merchant from time to time. Business and professional men were as much affected as farmers by the shortage of cash which was characteristic of Glengarry from its founding till at least the late nineteenth century. In the mid-1860's the *Freeholder* was begging farmers who intended to pay their subscriptions in wood to "bring it in at once." Even at the late date of 1888, when the cheese factories were already pouring their fertilizing streams of cash into Glengarry, we find a Lancaster doctor seeking a $100 loan from a money-lender. "I find it impossible," the doctor wrote, "to collect... enough to meet my engagements this winter although I have fully a thousand dollars due me."

In more recent times the purchase of farm machinery has been a great and, in the opinion of some farmers, a cruel devourer of the cash produced by Glengarry farms, but it would seem that in 1871 Glengarry farmers were only beginning to advance beyond such age-old implements as the plow, harrow, sickle, scythe, and flail, to the use of such new inventions as mowers, rakes, and threshing machines. According to the census of 1871, Glengarry had at that time 212 "Reapers and mowers", 266 "Horse rakes," and 358 "Threshing mills." To see these figures in context, we must note that in 1871 Glengarry had 1,963 occupiers of land amounting to 50 acres or more, an additional 321 occupying 10 to 50 acres, and 145 occupying 10 acres and under. In an editorial puff of 1866 for the Buckeye Mower and Reaper, the *Freeholder* expressed a desire "to see our farmers throw away that relic of the dark ages, the sickle," which may be taken as evidence of the continuing use of the sickle in the area. There is a diary reference to the use of the flail in the Williamstown area in 1882 and doubtless later references can be found.

Farming in Glengarry of the 1870's differed from that of today in the times for two of the most important events in the agricultural calendar. Haying at that time began in mid-July or later rather than in mid-June. Threshing took place in early winter with December being a month especially favoured for it. The grain was put in a mow in September to be threshed on the barn floor in winter by flail or machine.

The *Witness* announced to its readers in 1871 that "The New York *Evening Post* is strongly in favor of retaining the primeval forests of America that remain, and connects with their removal in parts of Europe and Asia not only the decreasing fertility of the soil, but the degeneracy of the inhabitants." There is some reason to suspect that in 1871 a considerable part of these protective forests had been retained in Glengarry. Before the rise of the cheese factories, it may not have been worth the effort for most Glengarry farmers to clear their whole farms. The evidence is incomplete and unsatisfactory, with the census figures being, despite certain evident defects, the best guide we have. In 1851-1852, about 62 percent of Glengarry was "Wood Lands" and in 1860-1861, about 60 percent. No figures for forest land were reported in 1871 or 1881. In 1891 this category of information was re-established with 34 percent of Glengarry being described as "Woodland and Forest." Now it is clear that the views of individuals on whether a certain piece of unimproved ground is woodland or not may differ, so we cannot take these figures as being more than a rough guide. They do, however, correspond to certain traditions to the effect that the final push in clearing the forest off Glengarry did not occur till the late nineteenth and early twentieth century. They agree also with the description of the Maxville-St. Elmo area given by Ralph Connor and his aunt Margaret Murray Robertson in their novels. We need only cite Connor's reference to the little farms set here and there "in their massive frames of dark green forest," or Miss Robertson's "miles and miles of unbroken forest." When Connor's family moved to the agriculturally more advanced area of Zorra, he was disappointed to find that the forest there had been "reduced to little wood lots.'' J.E. McIntosh, who was born in 1876 and who wrote under the pen name of Sandy Fraser, mentioned that when he was growing up, nearly half his father's farm at Breadalbane was under forest. Sandy himself in his early years as a farmer cut down the forest till he was able ''tae get the plough into every square foot o' soil on the auld farm.''

Whoever wishes to read a horror story about nineteenth century Glengarry can hardly do better than to leaf through the pages of the Abstract Index books of the Glengarry County Registry Office. There he will find the entries for the mortgages which were placed with such reckless abandon on the nineteenth-century Glengarry farms, and a fearful tale they make indeed. It was a rare farm which never had a mortgage feeding upon it, and many unhappy farms were host to a remorseless succession of these bloodsuckers. A survey of a block of ten lots in the 1st of Kenyon tells a not untypical tale by showing that between Confederation and 1901,

—no lot had less than three mortgages
—a total of 79 mortgages was placed on the farms comprised in these 10 lots
—a total of 15 mortgages was placed on the most heavily mortgaged lot.

A few random comments from about the year we are studying here will give some insights into the world of the mortgage holder and mortgage victim. In the Confederation Debates of 1865, Sandfield Macdonald said, ''And I ask honorable gentlemen from Upper Canada...whether it is not true that an immense number of our youth, now in the armies of the United States, have gone away because the properties held by their fathers are so heavily mortgaged that they had no hope of retrieving them. Speaking for my own section, I can say that there is scarcely a young man who can now look forward, as was the rule ten or twelve years ago, to succeeding his father in the family homestead.'' In the same year his newspaper, the *Freeholder*, had some thoughts on the same subject: ''We hope it may not turn out, if oil be found in the United Counties, that Yankee speculators will have the credit of discovery and the profit of the enterprize, while our monied men [of Canada rather than the United Counties specifically, apparently] content themselves with quietly taking mortgages on their neighbours' farms at rates of interest which no laudable use of money will ever pay.'' In a business letter of the next year, we read that "in consequence of so many having mortgaged their land to The 'Trust & Land Company,' and such similar Companys, land can be obtained cheaper at present in Glengarry, than at any other period for these Thirty years past.'' Bishop Macdonell, it may be noted in passing, had made a similar observation in 1828 about the recent cheapness of land in Glengarry as sold at Sheriffs' sales. From the year 1866, an instance of generosity can be recorded. A Glengarry mortgage holder directed in his will that the interest on a certain mortgage be reduced from 16 % to 12 %.

By 1871, immigration to Glengarry from Scotland had for all practical purposes ended, though of course a negligible movement of emigrants from Scotland — so slight as to amount to almost nothing — has continued like an invisible thread down to the present. Between 1816, when we last discussed the subject of Scottish immigration to Canada, and 1871, the history of Scottish emigration to Glengarry is hazy, but we do hear about the arrival of certain individuals and families, and there are some hints of larger organized groups. There appears to have been a flow of immigrants in the years just after 1816, with a sizeable group perhaps coming to Indian Lands in 1817, and there are references to settlers from the Isle of Skye arriving in 1832 and about 1863; a ship called the Lizard brought settlers to Canada and Glengarry in 1849; and in the early 1850's a group from Knoydart in Scotland is supposed to have settled in Charlottenburgh. Probably one reason why the history of Scottish immigration to Glengarry after 1816 remains so shadowy is that most of the apparent groups were only ''apparent'' — just a few individuals. If one had to produce a date for the end of the age of Scottish immigration to Glengarry, the date would be as arbitrary and unsatisfactory as those which, in the larger world, mark the end of the Middle Ages and the beginning of the Industrial Revolution. But subject to these limitations, 1820 is the date which the evidence best supports. Before approximately that date, Glengarry still had vacant places to fill up. After 1820, immigrants were moving into a settled community.

With the one possible exception of Ireland, immigration to Glengarry from overseas countries other than Scotland remained negligible before 1871. As we have seen, the Irish made up the third largest group in the county in 1871, with 1,279 persons being described as Irish by origin. Only 215 Glengarrians are described, however, as having actually been born in Ireland. How far members of either group were divided into Catholic and Protestant is hard to guess. The Irish made their way so silently into Glengarry, that we must reluctantly pass over the history of their arrival as simply a blank. We cannot even say whether the arrivals came directly from Ireland, or merely migrated from other parts of the Canadas.

There was large-scale Irish immigration into Upper Canada even before the Irish potato famine of the 1840's drove the Catholic Irish by the hundreds of thousands from their ruined island to the United States and Canada. A cloudy tradition speaks of a mass burial of Irish at Lancaster — perhaps in the cholera epidemics, perhaps in the 1840's, when the disease-stricken refugees from the famine were dying at points all along the St. Lawrence. We do find more concrete evidence in a petition for land which Bishop Macdonell forwarded to the government in 1820 from certain Irish Catholic immigrants who had been residing in Glengarry since their arrival in Upper Canada. They were in Glengarry, the bishop said, ''more on account of the facility for exercising their religion than of any other advantage they could expect to receive here. And it is the same reason that induces them to petition for land in the most contiguous situation to this settlement.'' In the following year the bishop spoke of certain ''Irish families'' in the Front of Indian Lands.

Some Glengarry girls found employment as domestic

servants in Montreal. We get a half humorous, half serious glimpse of their world in some correspondence in the Montreal *Witness* of 1870. "A Housekeeper" wrote to the editor,

Sir...Allow me to ask housekeepers, through your columns, to join with me in stopping a most annoying nuisance, viz., the constant run of 'visitors' which Glengarry servant girls have during the day, interrupting their work, and gossiping in our kitchens. I once thought I would be content if I had a Glengarry cook, but I find her an intolerable trouble, and I hear nearly every other housekeeper say the same. Yesterday she had seven visitors during the day, and this morning three and the greater number are regaled with their meals at my expense. I do not object to an occasional visitor in the evenings, but I do not care keeping open house for the long string of visitors to my servants. "Do you consider I am right?"

To which the editor replied,

We were so much surprised at the statements contained in the above, thinking it a most exceptional case, that we made some enquiry before inserting it, the result of which is that this experience can hardly be called exceptional. Not only are mistresses who employ Glengarry girls annoyed by a long succession of visitors to their kitchens, but the other servants are annoyed by a continual and impetuous stream of Gaelic. Nor are the Glengarry girls the only ones who have many friends; New Glasgow lasses are in the same predicament. Some employers, we understand, seeing the impossibility of limiting the number of visits, stipulate for none; but this appears rather rigorous. The true way would be for servants to exercise discretion, and permit only very few and short visits.

To the supposed slur on the Gaelic language in these remarks, another correspondent objected, asserting that "My humble opinion is and I am sure you conscientiously endorse it, that it would be a stronger guarantee for the loyalty of this section of the Dominion were it possessed of a larger 'stream' of the

Gael—the harshness of his vernacular to the contrary notwithstanding."

To this the editor replied, "We endorse all the last sentence except that part which implies that Gaelic is a harsh language—an imputation which we could not for a moment allow. All must admit that Gaelic is a good thing; but then there may be too much even of a good thing, and that was all that was ever hinted at."

Even at the relatively recent date of 1871, we can probably obtain no accurate idea of the mentality of most Glengarrians. The 70's form, however, probably the last decade for which this is so. To the researcher, this is the period of the darkness before the dawn. After that there are glimmerings of light, and and by the 90's we may regard ourselves as being in broad daylight. Except for a few things, it is with the greatest hesitation that we attribute to the Glengarrians of the 1870's or earlier any of the tendencies which we consider the property of the Glengarrians of later generations. Constant emigration from the county must itself have helped to shape the "characteristic" outlook of Glengarrians, for one may suppose that between those who left and those who remained there were in general certain differences of character, and that as certain personality traits were removed more than others from the Glengarry "pool," a new type of Glengarrian emerged. How far, for example, had Glengarry "neighbour-liness" evolved in 1871?

Attempts to measure the "quality of life" in Glengarry at this time are difficult because we do not know what people's ideas concerning a satisfying life were.

In terms of material goods, most Glengarrians lived a life of what would today be called austerity or even poverty.

Among the various misfortunes that could befall a Glengarrian at this time, there was probably none (short of death) that involved more complete possibilities of personal ruin than did insanity. For families also, at a time when facilities for treating the mentally ill were all far away, insanity could present the gravest problems. "Poor—1st of Kenyon," we read in a letter of 1865, "has two of his sons deranged & his wife, he is really to be pitied they have to keep the young men tied & they say there is no hope of their getting better." The current practice was to commit the mentally ill from the United Counties to Cornwall jail to await the time, sometimes much delayed, when they could be removed to a provincial asylum. In 1850, the Grand Jury inspecting the Cornwall jail complained that "The persons said to be insane make such uproar that nothing else but their shouting can be heard sometimes for minutes." Throughout the next half century, Grand Juries often mentioned or complained about the holding of the insane in Cornwall jail. In 1878, the Montreal *Witness* reported the suicide in Cornwall jail of a man from "a very respectable Glengarry family." He had been confined on account of insanity, and it was believed that he had taken his life on account of his fear of his imminent removal to an asylum. In 1882 the *Freeholder* reported that a man who "came from Williamstown" had starved himself to death in a fast of 41 days while "confined in the Jail here as a lunatic." Some of the insane had the relatively good fortune to be privately cared for in Glengarry. According to the figures (perhaps suspiciously round) of the 1871 census, there were then in Glengarry 25 males and 25 females of "unsound mind."

We are accustomed to looking back at this period as virtually crime free. This view is reinforced by examination of the Grand Jury reports for the United Counties and such other nineteenth-century official criminal records as survive. In 1873 the Grand Jury found only one prisoner in the jail, and congratulated the United Counties "upon the almost total absence of crimes." Similar Grand Jury compliments to the people of the United Counties can be traced through the remainder of the century. It is not often that one comes upon anything to the dishonour of Dundas County, but a writer in the sprightly *Freeholder* went so far in 1868 as to claim wickedly that "about nine tenths of the total crime and immorality in the United Counties" came from Dundas.

Yet the reader of newspapers of this period will find himself confronted with evidence of crime that is inconsistent with this view of Glengarry as practically crime free. In 1862 a Montreal newspaper noted the arrest, by Dr. Allen, the Mayor of Cornwall, of members of a gang of thieves who had been plundering the countryside and depositing the booty in their lair in a swamp near St. Andrews. "In Martintown their repeated robberies passed unpunished from the fact that the sufferers entertained a dread of their vengeance against any person who sought redress. If they did so their houses were sure to be burned, their cattle killed or maimed, their property destroyed, & c." If the charge of a Cornwall newspaper of 1866 is true, it appears that the same, or a similar, gang was then busily at work robbing and intimidating the public. In another Cornwall newspaper of 1865, two swindlers by the names of Grant and McKinnon who had been operating in Glengarry and elsewhere are compared to what appears to have been the gang smashed by Dr. Allen in 1862. The Montreal *Witness* published an astonishing story in 1869 about the unwillingness of the authorities to punish a rape in Glengarry and the security and insolence of the perpetrator. No doubt most Glengarrians of this period were of an irreproachable honesty which would put to shame the city-dwellers of today. It was no doubt the honesty of a multitude of simple, plain people that we remember when we savour our image of this as an almost crime free period. Yet it seems clear from the foregoing that a lawless element did not live by this puritanical code.

The reader will suspect from the account of the activities of gang members that Glengarrians, like members of many other close knit ethnic groups in nineteenth-century North America, had an extraordinarily high tolerance level when it came to enduring the depradations of a small aggressive criminal element belonging to their own community.

The failure to prosecute crime existed partly because of a deficient law enforcement apparatus, but also, we think, partly because such a policy had self-cleansing elements in it.

The community did look after its own under all circumstances and the majority were loath to bring public shame on their neighbours who were often their relatives as well. The policy appears to have worked, for we have no evidence of ''criminal families'' developing and such is the character of the Scot that the young reprobate of the 1860's would die forty years later a respected pillar of his church and community. The method of reforming the criminal element in our communities a hundred years ago was probably at least as efficient as that of today, if not more so, and was certainly less costly.

# Chapter V
# Glengarry from Confederation to the First World War
1: Introduction — The Canada Atlantic and the Rise of Maxville — The First French Canadians

## Introduction

This chapter and the chapter following will cover the period of a little more than a generation between Confederation and the First World War. At the beginning of this period, there were many Glengarrians still hale and hearty who could remember the United Empire Loyalists. By the end of it, the first automobiles were churning their way through the proverbially bad roads of Glengarry, and people were already stirring on the Glengarry scene who would live to watch the landing of the first man on the moon.

Several features of Glengarry in these years will be discussed in these chapters. The building of the Canada Atlantic Railway revitalized Alexandria and to all purposes fathered Maxville. The French Canadians rose from a small minority to a large one. Foreseeably, they would soon constitute a majority in the county. This ethnic revolution was accommodated by all concerned with to all appearances little fuss or anxiety. The first Glengarry newspapers came on the scene to break the monopoly of the Cornwall and Montreal press. In politics the Sandfield interest, much belaboured as a tyranny by its Conservative opponents, was ended. The whole period remained one in which Glengarry was represented by politicians often of outstanding ability and reputation. If there was ever a Golden Age of Glengarry politics, this was it. The temperance movement, so strong in Canada and the United States in those years, prospered in Glengarry. The county was involved in an abortive experiment in prohibition in the 80's. By 1914, Glengarry had again made up its mind to be ''dry.''

Samuel W. Jacobs, M.P. (1871-1938). He was born and basically educated in Lancaster Township. He was a graduate of McGill and Laval and was called to the bar in Montreal in 1894. Author of *Railway Law of Canada* (1909). M.P. for Montreal-Cartier 1917-1938. A very interesting man in his own right, Jacobs also serves to represent a very interesting ethnic group, "The Jews of Glengarry". This group gave prominent men to Alexandria, Cornwall, Montreal, and in the person of Nathan Phillips, whose mother was a Glengarry native, a mayor to Toronto.

Other topics from this period will be covered elsewhere in the book. Beginning in this period, and for almost two generations, cheese factories were an essential part of the Glengarry way of life. The Munro and McIntosh factory and the Schell industries gave commercial prosperity to Alexandria, while Rayside's lumber business helped the whole county and the south end in particular. This too, was the age of the Glengarry shantymen and of the continuing use of Gaelic.

The *Freeholder* was undoubtedly still correct when it declared in 1884 that "The people of Glengarry are almost exclusively farmers, with just so many of other trades and professions as are necessary to minister to the necessities of those farmers." By 1914, the industrial growth of Alexandria would have required a slight modification of this sweeping statement, but agriculture was still, unquestionably, the economic basis of Glengarry, the enterprise on which, directly or indirectly, most of its citizens lived.

A visitor to Lochiel Township in 1869 spoke of the "slovenly farming" of the Glengarry Highlanders, and in 1894 an Ontario County M.P. jeered at the "ramshackle" Glengarry farming. These censures were harsh and perhaps undeserved, but it would seem certain that in many respects the agriculture of the county remained backwards in comparison with that of many other areas of the province.

The story of overseas migration into Glengarry overlaps with that of the pouring out of Glengarrians into the rest of Canada, the United States, and even the most remote foreign countries. There has always been a pronounced streak of nomadism in the Glengarrians, who have ever delighted in travel, and who for all their attachment to the old county have ever been ready to pull up their roots there and remove themselves to foreign climes. One is almost tempted to believe that the crossing of the seas by their ancestors broke the spell which had attached them for centuries to their small spots in the Highlands, with the result that, freed from old inhibitions, they were by nature wanderers and citizens of the world.

Speaking of the later meetings of the Great Revival, Mrs. Gordon wrote in 1866 that "no less than fifteen of the young men, who used to take the lead," were now "scattered from the hallowed centre; some to the States, in search of more remunerative labor than they could find at home, some 'to shanty,' and some as school teachers in our own, and the neighbouring counties.''

Emigration continued to be heavy throughout the period we are studying. It has been calculated that in the years 1901-1911 just over 40 percent of the males aged 25 to 29 years left the county. Of the many who went to other parts of Ontario, and to Montreal, we need say nothing at this point,

John D. McArthur (1854-1927). This Glengarry-born railway contractor, timberman, and builder as a young man in 1879 worked on the first railway in Manitoba arriving in Winnipeg via the Dawson Trail. Forty-eight years later he died in his private railway coach in Winnipeg. In those 48 years it is reliably said that he built more miles of railway than any other man in Canada. Certainly he built a lot and much of it, such as the line to the Peace River Country and the one to Fort Churchill, lay far beyond civilization.

Donald Grant (1837-1917), a native of the South Branch, was one of the major railway builders of North America. He made his base at Faribault, Minn., where he served as mayor. Even a bare listing of his building activities uses an impressive amount of space. We hope in our Glengarry dictionary (if that work is ever completed) to give an outline of the lives of John D. McArthur and Donald Grant—two of the ablest and most productive men produced by Glengarry.

but it may be useful to notice separately those who went to the United States and to the Canadian West.

(1) At all times there was a flood of Glengarrians emigrating to the United States. Glengarrians went to every part of the country, but perhaps especially to Michigan and Wisconsin, the Dakotas, the South West, and California. We get a glimpse of a concentration of Glengarry exiles in a Chicago newspaper report of 1888:

There are many ex-Glengarrians among the prominent citizens of Chippewa Falls, Wis. A.B.Macdonell, President of the Lumbermen's National Bank is from Charlottenburgh, and ex-Mayor Hector C.McRae is from Martintown. The county treasurer is 'Big' Alex McDonell of St.Andrews, son of Big John, slide master at Hull, Quebec. Hugh D.McDonell, proprietor of the Nicolet House, and his father, D.Mc-Donell, returning officer, are both ex-Glengarrians. D.A.McDonell, grocer, is from Alexandria; William McDonald, blacksmith and carriage maker, from the Eighth Concession of Lancaster, and Rory McLeod, blacksmith, hails from Kirkhill. At Fifield, 100 miles west of Chippewa Falls, John Grincell, ex-Mayor of Eau Claire, an old Bridge End boy, is putting 15,000,000 feet of logs on the Flambeau river, and John Stewart, ex-Reeve of Kenyon is putting in a large quantity. Among other busy loggers are 'Big' John McDonald and Hugh McPhee, Fourth Concession of Kenyon; 'Slim' Hugh K.McDonald, Fifth Concession of Lancaster; Ronald Campbell, Dunvegan, and the four Ermatinger brothers from east of Alexandria. Among the leading scalers and scale inspectors are Archie D.McNeil, formerly of Alexandria; Alex A.McDonell, Lochiel, John McPhee, North Lancaster; Archie R.McDonald, Glen Nevis; Colin McMillan and Norman D.McLeod, Laggan; John Christie, Dominionville; John D.McDonald, Fifth Concession of Lancaster; William John Angus McDonald, North Lancaster; John McDonald (Moidart), St. Andrews; Duncan and James McKenzie, Dunvegan.

For young men, travel to the lumber shanties of the states of New York and Michigan for employment was often the first step towards permanent settlement in the United States. From these states, the shantymen fanned out through the Mid West, South West, and California.

Some of the Glengarry exiles working in various parts of the United States would ultimately return to Glengarry, but many or most settled permanently in the United States. An impressive number of Glengarrians achieved success as contractors or other businessmen, or as politicians in the towns springing up in the American West. The experience Glengarrians received on their home farms and in the country schools seems to have served them well on the American frontier or in regions over which the frontier had recently rolled.

(2) From about the beginning of the 1870's, a flow of population to Manitoba is visible. Doubtless there was limited migration to Manitoba before this, but we have not noticed any names of earlier migrants, and significantly a newspaper report from Lancaster in the spring of 1872 described the departure of a group of emigrants to Manitoba with the words that "These are the first leaving here with the intention to settle in Manitoba." An enthusiastic Glengarrian wrote in 1882 from North Lancaster, "Large numbers of our young men are off to Manitoba. God bless the gallant lads ! They go from Glengarry — as their forefathers came to it — to lay the foundations of Britain's grandeur in a new country. *And they are the boys who can do it.*" Even the aged Donald Cattanach was caught up in the movement to Manitoba. In 1882 he left for Winnipeg to live with his daughter; three others of his children were settled in that city. Twenty-five carriages and two pipers escorted him to the railway station.

From the opening years of the present century till the First World War, and then again in the 1920's, there was a strong flow of Glengarrians to what are now the provinces of Saskatchewan and Alberta; and Glengarrians since the opening of British Columbia in the 1860's have been making their way to that province.

"The family was a large one, and was widely scattered." This quotation from the Montreal *Witness* was an apt description of many Glengarry families. As evidence of how widely some Glengarry families had become dispersed, we may take evidence from three obituaries of Glengarrians published in the years 1902-1907. In one of these, the subject was survived by six children, living respectively in (1) Chicago, (2) California, (3) on the homestead, (4) Iona, Indiana, (5) Alpena, Michigan, (6) Michigan. In another, the deceased left two sons in Portland, Oregon, one in Texas, one on the homestead, and a daughter in Maxville, and was predeceased by a son who was killed in Nevada, a daughter who died in Maxville, and another daughter who died in Seattle, Washington. In our third example, the deceased left five sons, two in British Columbia, one in Hoquaim, Washington, one in Port Arthur, and one at home.

Two of the circumstances that made life in Glengarry easy to leave and hard to return to are spotted in a letter of 1887 which a Glengarrian in Victoria, B.C., wrote to an Alexandria money lender: "Sir...I am now too old to stand the winter storms in Glengarry and my lot is (as you know) mortgaged."

That the emigration of women from the county was for a time slightly less than that for men is shown by the ratios of males to females given in the census data. In the three censuses from 1871 to 1891, the ratio stood constant at 97 males to every 100 females. In 1901, the ratio rose to 99 males to every 100 females, and in 1911 there was an exact balance with 100 males for every 100 females.

A gifted historian of our county, who was often factually inaccurate but who almost invariably spotted those historical developments which are most deeply significant, has said that "In the first quarter of this century practically every family in Glengarry had one or two, or three old maid aunts. Not that they were objects of charity, they worked their fingers to the bone. They well earned their keep and the few clothes their relatives bought them. There must be a very special place in Heaven for the unwanted Old Maid Aunts of

Martintown and in fact of all Glengarry." The existence of these ladies, though perhaps in smaller numbers than our historian indicates, seems well authenticated, but it is necessary to dissent from the reason he gives for their single status. The young men, he says, left Glengarry, the girls stayed behind because there was no employment for them — but found there were not husbands enough for them all. The above census figures, however, show that there was no overwhelming lack of men. We must doubtless find the real reason for the spinsterhood of the spinsters of Glengarry in the addiction of so many Glengarry men to bachelorhood.

Employment opportunities were certainly poorer for women than for men, but the number of females leaving the county was kept high by the inclination of Glengarry men to return temporarily from exile to Glengarry to find wives and by married couples giving up their home in Glengarry and emigrating together.

Most emigrating Glengarrians would maintain a link with their relatives at home by letters and even occasional visits. As emigration continued, a network of Glengarrians was built up throughout North America such that no matter where a Glengarrian settled, he could nearly always find other Glengarrians nearby to fraternize with. These other Glengarrians would provide companionship and any kind of necessary aid, including aid in finding employment. Their links with their relatives back home would serve to direct back to Glengarry information about the whereabouts of anyone who was too disinclined to letter writing to keep his own family informed about him. Despite this system, nevertheless, a few emigrants dropped wholly out of sight. Some, doubtless, were struck down by sudden death, or felt themselves tainted by disgrace. Others no doubt for emotional reasons no longer cared to retain a connection with their relatives.

Now and then a voice of protest was raised about the constant loss of population to the county. In one such case a writer in the *Freeholder* in 1883 used the issue of emigration as a stick with which to beat the National Policy of Sir John A. Macdonald's party. Glengarry's present M.P., this writer charged, used to promise that the National Policy would "soon bring all Glengarry's sons and daughters, that were away from this County, back to their homes; and that no more Glengarry girls would need to leave their comfortable homes to hire as servant girls in the cities; that none would leave their parents for hard work in the [Cornwall] cotton factories; also that none of our boys would, after this great National Policy commenced, leave for Michigan or elsewhere, but would all stay at home and be happy." But has any of this, he asked, really come about? Let those who should answer begin in the writer's own Alexandria, "and see how many wives are left at home while their husbands are away in the States and in Manitoba."

Almost no organized effort was made to persuade Glengarrians to remain at home, though a Highland Society of Glengarry founded at Alexandria in 1909 had as one of its aims to encourage Glengarrians to remain on the homesteads their ancestors had hewed out of the wilderness.

The importance of emigration in Glengarry life at this time may help to explain a phenomenon which must inevitably both astonish and puzzle the reader of the Cornwall and Glengarry newspapers of this time. In our survey of Glengarry in 1871, we have noted that there was much evidence to show that Glengarry had a good deal of crime. This continued to be at least intermittently so till the end of the century or later. About the end of the 1880's, there appears to have been a serious wave of rural crime in the Summerstown area. The theft of the corpse of a wealthy Summerstown resident, Pat Purcell, caused the Montreal Star to moralize: "It is rather curious that the state of outlawry existing in parts of the counties of Stormont and Glengarry should only be made public through the robbery of the grave of P. Purcell, although highway robbery and violence are alleged to have prevailed there for some time past." The Star blamed this on the strong family attachments which made people protect evil-doers. Despite the Star's interpretation, one wonders whether a large part of this cannot be explained by the influence of the unruly conditions of the American West and South West being brought into Glengarry by the repeated comings and goings between that area and Glengarry.

At various times in the century, Glengarry men left the county to mine for gold. At least two soldiers of fortune went all the way to the Australian gold fields. Others, including Cariboo Cameron and his brother Allan, went to the California gold fields. When the Cariboo gold rush began in the 1860's, Glengarrians were soon involved. At this time George Macgillivray, near Williamstown, wrote to one of his brothers, "We have been in a state of excitement here all week, occasioned by the departure of so many fellows for Cariboo." And describing the several hundred people who attended the departure of two groups of men for Cariboo, he said, "If they had all been leaving on one day and the roads had been even passable half the country would have been at Lancaster to see them off." By this time, Cariboo Cameron's success in the gold fields had stirred all the adventurous breasts of Glengarry. In the 1890's, Glengarrians made an enthusiastic foray into the Klondyke gold fields. For several years from 1897, the *Glengarry News* and the *Glengarrian* tantalizingly reported the activities of the Glengarrians in the gold country. Some of them took their feats coolly. Two partners from Dominionville who were back from the Yukon by the fall of 1898 found "little difficulty in making the trips either going or coming. In fact they were pleasure trips."

In 1900, the St. Elmo correspondent of the *Glengarry News* paid a graceful tribute to a departing resident: "Hugh D. Sinclair, another of St. Elmo's young men, left for Dawson City on Tuesday. We hope he will arrive safe at his journey's end that he will not forget this place, and will be successful in procuring a large amount of yellow metal. His uncle C.R. Sinclair, and son, have been in the Klondike for nearly two years and have been very successful."

In 1902, the wedding in Dawson of Neil Stewart of Dunvegan was attended by at least 15 other Glengarrians, and gave occasion to what seems to have been a celebration memorable even by the gargantuan standards of the Yukon:

> The wedding of Miss Kate M. Crowley and Neil Stewart, of Dunvegan, Glengarry County, on July 12th, was the most notable event the old Klondyke has chronicled. The happy couple were joined in the tender bonds of wedlock at the Methodist Church at 10:30 in the midst of the most splendid gathering ever assembled in the city to honor a bridal party.
>
> Immediately after the service, a few of the more intimate friends discussed an elaborate luncheon at the home of Mr. and Mrs. McDonald until midnight. The bride and groom were then escorted to their new home. Soon afterwards 100 jubilant employees of the Orr and Tukey Co. of which Mr. Stewart is an employee, visited the home and presented Mr. and Mrs. Stewart with a purse of $500 and serenaded the life mates with song and music, making the heavens ring in echo and Neil to respond in the most heartfelt speech he has ever made.
>
> The town was agitated more than two-thirds the night, showing honor to the new man and wife. Many splendid gifts were given by friends.
>
> The wedding ceremony was witnessed by hundreds of friends and the following Glengarry boys: Alex McLennan, Rod Cameron, Jack Cameron, Norman Cameron, Dan McPhee, Tom McRae, K.G. McRae, Alex Grant, Peter Kennedy, Dunvegan; C. Franklin, H. McDermid, Maxville; W.A. Calder, H. McKenzie, Lancaster; Angus McMaster, John D. McMaster, Laggan. Nearly 1,000 invitations were issued and the church was almost filled with a brilliant gathering of the people in all callings, with whom Mr. and Mrs. Stewart are favored.

The church was prettily decorated about
the altar, and the chancel with potted palms,
evergreens, roses and wreaths. The soft,
dim light of the long arctic day fell in
a mellow flood through the great arched
windows, and bathed the bridal party in a
strangely fascinating light throughout the
ceremony, thus increasing a charming picture
of the nuptial service.

The groom arrived first attended by Jim
Laden as best man,...A few moments later the
bride elect arrived at the front entrance,
preceded by Miss Mary Donovan, as maid of
honor, and escorted by Mr. John McDonald.

The recital of brief verses by the preacher
ended the ceremony and the groom sealing the
sacred obligations with a kiss, led his
charming, gently blushing bride and the one
altogether lovely in his heart, down the aisle to
the sweet strains of Mendelssohn's inspiring
wedding march....

The bridal party entered carriages, and
with the bride and groom in a closed cab,
drawn by horses gaily decorated in ribbons,
was driven to the home of Mr. and Mrs.
McDonald, where the wedding feast was next
in order.

During the dinner the various toasts were
proposed and drunk to the health of the happy
bride and groom and the host and hostess, to
absent ones and others, and the evening most
delightfully and gleefully spent.

Everything up to midnight proceeded in the
more regular and methodical way of conventionality
[conviviality?], but the scores of good fellows who are
on Neil's long list of acquaintances, particularly the
Glengarry boys, whom we have already mentioned,

would not let the opportunity pass to serenade
the bridal couple in a way most particularly
peculiar to itself, like Neil yelling at his
six horse team at the very witching hour of one.
They were not all soft classic strains this time.
Not as the gentle dove of love but as the
jubilant conquerer came the hosts, with tin
cans, horse fiddles, base drums, cow bells,
ship bells, cymbals and psaltry, the harp and
the fish horn, and with other sacred instruments they came, and played in such sweet dis-
cordant harmony that bride and groom trembled
for their lives. Crossing the Chilkoot trail
was nothing to this bedlam. Soon the noise
subsided and clear upon the unending twilight
rose the words of a southern plantation melody
sang in full deep bass solo. Then came the
swelling harmony of the chorus and then the
frantic interlude of the orchestra. Another
solo and another chorus rolled gently over the
city, and then the atmosphere again was staggered
by the orchestra. After several relays in this
manner, the overjoyed Neil opened the door and
his beaming countenance shone like the full
moon. Beside him stood the radiant bride.
Neil began to think that was enough. The crowd
went in a spasm and the great instruments pealed
again and voices as of many waters, hot seething,
babbling waters, charged with drug store water
dynamite, joined the clamor. After multiplied
vocal and instrumental bombardments, the crowd
allowed Neil a word. He said: "My friends."
The crowd went wild again for five minutes.
Neil tried once more. He said: "We are
pleased." That was a tremendous hit, and for
three minutes, applause and orchestra waves
battered the hills and sky.
    "We are glad you are here," continued

140

Neil. "If it weren't for us, you wouldn't
be here."

Oh! He's a jolly good fellow, sang the hundreds
and the hills echoed the song.

Several more salutations and expressions
of good cheer were made and Mr. and Mrs
Stewart bowed a good night to their tumultuous
friends and retired. As the door closed the
noise subsided and the great crowd sang in chorus:
"Good night, Neilly, we're going to leave you
now." This parting song was one of the prettiest
features of the wedding honor.

People on the hills awakened from their
cabins and went to the doors to listen to
the serenade.

From 1899 to 1902, the South African or Boer War caused
much interest among Canadians. At least 20 Glengarrians
served in the Canadian forces in the war. In 1900,
Alexandrians loyally and vigorously celebrated Lord Roberts'
capture of Pretoria. A procession of boys paraded the streets
in triumph, and "Mr. J.A. Macdonell, Q.C. treated them to a
dish of ice-cream at Jno Boyle's ice-cream parlor."

About the beginning of this century, the harvest
excursions began to open a new avenue of adventure and
experience for young Glengarry men. For a conveniently small
sum, one could travel by train in late summer or early fall to
the prairie wheat regions to take part in the harvest as a
labourer and return home to Glengarry with one's wages in
one's pocket before the beginning of winter. Some of our
readers will have affectionate memories of the harvest
excursions they have gone on. Many others will remember
how fondly the older generation of Glengarry farmers dwelt
on these adventures of the bright days of their youth.

The years between the opening of the Canada Atlantic
through Alexandria in 1882 and the beginning of the First
World War were prosperous years for Alexandria and the
success story of the rising hamlet is told by the population

figures. As we have seen, the population in 1871 was between 600 and 800. By 1891, just twenty years later, when the census first reports the population of the village, the population had more than doubled to 1,614. By 1901, the population was 1,911, and by the year 1911 it was 2,323. Buoyed up by this expansion, Alexandria was incorporated as a village in 1884 and as a town in 1903. In 1882 the parish of Alexandria was described as the richest in the Diocese of Kingston.

Fr. John McDonald (1783-1879). He was ordained a priest at St. Raphaels in 1814 where he was curate 1814-1823. Then he spent 5 years as the first parish priest at Perth, Ontario, after which he returned to St. Raphaels as parish priest and Vicar General of the Diocese of Kingston. He retired to live in Lancaster in 1871. When he died, aged 96, he was buried under the altar at St. Raphaels where his body still rests inside the walls of the ruins of the church. He was a stern priest and memories of his severe penances still exist at St. Raphaels. When local historians refer to Fr. John's Diary they are referring to the records this man kept as a parish priest at St. Raphaels, not all of them impersonal.

In this period, achievement followed achievement, in a way that must seem astonishing to anyone who has known the unprosperous Glengarry of the 1930's, 40's or 50's. In 1884 the splendid new St. Finnan's Church, soon to be a cathedral, was dedicated. In 1890, the Diocese of Alexandria was formed out of the easternmost portion of the Diocese of Kingston, with Alexandria as the seat of the bishop. Within little more than a decade, an impressive palace was built for the new bishop. Meanwhile, the large carriage factory of Munro and McIntosh was doing a nation-wide and to a limited extent even an international trade; and its role in the industrial economy of Alexandria was ably seconded by the various enterprises associated with J.T. Schell. At the beginning of 1914, it was stated that Munro and McIntosh employed upwards of 200 hands, while the J.T. Schell Company and the Schell Foundry and Machine Company employed 125 hands. In this period, Alexandria also acquired two newspapers, a new post office (which was soon destroyed in a fire and rebuilt), the present building of St. Margaret's Convent, the Sacred Heart Church, and a new Presbyterian Church. The town installed a water system and its own electric plant but no sewers or drains. For a time it seemed, as we shall see later, that the fortunate town was about to become the site of a big all-Canada reformatory.

The ebullient young Alexandria was also the home of a striking group of able and well known men.* The rector of St. Finnan's, the Rev. Alexander Macdonell, became the first Bishop of Alexandria. The Rev. W.A. Macdonell, pastor of St. Andrew's, succeeded him in 1905 as the second bishop of the diocese. An Alexandria physician and resident, Dr. Donald McMillan, was a senator for thirty years (1884-1914). R.R. (Big Rory) McLennan, athlete, banker, and politician, was established in Alexandria for some years. J.A. Macdonell

*The Hon. D.A. Macdonald (d. 1896) lived in Montreal in his later years but often revisited Alexandria. A newspaper in 1885 said that his love for the old town "seems to increase with his years." Garry Fen at Alexandria seems to have continued to some degree to be his home. Presumably we are entitled to regard him as being *in some sense* a continuing Alexandria resident.

(Greenfield), commonly known as Jack Greenfield, who began his career as a law student in Sir John A. Macdonald's office, settled as a lawyer and political organizer in Alexandria. While in Alexandria he published a life (1890) of the Bishop Macdonell who featured so prominently in the early pages of this book, and the *Sketches* on the history of Glengarry (1893) which is still a recognized historical source and a valued book in the second-hand trade. E.H. Tiffany, another Alexandria lawyer, seems to have enjoyed a wide reputation. He was the author of a legal treatise on the registration of deeds (1881) which was described by a fellow lawyer-writer in 1946 as "still a very useful book of reference." Lockie Wilson was known far beyond Glengarry in the 90's as one of leading men of the farmer's movement called the Patrons of Industry. In the years 1900-1917 two Alexandria businessmen (J.T. Schell, J.A. McMillan) served as M.P.'s for Glengarry, and from 1911 to 1919 the Alexandria manufacturer Hugh Munro was M.L.A. for Glengarry.

Nevertheless, the progress of the town was insufficiently

Village brass band. Every self-respecting village, including Dominionville, had one of these in the gay 90's.

rapid, or insufficiently continuous, to please an ardent spirit who wrote in the Vankleek Hill newspaper in 1894 that "Alexandria has been in a dormant state for some years, but is now casting off some of its old-time sluggishness."

A legitimate subject of complaint for some years around the turn of the century was the lack of a grist mill. The old mill had been closed (1896-1902) by a fire and subsequent litigation, and the town lost trade when farmers no longer brought their grist to the mill.

If Glengarrians of today could return to Alexandria of the later part of the nineteenth century, they would find it a rough but vigorous town falling far short of the ideas of neatness, elegance, propriety, and convenience commonly held in the 1970's. Glengarrians returning in the last years of the century from Michigan, Wisconsin, or the American South West, probably found in Alexandria a town little different in physical appearance from the raw frontier towns they knew in those states. An Alexandria correspondent of a Cornwall paper in 1882 commended one of the citizens for his display of flowers, but added, "We are sorry to say that in this Village of ours such chaste and pleasing exhibitions as this are few indeed." However, a cautious advance in amenities was shown by a comment in the same column a few months later that the manufacturer Hugh Munro had become the first to introduce iron fences in Alexandria. The unpaved streets, alternating with the rains between mud and dust, remained a problem. In 1890 an informed traveller was quoted as having called the Main Street of Alexandria the worst piece of road in Glengarry. In 1897 the editor of the *Glengarrian* lamented, "The grass and weeds are growing very fast upon our streets. Those on the edges of the sidewalks, should it rain, will make it very disagreeable to pedestrians, and when the burdock ripens, the patience of many will be severely tried, and words not in the dictionary may fall from gentle lips. This ought not to be, and the sickle brigade should be at work, and soon give our town the appearance of a business place." Public drunkenness and street corner loafing were noted by the press; in

1896, impudent loafers on Main Street were said to be insulting church-goers. Against the turbulence and disorder of late Victorian society, Alexandria struck back, albeit perhaps not very effectively. A "lock-up" was provided in the 80's; while it was delayed in construction, an Alexandria writer in the *Freeholder* complained that "meanwhile rowdyism is rampant and the small boy rejoiceth." In 1890 Glengarry obtained its first paid policeman and in 1904 its first police magistrate.

We have seen that an early bank in Alexandria, the Ontario Bank, had closed leaving the village bankless in our sample year of 1871. From 1877 to 1879 a branch of the Mechanics' Bank operated in Alexandria. It would appear that the main demand in the area at the time was for mortgage money and this need was catered to by such as Dr. (later Senator) McMillan, representing the Western Loan and Saving Co., and J.A. McDougald, representing the Canadian Loan and Agency Co. Big Rory McLennan, in partnership with a man called George Brown, operated a private bank in Alexandria 1882-1886 which was bought by the Union Bank of Canada which continued it as its Alexandria branch. In 1898 the Bank of Ottawa came to Alexandria. In the years just after the turn of the century chartered banks established branches at Maxville (1902), Lancaster (1903), and Martintown (1905) in response to petitions from the inhabitants of those places who had evidently had enough of the Loan Companies and their equally grasping counterparts, the local usurers.

There is hardly a village or hamlet in Glengarry that has not had several bad fires in spite of the best efforts of the bucket brigades and prayer. This led to the formation of local fire brigades. The one formed at Martintown in 1894 seems to have been the first one, followed by Alexandria in 1896. Though their pumpers were hand operated and wells and ponds were depended upon for a supply of water, the value of these brigades was recognized and the system was developed until after World War II every township had two or three fire brigades strategically located to get to fires promptly. The

146

volunteer members of these brigades all had a bit of training and they cut down fire losses greatly. Because of distance and a strictly limited amount of equipment, buildings still burn, but today the fire loss is usually confined to the building in which it started.

Glengarry's fire losses in the nineteenth century did result in the beginning of the most successful and longest lasting business yet developed in Glengarry—The Glengarry Farmers' Mutual Fire Insurance Company.

Thirty-one ratepayers of Lochiel attended a meeting in the Lochiel Township Hall on 19 January 1895 to discuss the formation of an insurance company under the Ontario Fire Insurance Act of 1887. The organization was completed at a meeting on 28 March 1895. Today this company, covering all of Glengarry and part of Prescott and Stormont, is very much alive and prospering and so well are fire protection and precaution established that a 1977 announcement says the company is reducing its rate ten % for the next three years. Many local men have served on the board of this company, but one must be mentioned, Valentine Chisholm of Lochiel. Mr. Chisholm served as secretary-treasurer of the company from the time it was founded until his retirement in 1949—a period of 54 years.

Only some of Glengarry's churches, its municipal organization, and Williamstown and Maxville Fairs have a longer history then the Glengarry Farmers' Mutual Insurance Co. None have been more successful in their aims over the years and none still show the same ability to keep growing that the Glengarry Farmers' Mutual does.

## The Canada Atlantic and the Rise of Maxville

D.A. Macdonald had been involved as early as the 1850's in a project to build a railroad through Alexandria, but it was 1871 which saw the beginning of what was eventually to be the Canada Atlantic line through Alexandria. In 1871 he and a group of 13 other gentlemen (at least seven of which were

Glengarrians) obtained authorization from Parliament to build a railroad from Ottawa to Alexandria, and from Alexandria to the Grand Trunk Railway at some point at or near Coteau Landing. The projected railway was to be known as the Montreal and City of Ottawa Junction Railway. In 1872, D.A. Macdonald and six other gentlemen (at least three of which were Glengarrians) obtained **authorization** from Parliament under the name of the Coteau and Province Line Railway and Bridge Company to extend the line to New York state, where it would be able to connect with American lines. The projected line of rail would connect the lumbering regions of the Ottawa Valley with American lumber markets and the American ports. The Ottawa to Coteau Landing portion of this route was surveyed in 1871. In 1872, the American firm of A.L. Catlin and Co. was given the contract to build this portion and work was begun in September 1872.

A Canada Atlantic engine. The smokestack identifies it as a coal-burner. Those who know about such things agree that Booth operated the Canada Atlantic efficiently and used only the best and most modern equipment. —Photograph courtesy of Mika.

But the desire of northern Glengarry to have a railway was to be cruelly mocked by long delay. North America was struck in 1873 by financial panic, which in turn began a long period of depression. The contractors were forced to stop work at the beginning of 1874. For the next six years the strip of roadbed which they had prepared stood idle. In July 1878, the Montreal **Witness** reported a rumour that certain Glengarry farmers were preparing to take legal action to destroy the "plentiful crop of thistles and other noxious weeds that serve to mark out the 'line' " of the railway. Sharper than any thistles, however, must have been the pained indignation of northern Glengarry farmers that they were paying every year through their taxes for the building of this useless roadbed. As part of the system of financing the railway, the Townships of Kenyon and Lochiel had each granted $40,000 bonus towards the cost of construction. Of this money, Lochiel had actually paid $30,000 and Kenyon $20,000.

The day was saved for the Glengarrians by the intervention of J.R. Booth, the great lumberman of the Ottawa Valley. The projected railroad would provide a tempting means of marketing his timber from the Ottawa Valley. His wealth helped to provide the financing for the railway. Under his direction, the two previous companies were amalgamated in 1879 to form the Canada Atlantic Railway Co. D.A. Macdonald, the president of the previous companies, remained president of the Canada Atlantic till he resigned in 1881. He was replaced with another native of Glengarry, Edward McGillivray, a businessman and former mayor of Ottawa. In the following year, D.A. Macdonald disappeared even from the Board of Directors of the company. Work on the railroad was again in progress in 1881, under the able direction of the new contractor, D.C. Linsley, of Burlington, Vt. By January 1882, regular passenger and freight trains were running between Coteau and Casselman. In September, the first through service between Coteau and Ottawa began. Northern Glengarry had its railway at last. Glengarry politics had also been embittered by the charges and counter charges among the politicians and their partisan newspapers over the causes for the long delay in the completion of the railroad and over the honesty (or lack of it) with which the Kenyon and Lochiel bonuses had been used. But discussion of this topic may more conveniently be reserved till we come to discuss the politics of Glengarry.

Sir Francis Hincks (1807-1885) promoter of the Grand Trunk Railway.

As a by-product of the railway, Glengarry got a substantial new village, though only as an enlargement of a nucleus which already existed. On the swampy, wooded site of what is now Maxville, a saw mill and house are said to have been built as early as 1869. Thereafter, a few other businesses and buildings accumulated, and in due time the infant settlement was given a name; a Cornwall newspaper of November 1880 refers to it as "Macksville," and soon after the name was standardized as Maxville. According to legend, a group of local men assembled at the saw mill to decide on the name for their settlement, and agreed that it should be named in honour of the many Mac's in the district. A proposal that the name be enlarged to Macksville Anne to honour the female element was rejected. In the original plans of 1871 for the railroad, it was plotted to pass through Indian Lands just south of the Congregational Church at St. Elmo. In May of 1881, it was reported that the railway line was unlikely after all to go through the 17th concession of Indian Lands, the approximate site of Maxville, though some people had built their hopes on its doing so; and in June the line was being tentatively plotted to run north of St. Elmo. But by July this difficulty must have been cleared up, for it was stated that "Preparations are being busily pushed forward for the erection of buildings at Maxville. Village lots have been in brisk demand and the

John R. Booth (1827-1925).

prospects promise fair for this being quite a trade-centre. A number of lots have already been purchased for the purpose of starting stores,'' but, the writer gloomily concluded, ''as is too often the case in this respect the supply is likely to be greater than the demand.'' As the lucky possessor of a railway station on the Canada Atlantic and with the station operating, the hamlet quickly expanded. Under the pull of the powerful magnet of the station, the old settlements of Dominionville and Athol began to break up. Today, only a small cluster of houses survives to mark Dominionville, which was killed by the Canada Atlantic just as surely as the Canada Atlantic made Maxville and there is no trace of Athol.

Johnson Hoople (1859-1913), an early Maxville businessman. A native of Stormont, he began his business career driving a pedlar's cart from which he sold tinware to the housewives of SDG. In 1882 as a young man of 23 he saw the railway go through Maxville and he decided his future was there. By 1895 he was operating a tinsmith shop employing a number of men and a store from which he sold and installed roofing, furniture, agricultural implements, and acetylene gas machines as well as carriages. Shortly after 1900 he also became an undertaker. He grew with Maxville.

To have lived in Maxville in the first years after the station was established must have been an exhilarating experience.

"This village is growing every day," a Maxville correspondent exulted in the *Glengarry Times* early in 1882. He pointed with pride to the commerce of Maxville station in timber, potatoes, and grain. In the spring of 1882, a Cornwall newspaper honoured the achievement of the rising village of "Maxwell," which "has jumped into prominence and already taken the lead of the Town Hall [Greenfield] especially as regards business. Mr. Kennedy has built a commodious Hotel near the station, and having obtained a license intends running his house in good style. A number of stores are being built and its success as a business centre is undoubted. Since the opening of the Canada Atlantic the amount collected for freight there exceeded by $80 any other station along the line, not even Alexandria excepted." In August 1883, Alexandria was properly snubbed: "Maxville, nearly midway between Ottawa and Coteau, is now perhaps the principal intermediate station on the Canada Atlantic Railway. A great amount of traffic is daily handled. Houses in course of erection are numerous." In the following year, a newspaper correspondent from Maxville boasted, "Maxville has sprung into existence within the last three years, and promises to become of considerable importance." And in the next year, another boast followed, "Maxville, the ambitious capital of north-west Glengarry, is extending its borders, houses of all descriptions being erected or in course of erection." In 1891-1892, Maxville was incorporated as a village. A traveller of 1904 revisiting his boyhood haunts in Glengarry was said to be "pleasantly surprised" with the "thriving village" of Maxville, "as the site was nothing but a swamp when he left 50 years ago."

In 1901, when it first appears as a separate division of Glengarry in the census reports, Maxville had 749 inhabitants and was exceeded in size among Glengarry's villages only by Alexandria. By this time, its age of expansion had passed, and it was to be forty years before Maxville's population pushed above the 800 level.

A few words about the later development of railroads in Glengarry. In 1887, the Canadian Pacific Railway line through

Maxville Railway Station today.

Green Valley and Apple Hill opened, connecting these centres with Montreal and Toronto. In contrast with the exasperating delays, long frustrated expectations, and bad feelings that accompanied the coming of the Canada Atlantic line, this line seems to have slipped into place across Glengarry so silently and efficiently as to produce almost no "history" at all. Lancaster was now deprived of its old commercial hinterland in central and northern Glengarry by two roughly parallel rail lines through the county, and its old commercial hegemony was in ruins. Henceforth, like Maxville, it was to be only one of the two Glengarry villages which had come closest to rivalling the triumphant Alexandria. As early as 1871, a plan had been afoot to build a branch line from the projected Montreal and City of Ottawa Junction Railway to Hawkesbury on the Ottawa River. In 1892, a 21-mile line from Hawkesbury to Glen Robertson, by way of Dalkeith, was opened. By the end of this year, a total of 15 railway stations were operating in Glengarry. The Canada Atlantic had been operated by the Grand Trunk since its first year, and in 1904 the Grand Trunk bought it. In 1914 Glengarry received its final railroad when the Stormont and Glengarry line connecting Cornwall with the CPR main line at De Beaujeu station was completed and opened five more railway stations in Glengarry, making 19 in all: Dalkeith, Glen Sandfield, Glen Robertson, Alexandria, Dornie, Greenfield, Maxville, Apple Hill, Glen Roy, Green Valley, Glen Norman, Summerstown Station (Camerontown), Lancaster, Bainsville, Bridge End, North Lancaster, Glen Gordon, Williamstown, and Glen Brook.

## The First French Canadians

The early history of the French Canadians in Glengarry is a subject of uncertainty. It has been suggested, though not as far as we know on the basis of any evidence, that there may have been French Canadian families in Glengarry even before the coming of the Loyalists. That French Canadian traders and labourers were known in Glengarry from the beginning of Loyalist settlement or that the earliest Scottish settlers bought their farm animals from the nearby French Canadians is not improbable. We do come upon a valuable and indeed rather surprising piece of evidence in a letter of 1806 from the future Bishop Macdonell. In Glengarry, he says, there are 250 Scotch Catholic families, upwards of 200 Presbyterian families, and "about forty French" families. In the 1830's the records mention French-Canadian day labourers at Fraserfield. Also in the 1830's, Bishop Macdonell speaks of "the poor Canadians about Williamstown," and "the poor Canadians of the Indian Lands and other parts of Glengarry." We may assume that after the usual practice of English-speaking Canadians of his time, he was using the term "Canadian" as equivalent to "French Canadian." Glengarry records of most kinds from the first half of the nineteenth century yield a thin, but often only a very thin, trickle of French names. One of the more curious examples of this comes from the notes of the agent of King's College who inspected the college's Glengarry properties in 1840. Two miles east of what is now McCrimmon, he found one of the college half lots occupied by "a Frenchman whose name I cannot spell," who could speak only French, and his wife, who could speak only Gaelic.

The French Canadian population in Glengarry grew rapidly in the generation after Confederation. In 1861 there were only 1,371 French Canadians in Glengarry, making up 6½ % of the county's population. By 1901, the first year of the twentieth century, there were 7,219 French Canadians, who now made up close to a third of the population. And by 1911, the French Canadians numbered 8,710 and made up 41% of the population.

The increase in the French Canadian population took place more rapidly in some areas than others. Yet there was no township or village and probably no hamlet or neighbourhood in Glengarry which did not receive French families in these years. Perhaps the Scottish Presbyterian community around Dunvegan acquired fewest. Maxville has often been thought of as one of the most Scottish and Protestant areas of Glengarry, but even as early as 1901, when Maxville first appears as a separate subdivision in the census, Maxville's population was just over one fifth French Canadian. Closeness to the Quebec border does not seem to have been a major factor in the extent to which municipalities attracted French Canadians. In 1871, Charlottenburgh, which did not border on Quebec, had more French Canadians than Lochiel and Lancaster together, though these lay next to the Quebec border.

Charles Leclair (1805-1886). Born in Lower Canada, he settled on 24-6 Lancaster Township in 1828. An enterprising man, he became a storekeeper, postmaster, justice of the peace, and officer in the militia. Dun's the credit reference people in 1865 gave him a credit rating of up to half a million and a net worth of more than $25,000. Mr. Leclair is of interest not only because he was the first recorded Francophone to do well in Glengarry but because he founded a remarkable family. The town that grew up around his enterprises was called Clairville, later North Lancaster.

In this revolution in the affairs of Glengarry, nothing is more remarkable than the lack of fuss with which it took place. In the course of approximately one working lifetime, the number of French Canadians in Glengarry had increased over 500 percent, while the number of Scots was declining. By 1911, the French Canadians had come within sight of being the majority group in the county. To anyone who was aware of the figures, it must have seemed inevitable that before long they would be the majority. Everywhere in the world good relations are painfully difficult to maintain between groups which differ markedly from each other in race or religion, or differ at all in language. Yet these newcomers differed from all the Scots in race and language, and from half the Scots in religion. One would expect that so quickly fitting so large an alien population into the established Scottish settlement of Glengarry would create explosive tensions. Yet the reader of the nineteenth-century Glengarry area newspapers will search them in vain for evidence of such tensions. Nor does any tradition suggest that such tensions were developing uncommented upon by the newspapers. The Toronto *Mail*, viewing Glengarry from afar, noticed in Glengarry in 1886, "the steady aggressiveness of a creed and race which are rapidly impressing a new character on the community," and added that "this new element...is already perceptibly undermining the old order of things." The apprehensions with which these words are heavy, may have been quietly shared by many Scottish Glengarrians, but if so, the essential fact is that they did not act upon them significantly even to leave us clear evidence of their views. At the same time, the French Glengarrians quietly and unassumingly accepted what must have been in most matters a subordinate rank in the community. The fact that this great increase in the number of French Canadians has left so little historical evidence is itself a tribute to the common sense and neighbourliness of both groups; unlike strife, peaceable relations leave few historical records.

Among the most prominent Glengarry families of their day were the Leclairs. Charles Leclair was born in Lower Canada and came to North Lancaster, Glengarry, in the 1820's. Combining a variety of enterprises after the manner of many of the more successful rural businessmen of his day, he was a hotel-, store-, and ashery-proprietor, postmaster and mail carrier, loaned money, and owned farms and tenant houses, in addition to serving the public as a justice of the peace and as a militia officer. In 1881 there was speculation that he might be made a senator. His son Napoleon Leclair graduated in medicine at McGill in 1861, and in the 1860's

Fr. Louis William Leclair (1837-1906), third son of Charles Leclair, was ordained a priest in the order of St. Sulpice in Rome in 1861. He did parish work in Canada 1861-1885, then was sent by his order to Rome to establish a Canadian College there. The college was completed in 1888 and Fr. Leclair remained as assistant superior at the college till 1896 when he was appointed superior which office he held till 1902 when he retired to Notre Dame de Montreal. This outstanding cleric, administrator, and educator seems to have been the first Glengarry-born Francophone priest.

was in practice in North Lancaster and then in Alexandria, where he was on the first board of trustees of the Alexandria high school. Later he practiced medicine in Montreal. He died in 1884, two years before his father. He was probably the first French Canadian doctor to practice in Glengarry, and was coroner for the county for some years. Another son of Charles, Louis William, was ordained a priest. He achieved the distinction of being chosen to supervise the building of the Canadian

College at Rome. Afterwards he served successively as its assistant rector and its rector. Barely remembered though he is on the roll of distinguished Glengarrians it seems fair to say that few Glengarrians of any time have achieved higher honours in life. He died in Montreal in 1906. He was the first Francophone Glengarrian to be ordained to the priesthood.

Charles H. Gauthier (1843-1922). A native son of Glengarry with a French Canadian father and Scottish Canadian mother, he was an outstanding representative of the two races from which he sprung. Ordained in 1867, he served as professor of rhetoric at Regiopolis College and as priest in several parishes, and was appointed Vicar General of the Diocese of Kingston in 1891, Archbishop of Kingston in 1898, and Archbishop of Ottawa in 1910.

The only Glengarrian who ever achieved the rank of Archbishop, Charles Hugh Gauthier, was born in Kenyon in 1843. He was of both French and Scottish extraction, being the son of Gabriel Gauthier, one of the earliest French Canadian farmers of Kenyon, and his wife Mary MacKinnon. He studied at Alexandria and at Regiopolis College, and was ordained to the priesthood in 1867. Among the pastorates which he held was Williamstown, where he was priest from 1875 to 1886. In 1898, he was appointed Archbishop of Kingston, and in 1910, Archbishop of Ottawa. Unhappily,

Dr. Napoleon Leclair (1836-1884), second son of Charles Leclair, graduated in medicine from McGill in 1861. Almost certainly he was the first native-born Francophone doctor in Glengarry. In 1863, SDG Council appointed him to the first board of trustees of the about-to-be-formed Alexandria High School and in 1864 he was appointed a coroner for Glengarry. He practised at North Lancaster and Alexandria till 1873 when he moved to Montreal. He is buried in St. Raphaels cemetery.

the latter appointment raised what one historian has called "a storm of controversy." French Canadian nationalists objected to his supposed identification with English Canada, and feared that his appointment would be the first step towards ending the French Canadian tenure of this important archdiocese. It is more pleasant to be able to record that Sir Wilfrid Laurier called him "a saintly man." He died in 1922. The well known and much revered Father Charles Gauthier of the Diocese of Alexandria, who died in 1976, was his nephew.

In elections for M.P.'s and M.L.A.'s the French Canadians' numbers began to tell, and political organizers began to notice their preferences. In 1882, the *Freeholder* saw a reason for D.A. Macdonald's recent defeat in the federal election in the fact that there were now nearly 400 French voters in Glengarry. In 1893, Senator McMillan believed that the French voters were disenchanted with the Patrons of Industry movement because of its supposed connection with the Protestant Protective Association. In the provincial election of the following year, Donald Macmaster was concerned with inserting suitable political writings in the French-language press. In 1900, Big Rory McLennan wrote that he was having a hard election contest in Glengarry and expected to lose many of the French votes because his opponent, Schell, was a Laurier man. No French Canadian was a candidate in a Glengarry federal election till 1921 or in a Glengarry provincial election till 1934.

Gradually, the French Glengarrians began to establish institutions for their own use as an ethnic group, beginning with a branch of the St. Jean Baptiste Society which was in existence at Alexandria by the fall of 1881. The founder and first president was an Ottawa-born law student called J.A. Valin, who many years later was a judge in North Bay, Ontario, and one of the board of guardians of the Dionne Quintuplets.

The second institution to be established for the use of the French Canadians was the Parish of the Sacred Heart of Alexandria. By 1977, this parish had the largest congregation in Glengarry with an up-to-date modern plant in the south end of Alexandria and was sponsoring the only credit union in the county, the very successful Caisse Populaire du Sacré Coeur D'Alexandria Limitée and church oriented groups of several kinds.

Alexander Leclair (1843-1914), fifth son of Charles Leclair, shown here with his second wife Catherine Forestell (1863-1938), a niece of the contractor and M.P. Pat Purcell. Owing to the death of his eldest brother in 1863, and the avocations of his other brothers, Alexander took over his father's business in Lancaster Township as well as some he had started for himself, such as the first store at Lancaster Station in 1856. But Alexander was the last of the family to have extensive business interests in Glengarry.

It all began in 1896 when representations to the bishop

asked for a French speaking priest and the bishop having none among his own clergy borrowed Father Poitras from the Diocese of Montreal so that one mass at St. Finnan's each Sunday could be in French.

Not only were these masses in French appreciated, they acted as the germ of an idea — why not have a French church in the diocese, and the place for it was clearly Alexandria, where the greatest concentration of French families in the county lived.

So the leaders in Alexandria's French community put the idea to the test. At the turn of the century there were about 150-200 French speaking families in the Alexandria area, few of them with big incomes and many of them with incomes well below average. Building and supporting a church looked like a formidable task yet the idea's time had come. It could be done, IF....

The first positive step was to hold a picnic in Alexandria in June 1907 for the benefit of the projected church. Nearly 5,000 people came to the picnic. In May, John McMartin, M.P., had pledged $10,000 to a building fund and the **Glen-garry News** was able to report "the building fund of the new French Church is growing apace" and official permission to build was given on 7 April 1909.

On 9 July 1909 a contract to build the church was let to V. Ladouceur of Ottawa. It was to be on the south east corner of Alexandria's Main and Lochiel streets and was to be of cut stone. The corner stone was laid on 14 April 1910. The bells were gifts of J.A. McMillan, M.P., and D.R. McDonald, ex-M.L.A. The bells were blessed on 29 July 1914. By early December 1910 it was expected that the church would be opened for midnight mass on Christmas Eve. It was, though there were no pews; in the winter of 1911 the interior of the church was decorated and the pews were installed in March. The first priest of the parish was Father J.W. Dulin.

# Chapter VI
# Glengarry from Confederation to the First World War
## 2: The First Newspapers — Politics — The Temperance Movement

**The First Newspapers**

Late nineteenth-century Canadian journalism was lively, scurrilous, and vindictive. The modern reader of the newspapers of that period will rarely be bored, but he will wonder at the liberty enjoyed by journalists to abuse whomever they chose. A sizeable part of the press was ferociously partisan, dedicated to representing its chosen party and politicians as uniformly good and wise, and the opposing parties and politicians as unreservedly wicked and foolish. Glengarry began to play its part in newspaper history when the first issue of its first newspaper, a weekly called the *Glengarry Times*, was published on 24 December 1880. The newspaper's offices were at Lancaster, but the issue was printed in Montreal. It was not until the newspaper had been in existence for about half a year that the editor got his own press installed and in use at Lancaster. In the first issue, the editor announced that the *Times* would be independent in politics and religion. To help bring the paper into being, D.M. McPherson the Cheese King, James Rayside the lumberman, and Neil McGillis had each contributed $100, and Alexander Glennie contributed $50. In an early issue, the editor congratulated the Glengarrians on the probability that the Canada Atlantic Railway would soon be a reality, and declared that that being seen to, the repair and macadamizing of the Military Road, which was probably the worst main road in Canada, "the incorporation of the villages of Lancaster and Alexandria, and the hearty and undivided support of THE GLENGARRY TIMES, are next in order." It was high time that Glengarry had a newspaper, for by the editor's count, Glengarry and North Leeds had long been the only districts in Ontario without local papers.

The editor, J.C. McNeil, was a Nova Scotian in his early thirties. According to a sketch which he wrote of his career, he began his working life as a general store clerk in Nova Scotia at the age of 15, worked in a customs house, taught school, and prospered for a time in real estate in Boston. He was reported also to have had a background of newspaper work in Montreal. A schoolboy from Alexandria who worked as a paid contributor to the *Times* remembered McNeil as "a kindly, serious and even a scholarly gentleman of the old school" who was in "a field which he was...little adapted to occupy." John McLennan, M.P. for Glengarry, who complained that he had been misrepresented by the *Times*, called McNeil an eccentric. And in fact, in reading the plump file of back issues of the paper which survives in the National Library, it is hard not to feel that there was, correctly enough, a faint yet distinct eccentric or crankish tone in the paper.

But however that may have been (and perhaps we are dealing with a fault of literary style rather than of personality), McNeil certainly gve his readers an entertaining and news-filled paper. Here we see the Glengarry cheese factories in their first flush of success, with their achievements mentioned with the same enthusiasm as if they had been sporting scores. And here too we see Glengarrians caught up in the rush to Manitoba. "Manitoba! Manitoba!" a Martintown correspondent wrote, "is the order of the day;" and from Martintown came the plaint, "Should the exodus continue our village will soon be deserted of young men." Letters from Glengarrians in the United States demonstrate the extraordinary dispersal of Glengarrians which had already taken place, and show that the exiles realized the importance of this paper as a link with their Canadian home. We get a glimpse also of the rough, disorderly life of the untamed Glengarry populace of this period, and the editor recorded among other disorders in his village a fight which was broken up by Father Gauthier, the future Archbishop of Kingston and Ottawa, the heartless teasing of an aged tramp, and a disgraceful assault, by two drunkards, on E. McRae of McRae's Hotel.

At one point McNeil had a nasty clash with local sentiment. Towards the end of his first year of publication, he boldly published a long and abusive article called "A Royal Skulker," denouncing Princess Louise and her husband the Marquess of Lorne. The Princess, who was alleged to have abandoned her husband, was the daughter of Queen Victoria, and the Marquess was Governor General of Canada. The slur on the daughter of their sovereign was too much for the explosive loyalty of Glengarrians, and indignation meetings were held at Lancaster and Alexandria to denounce McNeil's article. At Lancaster, according to a Cornwall newspaper, "The unfortunate, miserable, despicable fellow, who was guilty of publishing it, was soundly pelted with rotten eggs and apples when he came out of the meeting." An Orange Lodge assembled at Pine Grove, Lochiel, condemned the *Glengarry Times* as a Fenian rag. It would appear, however, that McNeil fairly quickly made his peace with his Lancaster enemies. Not many weeks later he was secretary of and prominent in the proceedings of a testimonial dinner held at Lancaster for a local worthy who was departing for the West. The fact that the local folks were willing to fraternize with him so soon after his disgrace is perhaps remarkable, but more remarkable is the fact that the man who was honoured at the testimonial dinner had the same name as and probably was identical with the man who had organized the Lancaster indignation meeting against McNeil.

Perhaps such mishaps do a newspaper more good than harm. But if so, the *Glengarry Times* failed all the same to survive. It may have been in financial difficulties as early as its first winter, when it missed some weeks of publication. And unhappily, after it had survived for about a year and a half from its first issue, a Cornwall newspaper had the mournful duty of reporting in July 1882 that the *Glengarry Times* had "succumbed to the Sheriff." This failure, the Cornwall paper declared, was "merely the proof of the opinion which almost every businessman entertained, viz.: that the field was not a remunerative one. We have nothing but good wishes for Mr. McNeil, and hope to hear of his exercising his talents in a locality where the solid gains will be much heavier than they were in Lancaster." The *Glengarry Times* reappeared briefly in the summer of 1883, but no copies from that time seem to have survived. After this renewed disappointment, McNeil declared that he was abandoning the *Glengarry Times* "forever." Describing himself as totally destitute and as having "to commence the world anew," he sought employment from Big Rory McLennan, then active as a railway contractor. We have not been able to discover anything about him beyond this point.

Perhaps one reason for the failure of his enterprise was that he had not been able or willing to secure a sufficiently rewarding alliance with a politician or political party. The Cornwall *Freeholder*, itself unflinching in its role as a party organ, had stated its view at the outset of McNeil's paper that he would not be able to maintain his political independence. Independent journalism, the *Freeholder* said with stark realism, had always failed in Canada. And, in fact, before the *Times* ended publication in 1882, it had become a full-fledged Conservative journal. As its collapse at that time followed shortly after a federal election, one wonders whether it was not buoyed up on its final stages by a share of the Conservative election financing.

Once the Canada Atlantic line through Alexandria was in operation, the superiority of Alexandria as the location for a Glengarry newspaper must have been almost incontestable. The next newspaper, called the *Glengarry Review*, began in Alexandria in 1883 or 1884. It was probably a Liberal organ from the beginning. It fell into the hands of an editor called C.J. Stilwell, who had been editor of the *Fort William Echo*. Under his direction the *Glengarry Review* became a Conservative organ about the beginning of 1886 and its name was changed to the *Glengarrian*. Big Rory McLennan has been supposed to have been the secret influence which financed this switch-over. The local Liberals, in their own defence, established the *Glengarry News* in 1892. From almost the beginning this Alexandria paper was edited by A.G.F. Macdonald, the son of the Hon. D.A. Macdonald. Today, after nearly a century of honourable service, it survives as the sole newspaper in Glengarry.

Eugene Macdonald, son of A.G.F. (George Sandfield) Macdonald, took over editorship of the *Glengarry News* when his father retired in 1944. For the next 32 years Eugene carried on his father's tradition of unbiased, accurate reporting on local events and people. Both he and his father devoted much time to community work through such media as the local council, service clubs, and personal example. The existence of the Alexandria Golf Club and the Glengarry Historical Society owe much to Eugene Macdonald.

## Politics

In these years, political contests in Glengarry were not the pallid affairs they are today. Political convictions were of the most intense kind; animosities and enthusiasms alike assumed their most extreme form. If one were able by magic to revisit just one Glengarry scene of the nineteenth century, one could hardly make a more exciting and rewarding choice than to attend one of the nomination meetings or other large political meetings in Alexandria.

As to the reasons for the zeal with which our ancestors

Lt. Col. A.G.F. Macdonald (1863-1948) probably liked to think of himself as a Highland Scots soldier and in this role he rendered valuable service to his country, culminating in his raising the 154th Battalion and taking it overseas in 1916. But we suspect he will be longer remembered as the owner-editor of the *Glengarry News* 1892-1944. In this role, "George Sandfield" as he was popularly known, kept and left a marvelous record of his friends and neighbours in Glengarry.

plunged into their political struggles, we can only guess. It is possible that in the Glengarrians of that period the emotions lay closer to the surface than they did in a later, more restrained era. Democracy was then relatively new, and must have had an impact, through its novelty, which it has since lost. In the narrow difficult lives many people led, politics must have provided a welcome emotional outlet; in this way, perhaps, intemperate politics gave some of the same relief as intemperate pioneer drinking.

As a young political candidate prepared for his first campaign, he must often have felt his heart sink within him. Looking about him, he could see other politicians who had been vilified without restraint and without fairness by the opposition press. Nevertheless, this need not necessarily be his fate. For whatever reason, this vilification seems not to have been fairly distributed. Some politicians took an unmerciful shellacking; others slid through their political careers with surprisingly little abuse. But the candidate could console himself with the thought that if he were one of the unlucky ones, his party's press would give good measure in return. And if the worst came to the worst, and he found himself staggering under a campaign of abuse of the most heartless kind, he would have the consolation that any real misdeeds of his that were exposed would lose much of their effect through being lost in a torrent of frivolous or imaginary charges.

For the candidates' humbler supporters in the country-side, there were the joys and apprehensions of battle. One can admire, though hardly envy, the man from Dunvegan who visited the offices of a Cornwall newspaper in 1882 "smiling as usual...Alex. is a plucky fellow. He lives in a bad Grit neighbourhood but he 'doesn't mind them at all.' " Also unenviable was the plight of a party worker from the Dalkeith area who wrote in 1891 that "often at dead of night parties passing the house months after the election would cry out boodle." (boodle — a favourite political word of the time, meaning "graft", "bribes.")

Stormy though Glengarry political life was, the results in terms of elected representatives did the county credit. As there will be much that is sordid or unhappy in the tale of politicking that will fill the following pages, it is well to emphasize at the outset the truth of this statement. In the period from 1841 to 1900, a total of seven representatives sat for Glengarry in the Parliaments of the United Canadas and of Canada. One of these became the premier of Ontario; another was a brilliant and successful lawyer who finally became a baronet in England; three had respectable careers in contracting; one served as President of the Montreal Board of Trade and had a reputation for able speeches in Parliament; and the least distinguished of the seven had a career quite successful enough in business and public life to satisfy most people's ambition. Of the seven, four are included in that convenient guide to historical importance, the *Macmillan Dictionary of Canadian Biography*, and at least one of the missing three, Pat Purcell, was as important as many people included in that work. From the establishment of the Legislative Assembly of Ontario in 1867, to the retirement of Hugh Munro in 1919, the representatives of Glengarry provincially did only marginally less honour to the county. It does not seem an exaggeration to say that the generation which followed Confederation witnessed the Golden Age of political representation in Glengarry.

In the years after Confederation, D.A. Macdonald was the M.P. for Glengarry, continuing there the Sandfield political empire which his brother had founded. Glengarry, it will be remembered, had been represented throughout the period of the United Canadas first by John Sandfield Macdonald and afterwards by his brother D.A.. It may be mentioned as a historical curiosity that after Confederation John Sandfield was both premier of Ontario *and* M.P. for Cornwall in the federal parliament, as was permitted by the political rules of the time. He died at his home, Ivy Hall, Cornwall, in 1872, half a year after he ceased to be premier of Ontario.

In the same year, 1872, an ardent young political worker

in Glengarry prepared an analysis of why D.A. had just been able to get himself re-elected. The reason first stated was that "no political lines have been drawn in this Co., for 32 years, it being purely a family matter, with the people." The second reason stated was "his great wealth, having as he said 1600 notes out in this Co., a lever no doubt used freely this time." At the same time D.A. was planning the Montreal and City of Ottawa Junction Railraod, and it was alleged by the young political worker that D.A. had used jobs and other favours in connection with it as a form of patronage. A Roman Catholic missionary who had recently gone through the county had attacked D.A., but this had had the result of driving the Protestants into his camp. To all of this had to be added a fatalistic notion in the minds of the people that D.A. simply could not be defeated.

Nevertheless, the analyst thought he saw fatal cracks in the structure of the Sandfield power in Glengarry. The county was naturally a Conservative one, and at the election the Conservative workers had succeeded in forcing D.A. to take up an unequivocal position on the Grit (Liberal) side of the fence. A good beginning had been made, and it was now up to the Conservatives to continue their effort till by persistence victory would be theirs.

Some years later another Conservative party worker wrote that on the night of the resounding Conservative defeat in 1872, he and five others met "and swore we would never stop working until we had changed the representation of the county." Events, he boasted, had showed how well they had kept their word. Whatever the precise facts of this may have been, ten years certainly sufficed to uproot the Sandfield interest. In 1873, D.A. became postmaster-general in Alexander Mackenzie's Liberal government. In 1875 he was appointed to the Lieutenant Governorship of Ontario, an office which obliged him to give up his seat in Parliament. He was succeeded as M.P. for Glengarry by Archibald McNab, of Breadalbane, who was regarded by the Conservatives as simply another representative of the Sandfield interest. But

in 1878 McNab was defeated at a general election by John Mc-
Lennan, known as "John McLennan (by the Lake)," a
Conservative. In 1879 Donald Macmaster, another Conservative, won Glengarry's seat in the provincial Parliament,
and his victory was considered by the Conservatives to have
completed the process of winning Glengarry out of the
Sandfield grip. But in 1882 D.A., by this time retired from
the Lieutenant Governorship, attempted a come-back.
McLennan had retired from public life, and Macmaster was
running to succeed him as M.P. for Glengarry. D.A. was
persuaded by his Liberal friends to enter the contest against
Macmaster, but was defeated.

To the Conservatives, this was the ultimate triumph.
In the "sound Conservative village" of Lancaster, M.F.
McLennan contributed eight cords of dry wood for a victory
bonfire. The Conservative Cornwall *Reporter* asserted that it
had no wish to crow over D.A.'s defeat, but "that it was the
height of impropriety and of folly for him to ask a people who
had done so much for *him* and for whom he had done so little,
again to place their necks under the family yoke, and return
to the state of almost terrorism in which they were for over
thirty years previous to 1878. Mr. Macdonald knew of course
that he was getting up in years; he has now realized the fact
that a generation has arisen who knew not Joseph, and he will
no doubt be content to pass the remainder of his days in ease,
comfort, and retirement. Indeed the stern logic of facts has
shown him that his hold upon the county is gone, never to
be recovered."

Part of the reason for this failure can no doubt be found
in the fiasco resulting from D.A.'s railway project. When
work on the Montreal and City of Ottawa Junction Railway
began in 1872, hopes were bright for the farmers of Kenyon
and Lochiel, who, it seemed, would soon have a much needed
outlet for their farm produce. But a few years later, work on
the project had ceased, without any certainty that it would ever
resume. And worse than this disappointment was the fact
that $50,000 of the total bonus granted to the railway by the

174

councils of Kenyon and Lochiel had already been actually paid out by the councils. Even if the railway were never to be built, the hardworking farmers would still have to repay this sum, with interest, through their taxes. One would like to know what was being speculated about this matter in country stores and at bees and wherever men gathered to discuss public affairs. To the gathering suspicions, new fuel was added when creditors of the bankrupt firm of contractors openly accused the railway directors a week before the election in 1878 of dishonest practices and an unwillingness to see work on the railway resumed. In 1881 D.A. McArthur, a political enemy of D.A. Macdonald, accused the directors of the railway company of embezzlement of the greater part of the $80,000 which by that time had been paid out by Kenyon and Lochiel townships. At a meeting at Kenyon Town Hall late in December 1881, D.A. Macdonald is reported to have been shouted down by the enraged ratepayers.

Not only were the Liberals stained by their association with the controversy over the disposal of the bonuses, and with the long delay in completing the road, but the Conservatives were now claiming the credit for having revived the railway project. Accusations and counter-accusations, barbed and envenomed, flew thick and fast between the two contending political parties after the manner customary in the furious political controversies of the time. This is one of the examples of an incident in which the nineteenth-century political habit of routinely making the most reckless political accusations makes it difficult even to guess at what the real truth of the situation was. Accusations of dishonesty did not have the weight at that time that they have today, when far greater restraint is exercised in making them. But D.A. had unwarily got himself and his party into a situation in which by the stern rules of the political game such charges could be made, and whether groundless or not, they mercilessly followed—causing perhaps pain, but hardly surprise, and possibly not even resentment, to this experienced veteran of many campaigns. By his final election contest of 1882, he had also indiscreetly added to his political liabilities by a scandal created by the high living and deep drinking of an official tour party, headed by himself as Lieutenant Governor, which had inspected the Ontario North West. Generous to itself in the matter of drinks, it was dubbed the "Corkscrew Brigade."

The Conservatives liked to emphasize the oppressive features of the Sandfield system they attacked, and thereby produced a tradition and a problem about the accuracy of the tradition. Years later, an Alexandria doctor of literary interests wrote in the *Glengarry News* (edited at that time by John Sandfield Macdonald's nephew) that "It has been said of the late Hon. John Sandfield Macdonald...that he would put a poor Scotchman off his farm, if that man would vote against him in the last election, provided, of course, that he could get the hooks into him, and a Glengarry jury to convict him. And then he would replace this poor Scotchman by a man who was sure to vote right at the next election." A correspondent of a Cornwall Conservative newspaper in 1870, raging against the Sandfields, had deplored the plight of the Glengarrians who went to the polls to vote, "not as they wish, but as directed, for fear of what! *the bailiff's hammer*." It was customary for contenders in election campaigns to claim that rival parties used mortgages and loans as a means of coercing voters, and no doubt such charges were often true; and if John Sandfield and D.A. did not apply pressure personally on their debtors, the debtors might still feel that they were not entitled to be independent voters. The present writers are inclined to think that if the Sandfields took any more advantage of their position as mortgage and note holders than did the other Canadian politicians of their time, more evidence of the fact would have survived. It is also admittedly true, however, that whatever was done to put pressure on voters was necessarily done in private and there in a state of uncertainty we must leave the matter — unresolved, and perhaps neither capable of being resolved, nor worth resolving.

Growing up in the shadow of the Sandfields was another

Senator Donald McMillan (1835-1914). A native of Lochiel, he became a medical doctor in 1865 and was appointed Senator in 1884. Though he practised successfully as a doctor in Alexandria, his activities as a local politician, sawmill owner, coroner, J.P., township and village councillor, director of the Sovereign Bank, Trusts and Guarantee Co., and Merchants' Fire Insurance Co., and Ontario Medical Association, tend to obscure his "bedside manner." An arch Conservative, he held that party together in Glengarry and made it a fighting force in a period of Liberal domination. He had an excellent command of Gaelic and took an informed part in Senate debates.

remarkable family. John A. McDougald, who was born on lot 5, 4th Kenyon, in 1838, was the business agent and "confidential friend" of the Hon. D.A. Macdonald. Later, he was local registrar of the Supreme Court and clerk of the County Court of SDG. One of his sons, Dr. W.L. McDougald, became a Senator in 1926; we shall notice him in a later chapter. Another son, A.W. McDougald, a businessman and one-time provincial candidate for Glengarry, wrote a good history of Glengarry which was published in the *Glengarry News* in 1932-1933. Another son, Duncan J., who was born at Alexandria, was a Toronto businessman and father of the famous John A. ("Bud") McDougald of the Argus Corporation. When Bud McDougald died in 1978, the *Globe and Mail* estimated his personal fortune at over $250 million. Duncan J., like his brother A.W., had historical interests, and was said in his obituary to have "compiled a most complete family history, profusely illustrated, which will prove of real historical value." We regret that we have not seen a copy of it.

In the upset of the Sandfields, no one perhaps played a greater part than an Alexandria physician, Dr. Donald McMillan. Born in Lochiel Township in 1835, he studied medicine at Victoria University (of Cobourg, Ontario), which is now a part of the University of Toronto. A devoted and skilful political worker, he ran for Parliament only once — unsuccessfully, in the federal by-election of 1875, against McNab. Early in 1882, the Cornwall *Reporter* summed up his contributions and his deserts: "Dr. McMillan was about the first man of prominence in Glengarry who undertook to combat the Beast of Grittism in Glengarry. Through good report and evil report — through circumstances adverse and circumstances prosperous — through storm and through sunshine, the Doctor had never halted in the good work; and he has seen his cause triumphant...we take it that the services which Dr. McMillan has rendered in times of trial and depression, speak in trumpet tongues in favor of his call to the Canadian Lords."

On the same day as the *Reporter* article, Sir John A. Macdonald wrote, presumably in reference to McMillan's appointment to the Senate, that if it were not made, then "Good bye to Glengarry." Nevertheless, the appointment was slow in maturing, and the claims of rival candidates were discussed in the press. Dr. McMillan was alleged to have the superior claim resulting from a written promise of the appointment by Sir John A.. In March of 1883 an Alexandria correspondent of the *Freeholder*, alluding to the written promise supposedly held by McMillan, asked somewhat satirically, "why doesn't the doctor take a parlor car to Ottawa and claim his seat in the Senate; also the $1,000 a year for life". But in the next month the same or another Alexandria correspondent put aside political malice to hope that his fellow townsman would get his well deserved honour. "As a servant to the Conservative party the Doctor has worked hard and honest[ly] in this County. In 1875 he opposed McNabb and although unsuccessful, still kept up a continued warfare for the interest of his party, and was chiefly instrumental in electing Mr. McLennan and Mr. McMaster in subsequent elections." There seemed, the correspondent concluded blackly, to be an attempt to secure the senatorship for Cornwall. It was not until January 1884 that Dr. McMillan received his call to the Senate.

Why this delay? Sir John A. was notoriously slow in doing things, and in this instance there were doubtless other candidates whose claims had to be closely compared with those of Dr. McMillan. There is evidence that John McLennan (by the Lake) was unenthusiastic about McMillan at this time and was not pushing his appointment. It may also be suspected that although Dr. McMillan's services were considered large and deserving of reward, they were not considered quite large enough for this particular reward, the luscious prize of a senatorship. If the discrepancy between the merit and the prize was not present to the minds of Conservative Party officials, it certainly became evident in an exaggerated form to posterity. In course of time, as new generations arose who had not witnessed Dr. McMillan providing his political services, there grew up a legend, quite incorrect but not very surprising, that there was something decidedly mysterious in the appointment to the Senate of this village doctor who had never before sat in any Parliament.

Dr. McMillan enjoyed his senatorship for more than thirty years, and it is good to be able to report that he seems, from his contribution to the Senate *Hansard*, to have been an able, conscientious, and well informed legislator and a credit to his county.

Sir Donald Macmaster (1846-1922), a native of Glengarry, was raised to the rank of baronet in England. An eminent lawyer, he served Glengarry as M.L.A. 1879-1882 and M.P. 1882-1887 and was in the British House of Commons.

Donald Macmaster who, as we have seen, played a part in winning Glengarry for the Conservatives, was one of the most successful men Glengarry has produced. He was born in 1846 at Williamstown, where his parents, or at least his step-father, kept a hotel, and he was educated at Williamstown Grammar School and McGill. Choosing the profession of law, he soon established a reputation as one of the most able and promising of Canadian lawyers. During his several years in the Ontario legislature, he had no chance of becoming a cabinet minister, as his party was in opposition. One may wonder perhaps why someone whose talents were so much praised by his contemporaries did not become a cabinet minister during his four years in the House of Commons, when his party was in power; but it was doubtless against the grain to make someone a cabinet minister during his first term in Parliament. Senator McMillan thought in 1888 that if Macmaster were in Parliament then he would become a Cabinet minister, but by then the Glengarry electorate had rejected him at the notorious election of 1887. Macmaster never again accepted a Canadian political nomination, but concentrated on his law practice. As he had distinguished himself in appeals to the Judicial Committee of the Privy Council, he went to England in 1905 to live there and to specialize in such appeals. He was elected a member of the British House of Commons and in his old age was made a baronet. To have penetrated into at least the outer ranks of the English ruling class when it was still revelling in the immense security and prosperity of the Victorian age and could fairly be called the most successful ruling class the world had ever seen was an impressive achievement for the boy from Williamstown. Sir Donald Macmaster died in England in 1922.

For someone of his talents, it must be conceded, however, that he approached the Glengarry election of 1887 with his copybook badly blotted. He had had the indiscretion to let slip a remark in the House of Commons about the barbarism of the ancestors of the Highlanders. A similar remark in the previous decade by Sir Richard Cartwright, who had no connection with Glengarry, had reportedly aroused Glengarry wrath, and a delegation of Glengarrians had presented an address of thanks to a Senator who had fittingly rebuked Cartwright. By the code of contemporary politics, Macmaster had committed an offence which he must expect to hear about again and again and again, and his political enemies, seeing that he had delivered himself into their hands, showed him no mercy. A much more serious matter, which seems, however, to have aroused, at most, no greater response than the Highlander remark, was Macmaster's acceptance of a $4,000 retainer in a Customs case which his own government was prosecuting; under these circumstances, the retainer, inevitably, looked like a bribe. To complete his liabilities, he had, allegedly, an exceptionally bad attendance record in the House of Commons.

Patrick Purcell (1833-1891) successful contractor on railways and canals. M.P. for Glengarry 1887-1891.

His opponent in 1887, Patrick Purcell, was a man of little education but of much talent. He was born in Glengarry in 1833. His father was a native of Ireland and his mother was Scottish. Beginning life in humble circumstances, he became one of the most successful Glengarry contractors of his generation. He built portions of the Intercontinental Railway and of the C.P.R., and built St. Peter's Canal on Cape Breton Island. By the early 1880's he was the owner and occupant of Cariboo Cameron's splendid house at Summerstown. From that base he carried on business as a money lender, and he was also the proprietor of a store and a sawmill in Glengarry. As early as 1880 he was reported to be a millionaire. Conceivably the report was never actually true of him, but he was certainly more wealthy than any other Glengarry resident of his generation with the possible exception of Big Rory McLennan. A man of aspiring ideas, he had acquired a tract of more than 50,000 acres of land in the early 1880's in what is now Saskatchewan. He retained an interest in his ancestral Ireland, and a contemporary newspaper rumour claimed that a visit which he made to Ireland about this time was for the purpose of getting tenants for this western tract.

Purcell had been a supporter of the Sandfields, but otherwise his background was wholly or mainly Conservative. Nevertheless, he was chosen by the Liberals as their candidate to oppose Macmaster at the election of 1887.

Purcell won the election, but Macmaster and his friends challenged the results in a court of law and had Purcell's election voided on the grounds that corrupt practices had been used to win it. The sensational trial at Cornwall in which this verdict was reached resulted in the press throughout Canada publishing the means that Purcell's agents had used to get votes in Glengarry. Before the election, the *Glengarrian*, mistakenly expecting Purcell's defeat, published a song about Purcell which began:

> In days of old, when nights were cold
> And Purcell came this way,
> This boodler bold, with purse of gold,
> Our Freedom tried to slay-ha-hay,
> Our Freedom tried to slay.
> A whiskey flask he bore.
> He went from door to door,
> And much he lied

And vainly cried:
'I've money in galore.'
    Yes, much he cried,
    And vainly lied:
'I've money in galore.'

Now the Montreal *Star* hailed the trial results in these words:

## GLENGARRY'S SHAME

Glengarry hides her head in shame
    When now the tale is told!
That her good name, once known to fame,
    Was changed for Purcell's gold.
Like hucksters on a market day,
Her sons that good name did betray
    And votes and honor sold.

And know ye not, ye sordid fools!
    Who held your rights so cheap,
And, dead to shame, and honor's rules,
    Were bought like flocks of sheep,
That by such acts you but attest,
And to the rich make manifest,
    Before them ye will creep!

Yea! creep the slaves! and lick the dust
    From off the rich man's shoe!
He knows his power and counts your lust,
    For gold will keep you true.
The precious rights which distant lands
Sigh to obtain, with reckless hands
    You prodigally strew!

And is that all we can expect
    Beneath the people's sway?
Will like cause show the same effect
    Forever, as to-day?
And must we ever governed be
By gold, or else by bigotry?
    For both our hopes betray?

If this be true! then I, for one,
　　My franchise will disown;
Nor value what our fathers won,
　　And wrested from the throne,
I'd sooner serve an autocrat,
Than see in power a man like that,
　　Raised by his wealth alone!

But as I write, there comes a thought
　　That in Glengarry still
Full eighteen hundred were unbought,
　　And grieved to see the ill
Done to the grand old county's name.
Who swore that they'd avenge this shame,
　　And did their oath fulfil.

*-Felix O'Hara*

The comment of the Huntington *Gleaner* was that "The
revelations at these election trials are enough to sicken
anybody with party and party government as developed
nowadays."

Fortunately, a transcript of the proceedings of the election
trial at Cornwall survives. To someone who has first read
contemporary newspaper comments on the election scandal,
the transcript must inevitably have disappointing features. It
is devoted principally not to unfolding the worst that Purcell
and his agents did, but rather to proving a number of incidents
of corruption which were often themselves not very grave but
for which sufficient evidence could be assembled. Once the
reader has got past this initial disappointment, however, he
will almost certainly agree that the trial trans-
script is one of the most sociologically and politically valuable
documents we have for nineteenth-century Glengarry history.
Here we see the relations between a rich money-lender and his
agents, and the application of money-lending to getting votes.
We also find some information on the extent of expenditure
involved. Macmaster, the unsuccessful candidate, cross-
examined Purcell at the trial:

Q. How much money had you at the time of this election in
notes and mortgages in the county of Glengarry? A. In the

county of Glengarry I should think about $200,000, I think, in notes and mortgages altogether. Q. Not more than that? A. We had $4,000 — Q. I am not asking you about comparison, I am asking you about the amount? A. I will have to give it to you roughly, say between $200,000 and $300,000. Q. That is all told? A. Yes, I think so, but some of it was ten years old.

One of Purcell's agents estimated that since November 1885, he alone had lent from $150,000 to $200,000 on behalf of Purcell. During the period of the election campaign, the agent had lent roughly between $25,000 and $30,000. The significance of these loans was that they could be used as a means of obtaining votes for Purcell, but unfortunately for the curiosity of posterity the trial did little or nothing ' to demonstrate precisely how the borrower was approached (if at all) to elicit the proper vote.

As an example of the close association between money-lending and politics in Glengarry about this time, we may mention that of the six M.P.'s who sat for the Glengarry constituency between Confederation and 1900, three were money-lenders.

One of the unhappy witnesses questioned at the trial was a former warden of the United Counties who had received $100 under mysterious circumstances. According to his testimony, he came on nomination day to Alexandria where at Macdonald's Hotel a man asked his name, then invited him to an upstairs room, in which he (the ex-warden) was given a promissory note to sign. Not having his glasses with him, the ex-warden could not read the note properly, but he signed it all the same.

Q. Did you ask him from whom the $100 were? A. No, nor did he tell me. Q. Had you any any idea then? A. No, not in the least. Q. And you accepted the $100 without asking him from whom it was? A. Yes. Q. And you did not ask him to whom the note was? A. No. Q. Did you see in what time it was payable? A. I thought it was twelve months, but I could not say. Q. You did not look to see whether it was payable with or without interest? A. No. Q. You signed it without saying a word? A. Yes.

The implication in this case was that the ex-warden was being given the money to use in bribing voters, and that the promissory note was to cover the transaction with an appearance of legality in case the election expenditures came to be questioned in the courts.

Another witness claimed that he had overheard Purcell stating that his election was the dearest ever contested in the County of Glengarry and that it had cost him $36,000.

Shortly after this election, Big Rory McLennan wrote a letter to Sir John A. Macdonald outlining what he believed to be the reasons for the Conservative defeat in Glengarry. At Confederation, he said, not 10 % of the people of Glengarry were Conservatives. Since then, the Conservatives had managed to get a majority for John McLennan and Macmaster. John McLennan and Macmaster were aided by their popularity in the south, and by the unpopularity McNab and D.A. Macdonald had acquired in the rear of the county through their connection with the railway project. The new recruits brought in to the support of the Conservative candidates were not, however, confirmed Conservatives. When the most recent election campaign began the confirmed Conservatives did not amount to more than 20 % of the electorate, while the Reformers (Liberals) claimed to have at least 45 % of the electorate committed to them. The balance of the electorate "was made up of a class of men having no particular political opinions and liable at any time to be changed by money and other influences." The writer thought that Purcell must have spent from fifty to sixty thousand dollars on the campaign, and he asserted that Purcell "in some cases offered as high as two hundred dollars for votes." Purcell also, the writer alleged, had promised men jobs in railway work. Finally, the Roman Catholic clergy "were not with us," and Father Duffus of St. Raphaels "not only voted but Canvassed against us."

A casualty of the bitter 1887 campaign was Stilwell, the editor of the *Glengarrian*. Just before the election he published a letter, signed Flora Macdonald, stigmatizing Purcell as a moral leper, unfit to represent "the pure homes and moral firesides of Glengarry." Purcell was accused of being a Sabbath-breaker and a tippler, the enemy of his home and marriage, and was alleged to have "dragged into the mire at least one of Glengarry's fair and frail daughters." The name Flora Macdonald was probably fictitious, taken from the heroine of the '45 Rebellion in Scotland. The letter went well beyond even the wildly generous limits allowed to personal abuse in the electioneering of the time, and Purcell had Stilwell charged with libel. Perhaps as a counter-move, the editor of the *Freeholder* was charged with libelling Big Rory. The *Freeholder* editor received a suspended sentence, but nothing was done to bring the Stilwell case to a trial. It became evident that Purcell was willing to let the matter drop. Stilwell then began a suit against Purcell for false imprisonment and malicious prosecution. It was perhaps because of this suit that Purcell revived the dying libel charge against Stilwell.

Stilwell was found guilty and was sentenced to a fine and a month in jail. It may be noted as a further complication in the case that while Stilwell's trial on the libel charge was pending, he was convicted and fined on a separate charge of assault and battery, and that Senator McMillan was arrested on the same charge. Stilwell on his conviction received no sympathy from one of the best small Canadian newspapers of the day, the Huntington *Gleaner* edited by the novelist and historian Robert Sellar. The *Gleaner* desribed the *Glengarrian* as "A grossly personal sheet" and asserted that "party papers like the *Glengarrian* are a disgrace to Canadian journalism and that a man, who, in a county of Highlanders, would associate the name of the pure and leal-hearted Flora with the dirt of Canadian elections, cuts himself off from sympathy." An order for Stilwell's release was obtained from the Governor General, perhaps through the intervention of Purcell, and he was released before his month's term was up.

But misfortunes awaited him on his return to Alexandria. He was soon writing to Big Rory to lament that the John A. McDougald we have already mentioned had seized his safe and other property for non-payment of rent, and that a $45 board bill in Cornwall had been ominously presented for payment. And what, he wondered, was the fate of the balance of a fund which the "great conservative party" had been collecting for him? Within a few weeks a new editor of the *Glengarrian* was in office, who informed his readers that "Mr. C.J. Stilwell, the late editor of this journal," had "seen fit to leave Alexandria for parts unknown without having given any previous intimation of his intentions." The new editor promised that under his management the *Glengarrian* would shun the personal abuse and intemperate language of the past.

Perhaps Stilwell had little cause to regret the collapse of his journalistic career in Alexandria. He had served his political masters too well for his own good. Even before his final troubles came upon him he had given vent to his professional agony by describing himself as publishing "a metropolitan paper, in a place which is actually too mean to support the poorest rural sheet." A few months after his flight from Alexandria he was reported to be doing well with a large poultry farm, and when he revisited Cornwall a decade later he was said to be a detective working on the "celebrated Fair will case in San Francisco."

Despite the embarrassments of the election trial, Purcell was able to continue his Parliamentary career after all. He appealed the verdict to the Supreme Court, where it was reversed on technicalities. Macmaster in turn tried to appeal the case to the Judicial Committee of the Privy Council, but he was refused leave by the Judicial Committee to do so. It may be suspected that in terms of the county's reputation, it paid rather a high price for the honour of having Purcell as its M.P. The opposition press liked to snipe a little at Purcell's ineptitude in the House of Commons, but there is reason to suppose that apart from the question of how he got there, he was a respectable enough M.P., and he could always fall back, if necessary, on his sound reputation as a contractor. He introduced a bill for the financial protection of railway construction labourers which his Conservative successor, Big Rory McLennan, succeeded in pushing into law a few years later. Within a few months of his election, a Conservative paper noted his tendency, though elected as a Liberal, to support the Conservative government of Sir John A.. He was a friend and admirer of Sir Charles Tupper, the Conservative politician, and while a Liberal backbencher sent Tupper a gift of money on Tupper's retirement from Parliamentary life.

R.R. (Big Rory) McLennan (1842-1907), athlete, successful contractor, private banker, militia colonel, founder of the McLennan Scholarship at Queen's. M.P. for Glengarry 1891-1900.

Immediately after his death in 1891, Purcell was again the subject of public attention when his body was stolen from its grave at Flanagan's Point, in the south-west corner of Glengarry. It was not recovered till more than three years later, when it was found floating in the St. Lawrence. The body appears to have been stolen by two young ex-convicts from the Summerstown area perhaps because of a grudge, perhaps with a view to holding it for ransom.

Purcell's successor as M.P. for Glengarry was R.R. McLennan, often known as Big Rory McLennan. The number of sharply varying fields in which most of us can shine during one poor lifetime is small, but Big Rory, a man of unusual gifts and unusual versatility, prospered as an athlete, railway contractor, banker, money lender, and politician. He was born at Glen Donald, Charlottenburgh, in 1842. As a young man, he was possibly the world's best athlete in throwing the hammer. Unhappily, he had the misfortune to kill a little girl by accident while throwing the hammer in Cornwall in 1877. He had a contract for building a section of the CPR north of Lake Superior, and it was presumably in this contract that he made his initial fortune, which provided the cash pool for his later business enterprises. He was a banker and money lender in Alexandria in the mid-1880's. The many business enterprises he was involved in included a large ranch in Alberta (N.W. Territories at the time) called the Glengarry Ranch, of which he was one of the proprietors. He was at least briefly the owner of the *Glengarrian* , and he appears to have been for many years the owner of the Cornwall *Standard* . He was an enthusiastic organizer and officer in the militia. His election in 1891 was contested at law and he was unseated, but he was again returned at a by-election in 1892.

We owe to Big Rory one of our best collections of nineteenth-century Glengarry documents. The great store of business correspondence which he accumulated during his years at Alexandria is in the Ontario Archives, and gives a day-to-day account of the activities of a money lender and Conservative party activist. Included are many letters from his friend and fellow Conservative, Donald Macmaster. McLennan's formal education may have been limited, but his letter writing shows that he had somewhere acquired correctness and fluency of expression. There is not much in the collection, however, that casts light on him as a human being. One wonders if he presented himself to his friends as any more of an individual than he appears in his papers. It is, however, pleasant to be able to report that he seems to have had a talent for good living. One can only applaud his orders to his secretary in 1891, when he was preparing to entertain two M.P.'s at Alexandria, to lay in "a barrel of English soda." Following a favourite Glengarry tradition, he was a lifelong bachelor.

Early in Big Rory's period as M.P., there arose a new political movement in Glengarry which challenged not only his career but the whole established system of Conservative vs Liberal politics. This was the development of a farmers' movement called the Patrons of Industry. The Patrons movement began in the United States, and entered Canada in 1889. It is not known when or where the first Glengarry branch, or "association" as the word was, of the Patrons was founded, but we read of an organizer from Aultsville, called J.B. Dafoe, briskly organizing Glengarry associations in 1892. On 23 August 1892 it was reported that he had organized the Highland Association and the Apple Hill Association, both at Apple Hill, the Elm Grove Association at Martintown, the Mono [Monro] Mills Association at Mono [Monro] Mills, the Glen Roy Association at Glen Roy, and the Peerless Association at Dominionville. Before long there was a network of associations, amounting to as many as 40, spread throughout the county. The Patrons' national platform included the abolition of the Canadian Senate and made a number of demands believed to be in the interests of the farming class. The associations also provided a welcome opportunity for social gatherings. Picnics were among the social functions sponsored by the Patrons. We read of the Dalkeith Patrons chartering a blacksmith to do the work of members on special terms. The Patrons of North Lancaster and vicinity were reported to have similarly chartered the store of an enterprising young merchant, J.F. Cattanach, and other Patrons' stores in Glengarry are mentioned. Perhaps local entrepreneurs sensed a danger in the Patrons developing a large scale system based on such arrangements. In 1893 it was alleged that some Glengarry merchants had formed a combination to boycott Patrons members.

The Glengarry Patrons boldly dashed into the political fray in the fall of 1893 by nominating candidates: D.M. McPherson, the Cheese King, for the provincial house, and J. Lockie Wilson for the federal house. The Toronto-based newspaper of the Patrons movement, the *Farmers' Sun*, called Wilson and McPherson "representative farmers, one having established a name beyond the limits of this Province as a successful breeder and prize winner, and the other being crowned as the 'cheese king' of Canada".

McPherson caused some suspense for the Patrons and one may suppose embarrassment for his sponsors, by delaying several weeks before agreeing to accept the nomination. In the provincial election of 1894 he was opposed by George H. Macgillivray, a Charlottenburgh resident and son of the Hon. John McGillivray of the North West Company. McPherson won, though not by a large majority, and found himself part of an impressive bloc of no fewer than 17 Patrons candidates returned to the Ontario legislature.

The attention of politics-watchers in Glengarry now turned to the Patrons' federal candidate, J. Lockie Wilson. Aged now just under 40, Wilson had been born in Alexandria and had a farm just west of the town. He had had a lucrative contract as a young man to provide fencing along the Canada Atlantic line, and had long been active in the lively social life of the little town. Dramatically, when he was tendered the Patrons' nomination at the Patrons' convention in Alexandria, he offered to refuse it if so much as one Patron present objected to him. Holding a high rank in the Patrons movement, Wilson was well known through this connection not only in Glengarry but throughout central Canada, and especially shone as an orator. At a meeting of Patrons at Prince Edward County in 1895, one of the speakers was Wilson, who we are told, "in his refined, cultured and finished manner, eloquently held that huge audience spell-bound for over an hour and a half." He was hailed with "frequent bursts of applause with cries of 'go on' — 'go on' — ", and at last "the people could be seen to rise from their seats, so interested were they with the arguments and language flowing from the speaker's mouth in the interests of the laboring and farming community."

As the election approached, it appeared that Big Rory McLennan had secured a splendid prize for Alexandria. The Conservative government had chosen Alexandria to be the site of a big reformatory which was to serve the needs of delinquent boys from all of Canada. According to the official description:

> The portions of this building now under contract will consist of a pentagonal hub or central portion, known as a rotunda (from which eventually the administration block and 4 cell wings will radiate) and one of the cell wings. The "rotunda" will be pentagonal on plan with a frontage of 100 feet, a depth of 115 feet and a height of 80 feet from the ground line to the top of the battlements. It is to be covered by a flat roof and surmounted by an octangonal lantern 50 feet in diameter and 30 feet in height surmounted by a ventilator 10 feet high with a finial 10 feet in length, making 50 feet from the top of roof...
>
> The outside walls of the building are to be stone, lined with brick, the facings of the cells, stone, the walling and vaulting of the cells brick.

Surviving sketches of the intended building show that it would have been a monumental structure featuring a gaunt and forbidding central building. An imposing landmark in the town to delight those who had no fear of being locked away inside it, it would have daunted all but the boldest of those who appeared as prisoners before its gates. Alexandria seemed a suitable location for the all-Canada reformatory because of the town's central location in Canada, its position almost on the border between Ontario and Quebec, its nearness to Ottawa and to Montreal, its good railway facilities, its reasonable remoteness from rivers and from the American border which would normally offer facilities for prisoners to escape; and — or so it was alleged — because of the Glengarry supplies of building stone and timber. It can hardly be doubted that the acquisition of this building would have given a new impetus and a new direction to the development of Alexandria. Above all, its flow of government cash would have been of inestimable benefit to the town during the bleak years of the Depression which was now just one generation ahead. If it had been built, it would by now be obsolete, and we should be speculating about how to arrange the financing to preserve this venerable piece of Victorian architecture as part of the heritage of our town.

But alas! The much desired reformatory was never, never to be! From an early date the Liberal *Freeholder* derided this project of the Conservative government, seeing it only as an election hoax never intended to be transferred from paper to reality. One of the most serious objections to selecting Alexandria as the site of the reformatory was the town's lack of a good water supply; and when the Alexandria council drilled in vain for water in 1895, the *Freeholder* burst into mockery. The well "was sunk, at the expense of the Dominion government no doubt, to make gullible people believe that something was really going to be done about Rory's reformatory. But there was no water and there will be no reformatory." Even the government's sampling of the local stone supply, the *Freeholder* thought, was only part of the confidence trick the government was attempting on the Glengarry electorate. Whatever doubts the *Freeholder* succeeded in raising must have been much reduced when the contract for building the reformatory was actually signed in March of 1896. In the federal election which followed three months later, Big Rory was re-elected as Conservative M.P. for Glengarry, defeating Lockie Wilson — but the Laurier Liberals were swept into power. It remained to be seen what the new Liberal government would do to realize a project begun by its Conservative predecessor and intended to benefit a constituency still represented by a Conservative. The project was not immediately ended, but over the next few years it was allowed to die a natural death. The *Freeholder* looking back on the fiasco in 1899, objected to the views of those who blamed the loss of the reformatory on the Liberal party and reiterated its claim that the Conservative government had never intended the project seriously in the first place.

Another casualty of the election of 1896 was the Patrons movement, which in the whole country only managed to elect three M.P.'s and was soon in breakup in Glengarry and elsewhere. The poor showing of the Patrons' representatives in the Ontario legislature no doubt also contributed to this result. The associations in Glengarry had been a mushroom growth, and as far as we know they vanished as quickly as they came. Nevertheless, when D.M. McPherson was denied the provincial Liberal nomination for the Glengarry election of 1898, there were still enough Patrons around to set him up as a Patrons or Independent candidate. He was defeated by D.R. McDonald, a Conservative and prominent Glengarry contractor. McPherson was again defeated, this time as a Liberal candidate, in the provincial election of 1902. For Lockie Wilson, 1896 must have meant the failure of the one supreme opportunity which life had put before him of making a breakthrough into a sphere where he would be able to exercise his undoubted talents. He later had a long and respectable career as a public servant. He is lost from our sight today as that most irrecoverable of historical phenomena—the man whose reputation is based on dazzling traits of character and dazzling feats with the spoken word.

From this point we may quickly summarize Glengarry political developments for the remainder of our period. McLennan was defeated in the 1900 federal election by J.T. Schell, a Liberal, who was succeeded in his seat in 1908 by another Liberal, John Angus McMillan, who held it till 1917. William D. McLeod, a cheese factory proprietor, one of several people sometimes called the Little Cheese King, was elected M.L.A. for Glengarry in 1902, as a Conservative. He was defeated at the 1905 provincial election by John Angus McMillan, a Liberal. In 1908, D.R. McDonald was again elected Conservative M.L.A. for Glengarry, and held office till 1911. In that year Hugh Munro, of Munro and McIntosh, was elected M.L.A. as a Liberal. In 1914, Munro was returned by acclamation and he held his seat till the dissolution of the Parliament in 1919, when he retired from politics.

## The Temperance Movement

It is easy to romanticise about the drinking habits of the pioneers of this province, but there can be no doubt that they often drank far too much and created grave social problems. Faced with a life of hard labour and monotony, and often of loneliness and disappointment as well, the pioneer farmer often yearned for "a little drink" as a solace. To satisfy such yearnings, and indeed to encourage them, the local shopkeepers sold whisky, and taverns and rude shebeens of every kind were conveniently available along the new-cut backwoods roads as well as in the new hamlets and towns.

A man might quickly drink up his land or the money which was to buy the land. The worse consequences of this failing often fell on the wife and children of the drinker. To see the evil of pioneer drinking at its blackest, we have to remember how completely dependent on her husband a wife usually was, socially, legally, and above all economically at this time. A backwoods wife with three or four children (if not more!) and a husband too addicted to drink to support his family was in a helpless plight.

The idea began to grow that something might be done to contain this evil. At first, a few persons merely resolved to avoid the use of the stronger drinks. These sometimes banded together with other persons of similar outlook in small temperance societies. Before long, the dominating ideal of the temperance societies changed from the avoidance merely of the stronger drinks to the avoidance of all alcoholic beverages. The belief also began to spread that the authority of the government should be used to end the sale of drink. As this belief grew stronger and stronger in the temperance movement the movement turned into what was, in effect, largely a prohibition movement, but the old term "temperance," though no longer really accurate, continued commonly to be used for the movement. In the following pages, we will follow the usage of the times, and will refer to the "temperance" cause and "temperance" ideas, etc., even where, on strictly logical grounds, "prohibition" would be the more defensible word.

It is not very easy, at the time at which we are writing, to invite readers to view the temperance movement with sympathy. We know that almost all tendencies today are against that sympathy being given and indeed are against the appeal on its behalf being heard except with ridicule and impatience. The temperance movement in the United States and Canada has failed, and it has failed, not with tragedy and dignity, but with the hoots and sallies of its enemies resounding in its ears. Prohibition in the United States and Canada was a monstrous error, and the temperance movement made that error possible. It is hard to look back impartially past this disaster and appreciate the very real courage, idealism, and self-sacrifice of the early temperance reformers. Nevertheless, verdicts on the past have a habit of changing, and the time may come when these reformers will be seen to have been guilty of no worse faults than too optimistic a view of the possibilities of democracy and too optimistic a view of human kind in general, and when they will again be warmly applauded for their long fight against tenacious financial interests.

The temperance movement was important in Glengarry for several generations. Although the movement is all but extinct there today, its consequences are still with us. In view of these circumstances, we must ask our readers to summon up such tolerance towards the subject as they can manage and accompany us as we trace it as far as the First World War.

We are able to begin the story with one of Glengarry's claims to a "first." According to tradition, the clownish behaviour of drunken men at a logging bee at Breadalbane in 1820 caused such disgust in the neighbourhood that the first temperance society in Canada was immediately founded. This was seven or eight years before the accepted date for the founding of the earliest Canadian temperance society. Unfortunately we have not noticed any evidence to verify this story, though lack of evidence in a period when the sources for Glengarry history are so limited can hardly be used very strongly against it. If the society existed, it was probably dedicated, like the other early temperance socities, to opposing the use of strong drinks rather than to total abstinence. But whatever the exact truth about this society may have been, it is at least certain that the temperance movement was active in Breadalbane at an early date. In 1876 John Stewart of Dalkeith wrote to the Montreal *Witness* that "The temperance reformation was early espoused in Breadalbane, and the use of intoxicating liquors as a beverage, at any parties such as marriages, funerals, bees or socials, has been unknown in the place for more than forty years." This agrees with the statement of the Rev. William Fraser, minister of the Breadalbane Baptist Church from 1831 to 1850, who said that "I never heard an oath or saw a glass of liquor drunk in Breadalbane."

Passing reluctantly by Breadalbane's claims to priority, we must report that the earliest known proof of a temperance society in Glengarry comes in a newspaper announcement of 1834 stating that the "Temperance Society" at Martintown would hold its annual meeting.

In 1844 a Cornwall newspaper reported an interesting event and included some sharp words for the Glengarrians: "Father Clark, the Canadian Matthew [Father Mathew, 1790-1856, was an Irish temperance reformer], administered the pledge to 450 on Sabbath last at St. Andrews. This is a noble precedent which we hope to see followed by his brother-clergymen throughout the Province, and particularly in Glengarry, where intemperance prevails to an alarming extent."

Whatever the truth of this slur on Glengarry may have been, and whatever the exact history of the early temperance movement there, the Glengarry temperance movement seems to have been reasonably well established in the 1850's. A temperance society was established at Breadalbane in 1851 and lasted till 1854; it doubled as a literary or debating society, and was on friendly terms with a temperance society at Vankleek Hill. In 1852, a Glengarry temperance petition 32 feet long is said to have been presented to the legislature. The Peerless Division of the Sons of Temperance, Notfield, was founded in 1854 and was still in existence in the mid-1860's. In 1859 the Sons of Temperance were reported as holding a soiree at Lancaster, and there were doubtless other Glengarry temperance societies at this time which have escaped our notice.

In the present century, the temperance movement has been strongly associated in the public mind with the Protestant clergy, but in the nineteenth century, as we must emphasize, it was also strongly promoted by the Roman Catholic clergy. In 1871 Father J.S. O'Connor, the parish priest at Alexandria, established a total abstinence society in his parish. Soon thereafter similar societies were established by the parish priests at St. Raphaels and Lochiel. In 1881 it was reported that Father Gauthier had preached a temperance sermon at Lancaster and intended to revive the local temperance society. The St. Finnan's Temperance Society at Alexandria was active in the temperance cause from the beginning of the 90's onwards. Both the first and second Bishops of Alexandria lent their influential support to the temperance cause.

The support of the clergy, both Protestant and Roman Catholic, was of critical importance to the temperance cause, but the adherence of laymen of standing in the community must also have helped to sway the public mind. We read the following in an obituary of Col. Alexander Chisholm, of Alexandria, a Roman Catholic: ''Of the temperance cause he was an enthusiastic advocate, practically carrying out the reform doctrines he promulgated, by refraining from all intoxicating liquors under every circumstance." Donald Cattanach also adopted the principle of total abstinence. "As soon as he saw his duty," his biographer writes, "he accepted it, and this involved no small sacrifice. From his hospitable nature, and the customs of society then, it cost him a greater struggle to have the courage of his convictions than we of the present time [i.e., 1884] can realize. To abstain from social drinking, to abstain from offering strong liquors to his guests, or using wine at his own table, required strong courage, and he had it... In his capacity of squire, he saw...many troubles which needed the intervention of the magistrate before they could be settled, which never would have arisen but for strong drink; he saw death and destitution arise from its use; he saw the fair gifts of the new world made of no effect because of it,...he was the uncompromising foe of drink in all forms during the rest of his life."

It is evidence of the growing temperance sentiment, but equally of the continued strength of the evil that the temperance people were struggling against, that a Cornwall newspaper reported from Alexandria in 1882 a growing feeling that the facilities for the sale of drink in that town were excessive, "there being in Alexandria no less than six hotels and two stores for the sale of the 'accursed spirit' for a population of only eight hundred souls." Presumably none of these establishments were as innocent as one at Dunvegan, where a man denied the charge that he was selling "Strong Liquors" and explained that he sold "only temperate Liquors such as Pipperment Ginger Cinnamon and Lemond Syrup."

A consequence of the growing temperance feeling was that Glengarrians soon got their first experience of prohibition. The Canada Temperance Act of 1878, usually known as the Scott Act, made it possible for a municipality to vote itself completely "dry" through a referendum. Voting on the Scott Act took place in the United Counties of Stormont, Dundas, and Glengarry in 1884. The drys won a majority, and the Act came into effect in 1885. By the terms of this Act, the result could not be reversed by a further referendum till three years had passed.

We soon begin to hear of prosecutions under the Scott Act, but also of serious violations of the spirit and the letter of the Act. A contributor of Glen Robertson news to the *Freeholder* complained in September 1885 that "Several drunken men can daily be seen on the streets here, notwithstanding that Glen Robertson is strict in its observance of the Scott Act as any village or town in the United Counties. The province line is quite nigh, consequently the 'crater' can be obtained at any time, and in any quantity." In November, a correspondent from Martintown thought that "The Scott Act is making this place very quiet," but added that "Occasionally a party comes round with a barrel said to contain coal oil, and is well patronised. Where is the committee?" From Lancaster in the same month it was reported that the established way there to evade the Scott Act was to send a chap to Beaudette to buy supplies. In February it was reported that a bootlegger visiting Williamstown had had his hooch stolen. From Alexandria and Skye came suggestions that the Scott Act could not succeed in Glengarry unless Prescott went dry, but the United Counties of Prescott and Russell voted down the Scott Act in 1885.

Late in 1886 a Toronto daily published a lengthy report on the workings of the Scott Act in SDG, which is valuable not only for its information on the progress of the anti-drink cause in Glengarry but for its outsider's view of the county — comparable to those travellers' reports which cast so much light on the first decades of the county. As to the prohibition of drink, the writer's expectations seem to have been but modest, and he accordingly applauds the success with which the Scott Act had been enforced in Glengarry while admitting that a certain amount of selling still existed. The worst place in the county for the drink trade he thought to be Alexandria:

> In that town there are five or six taverns believed to be selling more or less liquor, and in the near neighbourhood groggeries and shebeening have always prevailed. Liquor selling seems to be taken to there as a last resort, when every other means of making a living fails. For instance, it is said that an old woman of 80, whose infirmities

prevented her from working any longer on the farm, removed to Alexandria, where she makes her living by a groggery. In the same town are to be found the halt and the lame privately selling liquor. The benevolent people, who on market days patronize them, exclaim, 'Poor people, what else is left them to do?' Yet here, in what is considered the stronghold of the traffic in the county, good has been achieved...At the late fair the principal hotel showed a marked change. Two years ago at the fair three bars could hardly accommodate the customers. At the fair the other day the landlord stood at the bar-room door with his hand on the key and admitted those whom he could trust two and two, and then only allowed them meagre fare. There is a decrease of open drunkenness, and very little treating is observed.

A temperance writer noted that all the Ontario municipalities that adopted the Scott Act later rejected it. In this, Glengarry and its two sister counties formed no exception. In the later part of 1887, a petition bearing 6,000 signatures asking for a referendum to repeal the Scott Act in the United Counties was presented to the government. The desired vote took place in the spring of 1888, and the Act was decisively rejected by the United Counties. The United Counties' majority against the Act was 2,143, and Glengarry's 715. A businessman at Alexandria wrote, "The Scott Act has been the great theme of conversation and the large majority by which the act was defeated Comes as a surprise to both friend and foe. I understand they had a great demonstration last night out here." It is hard to say whether the Scott Act had been a failure in Glengarry, simply because there are no fixed standards of success and failure by which it had to be measured. All in all, however, it does seem to have presented an unhappy early preview of what were to be the evasions and hypocrisies of twentieth-century prohibition in the United States and Canada. Before it was repealed, the editor of the *Glengarrian* stated his belief that it was extensively violated in Glengarry and actually harmed the cause of temperance there. And a few years after its repeal, the editor of the same journal almost certainly hit upon the right formula to sum up the history of the Scott Act in Glengarry by saying that the people had not given it "their moral support." Other forces at work in the functioning of the Scott Act are hinted at by the report that a few weeks before the voting on the repeal of the Act the hotel keepers of Glengarry met in Alexandria to organize the defeat of the Scott Act.

By the time of Glengarry's experiment with the Scott Act, the temperance or prohibition question had become an inescapable issue in politics. One gets the impression that most Canadian politicians of the time would have preferred to live in an earlier and simpler age, before such vexatious questions had been invented and when drink could be used freely by an open-hearted and open-handed candidate to lubricate the machinery of electioneering. In the provincial election of 1886, Rayside affirmed himself a prohibitionist. In the federal election of 1887, Macmaster was censured by the strongly anti-drink Montreal *Witness* for his hesitating attitude to prohibition, while his opponent Purcell had agreed without qualification to support prohibition. It would seem from the terms in which Senator McMillan, who did not have to be re-elected, discussed an anti-Scott Act petition from Glengarry in the Senate, that he had little love for the anti-drink people.

It is not hard to guess what must have been the thoughts and feelings of the temperance reformers of Glengarry in the years after the county had rejected the Scott Act. There was much evidence of the continuing vigor of the drink evil against which they struggled, much evidence, even, of weakness, vacillation, and lukewarmness among their professed friends. Yet was it not true also (we can imagine their thoughts continuing) that in Glengarry as elsewhere in Canada the temperance reformers had won to their side or reduced to neutrality nearly all the populace which had any claim to be religious or respectable, and that even their most venomous opponents could hardly defend their own position without seeming to be ashamed of it? Such reflections would largely have been true, and we distort history when we forget how much the anti-drink movement had captured of what was best and brightest in the last Victorian generation. Its opponents might struggle, but with enlightened opinion against them, could it be doubted that their defeat was inevitable, or that the day could be long delayed when a new and better society would flourish, in Glengarry as elsewhere, under the universal reign of PROHIBITION?

A liquor store in Glengarry. This one is at Lancaster; there are others at Alexandria and Maxville. The existence of these stores along with Brewers' Retail Stores and several sorts of licensed premises that sell alcoholic beverages by the glass are enough to make the ardent prohibitionists of not-so-long ago and their contemporaries the bootleggers wonder about the changes in Glengarry's drinking habits in the last forty years. These stores and modern licensed premises are even further removed from the inns and hotels of a century ago.

Having probed the temperance views of these years, we may now quickly list, and as it were set against this ideological background, the main events in temperance history as they relate to Glengarry County from the end of the 1880's to the First World War. In the Dominion plebiscite (the "Laurier Plebiscite") of 1898, the Glengarrians supported prohibition, though not by a large majority. In 1903 the temperance cause suffered a set-back when Maxville, dry since 1893, voted itself wet. By 1911, voting under the local option system had closed all bars in Glengarry except for those of two hotels in Lancaster Township. By 1914, Glengarry was dry everywhere. The county had therefore voluntarily imposed prohibition on itself even before the Ontario government established province-wide prohibition in 1916. That the Glengarry prohibition was far from foolproof (we dare not say watertight), we learn from a sombre statement made by Glengarry's M.P., J.A. McMillan, in Parliament in 1916: "The county of Glengarry, where I live, is dry, but we are close to licensed hotels in the province of Quebec, just a few miles away. There are some hundreds of soldiers in my town [Alexandria] at the present time, and there are most deplorable sights after every pay-day."

# Chapter VII
# Churches

Any church, anywhere, is a very complex thing. A tourist is perhaps more inclined to seek out and study the churches of a community he visits than any other buildings in the community. The historian visits them to consult their records, which in many cases are the most comprehensive, if not the only ones in the community. People who love music often attend church services to listen to various choirs. A lonely traveller often slips into a church, whether or not a service is scheduled, to find — whatever he hopes to find, be it a friendly voice, a place to meditate, or a place to mingle with people.

To the people who live in an area, this church is "our church" and that church is "their church." Yet these same people may farm or live side by side, vote the same way in elections, and drive the same sort of car. Another person may be able to say: My father went to "that" church, my mother's people belonged to "another" church, my wife belonged to "yet another" church, but we go to "this" church.

Any given church has to be considered from several different angles. One is the building itself, which must have size and space to contain people but is subject to all sorts of modifications to make it extremely elegant or extremely drab or anywhere in between. We must consider the age of the church: was it built to fill a need in a pioneer community? Is the church still filling that need in the community or has it been abandoned or torn down? Why does one church become "historic" and another a few miles away does not? If a church is being built what is the reason? Why is a church building here rather than there?

Finally we must consider the different aspects of a church in a community. One of the more obvious aspects is the building itself. The old log Congregational church at St. Elmo differs vastly from the little gem of a building that is the Roman Catholic church at Green Valley. The mighty pile of St. Finnan's in Alexandria differs widely from the simple elegance of the Covenanters Church at Brodie, yet all are churches.

Another aspect of any church is its social involvement in the community. A lawn social night at St. Mary's in Williamstown or the gathering outside any church door after a service will tell even the most casual observer that a church is a very important social centre. In time past, much more than today, they were cultural centres as well. Glengarry has had things such as Sunday School libraries, young people's literary and debating societies, as well as church sponsored temperance societies, tennis clubs, ball clubs, boy scouts and girl guides, glee clubs, and Bible Schools. Women's organizations connected with our churches have sponsored missionaries, catered to banquets, and provided help for all sorts of community betterment plans from public libraries to nursery schools; and their visits to "shut-ins" and hospitals, help to the needy and self-help programs of various sorts all are important aspects of church work.

The ostensible reason for any church's existence is its people's religion. This aspect the present authors will not go into very deeply, but we must note the different denominations that dwell among us, almost always amicably, while at the same time remarking that we have had some "good knock-em-down drag-em-out" church rows, almost entirely of the "family fight type" and confined to the Presbyterians. Though not so expressed in the Shorter Catechism, part of the religion of every Presbyterian Scot is his deep belief that his ideas about how to worship are as good or better than those of the next man. For some centuries now the Presbyterians have dispensed with Bishops, so have no umpire to call "time" on them when a difference of opinion has gone far enough. So our Presbyterians had a major division in 1844, a more minor one in 1875-76, and another major one in 1925. Each resulted in the building of some new churches, and incidentally in heated arguments that can still be revived in 1978, without too much trouble.

Since 1900 major population shifts, due to Francophone migrations into the county and a general exodus from the farms to the villages and the Cornwall area, have made changes necessary in the church structures in the county. Many of the older churches both Roman Catholic and Protestant have had their congregations reduced to the point where there is difficulty keeping some of our finest old churches open. This problem may become acute in the future.

There are several ways of "dating" churches, depending on whether we take the date of the opening of the present building, or the date of the dedication of the present building, or the date it was decided to build the present building, or even the date of the laying of the cornerstone. In most cases, however, we consider the most important date to be the date of the founding of the congregation who worship together in that particular area. This too can lead to confusion as many congregations now separate, both Catholic and Protestant, had a common origin.

Among the Roman Catholic churches, St. Raphael's is an outstanding example. From 1786 to 1833 it was the only Catholic congregation in Glengarry. It built its first church about 1789, was erected officially into a parish in 1802, and is said to have established its first mission in Lochiel in 1786 and its second in Alexandria in 1819. Every Catholic church in Glengarry can trace its roots back to this congregation at St. Raphael's. A similar case exists with the Presbyterian-United Church congregations, though here no one congregation can be said to be "the mother church congregation." But for instance, some members of the United Church at Maxville can trace their church roots back through St. Andrew's Presbyterian Church to the White Church, to the Beech Church, which church was ministered to by the

Presbyterian minister at Martintown. Others in that same United Church congregation trace their church roots back to the Maxville Congregational Church and from that to the St. Elmo Congregational Church.

So any list of churches and dates we may make has its weaknesses and does not show "the whole picture." The whole picture can only be shown by a rather complicated pattern of lines which meet for a space and then often diverge, and in some cases disappear, as is the case with Glengarry's Baptist, Congregational, Methodist, and Salvation Army congregations.

The story of the Roman Catholic church in Glengarry is a continuous one from the days of the first Catholic migration in 1786 to the present. As population spread to the north of the county, the Catholic church moved with it. At first it opened missions. Later most of these missions became organized parishes. As the ethnic structure of the county changed with the Francophone influx the Catholic church found it necessary to establish new parishes which are largely Francophone, though many of the people and all of the priests are bilingual.

In the years since 1900 when 13 Protestant churches have closed, the Catholics have organized eight new parishes in Glengarry. This is not as clear a gain as it may appear, as with one exception (Green Valley) the Catholic church had missions in these new parishes for many years before the parishes were formed. The extreme cases are Martintown where the chapel was built in 1885 and the parish erected in 1949, and Lochiel where the mission dates to 1786 and the parish to 1851, but Lochiel did not have a chapel building and Martintown did. Also in the years since 1900, two mission chapels which had served their communities for years and had come to be loved by the people in their communities were closed. These were the mission chapel at Loch Garry (26-9 Kenyon) which was in use 1870-1901, and the mission chapel at Avondale (24-9 Charlottenburgh) which was in use 1875-1949. The former was a mission from St. Finnan's in Alexandria, the latter a mission from St. Raphael's. Also in the past few years, two of the old parishes in the north of the county, Lochiel and Greenfield, have become mission churches for what were once daughter parishes. Lochiel has become a mission from Dalkeith and Greenfield a mission from Maxville. The Roman Catholic parishes in Glengarry in 1978 with the dates of their official erection are:

St. Raphael's - 1802
St. Finnan's, Alexandria - 1833
Nativity, Williamstown - 1847
St. Alexander, Lochiel - 1851
St. Margaret, Glen Nevis - 1882
St. Catherine, Greenfield - 1894
St. Martin, Glen Robertson - 1895
St. Joseph, Lancaster - 1904
Sacre Coeur, Alexandria - 1909
St. Anthony, Apple Hill - 1914
St. James, Maxville - 1946
St. Paul, Dalkeith - 1947
St. William, Martintown - 1949
St. Mary, Green Valley - 1956
St. Lawrence, Curry Hill - 1959

As stated above, the history of few of these parishes begins with their official erection. The Catholic church goes where its people are, whether or not a group in a given area can support a resident priest and maintain a church building. Several of these parishes maintained excellent chapels before they were parishes. One we will mention is St. Lawrence, Curry Hill. The chapel there, today a private residence with its exterior intact, is an exquisite little building on top of a hill. It is the sort of building a tourist stops to photograph. The church, a modern building on the north-east corner of the junction of the Curry Hill sideroad and 401, passes unnoticed.

Much more could be said of our churches. Each has a history of its own that tells of struggle to build, struggle to pay off debt, struggle to keep the church building presentable in the eyes of the congregation and the eyes of their neighbours, and, one hopes, in the eyes of the Lord. Each of these churches was ministered to by a succession of priests and ministers, rectors and pastors, some of whom were very human men with human weaknesses — some few approached greatness.

In many cases our churches have published their church history. In other cases it has to be pieced together from contemporary newspaper accounts, private letters, oral tradition, and human memory. In some cases cemeteries grew up around the churches and the tombstones therein are part of the history of that church community. In other cases, such as the Beech Church south of Maxville, both church and cemetery are so long gone and records so scanty that the exact site is cause for argument. There is a tradition in Lochiel that the Brodie Schoolhouse (S.S. No. 7, Lochiel) was once a Catholic chapel ministering to several Irish families in the neighbourhood. No one knows for certain what year the Blue Chapel was built at St. Raphael's (1786, 87, 88 or 89). Nor do we have any better knowledge of the date of the erection of the first church at Summerstown. It could have been as early as 1787; it could have been later than 1804. We do know the congregation got a deed for the land the church building stands on in 1804. But which came first, the deed or the building? Does it matter? People worship together, with or without a building, and people worshipping together constitute a church.

An example of the difficulty of dating a church is an extremely well documented one from comparatively modern times — that of Sacre Coeur in Alexandria. It is a Francophone church and came into existence to fill the need for such a church. Some highlights in its documentation are:

June 1896: French speaking priest, Father Poitras from Montreal Diocese, joins staff of St. Finnan's and announcements are made that one mass each Sunday will be in French.

May 1907: The building fund of the new French Church to be erected at Alexandria shortly is growing apace.

June 1907: Nearly 5000 people turn out for a grand picnic for the benefit of the projected French Church in Alexandria.

7 April 1909: Official permission given to 200 French

Canadian families in the Alexandria area to build a church. They buy land for a site on the south-east corner of Main and Lochiel streets from Abraham Markson. Father Dulin will be the first pastor.

14 April 1910: *Glengarry News*, reports the laying of the cornerstone of the new Sacred Heart Church by Bishop William Macdonell.

1912: Sacré Coeur church opens for midnight mass on Christmas Eve.

What date do we use for this congregation, which, although part of St. Finnan's, began to worship together as a Francophone body in 1896, became an official body in 1909, and opened their own church in 1912?

Most Rev. Alexander Macdonell (1833-1905), first Bishop of the Diocese of Alexandria. A native of Lochiel Township.

Practically all churches and the congregations who worship in them have a similar history at their beginning. It is the work of years to establish a church. It takes the work of generations to maintain it.

Though not a large diocese, ever since its formation on 28 January 1890 Glengarry has been proud to be part of the Roman Catholic diocese of Alexandria (now Alexandria-Cornwall) which comprises the counties of Glengarry and

St. Finnan's, Alexandria. A church has existed on this site since 1833 but this church was built 1884-1885. The present steeple, bells, and cross on top of the spire date to 1902. In 1890 when the Diocese of Alexandria was created St. Finnan's was designated its cathedral church. In 1971 population changes promoted moving the active headquarters of the diocese to Cornwall. In 1976 St. Finnan's was named co-cathedral for the newly named diocese, Alexandria-Cornwall.

The Bishop's Palace at Alexandria was built in 1900 and occupied on 29 April 1901. It housed the bishops of Alexandria and their staff till the diocesan headquarters was moved to Cornwall in 1971. Unofficially, the move began as early as 1968. In 1976 the diocese sold the building but the new owner is aware of its artistic and historical significance and at the time of writing it is still a landmark in Glengarry as it has been for three-quarters of a century.

Stormont and the City of Cornwall. Until 1976 it had Alexandria as its cathedral seat, the cathedral being St. Finnan's church. Population shifts made a change necessary in 1976. On Sunday, 5 December an official decree established Nativity Church in Cornall as a co-cathedral with St. Finnan's and the official name of the diocese became Alexandria-Cornwall.

In the 87 years of its existence the diocese of Alexandria-Cornwall has had six bishops:

Rt. Rev. Alexander Macdonell (1833-1905), bishop 1890-1905 (died), a native of Glengarry.

Rt. Rev. William A. Macdonell (1853-1920), bishop 1906-1920 (died), a native of Glengarry.

Rt. Rev. Felix Couturier (1876-1941), bishop 1921-1941 (died) (an import).

Rt. Rev. Rosario Brodeur (1889-        ), bishop 1941-1966 (retired) (an import).

Rt. Rev. Adolphe Proulx (1928-        ), bishop 1967-1974 (transferred to Hull) (an import).

Rt. Rev. Eugene Larocque (1927-        ), bishop 1974- (still in office 1978) (an import).

Has the quality of the people we produce dropped off or is the hybrid nature of our Scottish-French Catholicism at fault when outside men are needed for bishops?

St. Columba Church, Kirk Hill, 29 Dec. 1978 (one of those days photographers dream of, but seldom see).

The Presbyterian church in varying guises has been active officially in Glengarry since Rev. John Bethune entered our midst as the first Presbyterian minister in Upper Canada in 1787. Oral tradition insists that Presbyterian prayer meetings were held on the waterfront at Lancaster, in the open air, from the time of the first Loyalist landings in 1784, and the Presbyterians continued to use that spot as a meeting place until they built their first church building in Lancaster, very near the same spot, in 1796. Probably in winter they would find shelter in a nearby house. Tradition tends to forget such weaknesses of the flesh among our pioneer forefathers and mothers as would cause them to hold an indoor service merely to get away from an open air church service in Glengarry's winters.

St. Columba Church, Kirk Hill, from an engraving by Ed. Broomhall.

When Glengarry was being settled the Presbyterian Church in Scotland was enjoying one of its periods of comparative unity and all the early ministers were educated in

Scotland. So it is not surprising that our early Presbyterian churches were part of the "Church of Scotland," the official state church. An official religion implies some measure of state control as well as state support and both played some part in the formation of our early Presbyterian churches. Ministers were ordained in Scotland to be sent to a certain charge in Glengarry—some money came too. As part of the Church of Scotland, congregations were founded at Williamstown, Lancaster, Martintown, Indian Lands (Beech Church and the White Church), Kirk Hill, Dunvegan, the Second Concession of Lancaster (now Bainsville United), Summerstown, and Dalhousie Mills.

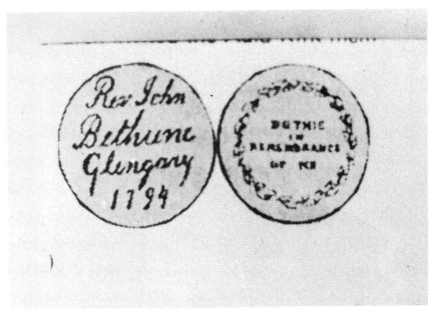

Bethune Communion Tokens. The periodic communion service was, and still is, an important and meaningful part of the Presbyterian form of worship. Especially in the early days in Glengarry, those who partook of communion were carefully screened by the elders and minister of the congregation who could and often did refuse communion to those they thought had erred and were not repentent. To be the possessor of this lead token, both sides of which are shown here, showed that the possessor was in good standing with Rev. John Bethune and the elders of his congregation in Glengarry.

In 1843 the Church of Scotland in Scotland divided sharply over the question of state control of its affairs. By 1844 the schism had spread to Canada and it opened a wide breach in Presbyterian solidarity in Glengarry. Despite the fact that many of the congregations in existence were in debt for new churches built in the preceding forty years a number of them decided to split up, with some of their members remaining with the old Church of Scotland and the others joining the new Free Church. Free in this case didn't mean that the collection plate wasn't passed. It was, and often those who left to form the new Free Churches had to continue paying on their pledges to the churches they left — believe it or not.

In the years after 1844, as quickly as the people could get the money together, new churches were built in Lancaster, Martintown, St. Elmo (the Gordon Church), Kirk Hill, Dalhousie Mills, and in the Second of Lancaster. Here the "Auld Kirk" and the new "Free Kirk" were so close together that it is said the ministers would argue with each other from their pulpits on summer Sundays when the church windows were open. Some of these new "Free Churches", under the circumstances, were quite humble buildings (Martintown's first Free Church built in 1848 was of logs) and so gave rise to a bit of a rhyme though the rhyme was imported with the Free Church Movement from Scotland:

The Free Kirk, the Free Kirk,
The Kirk without a steeple.
The Auld Kirk, the Auld Kirk,
The Kirk without a people.

In 1875 a union of the various branches of the Presbyterian Church was formally arranged and resulted in the formation of the Presbyterian Church of Canada. This union resulted in one church in Glengarry, St. Andrew's, Williamstown, splitting up and forming a second Presbyterian congregation there which eventually built themselves a church which they called Hepzibah, which continued to operate until 1951. However, all the "Auld Kirks" in Glengarry joined the newly founded Presbyterian Church of Canada, except the one in the Second of Lancaster, which joined in 1898, St. Andrew's,

Lancaster, which joined in 1899, and St. Columba, Kirk Hill, which joined in 1911.

The next problem the Glengarry Presbyterians faced was in 1925 after the central bodies of the Presbyterian Church, the Methodist Church, and the Congregational Church had voted to unite and form a United Church of Canada. Discussion of the pros and cons of this union in Glengarry were deep, serious, and eventually bitter, Part of the central body of the Presbyterian Church did not concur with the decision to enter the United Church and these "non-concurring Presbyterians," as they were known at the time, were numerous in Glengarry. Eventually each church voted separately on union and the church property went with the majority. Though this "union" only led directly to the building of two new churches in Glengarry, at Martintown and Maxville, both in 1926, its greatest effect, even if less obvious, was a wholesale rearrangement of the places people went to church, depending on whether or not they agreed with their old church becoming "United" or staying Presbyterian. Many of the partings were not friendly. Fifty-three years later they still go their separate ways and official union, of what is often two weak churches in the same village, is not a subject for serious discussion.

The Congregationalists built four churches, all at the west side of Glengarry. The first one, at Martintown in 1803, was sold to the Church of Scotland in 1811. The second one at Martintown was built in 1859 and closed in 1901. The log Congregational church at St. Elmo, still standing in 1978, was built after 1830 and was in active use as a church until 1881 when a larger church was built at Maxville. This church at Maxville flourished until 1925 when its people entered Church Union. The Maxville United Church of today stands on this site.

A Baptist group we have already had occasion to mention settled in north eastern Lochiel around Breadalbane in 1816. They built themselves a chapel in 1835 and a church in 1865, and this church is still in use in 1978. The Baptists' Notfield church, a log one, was built in 1839 and continued in use at

220

least until 1915. It was sold in 1925. In 1902 the Baptists built a brick church in Maxville which, because of dwindling numbers, was sold to the Anglicans in 1960. For a time there was a Baptist chapel at North Lancaster, perhaps for some forty years centred on 1900, and there was an active Baptist congregation in Alexandria in 1898, which, however, found it expedient to disband and most of its members joined the local Presbyterians to worship. The rest went either to Breadalbane or Maxville as suited them best.

A reformed group of Presbyterians, known familiarly by their original name in Scotland, "The Convenanters," established a congregation in the Brodie area as early as 1846 and in 1860 built a modest frame church just east of the Brodie Corner. There never has been a large congregation in this church but services are still held in it. Anyone wishing to see and think about the external trappings that are necessary for worship should visit this church. Its frame construction, plain white paint, well kept but unornamental lawn, along with its plain interior with only pews and a reading desk reminds us that men and women, rather than a building, constitute a church.

This church at Brodie is still open and is one of the few church buildings which are never locked. This in itself tells us the function of a church building is not to store things of earthly value but to stress other values.

The Salvation Army came to Canada in 1883, and in 1887 two members of it came to Maxville on the invitation of a Mr. McBain who made space available to them. All the churches supported the work of the "Army" at first and many nights the hall (later part of the Ferguson Threshing Machine Company's space) was packed with people standing in the aisles.

The interest in the Salvation Army was not confined to Maxville—people came from as far away as Martintown and the other churches realized that the Army was competing with them both for people for a congregation and for money. The

"Army" moved out of McBain's hall and in a matter of months had its own "Barracks" at Maxville and Martintown (the term "citadel" was not yet in use). By 1910 this movement had lost active support in Glengarry. However, the Maxville group founded the "Army" in Cornwall in 1888, where they are still active in 1978.

Few Anglicans were among the early settlers in Glengarry, and even though the Anglican Church was the church "the right people" belonged to for the first 50 years of this province's existence, no Anglican Church was built in Glengarry until 1888-89. This little gem of a church was erected by the MacLennan family of Lancaster Township on their own property, on the front of the township about a mile and a half east of Highway 34. Though erected as a private chapel by a branch of the family that had gone to Montreal and "done well" and become part of "the establishment" there, the church was open to any Anglicans in the neighbourhood who wished to worship with them. Today there are few MacLennans left in the area but the congregation is flourishing as people from other areas move into Glengarry, some of whom are Anglicans. The history of Anglican services in the north part of the county seems to begin in 1889 or 1890, when the Rev. F.W. Squire organized a short-lived Anglican congregation in Alexandria. By 1960, however, there were enough Anglicans in the north part of the county to form a congregation which bought the no longer active Baptist Church in Maxville (in 1960).

So since 1960 Glengarry has two active Anglican congregations, though neither is large in numbers.

About 1890 the Plymouth Brethren gained some converts and adherents in Glengarry and still have some members in the county, though they have never had an official church building.

In recent years, a Seventh Day Adventist Congregation bought the old public school in the Ninth of Kenyon (S.S. No. 20) at Fisk's Corners, and in 1976 made a nice·little church out of it.

222

Since 1900, thirteen Protestant churches have closed in Glengarry—Salvation Army at Maxville and Martintown, Baptist churches at Notfield, North Lancaster, Maxville, and Alexandria, Congregational Churches at Martintown and Maxville, the Presbyterian Church at North Lancaster, the Methodist churches at Maxville and Lancaster, Hepzibah Presbyterian at Williamstown, Burns Church at Martintown, and the United Church at Curry Hill. One minister now serves the three congregations of Alexandria, Glen Sandfield, and Dalhousie Mills, and another serves the three congregations of Summerstown, Knox at Lancaster, and Bainsville. These last six are United Church congregations. Also the United Church congregations at Williamstown and Martintown now share the services of one minister. The Presbyterians too have their problems. Their churches at Martintown and Lancaster share a minister as does the charge of Maxville-St. Elmo. Here the case is slightly different as the Gordon Church there, while still officially open, is only used "on occasion."

The active Protestant congregations in Glengarry in 1978 are:

### Anglican

| | |
|---|---|
| Maxville | dating to 1960 |
| Front of Lancaster Township | dating to 1899 |

### Convenanters

| | |
|---|---|
| Brodie | dating to 1846 |

### Presbyterian

| | |
|---|---|
| Dunvegan | dating to 1838 |
| Kirk Hill | dating to 1819 |
| Lancaster Village | dating to 1787 |
| Martintown | dating to 1803 |
| Maxville | dating to 1815 |
| Gordon Church, St. Elmo (officially open but not active) | dating to 1815 |

## United Church

| | |
|---|---|
| Alexandria | dating to 1863 |
| Apple Hill | dating to 1889 |
| Bainsville | dating to 1833 |
| Dalhousie Mills | dating to 1833 |
| Glen Sandfield | dating to 1882 |
| Kirk Hill | dating to 1819 |
| Lancaster Village | dating to 1787 |
| Martintown | dating to 1803 |
| Maxville | dating to 1815 |
| Williamstown | dating to 1787 |
| Summerstown | dating to 1787 |

## Seventh Day Adventist

| | |
|---|---|
| Fisk's Corners | dating to 1975 |

Private cemetery of the McIntoshes at Breadalbane. There are many of these small cemeteries scattered around Glengarry. Not all are as well maintained as this one. The very site of some have been forgotten except perhaps by some local history buff.

## CHURCH ACTIVITY IN RELATION TO POPULATION IN GLENGARRY

| Year | Glengarry Population | Roman Catholic Population | Roman Catholic Churches | Protestant Population | Protestant Churches |
|---|---|---|---|---|---|
| 1800 | NFA | NFA | 1 + 1 mission | NFA | 4 |
| 1820 | about 7,000 | NFA | 1 + 1 mission | NFA | 6 |
| 1840 | 12,397 | NFA | 2 + 1 mission | NFA | 10 |
| 1860 | 21,187 (61) | 10,919 | 4 | 10,286 | 18 |
| 1880 | 22,221 (81) | 11,758 | 5 + 2 missions | 10,463 | 27 |
| 1900 | 22,131 (01) | 12,731 | 7 + 4 missions | 9,400 | 33 |
| 1920 | 20,518 (21) | 13,579 | 12 + 4 missions | 6,939 | 21 |
| 1940 | 18,732 (41) | 13,388 | 12 + 4 missions | 5,344 | 21 |
| 1960 | 19,217 (61) | 14,129 | 16 | 5,088 | 20 |
| 1977 | 18,480 (71) | 13,540 | 14 + 2 missions | 5,940 | 20 + 1* open |

NFA = no figures available

Church numbers refer to churches in operation.

Missions refers to churches open but without a resident priest.

Parentheses refer to census year, for instance 1861, 1881, etc.

*Gordon Church, only used "on occasion."

The above table indicates the Roman Catholic Church keeps the numbers of its churches fairly well in step with the numbers of its people.

The Protestant churches respond to the same stimulus but not as quickly or as accurately.

225

CHURCH BUILDINGS USED OFFICIALLY IN GLENGARRY

| Place | Name of Church | In Use | Out of Use | Disposal | Denomination |
|---|---|---|---|---|---|
| Alexandria | Presbyterian Church | 1863 | 1912 | sold | Presbyterian |
| | Church on Hill | 1912 | active | --- | P/UC |
| | First St. Finnan's | 1833 | 1885 | torn down | Roman Catholic |
| | Second St. Finnan's | 1885 | active | --- | Roman Catholic |
| | Mission Roman Catholic | 1819 | 1833 | mill building | Roman Catholic |
| | Baptists | 1898 | ? | --- | Baptist |
| | Anglican | 1889 | ? | no building erected | Anglican |
| | Sacré Coeur | 1912 | active | --- | Roman Catholic |
| Apple Hill | Zion | 1889 | active | --- | P/UC |
| | First St. Anthony's | 1914 | 1917 | burned | Roman Catholic |
| | Second St. Anthony's | 1918 | active | --- | Roman Catholic |
| Avondale | St. Columbkill | 1875 | 1949 | sold | Roman Catholic |
| Bainsville | First Church | 1833 | 1886 | sold | Presbyterian |
| | Second Church | 1886 | active | active | P/UC |
| | Free Church | 1854 | 1898 | sold | Presbyterian |

| Place | Name of Church | In Use | Out of Use | Disposal | Denomination |
|---|---|---|---|---|---|
| Brodie | Convenanters | 1860 | active | --- | Presbyterian |
| Curry Hill | St. Andrew's | 1889 | 1942 | sold | P/UC |
| | St. Lawrence Chapel | 1909 | 1959 | sold | Roman Catholic |
| | St. Lawrence | 1959 | active | --- | Roman Catholic |
| Dalhousie | First St. Andrew's | 1836 | 1869 | torn down | Presbyterian |
| | Second St. Andrew's | 1869 | active | --- | P/UC |
| | Free Church | 1854 | 1876 | sold | Presbyterian |
| Dalkeith | St. Paul | 1913 | active | --- | Roman Catholic |
| Dunvegan | log church | 1840 | 1871 | torn down | Presbyterian |
| | stone church | 1871 | active | --- | Presbyterian |
| Fisk's Corner | Seventh Day Adventist | 1975 | active | --- | Adventist |
| Front of Lancaster Township | St. John Evangelist | 1899 | active | --- | Anglican |
| Glen Nevis | St. Margaret | 1883 | active | --- | Roman Catholic |
| Glen Robertson | First Church | 1895 | 1915 | burned | Roman Catholic |
| | Second Church | 1915 | 1954 | burned | Roman Catholic |
| | Third Church | 1955 | active | --- | Roman Catholic |

| Place | Name of Church | In Use | Out of Use | Disposal | Denomination |
|---|---|---|---|---|---|
| Glen Sandfield | Protestant Church | 1882 | active | --- | P/UC |
| Glen Walter | Precious Blood | 1907 | 1959 | parish hall | Roman Catholic |
| | Precious Blood | 1959 | active | --- | Roman Catholic |
| Greenfield | St. Catherine | 1873 | 1911 | torn down | Roman Catholic |
| | St. Catherine | 1912 | active | --- | Roman Catholic |
| | Protestant | 1896 | 1938 | sold | Presbyterian |
| Green Valley | St. Mary's | 1956 | 1957 | sold | Roman Catholic |
| | St. Mary's | 1957 | active | --- | Roman Catholic |
| Kirk Hill | St. Columba | 1820 | 1863 | torn down | Presbyterian |
| | St. Columba | 1863 | active | --- | Presbyterian |
| | Free Church | 1850 | active | --- | P/UC |
| Lancaster Village | St. Andrew's | 1796 | 1855 | torn down | Presbyterian |
| | St. Andrew's | 1855 | active | --- | Presbyterian |
| | Free Church | 1854 | 1874 | moved | Presbyterian |
| | Knox | 1874 | active | --- | P/UC |
| | Methodist | 1890 | 1920 | torn down | Methodist |
| | St. Joseph | 1904 | 1959 | parish hall | Roman Catholic |
| | St. Joseph | 1959 | active | --- | Roman Catholic |
| Loch Garry | St. Stephen | 1870 | 1901 | chapel - torn down 1914 | Roman Catholic |

| Place | Name of Church | In Use | Out of Use | Disposal | Denomination |
|---|---|---|---|---|---|
| Lochiel | St. Alexander | 1852 | active | ---- | Roman Catholic |
| Martintown | Reid's Church | 1803 | 1836 | moved | Congregational |
| | First St. Andrew's | 1836 | 1906 | burned | Presbyterian |
| | Log Free Church | 1848 | 1858 | sold | Presbyterian |
| | Burns Church | 1858 | 1910 | torn down 1977 | Presbyterian |
| | Congregational | 1859 | 1901 | sold | Congregational |
| | Salvation Army | 1888 | 1905 | sold | Salvation Army |
| | St. Andrew's | 1910 | active | ---- | P/UC |
| | St. Andrew's | 1925 | 1926 | rented | Presbyterian |
| | St. Andrew's | 1926 | active | ---- | Presbyterian |
| | St. William | 1885 | 1951 | chapel sold | Roman Catholic |
| | St. William | 1951 | active | ---- | Roman Catholic |
| Maxville | Beech Church | 1815 | 1828 | torn down | Presbyterian |
| | White Church | 1828 | 1900 | sold | Presbyterian |
| | Congregational | 1881 | 1925 | torn down | Congregational |
| | Methodist | 1886 | 1913 | sold | Methodist |
| | Salvation Army | 1887 | 1905 | sold | Salvation Army |
| | St. Andrew's | 1900 | active | ---- | Presbyterian |
| | Baptist | 1902 | 1960 | sold | Baptist |
| | St. James | 1910 | 1948 | chapel enlarged | Roman Catholic |

| Place | Name of Church | In Use | Out of Use | Disposal | Denomination |
|---|---|---|---|---|---|
| Maxville (con't.) | St. James | 1948 | active | --- | Roman Catholic |
| | United Church | 1926 | active | --- | United Church |
| | St. Michael's | 1960 | active | --- | Anglican |
| North Lancaster | Baptist | 1881 | c.1920 | sold 1947 | Baptist |
| | Free Presbyterian | 1881 | 1935 | sold 1949 | Presbyterian |
| | Leclair chapel | 1861 | 1906 | private chapel | Roman Catholic |
| Notfield | Baptist | 1839 | after 1915 | building sold 1921 | Baptist |
| St. Elmo | Congregational | 1835? | 1881 | historic site | Congregational |
| | Gordon Church | 1864 | officially open | | Presbyterian |
| St. Raphael's | Blue Chapel | 1789? | 1826 | sold | Roman Catholic |
| | Stone Church | 1826 | 1970 | burned | Roman Catholic |
| | present church | 1973 | active | --- | Roman Catholic |
| Summerstown | Zion | 1787 to 1804 | active | --- | P/UC |
| Williamstown | log church | 1787 | 1816 | sold | Presbyterian |
| | First St. Andrew's | 1803-06 | fell down | rebuilt | Presbyterian |

| Place | Name of Church | In Use | Out of Use | Disposal | Denomination |
|---|---|---|---|---|---|
| Williamstown (con't.) | Second St. Andrews | 1816 | active | --- | P/UC |
| | frame school | 1876 | 1878 | rented | Presbyterian |
| | Hepzibah | 1878 | 1952 | sold 1965 | Presbyterian |
| | St. Mary's | 1849 | active | ---- | Roman Catholic |

A former one-room school (S.S. No. 7, at Dominionville), now converted into a dwelling.

# Chapter VIII
# Schools, Libraries, the Gaelic Language

## Schools

The type of people who settled in Glengarry, the circumstances under which they settled, and the type of land in the county determined to a very great extent the form that educational facilities would take in the county.

Good evidence indicates that the leaders of the people who settled in the county had fair to good educations. Such men as Rev. Alexander Macdonell (Scotus), Aberchalder, Leek, Collachie, the Falkners, Rev. John Bethune, Alexander Macdonell (Greenfield), Donald Cattanach, and Alexander McLeod were undeniably literate by any standard.

Just as surely, other evidence indicates that many, if not the majority of the first two generations to live in Glengarry signed their name with an X. Old documents of many kinds bear evidence to this.

The circumstances under which they settled, often as penniless refugees, dictated they would first have to provide themselves with shelter and food. There would be no time or money to spend on anything not strictly necessary for survival. However, even before the end of the eighteenth century and before there was a vestige of a government grant to help defray the cost of education, we have pretty good evidence of private schools in operation in Glengarry.

The farm land in Glengarry, plus the thrifty ways of its citizens determined that even when in 1816 the province began grants to help the municipalities educate their children,

Glengarry's educational facilities would be of the "no frills" type.

So from John Bethune's probably very informal school in the log church at Williamstown which began perhaps as early as 1788, till the last one-room schoolhouse in Glengarry closed at Summerstown in 1973, the one-room all-classes schoolhouse was the focal point of our educational system. In the course of years, facilities for secondary education were developed. Williamstown began Grammar School work in 1846, Alexandria followed suit in 1866. Maxville's Public School became a Continuation School in 1914, and a High School on 1 January 1929. This completes the roster of "Higher Education Facilities" developed in Glengarry by the Public School System of Ontario.

Miss N.L. Mahon, first principal of Maxville Continuation School, 1914. This continuation school, which became a full high school on 1 Jan. 1929, filled a need for secondary school education in the northwestern part of the county. Modern transportation and a tri-county school board let this high school be closed in 1974.

However, beginning quite humbly at St. Raphaels with Father Alexander Macdonell's Iona Academy 1818-1826, which became a seminary to train young men for the priesthood 1826-1836, rather special schools connected with the Roman Catholic Church have made notable contributions to education in Glengarry. Maryvale Academy at Glen Nevis 1910-1950 must be noted as well as St. Margaret's Convent in Alexandria which began teaching in 1856. All these schools got government grants of some sort, so strictly speaking, were not private schools. Until the advent of High School Areas in the 1950's with their buses and in the following years an ever increasing flow of money from Toronto to help, only a very small percentage of Glengarry's young people could hope for a secondary education, even if they desired one. Distance from the schools, limited accommodation at the schools, and a strictly classical curriculum limited attendance to a select few.

Glengarry's rather sparse and mainly rural population did not permit the building of any institutions in the county for post-secondary school education. Those who desired post-secondary school education had to go to other centres. Glengarry developed no institutions in which to train doctors, lawyers, teachers, nurses, engineers, or clergy, with the exception of Bishop Macdonell's seminary at St. Raphaels. Nor did it do any better on the more prosaic level of carpenters, plumbers, electricians, machinists, welders, or mechanics until vocational training was started in Williamstown and Alexandria High Schools in the 1960's. Nor was Glengarry's main industry, farming, treated any better. No schools of any sort to train young farmers or teach agriculture ever existed in the county.

Such is the over all picture—a rather gloomy one to be sure, but not a hopeless one. Based on character derived from their surroundings and driven by need, Glengarry's one-room public schools and small high schools sent many students to universities and colleges all over North America. Its nurses trained in hospitals, often a thousand miles away, as did candidates for other trades and professions. Glengarry's schools gave good grounding in the basics and had a rather remarkable ability to develop character. Thus equipped, our young people, for six generations now, have not only held their own in institutions of higher learning all over the world, but on graduation from these institutions have more than held their own with their peers.

Can it be that Glengarry's youth valued a higher education because it always required real sacrifice, both from themselves and their parents, to get it?

Space does not permit an extremely detailed history of education in Glengarry, but we must examine it a bit.

We will begin with the first schools, which because there were no legislative grants, were supported entirely by those who sent their children to these schools. Today we would call them "private schools" and oddly enough perhaps, for the greater part of Glengarry's existence, one or more such schools have functioned in our midst.

The existence of many of these private schools is difficult if not impossible to document, as far as irrefutable evidence is concerned, but we feel that they should be included, partly as evidence of Glengarry's efforts to obtain education at a price it could pay and partly to give leads to anyone who feels he or she can document these schools definitively. Any school included here can, with a fair amount of confidence, be assumed to have existed in the location stated. In some cases dates are approximate.

The earliest school in Glengarry of which there is a trace is one taught by the Rev. John Bethune in the log church at Williamstown, probably beginning about 1788 and likely carried on until the first school building was built in Williamstown, where the North West Museum now stands, about 1809 or 1810. As evidence of this school we may cite traditions in the Bethune family and traditions in the Williamstown area.

In 1796 Archibald MacDonell of Lancaster, Duncan

Kennedy of Charlottenburgh, and 16 others entered into a six-year contract with Donald MacDonell, a schoolmaster from Scotland, to operate a school in the present Green Valley area, possibly on 1-9 Charlottenburgh, as descendants of this schoolmaster came into recorded history owning this lot. Here the evidence is a copy of the original contract, spelling out the terms of the contract in great detail, and the names on the contract, seven MacDonells, a Kennedy, two MacMillans, two McDougalls, a McGillis, a Campbell, and a MacDonald, which are all names in that area. The schoolmaster's salary was to be £30 per annum, half to be in produce, but they had to build two log buildings for him, one with a cellar and one with a loft, and with a chimney in each, and fence and clear two acres of land for his use. Also, modern teachers take note, both parties bound themselves to a maximum of 30 pupils. Unfortunately there is no evidence of precisely where this school stood or what was its ultimate fate.

In 1804 Rev. James Reid opened a frame church in Martintown and local tradition, oral and written, credits Reid with using the church as a school during the week. Reid sold the church building to the Church of Scotland in 1811, but is said to have taught school in it after the sale. Almost certainly he left Martintown before the battle of Crysler's Farm on 13 November 1813 as in a letter sent to Mr. Reid at St. Amand, Quebec, by Rev. John Bethune, dated 20 April 1814, Bethune describes that battle to Reid. Incidentally, the subject of the letter was payment for the church building, which had been "delayed."

Tradition dates the first school building at Williamstown to 1809-10, which is plausible as evidence indicates Rev. John Bethune was very interested in promoting educational facilities and the Grammar School Act of 1807 could have encouraged the people in Williamstown to believe that if they had a school in operation in a decent building, it would eventually become the County Grammar School, and so qualify for a government grant. To an extent they were correct in their thinking but it took time. The school qualified for a government grant under the Common Schools Act of 1816 and became a grammar school in 1846, while continuing to house the public school as well until 1861 when this school building was moved from its original site, where the North West Museum is today, across to the river bank where it served a variety of uses—Temperance Hall, Free Church, harness shop, and dwelling until it was torn down in 1935, 125 years after it was built.

The Misses Fraser operated a Girls' School at Williamstown, probably from shortly after 1818 until about 1850. These ladies were sisters of the wife of Rev. John McKenzie who came to Williamstown in 1818 and died there in 1855. It is possible, if not probable, that the Misses Fraser discontinued their school at the time or shortly after Williamstown got a Grammar School. It is also possible, or at least Grace Campbell believed it, that the Misses Fraser opened their school prior to Rev. John Bethune's death in 1815.

A Young Ladies' Seminary was operated in South Lancaster by a Miss Hibbard or possibly by two Miss Hibbards in the period about 1850-1880. Music was a specialty in this school. It to an extent, can be dated by the fact that the Rev. Thomas McPherson bought the Hibbard House sometime in the period 1880-1884.

For some years centred on 1850, a Mrs. Redmond operated a "Dame School" in Martintown, east of the bridge. Some fairly good evidence exists for the existence of these last two schools. The 1856 report of the Chief Superintendent of Education for Canada West reports two private schools in Glengarry with 40 pupils and two teachers between them (no names or places mentioned) and the 1860 report mentions one private school in Glengarry with one teacher who received $50 in fees. Once again, no mention of name or place but Martintown's new brick school, built in 1855 and opened in 1856, would probably make business rough for Mrs. Redmond, if she were still trying to operate her school, and she had probably closed it.

238

For two or three years in the 1860's Colin MacKercher (later Rev.) taught at Bethel Hill Seminary at what is now St. Elmo. The idea here was to bring the education of a few young men up to the standard needed to enter theological college.

The Sisters of the Congregation of Notre Dame operated a Convent school at Williamstown for young ladies and had both day students and boarders in the period 1865-1892. A private Roman Catholic Public School was opened in S.S. No. 14 Lancaster in 1916 and was later absorbed into the RCSS system.

Iona Academy at St. Raphaels, operated by the Sisters of the Holy Cross, became a private high school in 1914 and operated as such until 1924 when it became Iona Commercial College, still operated by the Sisters and continued as such until 1945.

Part of the Maryvale Academy at Glen Nevis, operated by the Sisters of Providence, became a private high school teaching grades XI, XII, and XIII from 1928 to 1950.

The Brothers of the Sacred Heart bought Fairfield, the former Cariboo Cameron house at Summerstown in 1946, and in 1978 it is still in operation as a Boys' School under the name Juvénat Sacré Coeur. In 1976 it had 15 students and a staff of five, and its course leads to university entrance. Waverly School for boys operated at the former Thornhill Farm between South Lancaster and Lancaster Village in the years 1950 to 1955.

These private schools perhaps take up more space than their number might seem to warrant but they are all special cases and they are not susceptible to being handled en masse . They were (and still are) important, if for nothing else than to demonstrate different forms that education takes in response to needs and circumstances.

Now we will consider our Common School System which began in 1816 and became the Public School System in 1871 and has developed into the system that today takes such a large share of our tax dollars. This system was designed for mass education in English and at the same time to teach Christian moral values, at first as the established Anglican Church saw them, but later supposedly undenominational. However, the Roman Catholics, co-operative at first in this system, in 1841 started to ask for their own schools, taught by teachers of their own faith, and in 1852 began demanding. In largely Protestant Ontario this started a long drawn-out series of moral and legal battles which in 1978 have not yet reached a final solution suitable to all concerned.

To complicate matters still further, from about 1905 on Ontario's French-speaking people, percentage-wise not a large group in Ontario but increasing in numbers rapidly and tending to form communities of their own, wanted public or separate school instruction in French. In 1978 this aspect of our educational system still is subject to hot and lengthy argument both on the street and in parliament.

Glengarry, at first a mixture of Catholic and Protestant Scots, had Roman Catholic separate schools as early as 1848 and a private French separate school by 1916, the result of what is known locally as "The Green Valley School Row." The famous Regulation 17 continued to be the enforced (but not always observed) school law of the province until 1924 when Premier Ferguson found a way of quietly killing it without arousing a fuss in the legislature. From then on Glengarry's Roman Catholic separate school system developed two branches, an English-speaking one and French-speaking one. In 1978 the French-speaking one is numerically strong enough in Glengarry to be in a position to demand that an ever increasing amount of the course work in our two high schools be taught in French. As of 1969 the law states that Francophone instruction may be permitted, on petition, if there are 20 or more Francophone pupils. Both Glengarry's high schools qualify for Francophone instruction—they have far more than the required 20 French-speaking pupils.

Now let us go to the townships and villages of Glengarry

to look at some of the detail of this revolution, which from no school system at all in 1816, by 1918 had every child between six and sixteen legally registered in public or separate schools and in actual fact did have a greater number present each day than had been the case twenty years before. By 1968 it had most of them going to high school as well, whether or not they had reached the legal school leaving age of sixteen.

As things stood in 1816 in Ontario, power of all sorts was in the hands of the Lieutenant Governor and his Council, that group which is known in our history books as "The Family Compact." Among this group, none spoke with a more authoritative voice than the Rev. John Strachan, the same who had operated the grammar school in Cornwall from 1803 to 1812. Naturally he was considered an expert on education and he had no doubt of his own qualifications. In 1815 he listed his priorities for education in Ontario and common schools were placed third, behind the establishment of a university and the continued support of the district grammar schools. So the ordinary people of the province won quite a battle in getting a Common School Act passed and approved by the Lieutenant Governor in 1816. The act (56 George III c. 36) let the inhabitants of any part of a municipality that could supply 20 pupils within walking distance of a school elect three trustees, build the school and hire a teacher who had to be (but often was not) a British subject. The Lieutenant Governor in Council appointed a District Board of Education to whom the local trustee boards reported and the reporting was mostly to provide data for distribution of the government grant which at first was £800 for the whole Eastern District (SDG). No course of study was laid down; there were no teacher training facilities and no building standards or length of school term laid down. The £800 was to be distributed among the schools according to proportionate enrolment but no school was to get more than £25. Government help had arrived but control of the schools was entirely in the hands of the people who used them.

For the period 1816 to 1846 information has only come

down to us in fragments. For one thing, at this time counties did not report to the government, only the districts did this. Also very few of our school sections have preserved their records. One of the few that did is S.S. No 6 Charlottenburgh, the Glen-Gore Section, south west of Williamstown. It was established in 1819 and Mrs. Jerome MacDonell wrote a very complete account of it in the 1964-1965 yearbook of the Glengarry Historical Society. A private communication from an old Charlottenburgh family tells us that in 1817 Charlottenburgh had seven common schools, more than any other township in Ontario. Williamstown we know had a school and local tradition tells us that Martintown had one that met in the basement of the house presently owned by Miss Emily McInnes. We have a definite record of a school on the South Bank of the Raisin in the McGillivray's Bridge area being formed in May 1820 with Charles Scrimgeour as teacher and 24 pupils of whom 16 are studying reading and spelling, four are learning to write, and four are learning arithmetic. From 1820 to 1835 the government grant was reduced to less than half what it was to begin with. Common school education was not prospering as can be seen from the fact that in 1827 in the whole Eastern District there were only 46 common schools, attended by 1,169 pupils, about the same number of pupils that went to the Alexandria high school alone in 1976-77.

Other schools whose history is fairly complete and date from this era are S.S. No. 1, Lochiel which was in existence in 1829, and S.S. No. 2 Kenyon which dates from 1835. The McCrimmon Women's Institute Tweedsmuir Book carries the history of these schools in full.

In 1838 the Eastern District Board of Education reported that teachers in the district had received £9/9/0 each for the past 12 months. The trustees felt that a good job was being done by both pupils and teachers but that more money would attract a better type of teacher. By now there were 89 common schools in the Eastern District attended by 2,460 pupils, who studied reading, writing, and arithmetic and in some schools, Latin, geography, and English grammar. This report was signed by Joseph Anderson and D. McDonnell, School Trustees.

This picture of Maple Leaf School (S.S. No. 13, Charlottenburgh) taken in 1838, gives us an idea of the raw material that produced Glengarry's doctors, lawyers, teachers, and farmers, and the school plant in which their characters were shaped. Obviously there was little style and no frills. In those days the teacher was directly responsible to the community she taught and was judged on her ability "to get kids through the entrance."

Perhaps the most interesting thing about this report is the attitude of the trustees. They seem quite satisfied that those who want some education are getting it, an attitude quite in accord with the thought of the times. There was no regret about those potential pupils who were not in school at all. They had nobody to blame but their own parents, had they?

But change is in the offing. The Duncombe Commission in 1836, Lord Durham's investigation in 1838, prodding of members of the Legislative Assembly, and the legislative union of the two provinces of Canada in 1841 brought forth new and improved school legislation and improved grants. Actually the years 1841-1843 saw several new school acts but apart from increasing grants their most potent deed was giving the central authority in Toronto more power to supervise and to suggest with more authority, though administration was still done on a local level and the parents of the pupils paid the schools costs, rather than all the taxpayers.

In 1844 Rev. Egerton Ryerson was appointed Assistant Superintendent of Education for Ontario, and in 1846 became Chief Superintendent of Education, a position he was to hold until 1876. Ryerson believed in universal education and was in a position to promote it.

During his term of office and the ensuing years Glengarry's school system was shaped. School sections were formed as the necessity for them arose. By the time the concept of school sections became obsolete and an SDG Board of Education took over in the 1950's Glengarry had formed just over 70 school sections with about 90 public and separate school buildings on them. Figures are of necessity inexact because in the late 1940's and early 1950's in some sections the Separate School system was building new school buildings at the same time as other schools sections were uniting and some one-room schools were closing as a consequence.

The conditions in these one-room schools can be judged from a report given by D.J. Hynes, Inspector of Public Schools for Glengarry, which appeared in the *Glengarry News* of 31 October 1952. Below are some excerpts from this report:
"In January 1948 only six schools in the County had electric lights and only one of these was fairly satisfactory."
"In 1948 almost all schools were equipped with outdoor privies and in 1952 fifteen schools still have them. (7 in Kenyon, 4 in Lochiel, 3 in Charlottenburgh, and 1 in Lancaster)."
"There are still two or three schools in the inspectorate with old fashioned double seats and desks."
"There is still a general shortage of good maps and other teaching equipment."

244

"The number of schools without a water supply on the school property is decreasing."

"Several boards have been able to undertake improvement of school grounds. Very many others have neglected and disreputable grounds."

This report by the Public School Inspector near the end of the one-room school era tells us that improvements and changes in the conditions in and around Glengarry's public schools had come very slowly indeed.

We will now note some of the more important changes in the public school administration. One of the major ones was the provincial school legislation of 1871 that changed common schools to public schools and at the same time did away with fees paid by the children's parents and put the burden of school support on all real property. This act made school attendance compulsory for at least four months in the year for ages seven to twelve though enforcement procedures left much to be desired.

At this time too, township school supervisors were eliminated and county inspectors appointed. They were given authority to enforce standards of teacher training and teaching as well as to enforce minimum standards for school buildings, which had to be large enough and numerous enough to accommodate *all* the children of school age in the county. The first inspector appointed in Glengarry County was A.W. Ross who had taught both high and public school in Glengarry for many years. He only served for about 2½ years (and then went on to greater things as an M.P.) and was succeeded in 1874 by Dr. Donald McDiarmid of Athol who served until 1910.

Some short extracts from one of Dr. McDiarmid's reports from Glengarry may be of interest. This from his 1877 report: "Instances are frequently met with in which the limited knowledge possessed by the teachers of the subjects of the advanced readers prevents them from giving the information demanded." "With the few exceptions, of the wretched structures which have done duty for years, comfortable school houses, fairly furnished are provided.''

Figures at this stage show that 724 pupils out of a possible school population of 5,062 did not attend school at all and of those who were enrolled, the average attendance was 2,033 out of 4,960 or 41%. Going to school was not a popular pastime among Glengarry's children, and if one can judge by Dr. McDiarmid's comment on the teachers' ability, they were probably not missing too much.

But to go back to the public schools of Glengarry in 1871 and the years following. The Act of 1871 made entrance to a high school possible only by passing an entrance examination, written under strict supervision in a high school. This ensured that only serious students entered the high schools and that the public school teachers did not promote pupils just to get rid of them. In 1926 school legislation permitted teachers to ''recommend'' pupils for an entrance to high school, a privilege which our Glengarry teachers used very sparingly. Indeed over the years Glengarry's ''entrance'' pupils and their performance remained fairly constant. In 1880 Glengarry had more than 5,000 pupils in its public and separate schools, by 1900 this number had dropped to about 4,000 and by 1945 to under 3,000. However, each year about 225 ''tried the entrance,'' about 150 passed, and about 90 entered our three high schools. As our Department of Education reports state, ''the rest resigned from the school system.''

We have not discovered when, if ever, the last log school house disappeared from Glengarry. In 1856, 49 of our 60 school houses were ''log.'' In 1860, the last year in which kinds of school houses were reported by counties, nine of Glengarry's 71 school houses are reported as being ''log'' but 56 did not report. Doubtlessly a fair share of them were still ''log.'' The Athol school, now at Upper Canada Village, was rebuilt of logs after it burned in the 1870's and was later covered with clapboards. No doubt many of our log schools became ''frame schools'' through the addition of a covering, and it is likely that a few such still stand *in situ*.

The 1918 Adolescent School Attendance Act raised the legal school leaving age to 16 and this meant that from then on Glengarry's schools would have all enrolled who were mentally and physically fit. In 1903 about 20 % of the potential school population was not enrolled in any school at all and average attendance was only 45%. By 1935 average attendance had grown to 88% of all the possible school population and by 1945 attendance had reached 93% of the possible school population in Glengarry. Regular attendance at school, by all those eligible to attend, is quite a recent phenomenon in our educational system.

School teachers' salaries by the standards of 1978 made slow progress in the years 1845-1945. We could lay out pages of figures but by 1945 the provincial averages were:

Male teachers in public schools - $2088.

Female teachers in public schools - $1457.

Male teachers in Roman Catholic separate schools-$1233.

Female teachers in Roman Catholic separate schools-$971.

In 1900 the same type of teachers had received $421; $306; $372; and $215 respectively. In 1848 the Eastern District did not report the salaries of its school teachers but the Johnstown District next door to us did so. There male teachers without board received an average of £35 ($140) per year while female teachers without board received an average of £19 ($76) per year. Very likely Glengarry's teachers' salaries were comparable.

Admittedly it is difficult, if not impossible, to compare the value of a dollar, as far as its purchasing power is concerned, over a hundred year period with simple figures. Suffice it to say that public and separte school teachers were about the lowest paid professionals in the Dominion, ranking well behind doctors, lawyers, and settled ministers. However, in the period we are considering the professional qualifications of most of Glengarry's teachers left much to be desired by modern standards.

A Normal School was begun at Toronto in 1847 but by 1877

only 17 % of Ontario's teachers had been formally trained. So the province set up "Model Schools" in each county. This was a sort of apprenticeship system whereby student teachers were put in the charge of a recognized good teacher who trained them in his methods. At first the course was only eight weeks long but was later extended to 15 weeks.

Glengarry's Model School was at S.S. No.12 (Martintown), Charlottenburgh, where Alexander Kennedy, holder of a first class provincial certificate and equipped with two assistant teachers, taught school for some 35 years. Typically he would have seven to fifteen student teachers for each term, and those who qualified would receive a third class county certificate. This for many years was the qualification of the usual Glengarry teacher.

County Model Schools were officially abolished in 1900, and Martintown's Model School closed. Practically, however, it was found necessary to keep some Model Schools open because distance and expense kept potential teachers from attending the Normal Schools (one of which opened in Ottawa in 1876). Cornwall's Model School trained many young Glengarry teachers until 1910.

About 1905, in Ontario, the school population was about evenly balanced between rural and urban schools. From then on the city, town, and village school proportion of the school population increased rapidly, while the rural school population declined. The movement of people to the cities had another effect. Glengarry's population dropped by about one-quarter and families got smaller in the twentieth century. Our public school population figure reflected this. In the late 1800's our potential school population was very close to 6,000, by 1900 it was just over 5,000, by 1935 it was 3,600, and by 1945 it was 2,814.

Half of Ontario's rural schools had closed by 1945 for lack of pupils, but in Glengarry the one-room school, often with less than ten pupils and an underpaid undertrained teacher, still carried the load of basic education. Fifty years previously many of these schools had more than 50 pupils enrolled, some came close to having 100 pupils which seems to be over-loading a teacher until we recall the less than 50 % attendance of those days.

In 1932, a School Act permitted township councils to make any part of a township into a school area by combining school sections. By 1945 only one small school area (three sections) was functioning in Glengarry, in Lancaster Township, though some school sections had combined unofficially. Even to the conservative Glengarry folk it had become obvious that the one-room schools (and counting the separate schools we had about 90 of them) had had their day. The cost per pupil, even with underpaid teachers, had become too great. The village schools and Alexandria schools were becoming overcrowded, the rural schools were almost empty.

Glengarry's Roman Catholic separate school system deserves more space than we can give it here. In many ways it was a branch of the public system, studying the same subjects and having on the whole the same type of teachers, though with some notable exceptions. For many years, in fact the situation is not full resolved in 1978, the official attitude in Ontario was that one school system was enough; and though the right to have denominational schools was built into the act that united Upper and Lower Canada in 1841 and confirmed in the British North America Act which created Canada in 1867, official Protestant Ontario, until very lately regarded the Roman Catholic school as a type of private school. Of course in a private school the whole cost is paid by those sending their children to it. The constitution of our country stated, however, that a government grant had to be given to our separate schools. However, until 1968 (and as some say even yet) the government grant was usually as small as a strict legalistic interpretation of the law would allow. This "dole" was usually given with a poor grace and it was often deliberately made difficult for the separate schools to collect their share of the taxes from those who chose to support the separate schools.

It is no part of a historian's task to take sides but even the most objective of us have to concede that the Roman Catholic church faced an "uphill job" building a separate school system in Ontario.

Glengarry's separate school system, originally based on its homogenous Roman Catholic Scots, began very soon after the Union of the two Canadas with schools in Sections # 16 and 17 in Charlottenburgh in 1848, in S.S. #10 in Lochiel in 1854, S.S. #12 in Lancaster in 1855, and S.S. # 10 in Charlottenburgh and S.S. #11 in Lancaster in 1856. By 1945 there were 20 separate schools teaching about 40% of the elementary school children in the county.

The majority of these schools were, like their public school counterparts, one roomed schools with undertrained teachers working with inadequate equipment to teach a small number of pupils. But there were noteworthy exceptions. The Alexandria separate school for girls, from February 1856 on was taught by the Sisters of the Holy Cross, and from 1854 until 1905 the Christian Brothers taught the boys. Then the Sisters continued to teach both sexes. This school, which developed into schools and became a boarding school as well as a day school, is worthy of a history of its own, for, if no other reason, its size. In 1910, for instance, there were 465 pupils at St. Margaret's Convent and Alexander School. At this time there were 47 pupils in the Alexandria Public School and 130 in the high school. So it can be seen the Alexandria Separate School system was carrying more than its share of the load. But it had more than size to recommend it—Sister St. Hilda was famous for "getting pupils throught the entrance" and pupils from the Convent School were doing well in music (Sister Rose was the music teacher), a very much neglected subject in the public school system.

In 1912, several sisters of the House of Providence arrived at Glen Nevis to take charge of the separate school there. With these good sisters teaching, what had been an ordinary separate school rapidly developed into an exceptional educational institution, with 100-125 pupils and known variously as Maryvale Convent, Maryvale Abbey, and Maryvale Academy. For a while (until the Tiny Case, 1928, brought an end to high school work in separate schools) it taught everything from "Baby Class" to fifth form high school, and in addition taught painting, fancy work, French, and vocal and instrumental music. The present Auditor General of Canada, James Macdonell, and others of his calibre are graduates of Maryvale. This school closed in 1950 as school buses to large central schools robbed the Sisters of their pupils. All in Glengarry who knew of the quality of work done in this institution regretted its closing.

Another Catholic institution that must be mentioned, with regretful brevity, is Iona at St. Raphaels, founded by Father Alexander Macdonell (later Bishop) in 1818 as a seminary to train young men for the priesthood. This function was later transferred to Kingston but Iona continued as a school until 1881 when it closed. It was re-opened in 1913 and functioned as a Roman Catholic separate high school until 1924 under the tutelage of the Sisters of the Holy Cross. Then "The Tiny Case" under adjudication at this time caused the Sisters to close it as a high school and it became Iona Commercial College until 1945, when high school work was begun again, and by 1949 Iona was once more a full-fledged private high school which continued until 1971. It was a day school but also usually had about 80 boarders as students. Once more government policy interfered and Iona became a continuation school until it was sold to the Roman Catholic Separate School System Board and in 1978 still functions as Iona Separate Public School.

As an example of the dedication that made places like Iona possible in spite of no government grants to Catholic high schools, the Sisters for the last 60 years of its existence (1913-1973) taught the senior grades WITHOUT salaries.

The Congregation de Notre Dame operated a boarding school convent in Williamstown 1865 to 1892. Then the building burned down and the Sisters withdrew from Glengarry to concentrate on a school in the Montreal area.

Sisters of the Holy Cross and Sisters of Providence taught in the Apple Hill separate school which was open from 1920 to 1970 but there seem to have been about as many lay teachers as sisters over the years and it was always a day school.

Four Sisters of Providence arrived in Lancaster in 1923 to take charge of the separate school there. More recently other sisters have taught at Williamstown and Martintown separate schools.

The Roman Catholic Separate School System owes much to the dedicated efforts of the sisters of various teaching orders and nowhere more than in Glengarry. Glengarry's separate school story is not complete without mention of a major complication. This is the growth in numbers of Glengarry's French-speaking population which is also entirely Roman Catholic.

The vigorous Francophone influx presented the Roman Catholic Separate School System with problems, especially as it was only gradually that the French became land owners and school taxpayers. Until they started to pay their share of the taxes, the Anglophones could maintain with good reason that they were paying for the education of the French children. Not only that, but a good deal of the primary education was being given in French, albeit illegally. The Scots, of course, had given up their own Gaelic to become English-speaking Canadians and the idea of paying for a French education for French children, illegal as it was, did not appeal to them. In most cases there was a lot of grumbling but no direct action.

However, one case, known locally as "The Green Valley School Row" did result in court action and periodically made the headlines of some of Canada's leading newspapers for about three years.

The school section concerned was S.S. # 14 Lancaster,

in the north-west part of the township, next to Green Valley. The trouble broke on 25 February 1914 when Donald D. McDonald, acting for himself and others, had a writ issued to the trustees of the Roman Catholic separate school in the section to restrain the teacher from teaching as "she is not a qualified teacher ... and allows the use of French as the language of instruction in the school." This issue came before the courts several times over the next few years, always to the disadvantage of the trustees. Early in 1916, the Francophones in the section opened a private school. For a building, Dolor Brabant contributed an old house, which had been serving as a granary. The teacher was Florence Quesnel, who, according to a writer in the *Almanach de la langue. française*, gave "aux petits Canadiens-français de la-bas l'enseignement des traditions de la race, fait apprendre la langue française et la religion catholique, apostolique et romaine." Later, a second private school for the French pupils at Green Valley was added.

Beginning in 1920, there was a struggle in Alexandria over the question of whether to introduce instruction in French into the separate school there. No private school after the Green Valley model was set up in Alexandria, but private evening classes were established for the Francophone students.

Emotions were high and it speaks well for the common sense of the local people of both tongues that such episodes were not much more numerous in Glengarry. The raw material of an explosion was present in Glengarry's separate schools. Some of it still is, as the Francophones ask for more and more teaching in French, but today the issue is joined on the high school level. The right to teach French on the public school level has been conceded and today there is no question of the Francophones not paying their share of the property taxes in Glengarry. Province-wide is a different matter as occasional headlines remind us, and Quebec's language bills will not let us forget.

The story of Glengarry's three high schools in the

100 year period 1846-1945 has the merit of being relatively uncomplicated. Williamstown began to teach grammar school work officially in 1846, though there is some reason to believe some work of this nature had been done from 1828 on. A new brick school house was opened in 1862 which the high school shared with the common school (after 1871 the public school) until the spring of 1901 when it moved into a new school house of its own which it still was in in 1945. It never became a large school. It began with about 30 pupils and in 1945 it had 88, though it had 119 in 1903 and 113 in 1935.

Wellington J.C. Barrett, Principal of Williamstown High School 1919-1955. At the time of writing he is a hale and hearty octogenarian, clerk of session at St. Andrew's United Church, Williamstown. Hundreds of his former pupils were able to pay their sincere respects to him at the High School reunion of August 1978.

Alexandria's high school opened its doors in 1865, holding classes in the old public school for a while and later in an old log building across the road from the public school, and then in the upstairs of the old separate school. In 1876 a new brick school building was opened which did duty until 1894 when a new brick school was built on an eight-lot site on St. Paul and Centre Streets donated by Big Rory McLennan. This school did duty through 1945 with the help of an addition built in 1909.

When the Alexandria High School was first started with an enrolment of about 20, often the teacher considered himself lucky if he had five or six to teach. In 1871 the high school inspector reported the Alexandria High School as being far below the standard of a high school and likely to remain so for years to come as the village in which it is situated did not have a public school in a sufficiently effective condition to furnish material for the support of anything worthy of the name "High School."

Again in 1878 the high school inspector's report has this to say of the Alexandria High School: "This High School was founded many years ago, closed in 1874, and re-opened in 1876. During 1876 and 1877, only one teacher was employed; now in 1878 there are two. It has until recently been of little service; but it is improving, and perhaps may succeed in falling permanently into line with the other High Schools. The two townships which constitute its district are well able to support a High School; *and a High School is very much needed there* for the instruction of teachers, because if we may judge from the qualifications of the Candidates for (High School) entrance in Northern Glengarry, primary education there is in a lower state than in almost all other parts of the Province."

Such was the state of education in the Alexandria High School district one hundred years ago — a year when there were 42 pupils in the Alexandria High School. But the school survived and prospered. James Smith, a real professional teacher, came to the school as principal in 1885 and was ably backed up by Duncan A. McDonald (Curly) who became Alexandria's first reeve in 1883. In 1885 the school had only 43 pupils. James Smith was succeeded by Robert Young who only stayed a couple of years and he in turn was succeeded in 1895 by Donald McKay, M.A., who remained as principal until 1934 when he was succeeded by J.T. Smith. Under these gentlemen and their successors no inspector could seriously question the academic standards of Alexandria High School. In 1903 there were 142 pupils in the school, a level maintained quite consistently until 1945.

C. Campbell Fraser, principal of Alexandria High School 1960-65. Mr. Fraser, of old Glengarry stock, may serve as an example not only of the teaching profession but of those who helped to hold Glengarry together. He took an active interest in politics, service clubs, and is "the authority" on the history of Lochiel Township. He is also an active United Church elder.

Maxville's High School was late on the academic scene in Glengarry. It opened on 1 January 1929, having grown out of a continuation school that had been in operation since 1914. Previously students from the area who wished to finish their high school education went to Avonmore, Cornwall, Vankleek Hill, or Alexandria. It will be convenient to finish Maxville High School's story here as it closed in 1974 and the building became a senior public school.

Donald McKay, M.A., Principal of Alexandria High School 1896-1934. Alexandria hired him away from Williamstown by offering him another $100 a year. His salary at Williamstown was $1100. McKay took his assistant at Williamstown, Robert Stewart, with him to Alexandria, also at a 10% rise on his $800 per annum salary. Williamstown was perturbed.

J.T. Smith, Principal of Alexandria High School 1934-1960. J.T. Smith came to Alexandria as part of the permanent staff of the Alexandria High School in 1921. In 1934 he succeeded McKay as principal and it was he who kept the school competent through the Depression and war years and almost unofficially introduced the driving of rural pupils to the school in the winter of 1945-1946. He also supervised the transition of the Alexandria High School from a small town high school to a larger, modern, district high school.

Here the outstanding principal was Miss Mabel White who was principal of the continuation school from 1925 and became first principal of the high school, remaining in charge until 1945 when she resigned the principalship. She continued to teach until her death in October 1952. The school had 115 students in 1935, 96 in 1945, and 305 when it closed.

The reason for its closing is more apparent when we know that in 1974 a single board of education administers all the public system of education in SDG and Maxville's pupils will help to fill a new high school between Avonmore and Monkland, known as ''Tagwi.''

Which brings us quite naturally to a consideration of what happened in Glengarry in the field of education after

1945. Several factors were involved. The first and most readily apparent at the time was the great number of one room schools, most with a very small number of pupils in them. The second was the availability of snowplowing equipment that was capable of keeping all necessary roads open (most days) all winter. The third was the know-how of moving people around by buses learned in World War II. The fourth, which became extremely apparent about 1950, was the sharp rise in the birthrate after World War II and most of these babies were not born to people who lived on the concessions, so the long term answer was not to rejuvenate the one-room schools. Perhaps the most potent factor of all was grant manipulation from Toronto, something governments had learned to do effectively in controlling all phases of the economy during the war. Furthermore, after six years of war—a war that had followed a ten year Depression—people were in a mood for change. They knew the system could be changed and hardly for the worse; the previous fifteen years had been about as bad as things could be. Such was the mood of the people, particularly the younger people, who had lived through the Depression and fought the war. They had nothing, so had nothing to lose from change or by change.

The change began slowly enough by the simple busing of pupils from the concessions to the three high school centres, thereby soon overcrowding the old buildings. Lancaster's public school area formed in 1943 proved so successful that by 1954 all of Glengarry was under one Board of Education. The building boom started in 1948 and continued through 1974. One by one the one-room schools closed and new schools were built in the towns and at central points in the townships as fast as money could be provided and even though Toronto provided most of it, the new schools plus the busing of the pupils drove the education part of the tax bill higher each year. The last one-room school in Glengarry, at Summerstown, closed in 1973, and Glengarry had almost a complete new set of school houses of every sort, high schools, public schools, and separate schools. But the number of buildings was smaller. There were nineteen elementary schools, eleven of which belonged to the separate school system, seven to the public school system, and a combined school for the retarded in Alexandria known as Harmony Glen. After mid-summer 1974 Glengarry itself only had two high schools, as Maxville reverted to a senior elementary school, leaving Alexandria and Williamstown and an interest in Tagwi.

The school administration too had changed. From 1969 on United Counties School Boards operated both Roman Catholic separate schools and public schools. The two boards are distinctly separate, though there is talk once in a while of sharing some of the expenses.

Part of Crevier's school bus fleet, 1978. Since the late 1940's every child in Glengarry no matter how far he or she lives from the school is taken to school each morning and delivered home each evening at public expense. For the most part the transportation is handled by contractors who arrange their runs in consultation with the schools concerned. This aspect of our educational system is a big business in itself and all roads on school bus routes have to be kept open winter and summer.

In the 1969-70 school year the total school population reached its peak and began a steady decline, noticeable first of all in the elementary schools. By 1976 teachers were being laid off and budgets tightened. As we write this, teachers have difficulty finding positions and there is space to spare, paricularly in the elementary schools.

In the years since 1945 almost every pupil who passed the entrance went on to high school and from 1950 on, when entrance examinations were dispensed with entirely, something over 90% of the public school pupils entered the high schools. In 1976, 83 pupils graduated from Alexandria High School and 33 of them planned to go on to college. So at the time of writing, the young people of Glengarry have as much education readily available to them as if they lived in a city.

Of course, there are problems remaining. One common to both the systems is the great expense involved. Another one is that education has become a matter of putting the needed number of hours in, in order to pass, even into college. As we write, a beginning is being made at rectifying this by means of stiffer courses and mandatory subjects. There still seems to be much room for improvement here. Also, in Glengarry we have the denominational school-language problem as much with us as ever.

A modern Glengarry school ( Laggan Public School), 1978.

The separate school system would like to operate its own high schools. The Ontario school grant system makes this very difficult economically. The Francophones would like more high school instruction in French, and the Anglophones claim it cannot be done and still give a sound education in English, the official language of Ontario and the business language of the world. The 1976 elementary enrolment figures in Glengarry show how evenly the question is balanced:

1. Pupils in Francophone schools — 1,567.
2. Pupils in Anglophone Roman Catholic Separate Schools — 516.
3. Pupils in public schools (all Anglophone) — 1,231.
   Total of 1 and 2 = 2,083   Total of 2 and 3 = 1,747
   1,567 to 1,747 — English have a small majority.
   2,083 to 1,231 — Catholics have a large majority.

In the thirty-odd years since 1945 the teachers have militantly approached the salary problem, and today Glengarry's teachers in every type of school are quite well paid professionals. As the salary paid is directly related to their professional qualifications, it pays them well to keep up-grading their qualifications, to the ultimate benefit of their pupils (we hope).

Education in Glengarry has come a long way since the beech gad and Bible days of the late 1700's. Though much more expensive, it is available to all. In contrast to those early days when the parents provided everything, pupils, school house, teacher, books and payment, today they provide the pupils and apart from that their only contact with the school is to pay the bill. And Toronto decides how big the bill will be.

## Libraries

If we define a library as a collection of books, then the history of libraries in Glengarry begins in the very early years of the nineteenth century. Bishop Macdonell wrote in 1834 that he had been "collecting all the books I could purchase for thirty years past." There is a reference of 1832 to his library being at that time at St. Raphaels. Rev. John Bethune and Rev. James Reid, both schoolmasters as well as clergymen, are reported to have had some books on their shelves. No doubt there were others, as the community leaders even in the very early days were quite well educated.

For our purpose here, however, by library, we mean a public library where any member of the community can borrow a book of his choice, read it and return it and then choose another to read.

Dr. Egerton Ryerson, Chief Superintendent of Schools in Canada West and Ontario 1844-1876, was a firm believer in the educational value of books, and he got his department into the book business as quickly as he could. As "man in charge" of schools he was in a position to promote libraries in the common schools that would not only be available to the teachers and pupils but to the community served by the school in which the library was. For a short period of time Ryerson also used his position to promote Sunday School libraries.

So it is not surprising that much of our knowledge of the early public libraries in Glengarry (and elsewhere) comes from the annual reports of the Chief Superintendent of Education. Here we find Glengarry's first public library appearing in the 1856 report.

In 1856 a new two-room brick common school was opened at S.S. #12, Charlottenburgh (Martintown) and in it the Department of Education placed £50 worth of books—454 different volumes. In the course of the first year 748 books were circulated to 40 different readers. The titles of the books are not given but the subjects covered were heavily weighted towards education, though 211 of the books are listed as "tales". (One would like to know how ponderous and moral those tales were.) At the same time, this report tells us that Glengarry had nine Sunday School libraries with a total of 1000 volumes. There is no listing or other indication of where these nine Sunday School libraries were in the county, so each reader may make his own guess.

Perhaps the breakdown of the S.S. #12 Charlottenburgh

school library by subjects will be of interest. If so, here it is: 40 volumes of history; 21 of zoology; two of botany; one of natural phenomena; 13 of chemistry; one of agricultural chemistry; 33 of practical agriculture; 27 of mathematics; 40 of literature; 22 of voyages; 36 of biography; 211 of tales. The teacher's library had one volume (not named) in it.

Four years later, in 1860, Ryerson's report shows there was little change. The Sunday School libraries now had 1,504 volumes, but S.S. #12 Charlottenburgh still had only its original 454 volumes, now valued at $200. Circulation had decreased to 374 books from 748, but the number of separate readers had increased to 100 from 40. One can suspect that the omniverous readers in the community had exhausted the library's resources but it is heartening to know that at least one hundred people around Martintown were looking for some books to read.

Martintown in 1860, with a decreased number of volumes in circulation, was early experiencing a phenomenon that was to become province wide in the next twenty years. In 1870 Ontario had 389 public libraries circulating 174,411 volumes. By 1875 there were only 164 libraries circulating 133,982 volumes. F. Henry Johnson's *Brief History of Education* attributes this drop in interest in reading to Ryerson's restrictive tastes in selecting the library lists—dull reading had resulted in flagging interest.

It is of interest to see how Glengarry compared with some other counties in Ontario in 1871. Glengarry now had three common school libraries (locations not given) with 650 volumes and a total value of $350.70, and its nine Sunday School libraries had 1,090 volumes, so there are 1,740 books in public libraries in Glengarry, *which was the lowest number in any county in Ontario.* The nearest competitor was Stormont with 3,015 volumes in 22 libraries. York County was at the head of the list with 40,258 volumes in 253 libraries. Huron County had 23,297 volumes in 196 libraries, and Prescott had 7,314 volumes in 34 libraries.

It is possible that the two additional school libraries shown in 1871 were in the Williamstown and Alexandria high schools as the report on Williamstown High School says the school has a library though there is no mention of one in connection with Alexandria.

An 1877 school report shows one new library at S.S. #9, Lancaster, giving Glengarry a total of six libraries with 796 books valued at $466.70. Evidently the Sunday School libraries have been "written off." But the new library is not a large one: it has 16 volumes worth $10.00, five dollars of which came from local sources and five dollars from a legislative grant.

On 1 January 1881 the Ontario Department of Education closed its book repository in Toronto, remarking that after thirty years in the library and school book business it no longer needed to compete with commercial sources that were well able to supply Ontario's books of all descriptions.

So ended the Department of Education's effort to make public libraries out of school libraries. There is no record of what happened to the books in these school and and Sunday School libraries. No doubt in time they were worn out, lost, destroyed, and probably a few of the volumes still exist, sitting on shelves in Glengarry homes, but the libraries themselves passed into history.

However, private interests in Glengarry were ready to start libraries. In 1871, Father O'Connor, the parish priest of Alexandria, was said to be planning to establish a circulation library in connection with his recently founded total abstinence society. A report of 1882 on the Annual Meeting of the Alexandria Mechanics Institute (President E.H. Tiffany) said that the Institute's library "contains an excellent selection of standard literature valued at upwards of three hundred dollars." Later in the year it was reported from Alexandria that "The energetic members of the Mechanics Institute intend adding to their already extensive library." In 1883 a Mechanics Institute was formed at Lancaster and it began to assemble a library which in time became the nucleus of the book collection in Lancaster which was turned over to the County Library Board when it took over in 1968, if such continuity has any meaning or merit.

Looking westward at Ontario we find that the first public library in Ontario was opened in Guelph in 1883 and the first free public library in the province was opened in Toronto in 1884. But Glengarry had to wait till the 1890's for its first true public library, which, largely due to the efforts of George H. Macgillivray, was established in Williamstown probably in 1894. Probably it developed out of a Mechanics Institute which had "a library and reading room" in Williamstown in 1889. It certainly was in full operation in 1896 and was housed in an old store building on the south-west corner of the old high school grounds (that is, the grounds of the high school that opened in 1901). James Brown, Williamstown's lawyer, was the librarian and in 1904 the Misses Elizabeth Raymond and Gertrude Snyder took over the librarians' duties.

By 1896 the Lancaster Mechanics Institute was calling its book collection a public library and it was housed in the Mechanics Institute building which stood between the McArthur and the Henderson blocks. Later it was housed in the Fraser block and Mrs. Edgar was one of the first librarians.

In 1902 Lancaster got its first public library building, the same one that houses the county library in the village today. The building was erected "by public subscription" and cost $3,000. However, quite a large share of this $3,000 plus an unknown amount for books came from one donor, a former Lancaster boy who had made good in Chicago, John D. Ross. Ross was approached by William Stewart and "Squire" Sandy MacLennan for a donation to the library building and he wound up buying the lot the building is on for $600 and giving a further $1000 towards its costs plus a cheque for books. However, Lancaster got a public library building to be proud of, and in the 1950's it was described by the Superintendent of Public Libraries for Ontario as one of the best buildings for library purposes in Ontario, outside the cities. When in the years immediately after World War I, Alexandria thought it should have a war memorial of impressive size, Lancaster too erected one at the front of the library. This cenotaph, along with the flower beds in season in front of the library building, creates a small focus of interest in the village even today.

The report of the supervisor of libraries in 1902 tells us Lancaster had 3,189 volumes in its library. In 1903 it had the same number of volumes and loaned 3,073 books to 246 subscribers. In 1908 Lancaster had 3,499 books and 223 subscribers, and the library also borrowed two travelling library boxes from the Department of Education in 1907. The 1909 report tells us Lancaster had about 3,667 volumes and issued 2,289. In 1910 Lancaster still had 3,667 books and issued 2,193. In 1920 Lancaster had more than 4,000 books and issued 2,388, and the *Glengarry News* reported that the Ontario Fish and Game Protective Association held a meeting in the Lancaster Library on 6 February 1920. In 1930 Lancaster had 3,295 volumes and issued 2,982. In 1935 Lancaster had 3,164 books, 155 borrowers, and a circulation of 1,618. In 1940 there were 3,120 books and a circulation of 1,980.

We hear no more of the Lancaster Public Library until the *Glengarry News* of 14 May 1953 reported, "The Lancaster Public Library somewhat dormant for many years is to be revived." The wires were crossed a bit somewhere because an article in the *Glengarry News* of 29 April 1954 states, "the Lancaster Public Library has re-opened and shaken off the dust of 24 years." As it definitely was lending books in 1940, the period it was dormant was no more than 14 years.

In 1968 when Lancaster Library's stock was inventoried prior to the County Library System taking over, it was reported that the stock consisted of a few up-to-date books in a locked case and some out-of-date encyclopedias. Apart from some old Canadiana, practically the whole stock was discarded. The report stated that prior to 1968 this library had been operating on a two-hour per week "open" basis.

We left the Williamstown Public Library as a functioning

unit back in 1904. In 1903 it had 1,322 volumes, 160 subscribers, and a circulation of 1,522. The 1908 report just carries the name of Williamstown as having a library; no figures are given, but the next year it is reported to have 1,990 volumes and a circulation of 2,106. That same year the high school library at Williamstown is valued at $311, but there is no breakdown at all. In 1910 Williamstown had 2,134 volumes in its public library and issued 2,340, and is reported to have bought 95 new books. In 1920 the Williamstown library had 2,449 volumes but had only circulated 1,280. In 1930 it had 2,592 volumes but circulation is down to 688. In 1935 there is no report from Williamstown, nor are there any later ones. Williamstown's library has faded out of existence after serving the community for about forty years.

We have considered the two most senior public libraries in the county, one dating to 1894, the other to 1896. Perhaps the next place we should look at is Alexandria because it got a library in 1902.

In that year Robert Wilson, C.E., a native of the area (brother of J. Lockie Wilson) and son of an Alexandria blacksmith, donated some books and some money to buy more to the trustees of McLaren Hall in Alexandria. This library never became a public library in the accepted sense of the word and no word of its existence appears in official reports of libraries in Ontario. But it must have been of some value to the community or at least to the church community that owned and operated McLaren Hall as this library was moved to the Church on the Hill in Alexandria in 1913 where the books were stored in the church school-room. And then all mention of it disappears. Occasionally in a home in Alexandria one can pull an old book off a shelf and the fly leaf is stamped "McLaren Hall Library," Alexandria.

Alexandria's efforts to get a functioning library in the next fifty odd years are of interest. On 20 February 1903 the *Glengarry News* reported that it was about to begin a circulating library among its correspondents in the Alexandria area. But no more is heard of that plan. For a regrettably short time beginning about the early 1950's, O. Detrait operated an excellent second-hand bookstore and lending library in the area of the Armouries. The *Glengarry News* of 23 November 1961 and 17 May 1962 carried editorials in favour of a public library for Alexandria. In February 1964 we read that the Alexandria Board of Trade had decided to make a public library for Alexandria its Centennial project. The *Glengarry News* of 19 November 1964 had an editorial in favour of a public library but commented a bit sadly "there seems to be a limited demand for a library."

In February 1966 the Glengarry District High School was expanding and it reported that a 2,000 square foot library was included in the facilities it planned. The *Glengarry News* of 16 January 1969 carried another editorial in favour of a public library for Alexandria, but when the County Library System took over they reported they could find no trace of a previous public library in Alexandria. However, "some years" after 1971 they received the collection that had been in "The McLaren Hall Library and Reading Room." There is no word of the disposition made of these books by the county library.

The good editor of the *Glengarry News*, Eugene Macdonald, seems to have known whereof he spoke when he said in 1964 that there seemed to be limited demand for a library in Alexandria. The "only town" in Glengarry got along without a public library service until 1968.

No community in Glengarry has preserved its history better than Maxville. This is due first of all to the fact that the first building at "the 17th crossroads" was erected only 109 years ago and secondly to the amount of work done on local history in the area by the local Women's Institute and preserved in their Tweedsmuir book. In this book Maxville is credited with getting its first library in 1920. We hope the Maxville Ladies will forgive us for finding a forgotten Library in Maxville which evidently was started in 1902 and received a government grant that year. The 1903 report credits the Maxville Library with 310 volumes, 115 subscribers, and 1,299 books loaned. The 1908 report just mentions Maxville and gives no data at all, and there is no further mention of it. So we may assume it either went out of existence or became completely dormant.

In 1920, however, the Maxville folk held various public meetings during June and July to discuss forming a library and in August 1920 it went into operation. At first it was housed in Hugh McLean's furniture store with Mr. McLean in charge of it. Very shortly the library moved to the Women's Institute Hall on Peter Street and until 1953 Miss Meta McKercher was the librarian. In 1930 Maxville's Library had 1,166 volumes and issued 1,380. In 1935 Maxville had 1,358 volumes, and 39 borrowers got 1,856 books out of it. In 1940 Maxville had 1,494 volumes and issued 762. There was no report from the Maxville library in 1945, but we can assume it was in operation as the local press carried an item about Meta McKercher retiring as Maxville's librarian ''after many years of service.''

In 1954 the Women's Institute Hall was sold and the books were taken to Fitzgerald's store where they remained until 1957 and were still kept in circulation. In 1957 Maxville's library books were removed from Fitzgerald's store to the Maxville Community Hall and thanks to the devotion of three local couples were kept in circulation until 1963 when they were donated to the Maxville High School. When the high school got the books, a book expert from the Department of Education looked them over and selected about half of them as suitable for school use and sent the rest to the dump. Maxville High School closed in 1975 as a high school but we trailed the books no further. Possibly they are still on the shelves of the Senior Public School now housed in the old Maxville high school building—possibly some went to Tagwi along with the Maxville high school pupils.

An interesting library appears in the Ontario library reports in Apple Hill in 1935, with 892 books, 65 borrowers and circulation of 1,645. In 1945 it had 1,359 volumes, 52 borrowers and a circulation of 877 books. It appears again in 1946 with

1,382 books, 49 borrowers and a circulation of 1,054. Then Apple Hill's library disappears from the public mention until the Glengarry libraries' resources were inventoried in 1968 prior to the advent of the County Library System. From this we glean that Apple Hill had a rather ragged collection (does that refer to the condition of the books or their inconsistency of theme?) of books in a private home, but did not operate regularly. No circulation figures were kept but it was assumed that a circulation of five per month would have been an exaggeration. In 1978 a few Apple Hill library books are in Maxville Manor Library.

Before we deal with the last public library to be formed in Glengarry that functioned until the County Library System took over, it may be of interest to see what efforts were made to start other libraries. These came to nothing, but it does show there was interest.

In 1907 Dr. Duncan McEwen, then the doctor at Dunvegan, tried to start a public library there and it is mentioned in the 1908 Ontario library report but no data are given and we hear no more of it.

In 1908 the Report of the Department of Education tells us that Glengarry has 19 public school libraries and in 1907 they had bought books valued at $38.15 and then they too disappear from official view. In 1947 we find an effort was made to start a library at McCrimmon, but it never made the offficial records.

In 1966 Charlottenburgh Township Council talked of making part of its $17,000 Centennial grant available for a township library, possibly in connection with the museum at Williamstown, but rumors of a county library in the offing put an end to that idea.

The public library at Martintown which began operation in 1914 has been saved to the last, partly because its documentation fits neatly into the present County Library System.

A Mr. Thompson and the local medical man at the time, Dr. McCracken, were the moving spirits behind Martintown's public library, and the Women's Institute were, as usual, very helpful with work and donations. In 1920 Martintown had 2,927 volumes and issued 1,974. In 1930 they had 1,890 volumes and issued 1,091. In 1935 they had 1,458 volumes, 23 borrowers and loaned 816 books. There was no report from this library in 1940, but in 1945 it had 1,646 volumes, 17 borrowers, and a circulation of 395. The 1946 report shows 1,643 books, 14 borrowers, and a circulation of 345.

The minute book of the annual meetings of this library from 20 January 1948 to 12 February 1966 exists and it shows the library was operating but had membership and circulation problems despite the best efforts of a devoted few, such as Rev. McKim, Rhodes Grant, Athol Edgar, Irene Jacques, and Jean MacIntosh.

A letter preserved among the Martintown Public Library records tells us much about the demise of the small local libraries. This letter is from the Provincial Library Service Branch of the Ontario Department of Education and tells the Martintown Library Board that the Public Libraries Act, 1966, Section 45, states that the assets of association (i.e. joint stock) libraries such as this will go to the regional library boards on 31 December 1966 unless they become a part of a county or municipal library or revert to private status, and no further grants will be paid to former association libraries.

Martintown reverted to private status as of 1 January 1967. The books of this library remained in the library building until 1970, where they were still available to readers, but circulation tapered off to zero. The building was sold in 1970 and the new owner requested that the books be removed. A select few were removed to the Women's Institute Hall, a collection of Churchill's works was donated to Char-lan High School (Williamstown), and the bulk of the books were donated to community of Iron Bridge on the north shore of Lake Huron. Moneys remaining in the Library Board's hands were donated to the local Masons who had provided the library quarters for many years and had seldom bothered to collect any rent.

In several places above we have referred to the County Library System which replaced all the local libraries in Glengarry beginning in 1968. Actually the first two or three years were devoted to "pilot programs" and the act that set up the Counties Library System was the Counties Library Act of 1970, which authorized the formation of a County Public Library in any county where at least 75% of the municipalities requested the county pass a by-law, or at least half the municipalities with a combined population of 25,000 so requested. The SDG County Library was funded by a government grant of $15,000 plus $1.50 per capita for each resident of the counties. The balance of the money needed came from local taxes. Land and buildings may be under the same ownership as previously if suitable arrangements can be made with the County Library Board. This board consists of the County Warden, three County Councillors and three other members appointed by the County Council. This board appoints its own chairman and meets monthly except in the summer. The chief librarian is executive officer and often secretary-treasurer of the board. In 1977 all branches of the SDG library in Glengarry were housed in buildings fully occupied and operated by the library system or in rented space, but only in Maxville is the rented space privately owned.

The pilot program which, as stated above, initiated the County Library System featured a bookmobile and some reading stations. The bookmobile started serving Alexandria in November 1968 and continued to do so until September 1971 when a branch library was opened in the former customs office in the old Alexandria Post Office. In 1971 SDG library system took over the Lancaster library building and the same year opened a branch in Maxville with Reeve Hubert Quart cutting the ribbon and John McKenzie's pipes creating a suitable atmosphere. On 24 May 1975 the system opened its fifteenth branch in the counties and fourth in Glengarry in the Johnson

Manor House in Williamstown. The Glengarry branches of the system in 1976 were Lancaster, with a circulation of 3,710 books, Alexandria with a circulation of 17,725, Williamstown with a circulation of 3,836, and Maxville with a circulation of 7,153. In addition there is a deposit station at Maxville Manor which circulated 6,830 books in 1976. One cannot help but be impressed by the amount of reading done in the Maxville area.

In a typical week in 1976 the bookmobile of the County Library System visited Apple Hill, Martintown, St. Raphaels, Curry Hill, Bainsville, North Lancaster, Glen Norman, Greenfield, Dalkeith (a small branch library is planned for Dalkeith in 1978), Green Valley, Glen Robertson, Glen Sandfield, McCrimmon, and Dunvegan. All branches, reading stations, the bookmobile, and the mail service for shut-ins provide inter-library loan service which fills 80% of its requests within 10 days and this service is well patronized. Inter-library loan transactions in SDG exceed in number those of the Ottawa Public Library.

Book borrowers who cannot go to the branches can meet the bookmobile at any of its scheduled twice monthly stops and the length of the stop depends on the volume of business. Occasionally new stops are added or old ones dropped, depending on demand, but the bookmobile will stop if there is one regular borrower. The bookmobile goes to some schools for the benefit of students who would not otherwise be able to attend the stop nearest home. The county library service also provides talking books on tape cassettes to those who, for medical reasons, cannot use standard books.

No person in Glengarry today need go without reading material of his or her choice in either French or English, and northern Glengarry at least is reading in quantity. We have already remarked on Maxville's turnover of books in 1976. Alexandria is perhaps even more remarkable. In September of 1976 the branch library there moved into new and larger quarters in the newly erected Sports Palace, and Osie Villeneuve, M.L.A., duly cut the tape. Some citizens protested the move, saying the new library was too far from the centre of town and too hard to get to, yet the Glengarry News of 26

October 1977 reported that the circulation of books in the new library, open for a year, is up 30% to 18,303.

We wonder if our good friend Eugene Macdonald recalls the day in November 1964 when he sadly wrote, "there seems to be a limited demand for a library in Alexandria."

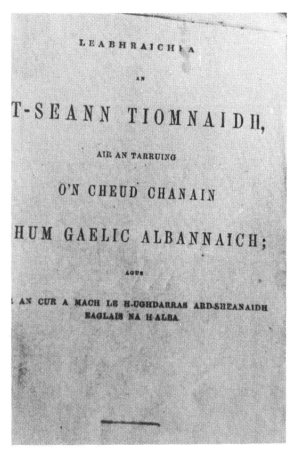

Flyleaf of a Gaelic Bible. A sine qua non in many Glengarry homes, for many a year in time past.

## Gaelic

It is difficult to write the history of the prevalence and decline of Gaelic in our county because so little documentary evidence exists on the subject.

Gaelic was mainly a spoken, not a written language. It is therefore impossible to trace the receding tide of the language through the written sources which, in Glengarry, were mostly in English from the beginning. When we add up, as well as we can, the evidence for the use of Gaelic as a written language in Glengarry, it amounts to very little. People owned Gaelic Bibles and a few other Gaelic books. Father John Macdonald of St. Raphaels used some Gaelic in the genealogical records he kept. He prepared a Gaelic catechism which was published at Toronto in 1871 and at Halifax in 1874, but no book in Gaelic ever appears to have been published in Glengarry. In the early decades of the Glengarry newspapers, they published occasional Gaelic poems or articles. In 1894 a Gaelic "paper" was being published at the Presbyterian Manse at St. Elmo, and it reached at least a second issue, but we have not found a copy of it. People who knew Gaelic were sometimes persuaded to write down a Gaelic song or poem. Gaelic was not used in Glengarry for legal documents, municipal records, advertising, or, so far as we have been able to discover, for account books, diaries, or business or personal letters. Its absence from personal letters seems surprising, but the present writers, who have turned over many hundreds of Glengarry letters, have to report that they have never seen or even heard of a Gaelic letter of Glengarry origin. Classes in Gaelic were never a part of the school system in Glengarry; hence in that area, too, there is no documentation.

Gaelic does produce an echo of sorts in the written sources, in the sense that one can at times find curiously distorted spellings which clearly arise from a clash between Gaelic pronunciation and English spelling.

The census did not list Gaelic speakers during the period in which the information would be of most use to us, but we do find that as late as the 1951 census 138 persons in Glengarry (70 male and 68 female) still claimed Gaelic as their "mother tongue."

Travellers and other casual observers occasionally commented on the use of Gaelic in Glengarry, but their knowledge was usually, necessarily, of an impressionistic sort; we shall see in a moment what some of these had to say.

It can hardly be doubted that in the first generation of the settlement of Glengarry the language normally used by the vast majority of the population was Gaelic and that many knew no English at all.

From the very beginning, however, the language must have been to some degree in retreat. And from the first quarter of the nineteenth century at the very latest, there can hardly have been a decade in which it did not disastrously lose ground.

The language declined earlier in the south than in the north. As early as 1825, a correspondent of the Glasgow Colonial Society rather disparagingly wrote that it would be advantageous for a Presbyterian clergyman at Martintown to be able to officiate in Gaelic for one half of the services "as that language is generally spoken by the lower orders of the old settlers." Despite this apparent dismissal of the old language as a dying relic, it was possible even in 1846 to describe Martintown, Williamstown, and Lancaster as "each forming the centre of a dense Presbyterian and Gaelic-speaking population." Similarly, in 1853 St. Andrew's, Martintown, resolved that any minister called must have both tongues, and the Rev. John Anderson, who was inducted as minister of the Lancaster and Dalhousie Mills Free Kirk congregations in 1854 preached to his people in Gaelic as well as in English. But an observer of 1861 drew an instructive contrast. At the religious services of the Presbyterians of Lochiel, he noted, an audience of some 800 during the Gaelic services would dwindle away to less than a score at the English services. But on the Front, Gaelic was "fast dying away, so that the comparative attendance at the English and Gaelic services is nearly the reverse of what it is at Lochiel." Even in Lochiel, he thought, its extinction was likely "ere many generations." In 1887, John McLennan (by the Lake), lately the M.P. for the county, wrote that "in some isolated sections" of the county "the Gaelic language is in some measure of use.'' His remark is vague, but it suggests that in the territory he knew best, his own homeland of the Front, the age of Gaelic was over.

The Breadalbane area may have been an exception to the rest of the north in the quickness with which it adopted the new language which was pressing in upon Glengarry from every side. From the early date of 1850, church services at the Breadalbane Baptist church were wholly in English.

Gaelic had its last stand in the north-west corner of the county, in the area around Dunvegan. At the Dunvegan Presbyterian church, one of the services each Sunday was in Gaelic till 1932. Then for the next two years, one Gaelic service a month was held. Finally, in 1934 regular Gaelic services were discontinued.

In November 1971 a Gaelic scholar, the Rev. John McKechnie, came to Dunvegan church as a minister and on very special occasions he would preach a Gaelic sermon. The last such was on 6 August 1972, and the authors are the proud possessors of a tape of that service. It is unlikely that there will ever be another such in Glengarry.

It is unlikely that one could assemble as many as half a dozen people in Glengarry today who could understand or carry on a conversation in Gaelic. However, many Glengarrians can remember hearing their elders speaking in Gaelic. For a long time a few Gaelic words, without English equivalents or more expressive than their English equivalents, continued to be used in Glengarry English speech, but even these have all but disappeared in the last few years.

During all the years in which Gaelic was giving way to English, many painful efforts must have been made by individuals to learn the new language. Many unfortunate people must have felt bewildered, frustrated and on occasion, isolated because their English was poor. According to one writer: ''As an example of heroic efforts at English, on the eve of a holiday a boy said 'no scush a morrow.' The experience of another boy was 'me see dhe bear, dhe bear see me, me make dhe sgriach, dhe bear made dhe sgriach crosgrach a craobh hemlock.'' These boys would in time improve their English, but for the elderly, inadequate English was merely another trouble of life to tolerate. A 92-year Glengarry woman was interviewed for the Montreal *Witness* in 1894: ''She speaks some English, and understands a good deal, but in the presence of strangers, would venture nothing but the Gaelic, her daughter and granddaughter interpreting for her.''

For those who knew no English at all, Glengarry long remained a place where they could hear and use the dear and good old language. A newspaper item of 1890 stated: ''A curious incident was noticed on the Canada Atlantic morning train at Ottawa. A Scotch lady, 78 years old, who has lived all her life in Canada, but never acquired a word of any language but Gaelic, was being taken to Alexandria to make her confession, there being no priest who spoke Gaelic nearer Ottawa. She returned to Ottawa in the evening.''

In the search for evidence of the extent and strength of the Gaelic language in nineteenth-century Glengarry, one field where enquiry seems most likely to be productive is politics. From Confederation onwards, a great deal more evidence exists about politics than about almost any other Glengarry activity. At the same time, one might expect that politicians, tireless in wooing the public, would make the most of any acquaintance they or their entourage had of the people's language.

Surprisingly, however, Gaelic seems to have played only a minor part in the potitical life of this period. Such references as can be found to its use are pretty small chaff. Speakers at political rallies sometimes greeted the crowd briefly in Gaelic. In 1887 Donald Macmaster issued an election manifesto in English and Gaelic. It was during the campaign of this year that the Toronto *Mail* commented with kindly satire: ''It appears by a Gaelic article in THE GLENGARRIAN that Maighster MachMaighster is a candidate in the county of Glenngaraidh for the representation of the constituency in Parlamaid.'' In 1900, Big Rory McLennan, facing a difficult contest, asked the provincial archivist, a noted Gaelic scholar, to lend him a helping hand by coming to Glengarry to speak in Gaelic. Gaelic songs, of course, were as much a part of political rallies, victory celebrations, and other political entertainments as they were of any other Scottish functions of the day. Dunvegan celebrated James Rayside's election to the Legislative Assembly in 1882 with speeches and Gaelic songs till 4 a.m. and a bonfire which was kept burning for three days.

An involvement of Gaelic in public affairs is found in the tumultuous Kenyon Town Hall meeting of December 1881 in which the Hon. D.A. Macdonald was abused by a mob angry over the supposed misuse of the railway bonuses. When D.A. attempted to speak, he was greeted with insults in English and Gaelic, hisses, yells, cat-calls, bahs, imitations of cork-drawing (in allusion to the Corkscrew Brigade episode), "and a perfect pandemonium of sounds, above all of which were to be heard the droning notes of a Gaelic song." The refrain of this song, "which seemed to contain some allusion which fitted the circumstances, was taken up by the crowd, and ere long was shouted out with more force than harmony by several hundred pairs of strong Highland lungs." A "burly farmer" shouted in Gaelic to one of D.A.'s political opponents, " 'You let us alone; you have had your say at him, and now we're going to take him in hand.' This sally provoked roars of laughter."

In connection with the involvement of Gaelic in politics, it is interesting to ask how many of the Glengarry M.P.'s spoke Gaelic. All of the six M.P.'s who sat for the Glengarry constituency between 1867 and 1900 had Highland Scottish names except Purcell, and his mother was a Grant from Argyleshire, but the present authors have found no serious evidence to indicate that any of these M.P.'s were Gaelic speakers. Obviously, negative evidence is always dangerous, but one suspects that in this particular matter it is practically conclusive. If a political candidate could speak a language as dear to the people as Gaelic is said to have been, would we really be left in doubt about whether he could or could not?

By contrast, there is ample evidence that Senator McMillan was fluent in Gaelic. (He is also said to have composed a number of Gaelic songs). Of the six M.P.'s, it should be mentioned that no less than five came from the south of the county, where Gaelic declined fastest; only McNab of Breadalbane came, like Senator McMillan, from the north.

For the M.L.A.'s from Confederation to 1900, the biographical information we have at hand is too small to make a similar scrutiny possibly, but we have not chanced upon any reference to any of them knowing Gaelic.

Why did Gaelic decline and disappear in Glengarry? We hesitate to answer this question, so obvious does the necessity of the result appear. In an English-speaking continent, the Gaelic of Glengarry was like an ice-cube melting in the August sun. There can, nevertheless, be detected several circumstances that aided the process, or increased the speed at which it took place. One of these was the position of English as the sole language of the schools in which the Gaelic-speaking Glengarrians educated their children. Nor was Gaelic merely neglected; it was sometimes vigorously reproved. A perceptive writer records that in the northern townships, "Gaelic was forbidden in school: if a scholar heard another boy speak it he would hand him the 'testra' (a round bit of wood) which meant that he must go to the teacher and be punished." The awareness that the more eminent people in the county knew English must have lent it appeal among those who desired the best for themselves or their families. By the final third of the nineteenth century, emigration to the United States had become standard for young Glengarrians, but in that country English was essential and Gaelic of no use at all. Finally, though it is hard to be certain in view of the probable scarcity of reading matter in nineteenth-century Glengarry, Gaelic may have been weakened by not being more fully represented in the written word and being therefore at a loss compared with the torrent of printed material available in English in Canada.

While Gaelic was still a living language in Glengarry, it had a flourishing popular literature there. Glengarry Gaelic speakers composed many songs and poems in Gaelic. Some of these have been preserved in manuscript or by being printed in newspapers or elsewhere, but many or perhaps virtually all have perished. With these there vanished many of the old stories which, it is said, were most effectively told in the old language.

While Gaelic was going out, French as well as English was coming in. An article in 1861 about the Lochiel Presbyterians said that "It is not a little amusing to strangers, traversing the junction of the French and Highland settlements in Glengarry, to note that the polite *Canadien* rattles out French and Gaelic with wonderful volubility, but is an entire stranger to the English tongue." A writer of 1884, looking back to a visit to Laggan at some undefined date, recalled the surprise she felt "when hearing a little child conversing fluently in English, French and Gaelic, and with equal facility."

About this time, we find some Glengarrians who were trilingual, that is to say they were fluent in all three of English, French and Gaelic. These included Archbishop Gauthier and his brother J.N. Gauthier, who was a farmer near Alexandria, Vicar General George Corbet of the Diocese of Alexandria, and Father Alexander Macdonell, the first bishop of Alexandria.

# Chapter IX
# Roads

Roads in Glengarry lead to someplace from somewhere for a reason. Just as there was no need for a highway like 401 in the days of the oxcart, neither will blazed trails through bush and swamp serve the people of today. The early settler for a variety of reasons was almost totally self-sufficient and he made or grew almost everything he needed for himself and his family, and as a consequence, his need for a road was limited. As his needs grew, so grew his need for roads. At first these needs could be served by a pedlar with a pack on his back, and a homemade toboggan could take his scanty spare produce to Lancaster or Summerstown on snow or river ice, or a sack of grain could be, and often was, carried on his back to the nearest mill, or in summer, a canoe would serve. Glengarry's first settlers all lived close to rivers and streams which had a much larger and steadier flow than they do today and in fact were natural highways.

One thing that influenced Glengarry's earliest roads and still has a bearing today is the fact that the county is on the direct route from Montreal to Toronto, which ensured that at all seasons of the year, people would be going to and fro across the Front. In the days of the French regime a mail courier passed through regularly and this continued when the British took over. People always have to go where the government is and governments attract businesses of all sorts. So it was inevitable that there would be a road across Glengarry as soon as there was a road anywhere in Ontario.

However, the form this road would take depended on both the land at the Front of Glengarry and the water beside it. Lancaster Township and the eastern half of Charlottenburgh are very swampy along their front and several large creeks and a sizeable river empty into Lake St. Francis. On the other hand, the water in front of Glengarry offered an easy passage by water from Coteau to Cornwall. In the winter the ice on Lake St. Francis provided a safe and convenient highway made by nature. So true is this, that there are people still living today who can recall regular steamer service at the Lancaster wharf and it is only sixty years (July 1918) since the "Chaffee," the last river steamer to call at Lancaster, burned at the wharf there.

As might be expected under such circumstances the road across Glengarry's Front remained a fair-weather road until the automobile age insisted on a through road, with no detours, and passage at all seasons.

From south to north Glengarry's terrain also presented problems for those who needed roads. The county is a succession of high stony ridges between swamps, some of them a mile or more in width. Some of these swamps had a small river in them that had to be bridged. Not all places where road allowances crossed these swamps and rivers were suitable for bridges or causeways. The problem of north-south roads in Glengarry is still not entirely solved in 1978. As we write this, word comes of a small bridge over the Raisin collapsing, east of St. Andrews. Every few years newer and larger bridges have to be installed over the Raisin, the Beaudette, the De Lisle, the Rigaud, the Scotch River, and their various tributary streams. Even today one cannot drive the full length of the county at its western border nor can one drive directly from Summerstown to Dunvegan. East of Highway 34 is almost as bad; the roads twist and turn and seek a compromise route between a straight line and what is practical.

A glance at a good map will show us that very few township roads, either concession or side roads, run the full

284

depth or the full width of any of the four townships. Each road has zigzags in it, either to compensate for surveying errors, or to avoid some particularly difficult piece of terrain.

The stage coach. This vehicle was basically a heavy duty wagon with a box suspended on it into which the passengers were packed, hopefully tightly enough so that they "wouldn't rattle." Luggage was piled and tied on the boot at the rear. The top was shared by outside passengers who paid a lower fare than those inside and the baggage. Four horses changed at about 15 mile intervals were necessary and even then on long steep hills and in swamps the male passengers had to get out and walk and sometimes even push.

Here let us say a word about surveying errors in Glengarry's roads. It has been said that the side roads zigzag to allow for the curvature of the earth, which gets smaller as one goes north. No part of Glengarry was surveyed originally under astronomic control (cadastral system). People who know how Western Canada was surveyed, with periodic offsets to compensate for degrees of longitude getting smaller, often think they see the same thing in Glengarry. But if they observe closely, they will find, if they follow any road from south to north, that it is as apt to jog east as jog west. In country surveyed under cadastral control all the offsets in any given road are always in the same direction and much farther apart than they are in Glengarry.

Glengarry was surveyed by many different people over a period of thirty years. All used the prismatic compass and Guenther's chain—the compass for direction and the chain of 66 feet for length. The early surveys in particular were hurriedly run under adverse conditions and the distance between sideroads varied on each concession, sometimes by a very few feet, sometimes by several hundred feet.

There is a theoretical grid in the layout of Glengarry's concession and side roads, dating back to Patrick McNiff's original survey in the south in 1784. Each farm lot was 1¼ miles long and a quarter of a mile wide. A side road was allowed for about every seven lots and there was a road allowance between every concession. Some of these roads are open, some are not. Some have been opened and closed again. Glengarry's concession and side roads are an interesting compromise between what is ideal and what is practical. Each township is nine concessions deep, even Charlottenburgh at the east side (the west side of Charlottenburgh has a little extra because of the bulge between the western boundary and Fraser's point, and this is taken up by a gore between the third front and the south branch, in which we have a couple of extra roads which we refer to as "the street" and the Gore Road).

Theoretically, all our concession roads are at the south end or the north end of every pair of lots and the road allowance between them is not open. Thus we would expect to find farm buildings only on the north side of the first concession road, and on both sides of the third and fifth concession roads, with no road between the third and fifth, and so on to the rear of the township. If this were so, each township would have a first concession road, a third concession road, a fifth concession road, a seventh concession road, and a ninth concession road. Once again, this is a rule that is broken many times. For a variety of reasons, mostly because of difficult terrain, it has been necessary in some cases to open part of the usually unopened head line roads and these roads are usually numbered by the concession to the south of them with the prefix "little." Glengarry has a fair number of "Little Seconds," "Little Thirds," "Little Sevenths" and so on. These are legal roads and usually more or less where the surveyors said they should be. Instances are not unknown, however, where the concession road or part of it, either the main one or the "Little One," have been displaced either north or south to avoid a swamp or a river.

Another type of road, very peculiar to Charlottenburgh, is "The River Road." To understand these it is necessary to remember that the very first surveys began at the St. Lawrence river on the west side of M. de Longeuil's Seigneury, at a point just west of the mouth of the river Beaudette. Patrick McNiff measured off 38 lots and this brought him to a natural landmark, the mouth of the Raisin River. Here he started a new township, which he called Township No. 1, after calling the one next the Quebec border "the Lake Township."

Township No. 1 presented him with a challenge. A sizeable river, the Raisin, flowed diagonally across the land he was to lay out for Township No. 1 and a few miles up stream the Raisin branched — happily the branch ran roughly parallel to the St. Lawrence.

McNiff solved his problem very pragmatically. He marked off lots west of the mouth of the Raisin and when one of these lots became a mile and a quarter long — about half way between Williamstown and Lancaster — he continued up the south side of the Raisin numbering lots as he went until he got to the east boundary of the Indian Lands which he (or some other surveyor) had run earlier in the spring of 1784, and there at the west side of lot 26, he crossed the river, started with lot 27 and came back down the north side of the Raisin numbering as he came to lot No. 60. We do not know why he stopped at number 60 as there are still two lots before he got to the eastern boundary of the township. These go by letters "K" and "L", "L" being the boundary lot.

At a later date when "Glengarry away from the rivers" was laid out in farm lots, a new numbering system was put into use at the east side of Charlottenburgh, facing Lancaster. The first concession north of the Raisin continued to be 1NRR, the one north of that the second and so on north. The seventh is the first concession to run across the whole township. As a consequence Charlottenburgh has a second concession front and a second concession facing Lancaster. It also has two third concessions — a third front and a third F.L. McNiff also laid out lots along the south branch of the Raisin. Then he laid out two concessions at the front of the township. So here we have the explanation of the strange nomenclature for some of Charlottenburgh's concessions — 1SRR means first concession south of the Raisin River and 1SSR means the same thing, first concession south side of the Raisin. We have the same type of name on the north side of the Raisin but only for one concession. On the south side today, we have 1, 2, and 3SRR, but 2 and 3 were laid out later. McNiff only laid out lots that were within a mile and a quarter of a water route.

We hope this explains the concession symbols that so many people ask about and also explains why the lots in 1NRR number from west to east, while all the other concessions in Glengarry number from east to west. McNiff just continued the numbering on the north side of the Raisin that he had started on the south. The turning point is just west of Martintown and east of Indian Lands.

These lots laid out along the Raisin and its south branch were accessible by water and the earliest houses were built at the ends of the farms nearest the water. In the course of a very few years trails were cleared along the river banks and in the course of time became accepted roads. The South Branch Road leads west from Williamstown along the south branch of the Raisin, the North Branch leads west from Martintown along the north branch of the Raisin.

"The River Road" runs from Lancaster to Martintown. Originally it left what is now Highway 34, just south of where the railroad tracks now are in Lancaster, and followed the river to Williamstown. The section from Lancaster to just east of Finney's Bridge was moved north to its present position in the early years of this century, an event we will note in due course. From Williamstown the road followed the north bank of the river almost to Martintown. It still exists as far as McGillivray's Bridge and can be traced as far west as 31-1NRR. It could have gone all the way to Martintown on 28-1RR. Well within living memory a barn still stood about a mile east of Martintown down near the river — part of a set of buildings that stood by this now non-existent road. One of the grandfathers of one of the authors of this book was born in a log house next door to this barn. The hearthstone of this old house now serves as a front door step at the house on 29-1NRR.

On the south side of the Raisin, the river road is open and in use today all the way from Martintown to Williamstown. From Glendale, just south of Williamstown, this river road can be followed to within a mile of Lancaster when it suddenly turns south to the Front.

The King's Road (west of Martintown it is called the Line Road — the road the telegraph and telephone lines ran along) in Lancaster and Charlottenburgh townships is another very early pioneer road that developed along with the county. In all probability a trail existed where the King's Road runs, long before white men saw what today is Glengarry.

It follows the first continuous ridge of high land north of the St. Lawrence from Coteau to well west of St. Andrews, where it divides and is out of our sphere of interest besides. Indian lore "experts" have traced this trail from the Glengarry border to the Ottawa, and certainly the east end of it strikes the St. Lawrence at the foot of Lake St. Francis, a logical place for an Indian canoe to safely cross. However, we will not plead the case for the King's Road beginning as an Indian Trail. Its existence as a white man's trail began very soon after Glengarry's first settlers arrived in 1784.

The second wave of settlement consisted of Highland Scots under the leadership of their priest, Father Alexander

Macdonell (Scotus) and they came up the river St. Lawrence in 1786. The probability is that they came up Sutherland's Creek from Lake St. Francis. Certainly they settled on the ridge of high land north of the swamp in which Sutherland's Creek rises. Here on the ridge they built their log cabins and their log church. At first the nearest grist mill was at Coteau and no doubt many a small sack of grain was carried on men's shoulders, along what at first would be only a blazed trail, from St. Raphaels to Coteau. In the next 15 years mills were built at Williamstown and Martintown, but getting to Williamstown involved passing through a long swamp—but of the road from St. Raphaels to Williamstown more hereafter.

Horse and Buggy. Buggies came in as many styles as cars of today and the style used very often reflected the owner's tastes and requirements. The one shown is a "utility" model, suitable for the "old folks" to go to town in to do the shopping and with ample space behind the seat for a couple of bags of flour or something like that. A young fellow would not go courting in this model, nor would his best girl ride with him if he did.

The settlers at St. Raphaels, the first settlers in Glengarry away from a river highway, with their necessary travel to church and mill, pioneered the King's Road as a white man's road. Government action on several different levels, in

290

the 190 years it has been in use, combined with an obvious need has constantly improved the King's Road and it still runs from St. Andrews to Coteau. Though far from straight, it is continuous across Glengarry and good paved roads lead into it at both ends which makes it unique among our county roads. For almost its entire length it is not on a road allowance that was surveyed as part of the county road grid originally. Only at its far east end does it coincide with such a road allowance.

Horse and cutter. Cutter styles too reflected their owner's tastes and as a consequence came in many models and styles. The style of cutter was judged by the curve of its body and dashboard and the height of body off the ground. The higher up and the more curves, the more fashionable the young spark who drove it. This young man's cutter tells the world, "I like to have fun but I'm really a solid citizen".

The other two roads that cross Glengarry and are awfully handy, are Provincial Highways 401 and 417. Both appeared in the last twenty years; both cross Glengarry simply because it is there, part of the distance 401 covers between the Quebec border and Windsor, and part of the distance 417 covers between Ottawa and Montreal. No part of them is part of Glengarry's original road system, though both have caused changes in Glengarry's road system by cutting off some roads (and parts of some farms) making service roads necessary. However, Glengarry has been given three accesses to 417 and four to 401, so from a traffic point of view they have been a benefit to Glengarry. Some land owners along their routes were not so happy when their land was divided by a four-lane highway. As we write this, it seems quite possible that one day Provincial Highway 417 will be Glengarry's north boundary. Discussions have taken place between the Glengarry townships affected and the Prescott townships affected about trading the small parts of Glengarry that are north of 417 for the small parts of Prescott that are south of it.

So much for the bird's eye picture of Glengarry's roads. Perhaps the detail will be of interest.

Glengarry's road building falls naturally into several stages which we will consider separately. The first stage, which for convenience' sake we will call the early pioneer stage, took our roads very little past the blazed trail stage, if any. No doubt some essential bridges were built and let it not be thought that bulldozers and cranes are essential for bridge construction. Half a dozen men with an axe and shovel apiece and with a supply of trees close at hand can bridge a stream or river whose width is less than the tallest trees available, in a matter of hours. Those of us whose occupations have taken us to the frontiers of civilization can vouch for that. Suitable trees are cut and manhandled into position across the river; other logs are laid crosswise on them for a platform and a bit of shovel work on the approaches is all it takes to make a serviceable bridge. Remember, in the early pioneer stage they did not have 50 ton loads to build for. Given a rope and pulley six men can put bridge timber into position that will carry a weight of tons. Given horse or ox power it is easier yet. Nor were the early pioneers stopped by a river that was too wide for the timber available. With no trouble at all they would construct a box-like affair of logs in the shallow water at the river's edge, put a log bottom in it and float it out to the centre of the river. Then they would fill it with stones. As it sank they would add rounds of timber, working from rafts if need be. Eventually the crib, as such a structure is known, would settle on the river bottom and logs and stones would be added until it was high enough to suit the site chosen on the banks, and it became a centre pier for bridge timber. Glengarry had lots of timber and stones and its settlers rapidly got acquainted with the axe.

So they could and did build bridges of logs two and three spans long. True, many of them would float away in the spring, but they were easily replaced. If they stayed in place for a few years the part of the stringers buried in the earth on the river bank rotted and replacement became necessary. This gave rise to the building of piers at the river banks to keep the ends of the stringers dry and ventilated. The first piers were simply big rocks buried in the ground to support the stringer. Gradually the piers became more and more elaborate. First of all they were built up of logs from below water level, then of square timber, then of masonry and finally of concrete with a mesh of steel rods buried in it. The early pioneer stage did not go beyond the log pier stage.

Perhaps a worse problem than bridges over well defined rivers and streams, to the early pioneer road builders, was swamps and marshes. They arranged the roads they used so as to miss, if at all possible, those that were hundreds of yards long, even if it meant adding miles to the route. No matter how roads were arranged some marshes and swamps had to be crossed. For instance, there is no way of bypassing the valleys of the Beaudette and the De Lisle in the full width of Glengarry, nor the extensive swamps where they rise. The Garry and its source lake, Loch Garry, and the swamps that feed Loch Garry were another barrier in Charlottenburgh and Kenyon. There were similar problems along most of the Front and even in places on the King's Road.

To build a passable causeway across these swamps the early pioneers resorted to "corduroy." Corduroy as applied to road-making was a series of logs placed side by side across the width of the road and as far along the road as was needed, sometimes for hundreds of yards. In effect they built a raft across this type of ground that as they said "was too thin to plough and too thick to drink."

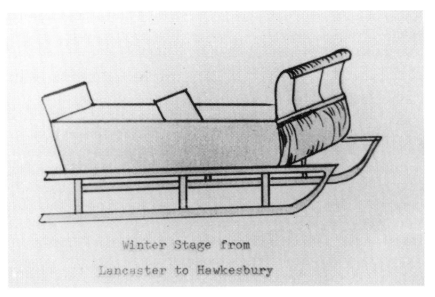

Winter Stage from
Lancaster to Hawkesbury

This drawing from the Glengarry Historical Society's Fifth Annual Volume (1965-1966) expresses better than a photograph the idea behind such vehicles which were simple, strong, low to the ground, and therefore hard to upset. Sooner or later all vehicles that ran on snow upset, so they were never built with a roof or cover. Every mailman who met the trains until the roads were plowed after World War II in winter drove a sleigh something like this one.

Corduroy roads were difficult to walk on and real bone-shakers to drive a wagon over; horses got their legs caught in cracks between the logs, and the corduroy itself rotted or became water-logged and sank. Repairs consisted of putting another layer of logs on top of those already there. The old-timers used to say that after 50 years of corduroying you were really driving on top of a wood pile. But it was the only answer until modern machinery made adequate drainage possible. Even today, as one drives on Glengarry's gravel roads, one often sees splinters of timber cut off by the grader blade. There are still wood piles under some parts of our roads.

The contracting company that builds roads is a phenomenon of the last seventy years. Prior to that, most roads were a "do it yourself" proposition. In some few instances contracts were let by government to open roads, a few of which we will note as we go along. However, for the most part our Glengarry roads were opened in the first instance by the people themselves who lived in the area where the road was needed. The system used was, and still is, referred to as Statute Labour.

As Statute Labour only vanished from our midst within living memory, we must explain something about it. The first Statute Labour Act that affected Glengarry, or might have, was passed by the Legislature in 1789, two years before Upper Canada was formed. Upper Canada continued the system, the control of which was in the hands of the districts and then the counties, until control was given to the townships in the late 1860's. This we will note later on.

No matter who controlled it, the system operated much the same. The controlling body appointed Road Commissioners, two or three to a county, and they in turn appointed pathmasters who were in actual charge of the road work in each locality. The commissioners determined what had to be done in the light of need and the available work force.

Every able-bodied male between 16 and 60 was liable to statute labour but the brunt of the burden fell on the landowners. Originally the formula was given in pounds, but maybe it is easier to understand in dollars, and the amount of work to be done by each landowner depended on the assessed value of his property:

| all under $200 | -2 days' work |
| $200 - $400 | -3 days' work |
| $400 - $600 | -4 days' work |

and so on up to $400 assessment when every $800 of extra assessment called for one day's work. (As usual the wealthy man got a break). The details of the formula varied from time to time but on an average a man and team counted for two men, and a man, team and wagon or scraper counted for two and a half days.

So it can be seen that a sizeable work force could be assembled, and their hearts were in their work as they were working on roads they needed for their own use.

We are told that the government placed canoes and row boats on the Raisin and the St. Lawrence for the use of the Loyalists. Likely the settlers soon made trails from one clearing to another but the first word of roads that we have comes in 1787 when the settlers of the Eastern District petitioned for a road to be opened between Montreal and Kingston. There is no record of any response to their petition, nor is it probable that there was any. In 1802, the Court of Quarter Session in the Eastern District ordered roads to be opened. This seems to have been a follow-up on a directive that the magistrates meeting as the Court of Quarter Sessions at Osnabruck had made at the first such meeting in the Eastern District in 1789. The only record of any action on this directive is the building of a bridge on the Raisin at Martintown by Malcolm McMartin, the mill owner there. Likely Malcolm was more concerned with providing access to his mill on the west bank of the Raisin for the St. Raphaels settlers, than he was in complying with the magistrates' order. It is very likely there was a bridge at Williamstown prior to the one at Martintown, but no record of it exists.

In 1805 Quarter Sessions ordered a road to be opened from Sir John Johnson's mill at Williamstown to the Lower Canada border. This led to the opening of the Johnson Road north from Williamstown, through land owned by Sir John, to the King's Road. Unfortunately no record exists to tell us whether this road system was usable the year around or only in winter and the dry part of the summer, but a start had been made.

We would like to know the details of this road. How many yards of corduroy? What did the bridge on the De Lisle look like? Did the builders dig out all the stumps and stones? Did they dig out any? We just do not know. And who presided at the official opening, if there was one?

When people travel they need food and lodging. No doubt many travellers in this early pioneer period carried their own food and slept under a tree or else stopped at a convenient cabin for the night. But an inn-keeping business was taking shape in Glengarry even at this early period. The records are not good and almost certainly far from complete, but in 1784 John Curry built an inn at the border of the Lake Township and M. de Longeuil's Seigneury. The family owned this inn until it was sold to the Bourbonnais family in 1885. The building still exists and in 1975 is owned by Anne Levac and Lisé Sauvé.

In 1792 Archie Stuart opened an inn at Lancaster. It too is still standing and has served the public under a variety of names—the latest being "The Moose Head Inn." John Cameron "The Wise" died at Summerstown on 10 September 1803, and in his will he describes himself as an innkeeper. Local legend tells us that by 1800 there was an inn at Haniman's Corner, today the cross roads at the north end of Apple Hill. From whence would an inn at that spot draw its custom in 1800? Yet it is possible—the fame of its home brew might have drawn thirsty souls for miles from the lonely cabins in the clearings in Charlottenburgh, Roxborough, and Kenyon.

The roads at the end of the early pioneer period in Glengarry probably seldom, if ever, were used by wheeled vehicles. The usual draft animal was the ox and it was used to drag loads. A stoneboat or jumper type of thing would be used in summer and sleighs in winter, with most heavy hauling done on the snow and ice in winter. The horse first appears as an animal to ride or to carry a pack saddle. The settlers found oxen to be by far the best animals for stump and stone pulling. They were not as mettlesome as horses, could find their own fodder by browsing most of the year, and as a by-product provided milk and meat.

The only road of which we have any written proof in Glengarry in 1805 was the road from Johnson's Mill at Williamstown via the Johnson Road — King's Road to Coteau. Perhaps a trail existed along the front; at any rate, in 1806 Quarter Sessions ordered a road opened along the St. Lawrence from 29-1 Cornwall to the Province Line.

Opening a road meant exactly that. A surveyor would call it "Opening a vista." The trees would be cut along a right-of-way but the right-of-way was not necessarily cleared of stumps, nor would any attempt be made at grading. Making a road along the Front of Glengarry was not a matter of a few weeks work in one year. It is not until 1812 that we hear of a bridge being built over the Raisin at Lancaster. No doubt the War of 1812 put some pressure on the local authorities to get cracking. At any rate, when the bridge was built, a blockhouse was built to defend it. This blockhouse stood south and east of the bridge and seems never to have had a formal name. It comes into our history as "Fort Needless," probably because it never had to fulfil its defense function.

That the road along the Front was not finished in 1806 and the builders had problems we can take for granted because in 1808 the Upper Canada government sent its "man for all seasons," the local schoolmaster John Strachan, along the Front to observe and report if it were practical to make an all-weather road there. Strachan reported that such a road was feasible, but as we have seen it took another four years and the threat of war before the Raisin was bridged.

By way of corroboration of the time it took to build roads in those days we have a record of the road between Cornwall and St. Andrews. Jeremiah McCarthy was ordered to survey it in 1808 and the road was opened in 1809. This road was only about four miles long and required no large bridge or extensive corduroying, yet it required two seasons before it was declared to be open.

The War of 1812 made it necessary to get military supplies and naval stores in large quantities up the St. Lawrence from Montreal to Kingston, the main British naval base on the Great Lakes. Most of this freight went up by water but there were a few incidents of the Americans interfering with the freight convoys on the St. Lawrence and there was constant fear that the Americans could and would effectively cut off the St. Lawrence route. In 1813 the government appointed a commission composed of Father Alexander Macdonell (later Bishop), Alexander McMillan, and Allan McDonell, and their task was to open a road between Upper and Lower Canada. This sounds much like the task that was started in 1805 when Quarter Sessions ordered a road opened from Johnson's Mill to Lower Canada. This commission was given £400 to get on with the job and we may assume the money was well spent as in 1814 Barnabas Dickinson established a line of stage coaches from Montreal to the head of the St. Lawrence rapids at Prescott. A fair amount of Dickinson's income came from his contract with the imperial government to carry the mail, but passengers were carried too. Pringle describes such a trip: ''A journey by stage wagon from Cornwall to Montreal in April or November would take twenty-four hours of steady ploughing through the mud, varied occasionally by the wagon sticking fast in a mud-hole, and the passengers being obliged to help the driver in prying it out with fence rails.'' Covered sleighs were used in winter, and in spring and fall strong wagons without covers, built to stand bad roads and deep mud. In summer the trip was very enjoyable. Travellers either went past Glengarry on a boat on Lake St. Francis or took a stage coach — a strongly built closed vehicle, the carriage part of it adapted to go through rough roads. Summer travelling time from Cornwall to Montreal was fifteen to sixteen hours. So speed over the road varied from about three to five miles an hour, depending on the season.

That Dickinson was fighting an uphill battle with the roads west from Montreal we can judge not only by Pringle's account but also by a note from 1820 that declares the road linking Montreal and Kingston is impassable most of the year. No details exist as to whether this applies only to the Front road or the King's Road as well. However, we know the King's Road was used fairly extensively at this time as inns at St. Raphaels, Williamstown, and Martintown date to the period of Dickinson's stage coach line.

The "Red House" at St. Raphaels was built in 1802. It became a stage coach inn (date not stated) and continued as an inn or hotel until 1914 when it became a store. It burned in 1952. Thomas Gray was a well established innkeeper at Martintown in 1823, as was Ronald McDonald at Williamstown.

Up until now we have had nothing to say about north-south roads in Glengarry, because there has been little to say. We know that from the very beginning of settlement in Glengarry, Lancaster was the entrepôt—our port town if you will—with Summerstown as a second, though less important one. We hear of the Rev. John Bethune using a row boat to cover his preaching circuit—Martintown, Williamstown, Lancaster, Summerstown, Cornwall—in the early years of his ministry in Glengarry. This may not have been due entirely to the lack of roads, particularly from 1805 until his death in 1815, but would also have been a convenient way to visit his parishioners who we must remember all had built their houses along the Raisin and the St. Lawrence. We can safely assume that Charlottenburgh's "river roads" were passable on foot or horseback by 1815, even though we know of no concerted effort to open them.

By 1815 most of the north part of Glengarry was settled. Indeed there had been extensive settlement before 1800 and the question arises as to how these people in the north part of Kenyon and Lochiel got what supplies they needed from Lancaster and got their ashes and pork out for sale. Part of the answer is that they did not. They went to Hawkesbury or L'Orignal and later to Vankleek Hill, which were supplied by the Ottawa River, but the pull to the south was strong. The Catholics looked to St. Raphaels for the consolations and sacraments of their religion and Martintown provided the initial Presbyterian impulse that eventually reached back through the Indian Lands to the Beech Church, to Dunvegan and even east to Kirk Hill. People tended to marry in their church community in those early days, and Gaelic we know remained as a family language for years after the first settlement, so ties of religion, family, and language, besides those of business would and did continue to keep the settlers in northern Glengarry coming to the south at all seasons.

The local post office. The pigeon holes, centre rear in the picture, were the most important part of the post office in a general store. A few post offices were in private houses. At the lower right of the pigeon holes can be seen the postmaster's scales. The cupboard at the left housed the necessary forms, stamps, and registered letters. There was no great problem involved in moving a post office as sometimes happened with a change in government.

Readers will remember the descriptions of early Glengarry by James Begg and by the Baptist visitor to Breadalbane, the Rev. F.A. Cox, from which we quoted at length in earlier chapters. To their pages we are indebted for a firsthand account, scanty as it is, of the first north-south road in Glengarry, along with definite dates. The road started at L'Orignal and in 1827 had just had the timber cut on it in north Lochiel. From Vankleek Hill the road led to Glen Elg (Kirk Hill) and thence to the Priest's Mills. From Breadalbane to Glen Elg, the minister needed a guide through the bush in 1835. Evidently, in spite of the corduroy in the

Priest's Mills area, travelling got better and the country more settled as he went south. It is to be noticed too that Begg mentions arriving at St. Raphaels and the Baptist minister passed through Williamstown on his way from the Priest's Mills to Lancaster. Evidently the road was not the road we use today to cover the route from L'Orignal to Lancaster and there seemed to be no choice of routes as late as 1835.

Various sources have helped us to define the route from the St. Lawrence to the Ottawa in those days, and for some years thereafter. This haulage road ran north from the present South Lancaster to just south of the present CNR tracks at Lancaster, then followed a slight ridge of high land to the bank of the Raisin between lots 55 and 56 in the 1st concession NSR of Charlottenburgh from where it followed the present road into Williamstown. Then the route went north on the Johnson Road to the King's Road, then east to St. Raphaels. From St. Raphaels the road went straight north, crossing the Beaudette at Frog Hollow, then north through Grey's swamp to the road that angles to the east to join the road allowance between Kenyon and Lochiel at Sandy Cameron's corner, at the south end of Alexandria. Then up Alexandria's present Main Street to cross the Garry at the bridge site, then northwest through the mill yard to the Registry office corner, then up the middle of lot 38 in the present 2nd of Lochiel (until 1818 the 11th of Lancaster) and then north on the road allowance, crossing the De Lisle at the site of the present highway bridge. Then east on the "14th road" (5th of Lochiel) to McPhee's Inn Corner, now Lochiel, and then straight north through Glen Elg (Kirk Hill) to Cameron's Corner, later McNab and today Lochinvar. Then east a bit on the road allowance between the 17th and 18th of Lancaster (now 8th and 9th of Lochiel) to the road allowance between lots 23 and 24 from where the road ran north to the Glengarry border and then on to Vankleek Hill.

A bridge had been built on the Garry at the Priest's Mills in 1817. Among Father Ewen Macdonald's papers in the Ontario Archives is a receipt from Kenneth McDonald, signed with an "X". The receipt is for £3 currency, being part payment for building a bridge on the river at 38-11 Lancaster, to the west of the mill. So we have good evidence of there being a bridge on the Garry at that date. The reason for teamsters keeping to the high land behind the present high school in Alexandria may not be readily apparent to those who know Highway 34 in 1978. Those who knew the Guaytown corner and "Lalonde's Sink" just north of Alexandria as recently as thirty years ago will remember it was no place to venture into with a load. Quarter Sessions allotted £6 to Duncan McDonell (Greenfield) in 1822 to chop out the part of this road between St. Raphaels and the Garry.

Kenyon's roads in the earliest days were, as they still are, best from east to west, so Kenyon's freight fed east to the main north-south road too. All in all a tenuous and round about way to Glengarry's entrepôt at Lancaster for those in the north-west of Kenyon.

When we come to consider mail routes, we will find them basing themselves on this same main north-south road through Glengarry, with mail going west to Skye and points beyond, from Lochiel post offices.

After the War of 1812 ended, Great Britain as was usual made elaborate preparations to fight it over again. Military surveyors covered the peninsula of Eastern Ontario and their plans and maps were sent across to England and solemnly discussed by the great minds at Whitehall and the various government offices thereabouts. Some of the results of this planning for a war that never happened affected our area. Locks were built to take shipping past the Long Sault of the Ottawa at Grenville, and the Rideau Canal was built. Then Fort Henry was built to protect the Rideau Canal. These schemes provided work for Glengarry men, many of whom worked on the Grenville canals, and a MacMartin from Martintown had a contract on the Rideau Canal. The main effect on Glengarry's roads was a formal survey of a military road from Lancaster to L'Orignal courthouse in 1841. In the north this military road survey came into Glengarry by the old haulage road, described above, and turned south towards McLeod's post office (now Kirk Hill) at the Bullfrog Tavern corner, once Cameron's Corner but in 1978 known as Lochinvar. Then it followed the old haulage road to McPhee's Inn corner (late Quigley's Inn Corner and Lochiel, and for a year, Glen James Post Office), then west to Fassifern, and then followed the present route of Highway 34 to Lancaster, crossing Dundas Street (the King's Road) at MacDonald's Corner (the Brown House). Also, it resulted in at least two maps.

The map we refer to as the William IV map is dated 1830 and shows roads and projected roads, some of which were certainly only dry weather and winter trails. It even shows a snug little harbor at lots 20 and 21, first Front Charlottenburgh, an area the present reeve of Charlottenburgh has declared would make a good seaway harbor. A much more realistic map is that made for General Rottenburg, commander of the British forces. This map shows the roads of the time in heavy black lines, quite often with a comment, as for instance, the road through Dunvegan east and west is noted as "bad spring and fall" and the third of Kenyon is "good road" and the North Branch road is described as "winter road to Bytown." Also the Rottenburg map notes some of the inns and comments on two good bridges; one over the De Lisle at Dalhousie and the other over the Raisin at Martintown. The bridge at Martintown had a bit of history attached to it. At the time of the "big flap" in Cornwall in 1813, when the Americans landed at Hoople's Creek and Crysler's Farm, anybody with any valuables and all the military stores in Cornwall were evacuated and sent off to Coteau via St. Andrews and Martintown. To block pursuit, the bridge at Martintown was torn down and cannon emplaced on the hill east of the river. The effort was not needed as the invading Americans were repulsed but Martintown lost its bridge. However, the military authorities helped with its immediate replacement and even provided plans to rebuild it from. A hundred and fifty years later, Charlie Grant, a skilled Martintown woodworker, working from these same plans, made a model (still in existence) of this bridge. The bridge we are speaking of served until 1861 when an abnormally high spring flood washed away all the bridges on the Raisin.

At that time, two brothers named Sylvester ran the saw mill in Martintown and in addition were master builders. They got the contracts to replace the bridges at Martintown and Williamstown. The result was Glengarry's two covered bridges, the one at Williamstown being only a single lane wide, while the one at Martintown had two lanes. It is getting ahead of our story to go on from here, but so well did the Sylvesters build that these two covered bridges of theirs served until the 1930's and were the last major wooden bridges in Glengarry. The one at Williamstown was replaced by the present steel one in 1934 and the one at Martintown was replaced in 1936.

The Raisin got a complete new set of bridges in 1861. In addition to those at Martintown and Williamstown, new wooden bridges were built at McGillivray's Bridge, at Angus Finney's, and at Lancaster. All of these were replaced by steel structures about the turn of the century, as we will note at the appropriate time.

The Eastern District Council from time to time felt itself able to give "grants in aid" for road building in the townships. In 1831 Charlottenburgh got £65, Lancaster got £32/10, Lochiel got £27/10, and Kenyon got £15. These grants were evidently based on population rather than need. However, roads were improving. In SDG in 1825 there were 12 two-wheeled pleasure gigs, one closed carriage, and 26 light wagons for pleasure driving. By 1835 there were 172 gigs and 37 light pleasure wagons, but no closed carriages.

In 1840 the first buggy with steel springs appeared in Glengarry. Prior to this invention, stage coach bodies had been hung on heavy leather straps and those who travelled by wagon had found they could cushion the jolts on the roads by laying two saplings from end to end of the wagon box and sitting on planks placed across the saplings. This type of seat remained in use as long as the lumber wagon, as it was quite effective and the lumber wagon did not disappear until the 1940's.

Blacksmith shop (D.C. McArthur). These small shops were a familiar part of every community and were expected to be able to make and repair almost anything their community needed. As roads and communications improved, one by one the local smithies were put out of business by competition from mass producers in the cities.

In the winter of 1840 William Weller, the man who operated the line of stages between Montreal and Toronto, had an opportunity to find out how quickly the trip could be made. Lord Sydenham, the Governor General, something of a sportsman himself and in a hurry to get to Montreal from Toronto, asked Weller to see how quickly he could get him to Montreal. The trip was made by sleigh; Weller drove the whole distance himself and changed horses every 15 miles. The trip took 35 hours and 40 minutes—an average speed of 9.318 miles per hour, and involved 23 changes of horses. We can contrast this with Pringle's trip from Cornwall to York (Toronto) by public conveyance in January of 1833. Pringle was 120 hours on the road, 86 of which were actually spent travelling. The elapsed time meant an average speed of little over two miles in an hour and actual travelling time was about three miles per hour. We hear of people walking from Glengary to York in those days— actually it was as quick a way to get there as any.

In 1854, when Rev. John Anderson became the Free Church Minister for the charges of Dalhousie Mills and Lancaster, he writes that though the charges were only 16 miles apart, at certain times of the year it was almost impossible to travel between them, even on foot or horseback. He was talking about travel in the south-east part of Lancaster township and Rottenburg's map of 1850 shows no through roads in that area at all. Dalhousie Mills had a road built to it from north of Green Valley (then called Greenfield's East Corner) in 1829 when Quarter Sessions gave William Roebuck a grant to open the concession road between the 8th and 9th of Lancaster. Roebuck had a saw and grist mill at the Quebec border on the De Lisle. The place was then known as Roebuck's Mills but later changed to Dalhousie Mills. Evidently at high water times, Anderson considered it impossible to cross the Beaudette anywhere in Lancaster Township in 1854.

By 1850 the main routes in Glengarry were fairly well supplied with inns. The Bullfrog Tavern had been operating for about 20 years at Lochinvar, there was a hotel in Alexandria (two by 1853 and five by 1864) and hotels at Loch Garry, Notfield, Dominionville, Dunvegan, and Greenfield's East Corner, and the Wildcat Hotel was functioning east of Glen Gordon. These in addition to the old established ones, supported by newer ones, along the Front and at Williamstown, St. Raphaels, and Martintown.

The secularization of the Clergy Reserves in 1854 made some money available for roads. In England John McAdam had discovered that gravel put on a well drained road formed a hard durable surface with use, and word of his discovery eventually got to the Eastern District of Upper Canada. Where gravel was readily available some was put on our roads but the poor state of the roads prevented it from being hauled far, even if money and help had been available to do it. So most of Glengarry's roads continued to be the natural soil until well into the twentieth century. However, the social forces that demanded better roads were present by 1860. The ox had given way to the horse for road haulage over any distance, and wagon and carriage makers had set up shops in every village in response to the need for moving crops to Lancaster and supplies of all sorts back out to the concessions and the local store keepers. Maps drawn about 1860 show Glengarry's road system to be much as it is today. The big difference was the quality of the roads. They were largely undrained and devoid of gravel. No hills had been cut down and no hollows filled. However, the pioneer phase was over.

Transition period. For many years Glengarrians accepted their bad roads as a necessary evil. In the 1890's farm newspapers and magazines preached the benefits of a "split log drag" for road maintenance. Then came the primitive horse-drawn grader such as is shown here but this one is pulled by a primitive tractor. In 1936 tractor and grader were combined in one unit. By 1948 this grader had become a road maintainer with rubber tires, heated cab, power-operated controls, and special snow plowing equipment. This machine let the townships repair their roads in summer and keep them open in winter.

The period 1860 to 1895 saw little major change in Glengarry's roads either in quality or quantity. Log bridges were replaced by bridges made of sawn timber and planks, and we can judge from road commissioners' reports that maintenance consisted of keeping the roads from getting any worse rather than improving them.

In 1849 the level of Lake St. Francis was raised by a dam at Valleyfield in order to operate the new canal at Beauharnois. This drowned out the old shore road along the Front of Lancaster Township and it was necessary to construct a new one along the new lake shore. By 1876 parts of this road had washed into the lake and in 1876 a new road was built, well inland, which in time became No. 2 Highway, the third road across the Front of Lancaster.

The railway age came to Glengarry with the Grand Trunk in 1855, and made a busy market town out of Lancaster and a lesser one out of Camerontown (Summerstown Station). Camerontown, because of the road layout and the now fast growing town of Cornwall, never was able to compete with Lancaster for volume of business. It remained a local service town, albeit a fairly busy one. With the opening of the Canada Atlantic and Canadian Pacific lines later in the century their stations became potential market towns which drastically cut down the amount of long distance haulage needed. So to this extent railways made expensive road improvements unnecessary. In place of a long haul to Lancaster with a load of pigs, now it was only a matter of taking them to the local railway station. In fact, at this stage and until trucks became common it was customary to drive livestock on their own feet to the local railway station stockyard. Though the railways eventually put up stations at a total of 19 Glengarry towns, they did not prosper evenly and as a consequence the roads into some of them became more important than the roads into others.

The railroads brought a new business to the larger centres — the livery stables. Outsiders who had business in the area came to town by railway and rented a horse and buggy to go about their business. Cattle drovers (buyers) visited each farm regularly. Drummers (salesmen) for wholesale houses came to town and stayed in a hotel and used livery horses to get about into the country to service their accounts. To this era we can trace all the ''Queen's'' and ''Commercial'' hotels in the county. Freight and express delivery became an organized business and the mail system got all shook up. As we said above, social pressures for better roads were increasing. Perhaps a few excerpts from announcements of the day will present the picture:

1857 - Alexandria connected to Lancaster by mail stage which also carries passengers. One way fare is $1.50.

1860 - three hotels in Martintown.

1862 - two hotels at Notfield.

1865 - six hotels in Lancaster, one in North Lancaster, four in Alexandria.

1870 - Glengarry townships assume responsibility for all roads and bridges inside their borders and each passes a statute labour bylaw to maintain them.

1874 - a typical tax bill shows a farmer with 150 acres has 8 days statute labor to do.

1879 - new hotels at Dominionville and Greenfield, and two at Dunvegan.

1882 - Munro and McIntosh establish themselves as carriage makers in Alexandria.

1885 - Ottawa and Commercial hotels operating in Maxville.

1890 - tavern operating at Hector Ross's Corner at junction of King's Road and Summerstown Road.

1892 - business is booming in Alexandria owing to recent arrival of snow. People can get to town now the mud is frozen and snow covers the ruts.

1893 - there is a hitching post in front of every Alexandria store and town council orders them removed as unsightly.

1894 - every village in Glengarry has a livery stable

and some have two. Many are run as part of a hotel's business.

1896 - bicyclists reminded that pedestrians have the right of way when they are on the road.

*Glengarry News* gives drivers of horses advice not to whip their horses when they see a bicycle but to treat them kindly, hold their heads if need be, and they will get used to them.

Many people questioning right of bicyclists to use public roads made for horses and vehicles.

There is an acute need for a street crossing in Alexandria on the west side of Main Street, between the Bridge and the Commercial hotel. The logs with one flat side that are supposed to serve have become lost in the mud. The children going to school, particularly the girls in their long dresses, have to use the picket fences to walk on. They face the fence, holding the tops of the pickets with their hands and place their feet on the 2 x 4 at the bottom through the gaps in the pickets to get past the worst puddles.

In 1898 the Alexandria Bicycle Club offered to tax its members $1 a head to help make Alexandria's streets passable for bicycles if the village would match that amount. No action reported.

Yet something fundamental had happened to people's thinking in Ontario about this time. It is difficult if not impossible to spot the beginning of it and more difficult still to understand why it took place, but suddenly, and almost as quickly as grassfire spreads, a movement for "good roads" spread across Ontario. Local "Good Roads Associations" were formed that recommended standards and methods for building these good roads. In August 1896 several meetings were held in different parts of Glengarry demanding good roads. In 1898 Lancaster township bought a grader and road roller, both horse drawn. Between 1898 and 1908 the township put a special levy on its tax bills to replace all the principal wooden bridges in the townships with iron ones, except the covered wooden bridges at Martintown and Williamstown, and even the United Counties got into the act by building iron bridges over the Beaudette at Green Valley and the Garry at Alexandria, after 1902. Though the beginning of the official Counties Road System was still in the womb of the future, in 1901 the province made $1,000,000 available to the organized counties for road improvements. Thus Glengarry spent its share.

"We will open that road." The province started to plow the snow on Highway 2 in 1926 "within limits." Soon the village blacksmiths and handymen were trying their best to contrive equipment that would keep the roads open between the main towns. Here we have a V plow mounted on the front of a Model T Ford truck. As can be imagined, auxiliary "armstrong" power was often needed with shovels. People in the Maxville area may recognize themselves or their neighbours in this picture.

From end to end of the county a chorus of wails about the state of roads continued, and the townships tried to contract some road building, with results that the editor of the *Glengarry News* commented on, "the same old method, mud from the ditches is piled on the centre of the road." Lochiel township discussed the abolition of Statute Labour in 1901 as a result of the clamour, but the rate payers wished to retain it and did. Lancaster township, however, gave up on Statute

Labour in 1902 and set an example which the other townships would follow, one by one, in the next twenty-five years.

Main Street, Alexandria, about 1900. The main streets in our important villages at this time had much in common. They were composed of the local ground and had no coating of gravel, much less tar or cement. The sidewalks were plank. Alexandria was unique in Glengarry in that it was already a major telephone exchange centre and had its own electric light system which it got in 1896. As a matter of interest the first street drainage in Alexandria was done north of the Garry in 1901, the first gravel was put on Main Street in 1910 and the first bit of granolithic sidewalk was put in front of the present Bank of Nova Scotia in 1900.

In 1902, N. Gilbert, the Superintendent of the Alexandria Carriage works, began driving a "rubber tired buggy." In November, the military road between Alexandria and its station was impassable and the road moved over into the field where the high school now is. That winter, in February, passengers who came into Alexandria station on the morning train, did not get up town to their hotels until evening, in spite of Archie McMillan's vaunted "station bus service." We have a blending of heavy traffic, all horse drawn, with roads and streets that can be impassable at any time of the year, even to horses.

In the next few years valiant piece-meal efforts were made to keep traffic moving. In 1903 we read "there are 20 'dagoes' working in the gravel pit at Maxville." In 1904 we find the Charlottenburgh township council meeting "on the spot" east of Finney's Bridge to decide where to move the River Road so it will not flood every time there is a heavy rain. They moved it to its present site, and the old road is now a pleasant lane. Also in 1904 we read of a certain Duncan McIntyre from Finch, driving east from St. Elmo, whose horse fell into a hole and broke its neck. We also read of another livery stable starting up at Alexandria station and the first automobile in the counties being bought in Cornwall. It was one of the first in Canada, as in 1903 there were only 178 motor vehicles registered in all of Canada.

In 1905 it was found expedient to send mail from Maxville to Apple Hill by train — down on the Canada Atlantic and up on the Canadian Pacific rather than by stage as had been the custom. In 1905, too, we read of a man from Williamstown driving to Lancaster, whose horse fell in a hole. The man tried to help the horse out of the hole and this time the horse fell on him, badly injuring him.

The winter passenger bus.

Perhaps the biggest permanent improvement in the villages in these early years of the century was the laying of "granolithic" sidewalks on some of the main streets. Alexandria built some in 1904, Maxville in 1905, and Lancaster in 1906. The iron bridges for which the special tax levies had been made were steadily going up, but the roads themselves seemed little improved. It was 1910 before Alexandria put the first gravel on its Main Street and 1918 before Martintown got its first gravel.

The horsemen could not get good roads built, the bicycle men could do no better, but in 1910 a different breed appeared — the automobile driver. The farmers had wanted better roads for a hundred years but were not willing to pay extra taxes to get professionals to build them. The businessmen in the towns were no different, if not worse. They wanted their trade to come to them, and in spite of the roads it had to, so they could see no reason to increase taxes to build good roads. The motorist was willing to pay a tax on every gallon of gasoline he bought, if it were used for road improvement and the Ontario government obliged in 1925. The results were spectacular. The number of cars in Canada increased from 5,890 in 1910 to 60,688 in 1915, to 251,945 in 1920, and to 1,060,500 in 1930. It would seem that the people who bought cars could and did talk to their political representatives as action on the roads became highly visible in short order.

In 1913 Ontario formed a Department of Highways. In 1916, SDG set up a Counties Road System, appointed a professional engineer to look after building and maintenance, and took over 340 miles of what had been township roads in the Counties.

In 1918 Ontario passed "the drive on the right" law, and in 1923 started to license drivers. In 1926 the Ontario Department of Highways announced "we will, to a reasonable extent, provide for through traffic on Provincial roads this winter." Snow plowing had begun.

The roads SDG took over in 1916 were much the same ones

they have today except that they included the Military Road which became Provincial Highway No. 34 in 1930 and the 3rd of Kenyon road which became Provincial Highway No. 43, formally on 13 April 1938.

Basically the Counties Road System in Glengarry, as it was planned and developed, consisted of five north and south roads, two on the west side of the county, óne in the centre (which became Provincial Highway 34), and two on the east side; and five east-west roads; though there are a few extra bits and a few gaps, such as the stretch from the King's Road to the 3rd of Kenyon and from Baltic's Corner to Fassifern and from Glen Norman to the north. Provincial Highway 34 provides the west end of County Road #10.

By standards of today, the road building efforts of the SDG Roads Department were not very effective. The bulldozer had yet to be invented (it appeared about 1930), graders were horse drawn, and the self-propelled, self-loading, self-dumping earth mover was even farther in the future. Nor was there much knowledge of suitable hard surfaces for roads. The years from 1916 to 1946 can be said to have been experimental. Hundreds and hundreds of man hours were put in on our roads with picks, shovels, and mud scrapers. Thousands of cubic yards of stone fences were put through stone crushers and crushed stone put on the roads, sometimes with a surface mixture of sand and asphalt, packed down with a steam roller. After a couple of years' use, the surface all broke up into an unbelievable mess of potholes, some of which were unbelievably deep. All our good county roads have been completely rebuilt since World War II and there is much yet to do. Modern methods, engineering, and materials, though costly, have given us a good and constantly improving county road system, some part of which is within a few minutes drive, no matter where one lives in the county.

SDG started in the winter of 1945-1946 to snowplow its roads. The first efforts only made them impassable for both cars and sleighs. To quote from a diary of a man who lived on such a road, "The road became like a canal with high banks on each side; the canal filled in and not even a team and sleigh could stay on top of it. We took to the fields to get to town.''

Nobody was aware then that an old truck unsuited for anything else was not the type of vehicle required to mount a snow plow on. The road machinery builders, after 1946, started to make heavy duty graders that maintained gravel roads in summer and had sufficient power to plow the snow off them in winter. By the mid 1950's all our townships had at least one of these all purpose road maintainers and SDG had several. In addition, SDG used extremely heavy duty trucks that hauled gravel in summer and could push a snow plow at high speed in winter. This meant that by the mid 1950's even the township roads on which school buses ran were plowed about as well as the county roads and the provincial highways. This made consolidated central schools practical and let our rural mail men use their cars to deliver mail the year round.

The bulldozer, the back hoe, the grader, and the skilful use of cement bridges have changed our traffic pattern completely. Cars became popular in the years 1915 to 1930. The motor truck came to each farmer's yard for his milk, his pigs, and his cattle for market. He began to use a truck or his car and trailer to take his grist to town and bring home feed. Little by little, people started to go to the larger centres such as Cornwall for their needs. Good all weather roads not only made this possible but a pleasure. As a result, Glengarry's villages have withered and today's roads serve mostly to take Glengarry's people to and from work and to let professional trucking concerns bring them what they need and take their produce to market.

We have had good all weather roads now for a bit more than twenty-five years. It took a hundred and sixty years to get them, and much hard work and money.

John Fraser (1852-1919), born and raised in the Loch Garry settlement in Kenyon Township. Auditor General of Canada 1905-1919. (At Loch Garry they learned to count pennies.) As we write this, another Glengarrian, J.J. Macdonell, is also Auditor General of Canada.

# Chapter X
# Communications: Post Offices — Telegraph and Telephone

## Post Offices

Glengarry's mail system had its roots in a system that is as old as civilized settlement along the St. Lawrence - Great Lakes Waterway. Before 1759 the French had a more or less regular courier system which connected Quebec City with Cataraqui, Detroit, and even Michilimacinac and Duluth. By means of canoe, dog team, and runners a tenuous line of communication was kept open. After the British took over in 1760, this line of communication remained open and a combination of military couriers and couriers for the fur trading concerns as well as private individuals who happened to be travelling in the right direction, carried what little mail there was.

In 1764, Britain's Deputy Post Master General for North America, Benjamin Franklin, established official British Postal Service in Britain's new Province of Quebec. The main post office was at Quebec City with branch offices at Montreal and Three Rivers. A monthly courier service connected Montreal with New York. A man named Hugh Finlayson was appointed Post Master for the province of Canada.

When the American Revolution broke out in 1775, Finlayson remained loyal to the British Crown and the postal service continued to operate under his direction, though at times service via New York had to be discontinued in favour of ports on Canada's east coast and British ships. During the revolution, Finlayson was given the title of Deputy Post Master

General of the Province of Canada and in 1788 Nova Scotia and New Brunswick were added to the area under his administration.

In 1789 a post office was opened at "Charlottenburgh" (then spelled "Charlottenburg") and in the next twenty years twelve more post offices were opened by the British Imperial Postal Service in Lower Canada and as far west in Upper Canada as Niagara-on-the-Lake. Charlottenburgh's nearest neighbours to the west were Cornwall and Matilda.

Charlottenburgh was thus the first post office in Glengarry. As we will see further on it was the practice to appoint a post office to serve a large area as long as settlement was light, and the settlers had to make local arrangements for getting mail such as neighbours picking it up for each other.

The Quebec Almanac lists this Charlottenburgh post office as being opened in 1789, but unfortunately gives no more details about it. We cannot even be sure where it was. Almost certainly it was at the present South Lancaster, but Summerstown is a possibility. Nor do we know who the post master was officially, though the Dunlop family in the present South Lancaster have a tradition it was to their store that the mail came. It could easily have been so. The Dunlops were on the spot and highly respected and trustworthy citizens.

This Charlottenburgh post office served an area of almost 500 square miles with a population density of about 1 to a square mile, though most people were concentrated along the river front and a few miles inland. So the duties of the Charlottenburgh post master would not have been too onerous, but many old letters survive, simply datelined Charlottenburgh.

Before we go into the details of Glengarry's mail in the 190 years after 1789, it might be appropriate to say a few words about mails at the time when this almost legendary Charlottenburgh Post Office was opened. Many or most people could not read or write; the stamp and envelope were a long way off in the future.

A letter in those days was a sheet of paper. As much as possible was written on it and as often as not, when the page was filled with writing in one direction, the page was given a half turn and the letter continued by writing across the previous writing. Then the page was folded, sealed with wax, addressed, and confided to the postal system. In those days the person receiving the letter paid for its transportation and the charges were heavy by any standard. Considering that cash was practically non-existent, a person had to be moderately wealthy to take delivery of a letter. Four pence ha'penny took a letter (a single sheet) 60 miles; 7 pence took it up to a hundred miles; 11 pence took it up to 300 miles; 2 shillings took it up to 1000 miles, to New York or Halifax, for instance. All the way to England cost 2 shillings, 5 pence ha'penny.

Penny postage was introduced in Britain in 1840 and theoretically was available in Canada. However, in Canada it was compulsory to prepay and stamp mail until the Province of Canada took over its own postal service on 23 April 1851. One of the most sought after stamps is "the three penny beaver" — Canada's first postage stamp. Though designed in Canada by Sandford Fleming, it was printed in Britain.

By 1855 our present Glengarry postal system had taken on the rough outline of what it would be for the next hundred years, that is until the post office department found it more economical to send mail by truck than by the railroads.

However, when Glengarry's Post Office system began to take shape, the railroads were still a few years in the future. Unfortunately the early Canadian Post Office records do not exist. They seem to have been at least partly lost when the parliament buildings at Montreal burned in 1849 and others got lost in the shuffle between capital cities before Ottawa became the capital in 1865.

The earliest complete records we have show us that Glengarry depended on mail service up the St. Lawrence and the Ottawa for its basic service. As early as 1855 (and probably earlier) there was a daily stage service each way between L'Orignal and Lancaster. From this basic north-south route post offices to the east and west were serviced. In the south west of Glengarry there was another service that originated in Cornwall and ran north to old Monkland. From Monkland, and later St. Andrews, a courier ran the mail to Lancaster via Martintown and Williamstown. Another courier ran the mail from Lancaster to Summerstown "on foot or horseback as required."

A convenient time to look at the detail of the early mail system in Glengarry is in the very representative year of 1869, immediately after Confederation. At this time the county was settled and even though the Grand Trunk Railway was in operation along the Front, its coming had not changed the pattern of mail delivery at all. Nor had it made it more regular. Stage coaches had been operating from Montreal to Prescott for 40 years when the Grand Trunk opened for business. That forty years only saw more stops for the mail stage men develop and these can be traced by the dates of the opening of various offices in the county. Thanks to lost records the opening date of some of our earliest post offices cannot be officially established. For instance, the official post office records for St. Raphaels state, "Date of opening: Prior to 1-1-1854. The exact date of opening is not known." This statement is duplicated for most of Glengarry's earlier post offices. Fortunately there are other sources such as the British Imperial Post Office records, business directories Gazeteers, and published reports of the Post Master General which annually list all the business of the Post Offices in Canada since Canada became responsible for its own postal system in 1851. Also there is a monumental work by the late Frank Campbell, called *Canada Post Offices 1755 - 1895*, published in 1972.

Campbell checked and rechecked post office lists of all

sorts and then checked his results with postmarks. Campbell's work has its limitations to be sure. Post Offices could close for a few years and he would not catch them; the only post office closings he notes are those prior to 1895, which was very little help in Glengarry. But Campbell is a wonderful check on independent work and we found when we disagreed with him, it was best to do our work over again. The lists at the end of the present section are, we are sure, as close to the facts as it is possible to come, but one area of possible disagreement still exists. This is the "unofficial" mail drop. It would seem that in the day when it was 15 miles or so to the nearest post office the post master would send mail to a given area with a known reliable citizen and his neighbours would get in the habit of picking up their mail at his place and leaving their letters to post with him. His neighbourhood came to think of his residence as a post office. As it happens, we have been able to check two of these "unofficial post offices" through the memory of persons of advanced age. One of these is the reputed "Clark Avenue" post office located on the South Branch Road at the Kinloch road corner, where the late Benjamin Clark (d.1899) acted as an unofficial post master for his neighbours. Another we have been able to check out is McGillivray Bridge where the late George Macgillivray (d.1912) acted as an unofficial post master for years before an official post office was placed in his house in 1908. It closed in 1913, a few months after his death, one of the casualties of the coming of rural mail delivery, and has the distinction of being the only post office opened in Glengarry in this century.

The post office services increased as time passed. Money orders and registration of mail came in 1855, though only a few larger post offices were designated as money order post offices. Those serving Glengarry in 1869 were *Alexandria Martintown*, and *Cornwall*. That it was not a big business we can judge as in that year Alexandria issued 23 money orders and paid 14. Martintown issued one and paid four. A parcel post system inside the Province of Canada came in 1859 and a post office savings bank was begun in 1868. Rural mail began in Ontario with a route from Hamilton to Ancaster in 1908. Glengarry's rural mail system was put into operation between 1912 and 1919 with most rural routes beginning in 1913, 1914 and 1915. Canada-wide parcel post came in 1914 and C.O.D. was begun in 1922. The first air mail in Canada was flown from Montreal to Toronto in 1918.

As can be seen by the appended list of post offices, by 1908 Glengarry had all the post offices it ever would have and in the next forty years the biggest change was the coming of rural mail and a rather steady if unspectacular improvement in service as more and more use was made of trucks and cars to get mail from the railroads to the sorting counters and into the hands of those to whom it was addressed.

A letter rate of two cents was established in 1898. It was raised to 3¢ during World War I and since then there has been a fairly steady rise to the present 14¢ (17¢ in April 1979).

But to return to our survey of the Glengarry mail system in the year 1869. Prior to 1869 the method of conveyance varied as circumstances demanded; canoe, foot, horseback, river steamer, stage coach, and railway were used at various times. After 1869, in 1882, 1885, 1891, and 1912, new railways played an increasingly large part in bringing mail to the main post offices but the distribution routes inside the county remained almost identical until modified by rural mail and almost completely changed by the mail truck and by township roads that could be covered by a car the year round. This last phase closed a few more post offices, leaving Glengarry with the fourteen it has operating in 1978.

In 1869 the mail came up the north shore of the St. Lawrence via the Grand Trunk Railway which dropped mail bags for Glengarry at Coteau, Lancaster, and Cornwall. Mail for Glengarry that had come via the Ottawa River route was dropped off at L'Orignal. L'Orignal and Lancaster were connected by a daily stage coach each way, which carried the mail under contract and also carried passengers. J. Murray Jr.

had the contract; it was for one year at a time at $860 per year. He could use any type of conveyance he liked, according to his contract, as long as the route was run six times a week in each direction and the route was 41 miles long.

Another basic supply route for Glengarry's mail in 1869 was from Cornwall to Monkland (old Monkland) at 6-1 Roxborough. On this route the contractor was P.D.McIntosh, the distance was 13 miles, and he could go on horseback or with a vehicle. He had to go three times a week and the contract was for 10 months for a total of $116.66. In this year the contract arrangement was changed and St.Andrews became the supply point or terminus of the Martintown route rather than Monkland, hence MacIntosh's ten months contract.

The supply route that served most of Kenyon in 1869 ran from Alexandria to Athol via Loch Garry and Notfield. C.MacGregor had the contract for 11 months and he got $160.41. J.Campbell had the contract for one month and he got $11.58. The route was 20 miles long, had to be covered three times per week and the mode of conveyance is specified as "horseback."

Another route that eventually took mail into the western part of Prescott county was designated as McPhee's Inn Corner to Skye via Laggan. Today we know McPhee's Inn Corner better as Lochiel or Quigley's. The contractor on this 13 mile long route was D.McMillan and he could travel by horseback or vehicle as long as he made three trips a week. For twelve months he received $112.

J.Campbell, who, we noted above, carried the mail from Alexandria to Athol, went on to Plantagenet, a further 16 miles, three times a week. For twelve months of this he received $112, but on this route he could use a vehicle.

From Lochiel post office at McPhee's Inn Corner, H.R. McDonald carried the mail east to Sandfield post office and then across the Quebec border to Mongenais. The trip was 12 miles, he went once a week, by horseback or vehicle as suited, and for this he received $50 per year.

Dalkeith got its mail from Vankleek Hill with the courier, William Robertson, dropping off mail at Breadalbane as he passed, though by 1869 Breadalbane post office was closed. It had closed in 1866 and it reopened again in 1874. Robertson's contract in 1869 was for four years for $275 for the four years. He could travel by horseback or vehicle as suited and he made the trip of 7½ miles on Tuesdays, Thursdays, and Saturdays.

This looked after all the post offices in the northern two townships, now we will have a look at the south.

In 1869 the mail was coming to Lancaster via the Grand Trunk railway, so as we may expect Lancaster was the terminus of a few mail routes.

One of these ran from Lancaster to Summerstown (on the river). The contractor for this route was D.Ross and he could cover the six miles by horseback or vehicle as suited. He had to go three times a week; his contract was for 12 months and for $78.

In 1869 the postal authorities still had an awkward way of getting mail from Lancaster station to the Riviere Raisin post office at South Lancaster. It was part of a route that started in Martintown, passed through Williamstown, picked up mail at Lancaster and then went on to Riviere Raisin. The contractor for this route, twelve miles, was M.McMartin; he could use a vehicle and went six times a week. His contract was for $222 for twelve months. The other end of this route, Martintown to Monkland, 9 miles, was under contract to R.P.MacIntosh. He travelled his route twice a week for $5.83 per month.

J.Murray's mail vehicle going north from Lancaster would find two couriers waiting for it at McDonald's Corner where the King's Road crosses the Military Road (The Brown House). One of these couriers would be A.Leclair who had the contract to take the mail the three miles to North Lancaster post office six times a week by vehicle or horseback. His contract was for $100 for twelve months. The other courier waiting at McDonald's Corner would be Mrs. M. McDonell from St.Raphaels, two miles away. Her contract was for $60 for twelve months and she could travel by horseback or vehicle as suited, six times per week.

The other two post offices in Glengarry in 1869, Glen Nevis and Dalhousie Mills, got their mail as an incidental part of a contract that had Coteau for its terminus and served all the post offices in Quebec along the border with a short side trip into Glengarry to drop off mail at those two offices in north-eastern Lancaster Township.

To an extent not perhaps always realized, the business a post office does reflects the business of all sorts done in a community. In 1869 Glengarry had 19 functioning post offices and the following list contains the name of each of those 19 offices, followed by its gross revenue for 1868:

| Alexandria | $519.41 | St.Raphaels | 70.74 |
|---|---|---|---|
| Riviere Raisin | 472.63 | Dunvegan | 67.38 |
| Williamstown | 268.08 | Dalhousie Mills | 61.77 |
| Martintown | 265.05 | Dalkeith | 61.37 |
| Notfield | 140.17 | Glen Nevis | 58.06 |
| Lancaster | 128.01 | Kirk Hill | 50.46 |
| North Lancaster | 101.42 | Loch Garry | 47.61 |
| Summerstown | 91.13 | Skye | 34.48 |
| Athol | 90.10 | McNab | 29.75 |
| Lochiel | 79.72 | TOTAL | $2637.34 |

By way of contrast, the busy and growing village of Cornwall gave its post office $2455.94 of business that year, which is only $181.40 less than all the offices in Glengarry.

But this is not the place to discuss Glengarry's economics, so we will pass on to the clutch of post offices that opened between the preparation of the 1869 report of the Post Master General and the one ten years later. In that decade twenty offices were opened, though five of these were merely a change in name and if we were to go into the figures of each we could find only two that counted for a great deal, Greenfield and Green Valley. Green Valley is still open in 1978 and Greenfield was one of the last to be closed by amalgamation of rural routes in 1970.

The main purpose of these many small offices was to give a mail service to all rural areas, within walking distance of each farm, and this object was accomplished. Though no one bothered to record it, we can suspect that having a post office close at hand—a place to gather and talk while the mail was sorted—went a long way toward ending the isolation in which many of our ancestors lived in those days of a century ago. A post office opening in the community must in its time have been an event equal to the coming of the telephone later on.

The contracts in 1869 give us a pretty complete picture of Glengarry's basic supply of mail to a fairly well developed post office system inside the county. The dates that the various post offices opened let us trace the development of the system, from the Charlottenburgh Post Office of 1789, when it was the only one in Glengarry. We can see the system push north into the county, extending branches to east and west as it does so.

Lest anyone think moving or opening a post office in the early days was an involved process, similar to what it is today, we must explain that all rural post offices consisted of a cupboard with the necessary number of pigeon holes in it, sitting in a corner of a store or a house. Usually the post master had a stamp, but hand cancellations from the early days are quite common. The first government-owned post office building in Glengarry was in Alexandria and it was opened in 1905. For about sixty years it was the only one that was government-owned in Glengarry.

But to go back to the beginning of Glengarry's mail system. Presumably, from 1784 on, some method of getting mail in and out Glengarry was in operation, but we can only assume how it functioned. We know a mail courier went up and down the St.Lawrence by whatever method of travel suited the season; and the Falkner settlement, later Dunlop's and later still South Lancaster, would be a central spot on Glengarry's front for mail to be collected by some responsible person and handed over to the courier when he passed through. The post office called "Charlottenburgh" was established in 1789, as we have seen, and it may have continued to operate until the Lancaster office was opened in 1816. In 1822 a second post office was opened toward the north of the county on the road to the Ottawa River. It was called Lochiel and that corner on the 5th of Lochiel is still so called. In 1823 an office was opened at St.Raphaels and in 1824 one at Martintown. In 1825 one was opened in Alexandria. Though we have tried, we can find no evidence that there was ever a post office where Alexandria now is called "The Priest's Mills," nor have we found any sort of a document datelined "Priest's Mills," either in English or Gaelic.

Williamstown had to wait until 1833 for its post office and North Lancaster got one in 1845. Before we go on, we must mention "McLeod's Post Office," which was just south of Kirk Hill. It is shown on the map of the survey of the military road in 1841 but is not mentioned in any list of post offices, official or otherwise. Yet it was there in 1840. We can only assume it was an "unofficial post offfice," or if official that its records have been entirely destroyed. One of the small mysteries of Glengarry's history.

A post office called Kenyon was opened in 1848 at what today is called Laggan and the then busy village of Athol got an office in 1851. Summerstown (at the Front) got an office in 1852 as did Dalhousie Mills, and the now lost village of Notfield got an office in 1857. An office was opened at Sandfield, now Glen Sandfield, in 1858, and Sierra, now Glen Roy, got one that year too. An office called Skye was also opened in 1858, but it was at the Dunvegan corner. James Fraser's busy settlement at Loch Garry got an office in 1860, and in 1862 there was a shuffling of sites in the north of Kenyon. The Skye Post Office was moved north and east to the locality we know as Skye today, on the Kenyon-Caledonia border; the Kenyon post office was moved to Dunvegan and the office that had been Kenyon became Laggan. Breadalbane and Kirk Hill also got post offices in 1862.

In 1865 the postal system finally took note that the Grand Trunk Railway had been open for about ten years and moved the Lancaster post office north to the railway. As the lower village was still a fairly busy port town, a new post office was opened there in 1865 under the name of Riviere Raisin. Even though maps of this era call Lancaster's lower village "Kirktown," there never was a Kirktown Post Office. In 1865 too, a new office was opened at Glen Nevis, and Dalkeith got one in Confederation year, 1867.

In 1868 a new office was opened called McNab — one wonders why it wasn't called "Bullfrog" as its nearest neighbour was the famous Bullfrog Tavern at the present Lochinvar corner. South La Graisse office on lot one in the 3rd of Lochiel was opened in 1869 and McNab became Lochinvar in 1872. In 1873 post offices were opened at Greenfield and Camerontown. Camerontown would one day be known as Summerstown Station and still later, in 1926, became the site of the Summerstown Post Office.

In 1873, the old Lochiel post office had its name changed to Glen James, but it did not catch on and in about a year its name was changed back to Lochiel.

The year 1874 was the biggest year for new post offices that Glengarry ever had. New offices were opened at Cashion's Glen, Curry Hill, Glen Donald, Glen Gordon, Glen Norman, Glen Robertson, Glen Walter, and Munro's Mills. In 1874, too, Sierra became Glen Roy and Sandfield became Glen Sandfield.

At this stage it is worth noting that Glengarry's member of parliament from 1867 to 1875 was Donald Sandfield Macdonald, and he served as Post Master General of Canada from 1873-75. During Mr. Macdonald's years as a member of parliament, Glengarry got 14 new post offices and three had their names changed to names beginning with "Glen." In fact that is when we got most of the "Glen" names in the county, and Glengarry got ten new post offices in the two years Mr.Macdonald was Post Master General, out of a total of 58 post offices that have existed in the county. One can suspect that all these new post masters were political supporters of Mr.Macdonald.

In 1877 Kingsburgh post office opened at a site that two years later would officially become McCrimmon, and in 1878 post offices were opened at Bridge End, Green Valley, and Dominionville. Those who are interested in the mile and a quarter long village that started as Notfield and became Dominionville and then disappeared, will note that for a few months the village had a post office at each end of it, until the Notfield office closed and left the scene to Dominionville.

In 1880 the new village of Maxville got its first official post office, though the courier had been leaving mail at the corner there for some years, when they could get him to stop. In 1880 too, the community of Bethel Hill got a post office which received the name St.Elmo, a name apparently picked by the minister's daughter, who had enjoyed a then current novel of that name. Baltic's Corners got a post office in 1881, and its name must have caused some confusion in Ottawa or else its post master was a poor calligrapher. Its post mark appears as Baltic, Baltie, as well as Baltie's.

Apple Hill got its first post office in 1882, and the name was chosen because the best site for the station seemed to be in Sandy Kennedy's orchard. These new post offices on railways always seemed to open three or four years before the railway they were built on was ready for operation. In those days everyone expected a railroad station town to grow into a city in short order, but this optimism was not justified in Glengarry.

In 1882 the Riviere Raisin post office became South Lancaster, and is one of the fourteen post offices open in Glengarry in 1978. In 1883 an office was opened at McCormicks and in 1884 one at Brodie. Bainsville and Fassifern also got offices in 1884, and Tyotown got one in 1887. In 1891 Camerontown became Summerstown Station and in 1893 the saw mill hamlet of Dornie had a post office open that only stayed open for a few months.

With the opening of the McGillivray Bridge post office in 1908 the total of Glengarry's post offices had been reached — 58 in all, though ten of these were due to name changes rather than offices in new areas. At the turn of the century, the county had 41 offices in operation. Nobody lived very far from a post office, and gathering at the post office and exchanging gossip while the mail was sorted was one of the recognized social activities of the times.

The coming of rural mail did away to an extent with the need to go to the post office but the older people particularly were in no hurry to break their custom "of waiting for the mail to be sorted." The rural mail driver, with his horse and buggy in summer and his horse and cutter in winter, became a standard part of the Glengarry scene and the "stages" that met the trains and took the mail to the various rural offices also carried passengers. A person coming home from a trip would try to arrive on a train that carried mail so as to be sure of a ride to his or her post office for a very nominal fee. This appealed to our Glengarry folk who, as was natural, would rather not spend money on a livery horse, the taxi of the day.

The rural mail driver in many cases became errand runner for the community he served, an important link with the people and the stores, and in the days before telephones in every farm house he was the community messenger service as well. The terms of the early contracts were strict — no matter how cold the day or how deep the drifts "the mailman" had to collect his mail and drive the first part of his route. And it was six days a week with only two holidays a year, Christmas and the 1st of July. As time passed, more and more rural routes were covered by car and by the middle of the 1950's the plowing of roads for school buses let the rural mail carrier use his car the year round. This let many rural routes be consolidated and led to the closing of a few more post offices as can be seen by the appended list.

In the fall of 1963 the post office department began its great switch from a railway based mail supply system to one based on trucks and by the end of 1963 only one train a day was dropping off mail in Alexandria. The rest came by trucks from Hawkesbury and Ottawa, and the shades of such men as Murray, Campbell, and Ross must have smiled as they saw the trucks following the same routes they had pioneered on foot and horseback.

The post office buildings in Glengarry show another modern trend. The local post office is no longer a few pigeon holes tucked in the corner of a general store or a private home. Since 1964 the postal department has been building its own modern style buildings, and Glengarry is now very modern in that respect.

## Dates of Glengarry Post Office Openings

| | | | |
|---|---|---|---|
| Charlottenburgh | 1789 | Notfield | 1857 |
| *Lancaster | 1816 | Sandfield | 1858 |
| Lochiel | 1822 | Sierra | 1858 |
| St. Raphaels | 1823 | **Skye | 1858 |
| Martintown | 1824 | Loch Garry | 1860 |
| Alexandria | 1825 | Laggan | 1862 |
| Williamstown | 1833 | Kirk Hill | 1862 |
| North Lancaster | 1845 | *Dunvegan | 1862 |
| **Kenyon | 1848 | Breadalbane | 1862 |
| Athol | 1851 | *Riviere Raisin | 1865 |
| Summerstown | 1852 | Glen Nevis | 1865 |
| Dalhousie Mills | 1852 | Dalkeith | 1867 |

| | | | |
|---|---|---|---|
| McNab | 1868 | Bridge End | 1878 |
| South LaGraisse | 1869 | Dominionville | 1878 |
| *Lochinvar | 1872 | Green Valley | 1878 |
| Greenfield | 1873 | *McCrimmon | 1879 |
| *Glen James | 1873 | Maxville | 1880 |
| Camerontown | 1873 | St. Elmo | 1880 |
| Cashion's Glen | 1874 | Baltic's Corners | 1881 |
| Curry Hill | 1874 | Apple Hill | 1882 |
| Glen Donald | 1874 | *South Lancaster | 1882 |
| Glen Gordon | 1874 | McCormick's | 1883 |
| Glen Norman | 1874 | Brodie | 1884 |
| Glen Robertson | 1874 | Bainsville | 1884 |
| *Glen Roy | 1874 | Fassifern | 1884 |
| *Glen Sandfield | 1874 | Tyotown | 1887 |
| Glen Walter | 1874 | *Summerstown Station | 1891 |
| Munro's Mills | 1874 | Dornie | 1893 |
| Kingsburgh | 1877 | McGillivray Bridge | 1908 |

\* Post offices opened earlier in same area, under a different name.

\*\* Location changes

334

# DETAILS OF GLENGARRY'S POST OFFICES

**Post Offices** - 14 open in 1978
- 58 all together over the years
- 41 open at once in 1900

*1.   Alexandria - open 1825
*2.   Apple Hill - open 1882
3.    Athol - open 1851, closed 19 November 1919.
*4.   Bainsville - open 1884
5.    Baltic's Corners (Baltic; Balties)-open 1881, closed 1882.
6.    Breadalbane - open 1862, closed 1866; reopened 1875, closed 1916.
7.    Bridge End - open 1878, closed 1914
8.    Brodie - opened 1884, closed 1 April 1915.
9.    Camerontown - open 1873, closed 1891 then became Summerstown Station.
10.   Cashion's Glen - open 1874, closed 20 August 1913.
11.   Charlottenburgh - open 1789, probably became Lancaster in 1816.
12.   Curry Hill - open 1874, closed 1 October 1887, reopened 1 August 1888, finally closed 30 September 1912.
13.   Dalhousie Mills - open 1852, closed 14 October 1944
*14.  Dalkeith - open 1867.
15.   Dominionville - open 1878, closed 17 December 1913.
16.   Dornie - open 1893, closed 6 May 1893.
*17.  Dunvegan - open 1862. Originally Skye Post Office opened 1858.
18.   Fassifern - open 1884, closed 17 February 1915.
19.   Glen Donald - open 1874, closed 23 August 1913.
20.   Glen Gordon - open 1874, closed 1876.
21.   Glen James—open 1873, closed 1874. Was Lochiel from 1822—1873 and Lochiel again 1874—1914.
22.   Glen Nevis—open 1865, closed 31 July 1914.
23.   Glen Norman—open 1874, closed 31 July 1914.
* 24. Glen Robertson—open 1874.

25. Glen Roy—open 1874, closed 16 December 1953. Originally opened as Sierra in 1858.
26. Glen Sandfield—open 1874, closed 1 November 1967. Originally opened as Sandfield in 1858-1860 and 1864—1874.
27. Glen Walter—open 1874, closed 3 December 1913.
28. Greenfield—open 1873, closed 1970.
*29. Green Valley—open 1878.
30. Kenyon—open 1848, closed 1862 (at site of present-day Laggan).
31. Kingsburgh—open 1877, closed 1879 then reopened as McCrimmon.
32. Kirk Hill—open 1862, closed 1916, reopened 1921 and finally closed 1928.
33. Laggan—open 1862, closed 1915, opened in 1848 as Kenyon Post Office.
*34. Lancaster—open 1816, moved from river to railway 1865 (had been Charlottenburgh).
35. Loch Garry—open 1860, closed 30 June 1898.
36. Lochiel—open 1822, closed 1873, was Glen James 1873—74 and became Lochiel again, closed 1914.
37. Lochinvar—open 1872, closed 1890, originally opened as McNab in 1868.
38. McCormick—open 1883, closed 15 July 1914.
39. McCrimmon—open 1879, closed 1919. Originally opened as Kingsburgh in 1877.
40. McGillivray Bridge—open 1908, closed 1913.
41. McNab—open 1868, closed 1872 then became Lochinvar 1872—90.
*42. Martintown—open 1824.
*43. Maxville—open 1880.
44. Munro's Mills—open 1874, closed 1915.
*45. North Lancaster—open in 1845.
46. Notfield—open 1857, closed 1879.
47. Riviere Raisin—open 1865, closed 1882 when it became South Lancaster. Originally Charlottenburgh 1789—1816 then Lancaster 1816—1865.
48. St.Elmo—open 1880, closed 14 June 1913.

49. St.Raphaels — open 1823, closed 1970.
50. Sandfield — open 1858, closed 1860, reopened 1864 — 1874 when it became Glen Sandfield 1874 — 1969.
51. Sierra — open 1858, closed 1874, and then became Glen Roy 1874 — 1953.
52. Skye — open 1858, closed 17 March 1915. Moved from site of present day Dunvegan in 1862.
53. South La Graisse — open 1869, closed 1879.
* 54. South Lancaster — open 1882. Opened in 1789 as Charlottenburgh then in 1816 — 1865 was Lancaster.
55. Summerstown — open 1852, closed 1925 (at river).
* 56. Summerstown Station — open 1891, closed 1 December 1926. Had been Camerontown 1873 — 1891, is Summerstown 1926 — 1978.
57. Tyotown — open 1887, closed 31 January 1913.
* 58. Williamstown — open 1833.

* still open in 1978

## Post Offices closed before coming of rural mail and probable reasons for closing.

Baltic's Corners, closed 1882 — railway opened to Maxville.

Dornie — saw mill moved to Alexandria, closed 1893.

Loch Garry, closed 1898 — railway through Apple Hill.

Lochinvar, closed in 1890 — road by-passed the corner. McCrimmon got its business.

Notfield, closed 1879 — Dominionville got its business.

South La Graisse, closed 1879 — lumbering settlement, timber gone.

## 1912 — 1919 — Post Offices in Glengarry closed by coming of rural mail.

Athol — closed 19 Nov. 1919.

Breadalbane — closed 1916.

Brodie — closed 1 Apr. 1915.

Cashion's Glen — closed 20 Aug. 1913.

Curry Hill — closed 30 Sept. 1912.

Dominionville – closed 17 Dec. 1913.
Fassifern – closed 17 Feb. 1915.
Glen Donald – closed 23 Aug. 1913.
Lochiel – closed 1914.
Glen Nevis – closed 31 July 1914.
Glen Norman – closed 31 July 1914.
Glen Walter – closed 3 Dec. 1913.
Laggan – closed 1915.
Kirk Hill – closed 1916 but reopened 1921 – 28.
McCormick – closed 15 July 1914.
McCrimmon – closed 1919.
McGillivray Bridge – closed 1913.
Munro's Mills – closed 1915.
St.Elmo – closed 14 June 1913.
Skye – closed 17 Mar. 1915
Tyotown – closed 31 Jan. 1913.

**Rural Routes begin**

1912 – one in Lancaster area to east
1913 – seven – 4 in west of Martintown, 2 north of Maxville,
      1 southeast of Martintown
1914 – four – all were east of Alexandria
1915 – five – 1 north of Maxville, 1 east of Apple Hill, 3
      east and north of Alexandria
1916 – two – both in Dalkeith area
1919 – two – 1 northeast of Alexandria, 1 north of Maxville

**Further adjustments in rural mail causing post office to close.**

Dalhousie Mills closed 14 Oct.1944
Glen Roy, closed 16 Dec. 1953
Greenfield, closed 1970
Kirk Hill, finally closed 1928.
St.Raphaels, closed 1970.
Glen Sandfield, closed 1969.
Summerstown, closed 1925.

**Glengarry's Postal Codes — effective 1972**

| | |
|---|---|
| Alexandria | KOC 1AO |
| Apple Hill | KOC 1BO |
| Bainsville | KOC 1EO |
| Dalkeith | KOB 1EO |
| Dunvegan | KOC 1JO |
| Glen Robertson | KOB 1HO |
| Green Valley | KOC 1LO |
| Lancaster | KOC INO |
| Martintown | KOC 1SO |
| Maxville | KOC 1TO |
| North Lancaster | KOC 1ZO |
| South Lancaster | KOC 2CO |
| Summerstown | KOC 2EO |
| Williamstown | KOC 2JO |

## Odd bits of post office data

1784 — Jacques Martineau carries mail on foot between Montreal and Kingston. Between Lachine and Cornwall he had to ''sleep out'' three nights.

1787 — Residents of New Johnstown area petition British government for a post office.

1794 — In winter there are two mails a month along the St. Lawrence, and only one in summer.

1800 — Mail along St.Lawrence once a month in winter and once in two weeks in summer.

1802 — Mail for England is dispatched from Quebec once every two weeks in summer and once a month in winter, to be put aboard the first packet boat.

1812 — Mails along St.Lawrence once a week.

1814 — Mail along the St.Lawrence three times a week.

1816 — John A. Dunlop, appointed first official Post Master in Lancaster, the first we have a record of in Glengarry.

1825 — Five post offices open in Glengarry: Lancaster, Lochiel, St.Raphaels, Martintown, and Alexandria.

1830 — Daily mail along the St.Lawrence.

1839 — Act of British parliament brings postal service to Britain and the colonies under government control.

1847 — McDonell family begin to operate the post office at St.Raphaels and will continue to do so until 1944 — 97 years.

1850 — Province of Canada takes over control of its postal system from the British Post Office.

1851 — Canada issues its first postage stamps; 3d beaver; 6d bearing portrait of Prince Albert; 12d bearing portrait of Queen Victoria (our rarest stamp). These stamps were engraved and printed in Britain.

1855 — Money orders and registration of mail become part of the Canadian Postal Service.

1856—Grand Trunk opened and there are two mails a day along the St.Lawrence.

1859—Parcel post begins in the Province of Canada.

1859—Only decimal currency is legal for stamps in Canada.

1868—Canada begins to engrave and print its own stamps.

1869—Post office begins a Savings Bank Service.

1871—Alexandria's post office opens a Savings Bank service and is the only one in the county.

1875—Use of prepared postage stamps made compulsory in Canada.

1895—Telegraph instrument installed in Alexandria post office.

1902—In one week of June, 2383 letters are posted in the Alexandria post office.

1905—Alexandria becomes a "Port of Entry" with the post master as customs officer. This office (customs) was closed in 1928.

1905—First government-owned post office building in Glengarry opens in Alexandria.

1905—In future, mail from Maxville to Apple Hill will go by rail via Montreal. The stage will run only as far as Dominionville.

1911—Angus Dewar, veteran mail carrier, stopped in the swamp east of McCormick's by two men. Dewar felled one of his attackers with an uppercut and whipped up the horse he was riding to escape the other one

1911 — First talk of rural mail in Glengarry.

1912 — Rural mail begins in Glengarry, out of Maxville and Lancaster post offices.

1914 — Canada-wide parcel post begins (10 February).

1918 — First official air mail flight in Canada. Montreal to Toronto.

1922 — C.O.D. orders now handled by Canada's post office

1928 — It is news when *Glengarry News* gets an air mail letter from New York via Montreal.

1943 — Storms block railways so horses called on to deliver mail north from Glen Robertson.

1954 — Attempted holdup at St.Raphaels post office foiled by post mistress, Miss Margaret Barry. Post office gave her a $500 reward eventually.

1963 — Daily mail service by truck to Glengarry's post offices inaugurated.

1964 — Postal department begins program of building and owning its own offices in all Glengarry towns that have a post office (14).

## TELEGRAPH AND TELEPHONE

In 1847 a telegraph line was built across Glengarry. It was built by the Montreal Telegraph Company and its object was to provide communication between Toronto and Montreal. It achieved its object in August 1847. This Montreal Telegraph Company, whose presiding genius was H.P.Dwight, got control of other telegraph lines in Eastern Canada almost as soon as they were built. This was interesting to us, as by a process of accretion all surviving files came into the possession of the Canadian National Railway system and some do still exist.

The Montreal Telegraph Company seems to have opened one station in Glengarry at Lancaster and one in Cornwall. The company sought and obtained permission to run its pole line along Cornwall's streets. There is no mention of such formality in the Glengarry townships east of Cornwall.

In 1855 the Grand Trunk Railway built across Glengarry with its own telegraph system which was eventually bought out by the Montreal Telegraph Company. The Grand Trunk opened a telegraph office at Lancaster and shortly after at Bainsville.

In 1868 the Dominion Telegraph Company started to build, among other lines, one from Montreal to Detroit that was in operation by 1870. This line followed the King's Road-Line Road (this is where the Line Road got its name) through Glengarry and it provided one station in Glengarry, at Martintown.

As we have seen in an earlier chapter, in 1871 the telegraph reached Alexandria.

In 1880 the Montreal Telegraph Company bought out the Dominion Telegraph Company as well, so it now owned three lines across Glengarry. The Canadian Northern Telegraph Company bought Montreal Telegraph in 1902 and in 1920 it became part of the Canadian National Telegraph Company, which in 1956 became a subsidiary of the Canadian National Railway Company. All of which may be of little interest except for the names of the first few telegraph stations established in Glengarry.

In 1881 Booth's railway, the Canada Atlantic, built its telegraph line across Glengarry and it seems to have put a telegraph instrument in each of its main stations--Glen Robertson, Alexandria, and Maxville. In those days telegraph lines were essential in working a railroad as they were the only means the dispatchers at divisional points had to keep track of their trains. The telegraph operator, who sometimes but not always was the station agent, reported each train past his station along with the exact time of its passing. Eventually the Grand Trunk system bought the Canada Atlantic and in time it too became part of the Canadian National system.

In 1886 Glengarry gots its last telegraph line when the CPR built its line, and provided instruments at Green Valley and Apple Hill.

So from 1847 on it was possible to send a telegraph message (or receive it) in Glengarry. Though there is little doubt that businessmen used the telegraph as a matter of course for placing emergency orders and even for routine business, to the ordinary citizen of Glengarry sending or receiving a telegram meant death or serious illness expected to end in death. In those pre-embalming days, a telegram was the only method of summoning family members home in time for a funeral. To the end of telegraph service (and it's not completely dead even in 1978) Glengarrians associated a telegram with bad news. Interesting but true.

The telephone became an usable tool with great rapidity after the first long distance call from Brantford to Paris in 1876 and it reached Cornwall by 1880. In 1885, in August, the first telephone service was established in Lancaster village under the management of A.R. McDonell. That same year the telegraph office in Alexandria was in Duncan A. (Curly) McDonald's store which also was the post office. In 1887 the Lancaster directory listed three telephones, all in Lancaster village — A.R. McDonell, merchant; D.M. McPherson, cheese; and D.A. McPherson, resident. By 1889 Williamstown too had a telegraph office.

The first telephones that can be traced in Alexandria appear in 1892 when E.H. Tiffany, the lawyer, connected his office in the old post office building with his home on the north east corner of Dominion and St. George Streets with a line strung on buildings and trees. It appealed to Tiffany's Irish sense of humor that his clients thought he was crazy because he would go and talk to it when it rang. In 1894 somebody connected Alexandria post office with the station by telephones that could be used by paying five cents. That same year McPherson and Schell connected their mill in the west end of Alexandria to this private system. At this time the Bell system was interested in building west from Montreal and their manager, Mr. McFarlane, met with "prominent Alexandria citizens" and sold them on the advantages of direct voice communications with Monteal. Bell would build west from St. Polycarpe if Alexandria would build east through Glen Robertson. So at a cost of about $500 Alexandria got connected to Montreal and the first call came to Alexandria on 12 November 1895. The Bell line went on to the west and installed one phone in Maxville, at the Canada Atlantic Railway station. In the next nine years Bell picked up only one more subscriber in Maxville, J.W. Weegar. However, Bell looked to the future and in 1895 made I.B. Ostrom its local manager in Alexandria, and in 1903 gave that position to A.H. Robertson in Maxville. Ostrom was able to line up 19 subscribers in his first year of business and Robertson in Maxville had 23 by 1906. Incidentally the charge in those early years was $15 per year and service was limited as to hours. Till 1913 hours were 7:30 A.M. to 9:00 P.M. weekdays and from 10:00 A.M. to 12:00 Noon and 3:00 to 5:00 P.M. on Sundays.

There seems to be no clear record of when Bell built a line into Williamstown, but it was likely to give service to McPherson and Schell's plant there and the office of this plant acted as the local telephone exchange in 1896. Evidently the idea is new as it was a news item in November of that year. What was perhaps the first telephone booth in the county was "fixed up" in the Alexandria telephone office (in Ostrom's drug store) in December 1896, "for the benefit of parties phoning direct from the central to points outside the town."

In March 1897 the sporting fraternity gathered at telegraph stations to get the round by round results of the Corbett-Fitzsimmons heavyweight boxing match. Alexandria's telegraph operator, James Taggart, left soon after the match though there is no traceable connection. By the end of the year long distance phone calls were being made and though people were surprised that phones worked, they admitted that they did.

1901 saw a fair amount of telephone inter-connection between places in Glengarry with the new type of metallic circuit. The first circuits were earthed -- one wire only with the ground serving for the other. Martintown and Greenfield were connected to Bell's system that year though as yet we must not look for any more than one or two instruments in those little villages. In 1903 Bell opened offices in St. Raphaels, North Lancaster, and St. Andrews, and in 1905 a line was run from Maxville to Dunvegan via St. Elmo and Athol. That same year the Roxborough Telephone System built into Maxville and connected to Bell's Maxville exchange. As a result of this, for fifty odd years, until Bell bought all the local systems out, many Maxville businesses had two phones—one Bell for service north and east, one Roxborough for service west and south west.

Dalkeith got phone service in 1906 via lines through Glen Andrew, Rigaud and so to Montreal. This was not really too handy as the people in Lochiel wanted telephone service to Alexandria rather than Montreal or even Rigaud, so in 1907 the people of Lochiel formed their own telephone system -- the Glengarry Telephone Company. They installed a central office at Lochiel and installed a five cent toll line to Alexandria. The system opened for business in 1907 with two subscribers on private lines, 12 on one party line, and five on another. They covered the township from Glen Sandfield to Laggan and Cuthbert's Corner to Lochiel. Their rules, published on the back of the list of numbers, contain some of interest: The company wishes to give good service to all but don't expect $25 service for $10. Three minutes is a goodly time to talk business, and should also satisfy those socially inclined. Also they took the view, repeated in five of their 21 rules, that "if you aren't paying for a phone, you aren't entitled to use one." The directors wanted everyone to install their own evidently. Eventually this system pretty well covered Lochiel and even reached into northern Kenyon and Caledonia townships with lines to Glen Sandfield, Brodie, Dunvegan, and Skye.

By 1910 about three-quarters of Glengarry's population could have phone service if anyone wanted it but one area around Martintown and Munro's Mills still just had the odd Bell telephone in its territory. In March 1911 a rural telephone company was organized in Martintown with a central office at Martintown and connected to Bell's lines. The Keir family provided central office staff and maintenance and Henry S. Kinloch was the first secretary-treasurer of the company.

1911 may well be looked back on as "the year the telephone caught on in Glengarry." When the year began there were 93 telephones attached to the Maxville exchange. At year's end, owing to a deal with the Roxborough Phone Company, Maxville's phone coverage area included about 200 subscribers stretching from St. Isidore to Newington and from Moose Creek to Apple Hill. Bell was stringing a direct line from North Lancaster to Ottawa and had a crew putting up poles and connecting new subscribers in Lancaster village and South Lancaster. This burst of activity in Lancaster by Bell was probably brought on by the formation of a Farmers Telephone Company in May 1911 in Lancaster Township. At any rate on 3 November 1911 the *Glengarry News* was moved to remark, "Decidedly the telephone has come to stay." Perhaps the editor knew too of the 17 miles of new line and 75 new phones that the Lochiel Farmers Telephone (Glen Tel Co-op) had added to their system in 1911.

The Lancaster Farmers never actually activated their telephone company but the noises they made and the actual formation of a Farmer's Co-Op Telephone System in the Martintown area got Bell moving out into the Concessions and kept it improving its service. In 1912 it put up lines east of Dominionville. In 1913 Bell began to give 24 hour, seven day a week service on its switchboards, and in 1914 it got busy on the concessions south west of Green Valley. By 1917 Bell covered north eastern Lancaster Township and proudly announced that the Bridge End Branch would have its local directory printed entirely in French.

In 1918, the Glengarry Telephone Co-Op in Lochiel found it necessary to raise its phone rates from $10 to $14 per year because of "increased costs of labor and material" but by 1920, it had 279 subscribers in place of the original 19.

The 'flu epidemic in the fall of 1918 gave many people a chance to try their hands at operating the local switchboards as regular operators got sick. Clarence Ostrom in his notebooks on the history of Alexandria remarks that there were times when there was no service at all because there were no operators.

Bell closed up gaps in its system. In 1924 it built lines into the area between Glen Norman and Glen Robertson, and in 1925 built into the 2nd and 3rd of Kenyon and in 1926 reconstructed its telephone line north of Lancaster, the original rural part of its system.

In 1928 the Martintown phone system was sold to Athol A. Edgar who operated it till 1952. Just before the system was sold to Edgar, it too went "modern" and started 24 hour, seven day a week service.

In June 1930 the farmers east of Brodie got telephone service and the telephone service in Glengarry had practically assumed its present form except for the Little Third of Kenyon — Bell completed a line in there in early February 1938 — and Breadalbane which did not get phones till 1948.

Many readers will remember the old wall phones, each with its own batteries and external bells, a rather cumbersome piece of machinery. Depending on circumstances there would be from 5 to 25 subscribers on each line, each with his own distinctive ring. "Listening on the phone" was a popular pastime and as every ring on a line was heard by all parties on that line, anyone speaking on a phone usually spoke to a large audience. One of the characters in J.E. McIntosh's

"Sandy Fraser" column disliked telephones because he "never was any good at speaking in public." The early telephones were far from impersonal instruments, they were an integral part of the community and used as such. But a man did not use the telephone to negotiate a loan with his bank manager. Perhaps the most interesting conversations were those held between courting couples. If a couple were known to be "going steady" rings to those households were especially carefully monitored.

Each line went into a central office which might have from 10 to 50 plugs on a board and the central operator could be summoned to "plug you in" by pressing a button on your phone and turning the ringing crank vigorously. If the operator was doing her nails, or talking to her boyfriend or engrossed in the conversation on another line the service at these small exchanges could be pretty awful. Many a person, after trying to get his own line clear, then getting Central only after a dozen or so tries, then finding the line he was trying to call was busy gave up in disgust and hitched up a horse and went to do his business in person. Yet these country lines, with sometimes exasperating switchboard operators, were an integral part of each community. In the event of a fire the switchboard girl plugged all the lines on her board in and "gave the fire ring," a very long continued ring which alerted everyone in the area and then she told the listening community where the fire was. At times of sickness or death the telephone girls acted as unofficial messengers. They almost always knew where the doctor, the priest or the minister or the local pump fixer or veterinarian could be found. And they always knew what time it was, if somebody's clock stopped.

The men got out to the cheese factory every morning; the women had just as good a colloquy over the party line which was well known to be their preserve at hours when the men were out of the house.

The first dial service in Glengarry came to the Lancaster exchange in February 1936. Alexandria's Bell exchange got a common battery system in 1949.

In the early spring of 1948 the farmers in the Breadalbane district asked the Glengarry Telephone Company to extend its lines into the area. In the course of a few months 65 phones were installed around Breadalbane and now it can be said that all those in Glengarry have telephone service that want it—63 years after the first phones were operative at Lancaster in 1885.

It is probable that that part of Charlottenburgh right beside Cornwall, particularly along the Front, received telephone service if they wanted it very shortly after the telephone came to Cornwall in 1880. Bell serviced the area from the South Branch Road to the river and on down to Lancaster and these people, while they had party lines, got big town central service. They got night service in 1893, common battery service in 1920, dial service in 1957, and direct distance dialing from one and two party lines in 1960. As a rule these people in south western Charlottenburgh got their improvements in service before the rest of Glengarry.

In 1948 the Glengarry Telephone Company had 375 subscribers and the Alexandria exchange had 575. Martintown hovered around the 200 mark and Maxville had slightly more. The Lancaster exchange, covering as it did all of Lancaster Township and the east side of Charlottenburgh, was about twice as big as any other exchange in the county.

1961 saw the beginning of the modern telephone age in Glengarry. J.A. Collette who had bought the system in 1952 sold his Martintown telephone system to Bell, and Bell installed a thoroughly modern plant, complete with some underground cable and dial phones, and the Martintown area was able to call Cornwall toll free. The change was completed on 18 March 1962.

Dial telephone service came to Maxville in November 1963 at a time when Bell was building a new dial exchange in Alexandria on Bishop Street near Elgin. Bell bought the Glengarry Telephone Company in Lochiel in 1966 and by November 1967 all of Alexandria and Lochiel had dial phones, though Alexandria itself got them in 1964. Some 1400 customers got "dial" in those two years in Lochiel, Kenyon,and Alexandria.

Though Bell now owned all the telephones in Glengarry and had exchanges serving Glengarry's less than 20,000 people at Cornwall, Lancaster, Martintown, Alexandria, Glen Robertson, and Maxville, there still was no exchange in the county that could call all other exchanges in the county toll free, a situation that exists to this day. Maxville seems to be most restricted in this respect as it can only call Moose Creek and St.Isidore without toll charges. Both Martintown and Lancaster can call Cornwall toll free but Martintown has to pay toll charges to all the other exchanges in the county except Lancaster. Of course the reverse is true too and the telephone continues to separate enclaves in the county. Though party lines still exist, very few, if any, have more than 10 subscribers, and only half the rings are heard on any given phone. Still not a private service, it is not as public as it once was.

In 1971 direct distance dialing came to Glengarry and the 1976 phone book records about 7000 telephone listings in Glengarry, about 2½ times as many as there were in 1948. The monthly rate reflects this, as Ma Bell's tariff is tied more or less directly to the number of phones that can be called toll free.

In an editorial in the *Glengarry News* of 18 November 1976, that shrewd, friendly and experienced observer and reporter on his neighbours, Eugene Macdonald, says "though we regret the personal touch of the Bell Telephone operator, after 10 years of dial service, changing to dial was a progressive move". The telephone subscribers in Glengarry seem to have agreed with him and there must be few householders indeed who are not subscribers. Many are multiple subscribers and have both homes and businesses listed, some in both French and English.

Our files show one reason why the phone is more popular than ever besides the more apparent ones of everyone being able to afford it and it being easier "to get the line". Phone service in Glengarry was badly disrupted by a big windstorm in August 1933, by a sleet storm in November 1935, and by the grand-daddy of all sleet storms on 30 and 31 December 1942. This storm put all phones in the area out of action for at least a week, some for ten days and some rural lines for more than three months. The telephone plant has improved since than In the following 35 years we have no major break in service recorded though there have been several fairly serious ones. The telephone seems to have won the confidence of the people in Glengarry -- a thing that is not easily won as the folk about Breadalbane demonstrated before they "put in the phone".

# Chapter XI
# Farming in Glengarry
# 1784 - 1978

From the time when the county was first settled until very recently, most people in Glengarry made their living off the land. The few who did not provided services to their farmer neighbours on the concessions. Thus the numbers and prosperity of our merchants, blacksmiths, school teachers, priests, ministers, doctors, lawyers, veterinarians, and even itinerant pedlars and beggars depended on the income of Glengarry's farmers. The only exceptions we have been able to note until

The stump fence. What more natural to do with the pine stumps the settlers dug out to clear the land than use them to fence the land cleared. Owing to their resin content pine stumps rotted very slowly and the stumps in this picture taken about 1930 must have been doing duty as a fence for about a hundred years.

353

the 1950's were Munro and McIntosh, the J.T. Schell Co., and Rayside and McArthur, all firms that started operations in the last quarter of the nineteenth century and were effectively finished by the end of World War I or very shortly thereafter.

Stone bottom—rail top. Fence lines were a suitable and handy place to deposit the stones taken from the fields during the land clearing process and each spring that the land was cultivated. Often there was not enough stone to make a suitably high fence so a rail fence was built on top of the stone bottom.

In our boyhood days in Glengarry it was often said that only one third of the land in the county was fit to farm. In the 1930's this could only have been a deduction based on instinct and shrewd personal observation. In those days of not so long ago, every one of Glengarry's 3000 or more 100-acre farm lots was owned by a farmer who expected (or hoped) that somehow it (the lot) would contribute to his total farm income or make it easier for him to make a living. In October 1976 Glengarry's long-time Agricultural Representative, Jim Humphries, stated that there were 500 dairy farmers in the county at that time, down from 1600 in 1967. Allowing these 500 farmers 200 acres of good land apiece, we come up with 100,000 acres, almost

354

exactly a third of Glengarry's total acreage, if we deduct built-up areas, roads, rivers, and lakes. (Glengarry has 481 square miles = 307,840 acres.)

Crossed picket rail fence. This type of fence was made from the same materials as the snake fence but it did require the use of wire to bind the pickets together at their hinge. This fence eliminated the awkward corners of the snake fence.

Without getting too technical about it, we can assume that each of those 3000-odd Glengarry farm lots was supporting a family by 1820. But perhaps it would be even more accurate to say that these farm lots provided a home for a family who "lumbered" a lot and farmed a little. As our section on lumbering will show, early records are more suggestive than detailed, but we do know all land that was at all suitable for farming eventually was cleared of its trees and many families had a potash kettle. In addition every village or hamlet beside running water developed an ashery, for which the raw material was the ashes of Glengarry's hardwood trees. Other local industries that made use of the forest products were the small tanneries with their constant demand for "tan bark" principally the bark of oak and hemlock. From the 1830's on there was a steady demand at Lancaster, Summerstown, and Cornwall for cordwood to fuel the small river steamboats. From 1847 to well into the twentieth century there was a steady demand for poles for telegraph, telephone, and hydro lines both for local use and export. The coming of the railroads brought a demand for ties and for cordwood to fuel the engines on the main lines (which started to burn coal about 1890 — all did by 1895).

Snake fence. This kind of fence needed no fence posts, no wire, and no holes bored. The rails as can be seen were piled on each other at such an angle that one panel of fence supported the next one. Moreover, the material for building the fence could be cut on the spot. In the days of hand mowing even the awkward corners of this fence could be mowed. With the advent of horse-drawn machinery the snake fence was of use only around pasture fields.

In Glengarry, quite a few acres of bush must have gone into the ''corduroy'' roads in our swamps and a great many more into the rail fences that surrounded each set of farm buildings as well as every three to five acre field and bordered most of our roads. The farm buildings themselves, whether of log or frame, also used timber. No matter what yardstick we use to measure early Glengarry farming by, we are driven to the conclusion that the men must have spent more time ''lumbering" than farming. To farm at all the land had to be cleared, and forest products as noted above would bring a necessary and much appreciated cash income, small though it was.

Undoubtedly there was a transition period that, in some unknown year, culminated in an equal division of man hours between Glengarry's forests and farming land. Each reader can guess at this date for himself (ours is 1880) but gradually the people on Glengarry's farms became a people who farmed a lot and lumbered a little. As our section on timber and timbermen will show, the sale of Glengarry's forest products was of significant value as recently as 1945. However, the "little heroic age" of Glengarry lumbering ended shortly after World War I, if not during that war.

What we are saying here is that Glengarry's forests played a significant part in keeping Glengarry's population rural and at first in keeping a family on each 100 acres. Later, after the timber was logged off, many farm lots now devoid of their timber value were bought by neighbouring farmers or incoming French families. The neighbouring farmers would buy the land for its rough pasture value and possibly a bit of work land. The incoming French families bought the land first of all for a place to live, and if possible make a living, supplemented by farm and bush work in the neighbourhood. When they "got their roots in," they too tended to "trade up" and buy better farms or more land.

A trend which we have noted, which began to be significant after World War II and has speeded up since, is the tendency for retired people and people who just want a quiet place to live to buy farmland in Glengarry. These people, "hobby farmers" if you will, very seldom try to live off their land. In any case, today, if the land in question cannot produce farm crops profitably it is either allowed to sit idle and reforest itself or is deliberately reforested either by the individual owner or the United Counties Reforestation Program.

As will be noted in our section on milk, the sub-marginal farm had a value because of its rough pastures which permitted summer milk to be produced cheaply for the cheese industry, which was entirely geared to summer milk. Even so, in 1967 when the cheese factories had just closed Glengarry's 3,000 farm lots were only occupied by 1600 serious farmers (a serious farmer in Glengarry was, and usually still is a dairy farmer). By 1976 those 1600 would drop to 500. In addition we recognize a few poultry men, beef raisers, and cash croppers, principally corn growers. In 1966 Glengarry had 250,000 acres in farm production, in 1975 only 165,000 acres.

A log barn. Every part of these barns was made or shaped with the axe, except the door hinges, and in a pinch these could be made too. The stable at the right end with a hay or straw mow around it would be quite warm in winter. Also it was very dark and had no ventilation.

So our tale of Glengarry's agriculture is really two sides of one coin. On one side, what happened to the greater part of the families that over the years thought there was a living to be made farming in Glengarry, on the other, efforts made to make farming a viable way of life in the county. These efforts culminated in some 500 or more farmers making a living from Glengarry's soil where once 3,000 had won a living.

Our chronicle will thus tend to concentrate on those efforts that tended or tried to make farming more productive. The reader will realize that the major breakthroughs in farming did not originate in Glengarry. The axe, the plough, the scythe, the seed drill, the use of fertilizer, crop rotation, improved breeds of livestock, threshing machines, tractors, and forage harvesters did not originate in Glengarry. Glengarry farmers adopted them and sooner or later made use of them and then very unevenly. One farmer might have a seed drill for instance and it the only one on the road. The assumption is also that there was a time lag, the north of the county being a bit behind the south in the adoption of new farming ideas. We do not feel we can prove this, nor do we intend to try. What is more obvious to us is a time lag in different sections of the same community, with a old-style dependence on lumbering coexisting with various advances in farming. Let us take some examples from the last twenty years of the nineteenth century. The Schell Co. was cutting timber in the north-east section of Kenyon, in the Dornie area, and Rayside and McArthur had shanties on farms in Lancaster Township. But in 1896 we note a steam-operated threshing outfit in operation at the barns of D.W. McLeod at McCrimmon, and in 1894 A.J. MacGillivray of Kirk Hill had a windmill installed to force water into his stables and the farmers around Picnic Grove (east of Glen Gordon) met to organize a plowing match for the first four concessions of the township. We know from these isolated instances, which attracted the attention of the media of the day, that these innovations were not in widespread use even in the communities where they were found.

There is a possibility that one farm implement that was very necessary in Glengarry farming originated in Glengarry or at least was independently thought up there. This was the stone lifter, a machine that most of our readers will have seen in museums in Glengarry and elsewhere. Basically it was a heavy duty windlass mounted high above a specialized heavy duty wagon frame. It was used to move heavy stone from the fields to fence or other disposal site.

In east central Lochiel there is a persistent story that a Jamieson from Brodie built such a machine, made sure it worked and then hitched a team of horses to it and drove it to

Kingston to apply for a patent on it. Kingston was at various times the Capital of Canada, so to that extent the story is plausible. Unfortunately the Canadian Patent Office has no record of such a patent or even an application for one by Mr. Jamieson. It could have happened. Eventually many communities in Glengarry had one or more stone lifting machines in them.

The reaper. Technically, the self-raking reaper, this machine cut the grain and the cut stalks fell on the table behind the knife. Periodically the windmill-like arms came around, dropped into position and raked the cut grain into a sheaf and onto the ground. The sheaves had to be bound by hand. In Glengarry not every farmer had one of these machines and those that did replaced them with a self-tie binder in about twenty years.

Perhaps the first and longest lasting effort to better agriculture in the county was the formation of Williamstown Fair in 1808. At first it was a copy of British events of the same sort held on the town street and designed to be an event at which livestock could be bought or sold, labourers hired, and ideas on farming exchanged. Over the years the idea behind the fair changed and it became a competition rather than an exchange but the twentieth century was well on its way before it stopped offering prizes for such things as fanning mills, knitting machines, churns, harness, and sub-soil plows. It did encourage local craftsmen, who in those days made needed farm equipment and supplied it to their communities.

Threshing oats with horsepower. The steam tractor was too big and too expensive for Glengarry farms so threshing with small threshing machines powered by horses on a treadmill persisted well into the 20th century. The portable gasoline engine and the coming of the small farm tractor (the Fordson and International 10-20) largely relieved the horses from duty on the treadmill.

Williamstown Fair, Ontario's oldest fair as it proclaims itself to be, was donated grounds for its fair, which it still occupies, by Sir John Johnson in 1815. It is the show day for a local agriculture society which over the years has had several names but one objective, helping agriculture in Glengarry. Beginning about 1854 a fair was staged at Alexandria every second year till 1908, usually by the same Agricultural Society that staged the Williamstown event. From 1908 to 1931 the Alexandria Fair was an annual event but it never seems to have been a huge success.

In 1889 Kenyon formed an Agricultural Society which held

its first fair in Maxville in 1890. Since then Maxville Fair along with Williamstown have been annual events of major importance to Glengarry's farming population. Though only a small percentage of the farmers are exhibitors, most turn out on "fair day" to see and be seen, to look and to talk, and to indulge in Glengarry's favourite pastime—discussion of their neighbours' doings.

The grain binder. A museum piece today, the grain binder in the late 1800's wrought one of the revolutions in agriculture. It enabled one man to cut and bind his grain crop doing about 10 acres a day. With the cradle, one man mowing and two binding did about an acre a day. The engine-powered combine replaced the grain binder in Glengarry in the 1950's.

In 1865 the Williamstown Fair Prize list offered among other things a prize for the best tombstone and the best bricks. Over the years these fair prize lists have encouraged "do-it-yourself people" and prizes have been offered for collections of knots, weeds and coloured slides; times change but this section of our fairs is still much in evidence. The type of quality of the livestock has changed much. In 1865 the Williamstown Fair Prize list offered prizes for "horned cattle," "Durhams," and "Mixed Cattle." Fifteen years later, D.M. McPherson giving evidence to the Ontario Agricultural Commission which appeared in its 1881 report, made statements such as these about Glengarry's "mixed cattle." "The Durham bull is coming into more general use. There have been Ayrshires for a few years back but latterly the favourite breed is the Durham. It is now quite common for our farmers to raise their best heifer calves to supply the waste in their herds." — "About 450 to 500 pounds of cheese is the highest average [as it took 10 lbs. of milk to make a pound of cheese this is a yield of 4500-5000 lbs. of milk per year] per cow in any herd. They were a select native stock with perhaps a sprinkling of Ayrshires and Durhams. Three hundred [i.e. 3000 lbs. per year] is a very good average but these cattle are very well selected and cared for" — "Ayrshires do not do well on Canadian pastures and are subject to milk fever" — "although it is quite possible that traces of Holstein blood are to be found here and there among the bovine descendents of some old Dutch importations, the Holstein Cattle are not, as far as any information before the Commissioners goes, represented by a single beast in Ontario today. But in the United States they have been bred for several years as well as imported largely from Holland."

Cows that D.M. McPherson spoke of as "the highest average" were just cows and would not find a place in a Glengarry herd today, let alone be taken to either of our two fairs, which have become as their prize lists indicate and newspaper accounts confirm show places for some of the best Holstein and Ayrshire herds in Ontario. Some few of these herds in Glengarry have international reputations as well.

The big upgrading in Glengarry's dairy cattle was done in the twentieth century but it began in the latter part of the nineteenth. With no apologies to our readers we will list some of the things that have made "cattle from Glengarry" as well known in the present as the Glengarry lumberman, contractor, and miner were a century ago. Though the list may be tedious to those not interested in this branch of our history, to no small degree this is the story of the use to which the good farmland of Glengarry was put.

1882 - Robert Hunter, an experienced Ayrshire breeder born in Scotland in 1850 came to Canada and bought property in the 4th of Lancaster (he soon moved to the Maxville area).

1900 - R. Hunter and sons William and Robert Jr. spend two months in Scotland buying Ayrshires.

1901 - R.R. Sangster, of Lancaster, offers an Ayrshire bull for sale at the Provincial Auction Sale (indicates Glengarry Ayrshires are felt to be as good as any in the province).

1901 - Peter Chisholm of Lochiel buys a registered Holstein bull of the famous "De Kole" strain.

1902 - J.D. McLeod of McCrimmon bought an Ayrshire bull calf from J. Lockie Wilson of Alexandria.

1904 - W.E. McKillican of Breadalbane has added three purebred Holsteins to his herd.

1905 - *Glengarry News* carries an article extolling the value of practical classes in judging purebred cattle and horses. Large and representative attendance at two meetings for this purpose.

1905 - Messrs. Hunter of Maxville send a carload of Ayrshire cattle to Toronto Fair (C.N.E.). They will visit several other large fairs before returning home.

1905 - R. Hunter of Maxville elected Vice-President of the Canadian Ayrshire Breeders Association.

1905 - At Maxville Fair Ayrshire prizes were won by Hunter, McMaster, McEwen and Cumming. Holstein prizes won by Bonnerville, McMaster, McEwen, Bourjon, Alguire, Anderson, McMillan, Munro. Jersey prizes by Cass, Sinclair, Cameron.

1905 - J.A. McArthur of Williamstown area has Jerseys, Herefords, and Ayrshires in his herd to compare them.

1907 - At Williamstown Fair, Ayrshire winners were Benning, McIntosh, Sandilands, Watt, and Mitchell. Holstein winners were Snyder, Burgess, McKay, Sangster, McLennan,

McArthur. Jersey winners were Munro, Harland, McCrimmon.

1909 - Robert Hunter of Maxville at Toronto Fair (C.N.E.) with his Ayrshires took 10 first prizes, 5 third prizes, 20 fourth prizes and others.

1909 - School fairs begin in Glengarry. This was an effort to interest young people in agriculture which lasted for almost thirty years. Prizes were offered for livestock and handicrafts.

1910 - D.C. McDougall of St. Elmo adds a number of pedigreed Holstein cattle to his herd.

1911 - D.E. McMaster of Laggan has a herd of some 15 registered Holsteins. They average 26.6 lbs. of milk per milking. (This was in June, the time of the flow of the milk, but we here are a long way from the "high average" cow of 1880, which produced 4500 - 5000 lbs. per year. The average cow in this herd is about twice as good).

1911 - R. Hunter and sons, Maxville, hold a dispersal sale of their Ayrshire cattle. Proceeds of the sale were $40,700.

1911 - Francis Trottier, well known Lochiel breeder of Holstein cattle, sold a 9 months old bull calf to J.McIntyre of Martintown.

1912 - D.F. McCrimmon, Dunvegan, bought a registered Ayrshire bull from McDonald College. Gordon Ferguson, Dunvegan, bought two pedigreed Ayrshire heifers at the same sale.

1913 - Holstein sale by Francis Trottier, 23 - 4 Lochiel; top price $245 paid by J.R. Sproule of Dominionville for "Corinne of Lochiel."

1914 - D.A. McLeod, Glen Norman, bought several head of purebred cattle at Inkerman to be the foundation of a herd.

1914 - W.E. McKillican of St. Elmo has a high producing 2 year old heifer on record of performance testing conducted by the Dominion Department of Agriculture (first mention of R.O.P. in Glengarry).

1914 - Peter MacGregor of St. Elmo installs a milking machine.

1915 - J.W. McLeod of Spring Creek Farm buys a Holstein bull from J.H. Taylor and Son of Scotland, Ontario.

1915 - David Munro of Lancaster will judge dairy cattle at Belleville and the other western Ontario fairs.

1917 - J.W. McLeod of Spring Creek Farm near Dalkeith sold his entire herd of 33 purebred Holsteins by public auction for a total of $4700. D.E. McMaster of Leggan paid the highest price for any animal $410.

1918 - Three young men from Glengarry win 1st prize in livestock judging at Kemptville, now go to Toronto to compete for Ontario Championship.

1919 - Professor Barton of McDonald College buys 5 purebred Ayrshires from A.Watt of Lancaster and 5 from Sandilands at Williamstown for the college farm.

1919 - Ayrshire herd of James Benning of the Glen, west of Williamstown, started in Beauharnois County, Quebec, in 1864 by his father, won a grand championship at Chicago World Fair in 1893. This herd moved to Glengarry about the turn of the century and is recognized as one of the best in North America (lots 9-10-11, 2nd Concession [Glen] of Charlottenburgh).

1920 - McNab Campbell of Dalkeith sold two purebred Ayrshire cows and two heifers to the Dominion Experimental Farm at Ottawa.

1920 - Highest price ever paid in Glengarry for a Holstein received by George Goodfellow of Lancaster for a 6 week old heifer sold to Senator A.C. Hardy of Brockville.

1921 - Eastern Ontario Ayrshire Breeders organize a club to improve the breed. James Benning of Williamstown elected President and Melvin Begg of Moose Creek, vice-president.

1924 - Neil S. McLeod of Dalkeith has his Ayrshire herd accredited (first mention of this which means the herd is guaranteed to be free of tuberculosis by the Department of Agriculture).

1929 - Large numbers of Glengarrians visited "The Better Livestock Train" which made stops at Lancaster and Glen Robertson on 29 and 30 May.

1925 - 2 young bulls from T.B. McAuley's Mount Victoria stock farm are bought in Glengarry by E.L.D. McMillan and J.D. McMaster of Laggan.

1928 - Stock judging team from Ontario Agricultural College takes 5th place in judging contest at the National Dairy Show in Memphis, Tenn. Ian McLeod of Dunvegan led the team in the individual competitions, also taking 5th place.

1929 - Plan worked out to test all cattle in Glengarry for tuberculosis and make the County a T.B. free area.

1930 - Glengarry Ayrshire breeders very successful at Ottawa Winter Fair. Cumming Bros. of Lanc. had female grand champion. Others who won were Wm. Gareau, Lancaster, W.G. McNaughton, and Murray Brothers of Martintown.

1931 - G.B.Holliday of Waddington, N.Y., bought 5 accredited and registered Holsteins from E.L.D.McMillan at Laggan.

1931 - Glengarry Ayrshire breeders form a Glengarry Ayrshire Club.

1933 - At sale of extra good herd of Wes Murray at Martintown cows average $30 apiece (Depression prices).

1936 - Neil Cumming, Lancaster, wins challenge trophy at Ottawa Winter Fair in the individual calf and heifer competition and cattle showmanship.

1938 - Glengarry breeders almost sweep the individual awards in Holstein and Ayrshire classes at the

367

Ottawa Winter Fair. Cumming Brothers of Lancaster in Ayrshires and Dan W. McLeod of Dalkeith in Holsteins were outstanding.

1940 - Cumming Bros. of Lancaster are informed that a cow judged to be "best uddered" at the American National Dairy Show at Harrisburg, Virginia, was from a dam raised by Cummings.

1941 - John MacLennan of Martintown was an important winner at the Ayrshire Cattle Show at the Ottawa Exhibition.

1941 - Record three hundred entries in Holstein and Ayrshire classes at Annual Maxville Fair.

1942 - Cow from Ayrshire herd of John McLennan at Martintown won a high production award and was rated a "gold seal Ayrshire", the 60th cow in North America to be so designated.

1943 - "Glengarry Sir Barton" herd sire of Cumming Bros. of Lancaster sells for $3600 at Buckeye Farm Sale at Lima, Ohio. This was the highest price paid for an Ayrshire since 1919.

1947 - Two meetings held in Glengarry in March to organize sub-units for an artificial cattle breeding unit in Eastern Ontario.

1947 - A. McNaughton of Bainsville was reserve dairy champion among senior boys at Kemptville Royal.

1948 - Ayrshire bull owned by Robertson and MacLennan of Martintown is Senior and Grand Champion at C.N.E. J.F. MacLennan won many other prizes with his Ayrshires.

1948 - For 18 months past the Eastern Ontario Cattle Breeders Association have been supplying semen from high grade Holstein bulls to Glengarry with good results. Now, if they can get 100 farmers to sign up in Glengarry they will start supplying semen from Ayrshire bulls as well. Only high quality bulls backed by high R.O.P. records are used (THE "END" for scrub bulls in

Glengarry.)

1951 - Cumming Bros. of Lancaster won the Premier Breeders Award at the Royal Winter Fair in Toronto for their entries of Ayrshire Cattle.

1956 - Malcolm Cumming of Lancaster presented with a life membership in the Ayrshire Breeders Association of Canada. John MacLennan of Martintown and Carlyle Watt of Lancaster elected directors of the Association.

1956 - George Goodfellow of Lancaster assembles 21 dairy cows from Glengarry for shipment to Puerto Rico.

1957 - Cattle from Ayrshire herd of Cumming Bros. of Lancaster form part of "State Herd" that won best state herd award at International Dairy Show in Chicago.

1960 - J. Carlyle Watt of Lancaster judges Ayrshires at the National Ayrshire show in Calgary.

1960 - Leslie B. Murray of Martintown awarded a Master Breeder's shield at the Holstein Friesian Annual Meeting at Toronto.

1961 - A 21-acre section of the farm of Clifford Wightman of Lancaster has been declared the best pasture land in Ontario. Wightman was selected Ontario pasture champion after winning Eastern Ontario Championship.

1961 - J.C. Watt of Lancaster elected President of the Ayrshire Breeders Association of Canada.

1963 - Lancaster bred cow "Kengor Ideal Aggie," grand champion Holstein at the Central Canada Exhibition, is first cow in Glengarry to produce more than 30,000 pounds of milk in one lactation. She is regarded as the top producer among current leading show cows in Canada (her production is about 6 times those that D.M. McPherson spoke of in the same area 80 years before).

1967 - A Holstein cow from the herd of Lloyd McRae of Bainsville will be one of the top type cows on display at the Canadian Pavilion at Expo in Montreal.

1968 - An Ayrshire cow owned by D.J. MacMaster of Laggan is awarded a diamond seal certificate in recognition of a life-time production of 150,000 lbs. of milk and 6000 lbs. of butter.

1969 - Canadian Ayrshire Breeders list 7 bulls as approved. Five of these 7 were raised by Cumming Bros. of Lancaster. This plan has been in effect for five years and to date only 47 bulls have been ''approved''.

1969 - Martintown farmer, Marland Murray, elected President of the Holstein Friesian Association of Canada after serving 12 years as a director (his farm is actually in Stormont).

1971 - A three year old Ayrshire cow owned by J.D. McMaster of Alexandria completes a Canadian Championship record. Milking as a 3 year old she produced 19,943 lbs. of milk with 705 lbs. of butter fat in 305 days and 22,266 lbs. of milk with 841 lbs. of fat in 354 days.

1972 - Tom Curran of Martintown has best Canadian milk cow in ''Sunny Dale Luck,'' an Ayrshire.

1972 - Glengarry has 42,485 cattle on 971 farms of which 21, 395 were milk cows; by contrast, 1,179 cattle were being fattened on 120 farms.

1972 - Carlyle Watt, Lancaster, honoured with a Life Membership in the Ayrshire Breeders Association of Canada.

1973 - Murdoch Arkinstall, of Dunvegan, presented with a Master Breeder's Shield by the Holstein Friesian Association of Canada, the highest award that a Holstein breeder can win. The Arkinstall herd was started in 1916 by Murdie's father, W.T. Arkinstall.

1973 - R.M. Roy, Bainsville, and D.J. McMaster, Alexandria, given awards for their high producing Ayrshire herds at Ayrshire Annual meeting in Montreal.

1973 - Kengor herd at Lancaster built up by Charles Naylor dispersed. 71 head of Holsteins brought $99,585, an average of $1,402. Clark MacCuaig of Lancaster bought the highest priced animal at the sale, a cow for $8,500.

1974 - Two of Canada's top producing Ayrshires owned by Tom Curran of Martintown.

1974 - Outstanding Ayrshire men in Glengarry are D.C. Murray, MacNaughton Cumming, Tom Curran, J.C. Watt, and Wilfred McNaughton.

1976 - At Ottawa Winter Fair in Holsteins Henry Krol, Williamstown, and Alma Smits, Lancaster, won prizes; and in Ayrshires winners were Mary McCrimmon, Dalkeith, Ian Vallance, Maxville, Allan and Ian Cumming, Lancaster.

1976 - Grand Champion Holstein bull at Royal Winter Fair, Toronto, was out of a cow raised by Campbell McDonald of Kirk Hill.

1977 - Bull from Ayrshire herd of Cumming Brothers of Lancaster sired the highest producing cow in the world "Middlebrook Fancy Madge."

1977 - A purebred Holstein cow owned by Murray Howes of Dalkeith and bred by John F. McCrimmon, Dunvegan, has received a Gold Seal Lifetime award from the Holstein-Friesian Association of Canada.

By far the larger part of the items cited above were taken from the files of the *Glengarry News* and the *Glengarry News* could and often did make things look as well as possible for Glengarry. But after making all due allowances for such a laudable attitude, we still find Glengarry's cattle breeders and their animals acknowledged as very good indeed by other breeders across the country. Also from the 1920's on we can see the type of item "that made the news" change. At first it was news if someone bought or sold a registered cattle beast, later it was news if Glengarry cattle breeders or beasts proved themselves in competition either in the show rings of the larger exhibitions or in the strong light of production figures, either of milk or quality progenitiveness.

While Glengarry's cattle breeders were making a name for themselves, every farm had its quota of other farm animals as well. As far back as 1793 it was found necessary to make arrangements for "pounding" stray animals and the scale of rates shows us that horses, horned cattle, sheep, and hogs were involved. Lord Selkirk's diary of 1804 tells us that the Glengarry settlement provided pork to the North West Company in Montreal and grew enough beef and produced enough butter for its own use. Selkirk was quoting Rev. John Bethune who most certainly knew the Glengarry settlement of the day from end to end.

In 1815 there were 1 stallion, 723 horses, and 136 oxen in Charlottenburgh. Lancaster had no stallions, 352 horses, and 80 oxen. There were probably sheep and hogs too but the District Treasurer did not include them in his accounts. The number of houses in Glengarry that had spinning wheels tell us that many families, if not most, kept enough sheep to clothe the family. John McGregor's diary, kept from 1877 to 1883, regularly mentions lambing, shearing, and doing things with the wool, but his references to his cattle indicate that he had only one or two milk cows, though he lived in the 2nd Concession of Charlottenburgh, today one of Glengarry's finest dairying concessions. In 1896 we read of the Glengarry beekeepers association meeting and the meeting was presided over by J.N. McCrimmon of Laggan in the absence of the President, J.G. Calder of Lancaster. We can assume, as their numbers were numerous enough to have an association and the two men mentioned were from opposite ends of the county, that beekeeping was a fairly widespread practice.

The 1851 Census record tells us that horses were on the scene in some numbers in Glengarry though we know little or nothing about their breeds. It can confidently be assumed that some of them were bred from the French Canadian breed of horses the Glengarry men brought back from their war-like activities in 1838. Certainly we know from personal knowledge that as late as the 1920's and 30's many Glengarrians both Scots and French were proud of their French Canadian teams. These horses were a medium-sized breed, 1200-1400 lbs. in weight, were good workers and thrived on ordinary hay with a minimum of grain. They were capable of putting up a good performance as driving horses too, as they were proud, well-gaited animals that looked good in a cutter or buggy and enjoyed a race on the way home from church or on the river ice any time that their owners disagreed on who had the fastest horse.

Making maple syrup in open pots. To anyone who has tasted maple syrup made by this method the modern product is tasteless and lacks character. The open pots and sap buckets attracted and collected mice, moths, leaves, twigs, bark, smoke ashes and various unidentifiable things. Though the larger pieces would be skimmed off, evidence of their presence remained in the taste. The evaporator made its appearance about 1895 but by no means every farmer bought one. Why should he? The kettles were still in good shape.

We do no know when the first of our modern heavy breeds of horses came to Glengarry, but K.A. McLeod of Laggan bought a "Scotch" Clyde at Ottawa in 1904 and by 1906 ads for heavy breed stallions for service appear and if at all possible, be the animal a Shire, a Clyde, a Percheron, or a Belgian, the fact that it was "imported" was stressed in the ad. Evidently, the horse breeders of the day were looking to Europe for good stock that was not available locally.

Mowing machine. Some 85 years ago this machine relegated the scythe to an implement used only for cutting weeds around the yard or a bit of hay for the bull.

By the start of World War I this had changed. In May and June 1914 most of one page of any issue of the *Glengarry News* is filled with ads for stallions for service and "imported" has become a rare word in these ads. In 1916 horse buyers for the French government visited Vankleek Hill and Alexandria and bought horses by the carload.

These scattered references show in some degree that Glengarry raised horses both for farm use and for sale. After World War II the tractor ousted the horse from Glengarry's farms and roads but a strange fact of chemistry kept large numbers of horses in Glengarry for the thirty years after the war. It had been found that a needed hormone for human use could be extracted from the urine of pregnant mares and several Glengarry horsemen found producing this to be a profitable business.

The horse is not yet gone from Glengarry however. Several breeders and trainers of hunters and jumpers have bought land in the south part of the county since 1965 and Williamstown now has several days of horse shows each year, good ones too.

The walking plow. This was Glengarry's basic tillage implement from days of first settlement to about 1950. It did turn over the ground efficiently and leave it so the winter frost and spring rains would help break up the sod. A man and team would plow about an acre a day which was not unreasonable with only 10-15 acres to plow, nor would it pay him to have a tractor to do it.

No one bothered to keep any record of Glengarry's early fowl or even mention them except in the most casual way. But we can deduce from old recipes that call for eggs that most people kept a few hens. Presumably these made their own arrangements for food and most of us with grey in our hair can remember finding hens' nests almost anywhere and taking the eggs to the house in our caps or hats. We also can remember that many of these eggs "had gone bad." We also can remember how quickly a chicken could be caught, killed, plucked, drawn, and put in the pot when unexpected company arrived. Most of us have slept under feather comforters our

375

great-grandmothers made, so poultry did exist at least in the last half of the nineteenth century, in Glengarry.

The farm well. Farm water supply over the years has ranged from a bucket dipped in the nearest creek or spring, through dug wells with a bucket on a rope, wooden pumps, cast iron pumps, engine driven pumps, to modern electric automatic systems. The picture shows a cast iron pump operated by man power discharging into a tub from which thirsty beasts and fowl could drink. Note the logs that cover the well and how the wooden stave tub has sagged to fit them.

The first trace of science we find in the poultry industry in Glengarry, however, is in 1900 when the Federal Department of Agriculture made arrangements with A.S. McBean of Lancaster to operate "an illustrative station for fattening poultry for export to Great Britain," with Mr. McBean undertaking to fatten about 1000. In 1912, Kenneth K. MacLeod won

376

1st prize at the Eastern Ontario Livestock and Poultry Show in Ottawa for a Brown Leghorn pullet. In 1921, and again in 1924, J.J. McMaster of Laggan won prizes for geese at the Ottawa Poultry Fair. In 1931, a White Leghorn hen owned by this same man was only one egg behind the winner in a 51 week-long laying contest sponsored by the Dominion Department of Agriculture.

Hauling ice. Some farmers "put up ice" each winter; those who shipped milk to the city dairies had to. The ice was cut on the nearest suitable river or pond with saws, hoisted out of the water with a "ginpole" derrick (hand operated of course), put on the sleigh as seen here, and then stored by packing it in sawdust. The ice could be used for cold drinks and making ice cream as well as cooling the milk. Nobody knew about pollution and bacteria so nobody worried.

E.S. Winter of Maxville was a prominent poultry man in the 1920's as were Alex McNeil and D.A. Gray of Skye, Pierson McIntosh of Martintown, and Angus Urquhart of Laggan. In fact in 1930, Angus Urquhart shipped breeding stock of Barred Rocks to both Ireland and Pennsylvania and in 1933 a pen of Urquhart's hens made the highest score in Canada in a year-long egg laying contest.

Since then the chicken and egg business along with the

broiler and meat bird business have become economical only if conducted on a large scale. Emile Bougie of Martintown was one of the first to make a business of "chickens" in the 1930's and his business flourished even after his death but was ended by a fire in 1954. Majors at North Lancaster were in the business almost as soon as Bougie and are still flourishing at the time of writing.

The hay loader. This implement which picked up the hay from a windrow and elevated it onto a wagon first appeared about 1895. It saved so much hard work that almost every Glengarry farmer bought one. The one shown here was probably made after or during World War II. The early models had a wooden frame, wooden wheels, did not pick up the hay cleanly, and were subject to many troubles, but they "were worth it."

A.G.F. Macdonald was fattening "stall fed cattle" for the Montreal market in 1901. D.D. McSweyn of McCrimmon bought a purebred ram at Arkell, Ontario, in 1910. In the 1920's Duncan A. Macdonald was raising mink and silver black foxes in Alexandria and consistently over the years we find honey being produced in Glengarry by such men as James Tombs of Alexandria, Emile Bougie, Bryce McNaughton of Martintown, and Lionel Levac of Green Valley. The last "economic" mention of sheep we can find is in 1942, when the Glengarry farmers were urged to produce more sheep to meet increased wartime demand for wool. There is no record of any response.

As we noted above, hogs were grown for market at a very early stage in Glengarry's history. When the cheese factories became common in the 1870's our farmers found the whey made good pig feed and for many years most farmers kept one or two sows. Apart from milk, pork was the main "cash crop," and a batch of pigs in the fall, ready for market, was expected to pay the taxes; a second batch, if there was one, was expected to make the mortgage payment. In those days "pigs were pigs," and it wasn't until hog carcass grading became part of the marketing system that our farmers began to realize there was a difference between a scrub boar and a good boar. One of the few Glengarry farmers that bred good pigs was R.J. McLeod of Kirk Hill who was champion bacon exhibitor at the Eastern Ontario Export Food Show in Ottawa in 1946. Since then some few farmers have specialized in pigs, one being Sam MacLeod of Martintown who in 1976 set up a 100 sow pig operation from which he expected to farrow 1800 - 2000 pigs and fatten them to market weight. Glengarry only marketed 8,344 hogs in 1976, so the scale of MacLeod's operation looms large in the county.

A man providing evidence for the Ontario Agricultural Commission Report of 1881 stated that "in Stormont, Dundas and Glengarry there were quite a number of good seedling apples cultivated up to 1863 when they were lost by a thaw followed by a cold snap. If they were looked up there should be some good ones still existing. The soil and the climate are very favourable to apple production and experiment could determine good new varieties. One of those lost in 1863 was an autumn apple of the size of the Golden Russet. Fifty percent of the so-called standard varieties are too tender for the district but a good deal depends upon location, soil, etc. It is important to get young trees from northern nurseries. A variety from Montreal will flourish here when the same variety from Rochester, New York, will not. Summer apples recommended are Red Astrachan, Early Harvest, and Tetofosky. Fall apples recommended are St. Lawrence, Duchess of Oldenburgh and Alexander. Winter varieties include Fameuse, Swayzie, Pomme Griese, Talman's Sweet, Spitzburg, Northern Spy, and Yellow Pippin.''

Apart from telling us that the area along the St. Lawrence was once regarded as ''apple growing country,'' the gentleman's report can be construed to cover a broader field. Our soils and climate actually determine what crops can be grown, no matter what the land owner would like to grow.

In the case of apples, Glengarry orchards did make a comeback after 1885 and until the winter of 1933-34 were pretty well able to fill local needs. That severe winter effectively ended all but casual apple growing in Glengarry, though all of us who remember pre-Seaway days will remember the orchards that were along #2 Highway between Cornwall and Morrisburg.

In the very early days of settlement, if oral history can be believed to any extent, spring wheat was grown in Glengarry and some was possibly exported. Over the long haul, though, Glengarry was forced by its soils and climate to be a county that grew hay and coarse grains such as oats and barley for its animal feed with buckwheat planted occasionally, usually when circumstance forced a field to be sown very late in the season.

Growing oats by force of circumstances was no great hardship for the Scots however. Along with hay it provided an adequate ration for their horses, and made into ''parritches'' (porridge) it supplied a substantial part of human diet as well. Potatoes have always been grown for home use and until a century ago were an easy crop to grow as there were no potato bugs. They appeared in 1874 and had spread all over the county by 1875, practically causing a potato famine as nobody knew of a method of controlling the pests except picking them one by one and then dropping them into a pail of water. Legend has it that some smart operator came up with a kit to kill potato bugs that sold like wildfire. When opened it consisted of two blocks of wood. The instructions read, ''Place bug on top of one piece, then bring the other down sharply; results guaranteed.''

Stooks of oats. After the grain was cut and bound, whether by hand or with a binder, the sheaves were set up on end in a shaped bundle called a stook to dry and await either the thresher or hauling to barn or stack. A well made stook shed rain and did not blow down, even in a high wind. Grain dryers were not needed or available on Glengarry farms when stooks were in use.

In 1894 we read of F. Major of North Lancaster shipping 50 tons of hay to Montreal and in 1901 W.S. Jamieson of Brodie is described as shipping an immense quantity of hay from Vankleek Hill station to the U.S.A. In 1903 J.G. McNaughton of Laggan sold 30 tons of hay to J.A. McRae, the hay and grain dealer in Alexandria. In 1911, N.D. McKenzie, the prototype Agricultural Representative for Glengarry, supervised an exhibit of Glengarry apples at the Royal Winter Fair in Toronto. In 1915 we read of the first sweet clover being grown in the county. A.J.McRae of Bridge End sowed three acres as a forage crop and it yielded 12 - 14 tons to the acre. Alfalfa began to be grown about the same time and field corn for silage became important to some farmers in some areas about the turn of the century, although many farmers did not feel ensilage was a necessary feed for their cattle and only about half of Glengarry's farmers as a result grew corn.

Hauling hay. For at least a century this is how Glengarry's hay moved from the field to the barn. The basic equipment was the high wooden-wheeled lumber-wagon with a hay rack on it with a team of horses for motive power. For at least half of that century the men pitched the hay onto the wagon with their pitchforks and then pitched it off into the mow in the barn.

John D. McLeod of Dunvegan was appointed special weed inspector for Glengarry (Eastern Ontario) in 1929. At the time there was quite an agitation for weed control in crops. In early February 1928 a group of Lochiel farmers met and discussed ''the installation of an improved fanning machine to clean all cereal seed grain.'' This resulted in the installation of a seed cleaning plant at Lochiel which was officially opened on 27 March 1931. The second such seed cleaning plant (and the 26th in Ontario) was opened in Maxville in April 1932 in McEwen's chopping mill with John D. McLeod the weed inspector in charge.

This movement for better quality crops in the north part of the County encouraged some outstanding efforts. In 1934, Keith McMillan and Francis McCormick of Lochiel were prize winners in barley and oats at the Central Canada Exhibition in Ottawa. Lyman W. McKillican and John Arkinstall of the Maxville area won 1st prize for red clover seed and 3rd prize for timothy hayseed at the Ottawa Winter Fair that same year. In 1936 Angus J.Urquhart of Laggan placed 20th in hard, red spring wheat at the International Show in Chicago. In 1941, McMillan Brothers of Dalkeith took 1st prize for spring wheat at the Ottawa Winter Fair Seed Show and D.L. McNaughton of Lancaster got 1st prize for fibre flax seed. That same year, McMillans were crowned "Timothy Kings" at the International Hay and Grain Show at Chicago while John M. Arkinstall of Maxville ran strongly in the field pea classes at the same show. The next time this show was held, in 1946, McMillans again were "Timothy Kings." John McMillan, Dalkeith, captured the World Championship in small seeds at the Royal Winter Fair in 1953 and Myles McMillan of McCrimmon won the world title for forage seed with his exhibit of timothy seed at the Royal in 1955. Lloyd McRae of Bainsville had the grand champion entry in hay classes at the Ottawa Valley Farm Show in 1963.

Even granting that these farmers were better than average, the above mentioned Glengarry-grown crops and seeds along with Wightman's best pasture in Ontario win in 1961, which we have already mentioned, demonstrate that some at least of Glengarry's farmers have progressed beyond the native grass and "bush browse" type of feed growing. But we note the marked improvement which began only about 75 years ago and has gathered impetus as it went along, part of the process that has resulted in good farmers occupying what good farmland Glengarry has, and making good use of it.

A crop that should be mentioned at least in passing is the fibre flax that was grown extensively in Lancaster Township during World War II, but that crop ended with the war and was only important for five years 1941-46.

For years, as we have stressed, the principal source of cash income for Glengarry's farmers was cheese factory milk. Happily as the cheese factories closed an alternative source of cash income became available. A type of hybrid grain corn has been developed that would ripen in Glengarry's relatively short frost-free growing season and in a matter of a year or two fields of corn and cribs for storing the crop became an accepted part of the landscape in rural Glengarry.

Making a stack. Many farmers with small barns found it necessary to stack part of their grain outside and move it into the barn as needed in the winter time. Others short of hay themselves would buy hay from a neighbour and stack it right in the fields to be hauled home in the winter. Still others in the south of the county went "to the marsh" (the marshes along the St. Lawrence) each fall to put up marsh hay to eke out their own. Glengarry's cheese factory cows depended on hay to live on all winter when there was no pasture.

The first year we hear of local experiments with corn as a grain crop was in 1941 when 12 different varieties were tested on the farm connected with the Counties Home, which was then on 11th Street East in Cornwall. It was twenty years later before any serious effort was made to grow it as a cash crop and it was not until 1968 that "corn became king of cash crops" in Glengarry. Along with milk, corn still holds that position in the county, in spite of discouragement by early frost and land too wet for harvesting.

The implements the Glengarry farmers used were determined by several factors, of which the two most important were availability and economics. Farming in both Britain and the U.S.A. had been a "labour intensive" operation till well·on in the nineteenth century As long as lots of cheap labour was available there was little concerted effort to get horse-drawn implements into use on farms. The plow and the wagon are the only two horse-drawn farm implements that can be traced back to antiquity. Even the plow came to America in a very crude wooden form whose wear points might be covered with iron by the local craftsmen who made it. Anything resembling the modern steel plow had to wait until the Bessemer and open hearth processes of making steel were invented in England between 1855 and 1865. The tale has often been told of how John Deere fitted a steel saw blade to the wooden mould-board of a plow of his day, about a century ago, thereby fashioning the first plow that turned the soil and was self-cleaning and founding the firm that is still in business today making farm implements. So recent is the age of steel and so recent is the plow that is more than a rooting implement.

Steel of a sort had been made prior to Bessemer's convector. Blacksmiths could heat and hammer a lump of iron at their forges and eventually have something that could be tempered. The product was very uneven in quality and not every blacksmith developed the skill to make such things as axe heads or scythe blades that would "stand up." As a consequence the scythe did not become popular till steel became plentiful and most crops were cut with the short-bladed sickle whose blade being shorter was less apt to break.

Donald Sinclair of St. Elmo, whose obituary is in the *Glengarry News* of 16 March 1906, said that prior to 1834 all grain in Glengarry was cut with a sickle. Sinclair would have first-hand knowledge, as he was born in 1817. One can imagine that on Glengarry farms the purchase of the first scythe would be remembered as a red-letter day, on which a big step forward was made.

So it was with other farm implements. People had tried to make satisfactory machinery of wood with the necessary heavy wear parts made of iron. A reaping machine that worked was in use in Britain in 1843 and Michael Partridge, the farm tool historian, tells us a few were exported to the United States. The same can be said of threshing machines. The basic threshing operation consists of beating the heads of cereal grain to loosen the seed from the stalk. Back in biblical times this was done by having oxen trample the grain, a threshing process that continued for many centuries. The same thing could be done by beating the grain with a stick (the flail). Someone discovered that a log with pegs driven into it and pulled over the grain by oxen or men would also thresh it and the cylinder and concave idea of threshing was born. The first threshing mills were no more than a method of loosening the grain from the straw. The grain still had to be winnowed, that is, the seed had to be separated from the straw and chaff. The straw would be lifted off the threshing floor with a fork and shaken to let the seed drop out of it, and the straw would then be disposed of. When only a pile of seed and chaff remained in a pile on the threshing floor, this would be thrown into the wind and the lighter chaff would be blown out of the seed, a process that got rid of the light material but left the seed grain mixed with a variety of weed seeds. To get rid of the weed seeds the grain had to be put through sieves of a suitable size to separate the wanted grain from the unwanted weed seeds. Then the seed had to be picked up and deposited in a suitable storage bin. Then a fresh batch of straw could be put on the threshing floor and the process repeated. It was a labour-intensive operation.

A satisfactory threshing machine driven by horse power or wind was in use from 1830 on (but presumably not in Glengarry). One by one attachments were added to the threshing machine, a shaker shoe behind the cylinder to separate the grain from the straw, a fan to winnow the grain, and sieves to separate good seeds from the bad ones. Eventually when enough power was available a blower to blow the straw away was added and an elevator to pick up the grain as it came from the sieves and deposit it in bags or a gin.

When did the first threshing machine come to Glengarry?

We do not know. But in 1835, a Bradalbane family received a threshing mill from Paisley, Scotland, and in 1841 the *Cornwall Observer* was advertising "Threshing Machines" manufactured in Toronto. John McGregor's diary 1877-1883 tells us there was a threshing machine in the neighbourhood which he used but he also mentions threshing small lots with a flail, if he needed grain before the threshing machine got to him. Incidentally, in 1881 McGregor threshed 179 bushels of oats, 38 bushels of pease, and 8 bushels of buckwheat. Prior to 1883, McGregor had evidently cut both his hay and grain with a scythe as he often mentions "mowing" and buying new scythes. In July of 1883 he proudly took home "a combined machine" (mower and reaper) for which he paid $30, and started it in the buckwheat.

Ferguson Thresher Co. Maxville, Ont.

FERGUSON STEEL THRESHER

2 SIZES 22" x 38" & 24" x 44"

★ SELF ALIGNING BALL BEARINGS
★ 36" LENGTH OF ADJUSTABLE SCREEN
★ PATENTED DOUBLE WIND BLAST

Threshing machine. This is one of the later models made by the Ferguson Threshing Co. of Maxville. The thing folded up at the right end is a self-feeder, a conveyor belt on which the sheaves were placed. Then they went through a revolving toothed cylinder that separated the grain from the straw. The straw passed over shakers that shook all the grain out of it and so to the blower at the rear which discharged through the pipe, here lying on the top of the machine. The grain was cleaned by sieve and by a fan in the lower parts of the machine and was delivered through the long thin spout at the centre of the machine.

Reapers had been available since 1851. Binders with the sheaves tied by hand were use in 1858 and the self-tie binders by 1876.

Filling the silo. The first silos for storing ensilage corn were built in Glengarry in the late 1890's, about 20 years before the gasoline engine and tractor appeared in the county. So a farm team on a treadmill provided the "horsepower" to operate the corn cutter and the cut corn was elevated to the top of the silo by an endless chain with cross cleats. The blower and the power to operate it were in the womb of the future when this picture was taken but our farmers, an ingenious group, had found a way to do the operation anyway.

Perhaps we would not be far wrong if we stated that by 1890 each community had the power implements it needed but that by no means every farmer in the community owned one of each. Economics dictated that several would band together to buy an implement or one man would buy one implement and someone else would buy another and yet a third would buy another and by a system of lending among themselves a suitable set of implements would be available to the community. From personal knowledge we know this system lasted at least till World War II in several communities.

The horse drawn implements that found their way into Glengarry farms in the 75 years between 1875 and 1950 are to be seen and marvelled at in many museums including the one operated by the Glengarry Historical Society at Dunvegan. By today's standards they were crude, cumbersome, and un-reliable and many of them must have been bought and used for their novelty value rather than their labour saving value as keeping them adjusted and in repair was no small task.

A dairy farm in Glengarry, 1978. Obviously this is plant designed to do a specific job and is as specialized as any industrialized process. It provides space for housing the dairy herd, space for housing replacement young cattle, space for milking parlour, an electrically operated bulk milk cooler, and storage tank, space for storing hay and straw, and no less than five silos for ensilage and haylage. Many of these farms even have their own feed chopping and mixing plant—a far cry from the log barn we have shown.

We do have a few dates when special implements appeared on the Glengarry scene. We have already mentioned the scythe, the threshing machine, the reaper-mower, and the stone lifter. The Rosses at Martintown bought a seed drill in 1886 and a binder about 1895. Evaporators for making maple syrup started to replace the iron pots and flat plans in the early 1880's as ads for evaporators testify. Wire fence was available in 1881 and John McGregor bought two rods of it. In the spring of 1897 the *Glengarry News* tells us "farmers along the military road between Alexandria and the Brown House are removing the old cedar rail fences and replacing them with wire." Binders had become common enough by 1898 for binder twine ads to appear, "which regret that this year twine is 14 to 17 cents a pound while last year it was 6¼ to 7½ cents." In 1899 the *Glengarry News* thought it worthwhile to send a reporter to the farm of John McCrimmon at Glen Roy to see a manure spreader "the only one in the County as yet" in operation. In March 1901, Massey Harris delivered three carloads of farm machinery to Alexandria which was picked up at the station by the 50 farmers who had bought it. They then formed a procession and paraded them down Alexandria's main street "following which the entire company sat down to dinner at the Ottawa Hotel."

In 1901, Dan McSweyn and his son John A. of the Mc-Crimmon area bought "a threshing machine that is up to date in every respect" and in 1902, A. Campbell and son had a threshing outfit operating in the Alexandria area "under their direct supervision." We can assume the flails were all left hanging in Glengarry by now, except perhaps to thresh a few beans or peas for home consumption.

We know nothing of the first horse power treadmill in Glengarry but Fergusons at Maxville were selling them of their own manufacture in 1901, and in 1904 N.F. McCrimmon and Malcolm Morrison were able to report that they had threshed 85 bushels of wheat in five hours with a Sawyer-Massey Separator (threshing mill) and a Ferguson horse power.

We read of the first windmill in Glengarry in 1894, and in the next fifteen years the first portable gasoline engines appeared. Corn cutters equipped with elevators to fill the new-fangled silos appeared in the first decade of the century; the blower had to wait until larger gas engines appeared with the first tractor. The first tractor we know of in Glengarry was one the government placed with A.A. McLennan of Lancaster in 1917 "equipped with a 3 furrow plow and a disc harrow to help the farmers in the area, in view of the shortage of labour and the need to increase production."

In 1905 Miss Annie McDougall aged 72 of 31-6 Lancaster slipped while getting water, fell into the boxed spring, and was drowned. This tells us that not every one had a pump, even a wooden one at that date. The first hay loader came to the county in 1905 and it was still news in 1908 when one was bought.

The first steel barn we can find was built by Norman Campbell of Athol in 1916 and at the same time he erected two silos and installed "iron stalls for 45 head of cattle." In 1918 the *Glengarry News* found it newsworthy that twenty auto-mobiles owned by area farmers came into Alexandria on Saturday to do business and remarked that the farmers are taking advantage of "the evolution of vehicle progress." In 1922 it was news when farmers bought tractors. Three were delivered to the Alexandria area that May. In fact, the *Glengarry News* mentions a person buying a tractor as late as December 1933, which shows they still were not too commonly owned. In 1941 there were only 399 tractors in Glengarry, or an average of 0.153 per farm (roughly one farm in seven had one).

Rather special equipment that deserves mention is Glengarry's mills. From time to time we have mentioned early mills, particularly saw mills, but grist mills were at least as important. The hulls had to be taken off the oats for the porridge, and when feeding animals became important oats and barley had to be ground for animal feed. As we noted elsewhere, the grist mill in Alexandria was out of operation for a few years at the turn of the century, and we were certainly impressed by the news accounts of the difficulty the community experienced as a result and the railway got into the act by advertising cheap freight rates on grist from Alexandria to Valleyfield. Even today when the only grist mill in the county is McEwen's portable one, it provides an essential service for animal feeds. Mills dealing with wool played an essential part in Glengarry's economy too, from 1801 when Malcolm McMartin built his mills in Martintown till McCormick's woollen mill at Alexandria, the former Tomb's mill, burned in June 1949. We can judge that people still did part of the work with wool at home as late as 1930, when a fulling bee was held at Brodie. However, the newspaper account goes on to say "the younger people of the community had never attended one before."

We have noted the seed cleaning plants being established in Glengarry in the late 1920's and early 1930's and ice was being put up from the turn of the century on—till artificial refrigeration gradually took over for cooling milk, but that had to wait till hydro came to the farms. The earliest refrigeration units on Glengarry farms that we have been able to trace go back to the early 1930's when two were installed by very progressive farmers east of Martintown (MacLennan and Urquhart).

The great revolution in farm machinery in Glengarry as elsewhere took place in the ten years after World War II. Light, high speed, economical gasoline engines had been developed for farm tractors in the 1930's and a suitable pneumatic tire for them had also been developed. Immediately after World War II, Harry Ferguson fitted his hydraulic system to the small Ford tractor and within a few years the armwork had gone completely out of farmwork. Front end loaders did all the farm lifting from loading the manure spreader to lifting a sick cow. The baler and forage harvester replaced the mower, hayloader, and pitch fork. The combine replaced the grain binder and the threshing machine, while the backhoe, bulldozer, and tile draining machine replaced the pick and shovel (the so-called idiot sticks). Even in the bush, the chain saw replaced the old bush fiddle, the cross-cut saw.

These modern implements had ball and roller bearings with either pre-sealed bearings or pressure lubrication points and were designed for constant high speed operation with a minimum of "down-time." Most were expensive to buy and only a good farmer on good land could afford to have them, another factor that speeded up the process of putting Glengarry's poorer farmland out of cultivation. But they also encouraged the owner of good land to buy more of the same, so as to make better use of his expensive equipment. The farmer in Glengarry today worries about paying for his machinery. His grandfather usually did not buy a machine till he could pay cash for it but then he had to worry about whether the machine would operate. Many still living can recall trying to start a one cylinder gas engine of about 1918 vintage in February to saw wood, or a Fordson tractor on a cold morning in the fall. We can recall one such incident when a balky Fordson tractor had played out every man on a silo-filling crew of about a dozen and still had not started. Dunkie James Tyo remarked "they done well when they put a crank on that thing!" Understatement, yes but perhaps it was preferable to the language we can recall hearing an elder of the Presbyterian Church using on one occasion when a bunch of chains had broken in his corn binder. We are sure the machinery of 1875-1950 is best in museums but it paved the way for today's mechanically minded Glengarry farmers, good farmers on good land; it either made mechanics of its owners or broke their hearts.

Though farming always played an important part in the economy (and still does, as it provides our food), until very recently it was left to the individual to provide himself with any technical farm training and in turn train his children to be farmers or farmers' wives. The results of this speak for themselves. In every generation since settlement occurred a significant number of young people (and not so young) have left Glengarry's farms for other occupations. Speaking as people who left Glengarry's farms ourselves we can see some of the formidable hurdles that had to be crossed by those who chose to stay there and farm. Lack of adequate methods of financing the operation was of course one and that has been remedied in the last 30 years. Lack of suitable education to help one to farm successfully was another. This one we feel we should say a bit about, mostly to describe what technical help was available over the years to Glengarry farmers and would-be Glengarry farmers.

First, and for years, the only technical help that was available was contained in a variety of farm magazines and journals. In 1837 the short-lived *Canadian Farmer and Mechanic* was published at Kingston and in 1842 the *British American Cultivator* was published at Toronto, followed by the *Canada Farmer* in 1847 and in 1848 by *Farmer and Mechanic* and the *Agriculturist and Canadian Journal* and in 1849 by *Canadian Agriculturist*. The *Farmers' Advocate and Home Journal* appeared in 1866. There were also a variety of American journals of the same type such as *The Agriculturist, Ohio Cultivator, Maine Farmer, American Herd Book, Working Farmer*, and *Allan's Domestic Animals*. We have no idea how many of these found their way to Glengarry but at least one very good book on farming methods was bought by a Grant west of Laggan about 1850 and is still in existence. With standards of learning as they were in Glengarry, described in some detail in our section on schools, we can doubt if ''book learnin' '' from any source played much part in educating Glengarry farmers in up-to-date technical matters until at least 1900.

The Ontario Agricultural School was opened at Guelph in 1874, with a two year course in practical farming. By the standards of the day its demands were stiff; entrants had to pass exams in reading, writing, arithmetic, spelling, and geography.Within four years it had 146 students. It is significant that this school was opened in Western Ontario rather than at Ottawa, Kingston, or Peterborough, yet Glengarry has always had a few students at Guelph, some few of whom returned home to farm. The first dairy school was also at Guelph but in 1904 the Kingston Dairy School was operating and three Glengarry men graduated from it in April of that year. In the course of the next 18 years most of Glengarry's cheese makers and the instructors hired by the various local cheese boards got their education at this school in Kingston. When the school at Kingston burned in 1922 the course was transferred to the newly founded Kemptville Agricultural College which in the fifty years since has given many Glengarry boys and girls the advantage of some technical training in agriculture, even if only on a three day short course. We must mention the availability of stock with good blood lines and expert technical information at the Dominion Experimental Farm at Ottawa and from McDonald College at Ste. Anne de Bellevue as soon as there was a need for such things in Glengarry.

In 1906 a Farmers' Institute was organized in Glengarry that was quite active for a time, discussing such things as the values of clovers as feed and the value of cooperatives to farmers. The Ontario Department of Agriculture opened an office in Alexandria in July 1910 and this office organized such things as field crop competitions and school fairs as well as giving technical help and advice when asked. The Junior Farmers movement in Glengarry started in 1916 when the first club was formed in Lancaster township and this group in co-operation with the agricultural representative's office formed a wide variety of calf, colt, and other clubs of that nature that from 1918 on sent judging teams to compete with others at Kemptville, Ottawa, Toronto, and Guelph. By 1930 girls were included in this program and Glengarry girls participated in clubs and classes dealing with home economics and domestic economy.

We have already mentioned the seed fairs that began in the county in 1933 and Maxville and Williamstown Fairs. They did play a part in promoting agriculture by at least making a public demonstration of what was available. Each farmer had to decide for himself, though, as to what upgrading it would pay him to do.

In January and February 1977, 20 Glengarry farmers received a five week course of instruction at Dalkeith in management of their farm business. The course was sponsored by the Kemptville College of Agricultural Technology, and John Gardiner of that institution was the co-ordinator of the course. The instructors however were all Glengarry farmers, Campbell Murray of Martintown, Sam Mac-Leod of Martintown, and Lloyd McRae of Bainsville — no outside help needed. We could not help contrasting this successful school with the results of a farm forum meeting at Quigley's (Lochiel) in November 1948. The subject for discussion at that meeting was "How a young man can get started in farming on his own." The meeting decided he probably could not and would be foolish to try!

Our summary of Glengarry's agriculture is 100 years of subsistence lumbering and farming and 75 years of transition when lumbering faded away and the expense and technology of horse powered implements discouraged many and would have discouraged more had it not been for the cheese factories, followed by 20 years of ruthless evolution that left comparatively few good farmers farming Glengarry's comparatively small acreage of good land.

The present authors, perhaps from personal bias, but hopefully from objective observation, must say that the most important product produced on Glengarry's farms was (and is) young men and women. There is a quality of life on Glengarry's concessions that instills character into children fortunate enough to be brought up on them and we can quote examples ranging from John Sandfield born in 1812 to Dr. Earl Lagroix, at present Superintendent of Separate Schools in Mississauga, Ontario.

# Chapter XII
# Milk

The *Glengarry News* of 24 September 1909 carried this statement, "There are seventy-seven active cheese factories in Glengarry." We were aware this was the lush "June" of the cheese factory industry. The market for "street milk" in Montreal, Ottawa, and Cornwall had not yet developed to any extent, nor had Borden, Carnation, Kraft, or Sealtest yet appeared on the local scene. So these 77 cheese factories presented a target to shoot for. Where were they all, when were they built, and what became of them?

Let us compare this statement with the census report of 1911, which gives two different kinds of figures for cheese factories in Glengarry. There are 65 factories producing cheese only, but there are 76 "Establishments making Butter and cheese." This therefore gives us a maximum of 76 cheese factories two years after the *Glengarry News'* statement, and thus agrees pretty closely with it.

The *News* gave no indication of the sources it used for its statement. No history of the cheese industry in Glengarry exists. Nor is there any cohesive documentation of the cheese boards that operated at different times for short periods at Lancaster, Alexandria, and Maxville. The Cornwall Cheese Board published its history to date, in 1919, but it was active only in south and western Charlottenburgh. So we were forced to comb the files of the local newspapers and piece together the scattered information in maps and other sources. A good deal of information came to light as we investigated the careers of D.M. McPherson of Lancaster, the Frasers of Vankleek Hill, and the

McLeods of Kirk Hill, all of whom owned several factories in the early days of cheese factories in Glengarry. Last but not least, we must mention Harvey MacMillan of Martintown, himself a cheesemaker all his working life, brother of cheesemakers and son of a cheesemaker, who spotted factories for us on a map as he knew them. The problem was confounded more than slightly by many factories having a trade name or a nickname. Who but a native would know that the King's Road Cheese Factory was not on the King's Road or that Aberdeen Cheese Factory was at the northwest corner of Little Russia? Or that "Glengarry Creams" factory was at Glen Brook when today most people have to ask "Where's Glen Brook?"

We came across evidence of the existence at one time or another of 25 cheese factories in Charlottenburgh, 25 in Kenyon, 18 in Lancaster, and 20 in Lochiel for a total of 88 in Glengarry. When we subtract those that we found were inoperative in 1909, usually because they had burned, and those that were built later, we found that the bald statement in the *Glengarry News* that there were 77 cheese factories operating in Glengarry in 1909 was probably substantially correct.

This number (77) is remarkably suggestive of the number of old public school sections in the county and spotting the cheese factories on a map showed that there was a remarkable coincidence between the locations of cheese factories and the locations of the old public schools. Which does not imply that the buildings were usually side by side because they were not. No sane cheese factory owner would put a factory so close to a school that the pupils would have easy access to it. School kids then as now, loved the curd and a handful apiece to forty kids every school day would have eaten into the profit. But many of us can remember a quick race to the cheese factory at morning recess, hoping to get there as they were salting the curd and hoping the proprietor would be in a good humour, or at least good enough to let us have a taste, if not a double handful.

For all practical purposes, cheese factories existed as an industry in Glengarry for one hundred years, 1870-1970. As a consequence of the number of them in the county and the cash income they provided, we have to consider the cheese industry as a separate factor in the general milk industry. We know cows came to Glengarry very shortly after the Loyalists arrived, as the British government undertook to supply a cow for every two families, though we have no record that this part of the program was completed. But we have independent proof that cows did arrive and that they multiplied. Rev. John Bethune told Lord Selkirk in the winter of 1804, that most settlers had three or four cows and that a good deal of butter was made. The will of John Haggard of Charlottenburgh, also dated in 1804, mentions two yoke of oxen and seven milk cows. Pringle tells us that in 1815 there were 1608 milk cows in Charlottenburgh and 1091 in Lancaster. If we assumed 3000 cows in Glengarry we probably would not be far wrong. In 1825, Pringle tells us, there were 7390 cows in SDG but in 1845 there were 13,118 milk cows in Glengarry alone. Cows and people were almost equal in numbers.

Nor must we conclude that because the last cheddar cheese factory in Glengarry closed in 1973, the cow had disappeared, or was in danger of doing so. Circumstances had changed and the small herd on every hundred acres had gone. In place of milk as a sideline the Glengarry dairy farmer of the 1970's was a highly skilled breeder and feeder who watched his cost-price ratio very closely, culled his herd ruthlessly, and used equipment that was almost completely automated to feed and milk his cows. Even the farm bull had disappeared with the coming of artificial insemination in the 1950's. Today's dairy farmer does not breed a cow simply "to have her freshen" in the spring. He breeds her to a bull from a line of proven milk producers and with every hope that the resulting calf will, if female, be in time a better and more efficient milk producer than her mother. If she is not, she will not be in production long, but will be "beefed", or perhaps more accurately "bolognied."

In its most elementary form, cheese and butter making came with the folks from the old country as an art that was ages old even then. Nobody knows who, in what land, discovered the basic properties of milk. It is refreshing and nutritious fresh from the cow. If allowed to sit quietly for a day or so milk separates naturally into two parts. A thick yellowish substance rises to the top of the container and comprises from 1/10 to 1/5 of the milk, depending on many factors such as the breed of the cow, the food she is eating, and how far she is into her lactation period. This thick part of the milk that we call cream was early found to be specially nutritious and if shaken up would produce globules of butter in time. Then if the liquid was drained off the butter globules, the butter could be stored and kept for use when needed. The liquid drained off (the buttermilk) itself made a refreshing drink. So here is the basis for a commercial use for milk — making butter from it, with buttermilk as a by-product.

D.M. McPherson (1847-1915), the man who brought the cheese factory industry to Glengarry in the 1870's and in the next 20 years developed it so a cheese factory was within easy driving distance of every farmer in the county. Still referred to as "the Cheese King." M.L.A. for Glengarry 1894-1898.

If milk is let stand, not only will cream rise to the top, but the whole thing will eventually go sour and most of the solids in the milk will flock together to form curds. It was found that these curds, if collected and squeezed a bit to get the liquid out of them, were a good tasty food and that the remaining liquid itself was a nutritious refreshing drink (whey), much relished by man and animals. This is the basic cheese making process.

Glengarry cheese box. These boxes were made by the tens of thousands and each held an 80 pound cheese. Properly covered they made excellent foot stools and sewing baskets. Knocked apart they made good kindling wood.

So it can be seen that we have three basic uses for milk. First as a food, used in the form it comes from the cow. Secondly, as a source of butter with its attendant by-products of buttermilk and the skim milk remaining after the cream is removed. Thirdly, as a source of cheese with its attendant by-product of whey. A fourth use, that never seems to have been practised in Glengarry, but is practised in many other parts of the world, is to let the milk ferment into a potent alcoholic beverage.

All four uses indicate a basic fact about milk. It is difficult (even with modern refrigeration) to keep milk for long in its natural form. Before refrigeration milk was milk for about 48 hours, so it was necessary to make a food product out of the milk as quickly as possible as butter and cheese, if properly handled, could be stored for fairly long periods of time. The problem of milk for table use in the towns and cities was quite simply solved. A lot of people in the towns and cities kept their own cows and those who did not bought milk from their neighbours. Right up until the end of the nineteenth century we read newspaper accounts of the nuisance cows are on city streets and in town gardens.

River Bank Cheese Factory, Summerstown.

When public health officers finally cleared cows out of the cities and the larger towns, a whole milk trade grew up in which Glengarry participated. Every railway ran a "milk train" which got milk to Montreal, Cornwall, and Ottawa within 18 hours of its being milked. These city dairies were fairly strict in their standards. They demanded an assured year round supply of good clean milk produced by healthy cows kept in sanitary stables. The milk from the night's milking had to be kept in clean cans in water cooled by ice and periodically the premises of the farmer who produced the milk had to be inspected by representatives of the dairy to which the milk was shipped—but a good price was paid.

Though figures are lacking, only a small percentage of Glengarry's milk ever entered this "street milk" trade as long as there were alternatives. Too much trouble, too much red tape was the excuse usually given by those who continued to send their milk to the local cheese factories and creameries.

The ostensible reason for not taking advantage of higher city prices for milk may have been fuss and bother. In actual practice there was a deeper and less obvious reason why most Glengarry farmers could not take advantage of city prices for their milk—they could not afford to produce milk the year around as their farms could not produce high quality feeds in large enough amounts to permit as much milk to be produced in January as in June, and this was a sine qua non of shipping to a city dairy. Most Glengarry farmers were in an ideal position to produce milk cheaply during the months of the year when the cattle could graze or browse on the rough pasture that comprised so much of Glengarry's rough workland.

Glengarry's farm cropland thus governed the number of those who could ship their milk to the cities. The basic requirement was enough cropland to produce enough high quality feed to produce enough milk the year around to make the high investment in better stables and milkhouses worthwhile. Glengarry farm cropland also governed the number of cows the farmer who shipped his milk to the creamery or cheese factory could keep over the winter. So in actual practice there was a strict upper limit to the number of cattle that could be kept on any given farm. The better the farm, the more cattle that could be kept. If the farm was good enough it permitted its owner to take advantage of higher city dairy prices. Otherwise his milk went "to the factory" or his cream to the creamery.

The only way a farmer could juggle his milk output at all was to decide whether or not he would raise his own replacement cattle. If he raised them he had to feed them for at least two winters before they became "production units." If he decided to kill all his calves at birth and buy milk cows he could keep three or four more cows on a hundred acres but that required a cash outlay which was generally about the profit that could be expected from a cow's milk for four years, and the cow could die or turn out to be a poor producer. Most farmers compromised by raising the odd calf from their best cows and buying the odd cow at a sale if the price seemed right.

To sum up, most Glengarry farms could produce milk at a nominal cost from May until November. Anything else, in most cases, defeated its own purpose as buying feed to produce milk cost more than the milk produced brought in. So Glengarry was in an ideal position to produce low cost milk for about seven months of the year, if there were a market for it.

Milk wagon with 40 gal. cans in a typical "lean to" shed at the back of the barn.

In early pioneer days Glengarry butter could and did face the Montreal market, and it is probable that the odd bit of what we would now call "pot cheese," "farmers' cheese", or simply "curd" found its way to the same market. This was not a true cheese in the modern sense of the term, or even the European sense of the term in the early 1800's. Even then many communities in Europe had developed distinctive true cheeses. These were milk curds with the whey completely pressed out of them and then the cheese allowed "to cure" under specified conditions. The names Camembert, Limoges, Edam, and Danish Blue come easily to mind today, yet it was Cheddar that developed as the cheese most representative of North America and Glengarry. Cheddar is a district in southwest England so we may guess that the method of making such a cheese was not a direct import to Glengarry and indeed it was not.

Irvine Cheese Factory, Martintown.

Fortunately for those of us who are interested in the history of things, in 1881 the Province of Ontario's Commission on Agriculture issued a book-length report on agriculture in Ontario. On page 404 this report states, "The manufacture of cheese in factories instead of private dairies may be said to have been inaugurated in Western Canada [that is Ontario] by Mr. Harvey Farrington of Herkimer County, New York, who settled in

Oxford County, Ontario, about the year 1864. In the year 1866 a great extension of the cheese manufacturing system took place in the Western Counties. In that year too, Mr. Ketcham Graham, after visiting the dairy districts of the States, put up the first cheese factory in the County of Hastings, now one of the greatest cheese producing centres in Ontario. The township returns give over five hundred cheese factories as being at the present time in existence in this Province and it is probable that nearly, if not quite five hundred are actually in operation. A large number are carried on upon co-operative principles by the farmers themselves. Others are worked either singly or otherwise by large manufacturers, and some, conducted by private persons, are designed to meet the wants of districts where the population is sparse, and only a limited number of patrons, consequently, can be found to share in the benefits."

Here we have the beginning of the cheese factory system in Ontario and that the factory system was producing more cheese than the small home dairy system used previously can be seen from these figures:

| Year | CWT of Cheese Exported from Canada |
|------|-----------------------|
| 1857 | 124 |
| 1858 | 117 |
| 1859 | 323 |
| 1860 | 1110 |
| 1863 | 466 |
| 1864 | 1138 |

In 1879-1880 Canada exported 387,867 cwt of cheese of which about 3,000,000 lbs. or 26,787 cwt was American cheese that found its way to market via Canada. So Canada (for which read Ontario) exported 361,080 cwt of its own cheese, or 317 times as much as in the year Harvey Farrington settled in Oxford County and started the first cheese factory in Ontario. The figure if expressed as a percent is almost 32,000 %, a truly spectacular increase in fifteen years. In that time herds had to be built up, factories built, men trained to operate them, and markets developed.

King's Road Cheese Factory.

Glen Walter Cheese Factory.

How did this spectacular development affect Glengarry? One of the earliest clues we have from local sources about a cheese factory in Glengarry is unfortunately not possible to date precisely. It is a sale bill, offering the Fraserfield property at McGillivray's Bridge for sale, and among its assets it lists a cheese factory and equipment capable of dealing with the milk of 1000 cows. Col. Alexander Fraser died in 1853 and the place was offered for sale for more than twenty years before Joshua Bowen bought it. However, if we date this sale bill to 1870 we will not be far wrong. In the fall of 1867 and the spring of 1868 the Cornwall *Freeholder* carried a news item, letters, and general information on a cheese factory being built and then opened by Mr. De Bellefeuille McDonald at Grey's Creek (presumably in Stormont). The tone of the information tells us that this venture into cheese making on a factory basis was at least comparatively new, if not totally new to the area. The newspaper accounts also lead us to believe these first cheese factory patrons in the area, whether in Cornwall Township or Charlottenburgh or both, were reasonably well satisfied with their returns from the new venture.

In 1871, the census report listed only two cheese factories in Glengarry, but the new system proved durable and popular, and in 1881 the census listed 16, and in 1891, 56.

By the end of the 1860's, Glengarry for one reason or another was ready for such a venture. In the first half of the nineteenth century its cow population had been building up. De Bellefeuille MacDonald's cheese factory at Grey's Creek had acquainted southern Glengarry with the benefits that could be derived from a cheese factory. At least one-third of the county's acres were unimproved rough pasture land, ideal pasturage for producing milk cheaply for cheese factories. All that was needed at that time was a man who could combine all the diverse elements into a business that would pay both him and his patrons.

Glengarry produced such a man in the person of a 23-year old Lancaster township farmer, David Murdoch McPherson. "D.M." as everyone knew him during his lifetime was born on 15-1 Lancaster Township in 1847, the fine farm occupied by

Lloyd and Tibby McRae in 1978 and by Lloyd's father "J.F." before him. When still a bit of a lad, D.M.'s mother died, and it is likely D.M., as the youngest of the family, had to look after the milk, which was considered "women's work" at the time. In the course of time D.M.'s father married a second wife, Phoebe Marjerison, and Phoebe probably knew more than the average woman about making cheese. Her folks were always well to the fore in the cheese and milk business in Glengarry. No name appears oftener in the newspaper accounts of any facets of the milk business over the years than Marjerison. We know D.M. was only educated at the local school so any education he got in cheese making he got at home or acquired by reading or by trial and error until he was a mature man.

In 1870 D.M. opened his first cheese factory—probably one of the first two cheese factories in Glengarry—on the family farm, and it was successful. That same year Charlie McPhadden started a cheese factory at Martintown but Charlie McPhadden was content to just operate one factory—D.M. believed in growth. In 1873 D.M. opened two more cheese factories, which he called Allan Grove numbers two and three. The factory on "Allan Grove," the home farm, became Allan Grove number one. By 1885 D.M. was operating five cheese factories in Lancaster Township, four in Lochiel, six in Kenyon, and nine in Charlottenburgh, a total of 24 in Glengarry. His operation had spread into Huntingdon County as well by this time and there he had an interest in 42 factories, but Clyde's Corner, Laguerre, and Dundee are outside our story.

For each cheese factory in Glengarry in which D.M. had an interest there would appear to have been two others in operation either owned by an individual who may or may not have been his own cheesemaker, or by a group of milk producers who had formed a co-operative to build a factory and hire a cheesemaker.

The Ontario Agricultural Commission which published its evidence in 1881 found only one man in Glengarry to give evidence and this was D.M. McPherson. We will quote his evidence at some length as it gives a picture of Glengarry's dairy industry about ten years after the first cheese factories had begun operation: "Mr. D.M. Macpherson [sic] of Lancaster (Glengarry), who was examined as witness is running no less than 13 cheese factories at the present time. Mr. Macpherson receives one and a half cents per pound, which covers, he says, 'all the work of manufacturing, selling, boxing, keeping the books and paying the dividends, everything, in fact, except drawing the milk.' His operations cover an area of about 18 miles square [note, not 18 square miles] and utilize the milk of some 4000 cows."

D.M. goes on to say: "One of my greatest difficulties has been to get the cheese of the different factories at a uniform quality; in that effort I think I have succeeded more this year than ever before. In order to attain that object generally throughout the County, I think it is better that one practical person should have the management of a section of factories, than that each factory should be managed separately. I think that system of management would be as great an improvement on the present factory system as the factory is on the private dairy. It would raise the standard of cheese everywhere. The great complaint at present is that there is a want of uniformity, as well as a great deal of inferior cheese."

D.M. goes on to give his observations of some other aspects of milk production, which because they are made by an interested eye witness are of more than passing interest to us almost a century later.

"Great improvements have been made in stables the last few years since factories were introduced, farmers having devoted more attention to housing their cows, keeping them comfortable and feeding them well. There are different kinds of stables, but the cows are generally tied with chains, very often facing each other with an alley between them. Stables are generally frame, closed in and made comfortable and warm, and well ventilated. There is not much bran or chopped feed used except that considerable is used when the cows come in (that is have their calves). Farmers are cutting their hay earlier than they used to, and when they do so their cows do not require so much grain. There is not much summer feeding. I consider corn excellent green feed for cows during the last of July or in August. I do not know that it increases the flow of milk, but it keeps up a uniform flow and also keeps the animal in good condition. Grass is the natural food for the production of milk. I have had some experience in bran feeding, and I find that it has not nourishment enough. It excites too much milk at the expense of the cow's vitality. A mixture of oatmeal and barleymeal with bran is good."

"All the feeding in the world will not secure an abundant supply of milk from every cow. If the dairyman is careful to raise his stock from a good beefing strain, such as the Durham [sic], he will not have so much occasion to put up with inferior milkers. Every one of the latter should be turned over to the drover or shipper as early as possible."

Though D.M.'s theory as quoted above is good, apparently in practice milk production left something to be desired in the herds of 1880, as D.M. goes on to say, "About 450 to 500 lbs. of cheese is the highest average per cow in any one herd. They were a select native stock with perhaps a sprinkling of Ayrshires and Durhams. Three hundred is a very good average, but these cattle were very well cared for and selected."

Though the next quote is not from D.M.'s evidence, it is from the same report, and is part of the evidence of a Mr. Malcolm, who went into the economics of milk production. "It will not be far from the mark to say that a cow that will give an average $40 a year will require, at market prices, $35 in food, leaving only $5 to pay for care and milking."

"But the profit is obtained, in the first place, by producing the food at less than the market price, and selling it through the cow, at the same time saving a large portion of its fertilizing value to the farm."

"In the second place, there is a profit secured by making use of the pasturage of land not fit for cultivation, also of bulky cheap produce, such as chaff, cornstalks, turnips, etc."

"In fact the cow should be looked upon as a medium or machine by which not only the coarse, cheap, bulky and unsaleable fodder may be turned into cash, but much that is of value, such as corn, peas, oats, barley and hay, may be marketed as remunerative prices."

Translated into more modern terms the above means that in return for feeding and looking after a cow for 365 days a year and milking her twice a day in season, each cow gave $5 reward and marketed otherwise unmarketable crops. A hundred acre farm could support from eight to fifteen cows, depending on "how good the farm was" so it will be seen that gross income was not great and net income was miniscule. But it was a cash income where none had existed before.

D.M. in this report explains at some length that care must be exercised in handling milk so it can be got to the factory "in proper condition." Milk utensils must be kept clean, milk must be removed from the stable as soon as possible so as to not pick up offensive odors. Milk must be cooled to 65$^{o}$ as soon as possible, "aerated" with a dipper as it cools, and then got to the factory once a day in a fresh, sweet condition.

The present authors must confess that at first they found the economics of the business of producing milk for the cheese factory industry unbelievable. Was it possible that a farm family would labour for a full year for a gross income of perhaps $500 of which only $60 might be considered profit? After all, this 1881 report reflected only the very early years of the cheese factory industry. Surely things improved later on. So we looked for further evidence at a later date. We found it in the form of a cheese factory record book from a cheese factory in central Kenyon (Baltic's Corner) for the year 1896. Here we found the story in detail and we found D.M. McPherson and Mr. Malcolm were exaggerating all right, but by making things look much better than they actually were.

In this book we found the largest income any patron had from his milk for a year was $278.56 and the lowest was $31.27. In the year 1896 the average was $118.70 and the median was $123.65.

The cheesemaker in this case was able to make a pound of

cheese from 10.16 pounds of milk and his pay for the months the cheese factory was open (May through November) was $589.88 based on 1¼ cents for each pound of cheese he made. Another observation we made was that nowhere in this cheese factory book was any allowance made for capital costs, depreciation, or interest on investment. By today's standards it was very much a "hand to mouth" operation.

As we followed the years along we found that the market kept asking for a drier cheese and at times it took eleven pounds of milk to produce a pound of cheese, instead of the 10.16 quoted above, which meant about a 10 percent cut in a patron's milk income, already small enough in all conscience. And we found that right up to the end of the cheese factory industry in Glengarry in 1973 the price of the milk the farmer sold was determined by the price of cheese, less the cost of manufacturing the cheese, although at times, such as during World War II, the government paid a subsidy to encourage cheese manufacture. We found it was possible to work out a rough formula to determine the price of milk delivered at the factory based on the price of cheese quoted on the various local cheese boards, on which Glengarry's cheese factories sold their cheese. If cheese sold for say 40 cents a pound, as it did once in a while in later years, and if we multiplied this 40 cents by nine (about the number of pounds of cheese made from 100 pounds of milk) we had an approximate idea of what a farmer received for his milk delivered to the cheese factory, in this case $3.60 per hundred pounds, less the cost of manufacture.

If we take the year 1951, when all of Canada's economy was expanding, we find in the Cornwall *Standard-Freeholder* that a fairly average selling price for cheese on the cheese board is 36 cents a pound. If we multiply this 36 cents by nine we find the farmer sending his milk to the cheese factory received a maximum of $3.24 per hundred for his milk. Few farmers kept books and fewer still of those who shipped their milk to cheese factories kept a record of their daily production of milk, yet from personal knowledge and many conversations with milk producers we can make a fair estimation of the income of a dairy farmer in Glengarry, who in 1951 sent his milk to a cheese factory.

Some few farmers sent more than 500 pounds a day in "the flow of the milk," the majority sent less, and "the flow of the milk" did not last beyond a month. Still let us say that it lasted the full seven months the factory was open, so 214 days x 500 pounds of milk at $3.24 per hundred pounds equals a maximum of $3466.80. This represented the return on a capital investment of land, stock, and machinery with a capital value of $15-20,000 and it also had to cover all operating costs, such as feed, fertilizer, gasoline, hydro, and the work 365 days a year of a man and his wife and usually his family. This at a time when a man working in a factory could earn $2000 per year with no capital investment, at least a week's paid holiday, every Sunday off, and several paid holidays during the year, and only a forty-four hour week to work, compared with the dairy farmers' eighty hour (or more) week.

The present work does not propose to be an exercise on the economics of farming but as a history of Glengarry it must note the forces working on the people of Glengarry and one of these was economic and for almost a hundred years the economy of Glengarry was very closely linked to the income from the cheese factories. The wonder of it is not that so many young people left Glengarry to make a living elsewhere but that so many stayed. Also we must note, and many of our readers will of their own knowledge know, that many farm families not only maintained a standard of living that they found to be agreeable on cheese factory income, but out of it as well some paid for higher education for their sons and daughters.

Nobody got wealthy sending his milk "to the factory." It did provide a steady, and if small, reliable source of cash, year in and year out, and the average Glengarry farmer adapted to it and "made do" without thinking that in any way he was imposed upon. He owned his land and he had few alternatives to the cheese factory as a source of income from that land. One of his alternatives was "to ship cream," or at least make some butter for himself from what milk he produced when the cheese factories were not operating in the winter months.

Prior to the invention of the cream separator in Sweden in the 1870's, the only way of separating the cream from the skim milk was to let the milk stand long enough for the cream to separate from the milk by gravity. This required about 24 hours. The first method used was to let the milk stand in large shallow vessels which required a lot of space, preferably in a cool place. The open pans were an invitation to dogs, cats, rats, and mice to help themselves, and if old tales be true they often did, with occasional drownings of the smaller creatures in the cream. This added variety to the taste of the butter, if not to the quality.

The next method used was "the cooling can"—a tall, small diameter can with a tap on the bottom and a sight glass in the side of the can so one could check visually when the skim milk was let out and only cream remained in the can.

There is no record of when the first cream separator appeared in Glengarry, and we would certainly like to know what brave soul ventured his hard cash to buy it. But we do know from a newspaper account in 1894 that R.J. Hayes was operating a creamery at Glen Roy and that Hayes won prizes for his butter at Ottawa Fair. A butter factory opened at Maxville in Nov. 1896 and the *Glengarry News* reported "it has given quite an impetus to winter dairying in the district." The manager was a Mr. Howey from Oxford Mills, which argues that local talent had not yet been developed.

In 1896 D.M. McPherson got on the creamery bandwagon and in the *Glengarrian* of 13 November 1896 we read, "D.M. McPherson, M.P.P. generally known as 'the Cheese King' is in the business of winter dairying on a large scale and will operate no less than 12 creameries this winter in Glengarry and Huntingdon."

The creameries of D.M.'s did come into existence, but they do not seem to have become newsworthy enough for the local papers to have given them much coverage. Alexandria Station, Williamstown, Glen Brook, Martintown, Dunvegan, and Green Valley each had one such creamery. In 1898 we read that the

Lorne Cheese factory (in Lochiel) is going to make butter in the winter months and is selling shares in the venture. In 1898 too we read that H. and P. Grant's butter factory at St. Elmo burnt in December.

The *Glengarry News* of 6 May 1898 carries a news item that tells us Croil and McCulloch of Montreal have erected a cheese factory and skimming station at Donald Roy Tailor's Corner, King's Road, Lancaster Township, and operations will soon begin for the season. That winter, too, D. Derbyshire and Co. of Brockville, manufacturers of dairy supplies, creamery outfitters, etc., appointed Ed Dever their agent in Martintown.

From the above we can judge there was a lot of interest in creameries in Glengarry just before the turn of the century. A small trade journal even appeared—the *Glengarry News* for 31 July 1898 reported that it had received the initial copy of *The Canadian Cheese and Buttermaker* published in Williamstown and Kingston by George F. Brown. "It is a 12 page journal devoted to dairying interests and is ably edited."

Very suddenly after 1898 mention of separate creameries disappears from the local newspapers and we hear more of "cheese and butter factories." In fact, it is not until 1923, when the Graham Creamery was established in Alexandria, that a creamery as such reappears on the Glengarry scene.

Evidently the production of winter milk on Glengarry farms was not a paying proposition and by combining butter making with cheese production in a cheese factory the profitable milk production season could be extended. Then too it was found that the whey left after the cheese curd had been removed had a butter fat content that could be separated from the whey and a more or less acceptable butter made from the resulting "cream." This made milk production more profitable and many farmers found "whey butter" would do on their own tables in place of the more expensive butter made from whole milk.

However, because "shipping cream" on the average paid about 10 percent better than sending milk to the factory, a fair number of farmers always shipped cream rather than milk. If there was no market for cream in Glengarry there would be in Cornwall and Montreal. Figures are impossible to come by but from personal knowledge we would say that about one-tenth of Glengarry's milk production was sold in the form of cream in the period 1894-1970. It could well have been less. Even if the skim milk was good pig food, turning the crank of the separator and washing it night and morning were monotonous jobs with little appeal when contrasted with the chance to swap gossip and news with the neighbours at the factory in the morning.

Another alternative open to a few Glengarry milk producers was a contract to sell "street milk" to large dairies in Cornwall, Montreal, and Ottawa. As stated earlier, this form of milk production called for extensive winter feeding of high quality feed, most of which had to be bought, even on the best Glengarry farms. When this feed cost was added to the extra capital costs of stabling and of milk houses that were good enough to pass inspection by the dairies concerned, this form of milk production became a comparatively expensive proposition. As a result it appealed only to those comparatively few farmers whose workland was a high proportion of their total land and of better than average quality. Though the returns were (this varied from time to time) about 50 percent higher than from the cheese factory, so were the costs. Part of the cost too required a cash outlay.

J.K. Galbraith, in his book *The Scotch*, though speaking of the Scots in Elgin County, might as well have been speaking of Glengarry when he said, "To spend either their own or borrowed money involved some risk of loss. The goal of their agriculture was a safe, one way flow of income, the flow being in their direction."

For many years few Glengarry milk producers seriously violated this basic equation. The good farmer on a good farm who could produce much of his own feed could afford to gamble with higher cost milk to secure a higher income. Most could not and did not. When in the years after World War II it became very apparent that milk for the cheese factory would not produce an income on which a family could live, Glengarry's farmers by the hundred simply quit milking cows and turned to "off farm work" for an income. By and large, those few with good land bought more, expanded their herds, improved their quality, and in 1978 are still producing milk which is sold through a milk marketing board on a "quota" per farmer basis. As a result, Glengarry still produces milk in large quantites but production is done by a few large operators who are coping more or less successfully with major changes that occur in their quotas, accompanied by price swings that make them prematurely grey, as government policies change. Only a few dedicated farmer-businessmen are willing to try to cope with the high cost and varying income from milk in Glengarry today.

Glen Falloch Cheese Factory showing the whey tank (what doesn't show are the flies around the whey tank).

One other major source of milk income in Glengarry deserves mention here. In 1915 the Borden Company built a milk plant in Maxville. By coincidence, this was the year Glengarry's "Cheese King," D.M. McPherson, died. It certainly marked the beginning of another era in milk marketing in Glengarry, as in a couple of years practically the whole flow of milk from the Maxville "milkshed" was diverted to Bordens. Much of Bordens' production was milk products such as ice cream and condensed milk, so pasteurization was an integral part of their process and they could afford to be not so rigorous in their inspection of premises as dairies that sold raw milk. As they paid a bit above cheese factory prices, in a very few years everybody in the Maxville area shipped to Bordens and continued to do so until the plant was destroyed by fire on 17 January 1957.

The Carnation Milk Plant at Alexandria. This modern milk processing plant opened in 1952, was enlarged in 1959, and officially re-opened on 2 Sept. 1959. Additional warehousing facilities were added in 1960-1961 and a spur line was built to the railway. Our readers will note the contrast apparent even from the outside to at least some of the factories we have pictured here.

Five years before the Borden plant burned, in April 1952 to be exact, the Carnation people had opened a plant in Alexandria and its success (and the need for such a plant) can be gauged from an item in the *Glengarry News* of 4 April 1952 which told us that the Carnation plant in Alexandria, on the first day it was opened, received more than twice the volume of milk expected.

Custom dies hard in Glengarry however, and cheese factories continued to operate. In January 1953, Glengarry's M.P., W.J. Major, asked the federal government to do all in its power to assist the provinces in protecting the dairy industry from the inroads of synthetic products (margarine) which were flooding the market. In 1954 H.S. Marjerison, president of the Glengarry Cheese Factory Patrons' Association, pointed out that the average return from a high grade herd last year was $1 per day (one hopes he meant net return rather than gross). Be that as it may, in the next fifteen years the *Glengarry News* chronicles the closing of one cheese factory after another, or else one burns and is not rebuilt as a factory but as a private dwelling or store.

The closing of the Glengarry cheese factories can be chronicled from the pages of the local press, but what need to do so? These factories closed within the memory of most persons still living, though it was such a quiet process that at the time it went largely unnoticed by the general public and was scarcely a cause for comment, though an elderly gentleman living east of Martintown did comment to one of the present authors about 1965, "In the fire miles east of Martintown there are only three farmers who milk cows anymore." If not absolutely correct, he was certainly close to the mark. A glance at the fences in advanced stages of disrepair or removed altogether told the story that crops no longer had to be protected from cattle, or rather that there were no cattle to protect them from.

The *Glengarry News* of 2 July 1970 perhaps printed the best requiem to the cheese factories, under the heading "Cheese Factories in Martintown Area sold to Kraft and are closed." The two factories concerned were the King's Road factory and the Burn Brae factory, and the writer of the article, probably the editor, Eugene Macdonald, himself of old Glengarry blood and a keen observer of his people, ended his article thus, "The closing of the factories brings thoughts of other days when they were important centres in the community where farmer met farmer discussing the weather, the crops, politics and news of the day while he waited with his horse and milk wagon for his turn at the weighing stand. On his way home he frequently stopped at a neighbor's gate for a morning chat."

"Gone are those more leisurely days and the cheese factory scene; gone the way of the blacksmith shop, the rural school and the country church or chapel."

But in spite of this requiem, the cheese factory industry was not yet quite dead in the Glengarry of 1970. The Apple Hill dairy owned by J.V. Guindon still continued to make cheddar cheese, and in March 1971 it was sold as a going concern employing 20 men to the J.M. Schneider Co. of Kitchener which intended to go on making cheese but a couple of years saw the end of the operation and the closing of the last cheese factory in Kenyon.

To witness the last struggle to produce cheddar cheese in Glengarry we have to go to Lochiel. There the descendants of the men who were beaten with Charlie at Culloden but not defeated, in 1963 girded themselves for a struggle to prove to themselves that cheddar cheese production was an economically viable proposition.

Their reasoning, quite well reported in the *Glengarry News,* was that a large cheese factory by using modern business methods and equipment to keep overhead low, could compete successfully for its share of the milk production and pay the producers enough to make it worth while to continue to send their milk to a factory.

In December 1963 we read that the foundations are being poured for a big six-vat cheese factory being built in Lochiel by the Quigley Cheese Manufacturing Association. The building will replace the factory destroyed by fire in March 1962.

In March 1964 we read that the "Big Cheese Factory" erected by the Quigley Cheese Manufacturing Company at Lochiel is ready to go into production.

In February 1971, Henri Gisoux, Cheesemaker and Plant Manager of the "Quigley Cheese Factory," reports that the Quigley Cheese Factory is being squeezed right out of business because the government quota will not let it have enough milk to make a profit on the operation in 1971. Its debt is $135,000 so it is likely the six year old plant will be sold to what he speaks of as a "viable concern."

In December 1973 an editorial in the *Glengarry News* is headed "No more cheddar cheese in Glengarry" and goes on to say "less than 40 years ago there were more than 50 cheese factories dotting the Glengarry scene, most of them patron owned. Today the Kraft plant at Williamstown is the only survivor.

"It is no longer economical for farmers to produce milk for cheese and cheddar cheese production is done."

In March 1974 the *Glengarry News* reported, "The Cheese Factory building of Quigley Manufacturing Company, Ltd., one mile east of Fassifern has been sold to Alexandria Moulding."

An era had ended.

In 1978 three large dairy plants process much of Glengarry's milk. Graham's Creamery in Alexandria at the date of writing has been in business for 55 years. The Carnation plant in the north-east corner of Alexandria has expanded several times since it opened for business in 1952, and today seems to be in equilibrium with its milk supply. In southern Glengarry Kraft Foods Limited operate a cheese plant that is modern in every respect, at Glendale south of Williamstown on the site of one of D.M. McPherson's first ten cheese factories, but cheddar cheese is not one of its products. Every day, huge refrigerated tank trucks haul milk out of the county to be processed into many different food forms from skim milk powder to baby formula. None of this milk is touched by human hands as it moves from the cow in its original form to store shelves in many forms. Machines milk the cows, pipes take the milk to bulk coolers which aerate it and cool it by machinery, and pumps load it onto the trucks and unload it at the plants. Anyone producing milk today produces it the year round and his cows are fed with "push buttons" that operate a variety of silo unloaders, augers, and conveyer belts. The cows are bred (since the early 1950's) by artifical insemination and the stables are cleaned by mechanical means. No stage of the operation is left to guess—breeding, feeding, and culling are carefully done.

The changes since D.M. McPherson's day would amaze him but one wonders if he would be too displeased. He not only was "the prophet" of a milk industry for Glengarry, he did much to encourage the mechanization of the industry. Well, there is no doubt the milk industry has become mechanized in Glengarry. There is also no doubt that Glengarry's milk production no longer depends on the efforts of the owners of its 3000-odd farm lots. It is in the hands of some 500 specialists who are hard-headed businessmen who happen to be in the milk business at the present time.

We hesitate to predict the future, if any, of the dairy business in Glengarry. As 1978 draws to a close we know there is an awesome cost-price squeeze on our dairy farmers and little hope of substantial financial reward.

Coal oil lamps. Left to right: an ordinary table lamp, a lamp with reflectors used in churches and public halls, a parlour lamp.

# Chapter XIII
# Light and Power

Tales from the early pioneer days about going to bed as soon after sunset as possible and rising at daybreak are probably only too true. Artificial light was a problem. As we know, our pioneer ancestors solved it in a variety of ways, ranging from the rush dip, through various forms of candles and torches made of cedar bark and pine knots, to the light from the fireplace, which also did their heating and cooking.

The rush dip was simply a bowl of grease from meat they had eaten, with a piece of bulrush stuck in it to hold and concentrate the flame. It gave little light and stank abominably. Candles gave more light and were made at home by either or both of two methods. The simplest methods required no special equipment. A length of cotton cord was dipped in a bowl of hot fat, pulled out, allowed to cool and then dipped again and again till the candle reached a suitable size. These dipped candles always came out to be different sizes along their length and lopsided. They were homemade and looked it but they gave a light and could be stuck in a candleholder and even in a lantern. The moulded candle was made in a mould—a hollow tube of metal—and these tubes were generally made into a cluster of six or ten. Cotton wicks were centred in the moulds, the moulds were poured full of hot fat and allowed to cool, and there was a handful of candles. A better grade of candle was made from beeswax but as this substance was rather scarce, wax candles were only used for "company" and on church altars. Wax candles had a decided advantage of not having an offensive smell. Torches need no particular description but were used for fishing and if light were needed in any wide open space at night. They had the advantage of being easily made of materials readily available to the pioneers.

Such were sources of artificial light for our ancestors. Until about 1860, indeed, there were no alternatives except the very expensive and, in Glengarry, almost impossible to obtain whale oil, which for some reason was sold as "train oil." But because a lamp had been developed to burn train oil, a lamp was ready to use the new-fangled "rock oil" or "coal oil" or "paraffin oil" that came on the market about 1860 as a result of commercial oil wells being dug (literally dug) in Western Ontario and Pennsylvania. In Glengarry the stuff was generally called "coal oil" though some insisted it was really "kerosene." By whatever name, it gave a very superior light to anything the folks had seen before. But it need not be thought that on that account Glengarry stopped making candles and torches. For one thing cash had to be paid for coal oil and few in Glengarry relished paying out money. For another thing, people, particularly the older folks, were scared of it. Coal oil lamps could and did explode—in fact we will note a fire started by a coal oil lamp in Glengarry that took a life in 1932. And then there were so many parts to be kept in tune—the burner, the wick, and the glass. So it was a rare Glengarry home that did not depend on candles for some part of its light right up to 1900 and even beyond. However, when electricity finally came to Glengarry it was the coal oil lamps and lantern that it displaced as a source of light. The candle eventually became a novelty or an emergency light.

Their primary source of power came to Glengarry with the first settlers—their own muscles. We can be sure that well before the nineteenth century began oxen were put to work to help move stumps and stones, pull the plough and harrows, and skid logs for burning. The ox lasted well in Glengarry too. Well within the memory of people who are in late middle age today, Glengarry folk died who had driven ox teams and for many jobs preferred them to horses. Ralph Connor, writing about the 1860's in the *Man from Glengarry*, mentions ox teams at the same stumping bee as teams of horses. The grandfather of one of the present authors who was born in 1852 had tales of ox teams to tell. Farm magazines of the period (none from or about Glengarry) debate the virtues of oxen as compared to horses. The ox was better in mud, the ox was less excitable in tricky spots in the bush or clearing land, the ox could find its own feed for most of the year, the ox required no special food, the ox could live on brush and twigs that a horse could not eat, the ox made beef when his working life was done, and so on. In fact, so well could a case in favour of ox power be presented that one could wonder how it came to pass that by 1870 everyone had switched to horses for their draft animals. As the farms were cleared it became possible to grow suitable horse hay and sufficient grain to work horses on, and the horse moved faster, meaning that more work got done in a day by a man and team. The faster moving horse brought church, mill, and market town closer to its owner and made its owner a bit more prosperous. So when the portable gasoline engine came to Glengarry farms about 1910, it replaced the horse on the treadmill for threshing and sawing wood and the ox was only a memory to middle-aged folks.

The earliest mills in Glengarry "went by water" and there was little difference between Johnson's mill at Williamstown built before 1790 and Christie's mill in the 9th of Charlottenburgh, still "going by water" in 1861, or for that matter mills that were in use 70 years after 1861. Water provided cheap power if there was a steady year round supply. However, even with a steady year round supply of water the wheel often "froze in" in winter and the family that had run out of oatmeal for "the parritches" was forced to use a hand mill or pound the oats in a hollowed out stump. Steady year round power was needed and this came in the form of the steam engine.

The steam engine both as a locomotive and stationary power unit had long been in use in the outside world before we hear of one being installed in a Glengarry mill in 1851. McIntyre's had this steam engine installed in their mill west of Williamstown and if it was not the first in Glengarry it could have been and we have no record of an earlier one. In 1856 Messrs. Vipond and Co. put a steam-driven saw mill into operation east of South Lancaster. In that year, too, D.A. Macdonald had a steam engine installed in his mill in Alexandria and to celebrate the occasion the people of Alexandria and area tendered their benefactor a banquet and a ball. On 14 January 1857 a special train brought guests from Montreal to Lancaster; a sleigh train brought them from Lancaster to Alexandria. A Montreal caterer prepared the banquet and a Montreal band provided the music between intervals of the pipes. *The Montreal Pilot* of 17 January 1857 carried a detailed description of this tribute to D.A. Macdonald, the man who made a mill in Alexandria run independently of wind, water, or frost. The account of this "do" has been republished several times since—many of our readers will be acquainted with it, without perhaps realizing what all the fuss was about. Power to turn Glengarry's millstones and saws was now under man's control and would be from then on.

In the 80 years after 1851 steam took over Glengarry's mills. If the mill was on a large stream with a fairly constant flow, the steam engine was auxiliary power. If, as in the case of Maxville or Apple Hill, there was no river at all or a river with an undependable flow, the steam engine was the only source of power. Also every cheese factory depended on its little steam engine for power for all its machinery and used steam to heat the vats and sterilize equipment as well. When stone crushers first came into use just after 1900, portable steam engines and steam traction engines ran them. Some may even have been used to thresh or run a buzz or drag saw but we have been unable to come up with any certain record of steam engines being used for farm purposes in Glengarry. Steam as a source of power for heavy equipment in Glengarry's mills and factories held its own till diesel power supplanted it in the 1930's and 40's.

In the almost 200 years since Glengarry was first settled perhaps as much power has been used to heat its houses as would have been used by all other power uses combined. Though that statement is impossible to prove, we all are aware that Glengarry's winters are long and cold and particularly in the far distant past when the laws of insulation were almost completely unknown and practised even less, a vast quantity of fuel was used (and still is in spite of insulation) to keep the houses, or at least some part of them livable in winter.

For many years Glengarry's wood lots supplied the fuel for household fires. At first fireplaces served both for heat and cooking purposes, but early in the nineteenth century stoves became available. The very oldest houses in Glengarry show good evidence that fireplaces were the main source of heat and holes for stove pipes were cut later. If wood was plentiful and help to cut and carry it was available, eventually a house would have a cook stove in the kitchen and a box stove in every main room. Even so, in the depths of winter all parts of the house not really needed would be sealed off and the family would occupy the kitchen and as few bedrooms as possible. It was taken for granted that on really cold nights "the pots" would freeze under the beds and as a matter of course there were at least two warmly dressed people in every bed under a mound of covers. The gravity furnace that appeared and was installed in many houses (mostly in the towns) just after the turn of the century used rougher and bigger blocks of wood than did the box stoves, but did little to make the houses more livable or cut down the amount of fuel used. Until after World War II the principal fuel used in the county as a whole was wood, though some few houses in the villages burned coal. We pick up advertisements for coal dealers in the *Glengarry News* in 1897 but coal was almost certainly burned before that.

During and immediately after World War II the *Glengarry News* carries stories of fuel shortages in the town of Alexandria. In the 1950's domestic oil ads appear and in a very few years oil furnaces, with forced air circulation, had taken over the job of heating Glengarry. As a whole, the county went from wood to oil for heat without an "age of coal."

Even today many farm homes have an old wood burning range in the kitchen, but for at least 25 years now, the electric stove has done most of the cooking in Glengarry homes.

In general terms the foregoing in this article brings us up to the start of what we like to think of as the modern era—that of electricity, gasoline, and natural gas. An era in which we like to think that a school janitor has as many conveniences as the school principal and lives in as warm a house, even if his house is not as big or his car as expensive. If the Sharps rifle and Colt revolver were the great equalizers in the American West, to no small extent cheap electricity was an equalizer in Glengarry.

Perhaps the earliest use of electricity for lighting in Glengarry came during the building of the Canada Atlantic, when a gravel pit a mile east of Glen Robertson was flood-lit. A newspaper writer who rode in an early train over this portion of the tracks in the fall of 1881 described the scene:

The drive was a delightful one. The beautiful
country through which the train sped was bathed
in the soft light of the full moon, in which
the hoar-frost twinkled and shimmered from
every tree, bush, fence-rail and bit of stubble.
Mountainous stacks of hay and grain dotted
many of the fields, showing that even the
capacious barns could not contain the bounti-
ful harvest, while the herds of cattle, un-
accustomed to the visits of the snorting
locomotive, scampered away as far as possible
from the track of the intruder. "But
what meteor is that which flashes intermittently through the tree-tops as the
train glides on at the rate of over 20
miles per hour?"
"That," the attentive Mr. Brown responds
"is the electric light at the gravel pit."
Worked, as it is by a steam-engine of about
8 horse power, it casts its brilliant rays
in every direction, so that the night gangs
who work at getting out the gravel for
ballasting, can see plainly how to labor, at
a distance of 350 feet from the incandescence:
Mr. Mountain assures us that the clerks in
the temporary office at a distance of 150
feet, can easily decipher manuscript or print.

There was something weird, almost uncanny, in encountering this triumph of modern science in what might be termed the back-woods of Glengarry.

Apart from this, the trend toward "modern" power and lighting began in our area in Cornwall in 1882. In that year Cornwall installed a plant to make gas from petroleum but Pringle tells us the gas was too expensive for private homes and only business places could afford it. In 1884 Thomas Edison installed an electric light system in the weaving shed at Canada Coloured Cottons in Cornwall and Wilbur Hitchcock, a local man who helped on the job, got the idea that supplying electricity to the town would be a paying venture and out of this idea Stormont Electric was formed. This company supplied light for domestic use in Cornwall for the first time on 24 August 1887 and in 1888 Pitt Street was lit with electricity.

In 1885 Ottawa got electric light and power and the ambitious citizens of Alexandria asked themselves, if Cornwall and Ottawa could have electricity, why can't we?

In 1894 Alexandria streets were lit to some extent with coal oil lanterns on top of posts on the main streets and Alexandria was engaged in putting in a water system for the town.

When Father Alexander Macdonell and D.A. Macdonald had been in the mill business in Alexandria they had tied up the water rights on the Garry River very tightly. The Garry, fed from its huge reservoir of Loch Garry, has a fairly constant flow even in summer, but under the circumstances the Garry was not available to Alexandria for a water supply so they were forced to go north to the River Delisle. East of the military road on the Delisle the first saw mill in Lochiel had been erected about 80 years before 1894 and there was a fair spot for a dam and a headpond. A good headpond was necessary as the Delisle's flow in dry seasons drops drastically. Even so there may have been enough water to supply drinking water to the population of Alexandria at the time. But the town fathers got ambitious and decided that their headpond and dam stored enough water to give the town not only drinking water but electricity as well. Alexandria got water in its taps in 1895 and in early 1896 the dynamo was put into position at the pumping station and Alexandria had electric lights on 17 January 1896. Nelson Smith was the engineer at the power house and Angus P. MacDonald was appointed collector of electric light dues. When first started up electricity was supplied only until 11:30 P.M. but in April the hour of shut off was extended to 1 A.M. When turned on there were 50 "beautiful" lamps of 35 candle power each on the streets and 300 lights in "mercantile establishments and private homes." Reeve Duncan A. McDonald and his colleagues were heartily complimented. Alexandria did have electric light and water, in some places at least. In October 1896 A.C. McDonald opened a shop for electrical supplies in the Harrison block in Alexandria and the *Glengarry News* reported in October that "it is expected that by Christmas upward of 800 lights will be in use in the town."

While Alexandria was getting water under pressure and building its own generating plant the people on the concessions and other villages had to make their own arrangements. Typical of these is a news item in November 1894: "Mr. Stubbs of Aultsville has erected a windmill on the farm of A.J. McGillivray at Kirk Hill to force water into his stables." But most pumps in the county were still hand operated and most water moved from one spot to another in pails rather than pipes.

1898 saw a telephone installed in Alexandria's power house and in February the Alexandria Council decided that so many people now were depending on electric light in their homes that power would have to be turned on in the morning as well as at night but it was December before that could be managed and then only from 5:30 A.M. to 7:15 A.M.

The first hint of trouble with Alexandria's power came in November 1898 when an expert from Ottawa (M.C. O'Donell) had to be called in as the lights were rather dim. He is reported to have "wonderfully improved the system" and the year ended with reports of four more houses being wired and Angus

McDonald, electrician, having a number of orders ahead.

On 14 February 1899, William Ritchie from Greenfield took over as engineer at Alexandria's powerhouse, a position he held until his death on 1 May 1931 when his son Duncan took over the job. Until H.E.P.C. took over in Alexandria in 1921, Mr. Ritchie's job must have been an interesting one.

While Alexandria was experimenting with electric light and power, over in the Maxville area James Ferguson was experimenting with a more primitive form of power—a treadmill for horses. In 1901 he patented his machine which was novel in that it had a reverse gear and in September he showed it at the Ottawa Fair. This was the beginning of the Ferguson Threshing Machine Company which for more than forty years was a major industry in Maxville and shipped its machines all over Canada. Ferguson's treadmill solved the power problem on many a Glengarry farm. With a team of horses on the tread, they would operate the tiny threshing machines of the day or run a circular or drag saw or in the pre-blower days when elevators were used to put silage in a silo they would run a cutting box. As late as 1935 one of Ferguson's treadmills was in use in the Martintown area, and there could well have been others.

In Alexandria the light system expanded. By November 1902, 300 more light bulbs had been added to the system and it was turned on every morning at 5 A.M. By 1903 Alexandria had $52,000 invested in its light and water system. With it, it was lighting about 1500 bulbs and was supplying water to the railroad for $800 per year.

The bicycle craze of the late 1890's had led to the development of a portable lamp. It had been found that if water were let drip on calcium carbide a flammable gas called acetylene was formed and this gas could be burned in a suitable burner to given either heat or light. A plant had been built at Ottawa to make calcium carbide and somehow the officials of this plant got together with the Maxville village fathers to conduct an experiment in street lighting by acetylene lamps. Maxville was on a direct railway line to Ottawa and it was simple enough to send carbide to Maxville as required. Maxville had been lighting its streets with large oil lamps placed on poles at intervals and was quite willing to try "gas lighting."

Kennedy Bros. in Alexandria were using a similar generator to fuel their laundry in February 1902 and the experimental building in Maxville seems to have been the Minto rink which the *Glengarry News* reported to have been lighted by acetylene gas in January 1903. The experiment was evidently a success because in August 1904 a carload of pipe arrived in Maxville and 20 men were put to digging a trench to lay the pipe. In November they were still laying pipe on Catherine Street and the generating plant was set up in a one storey tin building on the north side of the railway station, owned by John Smillie. Murdock Cather was the service man for the system but it seems he drew the line at charging the generator. John Smillie's son Walter had to do that job. (Acetylene generators had a nasty habit of exploding though Maxville's never did.) We have not been able to find any record of how many street lights and buildings were serviced by this gas plant, but it seems to have been satisfactory enough to stay in operation until hydro power came to Maxville. When the Presbyterians used it in their church to light "a circle of 50 lamps" and the rink used it, it must have been fairly economical as well as reliable. There was a by-product too. The used carbide was put in pails and sold to the farmers for 50 cents a pail. Apparently it made a good whitewash and in those days whitewash was used on the walls and ceilings of stables, hen houses, and cellars, and on the outside of the many log houses.

But out in the country there were still power problems. Finlay McEwen of the Maxville area erected a windmill in December 1904, and in September 1905, 27 windmills were unloaded in Winchester in one day.

On 14 May 1906 in far off Toronto an act was passed creating the Ontario Hydro Electric Power Commission. For all the good it did the United Counties for the next fifteen years, it might as well have been created on the moon. What makes this situation even less understandable is that the then Premier of

Ontario was James P. Whitney, a native of Dundas and sometime Cornwall lawyer. Indeed over the years one wonders why the Eastern counties were so well ignored by both the government in Toronto and the one at Ottawa. No place east of Brockville or Ottawa obtained any government building, institution, work shop, or anything else that provided a continuing payroll. This was true until the Seaway building was erected in Cornwall and its effect was largely negated by leaving Cornwall stranded from the seaway and with inadequate port facilities anyway. Did our members of parliament in both houses lack "power"?

We can guess that Alexandria had problems with an insufficient amount of water for drinking and electricity almost from the beginning because the *Glengarry News* of 31 July 1908 tells us that Alexandria is rebuilding its power dam on the Delisle with concrete and making it two feet higher "to ensure an adequate supply of water at all times." John Urquhart, acting town foreman, was in charge of the job. The *Glengarry News* of 11 September 1908 reports that "owing to unusually prolonged drought Alexandria's power system cannot deliver power to the town and town council is spending much time discussing the matter."

Perhaps in the next couple of years Glengarry's light and power situation can be best covered by a few dated entries:

1909- electric vacuum cleaners first appear in Eaton's catalogue. Very few Glengarry people are interested.
1910- portable gasoline one-cylinder engines appear on the market. In the next ten years probably at least half of Glengarry's farmers buy one. They were difficult to start in the summer and almost impossible in winter. They did supply power and they came in various sizes from ones small enough to pump water to ones big enough to run a fair sized threshing machine.
1910- Ontario Hydro inaugurates service at Berlin (Kitchener).

March
1910- Alexandria appoints a special committee to enquire into

feasibility of all-night electric power. The committee reported that the additional revenue would be insufficient to cover the extra expense and the matter was dropped for the time being.

October

1910-T.J.O'Shea installed a new gasoline lamp system in his store at Apple Hill—and in June 1910 a coal oil lamp exploded and the resultant fire destroyed the home of Nelson Larue, 19 Kenyon Street, Alexandria.

What with windmills, gas and coal oil lamps, acetylene lamps, gasoline engines, treadmills, and Alexandria's part-time electricity service combined with wood burning stoves, and horses, at the end of 1910 Glengarry's power requirements were taken care of. The most efficient of all these power producers was the horse and few would have predicted then that the days of the horse were numbered and those frustrating gas engines would drive the horse from the fields and roads. As for electricity, well just look at Alexandria—most of the town couldn't afford it and most of the time those that had it couldn't use it, because it wasn't turned on!

In November 1911 the Alexandria Water and Light Commission met to "further" discuss the question of the town's water supply. The town some time before had asked the owners of the mill on the Garry what terms they would ask to share their water with the town and the proposition was dropped as the mill owners were considered to be unreasonable. Now the town fathers considered artesian wells for drinking water. To make a long story short, several tries over 30 years gave the town no water from artesian wells.

In the meantime, in December 1911, the *Glengarry News* reported that Alexandria's electricity is shut off when "the powers that be" so decide each evening. Sometimes it is 11 P.M., more often 10 P.M.

Needless to say the local situation did not improve with the passing of time, but at the rapids of the St. Lawrence private power companies had developed electric power. In 1913 the

436

Cedar Rapids Power Company made noises suggesting they would like to expand into Ontario and in January 1914 Glengarry's M.P., J.A. McMillan, and its Provincial member, Hugh Munro, went to Ottawa to see the minister of railways about getting a power line run to Lancaster and then north to Alexandria. Nothing came of this move but the demand for electric power was increasing.

In March 1914, a letter to the editor of the *Glengarry News* said that electric light is used in 224 buildings in Alexandria and not used in 310. But as the ones that had it were rationed already no power expansion could be contemplated.

During World War I the first farm tractors appeared. They were unreliable, heavy, cumbersome, and awkward. When working they did do more work than a man could do with horses but they did not need to rest periodically. The first automobiles put in their appearance about the same time and bit by bit the reliability of the gas engine improved. This made another form of electric power possible—the home generating plant. Perhaps the first one to be installed in Glengarry was installed by Harry McLeod in J.R. MacLachlan's general store in Lancaster in August 1917. In 1918 at least two more were installed—one by Ed. J. McDonald on his farm in the 1st of Lochiel and one by D.D. McLeod at McCrimmon.

In the meantime Alexandria's power users and potential power users were getting desperate and at the town's annual meeting at the beginning of 1919 it was asked in plain English why Ontario Hydro was not in the town. About the same time (January 1919), the town fathers increased the electric rate 10 percent and the water rate 25 percent "with a view to meeting the deficit now existing between municipal receipts and expenditures". An Alexandria dentist, the very capable Dr. Cheney, headed the group that wanted to get Ontario Hydro in to replace Alexandria's "part time" system and eventually in November 1919 an engineer from the HEPC did appear before Alexandria's Town Council to tell them what was involved. It added up to getting the necessary by-laws passed and financing arranged after which, he thought, he could have Ontario Hydro at their disposal before the end of 1920.

At this time there seems to have been no thought of Ontario Hydro serving the farms in Glengarry and only Alexandria, Maxville, Lancaster, and the police villages of Apple Hill and Martintown voted, and Ontario Hydro was voted for by huge majorities—with only two against in Alexandria and one against in Maxville (January 1920).

By May 1920 nothing had happened and a delegation from Alexandria went to Toronto to interview the HEPC and were assured that their town would have HEPC power before the end of the year.

Ontario Hydro had made arrangements (not part of our story) to get hydro power from generating stations in Cornwall, and a line was built to Martintown, then north through Apple Hill to the 3rd of Kenyon with one branch going to Maxville and one to Alexandria. In August 1920 when the poles for the hydro line had almost reached Alexandria, the residents of Glen Robertson and the farmers along the 3rd of Lochiel tried "to get in on the act" and asked for estimates of the cost of supplying them with power, but they had to wait a while. In October the transformer sub-station was being built at the corner of Elgin and Margaret Streets in Alexandria, and Fred Gaby, Chief Engineer of the HEPC, told Dr. Cheney, now chairman of Alexandria's electric light committee, that power might be delivered to Alexandria by 1 January 1921.

They did not quite make it, but Ontario Hydro "came alive" in Alexandria on 18 January 1921, at 3:45 P.M. Joseph Laferriere, proprietor of the Union Hotel in Alexandria, gave everyone concerned a banquet.

A month later on 22 February, Maxville had Hydro power turned on, and they celebrated with a public meeting in the Women's Institute Hall that night. It was mentioned at that meeting, with a feeling of satisfaction, that Maxville's full complement of 5½ percent HEPC debentures were sold at par and all were sold in Maxville.

Nobody seems to have recorded when Apple Hill's big day was but Martintown and Lancaster got hydro power into their homes on 25 May 1921, "to the satisfaction of all concerned." We can reasonably assume Apple Hill was "lit up" about the same time.

Out on the concessions the power situation was as it had been. The *Glengarry News* in November 1920 reported the death of Laura Richer, aged 4, of the 4th of Kenyon, who received fatal burns "when her nightrobe came in contact with a lamp."

In November 1920 Albert Rowe east of Maxville installed a private generating plant at his farm, and in January 1921 Peter H. McEwen, 17th Indian Lands, also installed a private lighting system in his residence, barns, and outbuildings.

The farmers going into the villages and seeing them lit with electricity were now saying right out loud that "the folks must be better than the people." Finally Duncan A. Ross, M.L.A. for Glengarry and himself a farmer and member of the U.F.O., the governing party in Ontario at the time, called a public meeting in Alexandria in February 1920 to let the farmers discuss "cheap power for the farms and rural community." They did a lot of discussing but the HEPC was not ready to go out into the country yet. In fact it took a petition and a guarantee of three customers to the mile to get a line run to Glen Robertson from Alexandria.

In December 1922 we come across something that has been a recurrent theme with Ontario Hydro. The rates were raised. It was a raise we would not even notice today—a fifty cent per month increase on the minimum bill of domestic consumers, but it brought a powerful delegation from Alexandria to protest it before the Gregory Rate Commission in Cornwall, with the usual result of protesting hydro rate increases. They were necessary.

South Lancaster got electric light on 12 April 1923, Alexandria School in Alexandria installed electricity in February

1924, and by 1927 most farmers on a road on which hydro had a line had wired up.

Still only a favoured few lived beside a hydro line. Fred Vachon, 17-1 Kenyon, in December 1924 lost his barn from a fire started by an exploding lantern and the folks at St. Columba Church in Kirk Hill gave up waiting for hydro and installed a Delco home lighting plant in June 1927. In February 1928, William F. Campbell and Andrew Fisher dammed the west branch of the Scotch River at Athol hoping it would provide them with enough water power to generate energy for their own light and power needs. In November of 1928 a largely attended meeting in Kenyon Township Hall at Greenfield appointed a committee to solicit applications from farmers in the area for hydro as the HEPC had adopted a policy of going into rural areas if it could get three customers to a mile, particularly if the road the line is built on leads to a hamlet and both Greenfield and Dunvegan provided potential customers in this case. In November 1930 hydro employees built a line from Vallance's corner to Greenfield and there was talk of a line going west from Maxville on the 17th. At the same time another hydro crew was building a line north through Glen Sandfield to Dalkeith.

Hydro power had gone to Lancaster via Summerstown in 1921 and had worked its way up to Williamstown where Mr. Phillip Ross-Ross, then on the board of trustees, says the high school was wired and plumbing installed about 1930. The hydro seemed to be following the county roads as it penetrated Glengarry.

In December 1928, D.A. Campbell at Athol installed his own generating plant with Leslie Kippen of Maxville doing the job so the folks in that area were not hopeful of getting hydro service soon.

In 1932 the *Glengarry News* reported that a coal oil lamp exploded in Romeo Daprato's home in Alexandria and he died of burns in the resulting fire. This extreme misfortune of Mr. Daprato's shows that not everyone even in Glengarry's metropolis had hydro power. However, hydro was in enough homes that many people depended on it and a big windstorm in August of 1933 that knocked down many hydro poles and trees caused considerable hardship all over the county, not only in the villages but on the farms where many farmers had to milk and pump water by hand, something they had got out of the habit of doing.

In 1934, partly because industry due to the Depression was using much less power, HEPC reduced its rates. Also they commissioned Alexandria Reeve Edmond McGillivray and Louis Huot, an Alexandria businessman, to canvas Glengarry's townships to try to sell hydro to the farmers along them. This move had a touch of political porkbarrelling to it as McGillivray and Huot were both good Liberals, and Ontario at the time had a Liberal government under Premier Mitchell Hepburn, but the survey did show who was interested and where. Even if few farmers had money available at the time, in the next fifteen years hydro knew where to build.

The big sleet storm of November 1935 was only a minor setback for hydro and a boon to village store keepers. Many places were without hydro for 36 hours, and the stores in Glengarry got rid of their stocks of candles. No doubt the mice regretted the sleet storm—they loved candles.

In February 1937 hydro power reached the 4th of Kenyon and other lines were built around Glen Gordon and in Lochiel. Dunvegan church and manse were wired in July 1938, and the electricians were busy in Dalkeith that fall too. In February 1940 Glen Robertson got street lights and that summer a line was built across Glengarry linking Ontario Hydro to Quebec Hydro to cope with the demands of expanding war industries. 1940 saw hydro power come to the Loch Garry area and on 19 March 1941 an agreement to develop power from the Long Sault rapids west of Cornwall was signed at Ottawa. Seventeen years later that agreement bore fruit.

The biggest news in the light and power area during the war years was the damage done by the big sleet and windstorm of 30 and 31 December 1942. Most of the hydro and telephone lines in the county came down and many of the poles with them. Linemen were brought into Glengarry from Quebec and Western Ontario and it took the better part of two weeks to get "main line" service restored. The *Glengarry News* had to print with a hand press and it seemed the weather conspired to prevent permanent repairs as there were further blackouts on 15 January and again on 16 January. It was 22 January before power was restored to Martintown and even then many of the repairs were temporary. The local telephone systems of the day never really recovered from this storm. Five years later many of their lines were still strung on trees and fence posts.

But Ontario Hydro had strength and money, and right after the war got down to getting hydro into the concessions. A crew was building a line from Dalkeith into the Lochinvar area in January of 1946 and by 1950 almost anyone could have hydro in Glengarry that wanted it and could afford to pay for the necessary wiring, which a fair number could not afford.

A big snow and windstorm on 1 October 1946 cut off much of Glengarry's power and in the fall of 1948 Ontario Hydro, for lack of generating facilities, had to schedule power cuts all over the province at some time during the peak load period each evening from 4-8. By the fall of 1949 there was enough new plant "on line" to make these cuts unnecessary and since then the story of Glengarry's electric power is mostly one of expanding to close up gaps and tuck in loose ends.

Both Greenfield and Dunvegan got street lights in 1950 and Green Valley got them in 1958—just in time for Christmas, on 20 December. Alexandria put fluorescent lights on its Main Street in 1960 and South Lancaster got street lights in 1961.

As we come to the time of writing, Ontario Hydro is improving its plant and line in Kenyon and talking of new generating stations along the St. Lawrence between Brockville and the Quebec border, and the SDG council has expressed the hope one at least will be built in the counties because of the jobs it will create, at least during construction. Though the municipal councils keep trying and some industry has settled in Alexandria and in Charlottenburgh near Cornwall at the end of 1978, there is not much hope of improvement in Glengarry's tax base by industry in quantity coming in. To most Glengarry residents hydro power is a convenience rather than a real money-maker.

Before leaving hydro power we will note major breaks in the service in the area since 1942.

Glengarry took a bad beating from a sleet storm in early November 1951 and had another bad break in service on 30 December 1952 when 300 hydro poles were broken off in a storm in the Maxville-Apple Hill area. In March 1961 a weekend wind and rain storm disrupted service in north-eastern Glengarry for 36 hours, and in September of that year a deliberate cut-off darkened all of Glengarry and part of Prescott as a new regulating station was put into service and some necessary maintenance done. On 8 November 1965, a small safety switch overloaded near Hamilton, Ontario, causing safety switches to pop all over eastern North America. The break occurred in the early evening of 8 November and power was not fully restored until the next day. Battery operated radios and newspapers kept people informed and most people seemed to enjoy seeing the extreme confusion failure of a technical gadget could cause. And a follow-up on the "big hydro blackout of November 1965"—nine months or so later there was a big upswing in the birth rate in the blacked-out areas of the continent. With no T.V., people reverted to more primitive and less technical ways to pass the time that did not require light.

Natural gas as a source of power came to Glengarry in a very limited way. In 1958 a natural gas line was built across Glengarry crossing Highway 34 at Glen Gordon. The Carnation Milk plant in Alexandria wanted gas for fuel supply and would be a large enough user to make it worthwhile to build a line from Glen Gordon to Alexandria. Such a line was built, and a substation was erected in Alexandria east of the station and north of the railroad tracks. Gas was turned on on 10 February 1959. Having gas available in the town, in 1960 the Ottawa Gas Company canvassed Alexandria for potential customers and the first fifteen customers, eleven of whom were private home owners, got gas service between 7 and 24 September 1960. In 1961 the gas pipe line was continued on to Hawkesbury via Vankleek Hill.

Since the 1950's tractors supply all the mobile power on Glengarry's farms. The horse as a prime mover has disappeared from the scene and the working windmill is a rarity. Electricity cooks Glengarry's meals, oil heats its homes, and not many Glengarry women under forty would feel qualified to operate a "wood" cook stove. Most of those over forty have forgotten how.

As we write this, it even seems possible that the North West Museum in Williamstown will be the subject of an experiment in solar heating in the near future. It is enough to make all those old fellows who got two heats from every stick of wood turn over in their graves—the first heat came from cutting and splitting it, the second from burning it.

As we write this, the second municipality in Glengarry to install a municipal water and sewage system has it almost completed and ready to use. This is the village of Lancaster and perhaps before this is published we can record the date their system is officially activated.

# Chapter XIV
# Timber: Shantymen and the Timber Trade — Rayside and McArthur

## Timber and Timbermen

A few years ago the late Clarence Cattanach of Williamstown, at one time a saw mill owner himself, remarked to one of the authors, "In a gathering of any sort around here, just mention the word shanty, and every member of an old Glengarry family will prick up his ears. The newcomers won't be interested, but there isn't an old family in the county that hasn't had men in the bush someplace, at one time or another." Clarence was quite correct; perhaps he himself did not know just how correct he was, as he was speaking only from his own knowledge, extensive though it was. A hundred and eighty-six years have gone by since Chewett's map of 1792 showed three saw mills in Glengarry—at 10-1 Lancaster, 22-2 Lancaster, and Johnson's mill at 48-1 NSR in Charlottenburgh (east end of Williamstown). In 1978 there is a sizeable commercial saw mill at Dalkeith and there are several very small ones still doing a local business in the county.

In this long span of years, reaching right back to the days of first settlement, naturally there have been changes in the type of wood products that have been in demand. Lumber is still used for building today, just as it was two hundred years ago, a need that our first saw mills were built to fill and that they are still filling today. At the end of the eighteenth century there was also a demand for large timbers in Britain and in Lower Canada, a demand that Glengarry's men set out to fill, and in pursuit of this quest they followed "big timber" wherever it was to be found in

North America. Thanks to Glengarry's mixed forest, much of it on land that even the most optimistic farmer would not consider to be potential crop land, a lumber industry has persisted in Glengarry. When the first forest was cut off such land, it was allowed to reforest itself and today's forest products are cut from "second" and "third" growth trees.

A lumber shanty. Every lumber shanty consisted of at least three buildings—a combined bunk house and "cook's corner," always called a camboose in the Ottawa Valley, a horse stable, and a blacksmith shop. The gang foreman would have a corner partitioned off somewhere and this corner would also be the storeroom. It was a life for men who were men—no others could take it.

As we go along we will note saw mills and lumber firms in the county that became important enough to be considered "commercial mills" and we will note "shanties" in Glengarry, even in the twentieth century.

The word "shanty" to most twentieth-century citizens means a shack, a poor type of house. To an eighteenth century Frenchman the word "chantier" meant a timber or lumber yard, a place where timber "was made." The word came into English, spelled phonetically, with exactly the same meaning. Thus a typical shanty was a huddle of temporary buildings, almost always built of logs, where men lived and worked to make timber (and that was the term used: "make timber"). The buildings would consist of a bunkhouse, a stable, a storeroom, and a blacksmith shop. The bunkhouse would have bunks two or three tiers high around three walls of the building—the fourth wall was the "cook's corner." The fire for cooking and heating was built on a hearth in the centre of the bunkhouse (always called the camboose or caboose in the Ottawa Valley) and there never was a chimney—the smoke escaped through a hole in the roof. On benches around the fire, the men sat to eat their meals—porridge, potatoes, salt port, beans, and molasses were staples—and on these benches at night they placed their clothes to dry. Several writers such as Joshua Fraser and Sandy Fraser (John E. McIntosh) have described shanties based on their own experiences in them—none mentions bathing facilities but all speak with nostalgia of talking, singing, and music by the fire at night.

The contractor or a man he trusted would go into the timber limits he had bought rights to, in October, and select a spot for the buildings, with a stand of suitable timber within an hour's walk, a suitable stream to float the timber out on in the spring, and a suitable place on the stream's banks for a skidway from which the logs or timber could be easily rolled into the stream when the ice went out. An advance party would erect the buildings from material found on the spot, a few main trails would be brushed out, and with the first real snow a procession of already hired men, teams and sleighs would make their way to the shanty—the sleighs loaded with the hay for the horses and provisions for the men.

Then the men went to work. Work began as soon as it was light enough to see in the mornings, and continued until it was too dark to see at night. Sundays, Christmas, and New Years were the only holidays and blizzards meant nothing in the shelter of the bush. The owner or a close relative of the owner would be the foreman or "Boss" in a shanty, and his fists or moral supremacy was the only board of arbitration. In most years, if money were to be made, production had to be high and the overhead low.

Building the skidway. After the logs were cut they were skidded into an orderly pile built on small logs. This facilitated loading the logs onto sleighs or if the logs were to go "by water" the skidway was placed so the logs could be rolled from the skidway directly into the river as soon as the ice went out in the spring. This is a very old picture. Note that the logs were chopped rather than sawn at their butt ends, a technique preferred by the skilled axemen till quite late in the nineteenth century.

So a man who had done a winter's work in a shanty and came home with the approval of his boss and the respect of his fellow workers was entitled to proclaim himself "a man." This was the tradition that made a Glengarry family proud of its "shantymen" relatives and ancestors and also fostered the Glengarry "mystique" across America. We all remember that for more than a hundred years the men from Glengarry "made timber" with the best the rest of North America could produce, be it in Michigan, British Columbia, Northern Ontario, Wisconsin, New York or Quebec. Such was the reputation of the men from Glengarry in the shanties, that few would pick a fight with one of them or try to best him at any of the skills of making timber or river driving.

448

The man or men who could walk out on a jam like this, find the key log and after the logs got moving either get back to shore safely or ride a log down river were very valuable men. Sometimes dynamite was used to break the jam. Sometimes the men who broke the jam were either drowned or crushed. Many of the folk ballads of the lumber woods have "breaking the jam" as their subject.

It is probable that from the very beginning of settlement Glengarrians went to work in the lumber camps. At first these camps would be right around home or possibly within daily walking distance of home. Early references are scanty but suggestive. We know that in 1795 Jeremiah French contracted to deliver the hewn oak timber for the Cornwall jail and courthouse at 2½d a square foot, none of the timber to be less than 12" thick. That French could make such a contract argues that he had skilled hewers at his command or knew where he could find them. Squaring timber with a broad axe and chalk line is not an art that is learned in a day or two or even a month or two. Again in 1797 an old account book of the Molson family in Montreal tells us that John Molson bought a raft of logs and square timber from "up the St. Lawrence." It is not stated that this raft came from the Glengarry settlement but it is possible. Malcolm McMartin had mills operating in Martintown by 1801

449

and nothing can be more certain than that the timbers for his mill buildings and the bridge he put across the Raisin at that time were hewed either on the spot or up river from Martintown. By 1815 there were three saw mills in Charlottenburgh-Kenyon and three saw mills in Lancaster-Lochiel, all driven by water power. Anyone who has ever inspected the beams in any of our old buildings with the axe marks still plainly visible will join us in saying that Glengarry developed skilled broad axe men at a very early stage—in fact they built the mills and even after the mills were in existence and fairly easy of access, we read in the diary of James Cameron of his "making a timber." It was easier to do it at home than haul it to a saw mill whose carriage likely could not handle anything longer than about thirty feet anyway. So not all timber was made in distant shanties; some was made near home.

Hauling logs from the swamp. We have records of log drives in Glengarry on the Raisin, DeLisle, LaGraisse, and Sutherland's Creek. Nevertheless many logs moved from the bush or swamp as is shown here, four or five at a time on a bob-sleigh drawn by a team of horses. The binding pole that kept the chains tight that bound the logs to the sleigh can be clearly seen bent into an arc on the right side of the load.

But we can suspect that the most dedicated shantymen scorned to go to a shanty within easy reach of home. In the first half of the nineteenth century they swarmed to the Ottawa Valley, following its timber north and west, and in the 1870's Glengarry's shantymen were out in force in Michigan and Wisconsin. The obituary of a substantial Glengarry farmer who died in 1936 recalled that as a young man he "went as was customary with all the young men in his time to the Michigan bush for winter-work." One of the authors of this has a nice series of pictures of his Ross relatives in the Michigan woods in this period. In the last years of the nineteenth century and the early years of the present century, some of our Glengarry shantymen went to the "South Woods" as they called them, actually the foothill area of the mountains south of the St. Lawrence River in New York State. Both the *Glengarrian* and the *Glengarry News* carried news items about men leaving for and returning from "the South Woods," of which more later.

While the more dedicated shantymen travelled to distant timber there was still much timber to be dealt with on Glengarry's concessions and small scale timber operations multiplied in Glengarry. In 1816 the court of requests for Lancaster Township was to meet "at or near Alex Ross's mill" (probably it depended on the weather whether they sat on logs inside or outside the building). The will of John MacDonell of Charlottenburgh, made on 5 July 1816, leaves his grist and saw mill on 31 and 32-10 Lancaster to his brother Peter. Allan Cameron built a mill in north-east Lochiel in 1817, possibly on the site later occupied by Robertson's mills north of Dalkeith. In 1829 William Roebuck was given a grant to open a road through the 8th and 9th of Lancaster to his mill at what is now Dalhousie Mills. About 1840 Urquhart's built a saw and grist mill on "the Athole River," a short distance west of the Maxville-Scotch River Road at a point now the 20th I.L. James Craig (1823-1874), Warden and M.L.A., as a young man engaged in lumbering and supplying wood to the Grand Trunk Railway. George MacDonell ran a saw mill at Athol in the 1850's, 60's and 70's, and this mill was the nucleus of a busy townsite that disappeared when the good timber in the area had all been processed. As a matter of interest, this George MacDonell, when he left Athol, became Post Master in Cornwall and built a big house on the north-east corner of Second and Sydney streets. This house was later owned by Big Rory McLennan and by John McMartin, M.P., and then became the Nazareth Orphanage. Cornwall's present post office stands on the site.

Lumbering in Michigan with oxen, 1888. Very little of the work done by Glengarry men in the lumberwoods was glamorous. Most of it was monotonous hard work entailing long hours outside in the cold weather and deep snow. In this picture the ox driver is a native of the river road east of Martintown, John Ross. He stayed in Michigan and has many descendants there today. Many men preferred oxen to horses in the bush. Oxen were surer footed, less excitable, and did not need feed of as high a quality as horses.

Robertson's mill at Dalkeith appears in the 1852 census. In this section of Lochiel too Cosmos Kerr, later a prominent businessman in Alexandria, prior to his going to the California gold fields in 1852, lumbered in the 18th of Lancaster (9th of Lochiel) driving his timber to the Ottawa River and on occasion rafting it to Quebec. Kerr also lumbered along the Beaudette River and no doubt made use of its water to drive timber to the

St. Lawrence. In this period too, prior to 1852 a young man named Donald McIntosh who had been born in the Gore of Lochiel about 1833 was serving an apprenticeship in making timber. In the next 32 years Donald was with different concerns up the Ottawa and in Western Ontario and then spent 16 years as the "woods expert" of Rayside and McArthur of Monkland, Coteau, Williamstown, Lancaster, Martintown, and Maxville (Rayside and MacDougall in Maxville) whom we shall mention again later. Donald took up residence in Dalkeith in 1893 from where he operated his own business, as well as helping out Rayside and McArthur. He retired in 1912 and moved to Vankleek Hill, where he died 7 December 1918. Here we can only profile Glengarry's timber industry and the men connected with it but if a comprehensive history of it is ever written, Donald McIntosh will figure in it prominently.

For those who worked in any shanty, be it in Glengarry or anywhere else, the winter's work might conclude with an arduous but exciting trip down river to the point of sale, or to the mill the timber was destined for, on the timber raft. Of all the phases of lumbering, river driving is perhaps our most poorly documented. An agent of King's College, inspecting the college's properties in Lochiel in 1840, recorded that the occupiers of one of the college's lots were absent, being on a raft bound for Quebec. Cariboo Cameron's youngest brother Allan (d. 1903) spent several of his younger years in the lumber shanties and took rafts of timber to Quebec on nine different occasions.

Both Ralph Connor and Dorothy Dumbrille have paid literary tribute of the finest kind to Glengarry's timber men and river drivers. In "The Seven Mile Run" Dorothy Dumbrille had a Glengarry river man in action far from home (but very much at home in his surroundings) and Connor described them at their own backdoor "where the Scotch River joins the Nation."

Connor wrote fiction admittedly, but he remarked in his autobiography that "the tales of the lumbermen in *The Man from Glengarry* are from real life." Connor, born in 1860, said, "often I rode to school on the big timber sticks, 60' long and more, which were being hauled to the Scotch River to be floated down to the

Ottawa and thence to the St. Lawrence and Quebec."

De Boss Bully on de Reever Raisin. The ages of the people in the picture determine that the picture was taken about 1871 when the man centre front, Big Jim Rayside, was getting started in the lumber business. Years later he would be an M.L.A. and dress like a gentleman but here he is bossing his own river drive and he looks capable of doing so. In the rear, left to right, are Murdoch McGregor and Adam Thauvette.
At the left in front is Alex D. Ross and at the right is Frank Tyo.

This remark of Connor's is of interest as it shows that two different timber operations were going on in the area north of Maxville at the same time. George MacDonell's mill at Athol was going full blast in 1865-1870 and at the same time the Glengarry men were hewing timber right at home but destined for Quebec and the British trade.

454

We have two different views of our timbermen in the 1850's. One is by Ralph Connor: "A wild and colorful life was the lumberman's, full of danger and adventure, making the square timber, collecting the great sticks into rafts, breaking up jams, and running the rapids."

"Gay and gallant youths were these young Highlanders, quick as a wild lynx on their feet, fearless to meet the boiling waters, loving a fight for river right or for the honor of their clan, generous with their hard won pay to a new friend, or to a wily pimp, gambler or harlot. But the Great Revival...changed all that. The mighty sweeping of that religious upheaval [c. 1865] tamed the fighting, drinking, lusting Glengarry men into the finest river men that plied their adventurous trade on the Ottawa and the St. Lawrence.

"But the tales of the fierce old days survived down into my time, stirring my youthful heart with profound regret that deeds so heroically splendid should be all bad. For in spite of the Great Revival we were of the same race with ancient lust of battle in our blood."

Pringle, to an extent quoting Croil, or at least agreeing with him, says, "the lumber business appeared to be a very fascinating one, many were engaged in it either as employers or woodmen; the labor was hard, the winter was spent in the woods cutting and hewing the timber, the spring in getting it rafted and taking the timber to Quebec, where the men were paid off and too frequently verified the saying 'earning their money like horses and spending it like asses'."

"Large profits were made in favorable years, and were almost invariably lost in unfavourable ones, which unfortunately were by far the most numerous...of course the lumbering helped to clear the country, but it had a bad effect on agriculture, as many who were engaged in the work never attended properly to their farms. The farmers who remained at home and worked steadily there, were the best off in the long run."

Connor's florid prose written from the point of view of the social reformer he was, would bear more weight as to the high morals of the Glengarry timberman after the Great Revival if his scenario had not been restricted to one corner of Glengarry and one religious group in it. His Great Revival, really one of the big social events of his early childhood, impressed him out of all proportion to its extent and permanent results. Its effects lingered on for at least two generations in the area Notfield to Athol but it was confined to the Free Church Presbyterians and the Baptists.

A traveller named Adam Ferguson who visited Canada in 1831 criticized what he regarded as the backward farming of the Glengarrians and said "much valuable time is expended in the depths of the forest, in a demi-savage life, cutting and preparing timber for the lumber merchant, which, if steadily devoted to the cultivation of land, would certainly be attended with infinitely greater benefit, both in a physical and moral point of view."

In point of time Ferguson's dry comments about how cutting timber interfered with Glengarry farming should have come first. In point of fact, his view, though superficial, more or less agreed with Pringle's made some sixty years later. Ralph Connor's view we can leave to literary critics and sociologists (and possibly theologians) but we can agree with him that "shanty work did make men." We can also agree that there is a possibility, if not a probability that shanty work did to some degree at least interfere with farm work. We suspect that Ferguson the traveller, lawyer and gentleman farmer and Pringle the lawyer and judge just did not realize what a terrible scarcity of money existed on the (mainly) mortgaged farms of Glengarry and how few, if any alternatives the Glengarry folk had of earning cash money—the only thing that would pay off a mortgage, or buy such necessities as salt, nails, or tea.

It would be folly to suggest that shanty life never did ruin any Glengarry man for farming or spiritually or make an alcoholic of him. Glengarry Scots always had some of their number who drank with enthusiasm. They always had some who abstained with equal enthusiasm. Many people still living were privileged to know nineteenth-century Glengarry shanty-men and listen to their tales and they will completely fail to identify the shantymen they knew with such wastrels as Ralph

Connor speaks of in the early pages of *The Man From Glengarry*: "many a poor fellow in a single wild carouse in Quebec, or more frequently in some river town, would fling into the hands of sharks and harlots and tavern keepers, with whom the bosses were sometimes in league, the earnings of his long winter's work and would wake to find himself sick and penniless, far from home and broken in spirit."

Glengarry River Drivers. Though this is a fairly recent picture, c. 1905-1906, the quality has defeated attempts at total identification. The men are at Martintown waiting for a head of water to build up behind the dam so they can flush some more logs through the low water below the dam. D.T. Cresswell the mill and dam owner is in white (centre row right). Note the pike poles and cant hooks. This would be one of the last drives of McArthurs at Lancaster.

If further refutation of "the bad man image" of our Glengarry shantymen is necessary, one has only to consult the files of the *Glengarry News* from its beginning almost a hundred years ago through the 1950's and read the obituaries. The families of a surprising number of the men who died in those many years evidently made a point of having in the obituary the fact that their father had been a shantyman; they were proud of it. Equally surprising is the number of these ex-shantymen who "made good" in many walks of life, from members of parliament such as James Craig to James Ferguson of Maxville, founder of the Ferguson Threshing Machine Company.

In other words and words that can be proven, the roles of the shantymen in the later stages of their lives were various. Sometimes they used their savings to buy land or stock to establish themselves in farming or some other business in Glengarry. The death of such a shantyman was poignantly recorded by the *Glengarry News* in 1892: "Through his hard earnings in the shanties on the Ottawa River he saved enough money to buy the homestead on which he met his untimely end." While shantying was primarily a young man's activity, some men continued to go to the shanty winter after winter into middle age or even later. We sometimes hear of fathers and sons working in the same shanties such as Tom Ross (1795-1849) and his son Dan (1823-1906), and in his turn Dan's son Tom (1852-1944) worked with his father both in the South Woods and on Bear Creek. All were left-handed hewers and left-handed hewers were traditionally paid premium wages as they made it possible to work a stick of timber on both sides at the same time. Their broad axe with its left-handed handle and edges, is owned by Tom's grandson, one of the present writers. The Urquhart family from Martintown also provided at least three generations of left-handed hewers.

For many Glengarrians, the winter trips to distant lumber woods were the first step in what was to become, sooner or later, permanent residence in the U.S.A., British Columbia, or Northern Ontario; and often they were founders of families whose descendants write to Glengarry historians today asking for details of their grandfathers or great-grandfathers who left Glengarry to work in the shanties and then went into business or bought a farm—and if they did not prosper (but most did) they did not provide many welfare cases or criminals either.

Typical of one who went away and prospered was Sandy McDougall, born in Alexandria in 1844. He spent his early days at logging operations in the Ottawa Valley and went to British

Columbia in 1898 and went into the lumber business at McBride, B.C. Sandy died at McBride on 20 October 1934, aged 90. His obituary is in the *Glengarry News* of 7 November 1934.

Log drive in Glengarry 1906. Here they are shepherding the logs over the dam at Martintown and through the shallow water below the dam. The technique was to open one side of the dam, as is shown here, and flush the logs through the shallows a few at a time. 1906 was a disastrous year for McArthurs' drive. There was not enough water and about half the logs went aground and had to be hauled out of the river with horses so that they would not go out with the next winter's ice. For a variety of reasons this was the last year McArthurs "drove the Raisin." Campbell and Graham had a small drive in 1913.

Among those who stayed home and prospered was James Clark (1837-1915) of Dominionville, a shantyman from his youth up and with enough capital at his command in his forties to take a contract on the building of the Canada Atlantic Railway and to win the respect of his neighbors, who made hime reeve of Kenyon and set him on his course to being Warden of the Counties in 1877.

We have used a bit of space so far to deal with what is, thanks to Ralph Connor and to lesser extent, Dorothy Dumbrille, the "heroic age" of the shantymen. However, the 1870's, while they did not cut off the flow of Glengarry's young men to lumber woods in far off places, ushered in what we may call a "little heroic period" in lumbering right in Glengarry. For the first time we have evidence of local entrepreneurs buying or building mills and investing money in them right in the county and using timber from the county. Perhaps the foremost of these men and the earliest was Big Jim Rayside of whom more later.

J.T. Schell, an Oxford County native, appeared on the Glengarry scene in 1877 and for the next 39 years was much involved with lumbering in Glengarry, though he had other interests as well.

Other men of importance in Alexandria and area in the years 1880-1910 found it worthwhile to invest money in timber tracts and saw mills, among them Senator McMillan, Duncan Macdonald, storekeeper and post master in Alexandria, and Donald A. McArthur (1836-1918), Alexandria's first reeve. We have already mentioned Craig at Summerstown, Clark at Dominionville, and we must add Murdoch McRae (1855-1945), storekeeper and much else at Greenfield.

It is not fanciful to suggest that a fair share of Alexandria's prosperity around the turn of the century was based on the wood lots of northern Glengarry. The Canada Atlantic Railway had made it possible to get lumber to Montreal, New York, and Boston. Though big operators like Rayside and Schell stand out, there were many other smaller saw mills operating in Glengarry. In 1879 we are sure of 21 such mills, four in Charlottenburgh, eight in Kenyon, three in Lancaster, and six in Lochiel. There could well have been others too.

Some casual mention of timber and timber men in Glengarry will carry our story along. In 1896 McRae's saw mill at McCrimmon was totally destroyed by fire, and Glengarry's newpapers report men leaving for "the South Woods" in the fall and returning in the spring. An unusual news item in February 1896 is "upwards of 30 teams of horses passed through Alexandria on their way to the South Woods." We can assume that cutting was done and it was time to start hauling the timber to the skidways.

In 1897 D.D. McPhee's saw mill at Alexandria began to saw about the 1st of April and had 400,000 board feet of logs in the yard to start on. In November 1898 A.McArthur & Son, lumber merchants of South Lancaster, announced that they had bought a number of bush farms in Lancaster Township and they would have shanties on them during the winter months.

In 1898 Maxville seems to have been quite a mill town, with D. McKinnon and Sons' new saw mill advertising for 35,000 logs and Munro & McEwen of Moose Creek building another south of Smillie and Robertson's. In 1900 Colin McRae had a shanty near Fassifern, and in June of that year Donald, John Angus, and Finlay McSweyn, of McCrimmon, returned home after spending the winter in the Wisconsin woods. In November of that year Peter Grant, who was lumbering near Parry Sound, came to Alexandria to hire men to work in his woods.

In 1901, D.A. McDonald (Alexandria's post master, already mentioned) bought a timber tract in the 5th of Kenyon from John McMillan. In that year too Harlow G. Smith who had bought Rayside's mill at Martintown after Rayside's death sold the mill to Mathew Clingen and the Clingens would be in the lumber business for three generations in Martintown and in Apple Hill (after 1915). After Smith sold his Martintown mill he bought one of the ones at Greenfield and in 1901 he was buying timber lots in the Greenfield area. In 1901 D.J. McKenzie and John McLeod, lumbermen of Alma, Wisconsin, paid a visit to their native Glengarry.

In 1903 J.D. McArthur (whose father had been the Lancaster partner of Rayside) took a raft of square timber to Quebec from Lancaster and this is the last Glengarry record we have of "rafts to Quebec." We still find records of men working in the South Woods too. In his column in the *Glengarry News* of 9 April 1964 Angus H. McDonell, speaking of this period, says: "Men from Glengarry assembled at Summerstown with their horses and sleighs, provisions, cross-cut saws and axes, then headed across the ice bridge to the shanties of the South Woods in the Adirondacks." In this period, too, the *Glengarry News* found it worthwhile occasionally to carry a column of news headed "The South Woods."

In April 1905 McArthur and Son of Lancaster drove the largest lot of logs in half a century down the Raisin River, 63,000 logs compared to their annual average of 30,000, and that same spring Harlow G. Smith had some three million board feet of logs in his mill yard at Greenfield. In 1905 James R. Fraser and D. J. McPherson went up to the Madawaska to "cut off" Fraser's timber lands there, and this is also the last year we hear much of "the South Woods" (very last in 1912).

In 1907 Archie McPhee of the Thessalon Lumber Co. came to Alexandria to hire timbermen to work at Thessalon. No doubt he got several former "South Woods" men who would be glad to find an outlet for their skills.

An interesting news item of December 1909 is that "Ronald J. McDonald of Greenfield is manufacturing square timber for Jas. Cluff of Dominionville." Another item of interest is an ad in the *Glengarry News* of 19 November 1909 offering shantymen good wages of from $26-30 per month.

In 1910 we find H.A. McDonald and D. J. McDermid of Greenfield loading telephone poles for the American market and a gang of men cutting logs at Dornie for J.T. Schell.

In 1912 Angus J. Kennedy, formerly of Maxville but now a member of the New Liskeard lumbering firm of Grant and Kennedy, was elected Mayor of his adopted town. In 1913 Campbell and Graham took the last log drive down the Raisin River and the era of river driving was finished in Southern Glengarry.

In 1915 James Cluff built an up-to-date saw mill in Maxville and Duncan Morrison, from Dunvegan, was killed in a logging accident at Howe Sound, B.C. Perhaps the biggest lumbering news in 1915 in Glengarry was that "it was the first spring in 47 years that no drive of logs went down the River De Grasse [sic]."

In 1917 there were 19 saw mills in operation in Glengarry, compared to 21 in 1879, but none of these were large mills and they seem to have catered mostly to local trade and custom sawing. In the 1920's we find evidence that those Glengarry lumbermen who want to work at their trade have to go elsewhere, as for instance Edgar Irvine who (December 1920) "having secured the stumpage on some 1400 acres near North Bay will within a week have some 50 men working," and Neil McLeod of Laggan who in 1923 left for California to "accept a lucrative position with the Westlake Lumber Company." The 1920's too saw the close of the "little heroic age" of lumbering in Glengarry. In April 1922 Ethier's drove 18,000 logs   down the River de Graisse, a drive which is described as the largest in many years, and in the *Glengarry News* of 2 May 1925, we read: "Mr. Ethier, sawyer started his drive of logs this week from Lochinvar. He expects to float some 10,000 logs to his mill at Dalkeith." This is the last mention we find of log driving on a Glengarry river.

From 1925 to the present, items in our "lumbering file" tend to reflect the fact that Glengarry's "first growth" timber has about come to an end and the casual winter trips to shanties have ended. Here and there we find mention of Glengarry men working at timber, though. In March 1932 N.R. McCuaig, formerly of Dalkeith, was badly hurt in the northern part of Lanark County while running a saw mill. We can find evidence of only six saw mills in Glengarry in 1934, and in 1935 we find Malcolm and Neil Chisholm and Hedley Dawson returning to Maxville after a lumbering job at Lost River, Quebec.

In February 1940 Vogan Bros. at Kirk Hill completed cutting 400 logs for Fred McLeod. Log cuts are now in the low hundreds instead of the tens of thousands that we have previously noted. In February 1943 Alexandria had an acute stove wood shortage, only lumber slabs being available for firewood—shades of the days when the trees were burned for the sake of their ashes to make potash! In 1948, "Colin J. McPherson, age 21, a Glengarrian, drowned while engaged on a log drive on the Mississauga River, north of Blind River, Ont." The next item about Glengarry loggers abroad is from 12 April 1967, when Romeo Leroux, a native of Alexandria, drowned at Sioux Lookout, Ontario, where he had been engaged at lumbering for 14 years.

The last entries in our file concern the burning of MacLennan's mill at Dalkeith in 1971. It employed 22 men on day and night shifts. In June 1973 it was reported in full operation again, producing mostly rough hardwood lumber and employing 23 men—the last vestige of a major industry in Glengarry operated by a mighty breed of men.

### Rayside and McArthur, Lumber and Timber Dealers of Lancaster

This firm's story began at the beginning of Glengarry's "little heroic age of lumbering" and finished in a blaze well within living memory. The firm was run at first by James Rayside (1836-1895), then by a partnership between Rayside and Archibald McArthur, and then after 1889 by Archibald McArthur. Archibald McArthur died on 3 March 1906 and his son J.D. succeeded him as head of the business only to die little more than six months after his father. Then the firm was operated for a time by the Estate of J.D. McArthur.

So here is the story of men as well as that of a firm. All were involved in buying and processing local timber, a good deal of which was not sold on the local market but was sent across the lake to the U.S.A. and down river to Montreal and Quebec.

James Rayside, usually known as "Big Jim," was born in Montreal, a son of John Rayside and Janet Grant. At the time of writing, what became of John and Janet Grant Rayside is one of our unsolved but not forgotten mysteries. James was born in April 1836 and appeared in Martintown as a child living in the home of James Grant who was probably a relative, quite possibly his mother's brother, father, or uncle.

James got his education at the Martintown Common School and served an apprenticeship as a carpenter and millwright. In 1862 he went to the British Columbia gold fields where he was said to have made a small stake. He came back to Martintown and on 7 April 1864 married Margaret McDougall, daughter of Dave McDougall of the North Branch, west of Martintown.

James (Big Jim) Rayside (1836-1895), lumberman, business man, politican. M.L.A. for Glengarry 1883-1894.

Big Jim began married life as a farmer who did a bit of lumbering but he rapidly became more lumberman than farmer. He became well enough known and respected in this period before he became a full-time lumberman to serve six years on the Charlottenburgh Township Council for at least the last year of which he was reeve (1867-1872).

One of our treasured relics of old Glengarry is a picture of Jim Rayside taken with four of his river drivers about 1872. It is possible to date the picture within a year or two as one of the men in it, Alexander D. Ross, was a "teenager." Alex was born in 1855. All five men were tough, capable individuals and Big Jim looked quite at home among them.

It is very likely that Rayside bought the saw mill at Martintown from Sylvester's shortly after he returned from Cariboo. He was probably living in Lancaster in 1872 as his daughter Edith, born on 26 January of that year, was born in Lancaster. Rayside owned farm land in the Martintown area at least till 1879 and owned the saw mill till he died in 1895 when it was sold to Harlow G. Smith.

It is probable that Rayside moved to Lancaster in 1871 as that year he formed a partnership to go into the lumber business in Lancaster and build a saw mill there.

Rayside's partner was Archibald McArthur, born on the King's Road east of Martintown on 18 December 1831 and married to Janet McDermid. Almost certainly the two men had known each other from boyhood. The partnership would last until 1889 and the firm did a very large business in cutting logs and shingle bolts and exporting the resulting lumber and shingles.

As time went on Rayside either acquired outright or bought into saw mills at Monkland, Williamstown, Maxville, and Coteau. It will be noted that all these mills are either on a stream that was considered driveable or else on a railway. None of these smaller mills became part of the partnership with McArthur but evidently Rayside considered there was money to be made in saw mills.

Thanks to Rayside's great-grandson, Professor David Rayside, we were given access to what is, as far as we know, the only collection of business papers that are in existence on the Rayside operation. They consist basically of 63 cheques all drawn on Molson's Bank in Montreal and dated in the period October 1887 to December 1888. All are signed by James Rayside. Most of the cheques are for amounts under $150 and we can identify some of the people to whom they are made out as storekeepers and farmers in Glengarry at that time. These cheques are presumably in payment for logs delivered to one or more of Rayside's mills. The largest cheque in the collection is drawn to the order of the Commissioner of Crown Lands in the amount of $4815.50 and is almost certainly payment of stumpage dues. Several of the cheques ranging in size from $150 to $500 are to Donald McIntosh, whom we have mentioned elsewhere in connection with lumbering in Glengarry. On the basis of these cheques and other evidence we believe that McIntosh was a part-time timber buyer for Rayside. One of these cheques to McIntosh, dated 28 December 1888, carries the superscription—Donald McIntosh, Eau Claire, Quebec, and 30 miles back in the bush. Other cheques are to firms we know were in the lumber business in Glengarry at the time—McPherson and Schell in Alexandria, McDougall's at Maxville, Stewart and McRae at Maxville, and McNeil and McRae in Glen Robertson.

Incidentally Rayside's bank balance in Molson's Bank in May 1888 was $4512.76 but we have no way of knowing if this was his only account or just a business account, or even just one of his business accounts.

In addition to the cheques the collection of papers referred to above contains a few promissory notes made out in favor of Rayside by persons and firms who supplied him with timber. Evidently Rayside financed smaller timber cutters, at least to some extent.

In 1889 the firm of Rayside and McArthur dissolved in Lancaster, the business being continued by Archie McArthur who in 1891 took his son John D. (J.D.) into partnership. J.D. had been born in Lancaster in 1870, educated locally and grew up around the saw mill and is reported to have known the business thoroughly.

Though the firm of Rayside and McArthur had dissolved, Rayside still maintained an interest in lumbering. In 1890 Bradstreet had two listings for James Rayside. In Alexandria, Rayside McMaster and Company have an estimated net worth of $10-20,000 and in Lancaster Rayside and McArthur have an exactly similar rating.

In November 1894, W.H. Hill of Maxville went to Lancaster to superintend the building of a new mill for (as the *Glengarry News* puts it) Rayside and McArthur. Whether or not that was an exact statement about joint ownership of the new mill it eventually made little difference to Big Jim Rayside as he died on 1 November 1895 and was buried in St. Andrew's cemetery in Martintown.

Rayside or perhaps more exactly his money would be missed at the large Lancaster operation, now unquestionably A. McArthur's and Son, but the McArthurs carried on. In November 1898 they announced that they had bought a number of bush farms in Lancaster Township which they intended to log off and would erect shanties on them during the winter months.

In 1905 the McArthurs were employing about 100 men the year around and that year they bought one of the last stands of virgin timber in our area. This was the Stewart Tract of some 1100 acres, comprised of lots 2, 3 and 4 in the 6th, 7th and 8th of Cornwall Township, just west of the Glengarry border and north-east of St. Andrews. They planned to drive the logs down the Raisin River to the Lancaster mill (roughly the route of the Annual White Water Canoe Race which attracts such huge crowds in the 1970's).

On 3 March 1906, well before the first drive from the Stewart Tract could start, Archibald McArthur died. He was buried in St. Andrew's cemetery, Williamstown and his son J.D. became the head of the firm.

It was a bad year for a drive. The men got most of the logs as far as Williamstown and had to wait there for a really heavy rain to get even the small logs through to Lancaster. McArthur hired D.J. McPherson, now separated from J.T. Schell, to try to shift bigger logs down the river if need be one at a time. The Lancaster column in the *Glengarry News* of that summer quite frequently mentions McPherson's efforts, which the community was evidently following with interest. In October McArthur had to make arrangements to have the logs hauled out of the river before the ice formed.

Besides the problems McArthur had with the log drive in 1906, the people of South Lancaster were very interested in a steam driven electric light system that was installed in the mill in July. They were even hoping for a street light or two but in that they were disappointed.

John D. McIntosh (1858-1914). When he died, he had been for 31 years a partner of Hugh Munro in Munro and McIntosh.

J.D. McArthur died suddenly on 27 October 1906, at the age of 36, leaving a widow and three young children. He was buried (with full masonic rites) in St. Andrew's cemetery, Lancaster—and the firm was without a head.

J.D. McArthur's estate continued to operate the mill and log the Stewart Tract in the winter of 1906-7 and 1907-8. The spring of 1908 saw their last log drive, and in September 1909 the McArthur property was advertised for sale.

Copies of the sale bill are extant and give a good picture of what a large Glengarry saw mill was like at that date:

Parcel 1—the saw mill consisting of a tinned roofed building with a circular saw, trimmer, double edger, shingle machine and bolter, rip saws and tables, planer for tonguing and grooving, lath mill, etc. etc.

The mill is lighted by electricity generated on the premises. Capacity is 15-20,000 feet of lumber each ten hours with ample steam power and and a good custom trade to the mill from the surrounding district.

Parcel 2—about 1137 acres of Freehold timber land (the Stewart Tract) on which disinterested explorers make an estimate of over 36,000 saw logs, principally hardwood. The above limits are on drivable streams and not over 18 miles to the millpond.

Parcel 3 —about 2 million feet of sawn lumber piled in the vicinity of the saw mill consisting of maple, birch, ash, elm, pine, etc. Also, 2,000 cords of slabwood and a large quantity of shingles.

The great days of the mill at Lancaster were over. It was operated from time to time by various people. Campbell and Graham finished logging off the Stewart Tract in the winter of 1912-13 and the last log drive in the Raisin was in the spring of 1913.

The mill itself burned in the summer of 1921. By then it was of so little importance that no one bothered to record the exact date and it passed away entirely unnoticed, even as the local news item in the *Glengarry News*.

# Chapter XV
# Industrialists of Alexandria: Munro & McIntosh — J.T. Schell

These two firms were unique in Glengarry in their time and for many a year after the last of them stopped doing business.

They had much in common. Each of them depended to a large extent on Glengarry timber for its raw materials. Each of them depended to no small extent on markets outside Glengarry for sales, and profits were reinvested in Glengarry thereby providing more jobs. Each of them at the height of its prosperity employed a hundred or more men. When the principals in each firm died or retired the firm soon came to an end. The best business decade for each of these firms was 1901-1910 and both got underway at approximately the same time, in the second decade after Confederation.

## Munro and McIntosh

It may be almost forgotten today, but men from Glengarry were once able to compete very successfully in the carriage building industry. In the mid 1800's every Canadian town had at least one carriage maker; the larger ones had several. A firm headed by two Glengarry Scots, working in Alexandria, grew to be one of the largest in Canada, competing with success with such giants of the trade as Studebaker, McLaughlin, and Tudhope-Anderson as long as horse-drawn vehicles ruled the road. The firm of M & M did not make the transition to automotive power, which took over almost completely in road transport after 1925.

The story of the Alexandria Carriage Company is woven

around Hugh Munro and John D. McIntosh, a pair of cousins from the Apple Hill—Glen Roy area. Hugh became a super-salesman while John D. became an efficient and imaginative plant manager. Together they built up a business that for some years shipped more freight from Alexandria than came from all other sources in the area put together and this in a day when all the cattle, pigs, and milk moved to market by train. Their product sold well at home too.

Hugh Munro (1854-1939), senior partner in Munro and McIntosh.

Hugh Munro, son of Donald Munro and Janet McDermot of the 9th of Charlottenburgh, served his apprenticeship in blacksmith shops in Alexandria, Williamstown, and Martintown. As a young journeyman blacksmith he worked in big shops in Kingston and Napanee. When he was ready to start for himself he came back to Alexandria and started a general blacksmithing business on the south-west corner of Kenyon and Ottawa Streets. On 17 September 1877, five years before Alexandria got a railway and six years before it was incorporated as a village, we notice Munro going to Lancaster with a wagon and taking delivery of some blacksmith tools, bar iron, and coal that had been delivered there to his order by the Grand Trunk Railway. Munro's main interest at the time was repairing implements and vehicles but in slack times he began to do a little building. In 1878 he hired John D. McIntosh, a wheelwright by training, to do the woodwork repairs on the jobs brought to the shop. In 1880 McIntosh became a full partner and the team of M & M was born.

Their start was a shaky one. They had their skills but in 1881 the credit reference people gave M & M a net worth of $500 and "limited credit." In the period 1882 to 1885 they built 35 to 40 carriages a year and employed 15 men at the end of that time.

In 1885 M & M decided they needed more space and in October laid the foundation of a three storey building 60' by 40' at the north-east corner of Main and St. George Streets in Alexandria. For the next 50 years that block of Alexandria would be "Munro and McIntosh." *The Glengarrian* of 24 December 1885 reported: "The Blacksmith shop is on the ground floor with the furnace for setting tires. A carpenter shop and showroom each 30' x 40' are on the next floor with the upper one used for painting and trimming. The firm is doing an excellent business having many orders for the spring trade. The firm sells not only to Glengarry but in other parts of Canada. In the firm's showroom may be found single and double phaetons, timpkins, dexters, brewsters, McLaughlin gear carriages and many other styles of vehicles. Last fall M & M took 12 first prizes for carriages at Newington, Cornwall and Williamstown fairs."

The firm moved into its new building in 1886 and proceeded to make the most of its premises and equipment. No longer did the blacksmiths pump bellows, the forges were driven by a fan blast. Steam power hammers were in use and every possible machine was steam driven.

The secret of production is specialization, and M & M organized departments and a production line took shape. Henry Ford is generally regarded as the father of the production line but his did not start until 1903, long after M & M began theirs in 1886. On an assembly line each man does one job, or at most several related jobs. Parts are made in one place and assembled into sub-assemblies in an adjacent area, which in turn is beside the area where the sub-assembly is added to the vehicles being built. Then the finished product is inspected, painted, crated, and shipped. As the plant enlarges, each man becomes more and more of a specialist and more specialists are added. By 1900 M & M had all the departments, at least in embryo, of a modern assembly plant such as Ford's at Oakville. The purchasing department bought the right sorts of wood, iron, coal, paint, and tools. The blacksmiths made the iron parts, working to patterns. The cabinet makers made the bodies, the wheelwrights made the wheels (though M & M did buy many wheels ready made as we will note later), the cabinet makers made the bodies, the trim department made and installed the seats, dash, and leather work, and the plant engineer and his crew kept the engine running and maintained the shops with their hundreds of feet of line shaft, miles of belts, hundreds of pulleys, and hundreds and hundreds of wooden and babbit bearings. The paint shop did the painting and varnishing (by hand) and the shipping department did the crating and moved the crates by team and wagon to the waiting freight cars at the station. Good organization made it possible to produce vehicles for a net profit of about 10 percent while a small producer had to have 50-70 percent. The result was as it is today; the big firm got bigger and the small ones went out of business. M & M got bigger. In 1880 there were 13 small carriage shops in Glengarry; 3 in Alexandria, 2 in Lancaster, 2 in Williamstown, 2 in Martintown, 1 at Glen Roy, 1 at St. Elmo, 1 at Dominionville, and 1 at Athol. By 1900 there was one big one and several struggling ones—their credit ratings all the lowest possible. It can be suspected these lingering small carriage shops did more repairing than new building—M & M would not have time for repairs to damaged vehicles or to replace worn out or broken parts.

In 1894 M & M had the local market saturated and they set up agencies to sell "the buggy from Glengarry" all through the Ottawa Valley between Montreal and Ottawa. At first it was an uphill road as the firm had only a local reputation and Alexandria was not known as a manufacturing centre.

The quality of their vehicles and their prompt filling of orders soon gave them the Ottawa Valley trade and they looked for new fields. Glengarry's sons all over western North America no doubt helped M & M to establish a strong trade west of the Lakes and the company also established an agency in the West Indies. In November 1896 M & M shipped a "Solid Comfort" cutter to Dr. Hugh J. McDonald of Butte, Montana, a former Glengarrian, their first recorded sale in the U.S.A. In 1901 Walter Millar, one of Glengarry's sons in South Africa on account of the Boer War, wrote home that he had seen a "Glengarry Buggy" there (one would like to know its story).

In 1896 both Munro and McIntosh who lived close to the plant decided to run a steam line from the plant boiler to their houses and almost certainly these were the first centrally heated houses in Alexandria. Maybe it was the starting up of Alexandria's light and water system that year that prompted M & M to steam heat their homes. At any rate, they installed electric lights (Alexandria's small system only had power for lights—no motors or heaters) in the plant and in their homes and put one of the new-fangled telephones in the plant office—it was line 26 on the Alexandria exchange board.

We noted M & M's meagre credit rating in 1881; by 1890 they had an estimated worth of $5-10,000 and credit up to half a million. In June 1897 Munro returned from a two week trip to the Maritimes. While there he opened a new branch warehouse at St. John, New Brunswick. For the past two years they had had a warehouse to service the Maritimes and the West Indies, at Halifax but it was found to be too small for the present demand. They had to hire extra men in November 1897 and in December M & M went to the Alexandria Town Council to tell them that they needed a larger plant and would build it if the village would guarantee them no increase of assessment or water rate for ten years. The Council hastened to grant their request.

The big news in the fall of 1898 was that M & M received an order for a "handsome carriage from China, demonstrating the world-wide character of the firm's reputation," as the *Glengarry News* put it.

In 1899 the firm was receiving orders for "upwards of 50 carriages a week" and to expedite things they bought an interest in the Benjamin Company of Yarker, Ontario, who had previously supplied them with the wheels and other wooden portions of the running gear in emergencies. Now they could look to Benjamin's for a steady supply. The firm in 1899, though larger than it had been, and still growing, was still largely operated on a personal basis. Munro and McIntosh knew all their employees; their number at this time varied between 75 and 100 and they had one general foreman in the plant, a Mr. McNeil. John D. McIntosh personally superintended the upholstery department and Phillip McIntosh was in charge of the wood department. James Smith Jr. was the bookkeeper and in charge of the office and Felix Daprato looked after the shipping. In October 1899, M & M secured the services of E.J. Tarleton of Gananoque as a painter and he rapidly rose to foreman of that department—and there was not an activity in Alexandria that he did not participate in as long as he was in town.

We first hear of shipments by M & M in carload lots in November 1900 when a carload of cutters was shipped to British Columbia. In April 1901 there were 115 employees at M & M and the month's payroll was "between $2,500 and $3,000 the largest in the Company's history." Between the 15th and 20th of April, the firm shipped 8 carloads (246 carriages) and the factory was working overtime. That summer the firm made 2100 buggies and had 1000 cutters ordered for fall and winter work.

By comparison in 1899 they had made "about 1000" buggies.

The firm needed more space, so more was built in early 1902 and in April they were turning out a finished buggy in as little as 21 minutes and at a rate of 24 each day. In July the firm shipped two carloads of carriages to Winnipeg and two to Vancouver. In the summer of 1902 a prototype rubber-tired buggy was made and Ed Tarleton, the paint shop foreman and "man about town," tried it out in everyday use. In one day of November 1902, the firm sold 16 carriages and 64 cutters. The rubber tires on the buggy proved to be a success and in November M & M installed its own machinery to make rubber tired buggy wheels. Although the firm's advertising described them as "pneumatic" they were the type we find today on a child's tricycle and call "solid." In August 1902 M & M showed 6 cutters and 21 carriages at the Ottawa Fair, each one different.

We can see from the above that the small local firm, known variously and informally in Alexandria as Munro and McIntosh, or the Alexandria Carriage Co., or just "the works" had become big business—too big to administer on a personal level. So in 1902 the firm was incorporated as "The Munro and McIntosh Company Ltd" with a capital of $250,000 in $100 shares. Often firms were incorporated for far more than their value but behind the paper in this case were the factory producing carriages at the rate of 25 a day and sales coming in faster than the factory could build them. In those days when a dollar was backed by gold, Hugh Munro and John D. McIntosh were wealthy men.

Incorporating meant a shift in management methods. Nelson Gilbert, one of the best known carriage men in the U.S.A., was brought in as plant superintendent in July 1902. Sam Macdonell was hired as assistant to the head bookkeeper James Smith. M. Daprato became head of the blacksmithing department, F. Daprato became "traveling salesman," and Clem Daprato with his bay team and flat decked wagon delivered the crated vehicles to the railway.

In July 1903 M & M had completed their buggy orders for the season, nearly 4,000 of them, and were about to start to build

2,000 cutters. One of their men, M. Daprato, assembled "a double bearing buggy gear" and put it in a buggy that was exhibited at the Ottawa Fair. (Forty years later the railways would rediscover the advantage of ball bearings "to roll the load"). By the end of March 1904, M & M had completed the previous year's orders and had built some 4,000 more buggies.

9th April was one of the firm's shipping days and the growth of the firm can be seen by looking at shipments on that date for a few years:

| | | |
|---|---|---|
| 1895—40 | 1898—186 | 1901—  325 |
| 1896—75 | 1899—324 | 1903—1,274 |
| 1897—91 | 1900—308 | 1904—1,481 |

For the year 1901 the firm's payroll averaged between $2,500 and $3,000 per month. Work was still seasonal and 115 was the average number of employees, so the average wage was about $1 per day. This does not present an accurate picture as the comparatively few skilled craftsmen got $2.50 to $3 per day. The many apprentices got little or nothing, depending on how far along they were with their apprenticeship, and labourers got from 75c to $1 per day. The day was nine hours long and the work week was six days. Right from the start there seem to have been three unpaid holidays a year, Christmas, New Year's, and the 24th of May, though later the 1st of July was added. There were none of the fringe benefits we take for granted but Hugh and John had the reputation of being good employers who would dig into their own pockets to help an employee in an emergency. In return they wanted a day's work from every man, every day, and no waste, and no fooling.

The years 1902-1914 were prosperous ones for M & M. At the beginning of the period they had their key personnel and equipment and established dealers. The Canadian North West (Manitoba, Saskatchewan, Alberta) was becoming populated and every family had to have a buggy, a cutter, and at least one heavy wagon. Most families, as they could afford them, bought several of each. So these years can be covered with only a few highlights.

In 1905 Hugh Munro went on a selling trip along the north shore of the St. Lawrence as far as Quebec City and sent a big display of cutters, sleighs, and wheeled vehicles to the C.N.E. at Toronto with Felix Daprato to explain their virtues to anyone who showed interest in them.

In 1906 M & M installed a small steam driven dynamo to operate their sewing machines (seat covers and upholstery). Previous to this the sewing machines had been "foot operated". They also had a fire that burned their offices and storerooms and did about $40,000 damage but caused no delay in filling orders.

By the end of April 1907 the firm had already shipped 90 carloads of carriages from Alexandria station and they still had unfilled orders. But the big news was that Johnny Angus Mac-Millan, Glengarry's M.P. and M & M's local dealer, was going into the funeral and undertaking business and had ordered a special hearse from M & M. Its cost was $1,000. As a really well equipped buggy sold for $60 and a fairly good one for $45 it can be imagined what a stir this $1,000 hearse created in the community. In December 1907, M & M announced they had had their best year to date having completed 600 carriages and 3,200 sleighs and cutters and had more orders ahead than at any previous date.

In 1908 production was 5000 cutters for the winter trade and 6500 buggies, etc. for the summer business. The "etc." included light delivery vans, surreys, stanhopes, and other special jobs. There were 150 models available in carriages, all with numerous options. A few of these options may be of interest. No top, partial top, closed top, steel or rubber tires, a pole or shafts or both, special paint jobs, several different kinds of upholstery, whip holders and steps, lamps either coal oil, acetylene, or none, a variety of wheel sizes and widths, and a wide variety of seat type and arrangements, give some idea of what was available.

The firm as usual set up an elaborate display at the C.N.E. and while the C.N.E. was on, M.P.T. Legare of Quebec City came to Alexandria and placed a single order for 1500 carriages.

But they lost M. Daprato their foreman blacksmith who resigned to give full attention to his grocery store. M & M replaced him with a Mr. Cook from Chatham.

The story of Munro and McIntosh technically ended in November 1909, when the firm became part of a large amalgamation of carriage builders known as Carriage Factories Ltd.. It included Tudhope's at Orillia, E.N. Cheney of Montreal, the Canada Carriage Company of Brockville, and M & M. Hugh Munro became vice-president of the new concern, but nothing changed in Alexandria where the people still called the big plant on Main Street, "Munro and McIntosh." At the time of the amalgamation Bradstreet noted M & M as having a net worth of $150-$200,000 and credit up to a half million; by the standards of the day M & M had reached "big league."

In 1910 the firm found they needed something more than a bookkeeper and H. Williams became a director of the firm and comptroller. He is credited with making several technical improvements in the operation of the factory. Williams stayed with the firm until early in 1916 when he went to Canadian Vickers in Montreal. Having a competent staff left Hugh Munro free to get into local politics and go to Winnipeg and buy a block of stores—and the orders kept coming in. The firm needed 10 cars to ship their orders to the west in February 1911 and in March a Quebec firm ordered 1,300 cutters. By the end of 1911 the firm had the capacity to make 12,000 buggies and sleighs per year and that year had paid out $125,000 for supplies, a bit more than half of which was Glengarry timber.

A shadow of the shape of things to come passed over the firm beginning in 1910. Ed Tarleton, M & M's foreman painter bought a car in 1910, the first car in Alexandria. John D. McIntosh bought a "powerful" car in 1911 as did Nelson Gilbert, the plant superintendent. In May 1914, M & M bought a car for the plant.

The end of carriage making was not yet in sight however. In February 1912 the plant was shipping a carload of carriages a day, in May they were shipping two carloads a day. A fire in the plant in February of 1912 only did $3-4,000 damage and it was reported "that the new automatic sprinkler system helped confine the fire." All in all, 1912 was an extra good year, and the firm was steadily employing "upwards of 200 hands."

In 1913 for the first time in his life John D. McIntosh took a long holiday and with his wife went to Cuba. On 20 September 1914 John D. died.

War had broken out in the summer of 1914 and men and materials shortly became scarce and dear. Worse still, war promoted the use and development of the gasoline engine for road transport of both freight and people.

Neither Munro nor McIntosh had sons and there was no impulse to make the transition to gas powered vehicles as one of the firm's great rivals The McLaughlin Carriage Company of Oshawa did. McLaughlin's announced in November 1915 that they would no longer make any horse drawn vehicles. The McLaughlin plant in Oshawa in time became General Motors of Canada.

In Alexandria the story was different. During the war years we note good men leaving for other fields. William Forster, the foreman trimmer, became a factory inspector for the Ontario government in 1916, the same year Harry Williams left for Canadian Vickers. Leonard MacGillivray, faced with the prospect of a transfer to the Carriage Factories head office in Toronto, joined the army instead; and perhaps as hard a blow as any, Nelson Gilbert, the plant superintendent since 1902, left M & M in 1918 to go to Brockville where his sons were in the boat building business. Felix Daprato was appointed superintendent in Gibert's place and it is no reflection on Daprato's abilities to say the firm was never the same again. Times had changed and the great demand for horse drawn vehicles was over.

This will be a convenient place to take a look at some of the effects Munro and McIntosh had on their community besides the more readily apparent ones of making jobs, paying wages, and transforming Glengarry timber into goods that could be sold at a profit.

481

People came to Alexandria to work both for M & M and J.T. Schell. Many of their descendents are still there and very much part of the community their parents and grandparents helped to build. These people helped to build the churches, sang in the choirs, formed societies and clubs of all sorts, built houses, and paid taxes. Thanks to the efforts of these two large employers of labour, at least in part, Alexandria got the idea it should be a county town and twice led movements to separate Glengarry from SDG. That the efforts came to naught was no fault of Alexandria's or of "its leading citizen," Hugh Munro.

A quick rundown of the "extra-curricular activities of Munro and McIntosh and their employees might be of interest. For a time around the turn of the century, Hugh Munro was president of the Alexandria Driving Park. He was reeve of the village in 1900 and John D. McIntosh served as a councillor on Alexandria's first town council in 1903.

Nelson Gilbert, the plant superintendent, had a sailboat on the mill pond and Ed Tarleton had a canoe. Both were companionable souls who made friends and joined things and made them go. In 1905, for instance, the trimmers at M & M under their foreman W. Forrester played a game of hockey with Tarleton's painters, the painters won 4-2. In 1908 the following foremen at M & M donated a buggy to be drawn for at a St. Patrick's concert in Alexandria: Gilbert, Tarleton, Forester, F. Daprato, and M. Daprato. D.J. McIntyre of St. Elmo won the buggy. That same year the firm itself donated a buggy as a project at Williamstown fair and it was won by J. Barrett, but he had to go to Alexandria to get it. Both Hugh Munro and John D. McIntosh were on the committee appointed to build Alexandria's new Presbyterian Church (the Church on the Hill) in 1911 and the two gentlemen announced to the annual meeting of the congregation (30 January 1911) that they would match dollar for dollar all other voluntary subscriptions to the building fund of the church.

In 1910 M & M donated a buggy for a draw at St. Finnan's parish and the trimmers held a picnic at Fassifern in November (one wonders what they used to keep warm!). In 1915 Hugh

Munro bought a machine gun for the army; J.T. Schell also bought one and the rest of the town bought another.

In June 1920 interested people in Alexandria met in the M & M showroom to organize a brass band and in 1926 the second annual meeting of the Alexandria tennis club was held at the Carriage Factory.

We have already noted Hugh Munro as reeve of Alexandria in 1900. He was acclaimed Mayor of the town in 1908 and developed a liking for politics. He was the nominee of the Liberals to contest the provincial seat for Glengarry in the election of 11 December 1911. As a pre-election gesture and a demonstration of what he thought Ontario roads should be, Munro at his own expense built a sample mile of road on the driest part of the Military Road (Highway 34) that he could find, between Fassifern and Laggan. He had it black-topped and it was wonderful for the time—the drawback was that the mile cost $1000 and it would be many a long year before Glengarry would expend that sorth of money on roads.

As we said above, Hugh Munro contested the provincial election of 1911, and he defeated his Conservative opponent, Lt. Col. Donald M. Robertson of Williamstown and Toronto (mostly Toronto)by 1,988 to 1,724. As the member of parliament Hugh Munro was part of a delegation that went to Montreal in January 1914 to ask for better station facilities for Alexandria. The other members of the delegation were J.A. McMillan, M.P., J.T. Hope, M.D., Mayor of Alexandria, P.V. Massey, and J.A. Macdonell, K.C. . Hugh probably got some satisfaction from the knowledge that J.A. McMillan had become successful and widely known at least in part because he sold M & M's carriages and was the owner of that $1000 hearse he had bought back in 1907. Also there is more than a little truth in a statement that has been made, "that if it hadn't been for M & M, none of the rest would have been there either." M & M had done at least their share to make Alexandria a prosperous town.

Hugh did not have an opponent for the provincial general election of 29 June 1914 and so got the seat by acclamation. In

1915 the *Glengarry News* proclaimed that "Munro had got a front seat in the Legislature, 5 seats from the leader, Mr. Rowell—the 1st time in 32 years, that a Glengarry M.P. has had a front row seat." We do not know what that proved, if anything, but Col. A.G.F. Macdonald, himself a good Liberal, thought it worth reporting. Though Munro was not particularly active as an M.L.A., he presented a long-service medal to Wm. Murphy of the 59th in 1914, was president of the Citizen's Recruiting Leagues in Glengarry, and was appointed director of the Eastern Ontario Division of the National War Savings Organization at the end of 1918. Perhaps his best speech in the legislature was in March of 1916 when he spoke in favor of a more progressive farm policy and declared that Ontario was not developing her resources in a way to make for steady progress.

Munro did not contest the 1919 provincial election and he assumed the role of elder statesman and local historian. He was of United Empire Loyalist descent and he made good use of the Ontario Archives of the day to find out quite a lot about his folks in days gone by. Perhaps the culminating act in his family research was to erect a memorial stone on the Munro family plot in St. Andrew's Cemetery, Williamstown, where Hugh Munro and Catherine Campbell, his Loyalist ancestors (and Ewan Ross's too) are buried. Those of us who are Loyalists in Glengarry owe much to Hugh Munro's work and interest in them.

In June 1936, Hugh Munro went to Edmonton, to live with his daughter Grace, (Mrs. D.J.T. Hope) and Alexandria knew him no more. He died at his daughter's home on 7 November 1939, but to this day oldtimers in Alexandria think of the days of Munro and McIntosh as the Golden Age of Alexandria.

In 1918 the firm made a proto-type bus body for the passenger-express run between Vankleek Hill and Hawkesbury, and they did get some substantial orders for the bodies for military ambulances. They also got some orders for automobile bodies.

1918 was really the last year M & M had a decent business.

John McIntosh was dead, Hugh Munro was 64, and times had changed. The demand for horse drawn vehicles had fallen off and the men came back from the war expecting much better wages and living conditions, which meant increased cost of production. In 1919 Arthur Cook the foreman blacksmith at M & M left. In April 1920, the men at "the works" went on strike for more pay. The strike was settled in a little more than a week for 15 % increase in pay right then and another 10 % in August. A total of 93 employees voted, down quite a lot from the 200 or more of pre-war days. To rub it in, a representative of the American Federation of Labor arrived in Alexandria and invited all the wage earners of the town and vicinity to join a union. A tentative local was formed with Joseph McEwen of the Carriage Works as President. In 1921 the firm was on part-time till 26 September when it was reported "several good orders are booked and it is to be hoped employees now will have steady work." In 1922 R. Pimm left M & M for Kitchener, and in September Ed Tarleton left for Orillia with his family, 22 years after he had come—the firm was almost finished.

An article in the *Glengarry News* of 14 November 1924 suggests the Alexandria Carriage Works was still alive but struggling. In July 1928 the smokestack of the plant blew down, and a small order for grain wagon boxes from the West did not do much to revive the firm. Carriage Factories Ltd. kept a small staff in the plant till 1934 doing maintenance and odd jobs. The last carriage was probably made prior to 1930.

Alexandria got the buildings of the firm, apparently for taxes, in 1938 and Council in April discussed tearing them down but rejected the idea as financially impossible. But a way was found and in June 1938 a wrecking crew from Frankel Brothers of Toronto started to wreck the building and the site was clear by the middle of September.

In 1940 Shepherd Brothers started to build a cold storage plant on part of the site of M & M. T. Periard erected a gas station on another part of it and today there is nothing to evoke any memory of the Alexandria Carriage Works except the recollections of some elderly people.

More than memory lingered on, however. In 1942 Hormidas Seguin, who was perhaps the only carriage maker in Ontario still working, and who was still living in Alexandria where he had learned his trade with M & M, shipped a custom-made boot-body buggy to Brantford on the personal order of Col. Harry Cockshutt, President of the Frost and Wood-Cockshutt Company of Brantford.

J.T. Schell (1850-1916). He came to Alexandria in 1882 arriving by stage coach from Lancaster. For the next thirty-four years he made his home in Glengarry and engaged in lumbering, milling, house building, and the making and installation of office furniture for post offices and other public buildings. He also found time to operate a foundry and machine shop and engage in the manufacture of cheese boxes. He had several important railway building contracts. He was very active in local affairs in Alexandria and served as M.P. for Glengarry 1900-1908.

Requiem:

For display purposes in some of their larger stores, in 1968 Sears Roebuck ordered 12 replicas of the once famous M & M cutter from Rene Pigeon of Alexandria, once an M & M workman. A month long illness of Mr. Pigeon during September delayed delivery but the first one was shipped in time for display in the Chicago store at Christmas. The others were finished by the end of January. Mr. Pigeon was assisted by Bernard Jeaurond and by Francis Seguin who did the forging. Merile Desjardins was also in this team of Alexandria men, who as young men learned to build cutters at M & M and as old men showed they still knew how.

In Memoriam:

In May 1974, a letter to the Editor of the *Glengarry News* from the National Museum of Science and Technology says the museum has acquired a Munro and McIntosh cutter and would like information on the industry that produced it.

(We wonder how they made out?)

## J.T. Schell

We have been unable to determine exactly why Jacob Schell came to Glengarry as a young man. But perhaps the *Glengarrian* of 24 December 1885 sheds some light on the question. It said: "Mr. Schell has been cheese box making for the past fifteen years and was first to introduce the industry to Canada." As Schell was only 35 years old in 1885, the above statement would indicate he started making cheese boxes at the early age of 20. This is quite possible if his family had been in the business in Oxford County, where Jacob Schell was born on 27 December 1850. This could also explain how Schell found his way to Glengarry. In the 1870's D.M. McPherson was starting to produce cheese in quantity and it is probable that his search for suitable packaging put him in touch with the Schells of Woodstock, Ontario, who were producing cheese boxes. This much is certain—when Jacob Schell arrived in Alexandria on 1 November 1882, by stage coach from Lancaster, his first job was overhauling the saw mill on Kenyon Street West in Alexandria that D.M. McPherson in partnership with Mr. Merill and Son had recently bought from the Hon. D.A. Macdonald. This argues that Jacob Schell was a millwright by trade and had come to Glengarry at the urging of D.M. McPherson, who could have told the young man "we'll have lots of cheese to make boxes for, and we have lots of wood to make them out of." At any rate, Schell arrived in Alexandria just before his 32nd birthday and went to work overhauling a saw mill for McPherson, Merill and Co. on 2 November 1882, and one of Schell's jobs was to add a cheese box factory to the saw mill.

Jacob T. Schell was the son of Jacob Schell and his wife Catherine Smith, who was a native of Islay off the coast of Scotland. J.T. attended the public and high schools in Woodstock and his career in Glengarry argues that he had had excellent training in all phases of lumbering operations including the business end of it after his formal school days ended.

The former Donald Sandfield mill, complete with its cheese box factory, came into operation in 1883; and Schell, who started the year as plant manager, by the end of the year had bought out the interest of the Merills and had become a full-fledged partner in the operation, which would be conducted as McPherson and Schell for the next twenty-odd years. Schell however had energy to spare from this operation, and in partnership with Duncan A. Macdonald (Curly) built a saw and shingle mill on 6-4 Kenyon which was in operation by the spring of 1884. The site of this mill, on the Canada Atlantic Railway, where the first sideroad west of the Military Road intersects with the first east-west road north of Alexandria and the railway, became known as Dornie. Dornie became a busy mill town, complete with railroad spur line into the mill, a boarding house, and a hotel (also for a few months, a post office). The mill at Dornie stayed busy as long as the timber lasted in the area. When the mill moved to Alexandria, Dornie, except for its name and a cheese factory, died. Today few can even find the site of Dornie and fewer still can point out the former site of Schell's mill which was north of the railroad on the east side of the sideroad.

The *Glengarry News* of 29 December 1899 had some comments to make on J.T. Schell (among other prominent citizens of Alexandria). It reported that right from the start, Schell had done away with "the truck system" in all his business. This bit of information which means that Schell bought for cash and paid his help in cash, tells us in the first instance that Schell had markets for his products that paid him in cash, so he had cash to pay his creditors. In the second instance, this remark tells us something of the accepted standards of economics in Glengarry in 1883, and to an extent compares them with the economics Schell had been used to in Western Ontario. The truck system is really a form of barter, say logs exchanged for goods from a store, but with the account kept in terms of money by the storekeeper. This system worked very much in favour of the storekeeper who not only made a profit on the goods or services he bought but made another profit on the goods he gave as "truck." Schell's system of cash payments was evidently the one he was used to before he came to Glengarry. Earlier in the century it had taken two generations of struggle by the working men of Britain to get rid of the truck system there. As the *Glengarry News* thought Schell's cash payment system so novel as to be worth mentioning fifteen years later, it can be assumed that the truck system was an accepted part of the financial load Glengarry's farmers had to carry up to 1884. Indeed it was not unkown 40 years later as at least one of the present authors can testify from personal experience.

*The Glengarrian* of 24 December 1885 gives a report of Schell's Alexandria operation for the past year. "The Alexandria mill has a capacity of 1000 cheese boxes a day along with 2000 sets of box material which is shipped to the cheese makers and made into boxes by them. As well, the mill turns out 12,000 feet of lumber per day. Thirty-five men are employed in the mill and their number is increasing. In the past twelve months there were 240,000 sets of box material and 3 million feet of lumber turned out besides cheese-box making machinery which Schell also makes.[Everything except the saw and its shaft was made of wood in those days]. In the past year the firm paid out $16,000 in wages and $15,000 for logs. Thirty men are employed in the bush by the firm at present".

When the above was written, Schell had been in the county only two years and he was just nicely started. In the next few years Schell built up an organization that enabled him to widen his personal interest. Duncan Gray became Schell's expert on wood finishing and Donald Lothian became his general foreman. Adelard Lalonde, a native of Rigaud, became stationary engineer at Schell's Alexandria mill. These three men we find would spend the greater part of their working careers with Schell.

In 1890 Bradstreet rated Schell as being worth from $35-50,000 with a credit rating up to half a million. In 1891, Schell ran as the Liberal candidate for Glengarry in the federal election of that year but was defeated by Big Rory MacLennan. In March of 1894 Schell sold 24 carloads of timber to Raymond Belden, the contractor on Section Two of the Soulanges Canal Construction. In 1894 Schell built the first part of a new high school in Alexandria (St.Paul and Centre Streets) and that same year, a year before public telephone service came to Alexandria, Schell installed a private telephone line linking the mill on Kenyon Street West with the  post office and the Canada Atlantic station. As a public service, anyone could use the system for a fee of five cents a call. When Bell came to Alexandria in 1895, McPherson and Schell were in the first list of subscribers with line number 18.

In 1896 McPherson and Schell expanded their Alexandria plant to make "the Alexandria butter box" for which they had secured patent rights (but not the patent — a search of patent office records in Ottawa reveals that there were no patents issued to J.T.Schell, D.J.McPherson, or McPherson and Schell. Only one patent was issued to D.M.McPherson, for a steel cheese box hoop and that was in 1875. So much for local legend of many patents taken out by the above mentioned men).

In 1896 Schell was elected secretary of Alexandria's fire brigade and built Alexandria's new public school. Also in 1896 we find "the firm of McPherson and Schell have over 4 million feet of logs in their yards, 2,000 cords [8x4x4] of headings [material for tops and bottoms of cheese boxes] and about one million feet of elm at their veneer mills at Alexandria and

Monkland. The amount of stock turned over in 1895 was upwards of $200,000. There are now [April 1896] 124 hands employed in the different mills and their number will be increased in a few weeks". (The reference to veneer may be puzzling to anyone not acquainted with the old-time cheese box. To make the sides of the box an elm log was peeled in a huge lathe into thin strips of veneer, so a cheese box factory consisted of two main parts, a veneer mill and one that cut and turned circular cross-sections of logs for the tops and bottoms of the cheese boxes.) By 1896 too the firm was operating a sash and door business at their Alexandria plant and had a plant to make veneer in Williamstown. For a time this Williamstown plant with its telephone line to Lancaster was Williamstown's entire telephone system and McPherson and Schell kept a man on duty in the plant office "so that in case of necessity messages may be sent."

In 1897, J.J.McIntosh, a man who would later become well known as a builder in the area, became superintendent of Schell's wood work department and he held this job till 1903 when he started his own building contracting business. In 1898 Schell became a village Councillor in Alexandria, and maybe because he was now part of that village's executive, but more likely because suitable timber for milling had become scarce around Dornie, Schell and McDonald moved their saw mill from there to Alexandria and re-erected it near the station on a site leased from R.R. (Big Rory) McLennan on the north side of the track.

The building side of the business built complete creameries at Green Valley and Dunvegan in 1898. This was still the age of wooden vats and tubs, though tin linings were being installed now. McPherson and Schell were evidently equipped to build anything from wood and process the wood from the stump to the finished articles.

At this period we find less mention of D.M. McPherson in the business and more of D.M.'s son Duncan, usually known as "D.J." There is no evidence of how they divided their roles and responsibilities but as the people in Alexandria and area always spoke of Schell's mill, etc. and only mentioned "McPherson and Schell" when they were being formal, we can assume that the McPhersons, both father and son, kept a low profile and Schell moved in the public eye. By 1905 McPherson had severed all connections with Schell and D.J. eventually built a cheese box factory of his own at Lancaster in 1906.

During the spring and summer of 1898 Schell had a crew busy renovating Big Rory McLennan's Commercial Hotel in Alexandria and by the end of the year the saw mill at Alexandria Station was ready to go and in May of 1899 was employing 74 "hands" in the mill and its sash and door factory. The Glengarry News of 29 December 1899 reported that "McPherson and Schell are operating seven plants making veneer, doing machine shop work, windows, window frames and doors and they also operate a planing mill. Their plants are in Alexandria, Monkland, Dornie, Rimouski Quebec, Huntingdon Quebec, and a box factory on the Ottawa River". The statement is somewhat garbled as it does not mention cheese and butter boxes, nor does it tell that the Dornie mill is now in operation at Alexandria Station. This article however does add a list of some of Schell's more important building jobs either done or now (1899) in progress. It mentions the Alexandria public and high schools and the Commercial Hotel renovation, which we have already mentioned, and in addition it mentions the new high school at Williamstown, the Glengarry News Block and Boyle's store in Alexandria, three houses in Ottawa, a "mansion in Hawkesbury," Aubrey's laundry and dwelling, and Jos. Huot's residence. J.J. McIntosh in charge of the building end of the firm was evidently earning his salary.

At this time, J. Rowe is manager of the planing mill department, Duncan Gray is the salesman for finished lumber products, Archie Lothian is manager of the firm's Monkland plant, and C.F. Taggart is head bookkeeper and manager of the firm's main office in Alexandria.

To end the century properly, Schell announced the readiness of his firm to build saw mills and supply their machinery, or to build creameries complete with engine, boiler, and all machinery fitted up, and to provide other items made up to order in the machinery line. J. Cole was the firm's expert on machinery and foreman of that department.

A summary of 1899 reveals that in the past year Schell employed a minimum of 120 men in all his plants and in busy seasons up to 300. His operation was not all in Alexandria as was that of Munro and McIntosh, so Schell's operation did not seem as large or important to the casual observer but it bought logs and paid wages over a wide area.

In February 1900, M.F. McCrimmon, 8-9 Kenyon, went to the bush in the morning, cut nine logs, took them to McPherson and Schell's in Alexandria and by six o'clock the same day the lumber from those logs was in the firm's kiln. This was the sort of efficiency that got Schell the contract to build the new Bank of Ottawa premises in Alexandria in March of 1900. It also had impressed his fellow citizens who elected him a director of the local driving park in April and elected him as their M.P. on 7 November 1900. To win this election as a Liberal, he had to defeat the legendary Big Rory McLennan, who had beaten him in 1891; Schell did not contest the election of 1896 which was between Big Rory and J. Lockie Wilson. In February 1901 Schell was off to Ottawa "to attend to his parliamentary duties" and in May the firm was erecting a house at the corner of Dominion and St. George Streets in Alexandria. In September when the Duke and Duchess of Cornwall passed through Alexandria, J.T. Schell M.P. was presented to them, with Senator Donald McMillan doing the honours. The texts of Alexandria's official address to the royal couple was signed on behalf of the village by Senator McMillan, J.T. Schell, M.P., and E.H. Tiffany, who was secretary of the greeting committee.

In 1902, Schell lost his bookkeeper, C.F. Taggart, who was appointed manager of the newly opened Wood Export Company in Alexandria, and he was replaced by George C. Bradley who was with Schell till the end and was one of the group that bought Schell's business after his death in 1916. (Bradley was a native of Crysler).

Here we will not deal with J.T. Schell as a politician except to remark on his speech at the end of the Boer War jangle in Canada's parliament in 1902. Schell told the assembled House of Commons that "a higher percentage of the people who recently left Canada for South Africa were from Glengarry than from any other County in the Country." Glengarry's "mystique" had evidently entered Schell's soul in the twenty years he had lived there.

Schell believed in getting a good work crew together and then if at all possible keeping them together and he hit on the idea of having his men make furniture and interior fittings in slack periods, a branch of the business we will notice getting more mention from here on. In 1903 the firm got an order for 1700 large windows for the new locomotive works in Montreal but Taggart, Schell's former bookkeeper and now manager of the competing Wood Export Co., beat Schell out for the contract for the 56,000 sq. ft. of flooring needed for the locomotive plant.

We have noted that Schell had said his firm was able to supply complete sawmills including engine so he must have had a fairly good machine shop. However, in October 1903 he decided to build a modern foundry, 75' x 60', between his Alexandria factory and the machine shop, equipped with "the latest machinery" to supply his own needs in iron casting.

In November 1904 J.T. Schell again won the Glengarry federal seat, this time beating out his Conservative opponent, the well known contractor D.R. McDonald, by 464 votes. Maybe this spurred him to announce he was going to erect a new mill at Williamstown on McIntyre's Point to make veneer, and in February 1905 the Glengarry News reports, "only once in 22 years have more logs been taken in at Schell's where payment for logs, teams and wagons in January alone reached $9,404.67. The mill frame and machinery for the new Williamstown mill are ready to be taken down there and set up." And it is said "a large addition will be made soon to the machine shop in Alexandria." The new mill at Williamstown was reported in June "to be going full blast." Also the firm built a new house in 1905 for J.A. Macdonell, K.C., and had a couple of houses to build in 1906.

In May 1908 we read "that Schell's factory has sufficient orders ahead to guarantee work for the entire summer. In the machine shop the firm is making a special line of vertical engines (steam) which is greatly in demand throughout Canada." This was the "Auto Climax" engine, a real collector's item seventy years later.

Schell's office in Alexandria was struck by lightning on the 26th of May 1908. No serious injuries resulted (just some bad scares). He could have regarded the lightning as a warning from on high to get out of politics as Schell made such an announcement in August, but a more likely reason is that he had got involved with railway contracting. In December 1908 we read, "J.T. Schell has been a very busy man this year and will probably be busier in 1909. During the past summer the Hawkesbury-Ottawa line was virtually completed by Schell and Kennedy as well as other contracts in Quebec." In 1910 Schell got a good part of the contract to build the Waterloo and Woodstock railway and at the same time the woodworking part of the firm was busy making the interior fixtures for the central post office in Montreal. The job had to be finished by 1 November and three men from the firm, W.G. Rowe, P. McNaughton, and H. Deagle were busy in Montreal doing the actual installation of the fixtures. Another expert fixture installer with Schell was Paul Decoste who was not on the Montreal job but did work with McNaughton in 1911 installing the new fixtures in the main post offices in Winnipeg and Toronto. Back in Kenyon, M.J. Fitzgerald was in charge of the gang cutting logs, the raw material for Schell's mill. In 1911, too, Dan and Vincent McDonald installed the interior fixtures in the Victoria Memorial Museum in Ottawa.

1912 was a good year in J.T. Schell's life. Things were good in the woodworking end of the business but the machine shop and foundry "were doing exceptionally well." The largest timber cut in many years was in Schell's yard—more than 70,000 feet of elm from the Vankleek Hill area and 100,000 feet brought from Alex McEwen at Maxville. In May, Schell announced "that the present capacity of his plant is to be doubled and extensive additions made to the foundry and machine shop." The machine shop was turning out railway dump cars as fast as they could build them and orders were on hand for more, so in October Schell laid the cement foundations for an immense building for the foundry and machine shop extension and expected to have it closed in before the bad weather began. By the 1st of January 1914, Schell employed 125 hands in his machine shop and foundry, and later in the year the great war in Europe quickened the whole pace of Canadian industry: the *Glengarry News* records orders to Schell in July 1915 "for thousands of shell boxes."

Bradstreet in 1916, based on 1915's business, gave Schell's sash and door factory a value of $20-35,000 and the foundry a value of $50-75,000. Each branch had a credit rating of up to half a million.

But on 29 July 1916, J.T. Schell died, leaving a widow and one son, J.C. Schell of Trenton. Mention of the son is very rare in news items from Alexandria and evidently he had other interests than his father's businesses. In January 1904 the *Glengarry News* reports, "J.C. Schell for a time on the staff of the *Glengarry News* has gone to Montreal to work for Standard Photo Engraving Company." And in April 1905 we read that "J.C. Schell has installed a complete telephone system connecting the various departments at Schell's Alexandria's plant." J.T. Schell's body was taken to Woodstock for burial there and in November 1916 his house in Alexandria on Elgin Street East was sold to Hugh McMaster, a blacksmith: the Schell family had gone from Alexandria.

Some employees of the firm, perhaps as early as 1909 when Schell went into railway contracting, had bought an interest in the woodworking part of the firm. Now this small group headed by George Bradley and W.G. Rowe bought all the woodworking part of the business, and in July 1917 J.H. Cole opened up the machine shop to do general repair work. They did get some business. D.D. McRae on behalf of the firm installed fittings in the Port Colborne Post Office in 1918 and the firm built the new Alexandria Public School in 1921. By 1921 the town of

Alexandria owned the foundry, and the town rented it to William Lockridge of Clarence Creek, who planned to operate a woollen mill in the building—an operation that a local historian described as "a fly by night operation that soon folded up." This event took place in 1924.

In 1923 the Alexandria curling club gave the contract for lumber for their new rink to the "J.T. Schell Co." and that is the last mention we can find of the functioning of the company.

The final blow however came in a big fire on 18 October 1932. The building was owned by Archie Lothian at the time. The *Glengarry News* reported that his loss was heavy and the Edgar Irvine Construction Company and the town of Alexandria also had heavy losses in the fire as they had "valuable goods stored there."

J.T. Schell's monument in Glengarry—none, except a brief summary by Harkness and a few pages here, and many news items in the old files of the local newspapers. Also you can still kick up sawdust at Dornie—if you know where to look.

# Chapter XVI
# Glengarry from 1914 to the Present

When future generations wish to understand the impact of the First World War on the small villages of rural Ontario, they will find a superb guide in a Glengarry author, Rhodes Grant. The First World War sections of his *Horse and Buggy Days in Martintown* perform one of the most difficult tasks of the historical writer, that of bringing the reader back to the times and making him understand how ordinary people thought, felt, acted under the immediate impression of historical events. It is a misfortune that similar accounts do not exist for other Glengarry communities. In the present chapter we must, regretfully, concern ourselves principally with the basic facts without the possibility of revealing the fine texture of daily life as was done by Rhodes Grant.

When the war began in August 1914, no one in Glengarry or elsewhere could doubt the importance of the event. That great struggle among the European powers, for which preparation in war supplies, armies, and navies had been in progress on an immense scale for years, was at last underway. It was expected that there would be immense battles, tremendous victories, reprisals on a sweeping scale. But that the war would last for more than four years was a possibility that few persons in any country seem to have dreamed of. Nor could most civilians at least have expected that the death toll would be as enormous as it eventually became. But wars have a habit of developing unpredictably, and of few wars in recent times has this been more deeply and cruelly true than the First World War. Of this tragedy Glengarry was to have its full share.

As the Glengarry Scots in the early days of August read about the beginning of the war in their newspapers or heard about it from their neighbours, one of their foremost thoughts was that this was BRITAIN'S WAR—a war in which the loyal people of the Dominions were obliged by every tie of morality and interest to rally to the defence of the Mother Country. This way of thinking has so much faded out of the consciousness of Canadians in the last twenty years or so, that it is worth dwelling upon it a little here. Indeed, so great and so swift has been the change of opinion in this matter, that we are aware that in what we are about to say here, we are faced with the task of appealing with the same arguments to two radically divided audiences. To some of our readers, it will seem that when we say that Glengarrians of 1914 cared for Britain's interests and felt they should die, if necessary, to defend them, we are saying something so obvious that it is hardly worth spending paper on saying it. To other readers of a generation later than the present authors, the fact that this way of thinking once existed will itself seem so hard to believe or at least to understand, that this assertion will seem to need more facts, more arguments to prove it than we are permitted, for reasons of space, to give here.

The fact, however, is that in the last years of the nineteenth century, and in the early years of this century, there existed among English-speaking Canadians, and not just among them, an immense pride and satisfaction in being part of the world-wide British Empire—the greatest political unit that had ever existed. This attitude was not inconsistent with Canadian nationalism; rather, for a few years pride in the Empire and pride in Canada strengthened each other. A Canadian patriot, viewing with pleasure the opening of the prairies to settlement under the guidance of a free and self-governing Canadian democracy, saw these prairies also as among the jewels of the rich and farflung British Empire. Devotion to the Empire was industriously encouraged by the press, the pulpit, and the Ontario school system; and any reader who wishes to get the flavour of the imperial zeal of Ontarians in those days can do no better than to examine the Ontario public school readers of the period from the 90's to the First World War with their constant emphasis on the glories of the Empire and the need for Canadians to love and assist it.

Claude Nunney (1891-1918) came to Glengarry as a boy of seven or eight and adopted it as his home. In World War I he won the M.M., D.C.M., and finally the Victoria Cross.

Perhaps in their hearts some or many Scottish Glengarrians had doubts about the value of the Empire, and doubts about whether they should make any sacrifices for it. It was, after all, despite its name, basically an English empire and they were Scots. It has always, also, been among the admirable features of Glengarrians that they have had a high degree of resistance to outside ideas, popular fads, and over-emotional appeals. But it is also difficult for someone who wants to seem to be a good citizen and a right-thinking person openly to reject the orthodox ideas of his time—and devotion to the Empire was one of the most rigorous orthodoxies of late Victorian Ontario. So we may suppose that if there was inconsistency between what people thought and what they knew they were expected to think, the inconsistency was virtually always resolved in favour of acting in accordance with public expectations.

In the First World War, Canada first showed its maturity as a nation by the extent and vigor of its contribution, and in this contribution the Glengarrians played a full part. Glengarry men joined up in large numbers, and it was estimated in the *Glengarry News* of 9 November 1917 that there were by then at least 1200 Glengarrians and ex-Glengarrians overseas. Glengarrians joined among others the 21st, 38th, 59th, and 154th Battalions, all of which recruited in the area. The 154th, known as the Counties Own, went overseas under the leadership of Col. A.G.F. Macdonald, of Alexandria, the editor of the *Glengarry News* and son of the Hon. D.A. Macdonald. It had its own pipe band and had received permission to become a kilted unit, but unfortunately was broken up overseas to form drafts for other Ontario units. At home Glengarrians supported the Red Cross, contributed money to equip local battalions and for other war expenses, mailed parcels to the boys overseas, and tried to maintain their own morale as the death toll mounted.

One of Glengarry's heroes in the war was Claude Nunney, a native of Ireland who came to Canada as a child in 1905 and was raised at North Lancaster. He worked in different places in Ontario and the West but returned to Glengarry after the outbreak of the war. When he enlisted at Alexandria in 1915, he said "I could have enlisted out West, but I wanted to go with the old 59th Glengarry Regiment and with the fellows I know." He was later transferred to the 38th Battalion. He won the Military Medal, the Distinguished Conduct Medal, and that very high honour, the Victoria Cross. He died of wounds in September 1918.

Another Glengarrian who distinguished himself in the war, Father Ewen J. Macdonald, was born in 1883 in Lancaster

Township. He was educated in the Alexandria Separate Schools and the Grand Seminary in Montreal and was ordained a priest in 1910.

Except for service in both World Wars, Father Ewen would spend his entire career as a parish priest in his native diocese, Alexandria. He served in the parishes of The Nativity (Cornwall), Crysler, Lochiel, Greenfield, St. Finnan's, Dickinson's Landing, and as chaplain at the Alexandria monastery.

Fr. Ewen J. Macdonald (1883-1972), priest, army chaplain, diocesan administrator, Glengarry historian, genealogist, and conservationist. Perhaps his greatest legacy to us was his example in so many fields.

Father Ewen went overseas as Roman Catholic chaplain of the 154th Battalion in October 1916 and was sent to France in May 1917. In 1918 he was awarded the Military Medal for his splendid work with the wounded at the Battle of Amiens. On his return to Canada he went back to parish work but continued as Roman Catholic chaplain in the local militia, the SDG Highlanders. He joined the active forces again in World War II and went overseas in 1942 as senior Roman Catholic chaplain (with the rank of Major) of the 4th Canadian Division. He was returned to Canada and parish duty in 1943 (he was now 59 years old).

As a young man, before and after his studies at the Grand Seminary, Father Ewen was an outstanding lacrosse player on Alexandria's teams. When his own playing days were over he maintained an interest in the sport and was to a large extent reponsible for the Chisholm property on Main Street (where Alexandria's town office now is) being made available for the Alexandria lacrosse team to play in under its well known name of Chisholm Park. To make sure Alexandria had a lacrosse team to play in the new park, Father Ewen was President and team manager of Alexandria's lacrosse team in 1931. He was extremely interested in field sports, contributed some articles on conservation to *Rod and Gun Magazine*, and was the prime mover in setting up the Loch Garry game preserve in 1926.

As parish priest at Lochiel in the years after World War I, Father Ewen set up a small experimental farm project and even largely wrote and directed a very effective and well presented pageant "Bonnie Prince Charlie" in 1927, with descendants of many who fought and died for Charlie in the cast. The cast was from the parish of Lochiel and no doubt all of them had heard tales of Charlie and Culloden since infancy.

Despite the three careers outlined above, priest, soldier, and community improver, Father Ewen is well known and remembered outside his parishes as an able and active historian and genealogist. As early as 1924 he went to Albany, New York, to look at old records there of the ancestors of his Glengarry people, thus setting an example to those following after him: don't depend on folklore—go to the sources. How he found time in the midst of his parish duties to assemble documents and to work on as many different aspects of Glengarry history as he did is a mystery, but when he died in 1972 the Ontario Archives got the contents of his boxes which contain correspondence, newspaper clippings, printed material, telegrams, pamphlets, genealogical charts, receipts, letter books, work sheets, and subscription lists covering many things in the years 1761-1963. They occupy 3¾ feet on the Archives shelves and fill seven rolls of microfilm.

Edith Rayside, R.N., C.B.E. (1872-1950). A native of Glengarry, Edith Rayside was Canada's first matron-in-chief of nurses (World War I), and is one of the two Glengarry women (the other is Grace Campbell) listed in the *Encyclopedia Canadiana*.

Those of us who knew Father Ewen and have looked over the material he assembled know how many connecting links are missing from his material as they were in his head and are now lost. But we, would-be historians of today, walk on much firmer ground because of the work Father Ewen did in his lifetime and wish that once again we could have a drop of Teacher's Highland Cream with Father Ewen, watch him pull his glasses way down on his nose and with the hint of a twinkle in his eye begin to expound a lesson in Glengarry history, complete with detailed genealogy of those concerned and quite often very

504

interesting character sketches.

Father Ewen was not a great man—he was a good man, with all that that implies among his folk, the Glengarry Scots.

A woman from Glengarry also distinguished herself in World War I—Edith Rayside, R.N.

Edith Catherine Rayside was born in South Lancaster in 1872, a daughter of the lumberman James Rayside (see Chapter XIV) and Margaret McDougall. She was educated at Lancaster Public School and Williamstown High School from which she entered Queen's University in 1892. She is credited with being the first woman from Glengarry to go to university and probably was. In May 1896 she graduated from Queen's with her B.A. degree. She then entered the nurses' training school at St. Luke's Hospital, Ottawa, graduating in 1901.

After getting her R.N. she nursed in Saskatchewan till 1906 when she entered the employ of a mining company in Mexico as a nurse. She returned to Canada about the end of 1910 to nurse her mother who died in the following year. In 1914 Edith Rayside joined the Canadian Army Medical Corps as a nurse and in January 1915 went to England as Matron of Nurses with the second Canadian contingent. That spring she went to France as Matron-in-Charge of No. 2 Canadian General Hospital at Le Treport, France.

In October 1916 she was ordered back to England and her work in Le Treport was mentioned in dispatches. In England she was Matron of the hospital at Moore Barracks, Shorncliffe. In January 1917 she was awarded the order of the Royal Red Cross and was invested with the medal by George V. After the investiture, she and the others invested were entertained by Queen Mother Alexandra.

In August 1917 Miss Rayside was put under orders to return to Canada to fill the newly formed position of Matron-in-Chief of all Canadian Military Nurses. She served in this position in Ottawa till demobilization of the Canadian forces was completed. She herself was demobilized in 1919.

On 11 November 1919 the University of Toronto held a special convocation to honour some of Canada's high ranking war leaders and among them was Edith Rayside. She was awarded the honorary degree of Mistress of Household Science and was the first woman to be given an honorary degree of any sort by the University of Toronto.

In the fall of 1919 she went to Columbia University to take a refresher course in hospital administration which she completed in the spring of 1920. She then joined the staff of Montreal General Hospital as a teacher in the Training School for Nurses. In 1924 she was appointed Superintendent of Nurses and Superintendent of the Nurses' Training School at Hamilton General Hospital, a position she held till she retired in January 1934 (aged 52) because of ill health.

The New Year's Honours List for 1934 made Edith Rayside a Commander in the Order of the British Empire. In 1937 she was awarded the George V 25th anniversary medal and her decorations now were C.B.E., R.R.C., Mons Medal and Star. She was also appointed honorary president of the Nursing Sisters Association of Canada and appointed (not elected) to the Board of Trustees of her Alma Mater, Queen's University.

Edith Rayside died at the home of her older sister Isabella (Mrs. James McGillis) in South Lancaster in 1950. She had made her retirement home with the McGillis family and no doubt was pleased to read in articles published about her from time to time that she had been highly regarded as a nurse, administrator, and person.

An interesting feature of the Glengarry News during the years of the war was the many letters from Glengarry soldiers printed there describing their observations overseas. Usually these letters were written to the soldiers' families and then handed on by them to the editor. Actual fighting could not normally be described, of course, for security reasons, but there were many descriptions of Britain and, particularly, of Scotland. For many young Glengarry men, the war brought an opportunity to visit their ancestral homeland about which they had heard inherited stories but from which they were now separated by three to five generations.

The literary quality of these letters is impressively high. Assuming, as we almost certainly safely may, that they were not seriously revised or edited for publication, the letters stand as evidence of the impressive job done by the county and village schools of Glengarry. Faced with the new experiences of the overseas world, the young writers of these letters found themselves well able to organize their impressions and express them in correct, clear, vivid prose.

The comparison can hardly be made in a rigorous scholarly way, but the researcher in Glengarry history will be driven to compare these letters with an earlier collection of Glengarry letters. In the papers of Big Rory McLennan in the Ontario Archives, there are many letters written by Glengarrians to Big Rory in the 1880's in connection with his contracting and money-lending activities. These letters are often barely literate, and the conclusion follows, or seems to follow, that the quality of education in Glengarry schools must have been upgraded sharply in the generation preceding the First World War.

For Glengarry, the years of the war brought various developments. In 1915 a new weekly newspaper, the *Alexandria Times*, under the editorship of J. Albert Laurin, began publication. *The Glengarrian* had gone out of business in 1913, so the *Glengarry News* and the *Times* were now the two Alexandria newspapers. In 1916 David M. Courville became the first French Canadian mayor of Alexandria. In 1918 George Simon, a Jewish merchant, became mayor. The statement, however, that he "was the first Jewish mayor of a Canadian community," is incorrect. Alexandria's railway station burned in 1915. A gleeful tradition later reported that the citizen fire brigade, indignant at the delapidated state in which the station had been for a long time, refused to make serious efforts to quench the fire. A fine new station was completed in 1917. The Women's Institute had established itself in Glengarry during the years before the war. By May 1917, there were eight branches in the county, being Maxville, McCrimmon, Martintown,

Williamstown, Glen Brook, Apple Hill, Picnic Grove, and Alexandria.

When victory came in 1918, it was celebrated joyfully in Alexandria. The *Glengarry News* reported:

About half past three Monday morning [11 Nov.] the news was flashed over the wire that the Germans had signed the armistice and accepted all the Allied terms. A few moments later the fire alarm commenced ringing and shortly afterward the chimes of the Cathedral and the bells of the other churches joined in the chorus of sound. Realizing the significance of all this noise making our citizens lost no time in gathering in the Mill Square to commence the celebration of a victorious peace. A large bonfire was hastily arranged and the decorators lost no time in bedecking our principal streets and buildings in their holiday attire. Flags and bunting quickly put in their appearance so the town was transformed before 6 o'clock in the morning. Impromptu bands were organized by the younger element, choirs were formed and rejoicing became general. A public holiday was proclaimed by our worthy mayor, the schools were closed and everyone who could do so participated in the cele-bration.

In the afternoon about 2:30 a procession was formed which paraded the principal streets of the town. It was headed by one of our local boys arrayed as General Foch and mounted on a spirited charger, followed by Standard bearers, the Chief of Police, The Highland Pipe and Drum Band, Alexandria Fire Brigade and our local cadet corps, many of whom were mounted. Next came the returned soldiers and nursing sisters and the Mayor of Alexandria. A number of beautifully decorated automobiles and carriages followed by numerous pedestrians wound up the procession. On their return to the Square

Mayor Simon proposed the singing of the National Anthem in which all heartily joined.

The evening celebration began in the churches at seven o'clock where special Thanksgiving services had been arranged. These were attended in vast numbers, as the average citizen understood that there was much to be thankful for. After these impressive ceremonies, the crowds returned to the Square where the gigantic bonfire and a splendid program of patriotic songs awaited them. The choirs of all the churches combined to make the concert a success, and they are to be warmly congratulated on the program they rendered during the evening. The pipe band under the leadership of Pipe Major Stewart of Dunvegan had no small share in the success of the evening program. Shortly after eleven the crowd dispersed after a day of general rejoicing.

Rhodes Grant describes the end of the war in Martintown:
A false rumour was circulated on Nov. 7th that the War was over. No one believed it but a few children celebrated a little. Then Saturday, the papers announced that the Germans had asked for an Armistice. On Monday morning, November the 11th, 1918, I looked out the window and saw one of the neighbours hanging out the flag. I went out and asked him what had happened. He said that the Armistice had been declared for 11 o'clock that day. As European time is ahead of ours it was already in effect. THE WAR WAS OVER!
I can not explain how it felt. It had been going on so long it seemed as if it had always been going on and would always go on. Then a terrible black cloud seemed to lift off our shoulders. The War was over!
The church bells began to ring. The faint sound of St. Andrews church bell came to us on the west wind. Then the whistles of the mills and factories in

Cornwall and the stone crusher up the road. The War was over! No one who did not live through it can comprehend what that meant.

In the afternoon the people of Apple Hill came down to Martintown in carriages, waggons, buggies and on horseback. The Apple Hill pipers standing in a big open waggon played them up the street. Our piper, Archie McDougall, shouldered his drones and prepared to lead the victory parade. Poor man. He was old and he hadn't played them for some time and they had dried out and would do nothing but squeak. People teased the poor man. "Get a bottle of whiskey, pour half down the pipes and drink the rest!" That was an old remedy, pipers sometimes did give their pipes a dram and poured the rest into themselves. It worked until the piper got too much.

The poor man lost his chance to lead the Victory Parade and had to stand aside and let the Apple Hill pipers have the honour. After everyone was tired marching there were speeches and old women danced in the street. Everyone celebrated even if tears were flowing down their cheeks. Then the bitter wind increased, everyone got cold and went home for a time. That evening a great crowd, mostly young people, assembled on the Commons behind where Kenny McDermid now lives, and continued the celebration. They lit a huge bonfire and loaded and fired the old cannon as far as the amateur gunners could work it.

In those days every store kept a barrel of gunpowder for the old muzzle loaders which were still common, so there was plenty of ammunition.

As time wore on some of that whiskey which had been recommended to the piper appeared. Somebody rammed a stone down the barrel of the cannon and just missed Harry Nicholson's chimney. A little later the gunners, drunker and drunker, rammed the wadding down the barrel first and then the powder. Then they could not fire it so everyone staggered to bed and high time too.

War memorial at Alexandria. The war memorial was unveiled by the Govenor General of Canada, Lord Byng of Vimy, on 1 Oct. 1923 and dedicated to Glengarry's dead in World War I, whose names are on a plaque on the monument. A second plaque with the names of four who were omitted from the first plaque and those from Glengarry who died in World War II and the Korean War was unveiled by Governor General Vincent Massey on 6 November 1957. The gun is a World War II souvenir replacing the two original German Guns of World War I.

Glengarry's death toll in the war had been cruel. No official lists appear to have been kept in the armed services identifying the deceased soldiers by counties. It is certain, however, that no Glengarry neighbourhood was without its dead to mourn. We can get some figures from the lists prepared for the erection of war memorials after the war. The Lancaster War Memorial, unveiled in 1921, carried the names of 117 Glengarrians who died in the war. According to a statement at the time, "These are not all who have been born in Glengarry who fell in the war, for they are many, but only those who enlisted in the county or whose homes were there at the time." When the Glengarry War Memorial at Alexandria was unveiled in 1923, it carried the names of 175 war dead (5 more were added at a later date). However, a list of the dead read at the time of the unveiling listed 188 dead. Obviously, a satisfactory list would be particularly difficult to compile for a county such as Glengarry, where it had become almost standard practice for young men, on reaching adult years, to leave the county at least temporarily to work elsewhere. There was nothing in Glengarry's previous history to compare with this tragic loss of life.

War Memorial at Lancaster. Though Alexandria has often felt and acted as if it were the capital of Glengarry, the southern and western parts of the county have always stoutly resisted this claim. Lancaster erected this plaque commemorating the war dead of Glengarry in its library grounds on 18 November 1921, 23 months before Alexandria got around to it. Other war memorials in the county are at Apple Hill and Williamstown and several churches have their own Honour Rolls.

World War I—Ostrom boys and field gun. Everyone agrees that World War I was a battle of the wills and stamina of the front line soldiers of the opposing armies and that the strategy of the generals had been no more than a matter of trying to kill more of the enemy than were killed by the enemy—a war of attrition. The boys from Glengarry villages and towns played their part well in this unimaginative blood-letting in the mud. Some 1% of Glengarry's total population, all young healthy men, died in this mud, about 4% more were wounded more or less seriously. We paid our share of the price of victory.

Unhappily, while Glengarry was celebrating the end of the war in 1918, it was going, like the rest of Canada and many other countries, through another tragedy. The Spanish influenza struck with terrible consequences in the last months of 1918 and early months of 1919. It was a savage irony of history that just as the world was concluding so terrible a war, it was afflicted by an epidemic almost like the plagues of the Middle Ages. A month before the Armistice, a notice signed by the Chairman of the Board of Health, George Simon, stated in the *Glengarry News* that "The spread of Influenza in Canada and the prevalence of the illness in Alexandria having assumed alarming proportions," schools, cinemas, pool rooms, etc., were to be closed till further notice. According to Clarence Ostrom, 23 persons died in Alexandria of the influenza within a four-week period, being about 1 % of the population of the town. The Medical Officer of Health stated in a report in the *Glengarry News* of 20 December 1918 that 21 persons had died in Alexandria of the influenza. If these figures are correct, Alexandria suffered more severely than the province in general. No separate figures appear to exist for the death toll from the influenza in Glengarry as a whole. If we assume, however, that outside Alexandria Glengarry did not suffer distinctly worse than the rest of the province, it may be calculated from the figures published by the Registrar General of Ontario for influenza deaths and deaths from causes connected with influenza that Glengarry's total losses in 1918-1919 from the epidemic would have been a maximum of about 80.

The immediate aftermath of the war brought political changes to Glengarry. In the Ontario election of October 1919, Glengarry returned Duncan A. Ross, the candidate of a farmers' party called the United Farmers of Ontario. One week later in the same month, the Glengarry-Stormont constituency in a federal by-election returned J.W. Kennedy, also a nominee of the United Farmers.

For Glengarry as for so much of the rest of the world, the 1920's were a peaceful interlude between the toil and sacrifice of the First World War and the hardships of the Depression.

Prohibition, which had begun in Ontario in 1916, continued in force through most of the decade. Most Glengarrians supported it in theory as the 20's began, but it soon began to be evident that considerable numbers of people there, as elsewhere in Ontario, had no intention of living in accordance with its restrictions. When Quebec Province went "wet" in 1919, outlets were made available immediately across the Glengarry border, and the "road to Dalhousie" and to River Beaudette and other points in that province attracted drinkers young and old. In 1926 the Ontario electorate rejected prohibition by re-electing the Ferguson Conservative government. Glengarry concurred in this result by returning a Conservative candidate. Already in 1925 the government had introduced a watery 4.4 beer—"Fergie's Foam." In 1927 the Ontario Liquor Control Act replaced the

Ontario Temperance Act of prohibition. In 1928, Alexandrians voted by 688 to 97 to have a liquor store in their town. As yet, the rest of the county was dry. It was not until 1969, and after many "liquor votes," that all of Glengarry was wet. Kenyon Township was the last Glengarry municipality to permit beverage rooms for "men only," and it was not until 1976 that both sexes in all municipalities in Glengarry had equal legal access to liquor on licensed premises.

Modern technology pressed ever more insistently into Glengarry. The automobile, which had first appeared in Glengarry in 1910, continued steadily to find more purchasers. Staid elders wondered about the effects of the new mobility created by the automobile on the morality of the young. Ardent motorists longed for better roads than those which had served Victorian Glengarry. The automobile became part of the expense to be borne by more and more Glengarry farms. The Glengarry farms had traditionally been heavily self-reliant, with the individual farm producing much of the food, clothing, fuel, etc. of the farmer's family, but the automobile had needs which could only be satisfied from outside, and for money. The telephone and electric systems continued their cautious spread through Glengarry, but at the end of the decade most farms were still without the latter. In the early 20's ingenious people were constructing their own radio sets. Amid a barrage of static, and with a tinny note, music, songs, and speeches from far away could be entrancingly heard. Airplanes, apparently, were as yet a rare sight in Glengarry. One had been seen over Lancaster in November 1914, but Rhodes Grant says of Martintown that in 1928 "we saw the first mail planes fly overhead. We had seen only one or two planes before that...".

In the 1920's Glengarry got one of its finest buildings, that of the Monastery of the Precious Blood, at Alexandria. In 1918 and 1919 there had been a possibility that an Alexandria-born mining magnate, Archibald Mark Chisholm, of Duluth, Minnesota, would finance the building of a hospital for Alexandria. This plan was abandoned, and instead Chisholm built the monastery as a memorial to his parents. The cornerstone of the building was laid by the Bishop of Alexandria in the summer of 1925, and the formal opening of the building was in November.

The 20's were also the decade of the church union question, which has already been noted in an earlier chapter. There were now churches of a new denomination in Glengarry, the United Church of Canada, and some Presbyterians continued the Presbyterian church which had been one of the institutions of the county from the days of the Loyalists. Glengarry's most famous son, Ralph Connor, was prominent in the formation of the United Church of Canada.

Enthusiastic readers of Ralph Connor's novels, and there were many such in Glengarry, had a treat in 1922 when a recently made film of *The Man from Glengarry* was shown in Alexandria.

Another Glengarry writer, called J.J. Macdonald (1849-1937), who had long been a resident of St. Mary's, Ontario, revived his long interrupted literary career in the 20's with the publication of *An Ideal Courtship*, a verse romance set in Alexandria, and a collection of *Poems and Essays*. He had previously published a volume of verse about 1877. Unhappily, he was one of the worst poets ever to appear in print in Canada, and he had the misfortune to be heartlessly satirized for his bad poetry in W.A. Deacon's *The Four Jameses* (1927). Macdonald either generously forgave Deacon or, sadly, did not realize that Deacon's mock-serious criticism was a satire, for soon afterwards we find Deacon writing the preface to Macdonald's *Poems and Essays*. Macdonald had a brother W.J. Macdonald (died 1932) of Fort Macleod, Alberta, who set himself (but did not live to complete) the task of correcting and revising Euclid's geometry.

The Depression which broke in 1929 proved a severe trial for Glengarrians. For many, it darkened a lifetime, leaving lasting feelings of bitterness even after better times had returned in the 40's and 50's.

We wish to suggest a new interpretation of the impact of the Depression on Glengarry. We suggest that the Depression cut all the more deeply into Glengarry because it came upon a county which had in many ways already ceased to be the ebullient and resilient Glengarry which had made such a mark for itself in the world in the years before 1914. There are all kinds of collapses that an individual, or an institution, or a nation, or a community can undergo. Some are sudden and spectacular, others no less dangerous because, for a long time, their outward consequences are hardly visible at all. Let us see what evidence there is for supposing that Glengarry was in some sense already in "decline" before the Depression struck, what evidence there is for supposing that there had already been several kinds of inner collapse, of which the consequences were only beginning to show when the Depression struck.

In this respect, the population figures are striking. The Glengarry population reached its highest ever recorded total of 22,447 in the census of 1891. Thereafter, it steadily declined, amounting only to 18,666 in 1931. The figures for the townships show that the population decline in the countryside was spread pretty evenly among them. Alexandria had reached a population of 2,323 in 1911, but its boom period was ending, and its population was down to 2,195 in 1921 and to 2,006 in 1931. The population of Maxville remained almost static after it became an incorporated village in 1891, varying around the figure 750 throughout the four censuses from 1901 to 1931.

Behind these figures lay harsh and clearly visible realities: the decline of Alexandria as a manufacturing centre and the failure of the county to develop new industries, the end of the large families of children among the Scots, the continuing lure of foreign fields where opportunities were so much brighter than they were in Glengarry.

Perhaps these retreating figures were the outward sign of another kind of collapse that one dimly sees in Glengarry: a simple collapse of confidence, a crisis of morale. This concept is bound to be disturbingly vague and impressionistic; whether or not one sees it as a reality in Glengarry life will depend much on one's own system of values. Yet it seems to us that at some point and probably rather quickly, Glengarrians at least of the Scottish part of the populace lost much of that tremendous confidence that their Victorian fathers had. The world began to seem a more complex and baffling place than before; effort began to seem much less likely to bring certain reward. This crisis can only be known by its effects, but our guess is that the best date for it is somewhere around 1910—certainly, before the First World War began.

The war itself brought problems that heightened the crisis which was already under way. The extent to which the war unsettled people's ideas everywhere has often been mentioned by historians and other students of society. Indeed, it is summed up in the oft-quoted phrase, "How can you keep them down on the farm, now they've seen Paree?" Soldiers who had been through the fearful trench fighting in France, soldiers, war-workers and others who had seen a wider world, now looked with a critical eye on the ideas, values and achievements of the last Victorian generation which still ruled in Glengarry as it did in most of Canada. During the war most people in Glengarry as elsewhere had more money than before, and expectations as to what one should be able to afford rose. According to Rhodes Grant, the Glengarry society he knew after the First World War was more money-oriented than before: "after the War, Money became our God." After the war, people in Glengarry generally had more money than before it, but one senses that now their systems of values had changed. Before, their modest incomes had approximately balanced their sharply restrained expectations, but as the incomes climbed, the expectations climbed faster, with the consequence of—discontent, frustration, a slowly eroding faith in the possibility of the individual satisfying his own expectations.

Prohibition must also have created a new maladjustment between man and society in Glengarry. By being illegal drinkers, a multitude of people who a generation earlier would never have thought of themselves as lawbreakers now broke the law or connived at others breaking it. Others violated the spirit of the law by crossing into Quebec to do their drinking. To some degree, what people believed, said, and did with respect to alcoholic beverages now diverged and became three different things. Prohibition must also have increased the gap between children and their elders, and therefore the gap between children and that established wisdom of society of which elders are the representatives. With both the elders and the children entangled in their respective hypocrisies concerning the use of alcohol, what possibility was there of fruitful communication across this gap on any matter that related in any way to alcohol or law observance or the expected behavior of a good citizen? Seeking idealistically to purify society, the temperance reformers had unwittingly released an acid that ate away at the very sinews of society.

The Monastery of the Precious Blood, Alexandria.

In looking over the Glengarry past and trying to chart its hills and valleys, it is tempting, very tempting, to believe that one can more or less clearly see the outlines of a Glengarry Golden Age at the turn of the century, lasting perhaps from about the mid-nineties to shortly before the First World War. One seems to see there an age of shantymen and patriarchs, bearded and still often Gaelic speaking, men who "dwelt contented in a world they knew," who were equal to every opportunity or challenge that life put before them, and who were accompanied in their journey by wives equally heroic, majestic, masterful. These were men and women of the kind who inspired Ralph Connor, men and women from whose ranks there had, for some generations now, gone out such men as Big Rory McLennan, Sir Donald Macmaster and the eminent contractors J.D. McArthur of Winnipeg, and Donald Grant, of Faribault, Minnesota.

Archibald Mark Chisholm (1862-1933), born in Alexandria, son of a man A.W. McDougald describes as "a skilled master shoemaker" who employed five or six men in a sort of mini-factory in Alexandria. Archibald became a major force in the opening and developing of the iron mining in the Mesabi Range in Minnesota and also was involved in banking. Something of a philanthropist, he gave financial help to the area of Scotland his family came from. Chisholm Park and the monastery were among his gifts to Alexandria.

John J. Macdonald (1849-1937), poet. A native of Lochiel Township, he lived most of his adult life at St. Mary's, Ontario and is buried there.

Yet how far was this dimly glimpsed Golden Age a reality? Perhaps the answer is that is was partly a reality, for there were great men and women then—and afterwards for that matter—but also partly a historical fiction.

It is noteworthy that this period, which we so readily see as a Golden Age in Glengarry, was also something of a Golden Age, or at least as near to a Golden Age as good periods tend to get, in Canadian history generally. This was the age of the Laurier prosperity, the one period of prolonged and unstinting prosperity the Dominion had enjoyed since Confederation. It was also the first great age of Canadian national feeling, as Canadians began to rejoice in the great nation which was the envy of the world for its vast resources, and in which the new empire of the prairies was being opened up to civilization. So it is possible that when we see a great age in Glengarry at this time, we are really seeing a great age in Canada's history.

But also, as we look at the past, there are many optical illusions to deceive us, and one of these is the illusion that the past is better than more recent periods. We develop this mistaken notion about the past because we fail to see its unhappinesses and tensions as clearly as those of more recent ages; in history, as in our individual memories, time tends to filter out and preserve the good things and discard the bad. The period from the mid-90's to just before the First World War is probably a period which is for us today particularly apt to produce such an illusion, because it is just at the outermost fringe of human memory: we know it—we have or have had human links with it—but because it is so far away and its ways so remote from ours, it is also true that we do not know it.

We must therefore, no doubt, be especially cautious in forming our concept of a Glengarry crisis about 1910, that is to say, a crisis coming just at about the end of this supposed Golden Age and creating a society sharply in contrast with it. It is a period and a problem in which our own emotions, our own ideas, struggle to deceive us. Yet when all is said and done, the basic concept seems to hold firm: that something silently but dreadfully went wrong in Glengarry in those years before the First World War, and that other forces had made the crisis still graver before the disease of the Depression hit the enfeebled patient in 1929.

In connection with this concept of a Glengarry crisis, it is a striking fact that the ranks of the Glengarry contractors, who contributed so much to the fame of nineteenth-century Glengarry, were no longer being replenished as the new century began.* Nor did Glengarrians become important in any other business that could be considered a natural successor to contracting. It is tempting to see this as a sign of some failure of Glengarry morale, existing perhaps from a time as much as a generation earlier than 1910. It may also be supposed that when the ranks of the contractors were visibly diminishing, they no longer served to provide whatever inspiration they once offered to ambitious young Glengarrians. One of the explanations for what happened to the Glengarry talent for contracting is that business life in the United States, where many of the contractors flourished, had grown too complex by the end of the century for newcomers to work their way up easily from poverty to wealth without friends, technical expertise, financial "contacts," and business training. Significantly, the Glengarry contractors in the United States had flourished mainly in the developing areas such as the mid-west, rather than in the old established areas of the eastern seaboard. But after the late nineteenth century, there were no more developing areas in the United States; the frontier had finally closed, and the conditions everywhere, as far as business opportunities were concerned, were becoming like those in the long settled east.

This reflection touches on one of the factors in the situation in which Glengarry found itself early in this century, and that is that the closing of the American frontier, which ended one of the greatest and most dramatic chapters in human expansion, was itself an event in Glengarry history. Glengarrians no longer had the great, raw, exciting, undeveloped lands of the American west and south-west to spread out through: a whole world of adventure, of possibilities, of achievement, was cut off. The closing of the American frontier was of course a gradual process, but the traditional date for it is 1890.

*Since this paragraph was first drafted, we have had the satisfaction of learning that the present century has produced at least one eminent and wealthy Glengarry-born contractor, in the person of John L. McLaughlin (1895-1978), of Great Falls, Montana. See GN, 22 March 1978. McLaughlin's family emigrated to the United States in 1905 and he seems to have maintained little contact with Glengarry, where his achievements were unknown to the public till the year of his death.

By Archibald Browne, R.C.A. (1864-1948). This painting, to which black and white reproduction does not do justice, is of a scene along the Front of Glengarry. It is owned by Dr. and Mrs. Norbert Ferré of Cornwall. Many of Browne's works are in major art galleries in Canada and Britain. Browne lived and worked in Glengarry 1927-1948 and is buried at Lancaster. Once a genuine member of the Royal Canadian Academy of Arts lived and worked among us.

By a cruel coincidence, the Depression began just as the last of Alexandria's industry was disappearing. Brutally thrown back upon its original role as a merchandising and service centre for the local farming community, a community itself badly mauled by the Depression, the once promising little industrial town found it had little insulation left between itself and calamity. Twelve hard bleak years followed, and it was fully a generation before Alexandria had regained the prosperity which had come to seem natural in the lush days of the 90's.

Unemployment in Alexandria was a daunting and while the Depression lasted to all appearances insoluble problem. Unemployment registration carried out in Alexandria in August 1931 showed that this little town of about 2000 people had 236 men unemployed and that these men had 356 dependents.

J. Albert Laurin (1886-1959), editor of *Alexandria Times* 1915-1955, mayor of Alexandria 1923-1940 inclusive. When the *Alexandria Times* will have been forgotten, Laurin will be remembered as the man who did his best for the people of Alexandria as mayor through the grim years following the closing of Munro and McIntosh and of J.T. Schell and the onset of the country-wide Depression of 1929-1939.

The unemployed were given financial assistance called "relief." In the fall of 1933, the mayor of Alexandria, J. Albert Laurin, stated that there had already been over 500 people on relief at one time. In January of 1935, the council had the town clerk write to the Minister of Public Welfare asking that the Ontario government pay 90 percent of Alexandria's relief costs. Alexandria, the council explained, had lost its payrolls, assessment values had decreased along with population, and no relief work was being carried on here. The town had a population of 1950, but was caring for over 600 people. Of the families on relief, 20 % had come to reside in the town in the last three years for the purpose of getting relief. In the spring of 1936, the town council ordered that in future no relief was to be paid to families coming to Alexandria from other municipalities.

In 1937, Alexandria was requiring able-bodied relief recipients to work in the municipal bush or on farms to earn their keep. As an employment measure, 15 unemployed men were sent to northern Ontario to do bush work, but some of them shortly caused the town council embarrassment in its dealings with the Department of Welfare by deserting their place of work. In early January of 1938, approximately 500 persons were on relief in Alexandria, and "quite a large number" were entitled to be added to the relief roll before the end of the month. The Department of Welfare had also announced that it was considerably reducing its grant to Alexandria for this year. Faced with such pressures, continued year after year, Alexandria nevertheless avoided being forced into bankruptcy or being placed under Ontario government supervision. Under government guidance, a careful plan for the management of the town's finances was drawn up and followed. Then when prosperity returned to Canada with the opening stages of the Second World War, Alexandria's long ordeal came to an end.

During these years of Depression relief had been supplemented by private charity, including the donation of old clothes. Two small new industries had also been begun: a glove manufacturing plant, and a cannery located just outside the town on the Glen Robertson road.

Incomparably more elastic in the face of such misfortunes than wage earning communities, the Glengarry farming community adjusted itself to the new circumstances. Relief was given by the townships, but it was given sparingly. At a time when farm families still raised most of their own food, no farm occupants needed to go hungry. Few would refuse a neighbour who was evidently in need. For young men, work was normally available as hired men; board and lodging were provided, but the wages were often not much more than nominal.

Despite their own misfortunes, Glengarrians responded generously to the call of greater needs elsewhere. In the fall of 1937, Maxville and district filled a 40-foot freight car with fruit and vegetables for the relief of drought-stricken westerners. In the same fall a large refrigerator car was loaded at Lancaster for the same purpose by the effort of the Catholic and Protestant churches of Cornwall and southern and central Glengarry, while other Glengarrians contributed to the loading of two freight cars at Vankleek Hill.

Glengarry was no pit of gloom during the Depression years, nor did the people go into seclusion. Life had its joys, and in 1938 there was even, cheekily, a "Down with Depression Social" at Glen Robertson. In the north part of the county the present soccer league was in full operation and Alexandria always had a lacrosse team that held its own with other teams in the area that came and went. The United Church Young Peoples' Societies had a softball league and every hamlet had some sort of skating rink, even if only a pond with the snow cleared off it and ordinary fence posts frozen into the ice for goal posts. Hockey was played on these open-air rinks—one concession against another—one village against another—the boys against the men—anything for a game. Pads, helmets, and other such gear were practically unknown and there was no charge for ice time. If there was a bit of a crowd on hand to watch a game often a hat would be passed and the money collected used to buy pucks or balls. One collection we recall at a hockey game in Martintown's open-air rink resulted in a collection of 78 cents, two buttons, and a safety pin. In those days pucks cost 15 cents and the fellow who passed the hat had need of the safety pin to replace the nail holding the back part of his braces to his pants. Players and audience alike had enjoyed the game though.

Many groups in churches, Institutes, and clubs "got up plays" in the winter time, keeping the cast, director, and "stage hands" occupied and giving entertainment to their community when the play was presented. Often groups and communities exchanged plays.

And always there were the neighbourhood card parties, often with a bit of dancing and music. Those who did not dance or play cards might come to the party anyway just to talk and sing or hold a ceilidh of their own. Nor must we forget the radios that a few people owned. The neighbours would come in to listen to "Hockey Night in Canada" or Amos and Andy, Charlie

McCarthy, or any one of a dozen other shows that were followed religiously.

Both Alexandria and Cornwall had "picture shows"—on special occasions families went together, perhaps only once in two or three years. As a special treat to his best girl a young man would take her to the show, followed by a ten-cent sundae apiece. We did not have places like the Bonnie Glen but there were several open-air dance platforms in the county with local talent supplying the music but those who frequented such places were considered fast, nor were the dance halls above village stores considered much better, partly because the local bootleggers seemed to find crowds at public dances to be good customers. Lawn socials and tea parties were considered to be much more respectable and possibly were, though we have heard tales of a hostess' raspberry vinegar contributing to the entertainment—strangely, as raspberry vinegar was not supposed to be alcoholic.

The most popular young man in any group was the one who had a car or access to the family car. Though "joyriding" was frowned upon by the old folks, how were the old folks to know if the young fellow and a couple of friends put a gallon of gas in the car and drove around a bit with the girls. Oh the joy of four in a rumble seat and the cool breeze making the girls snuggle closer to keep warm!

The "Thirties" did have their pleasant moments for all ages and we must not forget one of the favourite indoor sports of the times, listening on the telephone. If a conversation was particularly interesting as many as four could get their ears close enough to the old wall phone receiver to hear. The only thing that was scarce in the Thirties was money—a bit of unsophisticated planning and the buoyancy of Glengarry nature made life bearable and at times quite pleasant.

The Depression had little political history in Glengarry. The Glengarrians were attached to their old political loyalties, or sceptical of the ability of political panaceas to alter conditions. They contented themselves with defeating their incumbent

Conservative M.P. in 1935 and joining with the rest of the country in creating the Liberal landslide victory which returned Mackenzie King to office as Prime Minister. A candidate of the Stevens Reconstruction Party, John A. Macdonell, ran in the same election but received less than one-eighth of the votes cast.

W. Clifford Clark, Ph.D. (1889-1952), deputy minister of Finance for Canada 1932-1952. Dr. Clark was a native of Glengarry. Those who know best about such things credit Clark with having the brain that found the way to financing Canada's amazing contribution to World War II and co-ordinating the even more amazing prosperity that followed the war.

In 1937, the United Counties obtained an important new facility with the opening of the St. Lawrence Sanatorium at Glen Walter for the treatment of tuberculosis. Having played a major part in beating back the scourge of tuberculosis in this part of

Ontario, the hospital began to phase out tuberculosis treatment in 1955 as many beds were vacant and by the end of 1968 was no longer a sanatorium. Now a nursing home, its new name is the St. Lawrence Estate.

In 1932 William Clifford Clark, a Queen's University professor and a native of Martintown, was made Deputy Minister of Finance for Canada. He held this office till his death in 1952. He left a mark on Canadian life through his influence on government policy during an important period in Canadian development and through his work in building up the Canadian civil service. John Porter writes in his widely known and much praised study of social class and power in Canada, *The Vertical Mosaic:*

> It is generally accepted by students of Canadian government that the senior public service has had a crucial position in the over-all structure of power, particularly after the appointment by R.B. Bennett, in 1932, of W.C. Clark, an economics professor from Queen's University, as deputy minister of finance... Sometime later, Bennett appointed Mr. Graham Towers as governor of the Bank of Canada. Gradually there was built up around the Department of Finance and the Bank of Canada an outstanding group of expert administrators who were to be the architects of the economic and social policies required by the war and post-war reconstruction. Clark's Department of Finance was described by one former deputy minister, who had earlier served under Clark, as "the central idea generating department of government." Clark did not see the task of the Department of Finance as simply controlling the purse strings. "His curiosity and energy found expression in the advocacy of policies touching every aspect of Canada's economic life." Among "Dr. Clark's boys" were R.B. Bryce, K.W. Taylor, Harvey Perry, A.K. Eaton, Ross Tolmie, David Johnston, John Deutsch, and others. Others from the Bank of Canada, and agencies tangential to the Department of

Finance, joined with "Clark's boys" to create the
golden age of Canadian public administration... "It
is sometimes said," one Ottawa journalist reported,
"that our national economic and financial affairs are
somehow settled at a long table with W.C. Clark at
one end and Graham Towers at the other."

When Clark died in 1952, Prime Minister St. Laurent
acknowledged that Clark had had "a decisive part in shaping
the wartime financial and economic policies which won for
our country such widespread admiration and respect
throughout the world." Taylor Cole, a student of Canadian
public administration, has written that Dr. Clark was "at the
centre of a small coterie of deputy ministers and of
permanent and temporary senior civil servants and officials,
mostly economists, who constituted the inner spring of the
governmental mechanism in Canada and largely determined
its economic policies from 1939 to 1945."

One of the policies that Clark was important in persuading
the government to accept was the beginning of family
allowances at the end of the Second World War.

Sandra Gwyn in an article in *Saturday Night* has described
the role of Clark in shaping the civil service as it existed up to the
mid-60's. This was:

An institution created by King [Mackenzie King] out
of Queen's. Queen's meaning the university, meaning
in particular a remarkable pair of former professors:
O.D. Skelton, who came to Ottawa in 1924 to run
Canadian foreign policy, and Clifford Clark, who
arrived in 1932 to get the finance department off
the Depression rocks. From there on in, there were
two main groups: Skelton's boys, like Lester Pearson,
...all at external affairs. And Clark's boys,
the money men like R.B. Bryce, John Deutsch,
Mitchell Sharp, and Simon Reisman himself. Which
is how the Ottawa Man was born.

In the spring of 1939 Canada had its first visit from a reigning monarch, George VI and his consort Queen Elizabeth. They toured Canada from coast to coast. Their only stop in Glengarry was scheduled to be at Alexandria for only four minutes on the afternoon of Sunday, 26 May at 2:35. The *Glengarry News* of 19 May had for its headline: "Glengarry will join in Welcome to Their Majesties"; and sub-headlines included such items as "School Children to have Special Provision"; "Roman Catholic hierarchy exhorts Catholics to show loyalty"; "Ottawa gaily bedecked for reception of their majesties; highway to be closed after 2 p.m."

Probably we cannot improve on the *Glengarry News'* description of the actual visit, even if we have to abbreviate it: "Eight thousand people were at Alexandria station on Sunday to give the monarchs a real Highland welcome. A jubilant roar rose from the crowd as the train pulled to a stop but a wave of silence succeeded it as the awe-struck crowd first glimpsed their king and queen. Anne MacIntosh, little daughter of Dr. and Mrs. D.D. MacIntosh and Master Lowell Ostrom were lifted to the observation platform of the train to present the queen with a basket of trilliums. Sgt-Major Dave Lalonde in charge of the guard of ex-servicemen had a chat with the King and Queen, while Glengarry's M.P., John D. MacRae, stayed discreetly in the background. The train was stopped at the station for a full seven minutes, instead of the scheduled four minutes.

"Probably never before in its history had Alexandria seen so many people within its limits. They came from the countryside and every town and village within a radius of thirty miles."

Though the *Glengarry News* carried no hint that everyone who could have been in Alexandria that afternoon was not there and the royal train either had stopped or would stop in Montreal, Ottawa, and Cornwall, still, the crowd was not large, perhaps only one half of what it could have been. Also we must consider the letter the Roman Catholic bishops felt it necessary to have published, exhorting loyalty.

As historians we feel we must ask the perhaps impossible to

answer question, "What kept so many people away from Alexandria on that May Sunday afternoon?" Had the traditions, symbols, and continuous reiteration of the glories and advantages of being a member of the British Empire become unreal to many of those who had just lived through some ten years of depression? Were most of the members of all the ethnic groups within a thirty-mile radius of Alexandria becoming aware of a present and a future, and possibly a past in which they did not share equally with others more favoured?

We can only report on what happened in Alexandria the day the King and Queen stopped there for seven minutes in May 1939 and go on to tell of the events of the next forty years but somehow the report of that day gives us a feeling that not only had an era ended but a new one had already begun—perhaps as much as thirty years before and perhaps, for some, 180 years before.

World War II came to a Glengarry that had been battered by nine terrible years of Depression. In 1938 the town of Alexandria's cheques had been dishonoured by its own bank and about a third of the town was on relief. The farming community were better off in that they could grow their own food but many of the farms had taxes owing on them, some dating back to 1929. Every municipality had relief bills to pay for indigent families. Farm equipment was well worn and largely obsolete and a fairly large proportion of Glengarry's young people had scattered all over North America in search of jobs.

When the time came to try to add up how many Glengarrians had worn uniform and how many died, the task would prove to be impossible because our young people joined the forces wherever they happened to be. We found them in the British Army and Air Force, in all branches of the American services, including nurses and merchant marine, and in Canadian units practically from coast to coast. There however are indications that Glengarry's young people gave their lives for the cause at a rate of least 1 ½ times the national average for Canada. Canada's population in 1941 was 11,507,000 (in round figures) and Canada as a whole had 41,992 fatal casualties in

World War II, which is 0.364 percent of the population. In November 1944, when the war still had six months to go, a count, which was certainly incomplete, of Glengarry's dead listed 88 out of a population of about 19,000, which is 0.463 percent of the population. The war memorial in Alexandria lists 126 names of Glengarry dead in the war, which is 0.663 percent of the population. So it is not fanciful to assume that Glengarry's young people paid more than their share of the blood price in winning the war.

The young folk who joined the services where they got regular pay, clothes, and medical care, got the limelight and the headlines but Glengarry's real battles in World War II were fought out on the concessions of the county. Not daring to trust our personal memories we reread the local papers of the war years and we confess for most of the war period it was a disturbing task. We found a middle-aged to elderly group left on the farms with no prospect whatever of being able to hire help and often enough with younger children still in school. One by one restrictions were put on their way of life—cheese and butter and hog prices were pegged, petroleum products restricted and then strictly rationed, as eventually were tires, meat, butter, liquor, beer, sugar, tea, and coffee. Taxes on everything that could be considered luxuries rose (which included theatre tickets, clocks, and radios), new car production was discontinued in early 1942 and even farm implement construction was restricted. And the government kept asking for more cheese, butter, and pork for Britain at pre-set prices that the Glengarry farmers constantly reiterated were below the cost of production. Then the government with an intensive, hard sales pitch in a series of nine Victory Loans borrowed every cent back "for war purposes." The salesmen were given a quota to fill and in only two of the nine victory loan campaigns did Glengarry not meet its quota.

From about the middle of 1943 on, we confess our initial feeling of distress because of conditions in wartime Glengarry began to give way to a feeling of pride, more than slightly tinged with awe at what our people on the farms accomplished. Glengarry was the fifth in rank of the counties of Ontario in cheese production in 1942, fourth in 1943, and third in 1944, and in those years it doubled its butter production as well. Also Glengarry in those war years, in Lancaster Township, had a flax industry that was very important to the war effort, producing both oil from the seed and fibre flax for linen. Britain normally got its flax from Russia, Poland, and Belgium, and the war had cut off these sources. The Cornwall *Standard-Freeholder* in November 1941 said Glengarry is producing much of the free world's fibre flax. What proportion "much" was we have been unable to discover but the Canadian government considered it important enough to help them get new machinery each time a flax plant burned. This flax industry did not long survive after the war ended.

Lt. Col. W.J. Franklin, M.C., V.D., C.D., a native of Glengarry, died in Ottawa in 1976 at the age of 83. He had joined the old 59th Battalion as a private before World War I and rose through the ranks till he was commanding officer of his regiment. He served in various capacities as a Lt. Col. in World War II, though wounds from the previous war prevented active service duty. He was appointed Sergeant at Arms in the Canadian House of Commons in 1941 and served in that capacity till 1960.

Brigadier Donald C. Cameron (1911-1970), Glengarry's most decorated soldier in World War II. A native of Lochiel, he began his soldiering career with the local militia. He became an able front-line soldier and was commanding officer of the Hastings and Prince Edward Regiment in some of its hottest fighting in Italy. Commanded the SDG's in army of occupation. Post-World War II his career continued to advance and he demonstrated great ability as an administrator. His last position before he retired was Commandant at the Staff College, Kingston.

Glengarry's major battle in World War II was fought on its concessions by the middle aged and the school kids. It must have been a grim one—more production each year and none of the tangible rewards. Just the sense of having done the job there was to do, doing it extremely well and not reckoning the cost either in worldly goods or in pleasure. When the war ended, Glengarry's farm buildings and machinery were not in good shape and few of its young people returning from the services could see a future on the farms.

Major General Donald J. MacDonald, C.B.E., D.S.O., M.C. (1889-1951) a native of Williamstown, attained as high a rank as any Glengarry man before him. He attained the rank of Lt. Col. (of Strathcona's Horse) in the field at the Battle of Cambrai in 1918 at the age of 28. He stayed in the permanent army between the wars, serving in high administrative capacities until he retired in 1945. Major General MacDonald is unique in that he is the 4th generation in his family to be newsworthy. His father D.R. MacDonald was a major contractor and M.L.A. for Glengarry. His grandfather Allan D.D. and his great-grandfather D.D. MacDonald were also major contractors.

As we read the newspapers from 1939 to 1945 we become aware of a very substantial war effort in Glengarry which was well enough documented at the time but which we have not heard mentioned since: that of the women and the Glengarry Red Cross Society. This group organized for war in September 1939 and never seems to have formally disorganized. What our women did (with the help of a few male "volunteers") is an epic. Their slogan seems to have been knit, knit, knit—sew, sew, sew,

537

and thousands of service people and refugees received the results of their labours. They sent off bales of sweaters, balaclavas, scarves, mitts, socks, cigarettes, maple sugar, and useful things of all kinds. They sponsored blood donor clinics, nurses registration, and household help to families that needed it. In addition to their work (on which they never seemed to place a cash value) they raised more than $100,000 in Glengarry in the war years. It should be added that the Red Cross also performed heroically in Glengarry in World War I. Mrs. Duncan McLennan, of "Ridgewood," Lancaster, organized and was President of the Glengarry Red Cross in 1914, and again in 1939. She died in March 1944.

Rt. Hon. William Lyon Mackenzie King, M.P. for Glengarry 1945-1949. Though he did little for the county and had no real connection with it, he was our most prominent Member of Parliament.

Dorothy Dumbrille (Mrs. J.T. Smith). In the 20 years after 1940, in poetry and prose she wrote of the mystique of Glengarry as well as of the problems of life there.

We feel that the Glengarry Red Cross well earned our salutation and thanks. They did a wonderful job.

The 1940's saw the appearance on the scene of two new Glengarry writers, Dorothy Dumbrille (Mrs. J.T. Smith), of Alexandria, and Grace Grant Campbell (Mrs. Harvey Campbell), a native of Williamstown, both of whom have left Glengarry works which will long be valued. Dorothy Dumbrille's works include a novel, *All This Difference* (1945), set in Alexandria of the 1940's, and Grace Campbell's works include two novels set in pioneer Glengarry, *Thorn-Apple Tree* (1942) and *The Higher Hill* (1944).

In June of 1945, between the end of the war in Europe and

the end of the war in Asia, a federal election was held which had the result, indirectly, of making Glengarry the constituency of a Prime Minister. Mackenzie King, who was at that time Prime Minister, ran in his old constituency of Prince Albert, Sask., but was defeated by a C.C.F. candidate. The problem therefore had to be solved of where to find a seat for the Prime Minister.

Grace Grant Campbell (1895-1963), author. Born in Charlottenburgh and wife of Rev. Harvey Campbell. Her creative writings, some of which are set in Glengarry, have made her one of the two women from Glengarry included in the *Encyclopedia Canadiana* (the other is Edith Rayside).

The Glengarry Liberal officials came to King's rescue with the offer that the newly elected Glengarry M.P., Dr. W.B. MacDiarmid of Maxville, would resign his seat to allow King to succeed him in a by-election. The deputation which brought this offer to King pointed out that Glengarry was conveniently close to Ottawa, presented few problems that would consume the Prime Minister's valuable time, and that there was "really no patronage to look after" there. To resign his seat in the only way recognized by the law, Dr. MacDiarmid had to go through the technicality of accepting a temporary government job, with an income of about $50. The Conservatives did not oppose King in the by-election, but he was opposed by an independent candidate, Dr. Richard Monahan, of no Glengarry connections. King won by a vote of 4,227 to 325. King visited Glengarry to attend the Liberal convention which nominated him, and on that occasion spoke for more than an hour at the Armouries in Alexandria. Otherwise, he was absent from the constituency throughout the campaign. "It was, of course," King thought, "pretty much a foregone conclusion that I would be returned." But remembering the general election which had just taken place in Britain, he added, "after what happened to Churchill in his own constituency where some ten thousand votes were cast for a crank who said he did not expect to win one could not tell what might have happened in Glengarry. However, the wisdom of the tactics of keeping out altogether was made apparent before Dr. Monahan had got very far in his campaign. He became a public nuisance and was a public annoyance. The first returns came in about ten past seven as I was sitting in the Prime Minister's office...It indicated from a limited number of polls the certainty of victory." The *Glengarry News* thought the election campaign was the quietest in Glengarry's history.

Mackenzie King had been connected with Glengarry at least twice before this. Back in 1919, when King had been first elected leader of the Liberal Party, he had needed a seat in Parliament, and the Liberal nomination for Glengarry-Stormont had been offered to him. He had refused, however, on the grounds that he was unwilling to run in a constituency where he would have to oppose a United Farmers candidate. King had also been caused much distress through his friendship with a native of Glengarry, Dr. W.L. McDougald (1881-1942).

Trained as a physician, Dr. McDougald preferred business and politics to the practice of medicine. He became Chairman of the Board of the Beauharnois Power Corporation, and a director of Hollinger Consolidated Gold Mines, Dominion Steel Corporation, British Empire Steel, and Canada Steamships Co.

In 1926 King named McDougald to the Senate, but six years later McDougald had to resign because he had been implicated in the financial and political scandals of the government-backed Beauharnois power project. King's own reputation had been gravely imperilled by these scandals, and a personal friendship which he had with McDougald was one of the threads that tied him to them. Dr. McDougald's adult years had been spent away from Glengarry, but in 1940, in a tight battle, he almost defeated Dr. MacDiarmid of Maxville for the federal Liberal nomination in Glengarry.

Title page of a Glengarrian's novel about Glengarry.

The reader is reminded how near Glengarrians just after the war were to the old ways of life by a report in the *Glengarry News* of 28 February 1947 that the Alexandria police were preparing to crack down on lightless cutters and sleighs.

The early post-war period saw the death of J.E. McIntosh, of Breadalbane, who is now, most unjustly, beginning to be forgotten, but who was once widely known and much admired for a column he wrote in Scottish dialect in the old *Farmer's Advocate* under the pen name of "Sandy Fraser."

This picture, at first glance of an ordinary farm family, is of the McIntosh Family of Breadalbane. It contains two of the outstanding "men of letters" that Glengarry has produced. The man in the middle of the back row is D.C. Macintosh (1877-1948), professor at Yale University's divinity school 1910-1942. Professor Macintosh's reputation as a thinker and teacher secured his inclusion in the *Encyclopedia Britannica*. The man at the left end of the centre row is Professor Macintosh's brother, J.E. McIntosh, who for many years was well known as the author of the "Sandy Fraser" articles in the *Farmer's Advocate*.

In this column, Sandy, a crusty old Glengarry farmer, was John's greatest creation, but he invented several companions for him—in the form of the Auld Meenister, who often came to the Fraser home to argue with Sandy on the meaning of life and of a farmer's life in particular; Duncan McGregor, Sandy's Scottish-born neighbour with a fondness for jokes and shanty-stories; and Sandy's sharp-tongued, argument-loving wife, Jean.

543

John Everett McIntosh was born 18 April 1876, on his father's farm on the south ½ of lot 14, 9th Lochiel—the farm where he would spend most of his life. John was the eldest child of Peter McIntosh and his wife Elizabeth Charlotte Everett. Peter's father, another John McIntosh, had emigrated from Killin, Perthshire, and in 1827 received the patent for the farm. Elizabeth Charlotte was the daughter of Cotton Mather Everett, of Pointe Fortune, and was related to the famous Cotton Mather of New England.

J.E. McIntosh's brother, D.C. Macintosh (who used a different spelling of his surname) was a Yale divinity professor well known in his time as a teacher, theologian, and philosopher. He published nine books and many articles on the subjects of religion and philosophy. In 1931 he attracted wide attention in the United States when the American Supreme Court denied him citizenship on the grounds that he refused to support the United States government in every war in which it might be involved. Only two twentieth-century Glengarrians have achieved the honour of entries in the newest edition of the *Encyclopedia Britannica*—and D.C. Macintosh is one of these (the other is Ralph Connor).

J.E. McIntosh's formal education was limited to the local primary school, but in later years he read deeply and widely. He also enlarged his experience of the world by going to the West at least twice on harvest excursions and by spending a winter in shanty in the Lac Tremblant and St. Jovite region about 40 miles north of Grenville, P.Q. By 1909, when Sandy Fraser first appeared in the *Farmer's Advocate*, John had settled down for life as a farmer at Breadalbane. Altogether he wrote about a thousand Sandy Fraser columns for the *Farmer's Advocate* during a period of nearly forty years, being paid more than fifteen thousand dollars. He also wrote less extensively for other journals.

J.E. McIntosh died 11 February 1948, at Dr. MacDonald's hospital, Vankleek Hill, after an illness of about a month and a half. His two columns of January 1948 were the last to appear in the *Farmer's Advocate*. On 26 February the editors announced to their readers the death of "this likeable and talented man." They noted that he was "rather shy and retiring, a good farmer,... and a man with a purpose in life." They also revealed to the readers for the first time that "Sandy Fraser" was only a pen name, that the author's real name was John McIntosh, and that Jean, Sandy's wife, was fictitious, John McIntosh being a lifelong bachelor.

John McIntosh had a philosophy which he outlined in the Sandy Fraser columns. According to him, the whole world, harsh and disappointing though it often is, is a place of education—similar to a school—where we learn from the cradle to the grave through experience. Life would be a futile business if this learning experience had no ultimate use, if death simply cut us off. But in all likelihood, death is not the end. Instead, there must be another world ahead of us in which we continue the learning process. In the present world, work has an outwardly forbidding aspect, yet rightly considered work is a blessing, not a curse. Work is the best road to such happiness as we can obtain, work tells us what we are worth, and work is an important part of the learning process by which we are prepared for the next "training-school world."

How good a writer was Sandy Fraser? This is a question to which the answer must vary depending on who answers it. But one of the present writers, who has made a special study of Sandy Fraser, has reached a conclusion which he hesitates to utter because of its daring nature, and that is that Sandy was in fact one of the best Canadian writers of his time. In lightness of style (in his use of Scottish dialect, though not, unfortunately, in his use of standard English, in which he was inclined to be a bit heavy), in wit, richness of material and constant flow of ideas, skill in the depiction of character, depth of thought in his articles, and above all in his astonishing richness of imagination, it is difficult to think of any Canadian writer contemporary to him who was markedly better gifted or more accomplished.

Well, there is a view so paradoxical that it is likely to darken rather than to improve whatever estimate the reader has so far made of the present book! But the reader has only to pardon it and to pass on. It would not have been uttered here if it could with honesty have been avoided. And perhaps one day Sandy will be "discovered" by the people who make literary judgements, and this view will seem only a statement of the obvious—or so let us hope.

It was a great misfortune that Sandy never bothered to publish his articles in book form. Such a collection was planned after his death, but for whatever reason the project fell through.

The Korean War in itself caused scarcely a ripple in Glengarry though a comparatively small number of Glengarrians did serve in Korea, perhaps 50 all told. In the years 1950-1954 Glengarry was more concerned with battles on the home front—two high schools or three, Sunday sports, liquor votes, school areas, community auction sales, "ban margarine" campaigns, and the price of milk products which lagged behind things the farmer had to buy, and industrial wages.

George Lanthier bought a small bake shop in Alexandria in 1932. In 1951 he found it necessary to make a major enlargement to his premises and had to do so again in 1961. Later he bought the bakery at Dalkeith. In 1978 the Lanthier family operate one of the bigger baking businesses in Ontario and are without competition in Eastern Ontario and neighbouring Western Quebec.

Canada's economy was booming and in spite of a tax on luxuries imposed in September 1950 Canadians were buying and building as they never had before—schools, houses, cars, roads, refrigerators, electric stoves—and Glengarry's old economy based on small dairy herds did not produce the cash needed. The factories of Canada needed men and would pay them. The Korean War economy in both Canada and the U.S.A. provided off-farm jobs and Glengarry's people took advantage of them to get the things they needed. By the time the Korean War ended Glengarry was well started on the path it has travelled since, which we describe in other places.

The ten years after the end of World War II saw the end of many small businesses in Glengarry that had depended on the area immediately around them for supply or custom as the case may have been. Roads were improved at an unprecedented rate and people used the roads with both cars and trucks to go to the larger centres to do business of all sorts.

From the files of both the *Glengarry News* and the Cornwall *Standard-Freeholder* we can chronicle the closing or the burning without replacement of general stores, bakeries, grist mills, saw mills, cheese factories, harness makers, truckers, blacksmith shops, plumbers, tinsmiths, and automobile and implement dealers. The large ones in all these categories that were being efficiently run tended to get larger; the smaller ones either sold out or stopped trying to compete and quietly close their doors.

The next stage of the process took fifteen years but the same forces, as well as others, were at work. By 1970 most of the general stores and blacksmith shops, all the cheese factories, harness makers and small truckers had gone out of business. Our files show very few names in Glengarry businesses in 1970 that appeared in 1945. But some did survive. In Maxville MacEwen's dominated the business scene with their feed and seed business, automobiles, fuel, and other interests. Georges Lanthier in Alexandria had expanded his bakery business to the stage where he was successfully competing with large bakeries from Ottawa, Cornwall, and Montreal. In Dalkeith, MacLennan's had the only large commercial sawmill in Glengarry. The Graham Creamery plant in Alexandria and the Kraft Cheese plant south of Williamstown were the milk processors in Glengarry. In Green Valley the Menards had made a name for themselves for competitors to conjure with and were active in the farm implement and supply field and had become major contractors able and willing to build a road, a house, or a factory. In the transportation field Gerard Lefebvre of Alexandria, ably assisted by his sons, had developed his Glengarry Transport line to the stage where it was ready to compete successfully with the biggest transport companies in Canada. In the road and bridge construction field, Chisholm Construction of Alexandria was getting contracts to build bridges and overpasses on Eastern Ontario's new four lane highways.

The paragraph above deals with the Glengarry businessmen who were able successfully to emerge from the post World War II (r)evolution in Glengarry business and in 1970 were poised to at least hold their own, if not to expand. Two municipalities in Glengarry took the initiative in trying to secure branch plants of already established industry. These were Alexandria and Charlottenburgh.

Alexandria in spite of its desperate need for steady wages for its citizens could do little to attract industry till it got an adequate water supply for the town. It had the other necessary attractions, a large under-employed labour pool, good transportation facilities, and no heavy demands on its electrical system. Finally, in 1952, the town got access to a reliable and adequate water supply (the Garry River) and in June 1954 finally got water enough for industrial expansion. In 1960 a natural gas pipeline came to Alexandria and by 1963 the town had a sewage lagoon in operation though it was not until 1971 that the water and sewage lines throughout the town were anywhere nearly complete and modern. But with adequate water and a modern sewage system Alexandria could and did go after industry.

Carnation Milk Co. established a small plant in Alexandria in 1951 that went into operation in 1952. In 1960 Carnation enlarged this plant to four times its original size and in 1968 increased its range of manufactured products. In 1978 it is still in full operation. In 1955 Alexandria was able to bring a branch of the S. Augstein Co. of New York to town. They were clothing manufacturers and obviously came to Canada because the town built the plant and leased it to them on very favourable terms. Also they must have expected cheap labour and Augstein's who employed about 80 persons in 1957 were very put out when their employees formed a union in that year. On 30 July 1959 they closed the plant "owing to a lack of reliable labour."

Fortunately, Perth Shoe Co. took over the Augstein plant at the end of 1959, began production in April 1960, and became part of the Brown Shoe Corporation of Canada as of 1 May 1960. The business prospered and was expanded in 1963. Brown's bought the plant in November 1965 and in 1978 are one of Alexandria's larger employers.

Consolidated Textiles established a weaving plant in Alexandria in 1964, which complete with a dye house opened in early 1965 with "over 100 employees." Though that quote is from the *Glengarry News* of 11 February 1965 in later years we find the payroll to be more modest, running between 60 and 75. "Square C," as the plant is known, is a good corporate citizen of Alexandria in 1978.

Alexandria was less fortunate with another textile plant that came to Alexandria in 1955. The Stotland Dress Co. of Montreal bought the Alexandria Glove works from George Barbara and sold out at the end of 1957 because of union activities.

In 1965 a former flax plant in Alexandria became the home of Galaxie Sportswear which in 1966 bought the old Armouries building. It prospered for a time, underwent a name change or two, and the *Glengarry News* of 1 March 1978 reported that 53 women had formed the Glengarry Sewing Co. Ltd. and rented space in the plant which had been closed since October.

A general hospital was opened in Alexandria in 1965 with the support of the neighbouring townships and at the time of writing is one of Alexandria's larger and steadier employers of labour both skilled and unskilled. Alexandria's large separate school plant and the high school must also be noted as large and consistent employers in the town in 1978.

In its issue of 20 March 1971 the *Standard-Freeholder* reported that Alexandria "has a 54 acre industrial park, serviced with a 10 inch watermain and an 18 inch sewer, storm sewer and electric power at a cost of $1500 per acre to prospective businesses." In 1978 most of this is still unoccupied though in November 1977 Elegance Kitchen Cabinets announced it would construct a plant there that would employ 35-40 people.

In the late 1970's Alexandria seems to have reached a level of prosperity hardly thought possible twenty years before. With the industries noted above and the attendant service stores and shops Alexandria enjoys a buoyant economy. However, it is quite possible that it has reached a peak. Sociologists recognize regional capitals that tend to draw people and industry to themselves. Alexandria and some of its more enterprising citizens at times of prosperity tend to think of Alexandria as "the capital of Glengarry". But a major part of Glengarry now as in the past refuses to recognize Alexandria's claims to be a "capital." North-east Glengarry goes to Vankleek Hill and Hawkesbury to work and shop. The thriving villages of Dalkeith and Glen Robertson supply many of the needs north-east and east of Alexandria. Maxville has a viable economy of its own which the residents of western Kenyon are more inclined to augment in Cornwall than in Alexandria. St. Isidore-de-Prescott has long been an important business and shopping town for the people of northern Kenyon. The southern two-thirds of Lancaster and all of Charlottenburgh except for the Green Valley-Glen Roy corner also look to Cornwall as their capital. In 1976 the administrative part of the diocese of Alexandria-Cornwall was officially moved to Cornwall, thereby removing prestige as well as income from Alexandria. There is talk of consolidating the small registry offices as well, a move which would affect Alexandria and the legal profession there as it would mean more real estate business would be concluded in Cornwall. So future expansion in Alexandria depends on more industry coming in and on its ability to supply it with labour. In the labour market Alexandria has to compete with Montreal, Ottawa, Hawkesbury, and Cornwall.

Only fifty years from now will historians be able to tell if in the last quarter of the twentieth century Alexandria realized its dream of becoming a "capital." As we write we can give it the status of the most flourishing locality in Glengarry. It is even developing a major suburb at Green Valley, but as we noted above Alexandria has to compete with Cornwall for prestige, industry, and labour.

Charlottenburgh Township, in the 1950's as in the past, rejected Alexandria's claims to being a "capital" and elected to become part of the Cornwall-centred industrial complex. The Seaway had left Cornwall without a harbour that was of any real value and the opening of Highway 401 meant Charlottenburgh had shipping facilities that were as good as Cornwall's, while at the same time Cornwall's labour pool was available for plants along the Front between Gray's Creek and Summerstown. These potential plants could also use south Glengarry's labour pool.

In February 1957 Charlottenburgh announced that it would get its first heavy industry. The EDO corporation of Long Island, New York, had purchased ten acres of land east of Gray's Creek and would build a plant in which to manufacture marine and aviation technical equipment. EDO went into production in the late winter of 1958 and maintained production until 1970 when the plant was taken over by Southern Deming Division Crane Canada, Ltd., the pump manufacturers, the present occupants.

In May 1967 the "Red Rooster" sportswear plant of Bantamac of Canada Ltd. officially opened at Summerstown Station, which encouraged Charlottenburgh to set up a "business plaza" at Summerstown in the years 1968 to 1970 with fully serviced land available for business sites, and in 1970 the township reported the plants operating represented an assessment of $385,000. But occupiers of the plants came and went. In 1974 we read of Summerstown Metals starting production and Richmond Metals starting tool and die production. Modernfold was manufacturing special wood products, Boutique Bagatelle was making clothing, and Cornwall Brass and Iron Foundry was busy on the east side of the Boundary Road. Pert Knitting was about to start production.

In December 1975 it was reported that Modernfold in the area since 1968 and employing 69 persons would close and Pert Knitting in operation for a year and employing 71 persons would close. In both cases the reasons given for closing were increases in material costs, lack of skilled labour, and transportation costs. Nesel's fast freight took over the Modernfold building and employed 60 persons and Marlin Yachts at Summerstown were working on a quarter million contract for the Dominion government. In the mid-1970's, too, an airfield of sorts was opened at Summerstown under the name of Cornwall Aviation. Alexandria has had an airfield since 1972.

Of course, writing at the time we are, when we comment about industry in Glengarry in the 1970's we are not writing history; we are merely reporting so historians of the future will have a place to start. The most significant thing is that both Alexandria and Charlottenburgh have developed industrial plazas and are prepared to make it as easy as possible for industries to work in these municipalites.

"The future is not ours to see."

The post-war years saw the establishment in Glengarry of a new and much respected group of Dutch farming families. The census figures from the 1880's to the 1930's show a "Dutch" population in Glengarry amounting usually to several score, but these figures are so difficult to reconcile with other data and common observation that we are inclined to suspect that these so-called Dutch were often in fact Germans of U.E. Loyalist descent. In 1941, the term used for census purposes changed to "Netherlands," and 151 Glengarry residents were described as being of Netherlands descent. In 1951, the figure for Glengarry residents of Netherlands descent rises to 192, in 1961 to 455, and in 1971 to 495. The post-war Dutch newcomers all or virtually all initially settled on farms. Later, some followed the example of their neighbours by seeking off-farm employment to better their livelihood. The settlement was practically all in the southern one-half of Glengarry.

The Dutch of Glengarry are today still a numerically small group, but they have made so deep an impression on the county that it comes as a shock to be reminded that they make up at the very utmost but 1/36 of its population. As good farmers, good neighbours, and good citizens, they appear to be universally valued. The children of the post-war settlers have now largely grown to adult years. It is to be hoped, and indeed may confidently be expected, that in years to come this active community will be as prominent in Glengarry business and political life as it has hitherto been in farming. The Dutch community has not tried to retain a separate existence in Glengarry, but has integrated itself fully into the life and customs of the Scottish-French community of which it is a part.

In Chapter XI on agriculture, the growth in Glengarry in the past few decades of a non-farming population of "outsiders" who have chosen Glengarry as a place to live was noted. Virtually all of these are Anglophones. Some of these are retired people. Others have jobs elsewhere, usually in Montreal or Ottawa, and commute daily or visit their Glengarry homes only on weekends. The opening of Highway 401 and Highway 417 has provided quick and easy access from these cities to Glengarry. Many of the newcomers have bought farms, and may rent their land to a neighbour who still follows the old Glengarry pursuit of farming. Others are content with a few acres of land on which they can enjoy the pleasures of country living without the vexations incidental to owning a full-sized farm. Others prefer Glengarry's villages. In the most recent years, these new settlers have grown in number under the impetus of the developing crisis in Quebec. They have the distinction of being the first "third group" in Glengarry County—the first sizeable group ever to exist and to preserve its identity in a county where, until recently, practically everyone was either Scottish or French or had chosen to identify himself wholly with the Scottish or French communities.

This is not to deny, however, in any way the indisputable fact that they have contributed much to the county: they have brought money into the county, they have improved many fine old homes and made them a delight to the eye, and they have often shown an interest in and a desire to preserve the long-established Scottish culture of the county.

It seems fair to say that with the old established Glengarrians their relations have been amicable, yet not close. Probably Glengarry is an exceptionally difficult community to get fully accepted in, yet it is probably true also that some comparable situation exists wherever "city folk" live in a rural or quasi-rural environment.

The French Canadians are now the largest ethnic group in Glengarry County. In 1911, according to the figures we have already cited, Glengarry had 8,710 French Canadians, making up 41 % of its population. Sometime between the censuses of 1931 and 1941, the French Canadians became a majority in the county. They reached their highest recorded total, 11,061, in the 1961 census. At that time, they made up 57½ % of the Glengarry population. By 1971, however, these numbers had dropped to 9,695 and 52½ %.

Let us see how these population figures look in terms of the separate municipalities. In 1911, the French Canadians made up 31 % of the population of Kenyon, 40 % of the population of Lochiel, 47½ % of the population of Lancaster (Township), and 37½ % of the population of Charlottenburgh. By 1961, these figures had risen to 47½ % for Kenyon, 59½ % for Lochiel, 66 % for Lancaster (Township) and 53 % for Charlottenburgh. By 1971, however, the percentages had dropped in all four townships to 43 % for Kenyon, 57 % for Lochiel, 56½ % for Lancaster (Township), and 46½ % for Charlottenburgh. The French Canadians made up 55 % of the Alexandria population in 1911, with a highest recorded total of 72½ % in 1961; the 1971 figure was 68½ %. In Maxville and Lancaster Villages, the French Canadian population reached its highest recorded percentages of 40½ % for Maxville and 56½ % for Lancaster both in 1941.

Being of French Canadian descent is not, of course, the same thing as being able to speak French. According to the 1961 census, in which 57½ % of the Glengarry population was recorded as being of French Canadian descent, only 47½ % of the Glengarry population listed French as their mother tongue, according to the definition of a mother tongue as being "the language first learned in childhood and still understood." In the 1976 mini-census, ethnic descent was not recorded, but 40½ % of the Glengarry population listed French as their mother tongue.

Since the end of the First World War, an impressive structure of institutions has grown up in Glengarry to preserve the French language and culture.

As to schools, first of all, to be exact, there is no French school system in Glengarry. What we do have is a Roman Catholic Separate School system that finds it necessary (or desirable, or expedient) to do much of its teaching in French.

In our section on schools we have presented the details of the schools, numbers of pupils, and the continuing struggle to get more teaching done in French in the high schools. Here we can only say as a supplement that a good education in French is available to anyone in the junior grades in Glengarry but as of 1978 English is still the dominant language in Glengarry's high schools for purposes of instruction, but that part of it is far from resolved to everyone's satisfaction. We predict there are changes yet to come.

Unfortunately, the school question is not being well handled and instead of bilingualism being regarded as a unique opportunity, it instead has created an "adversary" situation from which it is hard to see either side emerging as a winner.

But we can say this: good instruction in the schools by trained teachers, along with books in French, readily available through the Counties Library System and on sale at several outlets, have upgraded both the French language and culture in Glengarry in the past 20 years. This we are glad to see.

As English is the everyday business language in most of Glengarry, as we might expect we find many persons who speak French at home are members of a vast number of organized groups ranging from the Boy Scouts through the political organizations and the Women's Institute to the various livestock breeding associations. A few French language groups have been formed and among these we will mention Fraternité Alexandria Inc., the Richelieu Club, and la Fédération des Femmes Canadiennes Françaises. The French speaking teachers in Ontario have their own association and no doubt the meetings of the Catholic Women's Guild in those parishes that are predominantly French speaking will use French as their main language.

Raymond Lapointe became the first French-Canadian clerk-treasurer of SDG on 1 Sept. 1972, following a short period as assistant to L. Cameron Kennedy. Lapointe is a third-generation Glengarrian, completely bilingual, and very much in control of his exacting office.

No French language newspaper is published in the county, but the newspapers of Ottawa and Montreal are readily available, *Le Carillon* of Hawkesbury includes some Glengarry news, and *Le Journal de Cornwall,* a French-language weekly, began publication in Cornwall in 1977.

The immediate post-war years saw the transfer of the parliamentary representation of the county to the French Canadians. In 1948, Osie Villeneuve (Conservative) was elected as the first French Canadian M.L.A. for Glengarry. Today, at the time of writing, he is still M.L.A. for the provincial constituency of which Glengarry is a part. During the intervening thirty years, Glengarry has had only one other M.L.A., Fern Guindon (also Conservative), a French Canadian. In 1949 William J. Major (Liberal) was elected the first French Canadian M.P. for Glengarry, succeeding Mackenzie King, who had retired from public life. Since then, the federal constituencies of which Glengarry has been a part have been represented by French Canadians: Raymond Bruneau (Liberal), Osie Villeneuve (Conservative), Viateur Ethier (Liberal), Denis Ethier (Liberal).

In economic matters, the achievements of the Glengarry French Canadians have been particularly impressive. In a speech of 1928 on the status of the Glengarry French Canadians at that time, we are told that in Alexandria, Lancaster Village, Glen Robertson, St. Raphaels, and Green Valley, "the industries and the trade belong in large part to the French Canadians." Today we can simply say that the industries and the trade of the county are almost wholly in French Canadian hands.

The census figures tell a story of the numerical decay of the Scots in Glengarry. In 1911, there were 10,484 Scots in the county, making up 49½ % of its population. By the census of 1921, the Scots had come to number only 8,697 and made up only 42½ % of the population. The final year in which census figures were published for the Scots in Glengarry was 1941, in which there were 6,298 Scots in Glengarry, making up one third of its population. From the next census, 1951, the Scots population of Glengarry has been grouped with other nationalities in the British category but it would seem a reasonable guess that if the Scots category were revived for a census today they would be found to make up about one quarter of the whole Glengarry population. By 1901, the Scots were already in a minority in Alexandria and in Lancaster Township; by 1941, they were in a minority in all of the seven municipalities (4 townships, 1 town, 2 villages) of the county. The decline in their numbers in the county seems never, incidentally, to have caused the Scots any anxiety or alarm. Their characteristic of not getting excited was once more shown.

Gerard Massie. He was elected the first French Canadian warden of SDG at the first meeting of the 1973 Counties Council. He had served several terms as reeve of Lochiel and was the first warden from Lochiel in 30 years. He was nominated for warden by Albert Faubert, long-term reeve of Kenyon, and Harold Brown, reeve of Cornwall Township.

The relations between the French Canadians and the Scots in the period we are considering — from the First World War to present—have continued to be good. Perhaps good in this context needs to be defined. Clearly the association of members of different ethnic groups which feel their ethnic backgrounds to be sharply different, as these do, has normally been full of difficulties, and until we have a world far nearer to perfection than the present one, it will likely continue to be so. This being stated, we may go on to say that relations between the French

Canadians and the Scots in Glengarry have been amicable and neighbourly but have usually lacked that warmth of feeling and fullness of understanding with which members of each group in their best moods treat others within it. Between members of the two groups, conversation can never be as unguarded as when it is limited to members of the same group. It is a paradoxical result of this situation, that there are fewer social and personal restraints in the way of quarrelling with a member of one's own group than with a member of the other group. It will perhaps be only when a Glengarry French Canadian and a Glengarry Scot can quarrel vindictively without either of them feeling that their strife is likely to provoke wider ethnic rivalries, that perfect integration of the two groups will have come to Glengarry.

Osie F. Villeneuve. On 7 June 1948 he was elected Glengarry's M.L.A. Since then, with the exception of the one short period of June 1962 to Sept. 1963, he has served Glengarry continuously as either M.L.A. or M.P.

559

In the countryside, the usual neighbourliness of farm families has been an invaluable lubricant between the two groups. In the new styles of farming which have come to Glengarry in the last decade or two, neighbours are less important than before, and it is to be hoped that the result will not a be a loss of the good feeling created by the one-time need for all the people of rural communities to work together and to aid each other in distress.

Marion MacRae, native of Kenyon Township, is an instructor in Design and Museum Research at the Ontario College of Art. She was a member of the Advisory Committee on Design for Upper Canada Village and is an expert on architectural and historical research. She has three books to her credit with the promise of more to come.

Relations between the two groups have also been helped by the fact that most of the organizations in the county, other than those associated with Protestant religious denominations, have habitually contained members of both groups. Examples are the

Knights of Columbus, the Lions Club, the Women's Institute, the Legion, calf clubs, sports teams, political parties, snowmobile and CB clubs, and even the Richelieu Club. Such bipartisanship in these organizations seems to occur naturally and the fact that it exists seems rarely to strike Glengarrians as a remarkable or interesting fact, but perhaps at times wise and responsible members of the community take special care to ensure that the desired balance is maintained.

Intermarriage between the two ethnic groups has long been an established practice, and many Glengarrians can claim their descent from both groups. The census figures, therefore, which are based strictly on descent through the male line, are misleadingly clear-cut. Not many persons in the old Scottish families of Glengarry are now wholly without French Canadian kinfolk, though the relationship will perhaps more often be with remote cousins than with grandchildren, nephews, or nieces. The reports of weddings, funerals, family gatherings in the *Glengarry News* show that the overlapping of the two groups has already gone far.

Probably something which has helped the relationship of the two groups in Glengarry is that they feel themselves to be very different, while they are, in fact, in most respects very similar. The supposed dissimilarity prepares people to make extensive allowances; the real similarity provides plenty of common ground for agreement.

There is no scholarly study of this relationship in Glengarry, but there is an interesting novel about it by Dorothy Dumbrille. *All This Difference* (1945) is a love story in which she analyzes different kinds of Scots-French conflict in a Glengarry town which is in all but name Alexandria. In the end the expected marriage of Wencie MacMillan, Scottish and Protestant, to Raoul Faubert, French and Roman Catholic, is frustrated by Raoul's death while heroically saving one of the MacMillan children from drowning in the MacMillan family's mill pond. At about the same time the MacMillans succeed in keeping their economically shaky mill from falling into the rapacious hands of Raoul's anti-English father — a threat which is a tribute to the entrepreneurial qualities of the Glengarry French Canadians. In the course of the novel, a plot to replace Katie Macdonell, the high school principal, with a French Canadian is also defeated. All this takes place against the background of the engulfment of Glengarry by foreign invaders. The style and some of the flavour of the novel are imparted by an important passage in which one character confesses, albeit bitterly, that he is now reconciled to what he sees happening in Glengarry, "Katie," he says,

> "There's something I see coming, like rain across a field. We always thought we could keep this old County for the Scots—a little Scotland here in Canada, but we're losing out."

> She knew what he meant. Farm after farm had been bought by French-Canadian people. Thrifty and hard-working, they soon saved money on land which had failed to support English-speaking people.

> "We mustn't be too bitter, Katie," he went on. "In July 1939, I was in the highlands of Scotland. I saw only mounds of earth covered with gorse and heather where the homes and castles of our forefathers once stood...The wind swept through our Glen, bleak and desolate, and I knew an era had passed. As I stood there I changed my mind about a lot of things, just as you have had to do. I'd rather see this old County settled, filled with the laughter of happy children, no matter what their nationality, than have its homes forsaken, their dooryards grown up with burdock and bindweed!"

As we claim that this novel ought to be better known than it is as a revealing document in the social history of the meeting of the two Canadas, we have the responsibility, presumably, of pointing out that it paints what seems to us to be an excessively gloomy picture of Scots-French relations in Glengarry.

To many Glengarrians it must seem, looking back on the years since the end of the Second World War, that the changes

Glengarry has undergone in those years have been enormous, amounting to little less than a complete transformation of the county.

GLEN NEVIS

A sketch of a Glengarry beauty spot by a talented native son, Stewart McCormick.

Perhaps the most important change has been the greater availability of education for all young Glengarrians who desire it. Here, the great breakthrough was the high school bussing which began in the years just after the war. For the first time ever in Glengarry, country people were able to send their children to high school without the heavy financial burden formerly imposed by the necessity of boarding them in the school town for the five years of the high school program. At the university level, student loans smoothed the student's path.

Roads began to be kept open the year round. Hydro and the telephone at last were available to all the families in the county. For those who valued reading, an excellent library system became available.

Television made its appearance in Glengarry in 1952, when the first set went into operation in Alexandria. Since then the values, good and bad, of this medium have been imported into

Rhodes C.M. Grant (1900-1977), Martintown sage, was the author of two charming books full of the legends, tales, and folk history of the people around Martintown, covering the period from Loyalist days to the end of the 1930's. He was also the author of *The History of St. Andrews Presbyterian Church, Martintown.*

virtually every household in the county. With a persuasiveness of which newspapers were never capable, television nagged persistently at all the old established ideas and practices of the county.

Baby bonuses and a wider system of old age pensions brought a flood of government money into the county. The opening of the Glen Stor Dun Lodge at Cornwall, the Maxville Manor, and Villa Fatima in Alexandria provided the elderly with an opportunity for dignified refuge with excellent care from devoted staff members.

Church-going began to be less important than it had been since pioneer times. The long established puritanism of the county began to be replaced with the diverse codes of the outside world.

Neighbours and their opinions mattered less than before.

Glengarry Scots began at least sometimes to think of themselves as Canadians. Formerly, in their own eyes, they had always been Scottish, or as they said "Scotch."

How much Alexandria changed in these years we have already seen.

Charlottenburgh Auditorium at Williamstown. This building, a completely equipped auditorium and arena, was opened in 1974 and is being enlarged at time of writing. Part of Charlottenburgh as always goes to Cornwall for its recreation so there is only one arena in southern Glengarry. There are also covered curling rinks at Lancaster, Alexandria, and Maxville. We wonder do any kids anymore ever clear off some ice on the River Raisin for a pick-up hockey game or to go skating on it by moonlight?

Rae MacCulloch, Glengarry's dancing teacher 1950's to 1970's.

Elderly farm folk, who had devoted all their lives to farming, saw with dismay, indifference, or pleasure the collapse of the old-style farming of Glengarry. Farmers gave up their farms in mid-life to seek employment in town or city. Farms became fewer, their proprietors grew into businessmen. Recent ex-farmers saw new machines moving in the fields, and hardly could guess what they were used for. Almost miraculously, as it seemed, the surviving farmers grew ever more prosperous. By the 1970's they were living on a scale that astonished people who remembered the bleak Glengarry farming of the 30's and 40's. The unpainted farmhouse and the unpainted barn, so long familiar sights in the Glengarry countryside, gave way to the fine farm "spreads" of today—suitable company for the many old farmhouses tastefully remade by city folk.

Some desired changes did not occur. Glengarry remained a place where people grew up and went away. There was little local employment for the young men and women who had taken advantage of the new educational opportunities. The county still remained one of the poorer areas of the province. Economists, studying the face of Ontario, noted the laggard position of the famous old county.

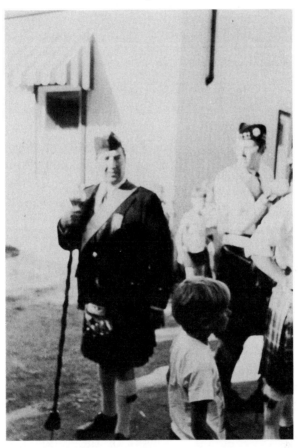

John MacKenzie had a long career with good pipe bands before he decided to settle in Glengarry and make his expertise as a piper and teacher of piping as well as his training as a pipe major available to pipers and would-be pipers in Glengarry. He along with David Danskin and Rae MacCulloch have established a solid basis of technical knowledge of pipe bands, Scottish music, and dancing in Glengarry in the last twenty years.

But there are more important things than wealth, and Glengarrians had every right to be pleased that there was much in the county which had not changed. The old neighbourliness continued, though the old neighbourhoods were increasingly threaded with "city-folk" newcomers who were unable or unwilling to accept the rules which had so long governed those neighbourhoods. Glengarry continued still to be a place where people mattered, where everything was on a human scale, where the chilling anonymity of big city life was kept at bay. Though much less intensely than before, Glengarry remained a place with its own systems of values, its own ideas, its own traditions, its own way of doing things. The little nation of Glengarry stood shaken, imperilled, yet still intact. To many of those who left Glengarry, it seemed that life elsewhere, though richer in mere possessions, has never been as emotionally satisfying as life in Glengarry. The way of life in Glengarry that created and seemed to support that point of view was often harsh and narrow, but if it dies completely, something of inestimable value will have been lost.

## A Glengarry Festival

For the past thirty years, on the Saturday closest to Ontario's civic holiday, Glengarrians by birth or blood by the thousand have foregathered in Maxville. Thousands of others who just could not make it are there in spirit. There they meet with thousands of fellow Scots from all over America and even across the seas. Thousands of people from Glengarry and within half a day's drive of it, rain or shine, head for Maxville too. Maxville's narrow and gaily decorated main street is a jam of nose-to-tail cars long before noon and the jam backs up for miles on all the roads leading to Maxville. Long before the buildings of Maxville are reached the skirl of the pipes quickens the blood and sets feet to keeping time, in the slowly moving massed cars.

Once in the approaches to the grounds, efficient parking attendants soon get the cars out of the way and a stream of people in kilts, trews, plaid skirts, plaid scarves and with Scotch in their souls (and often in their pockets and purses) march on the sound of the pipes, filling the road from shoulder to shoulder, as close as they can be packed. Inside the 50-acre grounds, friends and acquaintances from far and near greet each other and many a Gaelic salutation gets used that day, that has not been used for a year and will not be used for another.

Thousands keep adding to thousands in the grounds, the 3,500 seat grandstand fills and holds little more than a tithe of the average crowd; the raised embankment around the scene of activities grows colorful with men, women and children, not a few in Highland dress, and all with a touch of something Scotch about them. The roadway and walks get full of people, and as the day draws on and the individual piping and dancing competitions come to an end, an air of expectancy comes over the crowd. The time is coming for the first appearance on the field of the massed bands and a sight and sound it is—one to thrill the heart of any Scot and chill the blood of a Sassenach; hundreds of pipers in full regalia, playing and moving together with a precision that delights the hearts of all within sight or sound. The music that for over two hundred years now has played the Scots regiments into battle and at the same time put terror in the hearts of their foes—the pibroch of the Highlanders. Thoughts rise unbidden in each breast—thoughts of the message sent by the Cape Breton Highlander officer to his headquarters when his detachment was held up by a determined German strong point in Italy, "Send up three tanks or one piper"; thoughts of the relief felt by the besieged Britons in Lucknow when the skirl of the pipes with Sir Colin Campbell's relieving column was heard in the distance; thoughts of the pipers of Britain's Highland Division leading the hard bitten reconstituted Highland Division (it had been decimated before Dunkirk) through the mine fields at El Alamein, the beginning of a 2500 mile march home via Sicily, Italy, the Normandy beaches and on to the Elbe. For former members of the SDG Highlanders and its band, memories more personal and poignant still. Such is the quality of the piping at the Maxville Highland Games, held annually since 1948.

Athletic events are part of the show too, and "ferry gutt dey are too whateffer," though with one great exception they tend to get lost among the pipers and dancers, as far as the vast majority of the audience is concerned. The exception is the caber toss, an event competed in only by men of exceptional strength and skill who are dwarfed by the huge pole they must throw; they throw for distance, but the pole must also make a complete flip for a legal throw. The ordinary big, strong men feel puny and shy beside the caber tossers who draw admiring glances from the ladies, as they see broad-chested, hairy-legged Hieland men at their best, and a grand sight it is too.

Those of us who are addicted attenders of the "Games" have a rule of thumb for estimating the crowd. If people can walk without much interference with one another, about 20,000 are present. If shoulders and elbows must be used freely to move about, 25,000 are present; if the crowd is an immobile mass, somewhere close to 30,000 are present. Up to 1977 it has rained twice on the afternoon of the Games, in 1954 and 1974, and real downpours they were, but the rain only raised the spirits of the crowd and competitors. One gentleman well into his eighties, who had gone to the Games with his nephew, confronted his nephew after the pour was over to complain that his raincoat was locked in the trunk of the car. The nephew dutifully apologized and asked his uncle if he wanted to be taken home. The reply from his sopping wet uncle was, "hell no, I'm just beginning to enjoy myself!" He had only been there since 9 a.m. and it was now half past three! Many in the crowd, both men and women, removed their shoes and stockings, hung them around their necks, put on wider smiles, and the bands played on. Such is the spirit of the crowd at the Maxville Games.

The morning of the 1977 games dawned grey and pouring rain. One man who had a job to do appeared at 8:30 as he had promised and the rain quit as he arrived. An hour later he felt it safe to phone his wife to come and the long distance operator many miles from Maxville, realizing the call was being put through from the Games, badly breached all telephone operators' rules to ask, before she asked the caller for the number he wanted, "what's it like in the grounds?" Such is the interest in Eastern Ontario in the Games.

Angus H. McDonell. As Chairman of the Glengarry Highland Games, Angus is highly visible each year at Maxville. As sports editor of the *Glengarry News*, each week he hands a bouquet to Glengarry's athletes present and past. The debt we Gengarry Scots owe to Angus has been accumulating, however, for most of his life. At a time when Scottish games and concerts were few and far between and there was little public support, Angus kept organzing concerts, often little more than house parties that kept the spark alive. The present revival of things Scottish in Glengarry owes much to Angus.

One may well ask the story behind the Games. They began as the brainchild of Peter MacInnis, one of the handful of surviving Glengarry pipers of the 30's and World War II. MacInnis enlisted the moral help (and later the practical help) of

William McPherson, the long-time organizer of the Highland Games at Embro, Ontario. Back in Maxville, MacInnis enlisted the help of the Board of the Kenyon Agricultural Society and the Maxville Chamber of Commerce and work began to put together the first annual Maxville Highland Games. Peter MacInnis was President of the group selected to stage-manage the affair, John D. MacRae was secretary, Osie Villeneuve was ground committee chairman, Don Gamble, D.V.S., headed the sports committee, Clarence MacGregor headed the ticket salesmen, Clark Hoople looked after the publicity, Archibald S. Macdonald rounded up trophies, and Mayor Angus McDonald (Grove) (retired) was program chairman. Glengarry's M.P. at the time, the Prime Minister of Canada, Mackenzie King, was chosen to open the games, and the practiced "games stager," William McPherson, arrived from Woodstock to lend moral support and practical advice. On Games Day, 1 August 1948, the committee expected perhaps 5,000 to attend—at least 20,000 came. They ate all the food in Maxville, and drank all the drink (maybe thereby giving rise to the custom of bringing a supply of your own just in case). The eight bands present gave a sterling performance and everybody had a grand time greeting old friends and being greeted by them and just looking and listening and maybe conjuring up in their minds the shades of Bruce, Colkitto, Dundee, and Bonny Prince Charlie. At least something brought the people and the bands back; there were only 12,000 people and six bands in 1949, but 18,000 and eight bands in 1950 were well ordered by the now experienced committee, which had lost John D. MacRae as secretary and had gained the services of John Jamieson in that capacity, an office in which he would become a fixture. In time Angus McDonald (Grove) was succeeded by the able and affable Angus H. McDonell as Games Chairman. In 1963 a pre-games concert became an annual event, a magnificent bonus to those of us who drive hundreds of miles to be in Maxville on Games Day and the number of bands increased, all-girl pipe bands appeared, quality improved, and in 1973, more than 40 bands split the skies and thrilled the crowds with every form of pipe music and that year there were around 30,000 on hand to listen.

This is not a professional event, nor is it staged by professionals. Dedicated and able Glengarry people handle all aspects of the behind scenes organizing and planning, some 20-odd of them, and so quietly do they work that one has to almost be "on the inside" to know just who is responsible each year, and year after year, for the staging of this big-time event in a small Glengarry town. We hesitate to mention names but we believe those who work with them would be pleased rather than insulted, if we select for special mention, Peter MacInnis, John Jamieson, Angus H. McDonell, Dr. Don Gamble, and Benny Villeneuve.

A *History of Piping in Glengarry*, prepared by a group of Glengarry young people in 1975 as an OFY Project, on page 39 says about the Maxville Games, "The vision of a few men in 1948 has grown into one of the largest and most renowned highland gatherings in North America."

MacGillivray and Ross don't feel able to even try to improve on that, we can only thank them for saying it for us; we would have, if we had thought of it first.

We all know the grand finale of the big day is about to take place when here and there in the crowd, like islands in the sea, bands begin forming up for the mightiest presentation of the day—that second and last appearance of the massed bands. Eight or twelve abreast in a seemingly never ending column pipers and drummers pour into the infield and are marshalled by their pipe majors into ranks and files which eventually cover some acres of ground. The skirl of the pipes, the boom of the drums, the kilts and tall head-dresses give an impression of a force of nature, benign or deadly as occasion demands, a force not to be resisted in any case, a force that puts the best into and draws the best out of Scots' souls and brings us back again and again to the Maxville Highland Games.

# Chapter XVII
# Life as the Glengarry Folk Lived It

As an anatomist dissects a subject, so we have dissected Glengarry's history. We have tried to isolate and identify the things that happened from the days of first settlement until we got so close to the present that all we can isolate are general trends. Yet there was something lacking—the Glengarry people were more than the sum of the parts of their history. They loved and worked, hated and mated, raised families and in due course were buried, often in the shadow of the church they or their ancestors had built. They were carried to their graves by their neighbours and friends, and life went on. In a fairly well closed group such as that of the Glengarry settlement, work, play, amusements, and aspirations tended to be much alike all through the county and to vary in type very little over the years. The people's ideas of what was desirable in work and amusements changed very slowly. We found that when the Glengarry folk evolved something that suited them they were inclined to go along with it for generations, keeping change to a minimum. Few cared to be experimenters or innovators, as an innovation that failed brought derision from the neighbours and even an experiment that worked out, such as establishing a purebred dairy herd, would not gain general acceptance in the neighbourhood or be copied.

It would appear that "general acceptance in the neighbourhood," whether expressed or not, was the determining factor in Glengarry life, and to a large extent it still is. These folk who had intermarried for generations were related to each other for miles around and knew everyone by sight or reputation within two days walk of their homes, yet they said, "We can get along without relatives, we can get along without friends, but we can't get along without our neighbours."

So, as might be expected, from the earliest days we find Glengarry to have been composed of neighbourhoods. Sometimes these had a church as their centre but by no means always. In fact, the church-centred neighbourhood was probably the exception and would only exist if the whole neighbourhood was of one religious persuasion. Being neighbours meant that if a Protestant woman was about to have a baby, her Roman Catholic neighbour women moved in and attended to the midwifery and feeding of the family, until the woman of the house was on her feet again. In the earliest times, if there was no local Protestant minister, in due course the baby would be taken to the priest for baptism. If a Catholic home caught fire, the Protestant neighbours, often headed by their minister, showed up to fight the fire and if need be to rebuild the house. When in the course of time, French Canadians became part of the neighbourhoods, they too acted as neighbours and were treated as such.

The thing that got work done in a community and often led to a "frolic" was the bee. The Oxford Dictionary defines "bee" in the sense it is used here as "a meeting of neighbours to unite their labours for the benefit of one of their number." It goes on to state that the term is American in origin and can be traced back to 1809. This is almost a perfect description of the Glengarry bee and all indications are that bees became part of Glengarry life by 1809, if not sooner. Evidence is completely lacking to tell us if the neighbours got together to build their first cabins in the Glengarry bush, but it is likely enough that they did. Even if small logs were used for the cabin walls, putting them in place would have been heavy awkward work for a man and wife with only their own muscles for power. When bees do appear in written Glengarry records in connection with the building of our earliest churches, there is no effort made to explain the term. It is taken for granted that the term is familiar.

It would be idle to speculate on who thought up the idea but in the course of a few years we find any type of work that lends itself to mass participation being done by bees. There were stumping bees and logging bees, stoning bees and butchering bees, building bees and raising bees, hauling bees and threshing bees, woodcutting bees and fencing bees. Nor were the women folk behind the men in having bees. There were bees to deal with all stages of the wool preparation—shearing, washing, carding, spinning, and fulling. There were apple-paring bees and corn-husking bees, quilting bees and rug-making bees. If a neighbour had sickness at a busy time of the year the community made a bee for him or her and in a day or two brought that household's work up to the community standard.

A man named Dixon wove this bedspread at his own loom in Dunvegan about a hundred years ago. Perhaps when we examine the intricate weave, known as "overshot" and the complicated pattern, we can appreciate the great skill of Glengarry's best weavers. The loom was nicknamed "the four posts of poverty," and if we can imagine the time needed to make a bedspread such as this, we can see why a weaver's output was of necessity very limited as to quantity—quality was taken for granted.

In one sense a bee was a practical application of the old saying "many hands make light work." But the idea went further than that. It was early realized that some sort of organization was needed to prevent the people at a bee from working at cross purposes, so a bee often took the form of a "choose up sides" contest. The contest made it fun but what was perhaps most important, the persons chosen to lead the "sides" at a bee would invariably be the most capable persons in the neighbourhood which made for good management and effective work, something not everyone was able to do for himself. Many a man or woman who was a good worker was not an efficient manager. Bees ensured both good work and good management in a community.

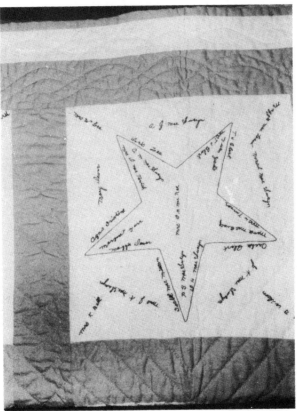

A Glengarry quilt. Names sewn into the pattern make this quilt outstandingly different, even among Glengarry quilts. Only a small part of the total quilt is pictured here so those who have not seen the quilt can imagine for themselves the minute details our ladies were capable of and perhaps appreciate the patience and skill required to make a quilt like this.

A Glengarry quilt. This thistle design is one of literally hundreds of designs that the ladies of Glengarry have painstakingly sewn into quilts both at quilting bees and in the privacy of their homes. To the hundreds of ladies connected with Glengarry who treasure their homemade quilts, each one a unique work of skill and art, the authors hasten to say, "we are presenting samples only," we are not presuming even to attempt to judge which is better than another. A display of Glengarry quilts is literally awe-inspiring even to us males.

The social aspects of bees were most important too. In a day when there was no public entertainment and the people had no money to go to such anyway, even if it had been practical to travel, they made their own entertainment. A very large part of this took place after a bee was over. If it were a women's bee the men appeared in the evening, if it were a men's bee, the women were often there all day, seeing that the men were fed. At any rate, when the day's work was done the sexes got together. Almost every community had a fiddler or a piper or both—if not, hand clapping would provide the rhythm for dancing. Between reels there would be story telling and singing. A good few of our ancestors are reported to have had an uncanny ability to compose a song on the spot. These songs could be about the old homes and times in Scotland or about the prowess someone had shown in the day's work just finished. Or the song might be about someone who had loafed on the job or done everything wrong that day. Exposing a person to public ridicule in a song that lifted long strips of hide from the errant was a most effective way of dealing with those who acted the fool or were lazy or who gave the grog boss too much trouble. Often there were a few fights among the young men, and those who thought they were men, as the evening wore on. These might be to decide who was going to escort a certain young lady home or to settle an argument that had been going on all day or even just to settle who was the better man. Many a staid and sober elder in both churches won his first claim to potential leadership in rough and tumble fights after bees. In "behind the barn brawls" such as these, the Glengarry shanty men served their apprenticeship in fighting—an activity that made them known and respected across North America for good or ill. Certainly fighting prowess won the acclaim of our most famous Glengarry author, the sober and sedate Ralph Connor, who stated categorically that a real Glengarry man would not be afraid to fight a man twice his own weight and size.

Since the 1830's, Glengarry's girls had been going to various cities to work as domestic servants. Some families have letters from these girls, most of them almost illegible, because of the childish spelling and unpracticed handwriting. The letters tell us these girls had little schooling as a rule. We also know when these girls came home to Glengarry to marry they had received an education in dress, manners, food preparation and serving, dressmaking and millinery skills that upgraded life in Glengarry. As wives and mothers these girls who had worked in the cities raised Glengarry's living standard. In many cases friendships grew between these girls' "families" in the cities and their families in Glengarry and visits were exchanged for years. From about 1850 on we find evidences of domestic skills and hobbies increasing—pillow slips get lace borders, quilts become works of art, horse hair pictures adorn the walls along with samplers and the odd pen and ink sketch or watercolor. An inborn Scottish talent for skilful work is beginning to be expressed by our womenfolk. Godey's Lady's Book still survives in a few Glengarry homes to prove that the women of the period were interested in improving their minds, habits, and skills.

The Sports Palace, Alexandria. This thoroughly modern arena and auditorium which also houses the local branch of the Seaway Library was opened in 1976. Maxville too opened a new arena and auditorium about a year later. These two arenas serve northern and north central Glengarry. It may be of interest to this age of affluence and comfortable covered arenas that the first covered hockey rink in Glengarry was opened at Maxville, with a box lacrosse game, on 17 Nov. 1931. It cost $9,900.

For the first three generations in Glengarry very few men and fewer women caught even a glimpse of the outside world. By 1870 there is definite evidence that the outside world was beginning to affect Glengarry. Kirk sessions and priests are becoming concerned with the "evils" of round, fast dances (square dancing and reels were all right) and those "devils" playing cards. There is some evidence too that the elders in the communities did not approve of the bright colours and modern styles the young people were affecting. In those days too, and for years thereafter (indeed into this century), the Kirk Sessions considered they not only had the right but the duty to hail people before them to be admonished or censored for what the elders considered bad behaviour, talk, dress or manners. Today we are better able to understand the social pressures that ended this tyranny of the community elders than we are to understand why several generations submitted to it. Yet church records prove that they did.

It could easily be imagined that this hardworking, frugal people dominated by a highly conservative clergy (in all churches) backed by the community elders led joyless, colourless lives. Yet oral history strongly denies that this was so. The basic ingredient for a Glengarry good time was (and still is) for two or more people to get together who had not seen each other for a few days. Sex seems to have had little bearing as such. In a mixed group each sex formed their own circle and talked of subjects of interest to them. But they did participate jointly in dancing and singing, both favourite forms of entertainment. Highland dancing does not require a partner to be well done; indeed, the contrary is true, and the dances of the old land came down to the present, handed on from generation to generation in the modest homes of Glengarry.

From the very earliest days until television broke them up, the Glengarry house parties, lawn socials, sleigh rides, skating parties, sugaring-offs, taffy-parties, house warmings, barn dances, and just plain "ceilidhs" with or without a formal reason for getting together were part of the way of life. The people made their own fun and most of the time at absolutely no cost. One great debt we owe to these "get togethers," formal and informal, that took place on every Glengarry concession at every conceivable opportunity from 1784 until well within living memory—they preserved our Highland folk culture with its dances, music, and folk tales.

For some reason or another one part of our folk tales has been "swept under the rug". Glengarry really has a rich store of tales of ghoulies and ghosties, bochdans and kelpies and tales of the second sight. Also there are stories of curses, some of which go back to Scotland and other stories of miracles worked and others seen in the sky. There are also tales of "doctors"—people who had miraculous powers to heal—and of charms to relieve or cure ailments ranging from toothache to cancer. Ralph Connor who must have heard many a tale of these "supernatural things" chose to ignore them in his Glengarry books, as did Grace Grant Campbell in hers. Dorothy Dumbrille and Rhodes Grant merely scratch the surface. The only book written about Glengarry that carries the tale of a full-blooded curse is Carrie Holmes MacGillivray's *Shadow of Tradition* (1927), in which the legend of Ann Fitheach Dubh—the Black Raven—and its curse on the Kennedy family provides the theme. Time has prevented us from delving very deeply into this aspect of the culture of old Glengarry, but we can assure our readers that the old Celtic, Pictish, and Norse folk beliefs came to Glengarry with its Highland settlers and co-existed quite peaceably beside Christianity. Today there is an embarrassment in speaking of them, and few indeed profess a belief in them, but a rich field awaits the researcher in this area who can persuade the Glengarry folk to talk to him or her.

Those two great events in human life, weddings and funerals, did not take place unnoticed in Glengarry. A wedding was a social event. Both sides of the newly-formed family got together for a wedding feast. In the case of the Catholics it was a wedding breakfast as their weddings were always in the morning. The Protestants married after noon and their feast as a consequence was in the later part of the day. In both cases the evening of a wedding was a big family get together, complete with the usual events of a Glengarry ceilidh. In the days before honeymoon trips the bride and groom would eventually be escorted to their new home by most of the community, showering loud jests and ribald suggestions on the newlyweds. It was considered to be essential that when the young couple were finally left alone and presumably on their way to bed that the assembled neighbours, relatives and friends, now outside the house, continue to make as much noise as possible. Guns were shot off, dish pans and pails were beaten, and everybody yelled.

Delvers into folk lore of course will recognize that all the noise was intended to scare evil spirits away from the marriage bed, but as it was practised it assured the newlyweds of the lusty good will of their friends and neighbours.

William J. Major (1896-1966). When Major became the first man from Glengarry of French descent to represent Glengarry in Ottawa, on 27 June 1949, those who knew the man and had followed his career felt he had earned his position. He began as a township councillor in Lancaster Township, then was deputy reeve and reeve. At the same time he was a hard worker in the Glengarry Cheese Producers Association serving there as Secretary-Treasurer and as President of the Glengarry Liberal Association. Though Osie Villeneuve was elected to represent Glengarry at Toronto a year before Major was elected,Major in the 20 years prior to 1949 did most to prepare Glengarry for Francophone representation in Parliament.

When in the late 1800's the honeymoon trip robbed the community of its chance to howl their good wishes to newlyweds on their first night married, it became the custom to arrange a "reception" for the young couple as soon after their return from the honeymoon trip as possible. These receptions (still very much a part of Glengarry life), with dancing, a good meal, and gifts for the newlyweds were pale imitations of the spontaneous, lusty celebrations on wedding nights. Much more decorous too.

However, the noisy celebration did survive for special cases. These special cases are hard to define but they include couples who were especially popular and couples, one or both of whom were unpopular. They also included cases where there was an unusually large age difference between the bride and groom. In these cases some night after the couple had returned from their honeymoon the neighbours would gather, completely un-announced, around the home of the newlyweds and give them what came to be called a "chivaree." The chivaree began after they were sure the couple were in bed and hopefully fast asleep. Then all the noise possible was made under their windows. From then on, how things were depended on the attitude of the couple thus suddenly awakened. If the window was raised a bit and a shotgun pushed out, the crowd merely retreated out of range and continued the noise. If, as sometimes happened, the window was opened and the pot emptied on the heads of those closest to the window, some minor physical damage might be done, such as breaking a window or two, but it was considered best in such churlish cases to force the door and escort the reluctant couple downstairs in their night attire and sit them beside those on whom the pot's contents had landed. Then they could enjoy the smell too. There was only one way to end the chivaree—the newlyweds had to feed the crowd and usually the whole thing ended in a good-humoured frolic. The more quickly the newlyweds got good-humoured about the whole thing and invited the crowd in, the better their chances were of being off to a good start in the neighbourhood.

Consciously or unconsciously a chivaree provided a good test for a newly married couple's future public relations.

The start a young couple got in life depended to a degree on the comparative affluence of the two families concerned. Presents from outside the immediate family were apt to be small but practical. What was most important, the young couple automatically became part of their community. The community would look after them in times of sickness, bad luck, fire and flood. In return they knew they had to be ready to help their neighbours when help was needed and that without being asked or prodded.

The Glengarry folk enjoyed their weddings but not nearly as much as they enjoyed their funerals, or to be more precise, the wake that was an essential part of every funeral.

The word "enjoy" may seem incongruous when applied to a funeral, so it needs some explanation. Death was a very real thing, a part of everyday life in any Glengarry community. Men were killed in the bush, men were gored by bulls and trampled by horses in the barns; men were drowned on the log drives and buried in gravel pit slides. Every woman who became pregnant had a grave risk of death through any of the many complications of childbirth or even the more dreaded "childbirth fever". Epidemics of smallpox, diptheria, scarlet fever, and typhoid swept the communities from time to time, even until well into the twentieth century. Old folks of course died natural deaths with their children's children and even great-grandchildren around them, but every family was well acquainted with death. The markers on the family plots tell us the story—here lie buried children, young parents, and strong youth as well as old age.

It is probable that some individuals existed whose death was a cause of quiet rejoicing to their community, but their number must have been small. In a Glengarry community each individual from the newest babe in arms to the oldest "grannie" had a place, and at a death the community immediately closed ranks to make the death bearable. The professional undertaker who is called in when a death occurs today is a comparative newcomer on the scene. He was hardly known a hundred years ago and it took a few years before his services were considered essential.

Here we speak of the funeral customs from the days of first settlement in Glengarry and for most families until well into the present century.

When a death occured word was spread by word of mouth with as much speed as possible. Someone in every community, usually a woman, was the one who did "the laying out", which consisted of washing the body and dressing it in its best clothes. Then it was laid on a bed with its eyes closed and its arms folded. The local coffin maker came and made his measurements and then departed to make the coffin. Along with the person who did the laying out and the coffin maker, the near neighbours, both men and women, arrived. The women took over the care of the house and its inmates, the men took over the necessary work in barn and fields and the family of the deceased were left free to be hosts to the ever increasing stream of relatives, friends, and neighbours who appeared as they heard of the death. Those from a distance came to stay until after the funeral. When the "wake house" was filled, the immediate neighbours took charge of the overflow. If it were a mother who had died in childbirth and the baby lived, in a matter of an hour or two some young woman in the neighbourhood with a baby of her own would be sharing her milk between the motherless child and her own.

When the coffin was made and installed in the "room" of the house of the deceased and the corpse put in it, the coffin was raised on a pair of saw horses and the formal wake began. Most, if not all communities considered it necessary to keep a permanent watch or wake around the coffin day and night until it was buried. Few, if any, realized they were acting on an age old custom, designed to prevent the Devil from stealing the corpse. The custom had become part of the ritual of death and around the coffin (not yet called a casket) voices would be low and muted and as visitors were ushered in to view the corpse they were expected to say a few words of sympathy to the family members present and when they actually looked on the corpse to say something like "my, doesn't he or she look natural" or "What a beautiful corpse." (Both remarks are still heard today.)

When the viewing was over, the people sorted themselves

into congenial groups. Very close friends and relatives of the deceased would install themselves in the room with the corpse. Those less closely tied would install themselves in rows around the kitchen walls, seated on blocks of wood from the woodpile or on planks over the blocks. Those a mite further removed from the family would set up in the summer kitchen or woodshed if any. When the house was full, the crowd spread outside and perhaps even to the barn.

The good name of the community demanded that food and drink be available to all guests and this the neighbour women attended to. They arrived with pots of tea and baskets of sandwiches, cakes, pies, and cookies. Inevitably at some wakes, if not at most, drink stronger than tea was available, if not openly, then with little effort at secrecy.

Not even an auction sale could draw people as a Glengarry funeral could. Relatives and friends appeared from far away who had not been seen since the last family funeral. Families in the community who had been "at outs" with each other for years appeared at funerals and gravely saluted each other, their feud forgotten for the time being. Estranged relatives and "disappeared" relatives appeared, all polite to one another in the presence of death.

So in a wake we had the basic ingredients for an enjoyable time in Glengarry, a group of people, more or less known to each other, gathered together with nothing to do but talk to each other, and they took advantage of the chance. Friendships were renewed, deals made, visits arranged and every aspect of politics, religion, and economics discussed. True, death had brought them together and the death was sincerely regretted but the family and the community still lived and would go on living.

Reading old obituaries and accounts of funerals of a hundred years ago in letters one gets an implication of a triumph in spite of the death, of a renewed hope out of the mourning. The community, by closing its ranks around the family of the deceased, had put into a very practical form the words the clergyman would utter at the graveside, "O, death where is thy sting, where grave thy victory?" And the community, while deploring the death, had enjoyed itself with lots of good food and good talk and for those who wanted it, a wee drappie too.

The mechanical part of the funeral in days past was governed by what was practical. Scottish custom demanded that the coffin be carried to the grave on the shoulders of relays of pall bearers. These pall bearers were always chosen because of some strong relationship to the deceased, either of friendship or blood. It was (and still is) considered an honour to be asked to be a pall bearer. Later, as roads permitted and people acquired wagons, a wagon would be used to carry the coffin the greater part of its journey. To this day there is a token "carry by hand" at each end of the coffin's journey from the place of the funeral to the grave.

As soon as possible after a death, or even before, if death seemed imminent, the family's clergyman would be called in. What he did depended on the religion involved, the clergyman himself and the family involved. As usual we will make no comments on the theology involved, but will content ourselves with remarking that as historians, we wish the Presbyterians had kept records of births, marriages and deaths that would bear comparison to those kept by the Roman Catholic parish priests.

In the earliest days the wakes and funeral services were both most often held in the home of the deceased or a near relative. As travelling (roads) improved, and cemeteries grew up around the churches, more and more of the funeral services would be held in the churches, though home funeral services were not uncommon as late as the 1950's.

The undertaking profession grew by stages from the local carpenter making the coffin to the local carpenter becoming a furniture dealer and furniture maker with coffin making as a side line. By 1900 most undertakers were also furniture dealers (or the other way round). One long established Glengarry undertaking family, however, seems to have got into the funeral business via the livery stable route—they rented horses, hearse, and wagons for funerals. The family a bit later became better known as saw mill operators and furniture makers, but Sam Clingen first appears in census records as a hotel proprietor and livery stable operator.

Embalming, at first a fad, after the American Civil War experience had made it a practical science became commonplace toward the end of the century and permitted more leisurely funeral arrangements, particularly in warm weather, and spelled the end of the old closed coffin with a glass plate over the head of the corpse. The funeral home was slow in gaining favour in Glengarry as people preferred the warmth of the community around them when a death occurred and it is only in the last 20-25 years that funeral homes have become fully accepted and there are those who say today funerals are not as friendly as they used to be. They are quite right.

It would be a pity to leave this topic without touching on the body-snatching which has given rise to many cherished Glengarry legends. One of the more lurid features of life in Canada at this time was that sometimes, under cover of darkness, medical students or those who profited by supplying them would stealthily enter a graveyard, quickly disinter a newly buried corpse, and carry it away to be used for dissection in a medical school.

Residents of Lancaster found they had been the unwitting hosts of body-snatchers in 1878. The *Montreal Witness* described the incident:

## MORE BODY—SNATCHING.
### WHAT WAS FOUND AT BONAVENTURE DEPOT IN A BOX AND BARREL MARKED "EGGS" — THE OWNERS OF THE "EGGS" DISAPPEAR.

The present cold weather gives a great impetus to the work of body-snatching. The three medical schools in Montreal are in full blast, and two bodies are wanted per week in each for purposes of dissection, consequently "prices are firm with an upward tendency," as a commerical reporter would remark, and a strong inducement is held out to unscrupulous men to steal "subjects" from quiet graves.

Last evening two French-speaking young men took
the train for Lancaster, Ontario, and duly got off
at that station. This morning, when the same train,
a local (usually known as the "Moccasin"), was returning, the same men got on board at Lancaster,
having with them a rough box and a barrel, marked
"F. Cardinal, Montreal; eggs." After the train was
in motion, the conductor and baggage man thought
they

SMELT A PECULIAR ODOR,
and applying their noses to a box and barrel of
"eggs," discovered that it emanated from them.
The smell was that of decayed flesh. The two
passengers appeared very weary, and slept nearly
all the way to Montreal, and this, with the other
circumstances, so aroused the suspicions of the
conductor that they were body-snatchers, and had
with them bodies stolen from Lancaster graveyard.
Accordingly he made his suspicions known to the
authorities here. Detective Murphy and Sergt.
Maher opened the box, and found a human body packed
up very tightly, while another (or perhaps two) is in
the barrel. The men, on arriving, had helped their
luggage out of the baggage car, but when the
officials wanted to open the articles they had a
private conversation, resulting in one of them
disappearing immediately, the other soon after
following him under pretence of changing a four
dollar bill in order to pay charges. Neither of
them has turned up since. The remains are now at
the depot awaiting information from Lancaster
as to where they were procured.

Though the bodies were put on the train at Lancaster, it was
found they had actually come from a burying ground at St.
Anicet, Quebec.

In face of this threat, what could relatives do? One answer was to bury the body near the house, on the home farm, where intruders were less likely to venture, and where barking dogs and restless sleepers would be protection. Then months or even years later, when the corpse had been rendered useless to medical students by decomposition, it would be removed to a cemetery. Such temporary burial at home was also used fairly commonly at this time because of the difficulty of transporting coffins over the bad Glengarry roads in some seasons. Occasionally, the family never got around to moving the body to its final resting place in a cemetery. Many a nineteenth-century Glengarrian still sleeps in the farmyard of his old home—the precise spot unknown, perhaps, to all but a few ageing neighbours. Another means of restraining body-snatchers was to bury the corpse in the cemetery the usual way, but to post watchers at the grave for some days or weeks after the burial. Angus MacMillan records in his diary for 1884:

16 August "Father died 20 min. to 12 o'clock"
18 August "Fathers funeral 95 carriages"
...
11 September "Stop watching the grave"

If the worst came to the worst and the body was known to have been stolen, a search of the medical schools might be necessary. In 1876 a farmer said to be living near Cornwall complained to the Montreal Chief of Police

that the remains of his wife had been stolen about a week previous from the churchyard in which they had been interred. The Chief placed the case in the hands of Detective Lafon, and that officer in the company with the farmer, searched several medical colleges, and at length found the body on a dissecting table, cut up by the students' knives. The farmer claimed the remains, and they were given up by the Dean of the Faculty, who was not, however, in the best of humor, complaining that the Government was neglecting its duty in not providing subjects for the use of the College. The students of the College in question are subjected to great loss from these seizures, as they state that they pay from $20 to $30 for each subject.

Both the law and public opinion seem to have accepted body-snatching with good-natured tolerance, thereby recognizing a need and demonstrating the coarseness which, like prudery and a need for respectability, was one of the strands in the makeup of the Canadians of the Victorian age. Nevertheless, the theft of Pat Purcell's body for, as it was supposed, purposes of extortion, seemed to add a challenging new element to body-snatching. Senator McMillan was sufficiently provoked to set in motion a bill on the subject which, however, died before becoming law.

It is difficult to set exact time limits to the Glengarry concern over body-snatching, but it would seem, from such evidence as we have been able to assemble, that the concern began about the 1860's and had faded out at least a few years before the beginning of the First World War.

Another facet of Glengarry life that deserves examination is the question of how the communities dealt with the everyday problems of food, shelter, and clothing in an almost cashless society.

We found the answer was twofold. One part was that very little cash was involved and the other part was that the community did it.

A typical Glengarry farming community had many farmers who at some early stage of their lives had acquired skills as artisans. Some of these skills such as working with wool probably came with a family from Scotland, others such as masonry could have been acquired working on the Ottawa, Rideau, or St. Lawrence canals. Skill with the broad axe and chopping axe probably came from an apprenticeship begun in their own clearings and continued in the shanties. The early barn framers could have learned their skills by working with the master builders who built the early churches. Every community had at least one blacksmith and possibly two or three who could and did make anything from a nail to a surgical implement that the doctor had need of. Somebody in every community had enough book learning to teach school, another could make dresses, while yet another knew a bit of law or how to do elementary surveying. Every community developed or attracted skills needed to maintain itself and to a large extent supply its own needs of every sort. This may sound ridiculous to us today who think only in terms of dollars to pay bills. But given the almost cashless and classless society that prevailed in Glengarry for much of its history, the almost self-contained community that did almost everything for itself becomes not only reasonable but inevitable. To get any sort of a job done it was only necessary for the community to know that an individual paid his debts—in the kind he did best. We can go into great detail on this but it is probably not necessary. The ladies who went around the communities knitting, sewing, patching, making clothes and hats, got what the community could give them in kind—food, fuel, cloth, yarn, and lodging. The barn framer, the timber hewer, the stone mason, and the doctor were paid the same way—with products of the community that they had to have to live. The millers took toll from the grain ground at their mills and it was accepted that when the clergyman called on his parishioners a bag of oats or a piece of meat or some preserves would be tucked in his buggy or cutter before he left. It was a pure and simple barter system and to quite an extent it worked very well for a long period. Some elements of it remained in existence until World War II.

Every community had its permanent members: the farmers on the concessions, the labourers both in the villages and in small houses here and there in the countryside, the artisans and shopkeepers in the villages, the innkeepers, the doctor and, if the community were fortunate, a saw and grist mill operator.

These permanent members of the community were visited now and then by various outsiders whom the community nevertheless made welcome for a variety of reasons. Some of these visitors performed a service, some were interesting in themselves, some, little better than tramps, were made welcome for a meal or a bed and breakfast simply because they were different faces and broke the monotony of everyday life.

County records and census records, as far as they exist, each year show a certain number of pedlar's licenses issued. The earliest pedlars were undoubtedly men who carried their goods on their backs but the genus continued until well into the twentieth century when they drove horses and wagons. Judging by the way the women tell it, these pedlars carried things mostly of interest to the distaff side of the family, who made them very welcome, as the women did not get out to the stores as much as the men did and out of the pedlars' packs they could buy needles and pins, mirrors and cloth, and other odds and ends that women folk are interested in. Teams of men, usually four in a group and often from Quebec Province, came around in the late fall and early winter looking for threshing to do with their flails, and men came around to repair chairs, mend and make shoes, repair pots and pans, sharpen knives and axes, and to buy ashes, horse hair, old sacks, poultry, and even various kinds of herbs for medicinal purposes. The folk were also glad to see the drovers and log buyers, people who were usually well known in the communities and whom they depended on to buy their surplus livestock or saleable timber.

Though many families organized themselves and had enough members to look after their own needs by picking wild fruits and berries in season, there were families that specialized in this operation. They knew where all the cherry trees, berry patches, and nut trees were, and often had them cleaned out before the owner of the land they were on got to them and he would wind up making a deal with these "professional pickers" to get his own fruit—but at least he or his family did not have to pick it. Though private property was respected, an unwritten law put wild fruit, berries, and nuts in the public domain, and the law of "first come, first served" operated.

People still living will remember McIntosh, the nursery man from north of Cornwall, making his rounds to sell fruit trees, and "The Daly Tea Man" from Maxville on his annual visit. Another came around selling Rundle's liniment (about 60 percent alcohol), good for man or beast, externally or internally, and Omar Fauteaux who would arrive with his horse and wagon, put the horse in the stable, sit around and talk and smoke for a couple of days, then move on to his next stop, where he repeated the process. Joe Besau would appear pulling his little hand wagon with his worldly goods on it and giving his legs, which he thought of as horses, named Jim and Charlie, a touch of the switch now and again. Joe would put on a show of "shying" when he met anything on the road or came to a bridge. He was of interest and few refused him a meal or a night's lodging or what he really appreciated, a drink of wine.

"Old MacKenzie" and "Old MacIntosh" were out and out tramps as was "Blue Tom", a well tattooed specimen who wandered around for years.

Many a Glengarry house still has samples of the magnificent handwriting of Phillip Roebakker, a partly crippled man who walked with two canes and was apt to appear winter or summer following a round of places that he knew would make him welcome and give him a chance to show his skill by entering names in the family Bible or in the title pages of books.

"Old Zeb" Leblanc made the rounds of the south part of the county with a barrel of coal oil in a cart and did a good business. Rumour, fostered by him, suggested that his coal oil was a bargain as he smuggled it in from the States, towing the barrel across the river behind a row boat. Then there was "Old Benton" and his whitewash barrel. He had two wheels, a pair of shafts, and a seat on the barrel, which was pulled by one horse, and he went from farm to farm with it. All he supplied was the barrel and pump. Each farmer supplied his own ingredients and did the pumping while Benton gave instructions. Nevertheless he was made welcome, though he and his horse had to be fed for a couple of days. He provided the initiative to get a necessary job done. In a day when whitewash was much more used than paint, on the outsides of buildings and insides too, stables, hen houses, and cellars all got cleaned up with a couple of coats of whitewash.

Thanks to Ralph Connor using him as a character in *Glengarry School Days* and a nice long write-up about him in the

*Glengarry News* in 1915, probably our best known character was the itinerant cooper and destroyer of unwanted dogs, "Allan Gorrach MacRae," also known as Allan the Dogs.

Allan McRae, also known as Allan Gorrach, Allan na Coin, Black Allan the Dogs. This man, an itinerant cooper and by repute a disposer of unwanted dogs in Lochiel and Kenyon Townships, is remembered by persons still living in 1978. For about 45 years or more (c. 1860?-c. 1905?) he roamed the countryside, staying where he could, doing what he could, attending wakes and weddings, and bringing with him the news of the day. He was only one of such colourful characters of his time and later. He is described in *Glengarry School Days*.

The Glengarry folk culture which, for the greater part of the nineteenth century tended to be rather ingrown, by the 1890's was drawing inspiration from the outside world. Photography, in the middle 1800's a strictly professional art, by the turn of the century had become possible for the serious amateur and Glengarry developed such serious photographers as MacMillan and Donovan, plus many "do it at home" photographers. Thanks to the leadership of such people as George Sandfield Macdonald and Dr. Donald McDermid, membership in the local militia became a force for social uplift and a matter of prestige rather than an excuse for a drinking binge on muster days. In the 1890's every village with any pretensions at all had a brass band; and our militia unit, the 59th battalion, developed a pipe band, the direct ancestor of the Glengarry Pipe Band of today. Singing schools became the order of the day in the last quarter of the nineteenth century, and "professors", many of them local people, conducted singing schools in nearly every community. Some artists of international stature such as John McCormick and Jessie McLaughlin were brought to Alexandria to give concerts, though McCormick did not hit if off with the county. The night he gave his concert there was a bad storm and the crowd was not up to his expectations. McCormick's remarks about lack of appreciation are still remembered sixty years later. However, others such as the Earl of Dundonald, Sir Sam Hughes, and Wilfrid Laurier, while not giving concerts, drew huge crowds in Glengarry on different occasions. The Chataugua, an educational variety show, came to various Glengarry towns on several occasions and there were even a few circuses at Alexandria, apart from the continuous one put on by the Alexandria worthies and their wives, who for some years thought of themselves as "society." The idea of a "society class" in this town of some 2500 inhabitants not only amused their relatives on the adjacent concessions but gave the practitioners of the ancient Celtic art of story-telling a theme to base new tales on. The wit and humour of the Scots can be a great pricker of bubbles and deflator of puffed up egos. One story may serve to illustrate the type of thing that went on.

The farmer brother of one of Alexandria's pretenders to society visited him one day when he had occasion to come to Alexandria. The hostess served him lunch with what grace she could muster and chatted on about the party that was planned for that evening. Hearing of the party and who would be at it, all relatives or acquaintances of his, made the farmer brother declare—"I'll just spend the evening here then and stay the night." His appalled hostess exclaimed—"Goodness, I hope you're not lousy"—to which the farmer brother replied, "Not yet I'm not."

Since man settled in communities and probably before, every community has produced a man (sometimes a woman) who had the knack of accumulating cash. This person was often a merchant, but not infrequently a lawyer, doctor, a blacksmith, or a mill owner or even a farmer.

In Glengarry the secret of amassing cash seemed to be for such an individual to use his credit as extensively as possible when buying in his community but to sell outside it for cash. He also tried, if he provided a service in the community, to pay as many of his debts in the community as possible with his goods or services on which he also made a profit. Thus he accumulated cash which he loaned to his neighbours on carefully secured loans, in their time of need. When there was difficulty about repayment he had no hesitation in taking possession of the security.

Every community in Glengarry developed one or more of these persons in the nineteenth century. Even today it is wisest to be careful with names in this connection, but readers from the county, no matter in what part of it their people lived, will have no difficulty supplying names for themselves.

To give these local usurers their due, their services were essential to their communities as for many years they were the only sources of credit and very often those who had difficulty repaying their loans or mortgages had only themselves to blame for their problems. But the local usurer would never have won a popularity contest had there been such things. Glengarry in fact had a continuing non-popularity contest, the results of which were evident the morning following Hallowe'en.

Hallowe'en in Glengarry was regarded as a legitimate occasion to even the year's score and the local usurer quite often received his share of attention. One such incident concerned the local "money bags" who was also the local mill owner. He always had his mill operating by first light and as a consequence performed his morning "toilette" well before daylight, a fact well known in the community. In those pre-indoor plumbing days, naturally the morning "toilette" involved a trip to the backhouse. On this occasion the young men of the community lifted his backhouse off its pit and then moved the structure four feet straight back. What took place in the pre-dawn darkness in that gentleman's back yard can be better imagined than described.

The Glengarry folk loved a good practical joke at Hallowe'en, or for that matter at any time. It was not unusual on the morning after Hallowe'en to see a wagon complete with rack and a load of sheaves on top of the covered bridges at Martintown and Williamstown. Of course it had to be taken down again, sheaf by sheaf and piece by piece, the same way it was put up there, but everyone concerned enjoyed doing it. Many a Glengarry farmer has put his cows in in the morning only to find them all "dry." The young folk in the neighbourhood had put his cows in two or three hours before they knew the man would be up, had milked them and put them out to pasture again.

Fire was an ever present hazard in all those Glengarry homes that burned wood, and until the very late years of the nineteenth century everyone in both village and country burned wood. The theory of insulation had not yet been developed and the only way to combat winter's frost was with lots of clothes and big fires in the stoves.

Quite often old newspapers were used over underwear and below the next layer of clothes to help keep out the cold when a long sleigh ride was necessary, and everybody had several top coats in various sizes to fit over the ones below and these coats were carefully handed down from generation to generation. In those days too people dressed to go to bed rather than undressed. Both sexes wore long woollen underwear as a matter of course. In cold weather this same underwear was worn to bed under a heavy woollen or at least flanellette night gown and every blanket and coat about the place was piled on the various beds and unlucky indeed was the person who had to sleep alone—even a dog made a better bed warming companion than none at all. But the main reliance against frost in the house (yes, the pots often froze under the beds) was the stove. There were several in each house, and once lit in the fall, they were not willingly allowed to go out until spring.

Burning wood tends to leave a flammable soot in the stove pipes and chimney and on an extra cold day when the stove would be operated full on, often the stove pipes and chimney would catch fire. Too often this resulted in the house catching fire and the family being left homeless. In a village or hamlet one house burning often resulted in several burning.

The Glengarry of the 1890's was obviously in a period of transition or perhaps a better description would be ferment. Older methods and forms were being questioned and many sooner or later were superseded. We have described the coming of libraries, hydro power, telephone, and the movement for better roads and schools. Even the way the people entertained themselves became more sophisticated. Formal horse racing became established at North Lancaster and Alexandria and fall fairs were organized at Alexandria and Maxville. Perhaps the biggest difference between 1900 and 1890 was the formal planning of events of all sorts rather than the mostly spontaneous things of an earlier age. By 1900 a list of the formally organized societies and clubs in the county would be very impressive indeed and most of these had taken form in the last ten years. The Sons of Scotland, the Sunday Schools, and some parishes held a big picnic each year. Literary and debating societies were formed in almost every community and political and farmers groups were organized. The literary oriented groups broadened the standard of the county's reading material which had been mostly "religion oriented" to include literature of all types. Even the Sunday School papers began to acknowledge that secular affairs had to be discussed at least a little bit. The people became much more aware of the world around them, partly no doubt because all had relatives scattered across the

600

continent, but also because of their reading, photographs, the stereopticon in every parlor, picture post cards, and Eaton's catalogues. The local newspapers carry samples of locally composed poetry and prose and mention the occasional oil painting done by persons in the county. The county became missionary minded, and several of our men and women became missionaries in far corners of the earth. Those at home both supported them and read their books and letters home with avidity. In 1978 this missionary spirit is still a potent force among the Roman Catholics, but by 1950 had spent its force among the Protestants and then even the Women's Missionary Societies began to decline in numbers and verve.

The early 1900's saw the beginning of church lawn socials, garden parties, and the production of amateur plays by all sorts of groups from temperance societies to Women's Institutes. The lawn social and amateur "play" were part of Glengarry life for many years, but few plays were staged after World War II and in 1978 the lawn social is largely a Catholic preserve in the south part of the county. However, lawn social night at St. Mary's, Williamstown, draws a crowd that is about as large as that which attends the fair there, and the one at Glen Nevis is the biggest annual event in Lancaster Township.

Examination day at the common schools, a big annual event until written examinations took over in the 1880's, gave way to an annual Christmas concert put on by the pupils and teacher of each and every one-room school in the township and these lasted until the one-room schools were closed in the 1950's and early 60's. By then everybody had television and except for some winter sports do-it-yourself entertainment came to an end. Gone was the ceilidh and the skating party on the pond—gone were the children's concert and lawn bowling— gone were the "pick up" hockey and lacrosse matches and ball games. As we write, even the venerable Women's Institute seems to be in difficulty and its future in the county seems doubtful.

Some few of our readers will never have come across or even heard of Glengarry nicknames. Very few indeed, if any, will be able to identify all the families or individuals appearing in the many pages of Glengarry nicknames which we have in our files and many have wondered about their origin and the need for them.

The need for nicknames or some sort of individual identification is obvious enough when we consider that there was a very limited number of surnames among those who settled in the county. Each of these few clans favoured a certain few Christian names that were repeated from generation to generation and sometimes were used twice in the same generation. For instance, John McMartin, M.P., left part of his estate to his brother John McMartin, and John Daniel McEwen left part of his estate to his son John Daniel McEwen. There is some evidence that as far back as the original Loyalist settlement nicknames were needed to distinguish individuals of the same name. There were three Thomas Rosses among the Loyalists—one was known as Thomas Ross Taylor, one was known as Thomas Ross Ban, and the third was plain Thomas Ross. Father John Macdonald, an early priest at St. Raphaels, kept parish genealogical records with a naming system based on the Scandinavian method—John son of John, son of Angus son of John, going back as far as needed to ensure he had a list of names that could be duplicated by no other individual. As time went on and the clans persisted in using the same Christian names over and over again, Fr. John's system got too cumbersome. Also, the folks gave their Scottish wit a chance and began to bestow names on families and individuals because of some characteristic of the family of the individual or the land they owned.

Often then an individual's nickname became a combination such as Little Alex Dunkie in the Swamp. This translates as Little Alex (who may have been 6'3" and weighed 250 and was sarcastically called "Little") son of Duncan (in this case MacRae) who farmed a piece of higher land in the swamps west of Maxville. Mary Margaret Hughie Angus Allan translates Mary Margaret daughter of Hugh, son of Angus, son of Allan McDonald who farmed in north-eastern Charlottenburgh. Nicknames such as Long Dan or Dirty Dan are obvious in their derivation, but one such as Archie the Schoolmaster refers to Archie Mcdonald, whose fifth great-grandfather was a schoolmaster in the very early days of Glengarry.

There was no consistent code contained in Glengarry's nicknames. Each was (or is) a separate name designed to distinguish one individual from another. By and large the system worked, but it had its areas of confusion as communication between the communities improved. At one time the McIsaac MacDonalds of the Loch Garry area were comfortably insulated from the MacIsaac MacDonalds of the Summerstown Station area. Today we who do genealogical work are glad one family was Roman Catholic and the other Protestant, and as a consequence buried their dead in different cemeteries and have their names on different baptismal rolls.

Fortunately cases were rare in which two Alex MacDonalds married girls with the same maiden name. One might marry a Margaret Kennedy (or some such), the other marry a Margaret Chisholm, which helps a great deal in tracing out Glengarry families. Today everyone agrees that the Glengarry nicknames are "amusin' but confusin' " but in their time they served their purpose, whether it was identification or mild insult or both.

As can be seen, in the old Scotch community in Glengarry the status of each individual was defined. His or her given name, plus clan name plus nickname placed anyone definitely by right of birth. If a baby were born mentally retarded or physically deformed, that baby still had a place in the family circle. When aged he still retained a place in the family circle. If he were hurt in an accident his place was still secure. If for some reason the immediate family could not cope with a given situation, the extended family of the community took over with a minimum of fuss. Nobody went hungry or cold. If help were needed and given, it was always given in such a way that it would not appear to be charity. An old woman who had lost all her immediate family in one of the epidemics would be told something like this by the nearest neighbour—"We're sorry your family is gone but it is good luck for us—with all our kids Mary can't keep up with the knitting, darning, and sewing—come away over to our place and we'll keep you out of mischief." And the old lady, blood relative or no, would be assured of a seat by the fire, a bed and a place at their table for life, and a decent funeral at the end of it.

This smooth-working community spirit was due at least as much to the women as to the men. Even today a few of the old-fashioned Glengarry women are ardent practitioners of women's lib. They know that for generations they have been "the keepers of the household gods," and on their laps and at their knees their children were taught how to be men and women and they passed on the tales that made them proud to be Scots. Who needed women's lib (which they had never heard of anyway) when they kept the household and community of today together while they trained the men and women of the next generation?

As long as the family and the community were the main units in Glengarry the status of the womenfolk was unquestioned. The women did not vote in elections, sit on school boards or municipal councils, or have a direct voice in church management. Yet the wiser men of the communities heeded well the advice of their womenfolk, if for no other reason than to keep peace in the family. As the women did at least their share of the work on the farm, and most did a lot more, a wife or mother on the warpath was something to be carefully avoided if at all possible. Unwritten laws and customs made divorce or even separation unheard of, so there was every incentive on the part of both sexes to keep a marriage working as smoothly as possible. Women had status in old Glengarry and not only did they earn it but carried it with a sense of responsibility to themselves, their families, and those who would come after them.

For a generation past now, educators and the media have been stressing that each one of us is an individual and entitled "to do his or her own thing." Then our society carefully collects a large share of the earnings of the more fortunate among us and redistributes a part of them (administration costs are high) in the form of welfare cheques of various sorts to those who are less fortunate, in effect paying them to stay out of the way of those who are earning.

We can't help but contrast this system of today with old Glengarry's system where everybody had a place in the community and the community made a place for them.

# Chapter XVIII
# A Glengarry Farmer and His Wife

One of Sandy Fraser's most inimitable achievements was his portrayal of the character and outlook of the Glengarry farmers of his generation. This present chapter is an attempt to reconstruct the life of a typical (though fictitious) Glengarry farmer of a slightly later date.

This chapter is in many ways a sequel to Chapter XVII but here we are on much more solid ground. We ourselves, or our parents, lived through the period in which Archie and Annie McAngus are living. Much of our information is as a consequence from personal knowledge. At worst it only suffered from one telling—our parents telling us. Much of what they told us has been confirmed by newspapers of the day and by many conversations with people as old or older than the Archie McAngus of our story.

Let no one bother trying to identify the McAngus family. They are typical but not real. We have even selected surnames that if ever used in Glengarry at all were extremely rare. They contain no code to connect them with any individual, living or dead.

There can be no doubt that we have the McAngus family living north of the "height of land" and probably in Kenyon, though north-western or central Lochiel is not impossible. This gave us an opportunity to point out some small differences in nomenclature and habits that existed between the north and south parts of the county. Even more it points out the similarities that existed.

A typical Glengarry frame farm house. This house, though larger and more ornamented than usual, clearly shows the three sections that Glengarry favoured in the frame houses built to replace the original log houses as financial circumstances permitted. The section at the right was the "main house" to which the family retired in winter, heating only as much of it as was needed. The middle section was the "summer kitchen"; the left section was the woodshed which often housed the family buggy or cutter as well. These houses were built with large rooms and high ceilings in reaction to the cramped quarters of the log houses they replaced.

We have laid particular stress on certain events in the McAngus family, largely because no one else has written about these important things in Glengarry farm life in this century. We hope, after due allowance is made for human differences in individual families and persons that our word picture of this family comes across to our readers as accurate. We believe it to be so.

Our readers will also note that in accordance with our established policy, we did not connect the McAngus family with any church group, though it was tempting to do so. Each of our readers can construct that part of the McAngus story for himself and the more adventurous can speculate about what could be written had we made a Roman Catholic of Archie and a

Protestant of Annie and had them marry, as in this story, in 1942. Or we could have switched the religions as stated above around.

What we felt was most typical and usual of life on a Glengarry concession we mentioned.

* * *

Archie McAngus was born in Glengarry on Thursday, 26 January 1905, and as was usual in those days the birth took place right at home. Before dawn, three of the neighbourhood women, headed by the recognized local midwife, had arrived at the McAngus home to assist at the birth and to take charge of the house. Their first act was to banish the children to the kitchen and the men to the barn and then they filled every pan in the house with water and got them boiling on the kitchen stove. The midwife confined herself to the bedroom where Margaret McAngus awaited "her time" and the other two women prepared sandwiches and tea which they took to the barn or served in the kitchen at appropriate intervals, cleaned the house and kept blankets warm behind the stove. Margaret's room was cold but this day Margaret must not be allowed to get a chill.

From time to time during that cold stormy day neighbours drove in with their horses and cutters to ask for news and if help was needed, and twice men hauling logs on the road, cousins of the McAnguses, rested their teams at the farm gate and walked in to ask for news. With delay, anxiety grew, and Grandpa McAngus began to think of his mother who had died in childbirth almost fifty years before. But just as the light was failing on that short winter day and the coal oil lamps had been lit, Norman McAngus was summoned to the house to be told that he was the father of another son and that both mother and child were well. He was even allowed to peek at his wife through the bedroom door and was allowed a glimpse of the bundle of clothes in which his new son was wrapped.

The house in which this child began its days deserves a few moments of our attention. It consisted of two parts. The front and largest part of the house was built of logs and had been erected some fifty years before, as the second house to stand on that

608

farm. At some unrecorded date it had been covered with clapboards but these had never been painted. The back part of the house was a large frame kitchen added in 1890. It too was unpainted and its boards had softened in colour to the silver of the clapboards covering the original log house. Each of these parts of the house served its own specialized role in the life of the family. The kitchen was used as a kitchen only in the summer, being too cold for winter use; about the end of September, the family, each year, moved into a very similar large room in the log part of the house, commonly known to them as the "dining room." The kitchen then for some months served as a storage space for frozen (home grown) meat, heavy outer clothing, winter boots, the children's sleighs, and the family's axes and saws. It was handy to store the wood-cutting tools there so they could be "edged up" on stormy days and winter nights. Also a large "wood box" was installed just outside the dining room door along with a supply of finely split cedar for kindling wood at one end of it. In really cold weather the stove in the main house had to be replenished during the night—occasionally it would even go out—and a trip to the woodshed in -20 degrees F weather with an east wind blowing was to be avoided in night attire, even though the night attire consisted of a flannel nightgown over "long johns" underwear. It was the never-ending winter task of the children of the house to keep that woodbox full with sticks of suitable size for every stove in the house. The wood supply came from a frame woodshed at the back of the kitchen which was filled every spring, usually by a "sawing bee."

The McAnguses would have found it uncomfortable to use the "dining room" as their kitchen the year around as the wood-burning cookstove, going at least sixteen hours a day to cook the family's meal and heat all its wash water in its reservoir, produced such quantities of heat that it would have made the low, cramped upstairs rooms unbearably hot in summer. In winter, this heat though inadequate for comfort upstairs, was needed and appreciated. The seasonal nomadism of the family was perfectly sensible: it gave them as much comfort as possible. For some years the McAnguses had moved their cookstove back and forth from kitchen to dining room but it was such a heavy dirty job that Norman and Margaret had recently bought a second cookstove so that one could be left permanently in each room.

The McAnguses had a large log barn, with the stable in the centre of it, a spanking new carriage shed with the granary above it (Glengarry granaries at the time were always upstairs in some building remote from the barn), a two-holer outhouse (variously called the backhouse, the House of Parliament, or the toilet), and a small log house, once the farm home and first building ever to stand on the property, but now demoted to serve, un-glamorously but usefully, as the hen house. A lean-to shelter for the sheep at the south-west end of the barn completed the farm buildings.

First in rank and dignity in the household, but no longer with the prestige that went with ownership were the grandparents of the newborn Archie. Grandpa McAngus was the youngest son of the settler from Scotland who had originally claimed this farm and begun to clear it of its forest. Grandpa McAngus had spent many winters of his youth and middle age in the shanties; he had drilled with the volunteers at the time of the Fenian Raids; he had seen the coming of the Canada Atlantic Railway, the cheese factories, the telephone, and a post office with daily mail only an hour's walk from his house. Perhaps what was even more welcome to Grandma McAngus since she had come to live in the concession, the bush had been cut back so they could see the neighbours' houses and not just the smoke from their chimneys. Grandma McAngus had been born in Scotland, having been brought to Canada as a baby by one of the last families of Scottish settlers. Gaelic was still the preferred language of this elderly couple but they were fluent in English and English was now the usual language in the home. Grandpa McAngus was a big, heavily bearded man, stooped with age and the effects of years of hard work. He was now able to do little of the real farm work but made a contribution of driving the cows out to pasture and making the odd trip to town with Old Nellie and the buggy when something was needed that would have taken the time of a busier member of the family. His prowling about the place, too, often spotted a piece of fence that was down, a broken pole in a gate, or a ditch the cattle had blocked up. Grandma McAngus has taken over all the household knitting, darning, and casual sewing and on bake days she could make the old kitchen stove behave as no one else in the house could.

The head of the household, as owner of the farm, was Norman McAngus. He was a short, lean man with a bushy black moustache, and at the time of son Archie's birth he was forty years old. As a young man, Norman had spent four winters in the shanties and had worked in railway construction gangs in Manitoba, Ontario, Colorado, Arizona, and New Mexico. His visits home in those years were infrequent—just frequent enough to keep a romance going with Margaret McDuncan, the daughter of a farmer about a mile away from Norman's home. When Norman told his parents of his approaching marriage, the old couple realized that if they wanted Norman to stay in Glengarry and farm, rather than return with his bride to the States as he intended, they had best give the farm to Norman and his bride. So making a virtue of necessity, the old man deeded the farm to Norman and though no word of negotiation passed between them, it was understood by all concerned that the old couple would have an honoured home on the farm till the end of their days.

Norman's wife Margaret had received the usual home training of a farmer's daughter in Glengarry, which meant that there was no farm task, indoors or outdoors, that she did not know how to do, and if need arose would do, but as a rule her house, garden, and hens kept her busy. She had had a few years' schooling at the local public school and could read, write, and do simple figuring with ease. After leaving school she had helped her mother with the housework till Norman married her. Except for a two-day wedding trip to Montreal, she had never spent a night out of Glengarry. Now in her late 30's she was getting plump and she was troubled by ill-defined illnesses which she treated by taking the patent medicines advertised in the press of the day. Margaret and Norman's oldest child Malcolm now 12 years old, was already doing almost a man's work. When the

611

farm work did not interfere he attended the local one-room school but this winter he was needed at home for bushwork. It was understood that if the farm work permitted he and his brother John 10, and their two sisters, Kate 6, and Mary 4, would probably keep going to school till they got into the "entrance class " but it was pretty well taken for granted that only John, already a great reader and thinker, would have a chance to go to high school but any decision on that would have to wait till he was "ready to try his entrance."

The McAngus household was completed by an elderly unmarried sister of Grandpa McAngus. She had worked as a servant girl in Philadelphia for most of her adult life. She was now retired from service, and everyone in the household and community believed she had saved a nice nest-egg from her wages which of course included board. She worked hard around the house, doing the endless tasks that had to be done and at times when the men were busy in the field or bush she could be seen pumping water for the cattle at the wooden pump beside the stable or busy milking. For this she received the same wages as all the other members of the family—her board and clothes. "Old Auntie Jane" was on amicable though perhaps not warm terms with her niece-in-law Margaret, but her relations with her sister-in-law Grandma McAngus were little short of venomous. The children she loved without restraint, and with a deep sense of the privilege of being allowed to do so. Only many years later, when the surviving children had come to count up the occasions for affection in their own lives, did they realize that this had been so. Auntie Jane, in turn, considered that she had had two pieces of good fortune in her life. The first was to have been for some thirty-five years in service in a wealthy and cultured household where everything was "nice" and she had been treated with respect that over the years deepened into affection and the second was in being allowed to finish her days among the people she knew, in the house where she was born.

It was in this household that young Archie formed his first impressions of the great world of which he was now a part, and indeed for his first years this household *was* his world. At the age of two he recovered, though just barely, from a disease that was doubtfully diagnosed as pneumonia; at five he had the whooping cough, and within the same year he along with all the other children in the community had the measles and the mumps. The next year chicken pox made its rounds of the community and young Archie got an extra few days' holiday from school as a result.

When Archie was growing up to school age, the family's only "outings" were the weekly trips to church with all the family members packed into the double buggy in summer and the two-seated cutter in winter. Once a year the family "took in" either Maxville or Alexandria Fair as was most convenient to their work schedule. The year Archie was five they went to Alexandria Fair partly because Auntie Jane had been wanting them to go to Donovan's in Alexandria to get the family's picture taken. Norman could not see the point of this at all but Margaret wanted the picture and when Auntie Jane said she would pay for it Norman stopped objecting and even Grandpa and Grandma admitted to themselves that they were curious to see what their "likeness" would look like. So on "Fair Day" with everyone dressed in "their other clothes" they appeared at Duncan Donovan's studio just as he was finishing breakfast. Donovan had started his career as a photographer in Glengarry wandering from farmhouse to farmhouse soliciting business but his particular talent for capturing character in his photographs of his subjects made it possible for him to set up a room in Alexandria equipped with the standard backgrounds of the time that effectively removed his subjects from their everyday backgrounds in the town or on the farm. Donovan's photography was good and his slogan of "City Work at Country Prices" no doubt helped the McAnguses and their neighbours to decide sooner or later to have their likeness taken by Duncan Donovan. The McAngus family likeness turned out well and all the kin and neighbours agreed that Archie with his lingering baby features was the one that caught their eye. Two generations later, Donovan's photograph of the McAngus family is as clear as ever and a prized heirloom.

In the fall of 1910 Archie's carefree life around the farm was abruptly changed, for one cool and sunny September morning he was started to school. On that momentous day, the first day of his life of which he was to retain a vivid recollection, he was dressed in baggy grey trousers, a white shirt, gold stockings, and a blue jacket, all of his mother's manufacture. Then with careful and elaborate warnings to all concerned, Archie was delivered into the keeping of his two sisters and into his hands was placed a lunch pail (an old honey pail) containing two cheese sandwiches and two doughnuts. Over his shoulder his mother hung his "school bag " recently ordered from Eaton's mail order catalogue, which contained a slate, a slate pencil, a scribbler, a pencil, and a bottle of water and a rag. Among the warnings Archie had received earlier was the admonition always to use the water and the rag to clear his slate—only "dirty" boys would clear their slate by spitting on it and then wiping it with their coat sleeve—and the scribbler was not to be used unless the teacher specially ordered its use.

So Archie walked off to school, or more accurately was walked by his sisters, half a mile down the dirt concession road and was formally enrolled by the teacher, Miss Mary Beth McNorman, the 18-year old daughter of a substantial farmer in the Vankleek Hill area. Everybody in the section knew her as Mary Beth but Archie had been told many times to be careful to address her as Miss McNorman or he would "get the strap." Actually, when he was escorted into her presence by his sisters, Archie was tongue-tied and his sisters had to give Miss McNorman the details of Archie's full name (Archibald Dougald McAngus), his birthdate, and his parents' names.

At recess in the bare little school yard, Archie met the other children, both boys and girls of all ages from 5 to 18. They gathered around the new pupils and teased them and Archie, already homesick, burst into tears and bolted for home. He was pursued by his two sisters while the whole school screamed unrestrainedly at the entertainment.

During his schooldays, when Archie was nine years old, World War I began, and its effects soon extended to the neighbourhood and family of the McAnguses. Young men joined up, there was less help at threshings and other bees, and the son of a nearby farmer was killed as early as 1915 at Ypres. The bright side of this anxious period was that farm prices began to rise and farmers began to find themselves prosperous. In the McAngus household, there had by now been a few changes. In 1912 another son, Donald, the last of the family, had been born. John, the second born, had left home to work in Montreal the same year. John, who seemed completely to have resolved against farm life once he had had a taste of independence, was only an occasional visitor on the old homestead. In 1916, he joined the army. The following year, he was wounded in action at Vimy Ridge in Flanders (Belgium), and for many months was a patient in a military hospital in France. Auntie Jane wrote to him every second day. When conscription came to Canada in 1917, Malcolm, the eldest son, was successful in securing exemption as a necessary farm helper to his father. One day, as the scholars sat at their desks in the little school, there was the sound of buggy wheels at the door; the teacher went to speak to the visitor, and a moment later returned to announce that an Armistice had been signed. The war was over, and the scholars were given a holiday till the following day.

By this time, the flu epidemic was striking down its thousands. The McAngus household had the good fortune to escape it wholly, but Archie and his father and brother did chores late into the night day after day for neighbouring farmers who were ill. And one sunless November day, Archie and his father drove in the buggy to the churchyard—and dug the grave for a young girl of the neighbourhood who had just died of the flu.

Archie's schooldays ended in December 1918, when he was a little less than 14 years old. If he could have pursued his course of studies, he would have "tried the entrance" as the phrase was, the following June, and if successful he would have found himself qualified to begin high school. His father's reasons for removing him from school at this time were not explained to him, but in later years he realized that his father must have been having difficulties in meeting the payments on an additional farm he had bought in 1915. So throughout the winter, Archie, Malcolm, and their father hauled logs from their bush, piled them on a skidway back of the barn, and as weather and roads permitted hauled them to Alexandria where they sold them to J.T. Schell. The income from the cheese factory, which was enough to live on in summer, stopped in the winter. The extra cash needed to pay the mortgage had to come from the logs.

Though Archie's schooling had not continued even to the limits possible in the little school house down the road, he had obtained a solid grounding which served him well during the remainder of his life. He wrote and spelled with reasonable correctness, could draft a business or personal letter, knew the basic outlines of Canadian and world geography, and enough of the narrative of Canadian history to enable him to grasp the background of Canadian national politics, understood as much arithmetic (including decimals and fractions) as 999 people out of 1000 ever find any need for, and had obtained from the school readers more than a glimmering of the difference between good and bad prose. Narrow though the training provided by schools such as the one Archie attended doubtless was, it took the big schools of a later date to produce adult illiterates. In the evenings he was often drafted to read the Montreal *Witness* to Grandpa McAngus, whose eyesight was now failing.

In the summer of 1919 John returned, still pale and shaken, and just emerged from his long period of hospitalization. To the family, he seemed hardly recognizable as someone they had once known. Nothing, perhaps created a greater barrier between the family and the cool young soldier than an awareness that every word he uttered seemed to be carefully measured. To Archie, it came as a surprise to find his father speaking to John as to an equal, as he never did to Malcolm or himself, and moreover, for the first time his father seemed to Archie to be *old*. There were private discussions between Norman and his returned son, and it was understood among the other members of the family that the possible transfer to John of the newly purchased farm had been discussed, and that the son had expressed a determination to "try something else", in place of farming. A few weeks later John left. A good job with a paint-manufacturing firm in Montreal soon offered itself and was accepted; in a few years a better job in the same line of business brought John to California. Though John was hardly ever to become truly rich by California standards, he enjoyed an ample executive's salary for many years, and when he died in 1945 as the vice-president of his company, his energetic and useful career was noticed very favourably in the *New York Times*. His sons and daughters still occasionally visit Glengarry, and one of them, a well known physician, is intent upon completing an extensive genealogy of the McAngus family which her father began.

Whatever feelings went through his parents' minds on the subject of John's rebellion, they were soon overshadowed by a terrible anxiety—how terrible, the children recognized, if at all, only years later, when they had suffered anxieties of their own sufficient to give them a basis for comparison. At the age of 18, Mary was evidently ill, and the dread syllables "T.B." began to be whispered among the neighbours—and the final pronouncement was uttered, in a terrible hour, by Dr. D.D. McDonald, of Alexandria, in a consultation with the parents. Mary died in 1920, in the spare bedroom off the parlour. Norman and Margaret, looking at the other children, and thinking of Kate, who had always been more delicate than the rest, and Donald, who was slow in his growth and seemed continually to have colds, were filled with fear. This was not the first death from tuberculosis in the family; two at least of Grandpa McAngus's sisters had died from it. But it was, mercifully, to be the last in the generations then living; and as the years rolled by, and no signs of the illness appeared elsewhere in the family, the parents' foreboding gradually melted away.

Archie remained at home several years working with his father and brother, but the long hours with no financial reward made him long for a change and money of his own. For many years, shanty-going had meant adventure but few young men from Glengarry went to shanty any more. The harvest excursions offered a tempting alternative, and Archie went west on them twice, when he was 18, and again, when he was 20.

On the first of these occasions, his decision to go on the excursion came when several other boys of the neighbourhood invited him to accompany them. When he announced his intention to his parents, they did not object, and the next day his mother drove with horse and buggy to the general store and bought a quantity of overalling, from which she made her son two pairs of overalls for his trip. Two weeks afterwards, carrying a small carpet bag that belonged to his father, and a box containing enough lunch to last him during the four days train journey, he was at the station at Alexandria, with an expectant group of other young men, when the excursion train, already loaded with Maritimers and Quebecers, stopped to take him on the first long journey of his life.

The second time he made the excursion to the prairies, he did not return to Ontario in the fall. When the harvest work was done, he found employment in construction work in Saskatoon. For almost three years, he worked for the same employer in that town; once , during a slack season, he dipped into his savings for a trip to California to visit his brother John. Always afterwards, he looked back on these as the most independent and carefree years of his life. They were also the years in which he had more money to spend than ever before, and more than he was to have for many years to come. Yet even when the passage of many years had left this era of his life increasingly rose-coloured, he never concealed from himself the fact that he had often been lonely, that he had found the boarding house life irksome, and that he had missed the warmth of being a member, as people always were in Glengarry at that time, of a neighbourhood where everyone was known to everyone else.

All this ended suddenly in early April 1928, when he got a telegram from home saying, "REGRET MUST INFORM MALCOLM KILLED YESTERDAY BUSH ACCIDENT CAN YOU COME HOME TO STAY?"

618

Archie had now to make the most important decision he had ever made, and when he resolved, after only a little hesitation, to return home, he thought he saw, for the first time ever, all the rest of his life planned before him. Unless Donald, who was still in his teens, would choose later to take his place, his role would be to live with aging parents, to take an increasing role in running the farm, to be at length, when his father was dead or very old, its owner—in short, to take up the laborious role of a farmer which his father had filled for so long, and against the prospect of which the placid and docile Malcolm had never been known even once to have revolted. In making the decision to return, Archie could be compared to a novice monk resolving to take his vows in a monastery of the severest kind where all self-indulgence of every kind would have to be set aside forever. As the desolate wilderness of northern Ontario slid past the train windows on Archie's journey home, it is not surprising that he found himself wondering whether he had made the right decision. Would this be life? *Had* this been life already?

We may now pass quickly over a long period in Archie's life. On arriving back at the old farm of his childhood, he comforted his parents, stowed his few clothes in his old bedroom, and in consultation with his father decided upon—or more accurately, received his orders concerning—the manner of doing the year's spring work. His aunt had died during his absence, and his grandparents died, a few weeks apart, in the summer of his return. The next year, the Depression struck brutally. The years of the 30's brought hard work and little monetary return for it. With the war, a modest agricultural prosperity began to be felt again. And in the spring of 1942, when Archie was 37 years old, he made a revolution in the affairs of the family by getting married.

His wife's name was Annie McNish. Born in 1914, she was 28 years old at the time of her marriage. Her father, who had been a substantial farmer, had been able to send her and her three sisters to high school at------for three years each; sending a child to high school was a serious expense for farmers because in those days, before school buses, the child had to be boarded in the high school town during the school term. After leaving high school, Annie lived at home with her parents for several years, helping her mother with the housework and her father with the farm work. Her father was one of the first farmers in the neighbourhood to own a tractor, and she had mildly startled conservative opinion by learning to drive it. In 1932 wondering eyes saw for the first time ever in that part of the township a field which had been plowed by a woman. In 1933-1936 she was employed in Montreal in a small factory which made school desks, but when the factory went bankrupt she returned to her father's farm.Of an enterprising nature, she read books from the small but good library in the nearby village of----, cultivated one of the largest and best gardens in the neighbourhood, and from 1938 spent a day every week keeping the accounts of the sawmill which her uncle ran in the hamlet of ----.

Archie had met her at one of the church socials which were part of every summer's entertainment. Despite the fact that her father's farm was the inconvenient distance of ten miles away, Archie began to call on her two or three times a week. It was probably for this reason that he persuaded his father to pay for the purchase of a used car, a reliable Model A Ford, which henceforth replaced the Munro and McIntosh buggy as the family's means of summer travel (in winter, the roads being unplowed, the sleigh and cutter retained their old importance). The courtship lasted for four years, and at one stage seems to have been broken off for seven or eight months. As the wedding date approached, Archie's father agreed with a readiness and cheerfulness that surprised his son to a division of the family property. Archie and his bride would settle on the second farm which had been bought during the First World War, and which had at long last, with much pain, been fully paid for, the last payment being made in the grim year 1935, when spending money was like shedding blood. The old couple, and Donald, who was now a grown man, would keep the home farm. Archie's was legally deeded to him, and so he found himself an independent landowner at last.

To this couple were born two sons: Desmond in 1944, and Martin in 1946.

Let us get an idea of what their new place looked like. The buildings were a frame house (unpainted), a log barn, a granary, a wellhouse, an outhouse, a machine shed, a henhouse, and a log building once occupied by a weaver but now used for keeping pigs. This cluster of buildings was almost a quarter of a mile from the public road, with which it was connected by a muddy and ill-gravelled lane impassable to cars at the wet seasons of the year when the Model A was left at the road.

Though disused for some years, the house was found by the newly married couple to be in good shape. As usual, it consisted of a main house and summer kitchen, but the summer kitchen had in this case been so solidly built that the McAnguses were able to occupy it even during the winter months. Downstairs, besides the kitchen, there was a large dining room, a pantry, a parlour, and a bedroom opening off the parlour. The parlour had the best furniture in the house, bought with Auntie Jane's nest-egg which had been preserved intact by her cautious heirs through many a bitter year; in accordance with immemorial custom, the parlour was rigidly sealed off from use except for the entertainment of the most formal visitors. Upstairs, there were three bedrooms, one of which shortly became a storeroom. A cookstove in the kitchen served for heating and cooking; in winter, the door to the dining room was kept open to allow some of the heat from the cookstove to circulate into other parts of the house, but it was supplemented by a box stove in the dining room from which the stove pipes passed through a hole in the ceiling and heated the upstairs (a little) before disappearing into the chimney. Towards morning in the winters, when the fires in both stoves had burnt to ashes, the house would become bitterly cold.

The stock on the farm in their first years of farming consisted of 14 Ayrshire cows, 1 bull, 3 work horses and 1 or 2 sows with as many young pigs of their offspring as might not yet have reached saleable age, and about a dozen sheep, a flock of three or four dozen hens, and in summer a flock of up to a hundred chickens.

The principal crops grown on the farm in these years were hay, oats, and barley, but Archie also usually planted a field of wheat and two or three acres of corn and from time to time he planted a half field or so of buckwheat. Annie kept a good kitchen garden, and she and Archie shared between them the labour of managing a plot of potatoes for household use.

Let us take a look at a few typical days in the life of this couple in the late 1940's.

First a summer day.

On Tuesday, 13 July 1948 (to take that day) Archie got up at 4 A.M., awakened by the alarm clock. Hurriedly slipping on his shirt, overalls, and socks he went downstairs, lit the fire in the cookstove and "made the porridge" then left the double boiler with the porridge in it towards the back of the stove and went off to the pasture to get the cows. By the time he had them up to the barn and tied in their stalls Annie his wife, who had risen shortly after him, had breakfast ready and on the table. Their breakfast, which hardly varied year in and year out, was porridge, boiled eggs, bread and butter, and tea. The maple syrup pitcher was always on the table and most of the time cheese was available in the house if it was wanted. This having breakfast before chores was one of the hardest things Archie's wife had had to get used to when she came into the McAngus family. In the community where she had been brought up, breakfast was eaten after all the morning's chores had been done and before the serious part of the day's work began.

After their hastily eaten breakfast, both the McAnguses went to the stable and did the milking, which they did by hand though there were a couple of milking machines in use in their neighbourhood. The milk was carried in pails from the stable to the well house where it was put into 8-gallon milk cans, the morning's milk not quite filling these cans. The milk from the night before, already in similar cans, had been kept cool overnight in a tank filled with cold water from the well.

In the recent past all the milk in the community had gone into 40-gallon cans but these required a winch to lift them, both at home and at the cheese factory, and by 1948 very few people in the community still used the big cans although the cheese factory still had the winch and used it when big cans appeared at the weigh stand.

The 8-gallon cans weighing when full one hundred pounds were easily loaded on the light express wagon with a practiced swing. When Archie had bought the light express wagon at an auction sale in Charlottenburgh a few years before, the auctioneer had called it a "milk wagon"; to Archie this was a misnomer, the sort of thing he expected among those Loyalists down there. Archie hitched Old Grey to the wagon and in 20 minutes was at the cheese factory and even though it was only 7 A.M. he found himself third in line at the weigh stand. Archie understood the etiquette of the daily trip to the "factory". It was the great centre for the distribution of news in the community and those ahead of him, elderly men taking their milk to the factory to save their sons some time for farm work, always came early and stayed late to pick up all the news of the community and redistribute it.

Once at the weigh stand, Archie was greeted by the cheese maker, who always tried to be affable to his "patrons", as the farmers who supplied the factory with its milk were called. If he offended them, he knew well they would start taking their milk to one of the other cheese factories within easy driving distance. Unfortunately, this had happened more than once. When the cans were on the weigh stand the cheesemaker lifted the lid from each can and immediately put his head right down to the top of the can for a good smell of the milk. In July he really did not expect a bad odour from the milk—such odours usually came in May when the cows might get into a patch of wild onions and in October when a few of his patrons would start feeding corn ensilage. But there was always a chance that a partly filled can would be kept at home till the next day, or that the night's milk had not been stored in a cold water tank and had started "to go bad". In that case, the cheesemaker rejected the can and back home it went with the patron, for pig feed. This morning however Archie's milk passed "the smell test" and all the cans were dumped into the vat on the factory scales. Then the cheesemaker took a small sample of the milk and put it in a bottle with Archie's "patron number" on it. He would do a butterfat test on it later and the price the factory paid depended to an extent on the butterfat content of the milk. Previous to the "Babcock test" coming into common use during World War I it had not been uncommon for the more thrifty patrons to increase the weight of their milk by the judicious addition of a little water or to skim a bit of the cream that had risen to the top of a can of the night's milk, before the milk left for the factory. In fact it was whispered that one or two of the cheese factory patrons who were Archie's neighbours had cream on their porridge even yet.

But this morning as usual, the cheesemaker after taking the sample of Archie's milk for testing, weighed his milk, marked the number of pounds down on the sheet tacked up beside the scale, and then put the same figure in Archie's "cheese factory book" which Archie presented to him, exactly the same as he presented his "pass book" to the teller in the bank when he made a deposit. It served the same purpose too; it gave a rough idea of where a patron stood at any given time. What the cheese factory book did not tell was the "test" of the milk. That figure came on the statement that was with each factory cheque and the cheque came roughly every two weeks or when "they sold the cheese". Sometimes the test was lower than usual (which could be explained by a variety of natural causes) but which the patrons usually attributed to the cost of some repairs in the factory, which they thought (out loud) the cheesemaker was recouping by lowering their test and thus paying less for their milk.

When Archie got the empty cans back on his express wagon, he drove around to the back of the factory and from a spout put roughly the same amount of whey in his cans as he had brought of milk. The cheesemaker knew the big pig raisers in his community and kept an eye on them at the whey spout as they were inclined to take more than their share, as whey was a good basic pig feed.

624

When Archie left the cheese factory, his next stop was at the general store, practically next door to the cheese factory, where he and Annie did most of their buying. All he wanted that day was a couple of pounds of bologna and to hear any news he might have missed at the cheese factory and to pass on the news that old Mrs.Alex Peter Dan at the Hill (Vankleek Hill) who had been ailing was a little better and that he had a cow he might sell as he had a couple of good heifers coming along. Johney Big Peter, a staunch Tory from over in the next school section came into the store just as Archie was leaving and Archie lingered for a few minutes to hear him denounce Glengarry's M.P., who was also the Canadian Prime Minster Mackenzie King, in vitriolic terms. Archie's people had been good Grits since the days of John Sandfield and he was very tempted to tell Johney Big Peter some of the real facts about Mackenzie King but the thought of his unfinished haying made him reluctantly pass up the opportunity for a good argument. As he drove home along the tree-lined concession road, Archie thought longingly of the things he should have said to Johney Big Peter.

On arrival at home he emptied the whey into the pig or swill barrels, and surrendered the cans to his wife, whose job it was to wash them. He then fed the pigs with a mixture of provender (ground oats) and whey, one of the swill barrels being reserved for this mixture and the other for the pure whey. Throughout the scorching summer day, if these barrels were disturbed by any intruder, there erupted from them a black mushroom cloud of thousands of flies.

All the activities so far had been but a preparation for the real work of the day. By 9 A.M., Archie and his brother Donald were at work in Archie's fields. It was always their custom to share the field work of the two McAngus farms. Archie was cutting hay with a mower drawn by a team of horses, while Donald, with a rake drawn by a single horse, was raking the hay of the previous day's mowing into long rows or "windrows". At 11:30, they repaired to Archie's house for dinner, the main meal of the day. This consisted of salt pork, from the brine barrel in the cellar, boiled potatoes, canned tomatoes, lettuce and radishes from the garden, bread, tea, and lemon pie. Except for the cooked vegetable and the dessert, which varied, this meal would be exactly the same every workday of the month. After this, the men immediately left the house, and were soon at work gathering the hay which had been raked that morning. For this, they used two implements: a wagon, drawn by a team of horses, and a hayloader, which was drawn trailer-like behind the wagon. It is a mere thirty years since the events we are describing, but we realize, with a certain sense of surprise, that it is already necessary in the interest of making things clear to all our readers to explain what a hayloader was. The hayloader consisted basically of a revolving toothed drum, which picked up the hay from the long rows in which it had been gathered by the rake, and an escalator which carried the hay up the back of the hayloader and poured it onto the wagon, as indicated in this sketch:

When the wagon was being loaded with hay, one of the brothers drove the horses, while the other spread the hay evenly over the wagon with a pitchfork.

The wagon was then driven to the barn, where a rope and pulley device known locally as the "big fork", though the agent who sold it from down at Martintown called it a "horse fork", was used to transfer the hay from the wagon to the mow. A large steel fork, with a hooking device on the end of its two prongs, was sunk to the hilt into the load of hay. The stout rope attached to this fork enabled the bundle of hay which the fork had grasped to be torn loose from the rest of the load and raised to a track at the peak of the barn when the rope was pulled by a horse. When the fork reached the track, the fork and load slid on a carriage along the track, and when the carriage had reached the mow into which the hay was to be dropped, a trip-rope was pulled to release the hooking device on the fork's prongs, and the load fell into the mow. One brother stood on the wagon load of hay to sink the fork, the other spread the hay in the mow, and Annie had the job of driving the horse.

When five or six loads of hay had been gathered and unloaded in this way, the brothers found to their dismay and disappointment that it was almost five o'clock, and they would have to stop their work for supper and chores. Donald returned to his home, and Archie and his family had their supper; the fare this time being fried eggs, more salt pork, warmed-over potatoes browned in the frying pan, tea, cake, and plum preserves. As in the morning, Archie and Annie did the milking. Afterwards, Donald reappeared, and to their great pleasure the brothers were able to put in two more loads of hay before the last light of the long summer day had faded. A snack of bread and milk and a glance at the newspaper concluded Archie's day.

Horse forks (big forks). The name depended on the part of the county you lived in but the idea was the same. Although each blacksmith had his own ideas about design as this picture illustrates, each fork was a single, double, or triple harpoon with a locking lug at the bottom end that was turned by a lever when the fork was stuck into the load. Once locked, the fork with its big bunch of hay was hoisted to the peak of the barn by a horse attached to a rope and pulley device and then it ran along a track to the mow. A pull on a trip rope attached to the locking lever let the bundle of hay fall in the mow.

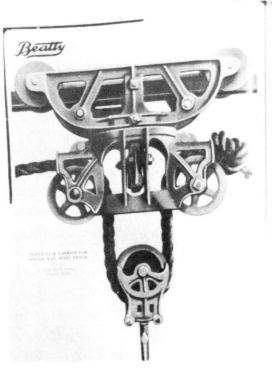

Horse fork car. This was the device that ran along a track at the peak of the barn and provided for lateral transportation of the hay from the barn floor to mow. A stop block on the track stopped the car over the barn floor and released the travelling pulley with its hook, to which the big fork was attached. These devices were so popular that farm implement dealers such as Beatty started to make and sell them.

Meanwhile, what had Annie been doing? One might well turn this question around, and ask what had she *not* been doing? Very truly had Sandy Fraser said that every farm wife gets the habit of hard work or dies in the training. We have already seen several things that Annie did on the day we are examining, and we will make no secret of what the reader has already guessed, that the meals we have described were all of her preparation, and that she did all the dishwashing afterwards. And how many steps she made after the children during the day, and how many tasks she did for and on account of them, we must pass over, as beyond the powers of historians to count. But we will add that in this one day, beyond the things indicated above, she made the beds, scrubbed the floor, washed some windows, did the laundry and saw it ironed before 3 P.M., fed the chickens three times and the pigs twice, snatched moments to weed her flower beds, and darned socks and sewed patches on a coat. And no one, not even as severe a judge of her achievements as herself, begrudged her the recreation of talking to her friends and relatives in several telephone conversations.

Thus a summer day in the life of this Glengarry couple, no more, but no less, industrious than most of their neighbours.

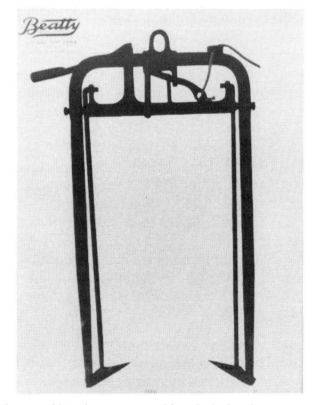

This is the actual big, horse powered hay fork that for some 50 years lifted the hay from the farmers' wagons to the mows. It was attached by the ring at the top to the travelling block on the car on the track at the peak of the roof. This one has a locking lever seen at the top left and a separate trip lever to which the small rope leads at the top right.

Passing onwards over a little more than a half year, we come to Thursday, February 24, 1949.

On that day Archie arose at the agreeably late hour of 6:30 A.M., and this time he had two fires to light—in the cookstove, and in the box stove. He trampled a path to the barn, through the new fall of snow of the night before, and fed the cows, horses and pigs, and trampling another path to the henhouse he also fed the hens before returning to the house for his own breakfast: the food at the breakfast table was the same as in the summer. After breakfast he returned to the stable, where he put four unweaned calves under their mothers to suck, and where he milked the only five cows that were currently in milk; the remainder of the herd were in the dry period as the birth of their calves approached. Having carried the milk to the kitchen in three pails divided between two trips, he poured it into the bowl of the machine called a cream separator; he then turned the heavy handle round and round while his wife tended to the stout flow of skim milk and thin flow of cream which issued from the separate spouts of the machine. At present, the cream was being saved to be churned into butter by the McAnguses when enough of it had accumulated; later in the season, and until the cheese factory now closed for the winter re-opened in May, the cream would be sold to the creamery in ----. When the "separating" was finished, Archie took the skim milk and a half pail of hot water to the barn where he mixed them with calf meal to provide a breakfast for the weaned calves, which he fed them in pails; meanwhile, his wife dismembered the pieces of the separator through which the milk had passed, and washed them carefully in scalding water.

Archie spent the rest of the morning till about 11 o'clock loading manure from the pile behind the barn onto his big, box-like manure sleigh pulled by a team of horses and spreading it on the field from which he had drawn the hay in the summer day we have just described. He then returned to the cow stable, where he released the cows from their stalls and let them file out into the yard, where he pumped water into the big wooden trough till every cow, however thirsty, had had enough to drink. Before he put them back into the stable, he cleaned out the gutter behind them and filled their mangers with hay. While they were out, the dog Laddie watched them restlessly, lest some disorder should require his services.

Dinner consisted of fresh pork, boiled potatoes, mashed turnips, a winter treat of curd (cottage cheese) made from skim milk, tea, and rice pudding with maple syrup.

Afterwards as pre-arranged Donald arrived and the brothers hitched the team, which Archie had already harnessed, to the bobsleigh. Today they had no rack on the sleigh as they would be bringing logs home from the bush for the drag saw. The binding chains for the expected load of logs were wrapped around the front and rear bunks of the sleigh and their two cant hooks were fastened to the rear bunk by a clever wrap of the binding chain. Each brother folded a horse blanket for himself to sit on and Archie who was driving the team put his blanket on the front bunk and sat on it. Donald did likewise for his seat on the rear bunk. As Donald climbed onto the sleigh he was carefully holding the crosscut saw and axes and had the saw wedge with its attached red rag (to keep it from getting lost in the snow) carefully stowed in a side pocket of his big coat. In another pocket he had a saw file with which they could, if they had to, resharpen either the saw or the axes in the bush. Trees sometimes contained metal objects that the wood had grown over. Sap spiles were sometimes left in maple trees, wires from fences of long ago could be met with, and traps forgotten by coon hunters could be found in hollow trees. If the axe or the saw ran into any of these things, completely invisible outside the trees, it was immediately dulled beyond effective use. A few minutes' work with the file would put things right enough to carry on with and save them having to call the day's operation off. Either of the brothers, like most of their neighbours, could file, joint, and set a crosscut saw right in the bush, using as their only tools the saw file as cutting instrument and straight edge, the saw wedge as a hammer to knock "set" into the cutting teeth, and a cut in a log or a split limb for a saw vise. But such repairs in the bush were not courted as they interfered with the work of the all too short winter day.

Today the McAngus boys selected four trees, two maples, an elm and a beech, growing in a fifty-foot radius. The team was tied to a tree, well clear of any chance of them being hit by a falling tree or limb and a horse blanket was thrown over each horse. Then the men held an almost wordless consultation about where and how the selected trees (selected because three of them had partly dead tops and the beech was handy) would be felled. That decided, each knelt by the selected tree, each holding one handle of the crosscut saw and with his axe in easy reach. Then they sawed a cut into the tree a foot and a half or so above the ground about eight inches deep on the side they decided the tree would fall on. When this cut was done, each brother took his axe (fortunately Donald chopped left-handed so both could work) and chopped out the kerf (vulgarly "natch") above the saw cut, leaving a V-shaped notch. Then they moved to the side of the tree opposite the notch and started to cut towards it with the crosscut saw. At this stage forces came into play that we cannot describe. It was possible by carefully cutting one side of the tree more than the other and angling the cut slightly up or down and judicious use of the saw wedge and wind to fell a tree in a selected spot. From years of practice and tricks of the trade passed on to them by that old shantyman, their father, Archie and Donald were "pretty good in the bush" and soon had their four trees on the ground, lying just as they wanted them for convenient sawing, with a minimum of walking, wedging, and prying. In an hour they had the large part of the trees sawn into 12-foot logs and while Archie brought the team and sleigh to a handy place for loading the logs, Donald chopped a couple of large limbs clear of brush to use as skids for loading the logs onto the sleigh. Archie unhitched the team from the sleigh and used them to skid the logs to the improvised skidway that Donald had set up beside the sleigh. In a few minutes the men had five logs in their sleigh, three big butt logs on the bottom and two of the smaller ones on top. While Archie was putting the team back "on the sleigh", Donald bound the load of logs with the chains they had brought to the bush, using a young ash tree as a binding pole. The big end of this pole had been slipped under the chain holding the logs to the front bunk of the sleigh from the front and then a twist of the chain was placed over the binding pole and as the pole was brought around toward the back of the load, pivoting in the twist chain, the front chain was pulled tight. The chain holding the load to the rear bunks had been formed into a noose, which surrounded the rear sleigh bunk and the logs above it. The free end of the noose of chain was put around the small end of the binding pole and as much tension as possible put on the binding pole which was now bent into a decided arc. Now, no matter how the sleigh twisted on the uneven bush road, logs and sleigh would stay together. Some of their neighbours used patented chain-tightening devices, usually called "bear traps", which worked on a lever principle to tighten the binding chains, but the McAngus boys could not see any reason for buying things to tighten their binding chains when their bush supplied binding poles just for cutting them down.

So the boys threw the horse blankets on top of the load of logs, carefully collected their saw, axes, and wedge and put them on top of the load too. Then they climbed up on the load themselves, Archie gave a cluck to the team, and they set off for the barn. Tomorrow if it was not stormy, they would come back for the other two loads of logs and while Archie was taking them up to the barn, Donald would brush off/out the limb wood and carefully pile it so that it would not be hidden by snow.

Today they rolled their logs off on the permanent skidway east of the barn, where each spring the gasoline-engine powered (or driven) dragsaw, with the help of a few neighbours splitting the blocks and hauling the resulting firewood to the woodshed, sawed up the "body wood" for the McAngus boys. Donald would bring his team over with the wagon each day when they were sawing and take a load of wood home with him when he went. Also we must mention that the McAngus boys, when they came across an extra good log of any species of tree, would set it aside and these logs they would take at their convenience to the local saw mill to be sawn into planks, boards, and scantlings for their own use. Then if they needed a couple of new planks for the barn floor, or had to build a new stone boat or hay rack or repair a manger they had the lumber on hand to do it with.

In the evening, all the chores which had been done in the early morning were repeated, including the separation of the milk. Only when these were all completed, did the family have supper. This meant that their winter supper, taking place after all the work of the day, could be a more leisurely meal than their dinner, or than any of their meals in the summer. The fare was home-made barley soup, cold roast pork, browned potatoes as in summer, some more of the curd, tea, and the remainder of the rice pudding. Afterwards, Archie read the newspaper and some copies of the *Saturday Evening Post* which a neighbour had recently left with the McAnguses. By 9:30 the house was in darkness. Archie had enjoyed two or three hours of well deserved leisure between supper and bedtime but not so his wife, who worked through till the moment she went to bed. What did she do during her long working day? Besides the usual tasks of meals, cleaning, and caring for the children, she had kept the two stoves fed with wood all the day, had ironed her laundry, which had been brought in in a frozen state from the line the day before and had since been drying on racks around the stove, had completed the stitching of a new dress, and had made an apron for sale at a church bazaar in March.

The typical days we have described in the lives of Mr. and Mrs. Archie McAngus could have been any one of the six working days of the week, but Sunday was different. On Sunday, the routine tasks of the farm and the house had to be done, such as feeding and milking the cows, making meals and doing the dishes, but no other work was to be done and most emphatically no field work and no bush work. By this rule the McAnguses and all their neighbours, Protestant and Catholic, Scottish and French, abided. By the 60's, this was to change, and Glengarry farmers were to be seen ploughing and seeding and harvesting on Sundays, but in the 1940's it still seemed unthinkable that such a state of affairs could ever come to be.

The McAnguses had good neighbours and were on good terms with them. Neighbours were still considered by all in this rural community of the late 1940's to be of the utmost importance. Everyone there had an intimate knowledge of the history and present circumstances of every other family. Anything of the least interest or importance done by anyone in any family was almost instantaneously—or so it seemed—known to the whole neighbourhood. Everyone's character had long since been acutely studied, and fixed opinions had been established concerning it; in the elucidation of character, accurate recollections of people's ancestors going back as far as three or four generations were sometimes called upon. No one felt this system to be oppressive, partly because it had existed as far back as memory went, and it was thus hard to imagine that any other system could exist, and partly because it did add a certain warmth to life. In this community, how was it possible to be a nobody, when even its humblest member was an object of unfailing interest to everyone else? And if the neighbourhood was sometimes harsh and intolerant in its judgements, it was also unfailingly elastic in its comradeship; no matter how unworthy someone might prove to be, there was no record of anyone ever having been cast out by the neighbourhood.

Neighbours helped each other with the work that could only be conveniently done by gangs of men. Every summer, the threshing machine made its round of the neighbourhood, and when it reached any one of the farms, 12 to 16 men of the neighbourhood would assemble there to help for as long as the threshing would take, normally ½ to three days but depending on the acreage of grain and the weather. Some of these men would bring their wagon, drawn by either horses or tractors, and in the wagons they could carry the sheaves from the field to the barn, where they pitched the sheaves into the threshing machine. Other men were assigned the duty of pitching the sheaves in the fields onto the wagons. Still others had the job of hauling the newly threshed grain from the mill to the granary. Similar gatherings would be held for certain special occasions, such as pouring concrete or erecting a building. And if any farmer was sick and unable to do his springwork, haying, or harvest, his neighbours would gather to do the work for him.

Among the neighbours there were also entertainments. If there was a wedding, neighbours would be invited to all the festivities connected with it. From time to time there was a dance in the nearby hamlet of ----; the dance might be in honour of a just-married couple, or for a wedding anniversary, or as a benefit for someone who had suffered a loss, as for example by a fire, and if the beneficiaries were from the neighbourhood, everyone in the neighbourhood would attend. In December there was always a children's concert, called a "Christmas Tree", in the local school house (called "the Christmas Concert" in Charlottenburgh).

Among the Scots of this neighbourhood, as in others in Glengarry, a peculiar system of name-giving had developed. Traditionally, boys and girls in Highland Scots families in Glengarry had received their names from among only a dozen or so names that were available, and resultant repetition and confusion was made all the greater by the fact that almost every Highland surname had a multitude of users in Glengarry. Thus Archie and his neighbour John MacIan had the same given name and surname as two other men who brought their milk to the cheese factory at ----. Custom had produced a way around this difficulty, however, for each of these men was given by his fellows his father's name as a second name. Thus John the son of Malcolm became John Malcolm; John the son of Murdoch became Johnnie Murdie; and John the son of Peter the son of Malcolm became Johnnie Peter Malcolm and combined three generations in his name. For a woman, the same system of distinguishing tags was used, except that after marriage her father's name was usually replaced with that of the husband. Thus Archie's sister Kate, who had married a farmer by the name of Donald in the next township, was known there as Katie Donald. At an earlier age, nicknames had been commonly used for this purpose of identification, but these had happily mostly died out with the owners. However, one of the few surviving vestiges of this practice could be found in the McAngus family. Archie's father had been known as Little Norman, and accordingly Archie and Donald were commonly called Archie and Donald Little Norman.

In the 1930's the local Scottish families began to choose the

636

names for their children from much wider range of names, and as we have seen Archie's children did not receive Scottish names at all. There had never before been a Desmond or a Martin in the McAngus family or for that matter in the neighbourhood.

In the case of the French families which made up about one-third of the neighbourhood, this system of adding the father's name was not normally used, as there was so little duplication of names in those families but was used when needed to distinguish individuals.

Besides neighbours, relatives were immensely important in Archie's life, and relatives he had in plenty: in the neighbourhood, in the township, in the county, and on the prairies (quite literally in Plenty there, for many Glengarrians had settled in Plenty, Saskatchewan), in British Columbia, and in practically every major city of the United States. Like so many Glengarrians, as he grew older he took an increasing interest in the history of his family, and he often regretted that he had not listened more closely in his youth to Grandpa McAngus, who had often traced the descent of the family for him from the days of its first arrival in Canada—but while the good old man talked on and on, it often happened that no one at all was listening.

We are afraid we must confess to those of our readers who are not Glengarrians that we shall not be able to explain to them in a fully satisfactory way why Archie took the attitude to his relatives that we are about to describe. We shall content ourselves, therefore, and ask them to be content, if they can, with a simple description of what this attitude was, so far as we were able to determine it through careful discussions with our old friend. To Archie it seemed that to every relative of his, he was tied with a bond which made his connection with that person quite different from his connection with anyone to whom he was not related. It did not follow that he liked all his relatives, and in fact there were some for whose company he did not care, and one particular branch of the family which he completely detested and of which he never spoke well to anyone—though to them also, he felt bonded in this peculiar way. The bond was mainly one of *feeling*; in most areas of life it did not normally except in the case of the nearest relations result in any actions different from those resulting from his dealings with his non-kindred. To a relative, however, one could speak with a little more freedom than to other people, because one had more in common with him (or her) than with people at large, and the nearer the relative, the greater the freedom. Also, if misfortune were to come upon one, relatives could be expected to assist one a little more liberally than other people, with the degree of liberality depending, of course, as before on the degree of relationship. Even a relative who happened to be an enemy could not entirely disavow his obligations in such a case. It was Archie's opinion that in these feelings he was identical with most of the Glengarry Scots, but that they would not nor be able to define this bond, depending as it did so much on emotion and custom, any more closely than he had done.

After further consideration of our questions, he added several observations which seem to us to be convincing, and which, whether they are fully correct or not, are worth recording here. One is that the Glengarry Scots never feel they know who anyone is until they know who his relatives are, and that the Glengarry French Canadians share, though to a lesser degree, in this attitude. Another is that one of the things that makes Glengarry so much different from the rest of the province is the extraordinary interest felt by so many Scots there for who was related to whom and how, and that this interest arises from the peculiar bond felt for relatives. Where else, he asked, would men working in a threshing gang in the field talk genealogy? He also observed that one of the lesser things which made it difficult for the Scots to adjust to the city-born families which have appeared in the county in such numbers in recent years is that these are families which cannot be identified as part of any web of kinship, being generally without any relatives in sight at all.

But to return to our narrative of Archie's life. In 1949 and 1950 his father and mother died, and Donald was left alone at home, a bachelor of 37, no longer young in feeling or appearance. While Archie had been single and at home, Donald had occasionally spoken of going to the West to live, but these stirrings of revolt had never developed into action, and after Archie's marriage Donald had found or at least had believed himself to be tied to the old homestead by the necessity of looking after his elderly parents. Old bachelors were a tradition among the Glengarry Scots, and after the death of his parents Donald slid without resistance ever deeper into all the customs associated with the tradition. Dust began to gather unresisted everywhere in the house; rubbish began to accumulate in the corners and to creep out glacier-like into the rooms. Donald still shared the farm work with Archie but sensing his danger of a loss of independence, became harder and harder to persuade to take meals with Archie and his family. As to what he ate, it must be reported on the careful testimony of the local general storekeeper that he lived for many years mainly on bologna and bacon,potatoes and white bread, and that as the 60's came in he was one of the neighbourhood's pioneers in the consumption of frozen TV dinners, frozen pizzas, and junk foods generally. Annie McAngus maintained the strongest discipline in one area of his life by doing his laundry (including the bedclothes) every week, and suppressing, with the severity and punctuality of a slave-driver, recurrent tendencies in Donald to avoid surrendering his laundry at all in favour of what were no doubt lamentable attempts to do it himself at home. Most of the time Annie had to go to Donald's home to get his washing over his loud protests.

Donald was left the home farm in his father's will, but subject to the payment of a number of small legacies to Archie's and Kate's children.

In 1950, Donald and Archie both bought tractors. Archie liked to tell his family that they were the only farmers in the neighbourhood who had switched from horses to tractors in mid-career. Elsewhere in the neighbourhood, according to his observations, farmers either began to use tractors when they were youths or drove horses exclusively to their dying days.

In 1950 also Desmond, Archie's eldest son, started school,

followed two years later by the second son, Martin. The school was the same one their father had attended, and he had no difficulty understanding what was done in the school for much had remained unchanged since his day. The school was still heated by a wood-burning box stove, and the students still found the ink in their bottles frozen on winter mornings. They still played in the same school yard, hauled their drinking water in pails from the same well a quarter mile away, used outdoor plumbing, and studied the useful basic subjects of spelling, grammar, arithmetic, science, and history. No one in the neighbourhood realized that this school system, which had survived with surprisingly little alteration from the days of *Glengarry School Days*, would be completely swept away by 1970 and replaced with a system which provided modern, big-city type schooling in large, multi-roomed schools for almost every child in Glengarry.

In this school the young McAngus brothers completed the 8-grade course of study in 7 years and proceeded to the high school at Alexandria in 1957 and 1959. The system of high school bussing had been in use for some years and the school bus picked them up every morning at their gate. The program of studies in the high school was rigorous and the teaching staff full of zeal, and the brothers were well prepared when they entered ---University in the 60's.

During the years in which Archie's sons were going through public school and high school (1950-1964) an almost bewildering series of changes took place in his neighbourhood. The farmers began to ship their milk to a condensed milk plant in ---, and the cheese factory closed down. Just a year or two later it was demolished, leaving only a nettle-bed to mark the site of what had been for two generations the economic power house of the hamlet and of the farming community around it. About the same time, the blacksmith died and left no successor. The combined grist mill and seed-cleaning plant burned to the ground and was not rebuilt. The storekeeper, feeling the loss of the custom which had been attracted to the hamlet by these vanished businesses, began to talk of closing his doors. In the farming community, ominous cracks were opening. Farmers were seeking off-farm jobs, and were either selling their farms or letting the land to neighbours while they continued to use the house as a residence. City dwellers from Montreal and Ottawa were buying up farms as weekend and retirement homes. Fewer and fewer horses were seen in the neighbourhood. Combines began to replace the old grain binders. Threshing bees and for that matter other bees came to an end. Archie began to feel that he was the last of a vanishing breed, the old-style Glengarry farmer. Yet with signs of disintegration all around, it was evident that the neighbourhood was, paradoxically, more affluent than ever before.

Even within Archie's house, there were many changes in these years. Home-made butter vanished, as did the pork from the brine barrel in the cellar. Like most of his neighbours, Archie stopped keeping hens and the family bought their eggs from stores. By the mid-1960's, all the food of the household except what Annie grew in the garden was store-bought. The hand-cranked phone was replaced by a wall-type dial phone. In 1948 Archie read a long article in the *Ottawa Farm Journal* by an astonished journalist describing the fad of television which was sweeping the United States, where more than a third of a million sets were said to be in use; in 1952 he read in the *Glengarry News* that a television set was in operation in Alexandria; and by 1958 he had a television set in his own home. In 1962 the installation of an oil space heater (for heating) and of an electric stove (for cooking) ended forever the use of wood for fuel in the McAngus household. That very same year, Archie sold off all the timber in his woodlot, using the money to pay for the new stoves and for installing running water in the house, but there was as yet no bathroom. Almost by insensible stages, the old off-limits parlour was invaded, encroached upon, despoiled of its joyless splendours, lived in, and at last turned into a plain living room where people of the household could be, and were, relaxed and comfortable.

In farming, Archie took a middle course between the large-scale modernized farming that a few daring younger men of the neighbourhood were attempting, and the old mixed farming which for so many years had supported his family, his father's, and his grandfather's. He enlarged his herd to 20 cows, and milked them with a milking machine. He sold off his horses, pigs, and sheep. He grew the same amount of hay as before, but converted part of his grain acreage to corn growing and erected a cement silo and a corn crib. He used far more artificial fertilizer than before, but still felt he was not using enough. He bought a better tractor, plow, disc and cultivator, but drew the line at buying a combine and baler; instead, he hired one of the neighbours, who had a baler and combine, to do his baling and combining for him.

As old customs crumbled, it became known that some enterprising young farmers and their wives actually went on holidays, but this innovation Archie and Annie rejected. He had begun farming at a time when Glengarry farmers never took holidays, and since his return from the West in 1928 he had never slept away from home for one night except for his honeymoon.

In 1972, Archie suffered a heart attack and was rushed to the Cornwall General Hospital. Before his release two weeks later, his doctor ordered him to give up farming.

Two years later, his brother Donald died suddenly. It had always been the practice that when there was a death in the family, the coffin would be placed in the parlour, as the best room of the house, and the relatives and neighbours would come there to pay their last respects. But by this time, the homes were no longer used for this purpose, and Donald's "wake" as it was still called, was at the undertaker's in---.

Now, in 1978, Archie and Annie still live on their farm but they no longer work it. The land is rented for $800 a year to a neighbour who needs fodder for his 80 head of dairy cattle. He crops the hay on about a quarter of the workable land and plants the rest in corn. In years when the hay crop is heavy, he uses the barn for storing bales of hay and he almost always shelters a few pieces of machinery there. The cow stables and the horse stables

642

stand empty, and cobwebs are growing across the mangers and the stanchions. There are no livestock on the farm, which is just as well since the fences have badly deteriorated—have been deteriorating since Archie's last years of farming. The McAnguses keep a dog, however, as they have always done, and a shifting population of half-wild cats frequents the barn, where Archie brings them a brimming dish of scraps every day.

When Donald died, Archie and Annie discussed the possibility of moving to Alexandria or Maxville; it seemed to them that as long as Donald was alive, they would have a responsibility to stay in the neighbourhood to keep an eye on his welfare, but that now they were free to do as they pleased. But the prospects of confinement to an apartment grew more irksome to Archie the more he thought of them, and the purchase of a house seemed too costly to be possible, and the outcome was that this old couple (as they now are, and as they now see themselves to be) have resolved that they will live in the country as long as they can, and that afterwards they, or the survivor of them, will go to live in the Manor at Maxville.

Their home has every comfort. From the sale of Donald's farm, which was willed to Archie, he was able to afford putting a bathroom in his house. The McAnguses now have two television sets, one of them in colour. A deep-freeze has joined the old refrigerator in the kitchen; the McAnguses who once butchered their own cattle and pigs for meat, now buy a quantity of some sort of meat they like, either from a neighbour who happens to be butchering when they need some, or else from a store that advertises a "freezer special." A good insulation job helps the oil heater keep the house warm through even the coldest and stormiest winter nights.

Archie has been getting the Old Age Pension since 1970, and now gets $153.44 per month and Annie will get it too once she has reached 65 in 1979.

Archie sold Donald's farm, the old McAngus homestead, to an Ottawa businessman in 1975. The new owner has stripped the clapboards from the old house to reveal the logs, and has completely remodelled the interior and added a handsome fieldstone fireplace. With the admirable freedom from sentimentality which goes along with the profession of farming, Archie was not the least depressed by the passing of the old farm into the hands of a stranger.

Archie and Annie's elder son is an industrial chemist in Hamilton and their younger son is a high school teacher in Toronto. Both married young, and have children of their own. Annie writes to them weekly, on behalf of herself and Archie, but no one expects Archie to write; though perfectly capable of doing so, he has never written a personal letter in his life. The sons and their families visit the parents several times a year, and Annie has several times visited them in Hamilton and Toronto. Archie, however, who has shown tendencies in his old age to be increasingly house-bound and even withdrawn, has always refused to do likewise. His daughters-in-law like him, but complain that he is difficult to talk to unless they find a subject he is interested in.

For the last time, let us follow Archie through one day in his life, choosing for this purpose Tuesday, 1 August 1978, a fine hot sunny summer day. Archie arose at 7:30, and Annie about half an hour later. Both would have thought these hours disgracefully late were it not for the fact that even some of their farming neighbours now slept as late as 7 A.M. In the cool of the morning, they had their breakfast in the kitchen: corn flakes, orange juice, bacon and eggs, coffee, and toast. Archie spent the morning on some of the multitude of small tasks that he always found to be busy at; in particular, there were few days when he did not take a hand at repelling the unwearying aggression of burdocks and other weeds in the farm yard and brush along the fences. At 11 o'clock, the postman left the mail in the box, and Archie went for it and found an advertising folder from a store in Hawkesbury, a copy of the *Glengarry News*, and a letter from a sociologist asking for permission to interview him on the subject of kinship ties in Glengarry. This letter was several times re-read and much discussed in the McAngus household in the next few weeks and was shown to a number of visitors but was never answered. Nor, it appears, were similar letters received at the same time in several other households of the neighbourhood ever answered. Archie immediately read all the leading items in the *Glengarry News* and returned to it at intervals over the following week, till he had read practically every line in it. Before it was thrown out, Annie took several clippings from it, and the McAnguses had consulted with several neighbours on a puzzling point in the genealogical data included with one of the obituaries.

Lunch was a light meal of tomato soup, boiled potatoes, new carrots from the garden, and a bit of cold pork. In the afternoon, Archie had a nap. Aferwards, he read for a while. He had never been fond of reading when young, and his busy life as a farmer had left him little time for books, but since his retirement he had re-read, for the third or fourth time in his life, *Glengarry School Days* and *The Man from Glengarry*, and now read about one book a week which his wife got for him at the library in Alexandria. Around 4 o'clock he went to the store in his modest used Chev. car to buy a few groceries his wife wanted. The store now seldom sees the throngs that had regularly assembled there on cheese-factory mornings years ago but still functions, if less efficiently than before, as a centre for the circulation of news. On the way home he had time to visit with a neighbour before supper. That meal consisted of a bowl of soup and warmed up things left over from dinner, and Annie had a bit of her own cake on the table. Afterwards he weeded the garden, work which in earlier years he would have left to his wife. The heat of the summer day was now waning, and accompanied by the dog, he enjoyed a leisurely walk to the far end of the place. By the time he had returned, the Ottawa daily newspaper had arrived, being left in its own separate box on its own post next to the mail box, and Archie leafed through it for a time. The balance of the evening he spent watching television; at 11:30 he went to bed.

It will be readily believed that although Annie was not as busy as she had been during the many years when she was the farm wife of a bustling farm, she still found enough tasks in the maintenance of her house to keep her busy all the day, and that it was only in the evening she was able to indulge in the leisure which had made up so much of her husband's day.

# Chapter XIX
# Conclusion: The Mystique of Glengarry

"In the minds of many Canadians," according to a writer in the *Canadian Forum* in 1942, "the word Glengarry evokes a great feeling of nostalgia."

To most Glengarrians or descendants of Glengarrians, this statement will still seem a self-evident truth; to many others without Glengarry connections, it will be more than a little puzzling. What has been special about this county? The present section will attempt to explain and trace the history of the "mystique " as it may be called, of Glengarry.

This mystique has historically been of two kinds. There has been the mystique of Glengarry as held by Glengarrians and descendants of Glengarrians, and this may be called the "insider's mystique." And there has been the outsider's mystique, held by those who are not of Glengarry descent.

First, to explain the insider's mystique. For Glengarrians, and particularly Glengarrians of Scottish descent, and for many of those descended from them, Glengarry has traditionally seemed a special, almost a holy place. It has simply not seemed like another Canadian county. In this respect, the sharpest contrast has existed between Glengarry and the counties bordering it, including Stormont and Prescott. On one side of the border, was the sacred fatherland of Glengarry, and on the other side was just another Ontario or Quebec county. The feeling of Glengarrians for their county has much resemblance to the feeling of the Irish for Ireland, of the New Englanders for New England, and of the old and modern Romans for Rome.

Behind this is the truth that the Glengarrians have been not just a random grouping of people, but a nation in the fullest sense of the word nation. For a people to exist as a nation, of course, we need not remind our readers, they need not have their own government, or any political structures whatever corresponding to their own sense of their borders. The Glengarry nation has been a very small one of course—far, far too miniscule ever to dream of establishing its own state, as the Irish did after centuries of foreign rule—but a nation all the same, with its own intense sense of cohesion and of separation from the outside world, its own customs and values, its own awareness of having its own heroic past separate from that of the country of which it has been a part, and for a time, even its own language. In accordance with its status as a nation, Glengarry is the only Canadian county from which it is possible to feel oneself an exile.

Within this insider's mystique, there has been the double attachment which has been characteristic of all nationalism, that is to say, an attachment to the people, and an attachment to the geographical area which the people consider their home. Traditionally, and perhaps invariably, in nationalism the attachment to the homeland exists mostly because of the people who live there, that is, the attachment to the homeland is a secondary attachment, gaining strength from the more important attachment to the people. When the Glengarrians' attachment to Glengarry is closely examined, it too can be seen to follow this rule. As a geographical unit, Glengarry is special, is sacred, because of the people who live there. If all the Glengarrians moved en masse to another part of Canada, all the mystique would undoubtedly be transferred with them. In the case of Glengarry, this situation is probably reinforced by the county's lack of any pronounced geographical features. There are no mountains, glens, deserts, moors, to linger hauntingly in the minds of exiles. There are many spots of great natural beauty in the county, but these are in no way different from similar spots to be found in the rest of Eastern Ontario.

Among the Scots, this insider's mystique has been strengthened by what we may as well candidly and without prompting call a racialistic conviction on the part of the Highland Scots of the superiority of Highland Scots in integrity, intelligence, charity, neighbourliness, and a number of other good qualities. Mingled with this has been a vague feeling that in pioneer times there flourished a race of Glengarry Highland Scots of qualities higher than any we can reasonably hope to equal in these feebler times and often of exceptional stature and strength.

Thus the insider's mystique of Glengarry.

The outsider's mystique of Glengarry is a gentler and far less passionate version of the insider's mystique. The people who hold the outsider's mystique recognize that there is something, though not necessarily a great deal, in the idea that Glengarry is a special place, and they value Glengarry as a place where people have formed their own rules for life and have tried to follow them despite the pressures of the outside world. The outsider's mystique no doubt derives from the insider's mystique, but the insider's mystique itself gains strength from being confirmed in part by outside opinion.

When the traveller John Goldie visited Glengarry in 1819 he referred to it in his travel notes as "Glengary of which the highlanders boast so much." This may be taken as evidence that even at this early date a mystique of Glengarry was developing among the Canadian Scots.

At the time of the Rebellion of 1837-1838 the Glengarry Scots were warmly praised for their loyalty, but in the longer run it is questionable whether they improved or blackened their reputation through their work in suppressing the rebellion.

Otherwise, our evidence for the existence of a mystique of Glengarry before Confederation is slight. This is a period for which all the historical evidence is so limited that lack of evidence on any particular topic is of little significance, but we are inclined to think that if the mystique had existed very strongly outside of Glengarry we would have come upon more signs of it.

Beginning with the 1880's, however, we have strong

evidence from the utterances of Glengarrians and of the Glengarry area press that the Glengarrians had a high opinion of themselves and of what they had achieved. We read, in an obituary of 1882, that the deceased "was a true specimen of the noble race to which he belonged." Another deceased of 1884 was called "the last of the old pioneers of this noble County of ours." In 1886, Big Rory McLennan uttered his tribute to the achievement of the Glengarrians:

> There is no county in Canada that has turned out
> so many successful railway men, and successful men
> in every walk of life, as the County of Glengarry.
> True, many of our young men start out in the world
> under many disadvantages,—without a proper edu-
> cation,—few friends, and no money. These dis-
> advantages are got over by energy and brains, and
> an honest determination to reach the front ranks.
> Men from this county are to be met with wherever
> you may go and as a rule you find them foremost in
> whatever position they have undertaken to fill.

A newspaper correspondent of 1888, reflecting on the humiliation the Purcell election scandal had brought to Glengarry, remembered sadly how much "has been said and sung in praise of this noble old county of Glengarry." A group of Glengarrians who had a reunion in Duluth in 1890 were described as fully sustaining "the reputation gained by the sons of Glengarry in the United States for integrity and ability in discharging the duties of any office or position they may hold." A trouble-struck Glengarrian pioneer in North Dakota affirmed in 1891 that "Had I not the grit of a Glengarrian I could not have stayed with it as I did." In 1892 an exuberant "Gael" wrote from Minnesota to say that in foreign lands Glengarry's sons "are chosen for their fine physique, integrity and respectability to be leaders of men, and to fill positions of honor and trust." The obituaries of James Rayside, M.L.A., who died in 1895, described him as "In person...a fine specimen of a Glengarry Highlander—over six feet in height and stout in proportion " and "In appearance...a typical Glengarrian. Tall of stature and broad-shouldered, he was a prominent figure in the legislative halls...". Another Glengarrian, who died the following year, was described as "a typical Highlander, a man of sterling qualities, upright, honest and generous to a fault." A Glengarry-born orator of 1897 spoke of "the glorious deeds of the sons of Glengarry" and hoped that, although he could not expect to equal them, he would at least not cast discredit on the fair name of Glengarry.

While these remarks reflect the idea that Glengarrians had of themselves, there is also evidence that the Glengarry mystique had already begun to infect people elsewhere. In 1885, the *Toronto World* published a tribute to Glengarry which presents so fully developed a heroic image of Glengarry that it deserves reproducing in full here:

> "The county of Glengarry is famous for at least two things: it is the eastermost one of the province and it is the home of the descendants of the Highlanders who settled there just 100 years ago. It has sent out more successful men than any other section of Ontario. They are all over the province; in Montreal they are thick and influential; the Northwest and British Columbia are full of them; and go where you will in the neighboring republic and you are sure to run across men who were bred in the old county; Toronto is rapidly developing a Glengarry colony. The men of Glengarry are more than famous as contractors and lumbermen. Most of the big pine forests have been worked by Macs, and more than half of all the contracting in Canada (railways, bridges, and canals) have fallen to these enterprising Kelts.
>
> "On Saturday afternoon at one of the leading hotels the following members of the clans were grouped together in earnest conversation: Roderick McLennan (Rory the mason), who was chief engineer on the Lake Superior section of the CPR; Alex R. McLennan (Aleck Rory), a brother of Big Rory, the contractor

who has the $250,000 suit with the CPR; Donald
McLennan (Donald Mason); John R. Macdonald, contractor; Angus Macdonald, VS; John D. McLennan (Rory the
Mason's son), of Conmee and McLennan, CPR contractors,
also in litigation with the company; E. McVeain, of
Martintown and George McSand, one of Otter's foot
soldiers in the late unpleasantness in the Northwest.
They were talking Gaelic at a great rate, and
were waiting for some others of the tribe to turn
up, who it was said had gone over to Kerr's
(another Glengarrian) hotel on Adelaide Street.

"Later on a World reporter interviewed Aleck
Rory, who is just home from California, where he has
spent a year. He expects a gang of at least 40 to
rendezvous in Toronto before Wednesday night, when
they will start east for the county. Like his three
brothers, Aleck Rory is over six-foot-four high and a
bad man in an election row. Aleck Rory was most
enthusiastic in his description of the Glengarry men
in the Golden State. At Stockton he met McDougalls,
Clarks and Macdonalds by the scores, and from one of
the former he received a gold-headed cane and from
another a diamond pin, both of which he had about him
and showed to the reporter with much demonstration.
All the Glengarry men on the Pacific are rich, or have
married rich wives and widows. But that whereon he
was most eulogistic was the Highland dancing that the
Kelts still kept up in that country. 'You ought to see
the girls dance the fling steps there; and the way
they play the pipes; some of them wear the kilts in
suits that cost over $600; I went 200 miles to a St.
Andrew's ball in Stockton, and it was the finest
gathering of clansmen I have ever seen.' And having
thus delivered himself, he again went off into
ecstacies over a girl of 16 that he saw doing the
gillie callum.

"In answer to the report Aleck Rory said he

was a nephew of Big Finnan Macdonald, the hero of
many a Northwest tale. Here is one of them: Fifty
years ago or more Big Finnan got separated from his
fellows in a big hunt on the plains of the Northwest
when the bison were as thick as now they are scarce.
He singled out a bull but got unhorsed; the bull
attacked him; Big Finnan grasped him by the horns
and the two struggled for hours, the desperate man
never letting go his hold; when his companions came
up the buffalo was found dead and Big Finnan lay
helpless and unconscious at its head still holding
by the horns. It was perhaps the greatest fight
between man and a beast ever recorded. 'Of such men do I
boast to be sprung,' said Aleck Rory as he
parted with the reporter."

So too in 1888 Rose's biographical dictionary praised the
Glengarry contractors:
While still a young man he [Patrick Purcell] was the
sole contractor on some important government works
such as great capitalists band together to undertake.
In this respect he is a worthy son of Glengarry. It
is hard to say what America, and especially Canada,
would have done to carry on its remarkable industrial
development had they not had such shrewd, hardworking,
responsible men as the great contractors who have come
out of Glengarry. Dozens of names could be mentioned,
and many will suggest themselves to the mind of the
reader who is at all acquainted with the history of
great public works in America.

These quotations bring us up to the most momentous events in
the confirmation of the high opinion Glengarrians and others
had of Glengarry, namely the publication of Ralph Connor's first
two Glengarry novels, The Man from Glengarry (1901) and
Glengarry School Days (1902). These novels were a superb
statement of the mystique of Glengarry and communicated the
mystique to an immense audience throughout the English-
speaking world.

We can see from the evidence already cited that the mystique of Glengarry existed before these novels were published. It was usually expressed, however, through the spoken word and newspaper journalism rather than through books. One can find traces of the mystique of Glengarry in the *Forest Flower* and *Shenac*, but they are not very pronounced traces. John Fraser's *Canadian Pen and Ink Sketches* (1890) is probably the first book to be strongly influenced by the mystique of Glengarry. J.A. Macdonell's *Sketches* of Glengarry history (1893) was full of the mystique of Glengarry and appealed to the general public to share the author's love for his county. William McLennan's novel *Spanish John* (1898) had Glengarry associations and A. Paul Gardiner's novel *The House of Cariboo* (1900) was set in Glengarry, but these authors neglected the opportunity, which was exploited by Ralph Connor so brilliantly immediately afterwards to apply the Glengarry mystique to the writing of a work of literature. If Ralph Connor had his aunt's novel *Shenac* to use as a model in writing about the Glengarry pioneers, he appears to have been a pioneer himself in the task of expressing the Glengarry mystique in literature in as full a form as the Glengarrians themselves held it.

Praises of the Glengarrians such as we have quoted from the period before the Connor novels continued afterwards. The obituary of Allan Cameron, brother of Cariboo Cameron and police chief of Cornwall, said that Allan "was a splendid specimen of the sturdy descendants of the Highlanders who came over from Scotland in the early part of the [last] century to make their homes in the Canadian Glengarry," and that "Although not a large man, as Glengarrians of his generation particularly were prone to be, he was gifted with remarkable muscular development, and in his shanty days used to lift a barrel of pork 'by the hoops,' a feat which baffled many brawny men of that time." The Toronto *Globe* remarked on the death of Big Rory McLennan in 1907 that "The Glengarry Highlanders were of a fine physical type, and he conformed perfectly to the typical ideal." In the obituary of another brother of Cariboo Cameron, the deceased was described as "a typical Canadian Highlander, warm-hearted, generous, outspoken and of sterling integrity." In 1909 the Ottawa *Citizen* called a recently deceased member of the Sandfield Macdonald family "this brilliant, brave and devoted daughter of old Glengarry." In a tribute of 1910 to a successful Glengarrian, *Saturday Night* spoke of "Glengarry county—whence come all the big Scotchmen who don't come from Nova Scotia." At the same time, a Cornwall *Standard* obituary described the deceased as "a man of splendid physique, a fine type of the stalwart sons of Glengarry, his native county."

We find an example of a visitor being captivated by, or fortified in, the mystique of Glengarry, in the person of the Earl of Dundonald, a Scottish nobleman who was in Canada in the early years of this century as the general officer commanding the Canadian militia. He was entertained by the Sons of Scotland at Alexandria in 1903. In his autobiography, he describes what he saw and felt:

> We arrived and were met at the station by
> Mr. J.A. Macdonell, K.C., Major A.G. Macdonald,
> Mr. Lockie Wilson, Lieut.-Colonel Morgan (59th Regt.)
> and many others, also a Guard of Honour of the
> 59th (Stormont and Glengarry) Highlanders under
> Captain Cameron. We then went to Major A.G.
> Macdonald's house for luncheon, and afterwards
> proceeded to the Driving Park, where the gathering
> took place.
>
> There were thousands present and the proceedings
> began by an Address to me read by Mr. J.A. Macdonell...
>
> I was deeply moved with the reception accorded to me
> by the people, and in the course of my reply to the
> address, I mentioned what my father had told me, that
> one of the most wonderful sights he had seen when
> fighting in Canada in 1837 was the Macdonald and other
> Glengarry clansmen formed up as volunteers, fathers
> in front, with their sons behind, and that when I had
> heard him tell me this story I little thought that
> one day I should be in command of the descendants of
> the very men he so admired.
>
> ........

It is needless to say that I was deeply impressed with the proceedings of the day. Some quite
old men told me that they had walked immense distances
to shake me by the hand. The faces of those present
were exactly like those in the Highlands: many were
dark, not tall in stature but very powerfully built,
most of them were talking Gaelic. Two MacKinnons
came up and shook hands; they were exactly like two
of my MacKinnon cousins in face.

There were also some dear old Highland women
present who came up and shook hands, one blessed me
in Gaelic with tears in her eyes; she and some other old
ladies wore old-fashioned bonnets with a sort of
white frill inside, typical of the days that are past.

Great numbers of the people of Glengarry are Roman
Catholics, amongst them my friend J.A. Macdonell, K.C.,
and most of the members of his clan, Bishop Macdonell
of Alexandria being their spiritual head, a man whom to
know was a privilege.

I saw some old pipes: they were brought from Scotland by the ancestors of men present and had played
the clans on at Culloden in the cause of the Royal
House of Stuart. Loyalty to the throne and the
British connection forms part of the very nature of
these Glengarry men; it was born in them, and
developed by the teaching of their forbears at the
fireside during the long winter evenings. When I
recalled to them what the men of Glengarry had done on
the battle-field for the British Crown the sea of
upturned faces showed how moved they were and every
reference to past loyalty was marked by deep murmurs
of approval. What a mighty force was here! What a
bond to bind Canada with the Motherland! Self-interest
is brushed aside by men such as these. I could see
these Glengarry men as my father saw them in 1837, in
two great columns, fathers in front, sons behind,

marching to offer their service to the King. How I loved this loyal warlike race!

I wished that I could have stayed on in Glengarry, where I felt the ties of blood relationship as well as the charm of natural surroundings. But as I was not in Canada to follow my own inclinations, I left for Ottawa by the night train, and was at work next day at the Militia Office.

Two questions can be asked about the growth of the Glengarry mystique. One is why did the Glengarrians create what we have called the insider's mystique for themselves? This question is practically unanswerable, but it may be mentioned that if we knew more about that impenetrably dark topic, the mentality of the Glengarrians of the first generations of settlement, it might be possible to trace some continuing nationalist feeling back to the homes of these people in Scotland. The second question is a good deal easier: namely why did the claim that Glengarry was a special place, deserving honour, reverence, and respect, find sympathizers outside the ranks of Glengarrians and descendants of Glengarrians?

From almost the earliest days of settlement, Glengarry was building up the basis for its claims to "special status." Bishop Macdonell, who must have been always closely associated in the public mind with Glengarry, was one of the greatest men in the province in his day, and we have already seen the names of a good number of other eminent men who were associated with Glengarry about this time. In order to see things in their true proportions, it may perhaps be suggested' that the North West Company did not loom quite as large in the memory of the later nineteenth century as it does today; still, when the company was in existence, it had strong ties with Glengarry, and many of its members cast lustre on the Glengarry settlement by their residence or connections there. Glengarrians won a reputation for loyalty and warlike prowess in the War of 1812 and the Rebellion of 1837. We have already seen that from the entry of John Sandfield Macdonald into politics in 1841 till the end of the nineteenth century, Glengarry made an especially impressive showing through the high qualities of its parliamentary representatives. By the later part of the nineteenth century, Glengarry contractors had come to be well known; and the Glengarrians who had poured in such numbers into the United States and Western Canada had provided ample evidence to support the growing belief that Glengarrians were a people who did remarkably well in the world.

These various achievements and claims to attention fell upon ears which were made sympathetic because of a trait in the Victorian mind to which we must now give a moment of attention. One of the aspects of the Victorian outlook, in England and in English-speaking Canada, and perhaps in a few pockets further afield, was an admiration for the Scottish Highlander and his simple, forthright qualities. In the eighteenth century, the very opposite situation had obtained, for then the Highlanders were as generally regarded with contempt. But the Romantic Movement, Sir Walter Scott's novels, and other factors had intervened, to produce what must be one of history's very few examples of a form of racial prejudice being not only abolished but turned into its opposite. As this attitude made its way from England into imitative and colonially-minded English Canada it made those who encountered it more ready than they would otherwise have been to appreciate the achievements and distinctiveness of the Glengarry Highlanders. Indeed, it is not impossible that this cult of the Highlander contributed to the development of the insider's mystique in Glengarry itself.

The great numbers of Glengarrians spread throughout North America no doubt spread the ideas of the Glengarry mystique by word of mouth in the same way that any other ideology may be spread. John Fraser must have been correct throughout when he wrote in 1890, "The sons of Glengarry are now scattered the world over, many of them filling high positions in distant parts; from all such response comes, with a pride of country—'Glengarry was my childhood's home'."

Two other factors may or may not have assisted the

growing cult of Glengarry. The fact that there were such great numbers of Scotsmen in Canada, including many of its leaders and wealthy men, must have encouraged writers to praise the Scots of Glengarry, knowing that such praises would be welcome even to those Scots who were not of Glengarry. The belief that Glengarrians resented Sir Richard Cartwright's and Donald Macmaster's criticisms of the Highlanders may have suggested to others that criticism of the Glengarrians was imprudent.

From not long after the publication of the Connor novels and the Dundonald visit of 1903, we can trace a divergence of the two mystiques of Glengarry. The insider's mystique has continued to flourish down to the present, though it probably took a more subdued form after the first ten years or so of this century. The *Glengarry News* has always played a noble part in sustaining this part of the Glengarry culture. But the outsider's mystique dwindled swiftly from a date which, although necessarily not very precise, can be set about ten years after the beginning of this century. It has never wholly died, of course. And in recent years, with an influx of English-speaking outsiders into the county, many of them interested in the Scottish culture so long established there, it has shown unmistakable signs of new life. As evidence of this, one may point, for example, to the books and paintings of Douglas Fales.

In 1922, at a time when the outsider's mystique of Glengarry was already in decline, we find a touch of the Glengarry mystique in no less a newspaper than the London *Times*, which said in an obituary of Sir Donald Macmaster:

> Glengarry is peopled by Scottish-Canadian settlers,
> men of Highland breed, holding firmly to their
> Presbyterian faith and Scottish customs, hard workers,
> simple livers, good friends, and fierce haters.
> Seventy years ago it was more Scottish than
> the Highland glens from which its settlers had
> come....From his youth Donald Macmaster was satu-
> rated with Scottish tradition.

It is a paradox in the decline of the outsider's mystique of

Glengarry, that it occurred so soon after the immense success of *The Man From Glengarry* and *Glengarry School Days*. As one of the causes of its decline, it may be noted that the age of the Glengarry contractors and lumbermen, whose achievements had done so much to feed the reputation of Glengarry, was ending; the older contractors and lumbermen were dying off, and few new recruits from Glengarry were joining their ranks. It may be argued that the achievements of Glengarrians and descendants of Glengarrians did not decline; but even if they remained constant, they were bound by contrast to seem less as Glengarry, with what was now its shrinking population, was ever more engulfed in the expanding population of North America. Outsiders, too, perhaps caught a glimpse of or sensed the fact that Glengarry was drifting into a period of economic stagnation and of failing morale—subjects we have already discussed. But more important, perhaps, than anything else, was a simple change in intellectual and literary fashions.

Nostalgia, romanticism, and sentimentality, all dear to the heart of the Victorians, had been important ingredients in the admiration for the Glengarry Highlanders and for Highlanders in general. By the early 1920's, these commodities were out of fashion among all but the older and more unchanging writers and intellectuals. The outsider's mystique of Glengarry had depended heavily on journalism for its survival and spread, and journalists everywhere, understanding that it was a new age and that the intellectual and literary climates had changed, must have adjusted their attitudes towards Glengarry accordingly. Similarly, ordinary members of the public must have adjusted their ideas of Glengarry to fit the new outlook. Authors continued to publish works based on the Glengarry mystique: Ralph Connor in his novels and autobiography of the 1930's, Grace Campbell in her Glengarry novels of the 1940's, J.E. McIntosh in the popular articles published under the pen name of "Sandy Fraser" from 1909 to 1948, Dorothy Dumbrille in her histories and *All This Difference*. But the Glengarry mystique could no longer have the general appeal it had had in the propitious era when *The Man From Glengarry* and *Glengarry School Days* were published.

Among Glengarrians and the descendants of Glengarrians, it seems unlikely that the mystique of Glengarry will die in the foreseeable future. Meanwhile, they can be proud that in a country as bare of legend as a new country such as Canada must necessarily be, their people created a vibrant legend that had for a time a wide appeal—the legend of Glengarry.

x      x      x

REMINISCENCE
[on the 150th anniversary of St. Andrew's, Williamstown]
1962

Could I stand once more, as I did of yore,
    In the choir of that old stone Church;
Could I finger again those organ-keys
    And the same old Hymn-book search
For "St. George's Edinburgh", "Martyrdom",
    "Dunfermline", "Evan", "Dundee",
"Kilmarnock", "Old One Hundred", "Jackson", "Duke Street,"
And "Coleshill" in minor key!

Could I sit with the choir in the corner there,
    In the hush of "Communion Day",
As the farmer saints distribute the Bread
    And the cup in the auld Scots way,—
G.H. McGillivray, "Sandy Cing",
    "Sandy Ossian" and "Alex Jim Roy",
"Hughie Donald", "the Colonel" and "Curly Mac",—
    No surnames these need employ!

Could I hear again the tones of the deep-toned bell
    For every service rung,—
One hundred and fifty years that bell
    In St. Andrews' belfry swung!
Could I hear again the beloved voice
    Of that saint in the pulpit there,
As the Spirit of God inspired his words
    In sermon and in prayer!

Above the pulpit a beautiful
    Stained-glass window says,
"Mine House shall be called an House of Prayer
    For all People", so he prays,
"Make us know Thy will and, when it is known,
    May no foolish pride or our self-will
Prevent us from doing it". Those words live,
    Though the voice is forever still.

On Sunday each family filled its own pew,
    In fancy I see from the choir
Robertson, Falkner, McKillop and Brown,
    Cattanach, Jamieson, "Archie Squire",
"Alex Philip", the Johnsons, Benning, Bethune,
    McCrimmon, Shiells, Farquharson,
Duguid, McKenzie, McNeil, McIntyre,
    Chisolm, Fraser and Murchison.
Sometimes McBain, McPherson, Dunlop,
    Though these were "Wee Frees", ye ken;
We might go to their church in the afternoon,—
    "Reverend Kenneth" was preacher then,
And Reverend Watson held, till his death,
    "Auld Kirk" in the Temperance Hall.
Three Presbyterian Kirk in one
    Small village! (Guid Scots folk all!) —

Fergusons,—"The Widow" and "Johnnie Bush",
    "Big William", the "Captain", Dingwall,
Mowat, McLennan, McLaren and Grant,
    Campbells and Burgess and Hall.

(The fathers bewhiskered and dignified,
　　Boys and girls so surprisingly neat,
I remember the bonnets the mothers wore
　　And how Curly Mac's shoes would squeak!)

McGregor, McMaster, Jack "skillagalee",
　　Kennedy, Raymond and Slack,
Smith, Snyder, Dickson, the Partridges,
　　(and Ed. Shinnett's bass at the back!)
McDougall, McArthur, McCulloch and Ross,
And McDonalds of course "effermore,"—
Macdonald, McDonnel and MacDonnell
　　From the South Branch, the Glen and the Gore.

From the Concessions as far as the Fourth,
　　From Finney's to McGillivray's Bridge,
They came to Church every week in the year
　　And deemed it a privilege!
They are sleeping now where they used to wait
　　After church with a greeting kind,
A smile and a hand-shake, warm and firm,—
　　Their names on those stones you'll find.

Long years have flown, but I'll ever see
　　Those beautiful maple-trees,
Hear the robin, song-sparrow and bobolink.
　　Smell the flower-scented breeze,
And hear those voices of long ago
　　In their soft "Glengarry drawl",
By the old stone Church with its sunlit spire
　　Pointing Heavenward over all.

Gertrude Wood

# BIBLIOGRAPHY

The present bibliography is intended as a brief introduction to research in Glengarry history and as a guide for those general readers who want to read some of the many worthwhile books relating to Glengarry.

Further references (mostly relating to specific problems in Glengarry history) can be found in the notes to the individual chapters of this book, and the present authors hope shortly to publish a book-length *Bibliography of Glengarry County* containing a more thorough treatment of its bibliography than is possible here.

This is the first attempt at a book-length comprehensive history devoted solely to Glengarry, but Glengarry has been treated in two histories of the United Counties: Judge J.F. Pringle, *Lunenburgh or the Old Eastern District* (1890), and J.G. Harkness, *Stormont Dundas and Glengarry: A History* (1946). The researcher who has at heart the principles of the historian's trade will perhaps at first value Pringle's book more highly than Harkness', because Pringle asks the kind of questions historians think most important to have answered. The present authors must enter a plea for Harkness, however. The more they have used his volume, the more highly they have come to esteem him. He has two outstanding merits: (1) he gathered in one convenient volume a vast mass of biographical and genealogical data which otherwise his successors would have had to search out for themselves at great expense of time and labour, and (2) he is a remarkably accurate historian, and what he has said in print is the result of an amount of painful sifting of the evidence which is not immediately apparent to the reader. All Mr. Harkness' years as crown attorney of SDG prepared him well for the judicial sifting of the history of Glengarry! One of the present authors admits that he undervalued Harkness till he had minutely re-examined the sources for the life of Cariboo Cameron while preparing a sketch of that hero for the *Dictionary of Canadian Biography*. He then found that although Harkness apparently did no archival research on Cameron, he had so carefully sifted the printed and traditional evidence, and had separated fact from fiction with such a master's hand, that every other passage of the book took on a new value in his (the present writer's) eyes.

Histories dealing with aspects of Glengarry include: John Fraser, *Canadian Pen and Ink Sketches* (1890); J.A. Macdonell, *Sketches Illustrating the Early Settlement and History of Glengarry in Canada* (1893); A.W. McDougald's excellent series of articles on Glengarry history published in the *Glengarry News*, 30 December 1932—29 December 1933; W. Boss's regimental history, *The Stormont, Dundas and Glengarry Highlanders 1783-1951* (1952); Dorothy Dumbrille, *Up and Down the Glens* (1954) and *Braggart in My Step* (1956); Robert J. Fraser, *As Others See Us* (1959), which has much on the Loch Garry area; Maxville Women's Institute, *History of Maxville and the Community* (1967?); *The Land of Plenty* (1968?), which has interesting sketches of the Glengarrians who settled at Plenty, Saskatchewan; *The MacLeods of Glengarry* (1972); Rhodes Grant, *The Story of Martintown* (1974) and *Horse and Buggy Days in Martintown* (1976); Ruth D. Mowat, *All's Fair* (1976) on Williamstown Fair; *Because People Came* (Laggan Public School, 1974); and Clarence Ostrom's lively and unfailingly absorbing manuscript history of Alexandria (copy in Dunvegan Museum).

Alex W. Fraser's *Gravestones of Glengarry* (Vol. I, 1976; Vol. II, 1978), will on completion be a superb collection in 10 or 12 volumes of Glengarry genealogical data.

J.K. Galbraith's *The Scotch* (1964) does not mention the Glengarry Scots but is about a group of Elgin County Scots remarkably similar to them.

Robert Sellar's superb *History of The County of*

*Huntingdon* (1888) has many references to Glengarry and describes pioneer conditions no doubt very similar to those of early Glengarry.

Much data on Glengarry is found in two small but good periodicals, the yearbook of the Glengarry Historical Society (published annually since 1962), and the newsletter of the Glengarry Genealogical Society, edited by Alex W. Fraser.

Among the articles relating to Glengarry history we especially draw attention to three influential early articles: John MacLennan, ex-M.P., "The Early Settlement of Glengarry" (1887), George Sandfield MacDonald, "The Literary Aspect of the Keltic Settlement in the Counties of Stormont and Glengarry" (1887), Archibald MacNab, ex-M.P., "The Settlement of the Township of Lochiel, Glengarry" (1892), all in *Transactions of the Celtic Society of Montreal.*

The following theses relate to Glengarry history: J.R. MacKay, "The Regional Geography of the Lower Ottawa Valley" (Docteur ès Arts, U. of Montreal, 1949); W.A. Douglas Jackson, "The Lands along the Upper St. Lawrence" (Ph.D., U. of Maryland, 1953); D.M. Ray, "Settlement and Rural Outmigration in Easternmost Ontario" (M.A., U. of Ottawa, 1961); P.K. MacLeod, "Gualainn Ri Gualainn: A Study of Concentrations of Scottish Settlement in Nineteenth Century Ontario" (M.A., Carleton U., 1972); D.G. Cartwright, "French Canadian Colonization in Eastern Ontario to 1910" (Ph.D., U. of Western Ontario, 1973); J.D. McRae, "Recent Changes in Land Ownership...A Case Study in Eastern Ontario" (M.A., U. of Guelph, 1977), based on Lancaster and Lochiel Townships.

Novels wholly or partly set in Glengarry are Rev. James Drummond, *A Forest Flower* (n.d.); Margaret Murray Robertson, *Shenac's Work at Home* (1866); A. Paul Gardiner, *The House of Cariboo* (1900), a highly ficitionalized treatment of the Cariboo Cameron story; Ralph Connor, *The Man from Glengarry* (1901), *Glengarry School Days* (1902), and *Torches Through the Bush* (1934); Robert Sellar, *Morven* (1911), about the coming of the U.E. Loyalists; Rev. J.D. McEwen, *Sandy McDonald in Brazil*

(1921); C.H. MacGillivray, *The Shadow of Tradition* (1927); John Harlaw (pen name of Rev. G. Watt Smith), *Glenlyon* (1936), an unfriendly look at the Maxville-St. Elmo area; Dorothy Dumbrille, *All This Difference* (1945); and Stephen Notar, *The St. James Quest* (1976), which the author tells us is not based on any personal acquaintance with the county.

Autobiographies by Glengarrians or containing material on Glengarry are: Rev. A.H. Scott, *Ten Years in my First Charge* (1891); Rev. John Anderson, *Reminiscences and Incidents* (1910); Daniel McLaughlin, *Chronicle of a Northern Pacific Veteran* (1930); D.C. Macintosh's chapter in *Contemporary American Theology: Theological Autobiographies*, ed. V. Ferm, Vol. I (1932); Ralph Connor, *Postscript to Adventure* (1938); Rev. G. Watt Smith, *From the Plough to the Pulpit: A Plain Pastor's Pathway* (1947); James Begg's autobiography published in Cornwall *Standard-Freeholder*, 7 instalments, 1 Dec. 1959 ff; J.J. Macdonald's autobiography in *Globe and Mail*, 14 December 1974; and Sir Edward Peacock's autobiography, 55 pp. typescript, unpublished. E.A. Howes, *With a Glance Backward* (1939), set in the Vankleek Hill area, and Al Lanoue's *The Funny Side of Farming* (1972), set in the Winchester area, are delightful memoirs of a kind of farming once well known in Glengarry.

Biographical dictionaries in which Glengarrians appear include the following: G.M. Rose, *A Cyclopaedia of Canadian Biography*, Vols. I and II (1886-1888); Rev. William Cochrane, *The Canadian Album: Men of Canada*, 4 vols. (1891-1895); H.J. Morgan, *The Canadian Men and Women of the Time* (1898 and, completely redone, 1912); biographical dictionary of Norwesters in W.S. Wallace, ed. *Documents relating to the North West Company* (1934); W.S. Wallace, ed. *The Macmillan Dictionary of Canadian Biography*, 3rd ed. (1963); *Dictionary of Canadian Biography*, multi-volume (1966-   ); J.K. Johnson, ed. *The Canadian Directory of Parliament 1867-1967* (1968), for lives of M.P.'s and Senators; and the various forms of *Who's Who*.

In the second half of the nineteenth century, many business directories were issued listing the businesses of the various Ontario towns, such as the *Canada Directory*. The Ontario Archives have conveniently put a collection of these on microfilm and have made a typed guide list to aid users of them.

A good many statutes from the earliest times to the present relate specifically to Glengarry. The present authors have what they believe to be a fairly complete list of them; the actual texts of the statutes can be found in the volumes of printed statutes accessible in large libraries.

The official printed debates of the Canadian Parliament begin in 1875 (a scholarly project is under way to fill the gap 1867-1874), of the Senate in 1871, and of the Legislative Assembly of Ontario in 1948. The contribution of Glengarry's M.P.'s to debates in the nineteenth century and of Dr. McMillan during his 30 years as Senator (1884-1914) proved unexpectedly interesting and contains bits and pieces of Glengarry information. Debates earlier than the above dates were often reported in newspapers, and see also the sources for pre-Confederation debates and proceedings cited in the notes to Chapters II and III.

Since Confederation, the Federal and Ontario governments have both published volumes of Sessional Papers, which contain a vast array of statistical and other information on the economy, education, and on almost every aspect of human life.

A major Canadian census is now taken every ten years (in the years ending in -1) and a minor census is taken half-way between the major censuses (in the years ending in -6). Ontario censuses in one form or another go back far into the history of the province. Usually the census findings are consulted in the printed census reports, but for the years 1851, -61, and -71, the manuscripts of the house-by-house findings of the census takers are available on microfilm.

Governments at various levels have sponsored reports of various kinds and of varying quality relating to Glengarry's area of the province. Researchers should not miss: *Ontario*

*Agricultural Commission Report* (1881); B.C. Matthews and N.R. Richards, *Soil Survey of Glengarry County* (Canada and Ontario Departments of Agriculture, 1957); *Background Information for the Glengarry Official Plan* (1973; revised 1974); and *United Counties of Stormont, Dundas and Glengarry Roads Needs Study 1970-1979* (n.d.).

Newspapers are one of the best sources for Glengarry history. Fortunately, as microfilming programs continue their good work, more and more back files of Canadian newspapers are made readily available to the researcher. For information on what newspapers have been microfilmed, consult a reference librarian at any university or other large library. The same librarian will also give you good clues on how to go about finding back files of newspapers which have not been microfilmed. Cornwall newspapers have always covered Glengarry news, though often with more attention to the front than the rear townships.

Cornwall has had newspapers since at least the 1830's but many early issues have been lost. The National Library and Ontario Archives have good collections (original and microfilm), mainly from the nineteenth century; for further information, consult their detailed directories of their holdings. Neither of these sources when we last checked had a copy of a 3-reel microfilm of the Cornwall *Standard* and *Freeholder* 1905-1910 made by Standard Microfilm of Scarborough.

In the above pages, we have already discussed the birth pangs of the Glengarry press in the 1880's. The National Library has one of the treasures of Glengarriana—an almost complete file (1880-1882, originals not microfilm) of the *Glengarry Times* of Lancaster, Ontario. The National Library and the Ontario Archives also have some originals of the *Glengarrian*, of Alexandria, which was published from 1883 or 84 to 1913; for these, see the detailed directories.

The *Glengarry News* began in 1892 and we are glad to say not only survives but flourishes as a cherished Glengarry institution. The editors have always given especial attention to making the *News* a newspaper of record for the events of Glengarry history. Complete back-files (except for one missing year, 1895) survive at the newspaper office in Alexandria, and the years 1892-1956 have been microfilmed in 39 reels for the Ontario Archives. We suspect that scholars ten years from now will not believe what we must now with shame and sorrow report, namely that at the time of writing not one library in Glengarry or Stormont had a copy of this splendid microfilm. Incidentally, the microfilm of the *Glengarry News* also includes a few years of the *Glengarrian* which have survived at the *Glengarry News* office.

The *Alexandria Times*, edited by J. Albert Laurin, was published from 1915-1955, but unfortunately no back files were preserved, and only a few copies in private ownership appear to survive.

The *Advertiser* (1904?-?) and *The Advance* (1908?-?) were published at Maxville but we have not found so much as one issue of them. *The Maxville Messenger*, edited by the Rev. George W. Allan or Allen, was a well got-up but short lived monthly magazine with a strong interest in the local history of the area. The Baptist Archives at McMaster University have five issues, all from 1920.

The Huntingdon *Gleaner*, edited by Robert Sellar, has been microfilmed for the years 1863-1900. It has good coverage of the southern part of Glengarry.

The Vankleek Hill *Review* began in 1893 and still flourishes. Students of Glengarry history will find it useful for the north-east corner of Glengarry. Back files are available at Vankleek Hill and have been microfilmed (copy in Ontario Archives) from 1893-1897. This microfilm contains much Glengarry material (more than the *Review* was to publish at a later date) and by a lucky stroke fills in admirably for the year missing from the *Glengarry News* files, 1895.

Ottawa, Montreal, Toronto, and other Canadian newspapers have always published a little Glengarry news from time to time. A useful source for Glengarry is the Montreal *Witness*, which has been microfilmed for the years 1862-1879. Its rival, the Roman Catholic *True Witness*, carried reports on some Glengarry matters, mostly religious; the Toronto Public Library has a convenient file of originals, 1850-1878. The *Farmer's Sun*, the newspaper of the Patrons of Industry, reported closely on Glengarry for a few years, 1892-1895. Otherwise, it is best to consult national newspapers only for their reporting on particular incidents in Glengarry history. It takes a lot of work to get through even one year of a newspaper, especially if it is a daily.

The present authors have prepared carefully indexed notes on the Glengarry material in the available Cornwall newspapers prior to 1910, in all the surviving Glengarry newspapers, in the *Gleaner, Witness,* and *True Witness* for the years named, and in the Vankleek Hill Review for 1893-1897, and in selected national newspapers, and they hope that at some time these notes will be microfilmed for the use of all students of Glengarry.

A detailed Auld Lang Syne column in the *Glengarry News* provides, over a ten-year cycle, a masterly summary of all the back files of the *Glengarry News* up to the beginning of the cycle, and is a valuable guide for all users of the *Glengarry News* microfilm.

The National Archives (Public Archives of Canada) and the Ontario Archives both have rich resources for researchers in Glengarry history; unfortunately, for reasons of space we can only give a summary here of the best they have to offer.

*National Archives.* For the early years of Glengarry, five huge collections of documents are indispensable sources: (1) the Haldimand Papers, which cover the U.E. Loyalist era, (2) the G Series, correspondence from the British authorities to the colonial officials in Canada, (3) C.O. 42, correspondence from Canada to the British government, (4) Upper Canada Sundries, internal correspondence of the Upper Canada government, (5) Land Petitions. For the use of these collections, and for the location of the calendars and indices which will simplify the task of spotting the Glengarry items, consult the archives staff. These collections sorely try the patience of researchers, but they are also very rich for our county, and when the researcher has stilled the last sobs he will find that the effort has been well worth while. Copies of some of these are also available at the Ontario Archives. The National Archives also contain papers of a distinguished Glengarry family, the Macgillivrays of McGillivray Bridge, or Dalcrombie, in 53 vols.—a superb source for nineteenth-century Glengarry history. Smaller but also useful Glengarry collections include the papers of John McLennan, M.P., and five notebooks (MG29c29) of data from interviews, other Glengarry lore in the 1880's, probably collected by George Sandfield Macdonald.

*Ontario Archives.* The several card indexes in the Reading Room provide a reasonably good guide to the many Glengarry sources here, but remember to check under all the possible Glengarry names: townships, villages, Mac-everything, etc. The bound inventories to specific collections are also important. The archives have an immense and varied collection of administrative and judicial records of SDG, which we cannot describe in detail here. We are afraid we must simply refer the researcher to the friendly and well-informed staff of these well-run and hospitable archives for guidance in the probing of this material. Absolutely essential for the researcher in pioneer Glengarry are the Township Papers, a collection of letters and official papers generated in the process of granting land. All kinds of material got stirred into this rich mass, some of it of great value for social history. We never see the pioneers more closely than we do in reading the Township Papers. The arrangement is by townships, with a separate file for Indian Lands; unhappily, the Township Papers for Conc. 14-21 of Indian Lands are missing. Among the collections of private papers of Glengarry interest, the following are especially important: (1) the typescript copies of the letters of Bishop Macdonell (originals in archiepiscopal archives, Kingston), (2) papers of Father George A. Hay, (3) papers of Andrew McBain—a small collection which gives us some of our most intimate glimpses of the mind of Glengarrians in the 1870's and 80's, (4) the massive collection of papers of Big

Rory McLennan, which includes some of the papers of his kinsman and fellow contractor, D.R. MacDonald, (5) the papers of Father Ewen Macdonald, the accomplished Glengarry genealogist and historian.

In Toronto, Glengarry researchers should also consult (1) the rich collections of the United Church Archives, at Victoria College, University of Toronto, where the nineteenth-century Presbyterian journals will prove especially rewarding, and (2) the King's College papers in the University of Toronto Library, for letters and other records concerning the King's College lands and their tenants in Glengarry.

The Centre de recherche en civilisation canadienne-française at the University of Ottawa has a good collection of material (correspondence, clippings, etc.) on the French Canadians in Glengarry and especially on those two unhappy subjects, the Green Valley School Case and the school dispute in Alexandria 1920-1922. We must however register our opinion and offer a warning to the effect that this collection reports much more fully and satisfactorily what outsiders thought than what the Glengarry French Canadians thought.

The Museums at Dunvegan and Williamstown in Glengarry have small but good collections of printed and manuscript materials—the nucleus, perhaps, of what will one day be the Glengarry Archives.

Glengarry County has its own Registry Office (for land ownership records) at Alexandria, but Glengarry wills are filed in the United Counties Surrogate Court offices at Cornwall. The nineteenth-century part of both these collections can be consulted on the microfilms made by the Genealogical Society of the Church of Jesus Christ of Latter Day Saints (copies in Ontario Archives). Wills which did not get into the Surrogate Court files can often be found in the Registry Office files, with the other papers for the deceased's landed property.

The records of the Glengarry municipalities are incomplete and we have found those we have consulted to be a disappointingly barren source. Lancaster Township has records only from recent years. The Kenyon records, once supposed lost, have recently been recovered, in whole or in part. Charlottenburgh's records (including a fine series of assessors' rolls) go back to the 1850's and are to be found in the township offices at Williamstown and in the National Archives (Macgillivray Papers and elsewhere). There is a microfilm of the early Lochiel papers in the Ontario Archives; otherwise, see originals at township office. Alexandria's records survive only from the 1920's and even after this the *Glengarry News* is the fullest guide to proceedings.

The Glengarry churches have vital records (births, deaths, marriages) and often other records as well. The Ontario Archives have a selection of these (usually copies)—see the indexes in the Reading Room. We confidently look forward to the completion of the project now in progress under the direction of our admired colleague Alex W. Fraser which will provide researchers with accurate transcripts of the vital records held by the Glengarry churches.

The diaries from Glengarry seem to be relatively few, but there are several excellent ones (all unpublished) which we have found most useful: James Cameron (of Cameron's Island)'s diary for 1854-1902, copy in Ontario Archives; Angus MacMillan's diary (continued by his children) for 1862-1889, 1881-1909, in National Archives; John McGregor's diary for 1877 to 1883, in the library of the University of British Columbia; and J.D. Ross's diary, kept about half the time 1917-1975, owned by Ewan Ross.

A considerable number of tapes of interviews relating to Glengarry have been made. One might well reply "Où sont les neiges d'antan?" in reply to the question of where many of these have gone, but there are two accessible collections:
(1) owned by the Multicultural History Society of Ontario which gave the present authors and Dr. Norbert Ferré of Cornwall grants totalling $2400 for Glengarry interviews. Dr. Ferré supervised the interviewers, who were Alan Haskvitz and Mrs.

Patricia Kulick. Sixteen Dutch Glengarrians, 25 French-Canadian Glengarrians, and seven Anglophone Glengarrians were interviewed.

(2) owned by Ewan Ross. He hopes to present this collection to some body in Glengarry as soon as a responsible body appears—which has not happened to date.

The most useful maps for students of Glengarry are the present-day ordinance survey maps and the Ontario government white-print maps, but maps of historical interest include: Patrick McNiff's map showing physical features and lot holders' names from 7th Charlottenburgh to Lake Front and from 2nd Lancaster to Lake Front, 1786; J.G. Chewett's map of Ontario east of the Rideau, 1825; Baron de Rottenburg's map of Glengarry area, c. 1850-1851?; F.H. Walling's map of Eastern Ontario showing landholders' names on lots, 1862; and maps in the *Illustrated Historical Atlas of the Counties of Stormont, Dundas and Glengarry* (H. Belden & Co., 1879).

Glengarry photographs are available in the large collection of Ewan Ross. A selection of the work of the Alexandria photographer Duncan Donovan has been published in *City Work at Country Prices*, ed. Jennifer Harper (1977).

# THE PROGRESS OF PATENTING AND
## LAND CLAIMS IN GLENGARRY
## COUNTY TO 13 MAY 1801

In the following tables, dates of patents are from Domesday Book, Queen's Park, Toronto (information also available in Registry Office, Alexandria). For the Clergy and Crown Reserves, Domesday Book was again our source of information, but see also the useful map of these in SDG in W.A. Douglas Jackson, "The Lands Along the Upper St. Lawrence," Ph. D. thesis (University of Maryland, 1953), Fig. 18. Information in col. E is based on a list of land certificates to 13 May 1801 in Ontario Archives, RG 22 Series 9. Parts of the list have been lost and consequently the figures in col. E could considerably understate the number of claims. Col. E. simply states the number of claims recorded on the list, without any attempt to eliminate those for lots covered by a patent. In the table for Lochiel, the lots A and the lots in the gore (all on the eastern border of the township) are omitted.

KENYON

| CONCESSION | A<br>TOTAL OF LOTS | B<br>TOTAL OF CLERGY RESERVE LOTS | C<br>TOTAL OF CROWN RESERVE LOTS | D<br>TOTAL OF LOTS PATENTED AS OF 13 MAY 1801 | E<br>TOTAL OF LOTS CLAIMED AS OF 13 MAY 1801 | F<br>TOTAL OF LOTS NEITHER RESERVED, PATENTED, OR CLAIMED, AS OF 13 MAY 1801 |
|---|---|---|---|---|---|---|
| 9 | 37 | 37 | 0 | 0 | 0 | 0 |
| 8 | 37 | 26 | 0 | 6½ | 7 or 8 | 2 |
| 7 | 37 | 3 | 0 | 14 | 29½ or 30 | 4 |
| 6 | 37 | 5 | 0 | 14 | 26 | 4 |
| 5 | 37 | 2 | 0 | 16½ | 29½ or 30 | 3½ |
| 4 | 37 | 1 | 0 | 17 | 28½ or 29 | 5 |
| 3 | 37 | 1 | 0 | 19 | 31 | 3¾ |
| 2 | 37 | 1 or 3 | 0 | 20 | 23½ | 6½ or 4½ |
| 1 | 37 | ½ | 0 | 21¼ or 21½ | 26¼ or 27¾ | 8¼ |

CHARLOTTENBURGH

| CONCESSION | A<br>TOTAL OF LOTS | B<br>TOTAL OF CLERGY RESERVE LOTS | C<br>TOTAL OF CROWN RESERVE LOTS | D<br>TOTAL OF LOTS PAT-ENTED AS OF 13 MAY 1801 | E<br>TOTAL OF LOTS CLAIMED AS OF 13 MAY 1801 | F<br>TOTAL OF LOTS NEITHER RESERVED, PATENTED, OR CLAIMED, AS OF 13 MAY 1801 |
|---|---|---|---|---|---|---|
| 9 | 37 | 0 | 0 | $18\frac{3}{4}$ | 29 or 30 | 6 or 6 $\frac{1}{2}$ |
| 8 | 37 | 0 | 0 | $20\frac{1}{2}$ | 23 or 25 | 9 or 10 |
| 7 | 37 | 0 | 0 | 9 | 13 | 18 |

## LOCHIEL

| CONCESSION | A TOTAL OF LOTS | B TOTAL OF CLERGY RESERVE LOTS | C TOTAL OF CROWN RESERVE LOTS | D TOTAL OF LOTS PAT-ENTED AS OF 13 MAY 1801 | E TOTAL OF LOTS CLAIMED AS OF 13 MAY 1801 | F TOTAL OF LOTS NEITHER RESERVED, PATENTED, OR CLAIMED, AS OF 13 May 1801 |
|---|---|---|---|---|---|---|
| 9 | 38 | 9 | 13 | 7 (all to Samuel Henderson) | 6 | 3 |
| 8 | 38 | 12 | 11 | 4 | 5½ | 7½ |
| 7 | 38 | 7 | 5 | 15 | 18 | 7 |
| 6 | 38 | 4 | 6 | 12 | 13 | 10 |
| 5 | 38 | 3 | 13 | 8 or 11 | 15 | 7 |
| 4 | 38 | 7 | 13 | 8 | 13 | 5 |
| 3 | 38 | 2 | 6 | 11 | 10½ or 11 | 14 or 14½ |
| 2 | 38 | 7 | 9 | 12 | 10 | 6 |
| 1 | 38 | 7½ or 8 | 7 | 12½ | 10½ | 6 to 7½ |

LANCASTER

| CONCESSION | A TOTAL OF LOTS | B TOTAL OF CLERGY RESERVE LOTS | C TOTAL OF CROWN RESERVE LOTS | D TOTAL OF LOTS PATENTED AS OF 13 MAY 1801 | E TOTAL OF LOTS CLAIMED AS OF 13 MAY 1801 | F TOTAL OF LOTS NEITHER RESERVED, PATENTED, OR CLAIMED, AS OF 13 MAY 1801 |
|---|---|---|---|---|---|---|
| 9 | 38 | 1 | 6 but some are incomplete lots | 10 | 15 to 19 | 11 to 12½ |
| 8 | 34 | 1¼ | 0 | 5½ | 15 or 15½ | 15 or 15½ |
| 7 | 29 | 1 | 0 | 8 | 17½ to 19 | 8 to 9½ |
| 6 | 31 | 1 | 0 | 2 | 18 or 18⅓ | 10 or 10⅓ |
| 5 | 32 | a little less than 4 | 0 | 3 | 10½ or 11½ | 14½ or 15½ |
| 4 | 32 | 6½ | 0 | 4¼ | 7¼ to 8¾ | 16¼ or 17¼ |
| 3 | 35 | 5½ | 0 | 9¼ | 14 to 16½ | ? |
| 2 | 36 | 4 | 0 | 8½ | 9½ to 13½ | ? |
| 1 | 38 | 0 | 0 | 8 | 9½ to 15 | 19 to 23 |

# NOTES

*Abbreviations*

AH      Anonymous history of Glengarry, probably by John Cattanach McMillan (1826-1913), stepson of Donald Cattanach of Laggan. Length: 21 typed pages, foolscap. Copies owned by the present authors.

BMacd      Bishop Macdonell Papers in Ontario Archives (typescript copies of correspondence in Archdiocesan Archives, Kingston).

FA      *Farmer's Advocate*

FH      *Freeholder* (Cornwall newspaper)

FS      *Farmer's Sun* (newspaper of Patrons of Industry)

Gl'n      *The Glengarrian* (Alexandria newspaper)

GN      *The Glengarry News*

GT      *The Glengarry Times* (Lancaster newspaper)

*Macg*      Macgillivray Papers in Public Archives of Canada (papers of Macgillivrays of McGillivray Bridge, Charlottenburgh)

McL      Col. R.R. McLennan Papers in Ontario Archives

PAC      Public Archives of Canada

PAO      Ontario Archives

Pringle      J.F. Pringle, *Lunenburgh or the Old Eastern District* (1890).

R'r      *Reporter* (Cornwall newspaper)

S      *Standard* (Cornwall newspaper)

TP      Township Papers in Ontario Archives

W      *Witness* (Montreal newspaper)

Unless otherwise identified, population figures are normally from the census.

CHAPTER I
"THE LAND WE LIVE IN AND THE LAND WE LEFT"

KNOYDART SETTLERS: Johnson and Haldimand, PAC, *Report on Canadian Archives...1896* (Ottawa, 1897), p. 76. Fr. Roderick Macdonell: *ibid.*, pp. 76-77.

PHILADELPHIA SHIP: A.M. Pope, "A Scotch Catholic Settlement in Canada," *Catholic World*, Oct. 1881, pp. 73-74; petition of 9 December 1835 in TP, Lochiel, con. 1, lots 31,32. In *The Shadow of Tradition* the ship is called the *Britannia*. Notes on the early history of St. Raphaels collected apparently by George Sandfield Macdonald in the 1880's (PAC, MG29c29) use the names *McDonald* and *Cochrane* for the ship(s) on which the emigrants of 1786 arrived, so perhaps the ship which went to Philadelphia was the *Cochrane*.

BRITISH QUEEN: PAC, C.O. 42/71/43v-45v.

ALEXANDER MACDONELL (GREENFIELD): J.G. Harkness, *Stormont, Dundas and Glengarry* (1946), p. 50; Rev. Brother Alfred, *Catholic Pioneers in Upper Canada* (1947), pp. 168, 170. However, an author descended from Alexander Macdonell seems a little doubtful of this tradition; J.A. Macdonell (Greenfield), *Sketches Illustrating the Early Settlement and History of Glengarry* (1893), p. 131.

1794 SETTLERS: Alexander MacLeod's petition, PAC, Upper Canada Land Grant Petitions, Reel C-2139; *The MacLeods of Glengarry: The Genealogy of a Clan* (Iroquois, Ont.) pp. 58-61 &c.

1802 SETTLERS: *Quebec Gazette*, 2-30 Sept. 1802. The reports of ship arrivals for 11 March 1802-20 Jan. 1803 have been examined in this paper. Customs officials: PAC, C.O. 42/330/161-161v. For the history of these emigrants, see also Lord Selkirk, *Lord Selkirk's Diary* (Champlain Soc., 1958), pp. 199-200, and Somerled MacMillan, *The Emigration of Lochaber MacMillans to Canada in 1802* (1958).

1st GLENGARRY FENCIBLES: "Account of emigration and services of Catholic Highlanders," in H.J. Somers, *The Life and Times of...[Bishop Macdonell]* (Washington, 1931); Fr. George Corbet, *A Retrospect* (n.d.); and Bishop Alexander Macdonell, "A Page from the History of the Glengarry Highlanders," *Canadian Literary Magazine*, April 1833; Lord Hobart's letters, PAC, C.O. 42/331/35-36v, and 42/334/19-19v, printed in *Report on Canadian Archives...1896*, pp. 78-79, and Hunter's Reply, *ibid.*, p. 79. Landlords...bill:43 George III c. 56. 16 men: PAO, TP for Glengarry; Father Macdonell to Bathurst, 1817: PAC, C.O. 42/360/195-196. John MacLennan, "The Early Settlement of Glengarry," *Transactions of the Celtic Society of Montreal* (1887), p. 118. Johnson on Lake Township: in E.A. Cruikshank, *The Settlement of the United Empire Loyalists* (1966), p. 101.

DIVISION OF CHARLOTTENBURGH: date from Pringle, p. 193, but where is the documentary evidence? D'Arcy Boulton, *Sketch of His Majesty's Province in Upper Canada* (London, 1805), p. 82, said that

681

Kenyon "is chiefly inhabited by emigrants from Scotland, and appears to thrive very fast." Kenyon was apparently named after Chief Justice Lord Kenyon. We have not been able to trace any connection between our Glengarry and Kenyon in Lancashire England, but one of the Glengarry founding families, the Falkners, are said to have been from Lancashire.

DIVISION OF LANCASTER: by 59 George III c. 3.

CLOTHING AND FOOD: *Mrs. Simcoe's Diary*, ed. M.Q. Innis (1965), p. 67; Cyrus Cuneo's painting of the Highlander is reproduced in PAO, *Report* 1930. A visitor to Glengarry in 1814 quoted in *A Family Memoir of the Macdonalds of Keppoch* (1885) said, p. 146, that "The appearance of the people is at all times respectable, but I was delighted on seeing them in church of a Sunday; the men clothed in good English cloth, and many of the women wore the Highland plaid." Lord Selkirk, *Diary*, p. 199, said the Glengarrians "made a good deal of Cloth—all of their own wear, except a little fine cloth which is bought for Sunday dress." Corn meal: historical notes apparently by George Sandfield Macdonald, in PAC, MG29c29. James Begg's autobiography, typescript in PAO, Misc. Coll. 1887, and printed in *Standard-Freeholder* (Cornwall), 1 Dec. 1959 ff.

WOODCUTTING: The Indians of St. Regis stated in 1784 that French Canadians had "paid considerable sums of money" to cut timber in the large tract these Indians claimed on the north shore of the St. Lawrence, Cruikshank, *Settlement*, pp. 58-59. BEAVER MEADOW: *W*, 4 Sept. 1894. FINCH SURVEY: PAC, Upper Canada Sundries, pp. 10283-86.

ESTABLISHING INDIAN LANDS: Correspondence in Cruikshank, *Settlement*, pp. 58-59, 62-63, 74, 80-81,88; R. Mathews to Sir John Johnson, 18 March & 20 May 1784, Haldimand to Col. Campbell, 22 March & 16 April 1784, all in PAC, Haldimand Papers, Reel 664; Sir John Johnson to Haldimand, 8 April 1784, Joseph Brant to Sir John Johnson, 4 May 1784, Sir John Johnson to R. Mathews, 6 May 1784, all in PAC, Haldimand Papers, Reel 685; Sir John Johnson to Wm. Claus, 18 May 1810, PAO, "Indian Lands" records, RG1-A-I-7, Vol. 7,8; Peter Russell to Hon. D.W. Smith, 13 June 1798, PAO, RG1 A-I-1, Vol. 3; Sir John Johnson to Major Foster, 22 June 1815, PAC, RG10, Vol. 1833, p. 181636; ownership in 1816: PAC, Land Petitions, RG1 L3 Vol. 267, Reel C-2116.

SCHEDULE OF 1812 and REPORT OF 1815: PAO, RG1 A-I-7 Vol. 7, 8. PETITION of 1821: printed in Clark Barrett, "The Glengarry Indian Lands," *The Ontario Genealogical Society Bulletin*, VIII (Winter 1969), pp. 5-6.

## CHAPTER II
## BISHOP MACDONELL'S GLENGARRY

Letters of Bishop Macdonell in BMacd, pp. 1194, 11,163, 579, 890-891, 154, 992, 628, 739 and in PAC, *Report on Canadian Archives...1896* (Ottawa, 1897), pp. 78-87; Somers, *Bishop Macdonell*, p. 145; Father Macdonell to Bishop Plessis, 30 March 1816, 24 June 1819, Archives de L'Archidiocèse de

Quebec; Macg, II, 560-563. Letter of 1806 cited from PAC, C.O.42/342/ff.5-7v.

EMIGRANTS OF 1815: Andrew Haydon, *Pioneer Sketches in the District of Bathurst*, Vol. I (1925); Jean S. McGill, *A Pioneer History of the County of Lanark* (1968); and H.J.M. Johnston, *British Emigration Policy 1815-1830* (1972); Robinson's letter, PAC, C.O. 42/356/69-72v.

SECOND GLENGARRY FENCIBLES: Depot, PAC, Upper Canada Sundries, p. 12882. Surveying, *ibid.*, pp. 13090-92. As late as the beginning of August, 1815, only the date had been set "for the Glengary's to draw their Locations in Lancaster." *Ibid.*, pp. 10283-86.

HARDSHIP AND FAMINE: *Ibid.*, pp. 13693-702; Journals of the Legislative Assembly of Upper Canada, PAO, *Ninth Report* (Toronto, 1913), pp. 344—345. There was also a petition in 1818 from distressed immigrants in Glengarry, *ibid.*, pp. 482, 487, 488, 539. These were probably immigrants who reached Indian Lands in 1817. BMacd, pp. 37-46. D.A. Macdonald in PAC, MG24B30, Vol. 2, p. 943; Bruce W. Hodgins, *John Sandfield Macdonald* (1971), pp. 32-33.

ALEXANDRIA: "about" 1818, date in 33 Vic. c. 72 (Ont.); receipt in PAO, Mgr Ewen Macdonald's papers; map of 1823 in GN, 11 Nov. 1965; insurance: BMacd, pp. 414, 264-265. See also A.W. McDougald, GN, 30 June 1933 on location of first mills. Princess Alexandrina Victoria, later Queen Victoria, was born in 1819. It would be interesting to know whether the village ever went through a stage of being called "Alexandrina".

DESCRIPTION OF GLENGARRY: Maitland in PAC, C.O. 42/361/115-116v; John Howison, *Sketches of Upper Canada*, 3rd edn. (1825), pp. 34-39; James Begg's autobiography, typescript in PAO, Misc. Coll. 1887, and printed in *Standard-Freeholder* (Cornwall), 1 Dec. 1959 ff.

NORWESTERS: Other Norwesters who retired to Glengarry were Donald McGillis, Archibald McLellan, perhaps Alexander Macdonell (MLA, Glengarry). In addition to Big Finnan, some or all of the following lived in Glengarry in their boyhood: Duncan Cameron, Paul Fraser, Hugh McGillis, Colin Campbell, John Dugald Cameron, John McDonald le Borgne, Angus McGillis, Aeneas Macdonell, Alexander Macdonell (MLA, Glengarry), Alexander, Donald, and William McKay. Alexander Ross taught school in Glengarry before entering the fur trade. Angus Bethune: Mary Larratt Smith, *Prologue to Norman: The Canadian Bethunes* (1976); Hilary Russell, "The Chinese Voyages of Angus Bethune," *The Beaver* (Spring 1977, pp. 22-31. Documents on William MacGillivray's struggle to obtain Indian Lands are found in PAC, Land Petitions, Reel C-2116. Bishop Macdonell and the Norwesters: BMacd, pp. 321, 1153, 845-846, 23.

HIGHLAND SOCIETY: J.A. Macdonell (Greenfield), *A Sketch of the Life of [Bishop Macdonell]* (Alexandria, 1890), pp. 41-49, 54-59; Macg. Vols. 5 & 6.

# CHAPTER III

## TOWARDS THE CANADIAN NATION 1837-1867

*The Rebellion of 1837-1838*

RADICALISM IN GLENGARRY?: Breadalbane petition in TP, Lochiel con. 7, lot 19. Mackenzie: *Colonial Advocate*, 10 Nov. & 1 Dec. 1831; clippings in PAO, Mackenzie-Lindsey Collection; petition in Macg., VII, 342. Bishop Macdonell: letters from in PAC, C.O. 42/428/407-408v; BMacd, pp. 1222-1223, 1418-1419; & in PAO, Fr George A. Hay Papers, GAH 176. See also Chisholm in *Seventh Report of Committee on Grievances*, p. 32. *Morning Courier*: repr. in *Montreal Transcript*, 2 Dec. 1837. *Witness*: cited in *GN*, Christmas number, 1903. Bishop Macdonell, 1827: BMacd, p. 232.

SUPPRESSION OF REBELLION: We are grateful to Mrs. Elinor Senior for permitting us to read her excellent manuscript on ''The Glengarry Highlanders and the Suppression of the Rebellions in Lower Canada 1837-38,'' subsequently printed in the *Journal of the Society for Army Historical Research* (1978). British officer: quoted by Mrs. Senior *op.cit.* Militia at Lancaster: *Cornwall Observer*, quoted in *Montreal Transcript*, 26 Dec. 1837. Hodgins, *op. cit.*

INTERFERENCE IN 1841 ELECTIONS: *Journal of the Legislative Assembly of the Province of Canada*, 1843, Appendix JJ; *Le Canadien*, 29 & 31 March 1841, 2 April, 1841; recollections of Dr. McCulloch's son in *FH*, 2 June 1899; PAO, Fr. George A. Hay Papers, GAH 112.

1849 TROUBLES: *Montreal Transcript*, 1 May 1849; Hodgins, *op.cit.* pp. 17-18; *The Pilot*, 10 May 1849; *Montreal Transcript*, 24 May 1849; *Montreal Gazette*, 3 July & 4 Aug. 1849.

*The North*

CATTANACH: PAO, letters in Pringle Papers, Series III-a, 1833-1845; Mrs. A. MacDougall, *Friendly Reminiscences of Donald Cattanach. Esq.* (1884); A.W. Macdougald in *GN*, 23 & 30 June 1933.

D.A. MacDONALD: *GN*, Christmas number, 1903. Beauharnois: *Montreal Gazette*, 10-20 June 1843; *Montreal Transcript*, 15 June 1843; R.P. Leon Pouliot, "Un conflit ouvrier au Canal de Beauharnois en 1843," *Bulletin des recherches historiques*, 62:3 (1956).

BREADALBANE: F.A. Cox and J. Hoby, *The Baptists in America*, 2nd edn. revised, with additions (London, 1836), first pub'd 1836. See *Dictionary of National Biography*, IV, 1336, for life of Cox.

*FOREST FLOWER*: Copies of the *Forest Flower* are owned by Mr. H. McKillican, of Pte. Claire, P.Q., and by the Presbyterian Historical Society, of Philadelphia. For dates of Drummond's preaching in Canada, see *The Ecclesiastical and Missionary Record, for the Presbyterian Church of Canada*, Nov. 1847, p. 4; Sept. 1858, p. 130. See also Dec. 1851, p. 28, for letter from J. D. (presumably James Drummond) in Cuba to friends in Glengarry. Other details of his life are in Rev. William Ewing, ed., *Annals of the Free Church of Scotland*

*1843-1900* (1914) I, 141, and *Alloa Advertiser* (Scotland), 5 Nov. 1898. In comments on the novel in *W*, 4 Sept. 1894, the date of Daniel's death is given as 1832, but McKillican family records say 1830. He is probably buried in the Baptist Cemetery, Breadalbane, but he has no tombstone there. Cattanach and tracts: *Ecclesiastical and Missionary Record*, Sept. 1858, p. 130 (letter by Donald Cattanach), also May 1855, pp. 102-103.

SECESSION MOVEMENT: Journals of the Legislative Assembly of Upper Canada, published in PAO *Reports*; Journals of Legislative Assembly of Upper Canada (microfilm, PAO); *Debates of the Legislative Assembly of United Canada* (Montreal, 1970-), Vol. II ff; 1837 petition in PAC, RG1E16 Vol. 5, No. 18; draft counter-petitions in PAO, Eastern District Municipal Records 1814-1850, MS-40(1-3) Reel 3.

*Ralph Connor*

SHENAC: The publishers of *Shenac's Work at Home* and the *Forest Flower* had offices on the same Philadelphia street. How far were they aware of each other's publications?

*FA*, 24 Jan. 1935.

REVIVALS: i. Rev. John Anderson, *Reminiscences and Incidents* (1910); *The Home and Foreign Record of the Canada Presbyterian Church*, March 1864, p. 155, May 1864, pp. 214-216, Oct. 1864, pp. 342-344. ii. "Revival at Notfield," in *The Canadian Baptist*, 24 Nov. 1864; "Revival in the Indian Lands," *W*, 12 Oct. 1864; "The Great Revival of 1864," *The Maxville Messenger*, Nov. 1920; Charles Sinclair's autobiography, p. 15; Rev. D.D. McArthur in *The Canadian Baptist*, 8 Sept. 1938; Maxville Women's Institute, *History of Maxville* (1967?). We are grateful to the Rev. Mr. William E.J. Toller of Edmonton for kindly sharing with us the biographical data he has collected on the Rev. Mr. Rainboth. Rainboth appears (with the wrong initial) in Connor's *Postscript to Adventure*, Chap. IV, and (in the guise of fiction) in *Torches through the Bush*, Chap. XI. He was probably born and raised in the St. Andrews area of Quebec. He died 14 July 1887. iii. Rev. D. Gordon in *W*, 19 Nov. 1864, and in *The Home and Foreign Record of the Canada Presbyterian Church*, May 1865, pp. 221-223; Mrs. Gordon, *ibid.*, 1886, pp. 186-188.

BETHEL HILL SEMINARY: *W*, 26 July 1867; Charles Sinclair's autobiography, pp. 7, 15.

CONNOR AND *SHENAC*: Mr. J. King Gordon has very kindly provided us with the following comments on the possible influence of Miss Robertson on Connor: "...I would doubt that he would be influenced by the contemporary writing of his aunt Margaret Robertson. I never encountered the book [*Shenac*] in his library in Winnipeg. But I can't speak with any certainty on this: it just doesn't seem to be the way my father worked and sorted out the past."

*Confederation and Its Background*

For the Sandfield brothers' opposition to Confederation, see Hodgins, *op. cit.*, *Confederation Debates* of 1865, and *FH*, 30 Aug. 1867.

CIVIL WAR: Macg, XIV, 839-840; *GN* 25 April 1941, on Dugald Macdonald, whose books were *The Heavenly Bodies: How They Move and What Moves Them* (1877) and *Ancient Science or Secrets of Pyramids, Walls and Temples* (1901).

FENIANS: *FH*, 23 March, 6 April, & 13 July 1866, 1 March 1867; *W*, 21 June 1866; W. Boss, *The Stormont, Dundas and Glengarry Highlanders* (1952); *GN*, 23 Feb. 1900 (rallying of Dr.McDiarmid's troops in 1870).


CHAPTER IV

GLENGARRY IN 1871

PESHTIGO FIRES: *Cornwall Gazette*, 18 Oct. 1871. Prize poem: *Gazette* (Montreal), 23 Nov. 1871.

CARIBOO CAMERON: bibliography of Cameron's life as in *Dictionary of Canadian Biography*. Corner stone: *The Advertiser* (Cornwall), 12 July 1865. Disinterment: *Montreal Herald*, 26 Aug. 1873, and Sister Claire MacDonald's scrapbook, from which together, but not singly, the date of 19 August can be calculated.

ANNIE CAMPBELL: *FH*, 22 May 1868; *Gleaner*, 30 April 1869; *W*, 9 Dec. 1872; *Gl'n*, 21 March 1890. We are informed that no parish registers for the Isle of Skye now exist for the period prior to 1800. A standard method of checking the reliability of claims to great age is to determine the consistency of the dates recorded in successive manuscript censuses. Annie Campbell's age was given as 121 in the 1871 census. She cannot be identified with any certainty in the censuses of 1851 and 1861, although an Ann Campbell aged 80 appears in the former and an Ann Campbell aged 90 in the latter. Annie Campbell was doubtless buried at Dunvegan, but she has no tombstone there and no Dunvegan burial records were kept then. Some judicious remarks on the unreliability of claims of great age are in the introd. to Vol. V of the 1871 printed Census Report. According to the *Guiness Book of Records*, the greatest authenticated human age is 113 years.

LANCASTER ACCIDENT: *W*, 13 Dec. 1871. POP'N OF ALEXANDRIA: Charles Legge, *Report on Survey of the Montreal & Ottawa City Junction Railway* (Montreal, 1871), p. 4, and *Lovell's Canadian Dominion Directory for 1871* (n.d.) pp. 165-166. CORNWALL COMPLAINTS: *FH*, 27 May & 4 Nov. 1881. CALEDONIA SPRINGS: *Montreal Transcript*, 30 July 1842, quoting *Cornwall Observer*; *Cornwall Observer*, 25 Oct. 1833, 5 Oct. 1837; Lucien Brault, *Histoire des Comtés Unis de Prescott et de Russell* (1965), pp. 199-202; list of Glengarrians who visited Caledonia Springs in the season of 1886, *Gl'n*, 3 June 1887.

*WITNESS: FA*, 26 Sept. 1946. NEWSPAPER CONNECTIONS: *W*, 4 March 1872, 12 Jan. 1870; Duncan McLaren, ed. *Ontario Ethno-Cultural Newspapers, 1835-1972* (1973), pp. 36, 55, 56; *Gl'n*. 7 Oct. 1887. *CANADA*

FARMER: *FH*, 29 Dec. 1865.

POTASH: TP, lot 35 con. 8 Lochiel; Pringle, pp. 93-95; Robert J. Fraser, *As Others See Us* (1959), pp. 218-220; AH.

OIL: *FH*, 9 June, 8 Sept., & 17 Nov. 1865, 13 July, 24 Aug. & 5 Oct. 1866; Macg, XIV, 820; Fraser, *As Others See Us*, pp. 27-28; Geological Survey of Canada, *Annual Report*, N.S., V. Part II (1890-91), pp. 21Q-22Q; *FH*, 15 Feb. 1867, cf. 12 July 1867.

LANC. STATION: *GN*, 30 Dec. 1932. DOCTOR AT LANCASTER: letter of Dr.Falkner, 1 Feb. 1888, McL. *EVEN. POST*, FORESTS: *W*, 4 Nov. 1881; *FA*, 6 Aug. 1925, 22 April 1937; 10 June 1943. MORTGAGES: *Confederation Debates* (1865), p. 739; *FH*, 9 June 1865; University of Toronto, King's College Papers, lot 19 con. 4 Lochiel; BMacd, pp. 390-391. IRISH: *ibid.*, pp. 51, 79.

SERVANTS: *W*, 8 & 12 Nov. 1870. INSANITY: Macg, XIV, 820; PAO, Eastern District & SDG Minute Books, Quarter & General Sessions, 1849-1948; *W*, 27 April 1878; *FH*, 4 Aug. 1882; PAO SDG Surrogate Court, reel G.S. Ont. 1-1255, will no. 274, and SDG Counties Minutes for private custody of lunatics.

CRIME: PAO, Eastern District & SDG Minute Books; *FH*, 17 April 1868; *The Montreal Daily Transcript*, 13 Nov. 1862, quoting *British Sentinel*; *The Advertiser* (Cornwall), 3 Jan. 1866; *FH*, 15 Dec. 1865; *W*, 1 March 1869; Rhodes Grant, *The Story of Martintown*, p. 143, and our chapter V.

CHAPTER V
GLENGARRY FROM CONFEDERATION TO THE FIRST WORLD
WAR: INTRODUCTION—THE CANADA ATLANTIC AND THE RISE
OF MAXVILLE—THE FIRST FRENCH CANADIANS

*Introduction*

FARMING: *FH*, 25 Jan. 1884; anon. author (perhaps James Croil?) in *The Presbyterian*, Nov. 1869, p. 339; *FS*, 19 Dec. 1894, quoting Toronto *Mail*.

EMIGRATION: Mrs. Gordon in *The Home and. Foreign Record of the Canada Presbyterian Church*, V (1865-1866), 188; Years 1901-1911: D.M. Ray, "Settlement and Rural Outmigration in Easternmost Ontario 1783 to 1956," University of Ottawa M.A. thesis (1961), p. 194; *Chicago Canadian-American*, quoted in *FH*, 28 Feb. 1908; Manitoba: *W*, 10 May 1872 cf. 11 May 1871, *Reporter*, 11 March 1882; Allan B. Cameron to R.R. McLennan, 11 April 1887, McL; protest: *FH*, 23 Nov. 1883; crime and Summerstown, e.g. *Gl'n*, 20 May 1887, 20 Dec. 1889; crime: *Star* quoted in *FH*, 29 May 1891. In 1895 the Vankleek Hill newspaper, which was currently printing a good deal of Glengarry news, reported the following from Glengarry: the slaughter of watchdogs in Alexandria by distributing poisoned meat, the burglary of a liquor store on Main Street, Alexandria, while the corpse of the recently deceased proprietor "was lying at his home," the activities of a Glengarry-based confidence man, burglaries at the Canada Atlantic freight-shed at Alexandria, and the blowing of the safe at a Dalkeith store; Cariboo Gold Rush: Macg, XIV,

13, 14; Klondike Gold Rush: *GN*, 7 Oct. 1898, 4 May 1900, 15 Aug. 1902 (wedding story).

Two highly articulate Glengarrians have left well written accounts of the harvest excursions and what they meant to them. See Rhodes Grant, *Horse and Buggy Days in Martintown* (1976), chap. 30, and Sandy Fraser, *FA*, 16 Sept. 1926, 26 Nov. 1942.

ALEXANDRIA: richest parish: *FH*, 14 July 1882; *Eastern Ontario Review*, 23 March 1894; *FH*, 11 Aug. 1882, 3 Nov. 1882, *Gl'n*, 18 April 1890. From the Dunvegan news in *FH*, 27 Nov. 1885: "The frost has dried up the streets [in Dunvegan] and pedestrians are not now in danger of losing their boots." *Gl'n*, 23 July 1897. *FH*, 24 Feb. 1882.

*The Canada Atlantic and the Rise of Maxville*

G.R. Stevens, *Canadian National Railways*, Vol. II(1962); A.W. Currie, *The Grand Trunk Railway of Canada* (1957); and many contemporary references in the Cornwall and Glengarry newspapers and *W*.

MAXVILLE: Name: *R'r*, 27 Nov. 1880, 14 May 1881. Location of line: Legge, *Report on Survey*, p. 5; *FH*, 6 May & 3 June 1881, *GT*, 30 July 1881. Growth: *GT*, 25 Feb. 1882, *FH*, 5 May 1882, & 27 April 1883, 3 Aug. 1883, 21 March 1884, 6 Nov. 1885, 5 Aug. 1904.

*The First French Canadians*

Fr. Alexander Macdonell to ecclesiastical superior, 3 Feb. 1806, Archives de L'Archidiocèse de Québec; PAO, St. Raphaels Parish records; BMacd, pp. 1363, 1374; University of Toronto, King's College Papers, B1 Group B, Vol. 132, lot E½29, con. 9 Lochiel.

*The Toronto Daily Mail*, 2 Dec. 1886.

LECLAIR: Dr. Norbert Ferré, "The Leclairs of Glengarry," *Glengarry Life* [yearbook of Glengarry Historical Society], 1977; Senatorship: *FH*, 4 Nov. 1881, *GT*, 31 Dec. 1881.

ARCHBISHOP GAUTHIER AT OTTAWA: Robert Choquette, *Language and Religion* (1975).

POLITICS: *FH*, 30 June 1882; McMillan and Macmaster: Macg, XV, 1549-52; R.R. McLennan to Alex. Fraser, 17 Oct. 1900, and Senator McMillan to same, 18 Oct. 1900, PAO, Col. Alexander Fraser Papers.

CHAPTER VI
GLENGARRY FROM CONFEDERATION TO THE FIRST
WORLD WAR: — THE FIRST NEWSPAPERS — POLITICS —
THE RISE OF THE TEMPERANCE MOVEMENT

*Newspapers*

Material from the file of the *GT* in the National Library has been used throughout.

BIOGRAPHY AND CHARACTER OF McNEIL: McNeil to R.R.

McLennan, 30 Sept. 1883, McL; *GT*, 31 Dec. 1880; A.W. McDougald, *GN*, 3 Feb. 1933: *R'r*, 12 Feb. 1881.

PRINCESS LOUISE EPISODE: *GT*, 12 Nov.-10 Dec. 1881, 21 Jan. 1882; *R'r*, 26 Nov. & 17 Dec. 1881, 21 Jan. 1882; *FH*, 18 & 25 Nov. 1881. Another article in the same issue as the Princess Louise article denounced the idleness and extravagance of the Prince of Wales and Prince Arthur.

FAILURE OF *GT*: *R'r*, 15 July 1882; *FH*, 6 July & 10 Aug. 1883, 3 Dec. 1880; McNeil to McLennan, as cited.

*Politics*

Cornwall, Glengarry and occasionally other newspapers have been used throughout.

HUMBLER SUPPORTERS...DUNVEGAN AND DALKEITH: *R'r*, 8 July 1882; McL, 14 March 1891.

1872 ANALYSIS: Dr. Donald McMillan to A. Campbell, 24 Aug. 1872, PAO, Sir Alexander Campbell Papers.

1872...SWORE: J.A. Macdonell to Sir A. Campbell, 7 July 1879, *ibid.*

FALL OF SANDFIELDS: *R'r*, 24 June 1882; *W*, 9 & 14 Sept. 1878; *R'r*, 12 Nov. & 31 Dec. 1881, 14 Jan. 1882; *Gl'n*, 21 March & 1 Aug. 1890; *GN*, 27 March 1914; *Cornwall Gazette*, 16 Nov. 1870.

DR. McMILLAN: *R'r*, 28 Jan. 1882; Sir John A. Macdonald to Sir Alexander Campbell, 28 Jan. 1882, John Hamilton to Sir Alexander Campbell, 1 Feb. 1882, PAO, Sir Alexander Campbell Papers; *FH*, 16 March & 6 April 1883, 23 Sept. 1881, 7 April & 16 June 1882, 17 Aug. 1883, 18 Jan. 1884.

MACMASTER, PURCELL: Senator McMillan to R.R. McLennan, 8 (May?) 1888, McL. *Mr. Cartwright's Insult to the Highlanders*, pamphlet collection, PAO. For the disputed text of Macmaster's remark about the Highlanders, see House of Commons *Debates*, 8, 15, and 17 June 1885. For Macmaster and Purcell's contemporary stature, see esp. their lives in G.M. Rose, *A Cyclopaedia of Canadian Biography*, I & II. Purcell's Western tract: A.N. Lalonde, "Colonization Companies in the 1880's," *Saskatchewan History*, XXIV (1971), *FH*, 28 July 1882, *S*, 17 Feb. 1887, cf. *FH*, 14 July & 4 Aug. 1882. Verses: quoted in *Toronto Daily Mail*, 17 Feb. 1887, and *Gl'n*, 27 Jan. 1888. *Gleaner*, 19 Jan. 1888; trial transcript, printed, in files of Supreme Court, Ottawa (Purcell v. Kennedy). R.R. McLennan to Sir John A. Macdonald, 26 Feb. 1887, PAC, Sir John A. Macdonald Papers, MG 26 A, Vol. 438, pp. 216525-29.

STILWELL: Flora Macdonald letter, *Gl'n*, 11 Feb. & 13 May 1887; *Gleaner*, 3 Nov. 1887; telegram D. Macmaster to R.R. McLennan, 16 Nov. 1887, Stilwell to McLennan, 5 Dec. 1887 & 30 May 1887, Senator McMillan to McLennan, 16 May 1888, all in McL; *FH*, 2 Dec. 1887, *Gl'n*, 30 Dec. 1887, *FH*, 23 April 1897.

PAC, Tupper Papers, Reel C-3204, pp. 2637-40.

Theft of Purcell's body: *The Montreal Daily Star*, for May 1891; Senate *Debates*, 26 June & 3 Aug. 1891; and other sources.

PATRONS OF INDUSTRY: Organization: *FS*, 23 Aug. 1892, 30 May 1894; *Gl'n*, 16 Dec. 1892. Candidates: *FS*, 10 & 17 Oct., 14 Nov. 1893, 19 June

1895. A previous speaker had also spoken for an hour and a half! For recollections of Lockie Wilson and the Patrons movement in Glengarry, see J.E. McIntosh in *The Ottawa Farm Journal*, 20 March 1945. An earlier farmer's organization, the Grange, is said to have been active in Glengarry in 1880; *The Journal of Commerce*, 29 Oct. 1880.

REFORMATORY: Broadsheet by J.A. Macdonell arguing Alexandria's suitability for reformatory site, in PAO, Papers of Father Ewen Macdonald; Canada, *Report of the Minister of Public Works...For the Fiscal Year Ended 30th June, 1896* (Ottawa, 1897), pp. 34-35; Estimates of Canada for the Fiscal Year Ending 1897, in PAC, RG 11, Vol. 3226, and same estimates 1896-1900; R.R. McLennan in House of Commons *Debates*, 15 Sept. 1896; etc. *FH*, 28 June, 18 Oct. & 1 Nov. 1895, 10 Jan. 1896, 31 March 1899.

*The Temperance Movement*

According to an old account book, on 10 June 1836 a storekeeper in Lochiel Township sold a "Cocktale," the price for this and ½ pint rum being 1s 3d. The transaction seems to have been on credit.

BREADALBANE 1820: Dorothy Dumbrille, *Braggart in My Step* (1956), p. 100; *GN*, 4 Jan. 1952; Sandy Fraser in *FA*, 21 Dec. 1922; *W*, 28 Sept. 1876; S. Ivison and F. Rosser, *The Baptists in Upper and Lower Canada before 1820* (1956), p. 95.

*Cornwall Observer*, 20 June 1834, 2 Oct. 1844.

BY 1850'S: Minute Book of Breadalbane temperance society 1851-1854, owned by Mrs. Ian Irvine; Pringle, p. 343; *FH* 15 Sept. 1865, 6 July 1859; D. Cattanach's obituary of K. McLennan in *The Ecclesiastical and Missionary Record*, Sept. 1858, p. 130; AH.

ROMAN CATHOLIC CLERGY: *True Witness*, 8 Dec. 1871, 31 May 1872; *GT*, 12 Nov. 1881. The well known "Father John" of St. Raphaels (Fr. John Macdonald) is said to have been a lifelong abstainer, *W*, 6 Jan. 1879.

ALEXANDRIA AND DUNVEGAN: *FH*, 7 July 1882; Macg, XXVI, 86-87. Maxville had a temperance hotel by 1883; *FH* 18 May 1883.

SCOTT ACT: *FH*, 4 Sept., 13 Nov., & 27 Nov. 1885, 12 Feb. 1886; *The Toronto Daily Mail*, 2 Dec. 1886; *Gleaner*, 13 Oct. 1887; David Fraser to R.R. McLennan, 20 April 1888, McL; *Gl'n*, 7 Oct. 1887, 14 March 1890; *FH* 17 April 1908. See also R.R. McLennan's remarks on Scott Act, House of Commons *Debates*, 3 July 1900. The proclamations beginning and ending the Scott Act in Glengarry are in *The Canada Gazette*, 24 Jan. 1885, 9 June 1888.

CHAPTER VII

CHURCHES

*GN* and *Gl'n*, church records, personal knowledge, interviews, printed church histories.

19th-century maps (Walling's and Belden).

Many personal letters to and from past and present governing bodies of

Glengarry churches and chapels and to individuals who we found had knowledge of records or dates of almost forgotten churches.

## CHAPTER VIII
## SCHOOLS—LIBRARIES—GAELIC

*Schools*

GN and Gl'n; Annual *Reports* of Chief Superintendent of Education, Upper Canada, Canada West, and Ontario, and of Ministers of Education, Ontario; personal knowledge; interviews; sources mentioned in text. For the Green Valley School contract of 1796; see W.J. Stewart, "Establishment of an Early Glengarry School," *The School* (Nov. 1935), pp. 189-191, and *GN*, 14 Sept. 1951.

GREEN VALLEY SCHOOL CASE: Green Valley files in collections of Centre de recherche en civilisation canadienne-française at the University of Ottawa; Joseph Gauvreau, "Green Valley," *Almanach de la langue française,* 2e année, 1917, pp. 20-27; report on demonstrations at Green Valley and Alexandria, in *Le Droit,* 29 & 30 June 1916; clippings from English-language press in PAO, Scrapbook Collection; Green Valley case 1914-1916 in *Ontario Law Reports,* XXXI, pp. 360-364, XXXIV, pp. 346-357, XXXV, pp. 614-625.

*Libraries*

GN and Gl'n. Annual Reports of Chief Superintendent of Education and Ministers of Education, as in previous section.

We are indebted to Mr. Herman Nylands of the Seaway Valley staff for up-to-date information on the county library system. Mrs. Jean MacIntosh was very helpful about the last days of the Martintown Public Library, and Mrs. Catherine Munro ferreted out the details of the last days of the Maxville Public Library for us. Our thanks to these people, and we must also express our gratitude to those who for many years kept the small public libraries of Glengarry open. One at least of the present authors cannot sufficiently express his gratitude to those who made it possible for him to indulge his love of reading in the small but good libraries of Glengarry, forty to forty-five years ago.

*Gaelic*

ST. ELMO PAPER: *GN*, 16 Feb. 1894.

SOUTH, NORTH: John Burns to Rev. R. Burns, May 1825, United Church Archives, Glasgow Colonial Society Correspondence, Vol. I, No. 17; *The Ecclesiastical and Missionary Record,* August 1846, p. 204; Rev. John Anderson, *Reminiscences and Incidents* (1910); *The Presbyterian,* Dec. 1861, p. 190; John McLennan, as in notes to Chap. I.

*The Breadalbane Baptist Church: 1816-1916* (1916?); Rev. Donald N. MacMillan, *Historical Sketch of Kenyon Presbyterian Church Dunvegan* (Alexandria, 1940).

AH; *W*, 4 Sept. 1894; *Gleaner*, 6 Nov. 1890; Toronto *Mail* quoted in *Gl'n*, 11 Feb. 1887; archivist: R.R. McLennan to Alex. Fraser, 17 Oct. 1900, and

Senator McMillan to same, 18 Oct. 1900, PAO, Col. Alex. Fraser Papers; bonfire: *FH*, 3 Nov. 1882; Kenyon Town Hall: *R'r*, 31 Dec. 1881; testra: AH.

FRENCH AND GAELIC: *The Presbyterian*, Dec. 1861, p. 190; Mrs. A. MacDougall, *Friendly Reminiscences of Donald Cattanach* (1884), p. 7. A Roman Catholic Newspaper, *The True Witness*, 2 July 1869, mentions recent religious services in Alexandria which included sermons in English, French, and Gaelic.

## CHAPTER IX
### ROADS

Most histories and memoirs relating to Glengarry contain some information on Glengarry's roads; Glengarry and Cornwall newspapers; reports of township and SDG Council meetings; post office records for mail contracts; statutes and bylaws; maps from McNiff's of 1786 to present day; tax bills of the MacLean family at Summerstown, complete from 1870's to present, for statute labour, special levies for iron bridges, etc.; *Official Automobile Road Guide of Canada 1912* (Ontario Motor League) for lamentable state of roads in Glengarry area; personal knowledge and personal inspection.

## CHAPTER X
### COMMUNICATIONS—POST OFFICES, TELEGRAPH AND TELEPHONE

*Post Offices*

Frank Campbell's *Canada Post Offices 1755-1895* and other sources mentioned in text; *The Quebec Almanac*, 50 vols. from 1780-1841; *Official Post Office Directories for the Canadas 1828, 1830, 1835;* Library of the General Post Office, London, Eng.; *Report of the Commissioners Appointed to Enquire into the Affairs of the Post Office in British North America* (1846), which lists all post offices in the above area open on 5 July 1840, sometimes with the date of opening; Post Office circulars listing new post office openings in the Canadas in the 1840's preserved in the Burton Historical Collection at the Detroit Public Library; Post Office *Annual Reports* which appeared annually after the Canadas took over their postal system in 1851 and appeared regularly till 1895; records of the Post Office Department of Ottawa which has excellent records from about Confederation to the present and in some cases earlier; Glengarry and Cornwall newspapers; 19th-century maps of Glengarry (esp. Walling's and Belden); Pringle; Mrs. N.F. Mossop (née Dunlop) re Dunlop's involvement with mail in days of very early settlement in Lancaster.

*Telegraph and Telephone*

The CNR Archives were helpful about early telegraph lines across Glengarry and *Canadiana* supplemented and corroborated their information.

The files of the *Gl'n* and *GN* were as usual extremely helpful with their weekly reports of changes in Glengarry's telegraph and telephone systems. By a stroke of luck Glengarry's newspaper age began almost at the same time as its telephone age.

We owe a special debt to the late Clarence Ostrom's manuscript history of Alexandria. His father was Bell's first manager in Alexandria and Clarence from early boyhood was interested in the telephone system and on his father's death became local manager in Alexandria, a post he held until 1944 when he became local business manager only. No fragment of Glengarry's history is better recorded than that of the telephone system's early days in Alexandria, thanks to Clarence.

Local phone books (perhaps because of their soft paper) had a very low survival rate. Those we were able to locate helped to establish sizes of the different exchanges in the county and toll free calling areas.

## CHAPTER XI
## FARMING IN GLENGARRY — 1784-1978

Glengarry and Cornwall newspapers and esp. the *GN*; printed and MS agricultural census; diary of John McGregor in University of British Columbia Library; diary of J.D. Ross, owned by Ewan Ross; *Smith's Canadian Gazetteer 1846; Canada Past Present and Future*, Vol. II (1852; republished Belleville, Mika Publishing, 1974), which has much useful information as the authors had access to the 1842 census records for the Eastern District which have since disappeared; Belden's Atlas; Government of Ontario, Ontario Agricultural Commission, *Report* (1881); H.M. Stiles, *Official History of the Cornwall Cheese and Butter Board* (1919); R.L. Jones, *History of Agriculture in Ontario 1613-1880* (1946); R.B. Gray, *Development of the Agricultural Tractor* (1956); Michael Partridge, *Farm Tools* (1973); Ruth D. Mowat, *All's Fair* [Williamstown Fair] (1976); Eaton's catalogues; personal knowledge.

## CHAPTER XII
## MILK

Glengarry and Cornwall newspapers; printed and MS agricultural census; Ontario Agricultural Commission, *Report* (1881); Baltic's Corner cheese factory book in possession of Mr. and Mrs. Archie P. Munro, R.R. 1, Maxville; Jones and Stiles as in notes to Chap. XI; H.A. Innis, ed. *The Dairy Industry in Canada* (1937), which has material on the rise of the Glengarry cheese industry.

## CHAPTER XIII
## LIGHT AND POWER

Glengarry and Cornwall newspapers and esp. *GN*, which fortunately for our purposes was in existence prior to the earliest attempts to install water under pressure and electric light or even acetylene lighting in Glengarry homes; Clarence Ostrom's notebooks, which provide an eye-witness account of the various installations in Alexandria and in other areas of Glengarry with some detail that did not get into the *GN*; personal experience; quotation on 1881 electric light from Cornwall *Reporter*, 15 Oct. 1881.

## CHAPTER XIV
## SHANTYMEN AND THE TIMBER TRADE

Glengarry and Cornwall newspapers and esp. the *Gl'n* and *GN*; sources mentioned in text; Adam Fergusson, *Practical Notes Made during a Tour in Canada, and a Portion of the United States* (1833), p. 265; Jones, *op. cit.*, p. 115; *Souvenir Book of the Stormont, Dundas and Glengarry Old Boys' Reunion* of Aug. 11-15, 1906, and information from Prof. David Rayside, for Rayside and McArthur; census and maps for saw mills and grist mills.

## CHAPTER XV
## MUNRO AND MCINTOSH—J.T. SCHELL

Glengarry and Cornwall newspapers and esp. the *Gl'n* and *GN*; interviews; personal knowledge.

## CHAPTER XVI
## GLENGARRY FROM 1914 TO THE PRESENT

We have not tried to document this contemporary chapter in detail. Our main sources are back files of the *GN*, personal knowledge, and interviews and discussion. We have also found Clarence Ostrom's manuscript history of Alexandria helpful. Statistics unless otherwise identified are generally from the census.

"RELIEF" IN ALEXANDRIA: *GN*, 4 Sept. 1931, 17 Nov. 1933, 3 April 1936, 7 Jan. 1938; Minute Book, Alexandria Town Council, 15 Jan. 1935; PAO, RG19 Series I-4.

John Porter, *The Vertical Mosaic* (1969) pp. 425-428, 432, 434; *Saturday Night*, July/August 1975, p. 27.

MACKENZIE KING: J.W. Pickersgill and D.F. Foster, *The Mackenzie King Record*, II: 1944-1945 (1968), Chapter 11; R. MacGregor Dawson, *William Lyon Mackenzie King...1874-1923* (1958), pp. 312-314. For a defense of King and condemnation of Dr. McDougald in the Beauharnois scandals, see H. Blair Neatby, *William Lyon Mackenzie King: 1924-1932* (1963). Harsher views of King were expressed in a renewed controversy about King's financial connections with McDougald in the *Globe and Mail* in January 1977.

FRENCH CANADIANS: Speech of 1928: University of Ottawa, Centre de recherche en civilisation canadienne-française, file C2/7/14 (author not stated).

## CHAPTER XVII
## LIFE AS THE GLENGARRY FOLK LIVED IT

BODYSNATCHING: *W*, 29 Jan. 1878; *Herald* (Montreal), 30 Jan.-1 Feb. 1878; Angus MacMillan diary in PAC, MG25 G 150; *W*, 19 Jan. 1876. The

*Witness* carried a number of articles on bodysnatching in its issues of Oct. & Nov. 1875. Senate *Debates*, 23 June - 10 Aug. 1891, for Senator McMillan's bill.

CHAPTER XIX
CONCLUSION
THE MYSTIQUE OF GLENGARRY

"Mystique—The atmosphere of mystery and veneration investing some creeds, doctrines, arts, professions, etc., or personages." *Concise Oxford Dictionary.*

*Canadian Forum*, Dec. 1942, p. 286; John Goldie, *Diary of a Journey through Upper Canada and Some of the New England States 1819* (1967?), p. 3; *R'r*, 2 Dec. 1882; *FH*, 18 April 1884; *S*, 22 July 1886 & 19 Jan. 1888; *Gl'n*, 25 April 1890; *FH* 12 June 1891; *Gl'n*, 2 Dec. 1892; *FH*, 1 Nov. 1895, & *Eastern Ontario Review*, 8 Nov. 1895; *FH*, 12 June 1896; *The Scottish Canadian*, Oct. 1897; *Toronto World*, 21 Dec. 1885, reprinted in *GN*, 23 May 1963; G.M. Rose, *A Cyclopaedia of Canadian Biography*, II (1888), p. 669; *S*, 24 April 1903; *Globe*, quoted in *S*, 15 March 1907; *FH*, 21 Feb. 1908; *Citizen*, quoted in *S*, 18 June 1909; *Saturday Night*, quoted in *S*, 11 Feb. 1910, *S*, 11 Feb. 1910.

The Earl of Dundonald, *My Army Life* (London, 1926), pp. 227-229, also 226, 269, 286-290, for more on the Glengarrians. Dundonald's visit to Alexandria was almost prevented by a hoax phone call, informing him that the planned celebration had been postponed on account of the weather. For this, see *ibid.*, and *GN*, 4 Sept. 1903, C.Ostrom's manuscript history of Alexandria, and C. Ostrom in *Maclean's*, 21 May 1960. In the London *Times* of 31 Aug. 1904 Dundonald denied a rumour that he had accepted the Conservative nomination for Glengarry.

John Fraser, *Canadian Pen and Ink Sketches* (1890), p. 328, and similar remark by Donald Macmaster, *GT*, 20 May 1882. See also the anecdote about the proud Glengarrian in Frederick Niven, *Coloured Spectacles* (London, 1938), pp. 220-226.

London *Times*, 4 March 1922.

Gerard Lefebvre. His name is synonymous with Glengarry Transport, in 1978 a very large transport firm with its head office in Alexandria. This transport firm is the largest business ever developed in Glengarry and Mr. Lefebvre is also a native of Glengarry. The business began with a couple of trucks in 1947; in 1952 there were 8, in 1962 there were 41, in 1973 there were 950 units and since then the size of the operation has increased by about 10% a year. Mr. Lefebvre's business and payroll are very important to the local economy at the time of writing.

The largest business ever to operate in Glengarry, Glengarry Transport, Limited was started and 'grew up' in the last thirty-two years. Data given here was either supplied or confirmed by the President of the firm, Mr. Gerard Lefebvre.

Resumé of Glengarry Transport Limited from the files of the **Glengarry News**. Questions arising from these news items.

Aug. 8, 1947 – Shepherd Brothers Transport and Cold Storage business in Alexandria is sold to Gerard Lefebvre of Rigaud and his brother-in-law Ovide Brabant of St. Clet. They will operate the business under the name of Glengarry Transport Reg'd.

Q. How many units were bought from Shepherds'?

A. Three old straight trucks, one tractor and one 22 ft. trailer.

Q. When did Mr. Brabant cease to be part of the firm?

A. Sept. 1st, 1948.

Q. Where was Mr. Lefebvre born?

A. Glen Robertson.

Q. How old was he in 1947?

A. 32 years old.

Q. Had Mr. Lefebvre a background in the trucking business?

A. For eleven years Mr. Lefebvre was employed by his father in Rigaud, Quebec as a truck driver.

May 16, 1952 – Gerard Lefebvre of Glengarry Transport is planning an extension of his business to include service between Cornwall, Alexandria and Hawkesbury. A huge new trailer van has been added and the firm now has eight units.

Q. When Glengarry Transport was started what were its 'Bread and Butter' hauls?

A. Hauling cheese from Glengarry County to Montreal and return with groceries, farm machinery and animal feed to the farmers.

Sept. 26, 1952 – Announcement that the Cornwall-Hawkesbury run is now part of Glengarry Transport's operation.

Q. Was there any local competition at this time?

A. One other trucking company competed at that time over the same routes.

Q. Who did do the freighting in Glengarry-Hawkesbury-Cornwall area if there were no local trucking firms?

A. No one.

Feb. 6, 1953 – Glengarry Transport this week instituted daily truck service between Cornwall, Alexandria and Hawkesbury.

Gerard Lefebvre of Glengarry Transport is erecting a warehouse and garage for his transport business on his property, Main Street, North in Alexandria.

Comments – It is made up of a two door garage, 55 ft. x 30 ft. and a four door dock platform 70 ft. x 50 ft. Prior to this date, Glengarry had been operating from the back yard of this residence and transferring freight directly from one truck to another.

July 7, 1960 – Glengarry Transport is adding daily transport service between Alexandria and Toronto. The new service will include Cornwall, Hawkesbury, Maxville, Winchester and vicinity.

Q. How many people employed at this time?
A. 20 employees.

Q. How many units on the road at this time?
A. 30 units.

July 28, 1960 – "Glengarry" will soon be a familiar name on the highways. Gerard Lefebvre's big transport vans are displaying their new paint jobs with Glengarry in big black letters across the front of the vans.

July 26, 1962 – Two new vans have been added to Glengarry Transport's fleet which now consists of 41 units.

Oct. 18, 1962 – Foundations are being poured for a big storage warehouse being erected by Glengarry Transport just south of the Alexandria town limits on the west side of Highway 34.

Comments – The new facility will consist of a 9000 sq. ft. public storage, a 14 door dock platform and 1200 sq. ft. of office space.

Dec. 17, 1964 – Production workers at Glengarry Transport will become members of Local 186 of the Canadian Transport Workers Union on Jan. 1, 1965.

Q. About how many employees were there in this bargaining group?
A. 35 employees.

Q. How big was the office staff at this time?
A. 5 employees.

Q. Did the firm have any sub-offices at this time?
A. Toronto and Montreal.

March 11, 1965 – Glengarry Transport will be renting a big terminal at Toronto.

Q. How big was this terminal?
A. An 18 door dock platform with offices. A portion will be sub-leased.

Q. Where in Toronto was it located?
A. 223 Bridgeland Avenue, North York borough.

Q. Is this terminal still in operation in 1979?
A. Glengarry has since moved to another larger facility at 90 Shorncliffe Street in the West End, but still retains the former location for its Broker Division. Today's larger facilities require 10 acres of land and larger buildings.

April 21, 1966 – Gerard Lefebvre, President of Glengarry Transport, is this year's Man of the Year in Alexandria.

Q. Was this honor given to Mr. Lefebvre for any particular activities or just because Mr. Lefebvre is such an important employer and businessman in Alexandria?
A. Primarily because of his great contribution and efforts as a leader in the social activities in the Town of Alexandria.

Sept. 1972 (date obscured) – Gerard Lefebvre, President of Glengarry Transport Ltd., turned the first sod at Ottawa, to signal start on construction of a new office, warehouse terminal and garage. It is being built in the new Hawthorne Industrial Park and will be occupied early in 1973.

A company spokesman says the new terminal will consolidate the Ottawa operation under one roof. At present operations are run from both the Hanson and Duncan offices of companies bought out by Glengarry Transport over the past two years. The new Ottawa service will serve the Ottawa-Montreal and Ottawa-Toronto-Hamilton runs.

Company headquarters will remain in Alexandria and the local payroll will not be affected.

Glengarry Transport now employs 250 persons, 205 in the parent firm and 45 in the two subsidiaries, Glengarry Quebec and Shawinigan.

Q. When did Glengarry Transport incorporate?
A. Sept. 9, 1956.

Q. Were the two subsidiaries mentioned above bought as 'going concerns' or were they developed by Glengarry Transport?
A. Purchased and eventually expanded.

Q. If bought, what were the dates of purchase?
A. Glengarry Transport (Quebec) Ltd. – Sept. 11, 1963.
Shawinigan Transport (1963) Inc. – March 1, 1966.

Nov. 29, 1973 – Glengarry Transport Limited, with its affiliates, now has 950 units on the road compared with 750 a year ago. The company employs 450 people, uses a computer system to synchronize operations. Its new warehouse in Montreal will open on Dec. 1st, 1973.

The President of the firm is Gerard Lefebvre; the Vice-President is Gilles Lefebvre (son of the founder of the firm); the Secretary-Treasurer is Jean Luc Caron, C.A. and Paul Poirier is Assistant General Manager.

Q. Mr. Lefebvre, an exceedingly able business man, recognizes the necessity of bringing good people into the firm and keeping them, but were there some factors in the business world that favoured or influenced the enormous increase in size and efficiency of Glengarry Transport in the 1970's?
A. It was mainly due to the fine reputation Glengarry had acquired for its service and its communication network between terminals that provided personal services to its customers.

Q. Where in Montreal was this new terminal established?
A. 151 St. Francois, Pointe Claire (street name has now been changed to rue Reverchon).

Q. Is it still in operation in 1979?
A. Yes, with a new addition to the garage and the purchase of additional land.

Q. How many employees does the firm have now?
A. 675 employees.

Q. How many units does the firm have on the road now?
A. 1700 units including 500 in Inter Can Leasing Limited.

Q. How many terminals are in operation?
A. 11 Terminals.

Q. Generally speaking, are most of the firm's employees from the Glengarry-Cornwall area?
A. No. Alexandria and Cornwall Terminals employ approximately 200 employees. Other employees are at Toronto, Hamilton, Ottawa, Montreal, St. Zotique, Ste. Therese, St. Hyacinthe, Shawinigan and LaTuque.

Q. Glengarry Transport is a major business and is the largest business ever operated in Alexandria. What factors have influenced the firm to maintain its headquarters in Alexandria rather than moving them to one of the cities which it services?

A. As Glengarry Transport commenced operation in Alexandria, County of Glengarry, it has maintained its head office in Alexandria due to the ideal location situated between the major cities it serves, as well as the sentiment Glengarry Transport holds for the people of Alexandria.

# LIST OF ABBREVIATIONS
# USED IN PICTURE SOURCE MATERIAL

C.C. and B.B. - Cornwall Cheese and Butter Board, Cornwall, Ont.

C.J. and C. - Clarke, Irwin and Company.

C.S.F. - Cornwall Standard-Freeholder, Cornwall, Ont.

F. and R. - Farrar and Rinehart, on Murray Hill, New York, N.Y.

G.N. - Glengarry News, Alexandria, Ont.

H.P. - Harpell's Press, Gardenville, Que.

M.G. - Mundy-Goodfellow, Oshawa, Ont.

M.H.S. - Minnesota Historical Society.

M.P. - Mosaic Press, Oakville and Ottawa, Ont.

M.P.C. - Mika Publishing Company, Belleville, Ont.

P.A.C. - Public Archives of Canada, Ottawa, Ont.

P.A.O. - Public Archives of Ontario, Toronto, Ont.

P.B. of P. - Presbyterian Board of Publications, Philadelphia, Pa. U.S.A.

R.P. - Rannie Press, Beamsville, Ont.

R.P.F. - Ross picture file - Ewan Ross, Goderich, Ont.

Ryerson - Ryerson Press, Toronto, Ont.

T.H. - Tower House, London England WC2

W.B. - William Briggs, Toronto

W.C. and S. - William Collins and Sons

# PICTURES FROM BOOKS

Mrs. John (Veronica) Bethune from **Prologue to Norman** by Mary L. Smith (M.P.)

Hon. John McGillivray from **History of S.D.G.** by John G. Harkness (M.G.)

Col. Alexander Fraser from **History of S.D.G.** by John G. Harkness (M.G.)

Hon. D.A. Macdonald from **History of S.D.G.** by John G. Harkness (M.G.)

Senator Donald McMillan from **History of S.D.G.** by John G. Harkness (M.G.)

Sir Donald Macmaster from **History of S.D.G.** by John G. Harkness (M.G.)

Patrick Purcell from **History of S.D.G.** by John G. Harkness (M.G.)

James Rayside from **History of S.D.G.** by John G. Harkness (M.G.)

Bishop Alexander Macdonell from **History of S.D.G.** by John G. Harkness (M.G.)

Sir Edward Peacock from **History of S.D.G.** by John G. Harkness (M.G.)

Rt. Hon. William L.M. King from **History of S.D.G.** by John G. Harkness (M.G.)

D.M. McPherson from **History of S.D.G.** by John G. Harkness (M.G.)

Rev. and Mrs. Daniel Gordon from **Postscript to Adventure** by Ralph Connor (F. and R.)

Ralph Connor from **Postscript to Adventure** by Charles W. Gordon (F. and R.)

John Fraser from **As Others See us** by R.J. Fraser (R.P.)

Samuel W. Jacobs from **Sam Jacobs M.P.** by Bernard Figler (H.P.)

Johnson Hoople from **The Hooples of Hoople's Creek** by Elizabeth Hoople (Ryerson)

Marion McRae from **Dundurn** by Marion McRae (C.I. and C.)

Making a stack from **A county Camera** by Gordon Winter (T.H.)

River Bank Cheese Factory from Official History of Cornwall Cheese and Butter Board by Harlow Stiles (C.C. and B.B.)

Glen Walter Cheese Factory (same as 100) from (C.C. and B.B.)

Rev. John Anderson from **Reminiscences and Incidents in the Life of Rev. John Anderson** by Rev. John Anderson (W.B.)

Breadalbane from **A Forest Flower** by Rev. James Drummond. (P.B. of P.)

Glengarry Beauty Spot from **Up and Down the Glens** by Dorothy Dumbrille (Ryerson)

Fly Leaf of Thorn Apple Tree from **Thorn Apple Tree** by Grace Campbell (W.C. and S.)

## FROM CATALOGUES

Horse fork and cars from catalogue of Beatty Brothers Farm Equipment, Fergus, Ont.

Ferguson threshing machine from Ferguson Thresher Co. advertising post card (from Maxville Women's Institute Tweedsmuir Book).

Stage coach;    135 Allan McRae.

## FROM NEWSPAPERS

Lt. Col. A.G.F. Macdonald (G.N.)
Lt. Col. W.J. Franklin (G.N.)
Brigadier Donald C. Cameron (G.N.)
Eugene Macdonald (G.N.)
C. Campbell Fraser (G.N.)
Fr. Ewen J. Macdonald (G.N.)
Gerard Massie (C.S.F.)
Osie F. Villeneuve (C.S.F.)

## FROM MIKA PUBLISHING COMPANY

Grand Trunk locomotive "Trevithick."
Canada Atlantic Locomotive

Winter stage
P.A.C.
John R. Booth
Sir Francis Hincks

## MINNESOTA HISTORICAL SOCIETY

Archibald Mark Chisholm
Donald Grant

## FROM PRIVATE INDIVIDUALS

Isabella McLean (Mrs. John McGillivray) from Mrs. Katherine Arnott
Finnan McDonald   from Mrs. Kathleen Emberg

Charles Leclair Sr.
Fr. Louis William Leclair
Dr. Napoleon Leclair
Alexander Leclair                          Dr. Norbert Ferré
Archbishop Gauthier
Claude Nunney, V.C.
Archibald Browne, R.C.A.

John Sandfield Macdonald
R.R. McLennan
Stone Church at St. Raphaels
Convent at St. Raphaels
Fairfield

A lumber shanty.
Building the skidway.
Log jam.
Sleigh load of logs.
De Boss Bully on de Reever Raisin.          James D. Ross
Glengarry River Drivers.
Stone bottom rail top fence.
Threshing oats with tread mill horsepower.
Hauling ice.
Making maple syrup in pots.
Milk wagon.
Kings' Road Cheese Factory.
Local post office.
Winter passenger bus.
Bishop Alexander Macdonell (the Big Bishop)
Village brass band.
Village blacksmith shop.

Major General Donald J. McDonald from Mrs. Florence McDonald.
J. Albert Laurin from Miss Josephine Laurin.
W. Clifford Clark from Mrs. D.R. Johnston.
William J. Major from Laurent Major.
Archie Cameron from Mrs. Velma Franklin.
George Lanthier from George Lanthier.
Rae MacCulloch from Rae MacCulloch.
Donald McKay from Miss Ethel Ostrom.
World War I: The Ostrom boys, from Miss Ethel Ostrom.
J.T. Smith from Mrs. J.T. Smith.
Dorothy Dumbrille from Mrs. J.T. Smith.
Early view of Stone Church, St. Raphaels, from Mrs. Nancy McMenamin.
Lumbering with oxen in Michigan from Mrs. Gladys Rojem.
Log drive in Glengarry from Mr. and Mrs. Finlay MacIntosh.
Glen Falloch Cheese Factory from Mr. and Mrs. Finlay MacIntosh.
John D. McArthur from John H. McKay.
Hugh Munro from Mrs. Helen Kaufmann.
John D. McIntosh from Mrs. Helen Kaufmann.
Walking plow from Mrs. Harriet I. MacKinnon
Old grader and steel wheeled tractor from Mrs. Harriet I. MacKinnon.
Main Street, Alexandria from Mrs. Harriet I. MacKinnon.
Snowplow in Model T. truck from Mr. and Mrs. Archie P. Munro.
Gerard Lefebvre from Gerard Lefebvre.
Fr. John McDonald from Edwin McDonald
Maple Leaf School from Mr. and Mrs. Howard Pattingale.
Grace Campbell from Mr. and Mrs. Howard Pattingale.
McIntosh private cemetery from Royce MacGillivray.
McIntosh Family from Kenneth Campbell.
Rhodes Grant from Mrs. Onagh Ross.
John J. McDonald from G.I. Douglas Cameron.
Angus H. MacDonell from Angus H. MacDonell.

Jacob T. Schell
Edith Rayside, R.N.
Raymond Lapointe
Miss N.L. Mahon
Wellington J.C. Barrett
Log House                              From Ross Picture File
Maxville Station                       (R.P.F.)
St. Finnan's

Bishop's Palace, Alexandria
  St. Columba Church
Former one room school
Modern public school
Monastery, Alexandria
Sports Palace, Alexandria
  Charlottenburgh Auditorium
  Liquor Store in Glengarry

704

Typical Glengarry farm house
Stump fence
Snake fence
Log Barn
Reaper
Grain binder
The farm well
Mowing machine
Hay loader
Hauling hay
Stooks of oats
Horse forks
Filling the silo                                    R.P.F.
Dairy farm in Glengarry, 1978
Glengarry cheese box
Cheese factory, Martintown
Carnation plant, Alexandria, 1978
Horse and buggy
Horse and cutter
School buses
Glengarry road sign
Flyleaf of Gaelic Bible
Coal oil lamps
War Memorial at Alexandria
War Memorial at Lancaster
Glengarry bed spread
Glengarry quilt
Glengarry quilt
John MacKenzie

# INDEX